CW01281941

A WONDERFUL GUY

EDDIE SHAPIRO

A WONDERFUL GUY

CONVERSATIONS WITH THE GREAT MEN OF MUSICAL THEATER

OXFORD
UNIVERSITY PRESS

OXFORD
UNIVERSITY PRESS

Oxford University Press is a department of the University of Oxford. It furthers
the University's objective of excellence in research, scholarship, and education
by publishing worldwide. Oxford is a registered trade mark of Oxford University
Press in the UK and certain other countries.

Published in the United States of America by Oxford University Press
198 Madison Avenue, New York, NY 10016, United States of America.

© Eddie Shapiro 2021

All rights reserved. No part of this publication may be reproduced, stored in
a retrieval system, or transmitted, in any form or by any means, without the
prior permission in writing of Oxford University Press, or as expressly permitted
by law, by license, or under terms agreed with the appropriate reproduction
rights organization. Inquiries concerning reproduction outside the scope of the
above should be sent to the Rights Department, Oxford University Press, at the
address above.

You must not circulate this work in any other form
and you must impose this same condition on any acquirer.

Library of Congress Cataloging-in-Publication Data
Names: Shapiro, Eddie, 1969– editor.
Title: A wonderful guy : conversations with the great men of musical theater / Eddie Shapiro.
Description: New York : Oxford University Press, 2021. | Includes index. |
Identifiers: LCCN 2020057885 (print) | LCCN 2020057886 (ebook) |
ISBN 9780190929893 (cloth) | ISBN 9780190929909 (pdf) | ISBN 9780190929916 (epub)
Subjects: LCSH: Singers—Interviews. | Actors—Interviews. | Musicals—History and criticism.
Classification: LCC ML400.S4804 2021 (print) | LCC ML400 (ebook) | DDC 782.1/4092511—dc23
LC record available at https://lccn.loc.gov/2020057885
LC ebook record available at https://lccn.loc.gov/2020057886

1 3 5 7 9 8 6 4 2

Printed by LSC Communications, United States of America

This book is dedicated to Alfred, Richard, John, John, Jerry, George, Robert, and all the spiritual ancestors of the men whose stories follow. It is also dedicated to the great men yet to come, and to those whose theater careers might have exploded were they not cut short by a plague.

CONTENTS

Foreword by Laura Benanti ix

INTRODUCTION 1

1 JOEL GREY 3
2 JOHN CULLUM 17
3 LEN CARIOU 37
4 BEN VEREEN 51
5 MICHAEL RUPERT 68
6 TERRENCE MANN 89
7 HOWARD MCGILLIN 105
8 BRIAN STOKES MITCHELL 124
9 MARC KUDISCH 142
10 MICHAEL CERVERIS 162
11 NORM LEWIS 186
12 WILL CHASE 206
13 CHRISTOPHER SIEBER 222
14 NORBERT LEO BUTZ 238
15 CHRISTIAN BORLE 254
16 RAÚL ESPARZA 275

17 **GAVIN CREEL** 299

18 **CHEYENNE JACKSON** 316

19 **JONATHAN GROFF** 333

Acknowledgments 349
Index 351

FOREWORD

I HAD THE PLEASURE OF being interviewed by Eddie for his hit book, *Nothing Like a Dame*. The first time I spoke with Eddie I was sure we had met before. Our conversation was so natural and comfortable it was like chatting with an old friend. An old friend with an almost encyclopedic knowledge of musical theater and the people who make it come to life! I'm delighted to say that we *are* friends now, and I was so honored that he asked me to write this (after the more famous people said no, no doubt).

Sometimes during an interview you can tell the person isn't interested in seeing you for who you truly are. They are more interested in presenting you to their reader the way that *they* want you to be seen. Eddie doesn't do that. That is one of the many reasons his writing is so compelling. His ability to capture the true essence of his subjects makes for interesting, heartfelt, funny, and honest stories! You can almost hear the cadence of each individual's voice as you read through the chapters. Eddie has a gift for being able to gently coax personal stories, hilarious anecdotes, and even some steamy gossip out of actors without even having to ask!

I know so many of the gentlemen featured in this book, and when I read it, I was struck by how clearly their voices came through. I could feel their trust in Eddie, and his genuine interest in presenting them as they truly are. I know you will enjoy it as much as I did!

INTRODUCTION

IN *NOTHING LIKE A DAME: CONVERSATIONS* with the Great Women of Musical Theater, I had the honor of talking with many of the greatest living female stars of the musical stage, collectively sharing sixty years' worth of Broadway's oral history. But, of course, the women only tell part of that story. For every Evita there's a Che, every Mrs. Lovett has her Sweeney Todd, Bess and Porgy will always share an ampersand. It was time to write the book my nieces insist on calling "Nothing Like a Dude."

As with the women, I wanted to sit down with everyone I could for career-encompassing conversations. Most articles I'd read about these men left me wanting more, so I wanted these chapters to have the luxury of length. Given the realities of publishing, however, long chapters meant a short roster. So once again, in order to cull the list of eligible men, I needed criteria.

The primary prerequisite was that all the men in this book have a robust and ongoing career in musicals. Theater had to be the thing for which they are best known. There are fantastic performers who have done extraordinary work in musicals, but Broadway isn't their primary residence (Hugh Jackman, Alan Cumming, Neil Patrick Harris). There are other greats who contributed more significantly as creators than performers (Tommy Tune, Lin-Manuel Miranda, Harvey Fierstein). And there are excellent working actors who may not yet have had the opportunity to shine as leading men, or to do quite as many shows (I love you, Ben Platt, but the list of shows we'd be able to discuss is a short one—at least as of this writing). The final, and not-insignificant qualifier, however, was saying "yes."

The nineteen men whose words make up these pages did more than just say "yes"; Every single one of them was incredibly generous with their time and their candor. They sat for hours. They shared food. They shared gossip. And they offered wisdom, sometimes in the form of life-lessons I never saw coming but will always cherish. In some instances, conversations happened over a period of months or even years, so you might notice an occasional time lapse. Have no worries, you haven't misread something. Hopefully, you will enjoy the opportunity to feel like a fly on the wall. With *Dame*, I was pleased to offer a picture of what it meant to be a woman in musical theater over the last half century. I am excited to add a companion with new colors and textures. These chats, while they can certainly stand alone, tell a fuller story when taken as a whole. They intertwine. These men have not only played the same parts, worked with the same collaborators, inhabited the same dressing rooms; they inspire and learn from each other. They are each other's role models. Together, they provide connections and insights to decades of ephemeral history created within a mere twelve-block span of Manhattan.

1

JOEL GREY

August 2017

JOEL GREY OFFERED A TOUR as soon as I entered his sunny loft overlooking the Hudson River. Thank God, because without it I'd have found myself making excuses to go to the bathroom just to steal glances at his gorgeous, airy place, a veritable treasure trove of a life in show business. The bedroom wall is covered from floor to ceiling with Technicolor close-up photos of flowers from his forthcoming book (his fifth art book and sixth publication). Crammed onto a windowsill are the awards—Oscar, Tony, Golden Globe, etc. The office area, full of shelves and shelves of books, features three large Hirschfeld pieces of Grey, practically leaping out of their frames. And in the bright, very tasteful, very modern living room, he's managed to find space for his show trunks, which toured the country with him decades ago. His rich history is everywhere.

Joel Grey is one of those very rare actors who arrived on Broadway having already made a name for himself appearing on TV shows and touring as an entertainer. He wasn't a star, but he wasn't a neophyte, either. He grew up in Ohio, the son of Grace Katz and the musician/comedian Mickey Katz, a headliner on the Yiddish Circuit. Grey got the theater bug, however, not at home but when, at the age of nine, he performed in *On Borrowed Time* at the Cleveland Playhouse. The experience of that show—the discipline, the rehearsals, the sharing of the stage—were tremendously influential and instilled in Grey the work ethic by which he still lives.

The Katzes moved to Los Angeles when Grey was a teenager, and it was there that he started performing professionally, like his father, as a variety performer. TV appearances followed and, when Grey moved to New York in the '60s, Broadway opportunities for him came fairly quickly, first as a replacement in Neil Simon's *Come Blow Your Horn* and then in the musicals *Stop the World—I Want to Get Off* and *Half a Sixpence*. But the call that changed everything came from director Harold Prince, who was a friend, and thought of Grey for the as yet undefined role of the creepy Emcee in *Cabaret*, the show that would make the careers of Grey, the composers, John Kander and Fred Ebb, and of Prince himself, who, though experienced on Broadway, displayed his unique, unconventional vision for the first time and had his first directorial hit.

Cabaret was, of course, a sensation, winning Grey the Tony and later, the Oscar and Golden Globe for the film version. His subsequent Broadway shows, *George M!*, *Goodtime Charley*, and *The Grand Tour* didn't measure up to the success of *Cabaret*, but in 1995, he returned to Broadway after a long hiatus in the historic smash hit revival of Kander and Ebb's *Chicago*. He had another blockbuster immediately after with *Wicked*, and then another success with the revival of *Anything Goes*. In between, he managed to squeeze in the aforementioned books (including a 2015 memoir, *Master of Ceremonies*, in which he very candidly discusses his sexuality for the first time). He also added directing to his résumé, with the 2011 Broadway revival of *The Normal Heart*, (a play Grey had starred in during its original 1985 run at The Public Theater) and, in 2018, a critically acclaimed and long-running off-Broadway Yiddish production of *Fiddler on the Roof*.

When I met Carol Channing, I was struck by how different stardom was for Broadway actors in the '60s as opposed to today. Channing knew everyone in show biz and Grey is much the same. His friends are luminaries (Grey casually introduced me to his buddy, Hal Prince, and Ian Holm called to chat during one of our meetings). But Grey himself is unassuming. He's got a twinkle in his eye, a seemingly permanent smile on his face, and an infectious, welcoming warmth mixed with just a dash of mischief. It is this Puckish quality that is his hallmark.

Giving regards to Broadway in *George M!* (Photofest)

You got started in *On Borrowed Time* at the Cleveland Playhouse.

Yes. I never thought I was going to sing or dance ever and, you know, as a matter of fact, I couldn't. I didn't really have the chops. I only was interested in acting. That's what made my life what it needed to be, gave it purpose.

But it took a while until you were able to act again. In your book, you described your way back to the stage via singing and dancing on the circuit, emulating people like Danny Kaye.

That was my father's world: vaudeville and music.

Joel Grey	
Borscht Capades	Broadway, 1951
The Littlest Revue	Broadway, 1956
Stop the World— I Want to Get Off	National tour, Broadway, 1962
Half a Sixpence	Broadway, 1965
Cabaret (Tony Award)	Broadway, 1966
George M!	Broadway, 1968
Goodtime Charley	Broadway, 1975
The Grand Tour	Broadway, 1979
Cabaret	Broadway, 1987
Chicago	Encores!, Broadway, 1996, West End, 1998
Wicked	Broadway, 2003
Anything Goes	Broadway, 2011

As you described it, you enjoyed the work but not the touring, not the clubs . . .

Nothing about it actually. I couldn't say that I enjoyed it. I found a place where I could make a living and I sort of made my parents happy. And my grandmother, Fannie. Someone just sent me footage of my family being interviewed about my career. My grandmother didn't speak English very well, but she sat down, and they were fixing her hair, the lights were on her, and it was like nothing she'd ever experienced. She says, "You want to know what Joel was like? Joel was the best." I was standing right there. It wasn't like I was dead. "He used to come to my house every Sunday for brunch. And he would have lox and bagels and cream cheese and bali [barley] soup, and I said to everybody"—little of this is true by the way. It was all bullshit. She was making it up to the best of her ability. "And I said to everybody let him sing, let him dance, let him do whatever his heart desires." It was fantastic. She was rising to the show biz occasion.

Well, even though you hated performing in the clubs, it got you to New York.

Took a while.

You were nineteen.

Yeah, but I couldn't get a job in the theater or be seen. There was so much negativity about anybody who performed in vaudeville or nightclubs. It was a very goyish kind of clan: The Theater Guild—it was about a whole other thing.

In your book you described going to a dinner party and hearing the word "kike" being tossed around fairly casually. That's so fascinating because these were theater people, theoretically more liberal and tolerant . . .

But not Jewish theater people. The Theater Guild was a very social deal. Emulating the British . . .

How did you pay your rent?

Going to the Catskills.

And doing club acts that you didn't want to do?
Mm-hmm. Hard work.

But they must have loved you.
That's beside the point.

Around that time, though, you became social with a lot of people who would go on to be very significant in the theater. John Kander, Larry Kert . . . How did you come across these people if you weren't working with them?
Larry Kert was my friend from Los Angeles back when we were sixteen. We knew each other just as gay guys who were not saying anything about that, but we knew we were brothers, and we acted like brothers. He was very important in my life. And I am still struggling with my sexuality. But I knew then from what I could see and feel that it was—to be gay was to be dead back then.

You finally got to do a musical in 1962 with *Stop the World—I Want to Get Off*. As you said, you never expected to go down that road. Once you did, did musical theater feel . . .
Well, it was a very offbeat, strange show. Highly stylized and almost avant-garde. Somehow I got that vibe. In order to be seen for that show, I put on whiteface at the theater [where *Come Blow Your Horn* was playing] and walked three blocks in whiteface.

Just to do something to stand out?
No, I needed to do something to cover up who they thought I was [a vaudevillian].

In doing musical theater for the first time was there . . .
You know, I was a stage actor because I didn't know how to sing or dance, and I just . . .

But clearly you did because you got the show.
I had to study. I went to this woman on 7th Avenue. Her name was Amri Galli-Campi. She taught me how to sing. Sam Waterston was also studying with her. Everybody needed to know how to sing then. It was just another way of getting a job.

And the dancing?
Studied. I didn't know how to tap and studied for months. I had to fool them. I had to make the audience believe I was the best. And I would go downstairs every single goddamn night before the show under the stage and run my first solo. Never went on without doing that.

In your next show, you REALLY had to dance; you replaced Tommy Steele in *Half a Sixpence*. That was just faking it?
Yeah. And studying like crazy. I only did that show for one week. That was his vacation. And they made ten or twelve costumes.

At that point, did you feel like you were making it? You were getting consistent work. Were you feeling . . .
A commodity of sorts. Hello. I'm a commodity of sorts.

Enough of a commodity that for your next gig, Hal Prince was calling you to offer you an integral role in *Cabaret*.

No, it wasn't. That's what it wasn't. It was not integral, and that was my struggle. There was no character. There were no words. No lines. I had to find the interior life that would flavor and color these songs so that you think that I spoke during the evening.

The Emcee's five songs were originally all lumped together. Back to back in one sequence.
It was a musical comedy turn. Five songs. Had nothing to do with the book.

So as you tell it in your book, you read the script, and you were quite apprehensive. It was your then wife who sort of convinced you.
I did not want to be a nightclub performer. That is what I had been struggling not to do for a career.

So you walked into rehearsal still apprehensive?
Yeah.

Hal Prince at this point in his career was already quite established, and John Kander and Fred Ebb are coming off of *Flora the Red Menace* **...**
That's not such a big deal. You think that was good?

I think the score's good.
Everybody was not at their pinnacle.

Boris Aronson? Patricia Zipprodt? And Lotte Lenya.
Never been on Broadway. Jill Haworth [who played Sally Bowles]. A nightmare.

Was she a nightmare?
No, she's lovely, but it was a nightmare for her. She was so horribly castigated for just not being up to it.

Let's go back to the rehearsal process, and you finding this role. You described in your book sitting at your wife's makeup table and finding the look. I'm most curious about that. You talked about the used eyelashes that had so much mascara on them that they were like cardboard.
And they were just old. But they did the job. They also made me look sort of like a dummy. If you put on regular eyelashes you'd look like a sissy.

There's certainly an androgyny to the look of the Emcee.
It's very complicated, when you're talking about something like that. It's not drag queen.

No. No, no, not at all. If anything, it's sort of asexual in a way. But provocative at the same time.
A word came to me that so describes who that character was just last week: promiscuous. In the deepest sense. Not caring about any of the pitfalls of your behavior, just, you know, doing it all ...

Hedonistic?
Hedonistic and doing a dangerous thing, come what may. He was promiscuous the way in which he pushed everybody around on the stage. I thought that would have been a very useful word to describe to an actor.

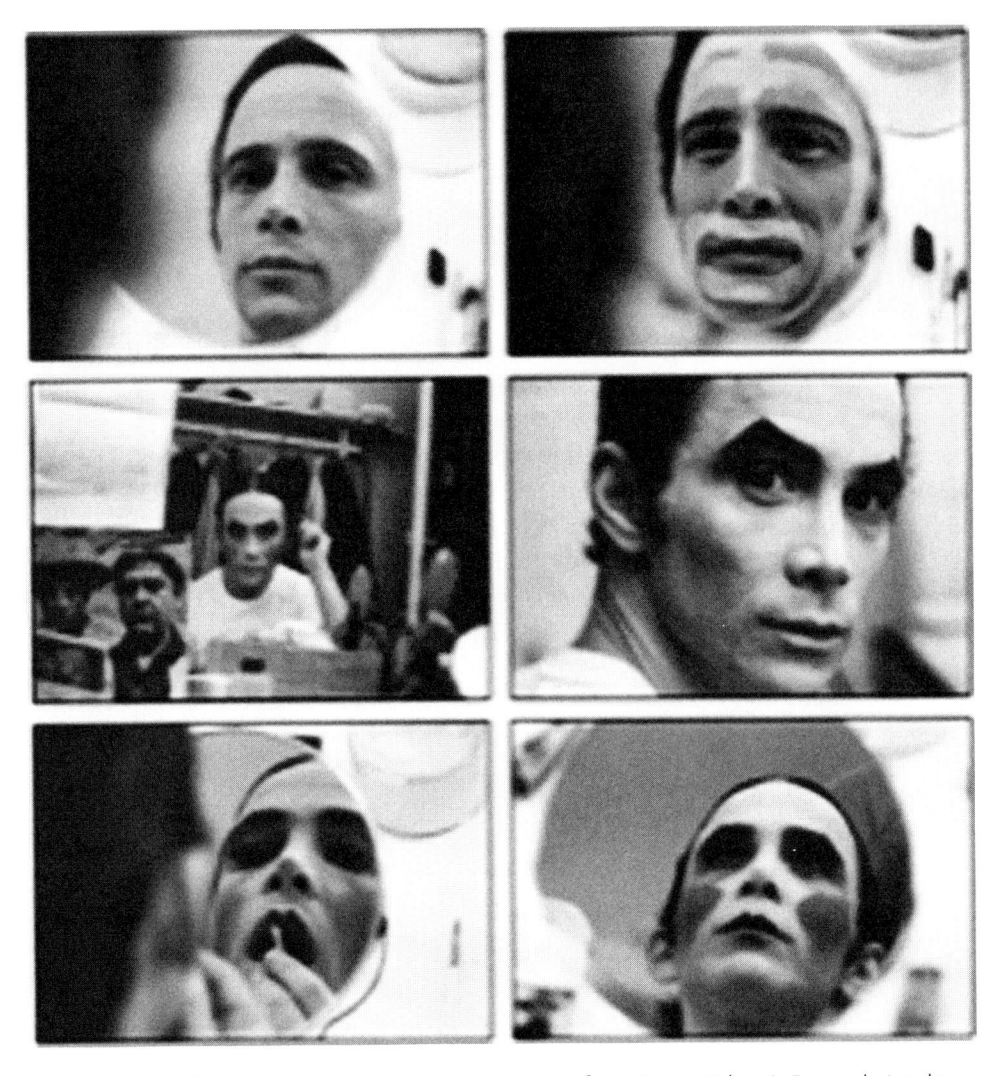

Grey allowed dear friend Raymond Jacobs to capture his transformation to *Cabaret*'s Emcee during the original Broadway run. (Raymond Jacobs)

Everybody I've talked to who's worked with Hal Prince says that he doesn't do a lot of directing of actors. He really trusts you to find it. So when you found your Emcee and he said, "That's it!" . . .

I was so embarrassed. [The characterization felt] raw. Who would ever want to see that on the stage? But I think if I remember correctly, it was "Thank God!" After many weeks of questioning what I was doing, all of a sudden I knew what to do.

When you were rehearsing this show that combines naturalism and symbolism and has this bizarre structure, do you remember whether or not it felt extraordinary? Did it feel special or did it just feel odd?

I couldn't tell you that.

Well, once the show opened, and it was getting the critical acclaim, did it feel special? Like you were in a hit? What do you remember about that?

It's one big "yes" that touches every part of your life. That's what that is. It's a yes from the community, from the director, from your collaborators. It's one big "yes."

So is that just a year of being on a high?
Well, I mean, nothing ever stays like that. There's maintenance. And there's, 'do I go to London, which I've always dreamt of doing? Or do I take a big fucking risk and play the greatest song and dance man [George M. Cohan in *George M!*], Irish, the greatest tapper, and put myself over the title? Do I allow that?' I don't know where you get the confidence or strength to do that if you've been afraid of everything most of your life.

So where do you think you got the confidence and strength to do that?
I don't know. I think if you love the craft and love the commitment to being an actor—a professional actor—and people are liking it, and you're being paid, and you're being respected, and—it's impossible not to be affected by that and happy about it and willing to take further risks.

Yes. I was just thinking after "one big yes," there would probably be a newfound confidence.
Yeah. I mean, it doesn't change your life totally. But it gives you a boost.

How was your experience working with Hal Prince? He is, of course, known as a visionary, and I wonder if being in the rehearsal room with someone who's envisioning . . .
In a way, even though he had done a few things before, and he'd been a successful producer, this was new for him, too. I think it was a first for both of us, and it defines itself in our friendship even today. He considers me a part of his beginning, and he knows how much a part of mine he is. I was at their house for nearly every show that is in *Prince of Broadway*: listening to the score before anybody anywhere had ever heard it. It was sometimes six people, sometimes a dozen people, and Steve [Sondheim] sitting at the piano, and Hal telling the story. I mean, amazing. And his wife and I are very tight. Their children and their children's children and mine, we're all a part of the work, and the life, and the challenges of both, and the heartbreak of both. We vacationed together, and while we were vacationing, he was working on X, and I was working on Y, but we had our children, and we had our lives, and our food, and our opinions, and our community. I would go to their house at Christmas and see the same people, their close friends—a lot of them became my close friends. It's very deep. It meant so much, and art means so much to me, and I know it does to him. So we would have—we would share that, and we would watch each other's successes and misses, and feel the heartbreak of the misses and the heartbreak of the life parts. What didn't go right. A kid was sick, somebody died, you know. There's—just everything. This was not arm's length, this connection. The awareness that both of us gave our lives and are giving our lives to the theater.

What do you remember about the night you won the Tony?
I guess it was the biggest moment of my life thus far, next to the birth of my children. It was like being home. Everything that I admired in those people at the Cleveland Playhouse and how serious we were, and how I was respected as long as I knew my lines, and I was quiet at rehearsal and taken seriously. . . . That's a big thing for a kid. And that was not really in my family. My aunts and uncles were kind of a rough group. "Kid, shut up. What are you? You're a kid." But when you were there, and you were doing what you were supposed to do and people thought I was not just a kid, that was something special. I look at that opening number from

the Tony Awards [Grey and the cast performed "Wilkommen"] and I think to myself, "Oh, my God, look at him. Look at how disgusting I allowed myself to be to tell this story, to be this character and how the risk of it ended up with me winning the Tony." It's cuckoo.

And yet, even after that, when it came time to make the movie, Bob Fosse didn't want you in the role.
It was horrible.

Did that make making the film unpleasurable?
I would say that. But I was already part of the reason for the film. I knew that. And I had to protect that. I was very watchful and focused, and I knew—because it had already been proven that I was that character. It was celebrated and stamped. I had him to fight all the time, all the time, although I could see him secretly smiling and getting it and liking it.

In the end, was there sort of a begrudging . . .
Never.

That's sad.
He had a sad life. And I was ready to forgive every second, but he was very fucked up.

Did you learn from him at all?
I think he probably made me very intense and in command, using all of my wiles and intelligence.

Did the character change for you at all for the movie?
Yeah. It became more dimensional. There was a backstage. There was a relationship with Sally, with Liza. There was a relationship with the audience in the club. They were real. And I had to prove that I wasn't Joel Katz from Cleveland.

Why did you feel you had to prove that in the film but not prior? I would think that by the time of the film . . .
Because those were actors in the audience—in the film. I had to make them real by believing in them. If you remember, there's a place where a woman reaches up to touch my hand and I reach out to her, and she starts to pull me into the audience. That was not planned. She just got all excited.

So after *Cabaret* on stage, and when you decided to leave at the end of the year, you said you had a choice, and you chose the scary one. You chose *George M!*
It was a killer. It never stopped.

You were also a father and a husband at the time, but did you find yourself exhausted by that? Invigorated by that? Both?
Both, both. You know, to get through a show that's that hard gives you kind of a boost. Like "oh, I'm alive!" But it was always hard.

In William Goldman's book, *The Season*, he says that the show was not good and really riding on you and you alone.
Those numbers were great. Joe Layton did great stuff. But it didn't have a particularly unique book.

After conquering *George M!* and having learned all that tap and choreography, did you feel you had an arsenal of different skills, that you were now capable of something new?

Yes, I did. I did. And there was no question that it was—when we were on the road, we made a bundle—just made so much money. And [I was able to] keep making it better. Joe Layton made it so fast. Number, number, number, number, number.

What was it like working with Bernadette Peters at the start of her career?

She's probably my closest friend in the business. She's my sister. I care deeply about her. And I am so proud of her accomplishments. I don't love anybody more. I am very protective of her, too.

***George M!* brought another Tony nomination, and then you did the film of *Cabaret* and at that point you were a minted musical theater star. The next gig was *Goodtime Charley*, and at that point, all indications are . . .**

Yeah. What went wrong? I think it was a case of overproduction. Taking a very charming idea—making real people out of these giants, Joan of Arc and Charles VII, and it was—when they played it for me, it was just so much fun. And then it ended up in the Palace Theatre with the most magnificent sets and costumes. Big. I think it lost its charm. Did you know that Patrick Swayze was in it? He was one of the ensemble dancers.

As this is happening around you, while you're working on it, do you trust the creators or do you speak up about what you see as not working?

It's very hard to see outside of doing the work. If you're looking into the character, you're not looking at the whole. And I wasn't the director.

Your next musical outing was back at the Palace. *The Grand Tour*.

Audiences loved it and I loved the character. I think both shows, *Goodtime Charley* and *The Grand Tour*, replaced the directors.

Well, Tommy Tune came in to help on *The Grand Tour*, right?

He did. And he did help. He's good. Musical theater is very tricky. You know, if one thing is off, a lot of things tumble.

I read that Jerry Herman actually thought that you were so good in *The Grand Tour*, it actually threw off the balance between your character and Ron Holgate's.

Meaning my role should have been more of a schlepper? Maybe. We did go out of town with *The Grand Tour*, but I don't remember anything. That's really strange. I remember I was shot out of a cannon. And there were a lot of changes. I think you start to lose confidence. And then there's a full house and you can't lose confidence. You've got to be totally confident. And by that time, the material is somewhat corrupted. Too much rewriting so it no longer has the vision that it had. You know, I don't like to say bad stuff about people because nobody gets into it to not make it good. I remember reading somewhere that somebody in the Jerry Herman camp said that I ruined the show. It's all hard. It's all very often not so clear why this or that didn't work.

After those two shows, you did a lot of TV and clubs, but you took a nine-year break from Broadway.

Seemed like a minute.

You came back with the 1987 revival of *Cabaret*. It was you, Hal Prince, Boris Aronson's sets all back again twenty years later. Why do you think it failed? Frank Rich, in his *New York Times* review, praised you but said the rest of the cast was weak.

I don't know that I agree. And there was also a movie in between. So maybe he liked the movie better. I thought it was good. Alyson Reed who was Sally, she could sing like crazy. I actually remember protecting myself in circumstances where things were not well received by just sort of stepping back and saying, "Time to move on."

You told me that you didn't like the Sam Mendes revival.

I thought that it missed the boat by being so outrageous. It was just so opposite of what we all originally intended. It begins with the world falling apart. That happened at the end of ours. The end was at the beginning in that production. I thought Alan Cumming was very good. I thought everybody was good. I just thought that the mystery and the build of the original, which is so much like what it was in Germany—nobody knew what the end was going to be. So I disagreed with the form and the attitude about it. It wasn't mysterious and therefore less frightening. It was frightening at the outset. We all have different stories we want to tell, and I was involved in a story that was told differently.

You bring up an interesting point because your next Broadway musical was *Chicago* and Chita Rivera says something not dissimilar about the revival of *Chicago*.

Yeah, I bet she does.

She says, with all due respect to your production, it's not the story that they were telling in 1975 . . .

That's true. It was more stylized. It was a concert.

So when you took it on, and when you were asked to do it for Encores!, just for five performances . . .

I didn't want to do it. I didn't remember liking [the original] much. I thought it was over the top. And maybe it had something to do with Fosse and me. I thought it was overdone. Chita and Gwen were magnificent performers always. I mean, queens. And I actually thought that poor slob [Grey's character, Amos]—I didn't have a real sense of compassion for him. Barney Martin was excellent in doing that but I didn't see myself doing that, and I didn't see myself as six foot two and 180 pounds. I couldn't imagine why they wanted me to do it. I didn't think I could play a dumb mechanic. I don't think I'm dumb. I don't think I play dumb well. It's not my sense of myself as an actor or as a person. I'm aware. He's not aware. But Walter Bobbie was really insistent and sweet, and Annie Reinking—this was the first time I'd really been with her since *Goodtime Charley*, and I had a lot of affection for her, and John and Fred are part of my family, and Fosse was dead, and I decided I wanted to do it. So I came in, and I said to Walter and Annie, "The only way I can imagine this guy allowing this woman to cuckold him is because he loves her that much. It's not dumb, it's that she can do no wrong." And that's what I based my character on.

And you did it for five performances at City Center.

And the audience went crazy. Went crazy. I stood backstage with Walter and Jimmy Naughton, and I heard the first number stop the show. And I heard the second number stop the show. The third number stopped the show. What's going on? How long can they [the audience] do this? And as it turned out, it was every number, every night. It was just phenomenal. It was like being at a rock concert.

"Lord knows he ain't got the smarts." With Ann Reinking in *Chicago*. (Photofest)

So the opportunity comes to then take this show to Broadway...
It was heavenly. I loved all the dancers. I mean, nobody had seen anything quite like it—that concert version. And it worked. Told the story. And it was new. And I had a great time. And I went to London and did it. I loved being a part of it and not being the center. Being part of a company.

It's unexpected that you'd find so much success again in the Fosse world, given how much you two struggled.
Never thought of it. Because there was very little Fosse in our production. I mean, in that original there were sets, and it was a big production—my God, how different could this be?

That's what Chita said about it. She said, "Nothing against what they've done, but what they did isn't *Chicago* as I know it."
Of course not. When you're an actor, the deep personal experience of creating it in the first place—that's how we get.

Territorial?

Emotional. Invested. You know what happened with the Tonys that year? The Weissler office neglected to put my name in. The person there that was supposed to do it forgot to do it. I was fucked. But it was so satisfying doing it every night. Being a part of the whole thing was great.

How was your experience working with Ann Reinking again?

It was an opportunity for me to—I just thought of it—to love her as Roxie and Annie. Because we were not connected during *Goodtime Charley*. The show was a problem, and she was Fosse's girlfriend. She's got a vulnerability and a mystery about her that is very appealing, and I never could see it then because I was struggling as an actor in *Goodtime Charley*. If you are carrying a show, or are expected to, you're so self-involved. It's sort of necessary. I think of George Cohan writing all these parts and playing all these leads and writing music and directing. I wonder what the quality of that work was, besides the star quality of George M. Cohan. I never heard of any of the people who worked with him.

Are you suggesting that because he had to be completely . . .

Self-involved.

That he wasn't focused on anybody else's performance or . . .

Not much. But I, as a future director and as a lover of the art and craft of it from nine years old, I was—that was the mystery and magic, as corny as it sounds. It never left me, not even today. It's the love of the possibilities of art.

You know, you speak of having to be totally self-involved for the work. But you had a wife and kids throughout much of your career and you were a devoted father.

I mean, I don't regret a second of it, but most actors spend their lives worrying about the work, and there's not much left for the rest of a life. That was always a challenge for me, because my family meant so much. And if you're doing a show like *George M!* you don't even speak.

Being equally committed to both, are you aware of particular sacrifices you made in either direction?

Always. The family was crucial to my being. And sometimes those things really bumped up against each other, and you had to make choices, and for the most part, I chose the family.

Did you ever take work solely in order to support the family?

Yeah, when theater wasn't happening, I had to take nightclub work that I detested. Vegas.

When you went to London with *Chicago*, did you find the West End different from Broadway?

It was surprisingly loose backstage. People would actually be drinking during the performances.

After the massive hit that was *Chicago*, your next Broadway show was another massively huge hit, *Wicked*. You replaced Robert Morse.

Who I idolized. I think he's a great comic genius and a wonderful actor. I thought there was something wrong with the fact that they let him go. They had offered the show to me a couple times before. [But I didn't think there was] dimension to the character. Then they wrote that song, I am "A Sentimental Man" about being a father and added a dance to "Wonderful." I loved those two girls [Idina Menzel and Kristin Chenoweth]. I was just enchanted with their talent.

They added that stuff before you said yes?
Yes. Out of town so much happens and I don't know whether or not it was just anxiety about how long it took [Morse] to own the Wizard. Maybe he just needed more time because he's a genius. But that character wasn't fully realized [when he played it], because they were focused on the girls. I came in and they started rehearsal again. And I fell under the spell of those magical girls.

You told me that you were "Daddy" between them.
I was. That's probably true. Because I'd been around the block. And because I did have genuine affection and admiration for both women.

They worked very differently. Idina told me that she likes to preplan a lot, and she likes to walk in quite prepared and knowing exactly what she is going to do. And Kristin . . .
Very improvisatory. But I could see that they were both so good. I just loved watching them.

As that show took off and became . . .
A rock concert. It was fun. It was like, "Oh, my God, listen to this." And this is in the overture.

When you're in a show that's selling out like crazy and is the hot ticket . . .
I'm just doing the work. [I am focused on] the quality of the work and the challenge. There was not a lot there. I mean, those two songs I liked very much, and *Wonderful* was so much fun to do with Idina, but it was a struggle; I have a quiet role and everything else is shrieking, blaring.

Your next musical was *Anything Goes*. How did that come about?
Oh, Kathleen Marshall.

She just called?
And called and called over a two-year period.

And why did she have to keep pursuing you like that? Were you initially not interested?
I very often don't think I'm right for the parts. But Kathleen and I kept talking, and thinking about [the character, Moonface] as a classic, almost Burlesque icon. Like those early guys.

What was the experience of working with Kathleen Marshall, Sutton Foster . . .
She and I had such a joyous time on stage together with that number ["Friendship"]. And it was staged great. And it's a classic. You live to sing a song like that on Broadway, right? But the second act song ["Be Like the Bluebird"]—I didn't know what that was. But it turned out to be just great. And Kathleen—she gets it. She gets the excitement of performing. And Sutton? She's my joy. She's a wonderful person and has come to find her own fullness as a human being. And unbelievably talented. I had one goddamn great number after another one.

Was it different for you in these last three shows, *Chicago*, *Wicked*, and *Anything Goes*, now that you no longer have kids at home? Did you experience the theater and the theater world differently?
Not much. It's still me. I was still the same guy. Still a dad.

Do you ever consider your place in the pantheon?
I'm another actor.

Is that all? You're one of the very few people in the world who has won a Tony Award and an Oscar for playing the same role. You've had a career in musical theater that has spanned the decades. You've gone from the classic Golden Age to contemporary theater. You've also directed and performed in one of the most grueling straight plays that there is.
That's nice.

Three Hirschfelds in the other room. Three, count 'em, three.
There are lots more. I have so many . . .

Well, I only see three on the wall, but yes. When you have an opportunity to sit down with somebody like me or to write your own book, and reflect on the totality of a career . . .
I'm very happy.

Anything else?
Mostly satisfied.

What are you unsatisfied with?
You know, there's always something that you're dealing with that isn't fulfilled. I wanted to be in *How to Succeed*. I auditioned for so many things I didn't get.

If you weren't performing what would you be doing?
Directing. Painting.

You talk about intimate relationships with a circle that includes Hal Prince and Stephen Sondheim, and Betty Comden, and Adolph Green, and Phyllis Newman, and Barbara Cook, and Ian Holm, and you even talk about how much you adore contemporary performers like Donna Murphy, and Sutton Foster, and Judy Kaye, and Idina, and Kristin, and Bernadette. . . . It's like everybody is a history maker. So many of the people who you call friend are singular historic talents. To be surrounded by that much creativity . . .
But you search it out. You're hungry for it. You have no patience for much else. You're not going to waste your time because you're too hungry to learn. And we learn from all these people. They give us so much. I am thrilled with greatness in the theater.

Do you ever have moments when you pause and consider that, with these people, greatness is all around you?
I don't think about it. I don't think about it as such.

So if I ask you to think about it as such, then what words come to mind?
Admiration and stimulation. And respect. People who make things happen wherever.

2

JOHN CULLUM

February 2017; February 2019

TO SIT AND LISTEN TO John Cullum reflect on his sixty-year (and counting) career as an actor, is an incredibly satisfying experience. He recalls names and details with an ease and specificity that a steel trap would envy; his colleagues include some of the theater's most influential and legendary people; he's sure of himself without conceit; and his southern charm, dating back to his upbringing in Knoxville, Tennessee, is as warm and inviting as hot cocoa with a splash of brandy. Our conversations have a tension to them, nonetheless, because his delightful and devoted wife of almost sixty years, Emily, is watching his calendar. She knows that given the opportunity, he can spin a yarn. Cullum hates rushing through a story (and he's got a lot of them) almost as much as he hates frustrating his wife who, he repeatedly tells me, does so very much for him. He's so conflicted, in fact, that he conspires with me to find time on the sly. "We'll figure out something sub rosa," he whispers. To call the dynamic between the two of them adorable could be considered condescending, but I am hard-pressed to come up with a better adjective.

John Cullum came to New York in 1956 and managed to get himself instantly employed in the theater. It's the kind of story that seems to happen only in Jimmy Stewart movies and would never be believable if it wasn't true, but the marriage of kismet and gumption got him his first job (as a spear carrier!) immediately after arrival and from then on, he never stopped. He wasn't particularly interested in musicals, however, so the idea that he'd do fourteen of them on Broadway (winning two Tonys along the way) would sound improbable to the young Cullum. The first was an auspicious debut: a featured role in *Camelot*, understudying both Richard Burton and Roddy McDowell. And while many of his subsequent roles, like much of his television work, have traded on his southern roots (*1776*, *Shenandoah*, *The Scottsboro Boys*, *110 in the Shade*, *Waitress*), his résumé includes playing urban sophisticates (*On a Clear Day*, *Aspects of Love*, *On the Twentieth Century*) contemporary straight plays (*Deathtrap*, *Doubles*, *August Osage County*, *Casa Valentina*) and classics (*Hamlet*, *Private Lives*, *You Never Can Tell*, *Cymbeline*). It is, perhaps, because of his great range that, like Judy Kaye with whom he starred in *On the Twentieth Century*, he is a star of the theater but not a household name.

At eighty-seven, while both he and Emily speak of slowing down, there is no sign of Cullum doing any such thing. At this writing, his role in *Waitress* coincides with recurring work on TV's *Madam Secretary*, and in his spare time, such as it is, he's putting together a one-man show. I am therefore that much more appreciative of his fitting me in, but now that I know him, I am unsurprised; John Cullum is truly a gentleman of the theater.

In *Shenandoah*, the second of Cullum's many roles to capitalize on his southern roots. (Photofest)

You were born in Knoxville, Tennessee, and you were a championship tennis player. When did the theater bug bite?

Oh, well, about the same time. I would say five or six years old. You know, I was brought up as a Southern Baptist in the church. We had to memorize different chapters, different Scripture, and say it out loud. Sometimes I would be called on to sing. I was kind of a show-off at home, so from the very beginning I was interested in showing my wares as far as singing or talking or telling stories. And then as I got older, there were pageants and that sort of thing in the church. I seem to have a vague recollection of playing a tree in the fifth grade. I know that the teacher put me in the back row because I was overacting. But those first formative years in junior high school were when I became involved in doing real plays. And I was also very interested in folk dancing and square dancing and country dancing. That had a strong influence on me. When I went into high school, that just continued. I played in school plays all the time, and I was a good athlete. My senior year in high school my drama teacher colluded with my mother, and they called the coach and got me kicked off the football team so I could continue my theatrical career.

Why do you think that she favored your being a performer?

Well, I think she knew I was going to get hurt in football. She followed my career. My mother was a constant supporter, and she loved what I was doing, but she didn't quite understand what I was doing. When I got into college, we did productions in a local theater, the Bijou, which was exactly like a New York house. I thought it was a crummy, old place. Dirty dressing rooms. I didn't know until I came to New York that I'd be playing in houses just like that. But my mother would come to see the productions. In those days, you weren't allowed to use profanity. She would sneak in and watch from the back, but she heard me say "damn" and that was a big deal. I did all kinds of productions at the University of Tennessee and really got very good training. And we got reviewed and all that sort of thing. The head of the department, Dr. Soper, would go to New York and see all the shows and then he'd come back and as soon as they were available, he would do them at the University of Tennessee.

Oh, so you were doing contemporary plays not classical plays?
I never saw a Shakespeare play until I came to New York.

But right when you got here you were doing *Saint Joan* and Shakespeare in the Park . . .
Well, that was because when I came here you could not get an audition for a contemporary play because the system was so different. The producer would find a piece of material, he would work with a playwright for a year, then he would pick a director and all the production staff and they would work with an agent. They would have the whole show cast without ever even auditioning anybody. They just picked people that they wanted. You couldn't get an audition for that. The only thing you could get auditions for were musicals. You could go in for the

---

John Cullum

Camelot	Broadway, 1960
On a Clear Day You Can See Forever	Broadway, 1965
Man of La Mancha	Broadway, 1967
1776	Broadway, 1970
Shenandoah (Tony Award)	Broadway, 1975
On the Twentieth Century (Tony Award)	Broadway, 1978
Shenandoah	Broadway, 1989
Aspects of Love	Broadway, 1990
Man of La Mancha	National Tour, 1995
Show Boat	Broadway, 1996
Urinetown	Off-Broadway, Broadway, 2001
Wilder	Off-Broadway, 2003
Purlie!	Encores!, 2005
Dr. Seuss' How the Grinch Stole Christmas	Broadway, 2006
110 in the Shade	Broadway, 2007
The Scottsboro Boys	Off-Broadway, Broadway, 2010
Waitress	Broadway, 2016

chorus in a musical or they had open calls for classics. I got into *Saint Joan* because I had a little letter of introduction from Dr. Soper to Norris Houghton. Norris was a theater notable. He established the Phoenix Repertory Company in an old movie house down on 12th Street and 2nd Avenue. I walked into his office, and it was bustling with activity. I showed this letter of introduction to the guy who was in charge. He didn't even look at it. He just said, "How tall are you?" and I said, "Five eleven." He said, "Sit down over there." He pointed to a bench. There were three other guys there. So I sat down and I said, "What's going on?" "They're looking for tall actors to be extras in *Saint Joan*, and this is the under-six-foot bench." They took us four in there to see Norris Houghton, and I showed him this letter of introduction, and he said, "I'll talk to you afterwards, Mr. Cullum." And then he told us they were looking for tall actors and if anything changes, "we'll give you a call" and he dismissed them. He said, "John, I'm very late to an appointment. I can't really talk very long. Which way are you headed when you leave here?" And I said, "Which way are you headed, Mr. Houghton?" And he said, "Uptown." And naturally I said "Uptown." So we jumped in a cab together, and I started showing all these pictures of me playing Golden Boy in *Golden Boy*, Dr. Sloper in *The Heiress* with a fake beard. I could see this was going nowhere. And so I just said, "Mr. Houghton, I know this is the beginning of your subscription season. I can type a little bit. I can file things. And I've got the time, and I enjoy doing it. It won't cost you anything. What do you think about that?" He said, "Well, we could use some help, John." I said, "What time does your office open?" He said, "10:00, but you can come in any time." So the next day I showed up before 10, and I was the last person to leave in the evening. And the same thing the next day and the next and on the fourth day, he came in and said, "John, I think we can use you in *Saint Joan* as a spear carrier if you don't mind carrying a spear." And that's how I got my first paying job after about four weeks in New York. It was a wonderful production with great actors. Siobhan McKenna played Saint Joan, and Ian Keith and Kent Smith, who were famous Hollywood people, were in it. Then I heard that they were auditioning for a production of *Hamlet,* and I asked [one of my castmates], "How do you get an interview?" And he said, "You pick out a section of the play, you work on it, and then you get an appointment, and you go up and do it." So I went over to the Strand bookstore and bought a dollar version of complete works of Shakespeare, and I picked out the gravedigger scene. But I had never seen a Shakespearean play.

You just went for the gold?

Well, I ended up—they called me "Tennessee" in the office. I had the Tennessee accent, see. They couldn't believe that I was even going to audition. I said, "I'll audition. In fact, I'll go right now." And I headed out the door. A guy named Phil Lawrence said, "Wait a minute. You don't even have an appointment." He called and he said, "I've got somebody here who'd like to audition. Is it too late?" They asked, "What are his credits?" And he asked me quietly. I said, "I don't have any." I thought he was going to hit me in the head with the telephone, but he started making up a bunch of things. Anyway, to make a long story short, I went in and auditioned, and even though I had never done Shakespeare, I was brought up on the King James version of the Bible, which was translated in 1604. Right in the middle of when Shakespeare was writing his great plays. So if you can read the King James version of the Bible, you can read Shakespeare, and I zipped through this stuff. And they hired me to play Rosencrantz and double as Marcellus. The people at the Phoenix couldn't believe that I had gotten it.

You were twenty-six-years-old when this internship happened?

Well, that's kind of a strange story. I was in Korea for a year as company commander on the 515's transportation corps. I made up my mind not to be an actor or a tennis pro because my dad had a beautiful little business, and he was going to turn it over to me. He and my mother would work for me. She was a real estate gal and he was a tremendous businessman. They were going to retire so they couldn't get a salary of over $100 or it would interfere with their retirement plan. So they were going to work for me for nothing. I was also playing in the local theater. I was partying a lot and drinking a lot, and I got picked up—well, anyway. What happened was they . . .

Did you just start to tell me that you got picked up by the cops?
That's right. And it got into the paper, and I used that as an excuse with my dad to say, "I think I'm going to get out of Knoxville because everybody was so glad to see me fall on my face." I think I used that as an excuse so I was able to leave. I just took off. And a couple of guys went with me. We drove up and that was like August the 22nd, I think, 1956.

Well, *Saint Joan* opened in September so that is an amazingly quick trajectory.
Within six weeks I had two paying jobs, one at *Saint Joan* and one with *Hamlet*. It was really extraordinary, but the—I don't like to tell this story, but we got to the tech week of *Hamlet*, and—well, the day before Art Larson had pitched a no-hit, perfect game—the only one that's ever been pitched in the World Series, and I got a call the next morning at the theater about 10:00 in the morning. I thought it was my dad, who loved baseball and played semi-pro ball. I thought he was calling about the no-hitter, but it turned out that it wasn't that at all. My mother had been killed that morning in an automobile accident. So I left New York and didn't come back until the next January, and of course things were a lot different then. There were plenty of good times ahead of me, but it was a very depressing situation for me. And then I did all kinds of stupid things, but one of the things I did was I got into a production of Greek theater, which I had never even read. It was the *Oedipus Cycle*, and I played in the chorus, but the producer had me understudying the lead. After we'd played for three weeks, he said, "If you want to do the matinee on this Saturday, you can go in and play Oedipus." I had never had time—there were three plays, and I was an understudy in all three plays, and so I had never learned the last scene of *Oedipus*. I actually started the play knowing that I didn't know the scene at the end of the show, but I said to myself, "This is the greatest part in classical theater. I'm going to play it come hell or high water, even if I only play part of it." So I got to the end of it, and I knew the scene I didn't know was in rhyming couplets. Can you believe it? So I had to improvise that last scene.

You improvised rhyming couplets?
Yes. Things like—what the heck did I say? "Oh, loving wife who was my mother, oh, loving daughters to whom I am a brother." Just very clever when you think about it. The fact that I got out the whole story in two lines. So we went off stage and got a round of applause, and nobody seemed to notice that I'd cut a dozen pages from the most famous play in Greek literature.

Did you perceive yourself at that time as having an inordinate amount of chutzpah?
No. I didn't think it was unusual. It never occurred to me that I was doing anything extraordinary, and that followed me through my whole career, even when I got the lead in *On a Clear Day*. I remember the company manger, when we were out in Boston, he dragged me out to the front of the Colonial Theater, and he pointed up, and my name was above the title, and he kept saying, "This is wonderful! Blah, blah, and what a great moment." I'm thinking,

"Listen I've got to learn this goddamn script." I only had five days to learn the script. It never occurred to me that it was anything . . .

Looking back on it now, do you recognize that that was kind of unheard of?
I was prepared to do these things. I mean, even in college, my mind was always on the tennis tournaments or something else in addition to theater. We spent two hours working on a show, and we just put the things together in a big, big hurry, and you had to come up with it. It never occurred to me that we were doing anything—I figured that's the way theater was. I think it was innocence more than bravura.

What were you doing for money?
I had about $500, and for awhile I got $25 a week severance pay from the army and I lived on it. And then the first job I had was $16 a week as a supernumerary [in *Saint Joan*], and then I got $24 a week for *Hamlet*, and they had to raise it to above $26 because the unemployment was $25, and so that—it wasn't that difficult. And I never went hungry.

Did you ever have to have a survival job once you were in New York?
I did. I took a job where we were supposed to be doing the inventory for a huge building on Varick Street, the headquarters for the city administration. They furnish all of the equipment for offices and everything. And we never looked at any of the equipment. We just initialed the cards as if we'd done it. And that's when I learned the *Oedipus*. I would sit there and go over the lines. I worked there for about six weeks maybe. That's the only job I ever had.

So from that time on, in sixty-plus years of acting, that's the only job that you ever had to hold down other than acting?
Yeah. And I didn't have to hold that down actually. I probably would have been able to get by, but I had time on my hands. And then I got into this kooky production of *Brigadoon*. I went in to audition, and I hated auditioning for musicals. I was very nervous about singing. I never got over that. I'm still—I don't like to stand up and sing a song. As long as I'm playing a role I'm okay, but . . .

You're not alone in that. You know, there are several—Angela Lansbury, Donna Murphy, they say the same thing. In a role they're fine, but they don't like to stand up and sing in a concert setting.
Well, that's good to find out that other people are the same way I am. I didn't realize that, particularly with Angela. I have to tell you a story. When I got into *On a Clear Day*, I got a knock on my door. It was about twenty minutes before half hour, and I open the door, and there was Angela Lansbury. I couldn't believe it. She just came by there. She didn't know me. She just heard that I was in this show, and she came by to welcome me to Broadway. She was doing . . . what would it have been, *Mame*? I have never ever gotten over that. She's extraordinary. Anyway, I went in to audition for this thing, and I had a few drinks to bolster my courage. I sang like I knew what I was doing, and I told them, "I've been in the chorus of other things. I don't want to be in the chorus. The only thing I'm interested in is playing Woody. I'm a hillbilly from east Tennessee, and I know more about Woody than any of you Yankee guys. If you let me read it, you'll find out." And they read me, and of course I am right for Woody, and I did a very good reading. But they thought I was some kind of kook. And so I didn't hear from them. But three weeks later they called and said, "We've lost our Woody. Would you be interested in doing this production?" I had five days. It was a ridiculous kind

of situation. But we had a good time and an agent signed me for musicals. And he kept putting me up for musicals even though I didn't want to go. When I was in Shakespeare in the Park, I auditioned for Joe Papp, and I prepared this rather extraordinary audition piece from *Lear*—Edgar—about seven minutes. He made me redo the audition for Gerald Friedman who was directing *Measure for Measure*, and for Alan Schneider who was directing *Henry V*. So I got a part in all three plays, and then Joe Papp insisted that I understudy the two male leads in each of those shows, so I learned, in that one summer, six major roles and three featured roles. Nine roles in that summer! And he came to me one night and said, "You're going to have to go on." "I said I don't know all the lines, Joe." And he said, "That's all right, just use your script." But I knew that opening speech. So he went out and apologized for me having to play it. Then I came out and tore that—"O for a muse of fire, that would ascend the brightest heaven of invention"—and I just tore the stage up. I chewed the scenery. And then of course I had to creep around [with a script for the rest of the show]. But Bud Whitney, Alan Jay Lerner's assistant, happened to see that performance. And when I went in to audition for *Camelot*, I sang this song, and they said, "Do you have a ballad?" And I said, "Yeah, I have a lovely ballad, "There But for You Go I" from *Brigadoon*. You may know it." I didn't know I was singing it for the guys who wrote it.

Seriously? You did not know that that was a Lerner and Loewe song?
No. And the guy who was talking to me was Moss Hart. Didn't know that either.

Had you seen *My Fair Lady*?
That was the only show I saw—no, two shows. I saw the baseball show.

***Damn Yankees*.**
Damn Yankees and I saw *My Fair Lady*.

Okay. So when you were going in for *Camelot*, you knew that you were going in for the *My Fair Lady* people?
No, I did not. It's kind of amazing to me that I ever got through any of this, but it all worked out. Lady Luck is the most important thing for an actor to have when he's doing these things, because there I was singing for these people. And Bud Whitney said to Alan Jay Lerner, "That guy Cullum is a very good Shakespearean actor." I left after the audition thinking "Well, I'll never hear from these guys," and then they called and said, "Would you come back in, Mr. Cullum, and sing a whole note scale?" I said, "Well, sure, I can do that." I had never even heard of a whole note scale. I didn't know what it was. I found out. It's very difficult to learn one. And it's impossible if you're trying to learn it on an out-of-tune piano, which is what I had. I went back the next day, and when I got there, there were all these big guys that I'd seen at auditions, baritones. I knew they probably couldn't act their way out of a wet paper bag, but they all could sing circles around me, so I started to leave without seeing anybody, and the stage manager said, "Mr. Cullum, you're wanted on stage." So I walked out there, and this guy said, "Mr. Cullum, my name is Moss Hart. Do you know who I am?" I said, "Oh, yes, of course, I do." I should have said, "I do now." But he said, "I understand that you're doing *Henry V* in the park for Joe Papp. Why didn't you mention that?" I said, "Well, I didn't think you'd be interested." He said, "Well, we are interested. Could you do something from it?" And I said, "Well, yes, I can do practically anything from Shakespeare." I had learned all these parts so I thought I knew the whole canon. But you talk about overconfident . . . He said, "Will you do something from *Henry V*?" I said I'd do the opening chorus, and believe it or not he said, "No, no, no, Mr.

Cullum, we've heard you sing. We want to hear you do a reading." I thought, "Oh, my Lord, Moss Hart thinks that the chorus is the singing part." I said, "I'll do the opening speech." I tore through it like crazy. And Alan Jay Lerner and Moss came up on the stage and said, "Mr. Cullum, we'd like for you to play the role of Dinadan, a very nice part, and consider doing the understudy to Richard Burton and Roddy McDowall." I was a smart ass in those days, and I said, "How long do I have to consider it?" He looked at me like I was crazy, and I said, "I've considered it. Of course, I'll do it." And so that's how I got into my first Broadway show.

There's so much history to the making of *Camelot*. The cutting and the reworking of the show again and again . . .

I could tell you a lot of stories. I was not considered a very good singer, but Alan came to me and said, "We're not satisfied with the understudy to Bob Goulet. I want you to sing for me again." I said, "I'm meeting myself coming and going in understudies as it is, and I can't sing as well as Bob Goulet. You give me a couple of months to work on my voice maybe I can . . ." "No, I want to hear you sing." And so I sang for him, and he came up on the stage, and he said, "John, you're absolutely right. You don't sing well enough." And they sent me to a mad Russian voice teacher, Seymour Osborne, and I studied with him for thirty-five years until he died. And gradually my voice got better.

Alan Jay Lerner and Moss Hart were both so colorful. Do you remember being influenced by them as men of the theater?

I had a great affinity with Moss. I liked him very much. And he liked me. Here's another story: I went on for Richard. He got sick and I went on for four performances. And Moss Hart went to the producer and said, "How much are you paying John Cullum." "$250 a week." And he says, "That's ridiculous." And he doubled my salary. Boom. Like that. And then later on—there was—Richard was a very perverse kind of actor in some ways, particularly with directors. He really made their lives difficult. Oh, God. I mean, there are so many stories about *Camelot* I could tell you. We left half the sets and costumes in New York. They never got to Toronto. And with all those adjustments and the cuts, the opening night was ponderous and interminable. The second act didn't go up until after midnight. Moss had a heart attack and went into the Toronto Hospital there. Alan said he would take over. Well, the first day of rehearsal, he wasn't there. We read in the paper that he was in California doing something. Anyway, he came back and then he ended up getting stomach ulcers so he never directed at all.

So who ended up taking the helm?

Well, nobody, nobody. We were on our own. It was a huge show that was in big trouble. Burton didn't like to fly so we took an overnight train ride to Boston. And it was a drunken ride. Then that night we all ended up at Richard's place drinking and one of the topics of conversation was we didn't have a director. The party started breaking up around 5:30 AM. But Richard didn't want me to go. He said, "John, love, why don't you lie down on that sofa over there and take a little nappy." And so I lay down and pretended to sleep. This is a story I never told anybody else. Richard was prowling, and I heard him pick up the telephone, and he said, "Julie [Andrews]. Of course, it's Richard. I want to come up. Yes, I want to come up now. You don't love me." Bam. He slams the telephone. I kind of peek out with my one eye. He's staring at the telephone, and it rings, and he picks it up, and he says, "Yes, of course, it's me. I want to come up, Julie. Why not? You don't love me anymore." He slams the phone down again. I said, "Oh, my God, Richard, it's almost 7:00 AM. We've got a rehearsal at 10:00 AM, and Alan's going to be there." And he said, "Yes, but Alan is no director." And I said, "Well, I think I better get some sleep anyway." So he escorted me out to the elevator, and I said, "Are you all right, Richard?" And he said, "I'm fine, love. You go ahead and get some rest." And I got on an elevator, and I said, "Well, I'll see you at 10." He didn't say anything. He just smiled. We all straggled into the Colonial at 10:00, and there was no Richard. And Alan got there an hour late, and then we all were getting worried because he wasn't at the hotel, and I knew I was the last person to talk to him, and I was just ready to say something when Julie piped up and said, "I talked to him at 6:30 AM." And Alan asked, "Were you with him?" She said, "No, I was on the phone." "Was he upset?" "He got upset when I said he couldn't come up." He said, "What do you mean? Why couldn't he?" "He wanted to come up, and I told him no." And Alan got very upset with Julie—she said, "I'm a married woman. I had to say no, but I left the door unlocked." And I never told Julie or Richard that I had heard that conversation from Richard's point of view. Richard showed up that night, made an apology, and the next morning, Philip Burton, Richard's foster father, arrived on the scene at rehearsal at 10:00. He was not a director, but he was a well-known scholar of the theater, and he knew good writing and good acting when he saw it. He took over, and he made a bunch of changes and got rid of some of the scenes. He tightened up the show and even gave a little direction, but not much. He pulled the show together, and we limped into New York. He was responsible for getting us there. And then he disappeared, and there's no record, as far as I know. People don't even mention his name. There's no reference to him having done all this work, and I hope he got paid for it. He certainly deserved it because we were in terrible shape, and he could handle Richard. Nobody could handle Richard if he didn't feel like it.

Did Moss Hart come back to the show?
Moss came back the next March in time to make some changes for the Tony Awards.

But not before opening?
No.

So as a young actor doing your first musical, did you have the sense that what was going on was atypical or did you think that this is just how musicals come together?
Well, I knew I was working with the top people in the business. Moss Hart and Alan Jay Lerner and Frederick Loewe were the top of the heap at the time because of *My Fair Lady*, and one of the reasons why *Camelot* was so difficult was that the shadow of that show was hovering over. So everybody overextended in every department in *Camelot*. The sets, the costumes . . . even the dance. I saw a rehearsal of a wonderful dance that Hanya Holm had created for the animals in the enchanted forest, and it was magical. And the minute they put on the costumes and the headpieces, the magic was gone. It looked like a cheap imitation of a Walt Disney cartoon. And nobody ever saw this wonderful piece of material that Hanya had done. The same thing happened to the quests of Lancelot. They were overdone, and some of them were just ridiculous, and gradually they dropped them one by one until none of them were left. That's why I said we left half the costumes and sets in New York City.

But again, you're new to musicals. You're working with the top of the business so was it your sense at the time that this is just the way it happens or did you know from other actors that this was not typical?
Well, I couldn't help but—I mean, I couldn't have been in a better position. I was in the best position that any actor in my category could ever be in. I was playing a very nice role in the biggest musical. *Camelot* was the biggest musical of its time. Everything was overdone, but it

was fantastic. And there I was understudying Richard Burton. He was very, very good in *Camelot*. That was one of the best things he ever did, and I was in his *Hamlet*, and I was in *Private Lives* with him. He was considered one of the top classical actors in the English-speaking world. He could do anything you wanted, but he only did it if he felt like it.

The stories go that he was inconsistent, and that inconsistency was largely due to alcohol, but you're saying it was sort of due to whim?

The only time I ever saw Richard inebriated was in *Hamlet*, and he had been taking medication all morning long for a condition that he had. He got kicked in the neck in a fight in England, and he almost got his eye knocked out. And when he and Elizabeth Taylor would talk about it, they would joke about the fact that his eye was hanging out, and she had to push it back in. And—why am I telling this story? That was the only time I ever saw him inebriated. In fact, he jumped on me one time when I played Mordred. He always held court in his dressing room, and everybody drank in his room during the performances. Richard drank, too, but he never got inebriated. When I played Mordred, he kicked everybody out of the room, and he said, "John, how do you think you did today?" I said, "Well, everybody's telling me how good I was as Mordred," and he said, "You weren't as good as you could be. You were inebriated. You know I like to drink, but have you ever seen me drunk on stage?" And I said, "No." And he said, "Well, if you can't handle it, don't do it."

Angela Lansbury talked about how during the run of *Mame* they'd go out and party at places like El Morocco all night long and then roll in the next day to do a matinee. And that's not the culture of Broadway at all right now. It's the polar opposite. People treat their instruments very carefully and very protectively. It's amazing to me that people were able to get through eight shows a week with that level of partying.

Well, you're absolutely right. It was a—not just among actors but among artists and writers particularly. Writers and actors were kind of expected to drink a great deal. And it just about ruined my career for a while there because you couldn't—and it eventually got to Richard because he kept drinking later in life and he went through a bad spell. It was killing him, and he finally tried to quit but that's a whole other story.

When you say it almost ruined your career, what do you mean?

Well, I was drinking all through *Camelot*. Everybody was. I had a bar in my dressing room, but I didn't need it because I would just go down to Richard's room, and everybody would be sitting around drinking drinks. And Richard got through it okay, but some of the other people didn't get through it. It was a stupid thing, but it was prevalent.

What do you remember about working with Julie Andrews?

Julie was exquisite. She could do anything you asked her to do that was within her range. She had an exquisite voice and perfect pitch and lovely sound. And she could play comedy, she could play the romantic scenes with Bob Goulet, and she could play tragic scenes toward the end of the show. She was not what you'd call a great actress, but I can't ever remember her making a bad choice on stage or in film. She always made good choices. And believe me, she had some tough guys to work with. I mean, with Richard Burton and Richard Harris and Rex Harrison and Chris Plummer—all these guys were volatile. And she worked with all of them and came out smelling like a rose. She was wonderful.

You played Mordred for a full year.

Well, it's not a very good role. It's not well written, and he is too one-sided. Good villains always have some very attractive quality and Mordred didn't have it. Roddy McDowell got by with it because people think of him as all the different roles that he's played. But I did not enjoy playing that. And the one song he has, which is a laundry list, "The Seven Deadly Virtues," is not the best writing that Alan did. I was glad when my contract was up. I did a musical with Bob Preston.

We Take the Town.

Bob Preston was extraordinary. He had the same qualities as Burton in terms of vocal power and magnetism on stage. He could do anything he wanted. He was not an extrovert like—Richard held court wherever there was a place to hold court, and even when there wasn't. Bob Preston was much more withdrawn. He hung out with the stagehands and that sort of thing. But when it came to doing things on stage, he could do anything you asked him to do, and he would try anything. He was very wonderfully cooperative and helpful of other actors. It was an extraordinary show. I had been in rehearsal about two or three weeks, and I remember saying to some of the other actors, "This is the most incredible show. I would put every penny I have into this show if I had the opportunity to do it." And then, of course, we closed in Philadelphia for lack of about $40,000 to get us into New York.

So what happened? I mean, Robert Preston was at the top of his game right then so that should have been enough to carry the show.

Well, it was a combination of things. We got very good notices in New Haven, but I think that probably the real trouble was that Pancho Villa was a very unsympathetic character in many ways. Bob played him beautifully, but the character . . . I know that Preston was very upset when we closed. I think the story was too dark. It had a lot of good numbers, and the choreography was good, and the company was good, and it seemed like it ought to work, but somehow or another the director couldn't get the writers and the composers to make any alterations.

You had an amazing thing happen next. You suddenly get tapped to replace Louis Jourdan in Boston to be the leading man in *On a Clear Day You Can See Forever*.

Yeah, how about that?

How did that come about?

I was in California and I got a call from Boston saying to come. They wanted to replace Louis Jourdan. And so my wife and I jumped on the plane, went to Boston, and I learned the show in five days. Nobody knew I was there except Barbara Harris and the director and Louis Jourdan. Louis actually thought he was going to go back in. But as it turned out, I stayed in it, and the rest is history. Alan couldn't bring himself to actually fire Louis, so even though he never did the show, they kept paying him through the run. $5,000 a week. More than Barbara and me combined.

How did you handle coming into the company and getting their support?

It wasn't easy. In fact, it was kind of uneasy the whole time. Barbara Harris was not the easiest gal in the world to work with. And she had just lost a leading man who was a star in film and was very good-looking and had a reputation. I was an unknown guy. And not only that, but the book of *On a Clear Day* was never really—They tried. I even tried at one time after the show closed to rewrite the script myself, and then of course they did a revival of it. I didn't see it, but I was hoping it would work. But I went through all that, and we closed. I think Alan could have kept that show running a little bit longer, but he couldn't rewrite it. He had written an awful lot for that show, and I came in with the idea that I would be able to make some suggestions, but every suggestion I would make, Alan said, "Well, we've already tried that." He had reams of paper. He would actually get his assistant to go and show me. There were 2,500 pages.

You went from being in a show that closed out of town to being a leading man with a Tony nomination. Did this all feel like you were on an unusual ride or did you think maybe this is just the way the business works?

Well, I think it was more of the latter. It was all such a flurry of activity, and I'd auditioned for them, and I was really—to tell you the truth, I was pissed off because they had been jerking me around for a year or more. I had to learn a Viennese accent because when they cast Maximilian Schell—they fired him, but they decided that Bruckner should have a Viennese accent. I guess because they figured any good psychiatrist had to come from Vienna. Freud was from Vienna or something. I don't know. But anyway, I was stuck with this Viennese accent, and Barbara was not particularly happy with the show. I was facing a very, very tough job. Emily was pregnant at the time, and she had helped me pick out these costumes because we weren't in contact with anybody except the director. I was working alone in a hotel room by myself. And so we went and just bought costumes off the shelf, and I was very comfortable in them. And then when we opened, the costumers and the makeup people and the director, everybody descended on me with their own ideas of how I should play this role, and they bouffed up my hair, and they gave me five different costumes—in each one I looked like an imitation of Louis Jourdan. I kind of lost my way there. I didn't think I was doing a very good job, and I wasn't probably. It took a long time to get that straightened out.

Well, you ended up with a Tony nomination so obviously you did.

Yeah, that's right. But I don't remember ever feeling comfortable in the role. I mean, I couldn't judge. You don't know what's happening to you because you're so deeply involved in the show itself. The show closed after eight months.

And you never feel like you got your footing?

No, no. In a way I blamed Bob Preston for letting *We Take the Town* fail. And then there I was in *On a Clear Day*, and there wasn't a damn thing I could do about the role because it was a flawed show. It became very obvious to me that you couldn't save a show if it didn't want to be saved. I thought if I were the star I'd be able to do something. No. You can't.

I do want to talk a little bit about Barbara Harris. A troubled person but such a talent.

Yes. Exactly. It's very easy to talk about her eccentricities, but the quality that she had on stage was irrefutable. I mean, she didn't even have to have dialogue to make people understand what she was doing. She was a natural talent. With Burton, I got the impression that he didn't feel that acting was an important achievement for a human being. That was very upsetting to me, but you see, Richard could speak three or four languages, and he went to Oxford, and he was, in a sense, a scholar. And yet he came from this low background, the thirteenth child. He was raised by his sister because they couldn't afford to keep him in his own home. So there was this dichotomy. He wanted to be best. Elizabeth Taylor was the best. When we did *Hamlet*, he insisted that we do 101 performances because Barrymore had done 100. And it killed him that he never won a Tony. I got the same kind of feeling from Barbara, that she didn't feel that acting was . . .

Important?

She didn't really. I could never figure her out, to tell you the truth. Because we never rehearsed. And then I read later on that she enjoyed rehearsals, but she didn't enjoy the performance. She enjoyed the work of the work. And I saw her in *The Apple Tree*, and she was marvelous. But after that, she just quit, and she went down to The New School on 6th Avenue. She started studying. And the next thing I heard that she was working in Bloomingdale's, just doing ordinary sales work. She was searching for something, which I don't think she ever found.

After *On a Clear Day*, you stepped into *1776*.

Yeah. I was doing out of town stuff at a reasonable theater and also off-Broadway, and I told my agent, "I want to get back onto Broadway." I had never played a southerner. I'd only been in tights and played Shakespeare and used Viennese accents and everything else to cover up my southern accent.

Well, later you obviously embraced it because you have peppered some amazing southern roles throughout your résumé.

Yeah, that's true. Once I did Rutledge [in *1776*], I knew—and *Shenandoah*, even though I was too young for it, it was the most comfortable show I ever did as far as understanding the role. I loved doing it. But there again, it was not a perfect show, but it had wonderful moments in it.

You've done other imperfect shows that didn't make it. This one hit big.

Well, it ran for two and a half years. John Simon wrote a terrible review of it, and there was a blurb that stayed in the *New York Magazine* for the entire run. In essence, it said, "If you like this show, you're kind of stupid."

But you took home a Tony Award.

That's right, that's right. Well, it was a great role. It was my best role, I think. New Yorkers didn't care for the show very much. They didn't even really come until much later, after we had been running for a while.

I remember that the TV commercial was what made me want to see it. It looked like a fun show, which, of course, it wasn't.

Did I tell you that years later Clive Barnes pointed out that we had cheated the public with our commercial because it was so different from what the show was? They shot it outdoors and it looked gorgeous. I said to him, "Well, you didn't help us out very much." He was very hurt by that. I never got around to telling him that he was my favorite critic and always would be because he loved actors and the theater more than any other critic I ever met. I developed a kind of a hard-ass kind of attitude toward critics.

You kind of have to, don't you?

When we opened *Hamlet* in Toronto, a critic said "Ophelia, Laertes, and Horatio are waxen figures." And then he came back weeks later, and he said "Ophelia, Laertes, and Horatio have deteriorated." That's when I stopped reading reviews. You gradually learn how to figure out what the review said by hearsay.

I do want to go back to *1776* for a moment because you got to do it on film with most of the original cast. And your song is like its own play. What do you remember about getting to do that on screen?

Well, it was a difficult shot. It was about a seven- or eight-minute scene. Peter Hunt wanted a sense of live sound so the orchestra was prerecorded and they recorded my voice from the stage. So it was a live recording. I did a take, and Peter Hunt came to me and said, "John, that was beautiful, but we had a little problem with sound." And they did it again, and there was another sound problem, and then there was a lighting problem, and then a camera problem. And they got to the fourth take, and I said to Peter Hunt, "I'm awfully sorry, Peter, but I've got one G left." And if you listen to the recording, you can kind of hear me squawk a little bit there. It was exciting but it was a long, seven-minute take with no breaks. I was very proud of the way it came out.

It's extraordinarily rare as you know to get to preserve a stage performance on the screen, let alone one that you didn't originate.

And that's one of the few [video] recordings that I have of me on stage. [There is also] the duel between me and Hamlet, but that's Burton's moment. A lot of times he almost killed me. That was a dangerous fight. He broke three swords and the metal pieces would fly, and they had sharp edges when they broke.

Between *1776* and *Shenandoah*, you stepped in for Richard Kiley in *Man of La Mancha* for a while.

Right, right, right. That was just an interim kind of thing for me. That was a very low point. I was thinking my career was going to be sailing like crazy, and it wasn't. I played villains on *Edge of Night* and *One Life to Live*, and so I was working all the time, but I hadn't been on Broadway for a while so I was glad to get to do it, and I love *La Mancha*. It's a wonderful show to play. That was an interesting situation because I walked on stage to work with [director] Albert Marre, and there wasn't anybody else in the whole auditorium. He was sitting in the front row, and he called me down and said, "Sit down." And so I sat on the edge of the stage. He took the script out of my hand, and he started going through the script verbatim without referring to the script at all. He just went through the entire script, gave me line readings for everything—exactly what he wanted, and then that was it. And then I played it that way.

After *Shenandoah*, obviously you were very much at the top of your game musically, and the next show that comes along happens because Alexis Smith recommends you for *On the Twentieth Century*?

Hal Prince was looking—see, Hal had seen me in *On a Clear Day*, and he denies this, but I had heard that he said, "Cullum is the dullest actor on Broadway." But he was looking for somebody to play this role, and he couldn't find anybody, and Alexis Smith was talking to him, and she said, "Well, have you thought about John Cullum?" Hal sent me three songs from the show and I wasn't that keen on them. I had seen a production of the play in Chicago and I thought it very static. I met with Hal, and I told him my reservations about the show, and he took me into the back office and showed me this enormous model of the set and the trains and how it worked, and I said, "Okay, I'll do it." There was a lot of [contractual] difficulty between Madeline Kahn and myself and Imogene Coca, about billing but we finally got it worked out. And then of course the whole thing with Madeline leaving and Judy Kaye coming in.

Hamming it up as Oscar Jaffe in *On the Twentieth Century*. (Martha Swope, ©Billy Rose Theatre Division, New York Public Library for the Performing Arts)

I heard from Judy Kaye that Madeline was really, really insecure about what she was doing, and you had to sort of prop her up?

Well, I did in a sense actually. I spent a lot of time with Madeline alone talking to her. She was very insecure, but they didn't treat her like a star. And she was very self-conscious. People think of Madeline as the kinds of roles that she played, but—in one of the scene changes, she had to change backstage, and she had to strip down. She was very well endowed, and they gave her just a little enclosure that was open at the top and the bottom. The stagehands would peer at her. That sort of thing contributed to her being insecure. And also, she had come into the show letting everybody know that she could sing, that she'd studied classical stuff. Then when Cy Coleman gave her a lot of difficult notes to sing in the "Sextet," she got very worried about her voice and she transposed some of those things herself. Cy just went ape shit. So just little areas here and there contributed to the difficulties. And she took refuge in a way that made the problem worse. When we got ready to do the final rehearsal in New York, Madeline didn't do it. I don't know why she didn't do it, but in any case, she came to me and said, "How was Judy?" And I said, "Well, Judy knows all the blocking. She certainly knew what she was doing." And then Madeline missed a big rehearsal in Boston, and she came to me and asked, "How was Judy?" And I said, "Well, she knows all the lines and the songs." And when she missed again and came to me, I said, "Don't miss any more."

The reports are that when she was on there was no touching her, but that she was not consistent, and she wasn't always on. I read that on opening night she was genius, and reportedly Hal Prince came back to see her and said, "That was it! That's what I've been looking for!" And she said, "You don't expect me to do that every night, do you?"

Hal came to me and he was worn out, and he started talking about Madeline, and I said, "Wait a minute, Madeline is my starring lady and you're not going to get me to say anything negative about her." I wouldn't take any criticism of her, and so I guess I got cut out of the loop because I didn't know what happened after that. I was just being loyal to Madeline. Madeline had a magic to her performance. It was like Barbara Harris, but Madeline was more extraordinary in the sense of you—you didn't know what it was—the quality that made her into this extraordinary performer. But the thing about Judy—Judy had a terrific figure, she was good-looking, she could sing like a diva from the opera, and she could dance. And you put all of those things together, and weigh them against somebody that's giving you a hard time, what the hell are you going to do? And that's why I said, "Don't miss any more" because Judy was always ready to step in and play the leading role. And Madeline was—I didn't think of her as floundering, but she was under a lot of duress and it affected her. I was tremendously surprised when they decided to replace her. I always understood that it was a mutual kind of thing, but as I say, I was out of the loop.

Just as with *Camelot*, once again you were working with titans of the musical theater: Betty Comden, Adolph Green, Cy Coleman and Hal Prince . . .

I was never into the musical comedy scene. I was much more intimidated by Arthur Miller and William Inge and Tennessee Williams because I thought of myself as a straight actor. But these people, there was no question, once you saw them and watched them operate, you knew you were watching the best in the business. I always found that the better the people that you've worked with, the easier it is to do it. Most of the time, the better the quality of people you work with, the more you shine if you've got the goods.

You said that at the beginning you weren't crazy about the songs. Did you end up warming to them?

Well, yes. I worked alone on my solos and figured out choreography. Same with Kevin Kline. Kevin and I had an unspoken kind of competition going on. Believe me, he was tough to keep up with. He would pull out all the stops when he was doing things. And my numbers were tough numbers. I worked them out by myself because Larry Fuller had his hands full. And the more I worked on them by myself, the more I became attached to them. Yeah, it was a big, big, difficult, complicated, but I think successful, show.

I heard from Angela Lansbury and others that Hal Prince is not an actor's director. He really trusts you to make your own choices, and he wants you to deliver a certain product, but he's not eliciting performances from you. Was that your experience?

Yes. Hal was a New York director. He had a sense of what New York theater should be, and the bigger the project, the better he liked it. I always got the feeling it was like a big toy to him. That's when he worked the best—when it was all a big toy for him to play with. Once it got down to the nitty gritty of the actor, he didn't want to contribute that much. But he was very aware of the quality of people, and if you didn't deliver, you could tell he was upset.

But he counted on you to bring it?
I can give you an example. We had huge rehearsal studios with mock-ups of the sets. We would read through, and then we would walk through, and then he would bring in all the production people and we would run the scene, and then he would dismiss us. We'd come back twenty minutes later and he would have done cuts on the scene, and then we would go to the next scene. Well, by the third scene, people like Kevin and Imogene and I were trying to give top-flight performances because we didn't want to get cut. That's the way he worked. You were giving as close to a performance as you could get. You were fighting for your roles. So that was the first day of rehearsal.

You took home another Tony Award. That's two more than Burton.
Yeah, I think Richard was jealous.

After *On the Twentieth Century* you went almost a decade without doing a musical on Broadway. You did a lot of plays and you did a lot of TV. And then you came back in *Aspects of Love*.
I wanted to do that show but I never felt very much at home in that. I really felt like a replacement. I think it had to do with the star [Sarah Brightman], and it also had to do with the composer [Andrew Lloyd Webber]. I never met him and I seldom ever talked to his wife. I have very little memory of that show.

After that was *Show Boat*. You must have been called by Hal Prince for that.
Yes. And I enjoyed doing it. I made as much out of that role as I could. I replaced John McMartin and he came back and replaced me.

Did you still have Elaine Stritch as your Parthy?
No, no. Carole Shelley. She's a wonderful gal and very easy to get along with. I wanted to work with Elaine Stritch, but there was a part of me that was scared to.

And after that, you came back in a very big way, originating a role in a small off-Broadway show that went big: *Urinetown*.
That was interesting. They sent me the script, and I looked at it and I thought, "What the hell is this about? I can't figure this damn thing out." And I called my agent. He had deliberately thrown out the front page that said *Urinetown* on it. Finally, I said, "I've got to talk to the director." I was in California, and I called the director, John Rando. Within ten minutes we were hooting and hollering, and the next day I was on the plane. We were all in one dressing room with a sheet on a wire between the men and the women. It was like a dance company. You didn't pay any attention to people being naked or anything. There was a bathroom—the top was open, the bottom was open so you could see everything that was going on. It was a wonderful company. They were all stars.

So when a little show like that makes it to Broadway and is really the toast of the town, what's that wave like?

Well, it was a very calculated kind of thing. I think they knew that they had a good show, and they deliberately wanted to keep it in that little theater because there was such a demand for tickets that it built up a kind of a pressure for it. It was a great show to be in and I loved doing it.

You played villains before but this one was really twirling the mustache.

Yeah, he was a villain. There was no question about it. He was the bad guy. And I played him as bad as they wanted me to. There's a certain barrier when you're playing comedy and I find that if you go beyond it, it becomes almost like you're talking to the audience. It's a style. Any good actor loves to play those kinds of things.

Your next show was *110 in the Shade*. What was your experience like working on that show?

Audra McDonald is a phenomenon in herself. I've watched her since she was young, and she's what I would call an elemental force. I had auditioned for the original production [1963] with Inga Swenson and Robert Horton. He was a good singer and actor and very right for it. David Merrick hired Horton and hired me to be the understudy to the two male leads for the rehearsal period. Merrick called me to his office. He offered me the understudy to Horton [for the run]. He said, "I can only pay you $225." I said, "You're paying me $250 right now!" He said, "Take it or leave it." So I left it.

You remember how much you were paid for every show!

Either that, or I make it up!

Reacting as Lizze (Audra McDonald) describes the ways in which she will be "Raunchy"—"wearin' Maybelline," in *110 on the Shade*. (Joan Marcus)

Fast forward to the revival.
Working with Audra, my big moment was when she did her number "Raunchy." I looked forward to that every night. I had no lines but she made me part of that number, which she could afford to do. I just had to react to her. I always knew she could sing beautifully but it hadn't dawned on me what a terrific actor she is.

And then, *The Scottsboro Boys*.
The thing that was so surprising to me was that it was misunderstood by a lot of people. The very concept—a takeoff of a minstrel show. They didn't get using a particular kind of storytelling in order to convey something that was too difficult to talk about in simple terms. Deep down they were trying to express something very, very personal about black people and how they are mistreated, misunderstood, taken advantage of, and accused of things. We were picketed by people who thought that we were anti-black, that we were doing stuff that was putting down the very thing that we were trying to illustrate. And those people had never seen our show. Some of the people came back and saw the show later and apologized for having criticized it so much. We had a wonderful show.

That's a show where you are up there presenting really, really raw pain. What was it like dealing with the material nightly?
Well, I was the only white boy in the show and dressed in white. Fifteen minutes before curtain time, we would all congregate downstairs, and it was like a prayer meeting with individuals giving witness or telling stories of themselves. We were a company determined to present, as best we possibly could, these Scottsboro Boys that had been misunderstood for so long. That company was dedicated to giving the Scottsboro Boys a place in history that was honest. It made me uncomfortable to play that role because I understood the character very, very well. I was not proud of the character. I was proud of the way I played it because I knew what I was doing, but it was uncomfortable.

That was the final Kander and Ebb show.
I was very aware of the absence of Ebb and very aware of his presence in spirit. And Kander—he represented years and years and years of wonderful productions, and he was just as excited as any newcomer to the scene. Everybody worked as if they were doing something important. I missed Ebb in that I wish I had known him. Kander hasn't aged in terms of his dedication to the theater. He's totally involved and holds his own with anybody—the young people or Susan Stroman or Tom Thompson or whoever's working with him. They all pay attention to him. And yet he doesn't steal the limelight at all. He just wants to participate.

Recently, you went into *Waitress*.
I enjoyed it. I had read for it originally. I was actually the first person to read for it. They didn't even have the song yet. But I was committed to *Casa Valentina*, and they wouldn't let me out. [Going into it as a replacement] was perfect because I was feeling weak at the time and this part is small, although it has some wonderful songs. The company was wonderful. They could do everything.

Do you notice a difference between a typical Broadway company these days versus when you started?
The people have gotten a lot younger!

Your career spans so many different eras and styles of theater . . .

I've just been rereading the Greeks, and I find flaws in their writing that annoy me the same way flaws annoy me in scripts that I read today. And yet I'm reading the best of the Greek theater. And I'm reading contemporary stuff and trying to compare them and it's just wonderful. Theater keeps going. Theater, as far as I'm concerned, will never die. It will just change its shape. And I think essentially the very essence of theater is communication with God. I know that sounds silly or too highfalutin', but the truth is it's man's relationship to his existence. It will never die because it's human nature. I remember in *Shenandoah,* at the end of the first act, I was singing a big number and thinking, "What in the hell am I doing? I'm standing up here. These guys are down there playing musical instruments, and a bunch of people are sitting down there watching me imitate somebody else. If somebody came from outer space and saw this, they wouldn't know what the hell to make of it." But this is what theater is. It's the essence of somebody getting up, pretending to be somebody else, and doing something that that person did, whether he was a hunter or a southern farmer in Shenandoah Valley or a sophisticated director of Broadway musicals who was down on his luck. It's always about people and their existence. And so how could it die until people die?

I should let you get back to work unless there is something else you want to say.

What I'd like to say is that I don't feel like getting back to work!

3

LEN CARIOU

January 2019; March 2019

THERE ARE BROADWAY MUSICAL THEATER actors who have done some classical theater. And then there is Len Cariou, the only leading man of musicals whose résumé includes the likes of Macbeth, Prospero, Iago, Lear, Petruchio, Oberon, Coriolanus, and Brutus. While his first professional show in his native Manitoba was *Damn Yankees* in 1959, he quickly focused on the classics, at the Stratford Shakespeare Festival and later at the Guthrie and theaters around the country. The season he made his Broadway musical debut, he also played Henry V right across the street.

That musical debut was an auspicious one, as the male lead opposite Lauren Bacall in the smash hit adaptation of *All About Eve*, *Applause*. The show won the Best Musical Tony and Cariou received both a Tony nomination and a Theatre World Award, given to the season's most promising newcomers. It was at the *Applause* "gypsy run through" (the last invited rehearsal before the public sees the show, performed for actors and other guests) that he caught the eye of Harold Prince, who cast him as Fredrik in *A Little Night Music*, a role Cariou reprised opposite Elizabeth Taylor in the film. *Sweeney Todd* followed, in 1979, and Cariou made history originating the vengeful, smoldering, blood-thirsty demon barber of Fleet Street, a role that, for many actors, has become a career Everest, waiting to be conquered, like Hamlet and Mama Rose in *Gypsy*. He took home the Tony and Drama Desk Awards and cemented his place in theater history.

After those three big hits, Cariou's musical career was followed by three disappointing flops: the Alan Jay Lerner/Charles Strouse debacle, *Dance a Little Closer*, which closed on opening night; *Teddy and Alice* in which Cariou, as Theodore Roosevelt, sang a John Philip Sousa score; and *Ziegfeld*, a West End bio-musical extravaganza that was more sparkle than substance. But Cariou, undaunted, was everywhere: film, television, regional theaters, and both on and off Broadway in straight plays including *Proof*, *The Speed of Darkness*, Neil Simon's *The Dinner Party*, and *Papa*, in which he played Ernest Hemingway. In 2004 he was inducted into the American Theater Hall of Fame. At the time of our meeting, he was in production on his eighth season of the CBS drama *Blue Bloods*, while simultaneously rehearsing a tour of his one-man, off-Broadway show, *Broadway and the Bard*.

Our conversation is, in some ways, the most difficult conversation I have had for these books, not because Cariou wasn't lovely (he was—funny, gracious, and not at all shy about dropping expletives with a throaty laugh), but because he didn't strike me as much of a talker. His answers were short and often lacking detail, but I never got the feeling that Cariou was holding back or that he was forgetting his past. Rather, I think that he is a man whose way is

"You're One of a Kind." With Lauren Bacall in Cariou's Broadway musical debut, *Applause*. (Photofest)

to simply do the work more than consider it. He is not one for navel-gazing or analyzing; he just does his thing. And at seventy-nine, he has no intention of slowing down one iota.

You went from a career of doing classics in Canada to a big Broadway musical, *Applause* on Broadway. How does that happen?

I was doing *Henry V* at Stratford, Connecticut. My agent called me and said there was this musical based on *All About Eve* and they want you to come in and audition. They were doing the auditions at the Alvin Theatre, which is now the Neil Simon. The work light was on, [director] Ron Field was in the house and he's talking to me. I couldn't even see him. He [had me read with] the stage manager [playing Margo] who was the dearest man in the world, six foot four and a screaming queen. It was all I could do to not laugh out loud. I do the scene, and Ron says, "Thanks very much." A month later, they want to see me again. [Composers] Strouse and Adams are going to be there. I said, "Okay. But could we have a woman for me to read with?" I do the second audition and they're out there, and I hear voices, but I still don't see any faces. And they call me a third time. What the fuck is going on here? This time it's because Bacall is going to be there and she has to approve her leading man. And the producer's going to be there, and [book writers] Comden and Green . . . So I come in, and I do the final audition. By that time, *Henry V* was going to be playing at the ANTA Theatre when we were through in Stratford. So I do the final audition and everybody comes up to introduce themselves to me. Ron says, "If it were up to me, you're my choice. But it's not up to me. Remind me what you're doing again at the moment?" I said, "Come with me, Ron." We walk out the stage door and the Alvin's right across the street from the ANTA. There were three six-foot photographs of me as *Henry V*. And I went, "That's what I'm doing. Bring them out and show them. Just point that out to them, just for my satisfaction." Doing *Henry V*, the voice was in good shape. And they were impressed. I was at the peak of my power. So I finally got the job, and we're going out of town for tryouts. We were the first people in the Mechanic Theater in Baltimore. We do a gypsy run-through at the Shubert, and I'd never done one before. The joint was packed, of course. And they all went nuts. A lot of them came up on the stage afterwards and I was cornered. I'm standing there, saying thank you to a lot of people I've never met and Ron comes up and says, "What did Hal say?" I said, "Hal who?" "Hal who? Hal Prince!" "I don't know who Hal is." [He pointed him out to me] and I said, "Do you really want to know what he said? He said, 'Congratulations on one of the best leading men I've seen in a long time. I hope we work together sometime.'" I didn't know who he was.

Len Cariou	
Applause	Broadway, 1970
A Little Night Music	Broadway, 1973
Sweeney Todd (Tony Award)	Broadway, 1979
Dance a Little Closer	Broadway, 1983
Up from Paradise	Off-Broadway, 1983
Teddy & Alice	Broadway, 1987
Show Boat	National Tour, 1997
Ziegfeld	West End, 1998
No Strings	Encores!, 2003
Broadway and the Bard	Off-Broadway, 2016

That's probably for the best.

Yeah, right. Exactly. All my family, all my brothers and sisters and their husbands and wives, and my mother, and my mother's sister, all came to the opening. There were thirteen of them.

Lauren Bacall was a huge star doing her first musical. What was it like navigating those waters?

It was an enormous undertaking for her. She wasn't a singer. She was nervous all the time and I just said to her, "Betty, you're going to be wonderful. You forget how sexy you are and how you've got this thing by the throat. You don't have to worry." She wasn't a great dancer and she banged up her leg pretty good, but she got by. And we became lovers during the run of the show. She had a lot of responsibility. I then realized what that was.

You mean leading a company?

Yeah, right. And what it meant. I think I was helpful to her in that play. I said, "You've got to be good and strong, but you don't have to be a bitch. You can be good and strong and spoiled, too." And I think for the most part that's how it went.

What can you tell me about working with Betty Comden and Adolph Green?

Adolph was the outgoing one of the two. Betty had a great sense of humor, but Adolph was always kibitzing around. They were a great deal of fun to be around. I was a bit of a rookie, but I thought, "Well, I am going to go in there as if I have been doing this my whole life." They were all very positive people. When I had my nightclub act in Winnipeg, I sang "Put on a Happy Face." It didn't occur to me until I was in rehearsals and Charlie Strouse was playing the piano, and I thought, "Jesus, this guy wrote that song." Didn't seem possible. It was very heady stuff. And you think, "This is going to be really good!"

You won the Theatre World Award and were nominated for a Tony.

They announced the Tony nominations just after the opening, so my folks were still here. It was pretty exciting. And Betty was nominated and the show was, and so it was great. I had won the Theatre World Award for doing *Henry V* and doing *Applause* in the same year, so that was pretty exciting, too. It was very exhilarating. It's everybody's dream to be in a hit on Broadway. It changes everything. You walk with a little more pep in your step. You've got a smile on your face and you're living the life. And then at the end of the year, I went back to the Guthrie.

And was that just because you were ready to move on?

Yeah, I just wanted to do Shakespeare again. That's really my first love.

I think that a lot of actors who had made a mark in New York as you had would want to stick around and try to build on that. Going off to do Shakespeare at the Guthrie is an unusual move. Did you perceive it that way at the time or . . .

I didn't. Betty did. My agents, of course, said, "What the fuck are you doing?" And I said, "C'mon, guys, I don't see people running up to me saying 'I've got another musical for you.' There's an incredible, wonderful theater saying 'C'mon back, c'mon back.' And so I'm going back. Everybody knows what I did in *Applause*, and you're my guys that are here. If something comes up, I can fly from Minneapolis or anywhere else in the world."

Well, your next New York musical was *A Little Night Music* so that chance meeting with Hal Prince bore fruit.

Yeah, it did. He sends me the script in Minneapolis and says, "We'd like you to consider playing Carl-Magnus." There are no lyrics, but this is the script by Hugh Wheeler. It read like a novel. And it was just gorgeous. Really strongly written. Great book musical. And Sondheim. I didn't want to miss the chance to sing for Sondheim, but I didn't want to play Carl-Magnus. That's a role I played twenty times in my life, but I thought, "I've got to sing for Sondheim." So I came and I sang. And Hal said to me, "We've got a new version of the script, and we've got some lyrics in it. Why don't you take them home and read it and we'll talk tomorrow." I read it, and "Now/Soon/Later" is in there. I knew it was going to be good, but I didn't think it was going to be that good. It's really good. Hal calls me and says, "How did you like it?" I said, "It's outrageous. The opening number that Fredrik has?" And he said, "Yeah, that's who we want you to play." "What?"

Famously, *Night Music* started rehearsals with only half of the score done. Did it feel unsettling that so much of the score wasn't there yet?

Oh, yeah. And my character was to have the eleventh-hour song and it wasn't being written. Steve couldn't write it. He would be up for twenty-two hours writing stuff. But anyway, we're going along in the rehearsal process, and there's nothing left to rehearse except this scene, which we've been avoiding, waiting for the music. It still wasn't there. So we do a rehearsal of this scene and we improvised a little. We kicked that around for about an hour or two, and honed it, and improved it. We play the scene for Steve, and I remember he looked like death warmed over. I mean, he had a cold, and he was—he really looked miserable. He said, "That's interesting." And he got up and left. And Hal said, "That's Steve." So about three or four days later, he comes in and the whole company is there. He says, "Sorry, Len. You don't sing this song anymore. She does." And he proceeds [with "Send in the Clowns"]. "Isn't it rich? Are we a pair?" So it's my song. When we were in New York, about to preview, Victoria Mallory and Glynis Johns and I go out to dinner, and the next day, we get a phone call. Glynis is in the hospital. What? I just said goodnight to her ten hours before. But what nobody had told me was that she had a drinking problem. She didn't say anything and nobody had told me that we can't let her drink. She fell off the wagon and it poisoned her. She was bedridden at the hospital. They approached Tammy Grimes [to replace her].But Glynis rebounded.

What do you remember about working with her? It was an interesting choice to cast a woman with the perfect essence but not much of a singing voice and then write around that, although I guess you had just gone through that with *Applause*.
I did. Glynis had—Glynis's is still the best recording of "Send in the Clowns" that there is, no matter who does it. When we were recording it, everybody leaves and Glynis is going to record "Send in the Clowns." I stick around because I'm going to do the reprise. And Glynis is terrified because it's going to be on a record. It's not like we're doing it every night. She's wired. I said, "Glyni, I'll stay here, and you can sing it to me like we do it in the show." She does it on the first take, and it's good, it's good. Nothing from the booth. And I'm looking at [musical director] Gemignani, and I'm looking at [album producer Thomas] Shepherd. And then we hear "Glynis, it's Goddard Lieberson [legendary former head of Cast Albums at Columbia]. I'm coming in. I just have a note for you." He comes in, and he walks up to her and says. "It's a torch song." It's not a torch song, but that was his note. He turned around and walked away. In her head, that seemed to relax her. And that's the recording.

After that, did you notice a difference in her performance on stage, with that note in her head? Did it change anything in her performance?
I think it may have.

From what I understand from others, that's not the kind of note Hal would ever give. He's not one to direct actors in their interpretations.
That, I think, was one of his great talents. Let the actors take care of that part and I'll take care of the rest. So that was absolutely true. I don't think Stephen ever would have thought of that [note] either. But obviously Goddard . . .

Do you remember the process of putting that show together as joyous? Or arduous? Or simply as just work?
Oh, no. It was genius stuff. It was joyous.

And you knew it was genius as you were doing it? Because sometimes I think people don't. Sometimes you're just doing a job, and only in retrospect do you go, "Wow, that was amazing."

"You must meet my wife." "Yes, I must. I really must." With Glynis Johns in *A Little Night Music*. (Photofest)

I knew as soon as I had the lyrics to "Now/Soon/Later." I thought, "Oh, this is fucking unbelievable."

Broadway in the '70s was very different, wasn't it? People partied a lot after their shows.
We were all hanging out at bars; Joe Allen's and Jimmy Ray's. That was where all of the hard-nosed actors went to drink. I got in with that bunch. We had some knock-down drag-outs there. Booze battles. George C. Scott used to drink there and he got into it a couple of times. It was like that. On Tuesdays and Fridays, because of the matinee the next day, it became sort of an unwritten law that you stayed until 3:00 in the morning, and then you had to show up sober and on time for the matinee.

To prove that you could handle it?
Yes.

That sounds insane!
It was insane. Everyone was doing it so I went along for the ride.

No one would ever do that now.
And yet, I was talking with Penny Fuller the other day and she was telling me how young people in her cast [*Anastasia*] take "personal days." We would never do that. Ever. There was something about not missing a show, and I didn't. Never missed one. I was pissed when people took vacations.

You never took a vacation?
Never.

With *Night Music*, you got another Tony nomination in another show that won Best Musical. Two for two.
Three, if you count *Sweeney* [his next show].

At a certain point, do you start to feel like this is just the way it goes?
Well, I was really disappointed when I didn't get the Tony for *Night Music* because when we arrived, I was able to see the competition [Ben Vereen, Robert Morse, and Brock Peters]. It was all playing already. And I thought it's a shoo-in. Whereas with *Applause*, I thought, "I don't deserve this."

But it was a happy run for you?
Oh, very.

And then, of course, you're off doing the classics again when Hal calls to say . . .
I'm offered the job of artistic director at the theater that I began at in Winnipeg. I take the job with the proviso that the only thing that can break the contract is a musical. That's in the contract. I'm in Winnipeg and we're going to do *Company*. So I called Hal and said, "Would you mind sending me a copy of the stage manager's book from your production?" And he said, "Okay. Sure. And by the way, Stephen has a written a musical for you." By the way?????

Before we get to *Sweeney Todd*, we should talk about the film of *A Little Night Music*.
Oh, that phone call! Wakes me up in the middle of the night. "Len, it's Hal. Can you get a plane and come over here [London]? We need you to come and be in the film of *Night Music*." So I get on the next flight that I can get on and [book writer] Hugh Wheeler meets me. He says, "They're in there recording with the symphony. And you've got to go and meet Elizabeth Taylor." So we get in the cab, and I arrive, and Steve and Hal are there, and they're doing "Send in the Clowns." I'm introduced to her. We go into the booth. And she's not a singer either and doesn't know music. She's a little nervous, obviously. I said, "I'll help you. When it's time to come in, I'll tap you." So we did that. She was very appreciative. And there I was playing Fredrik again.

Gaining her trust as soon as you got off the plane probably served you well throughout the shoot.
It did, yeah. It did.

And I read that you were bored out of your mind in Vienna.
It's a pretty boring place.

Hugh Wheeler said of Elizabeth Taylor, "[She] is such a complicated personality. She could easily drive you crazy. You could fall madly in love with her, and then you want to kill her, and then you fall madly in love with her all over again." Was that your experience?
Yeah, pretty much, pretty much. She had a luncheon party where she was staying, and she had Iranian gold caviar—gold-colored caviar that's so ridiculously expensive. Elizabeth has not an ounce of makeup on and [after the party] she's going to go shopping. She sits down and starts piling on the makeup. I said, "Elizabeth, what are you doing that for?" She said, "It's my mask. I can't go out without makeup on." So she does the full Kabuki makeup and gets in the car. She felt she couldn't go out the door without having full eye makeup and all that.

What did you think of the film?
I thought it was pretty damn good, but they wanted them to remake *Smiles of a Summer Night*. And they were gunning for her. They weren't very kind or didn't want to be kind to her.

Did you feel happy to have your Fredrik preserved?
Absolutely. It was never meant to be. First, it was Peter Finch. He was a drunk so . . .

That's the second time you've brought up alcohol, and it does seem accepting the addictions of actors who are legendary drinkers like Richard Burton or Peter O'Toole is a thing of the past. It's not part of our culture now.
Oh, I think it is still. Not to that extent perhaps. I think that turnaround was when I came on the scene, when a lot of actors who worked in the regional theaters came to Broadway. They had this classical experience that nobody else here had. We'd all come out of the regional theater movement.

That movement that you're talking about could not happen now because there isn't really a lot of opportunity for classically trained actors to come to New York and do *Henry V* on Broadway any more. But being trained in drama of Shakespearian proportions is likely what made you the person to get that call from Hal Prince saying, "By the way, Steve's written a musical for you."
"It's called *Sweeney Todd: The Demon Barber of Fleet Street*." Really? Okay. I was in rehearsal for *Equus*, and I read it, and I go, "Holy shit. They've lost their minds." I re-read it and thought that if Steve writes a romantic score, it might work. They're going to go into rehearsal at the end of November, so I had no work for like six or seven months. I got an offer to do a film and shoot it in Alberta and that would mean me missing the first week of rehearsal. I went to Hal, [who agreed to that] and asked, "Do you think Steve would give me music so that I'm not behind the eight ball when I get there, and I can work on it while I'm in Canada?" Steve agreed. So I go to Steve's home, and I'd been there before but only at parties. I'd never been in the composing room. There we are in the composing room and he's nervous. I'm the one who's supposed to be nervous. He was just nervous, fidgety. He said, "Excuse me," and he leaves the room. He comes back with a joint, and he lights it, takes a couple of tokes, offers some to me. Then he says, "You know the Catholic Mass for the Dead?" I said, "Steve, I'm a Catholic, French Irish, (singing 'Dies Irae')." He says, "Listen to this." [hums]. "I don't get it." He says, "That's "Dies Irae" backwards." I said, "Oh, you're a sick fuck; aren't you?" He laughed. So he plays that for me and "Barber and His Wife." I was in tears. It took me about two weeks to not cry when I sang that. It still does that to me. And then he hands me what I thought was a New York phone book. It's "A Little Priest," and I'm on the floor. That was some afternoon. So I take this music with me and I go to Canada.

I can't imagine having heard that music for the first time and thinking anything other than "I am the luckiest fucker ever."
That's exactly right. That's exactly what I said. I told myself, "This is fucking incredible." I'd met Angela Lansbury before, but we'd never worked together. There was instant rapport there.

She was actually the first person to tell me that Hal Prince leaves the performance choices to the actor. But this is a script that actually calls for you to go outside the boundaries of sanity. I would imagine that modulation could be a real challenge.

We were really proud that we didn't go [over the top]. I said, "We've got to be really careful that we don't or it'll turn to rat shit." We had to be conscious of it. We kept each other in check. We were pretty proud of toeing that line for that whole year. And I think Hal was astounded by the consistency of it. I know Stephen was. At the end of the first preview—and we lost some people at the intermission, but at the end of it, they were on their feet. We took our bows and congratulated one another and I go to my dressing room. Steve is standing outside the dressing room and he says, "They understood it! They fucking understood it!" And we had a great hug. He was just beside himself. I said, "Now if we can get the Goddamn set to work we'll be all right." But that was pretty joyous. [One night, during the scene] when we discovered that Toby knows what we're up to and we go looking for him, the stage is bare and floodlights are on me and Angela. Can't see a thing. [I hear] "click, click, click, click, click." The music is going strong. We walk downstage, making kind of a serpentine movement. I hear this clicking sound. I look up and the bridge is coming down. I grab Angela and bring her downstage. And "wham," behind us. The fucking set fell. Would have killed anyone. We had to stop the show. That was something.

What was it like to maintain both vocally and emotionally for the year?
If you're singing properly, it's no different than [anything else]. People would say, "How the fuck did you do that eight times a week?" Once it's in your voice, it's there.

I think there are other actors who would find it challenging.
Then they're not singing properly. If you're singing properly, you can sing anything for any length of time.

Or at least, perhaps you can.
Yeah. I was one of those people. I mean, recording *Sweeney Todd*, I had diagnosed strep throat.

And you didn't ask to reschedule?
Couldn't. I was just singing properly. I went to Wilbur James Gold, who was the preeminent nose/throat guy at that time, and he said I should be on vocal rest. I said, "As long as I'm alive, nobody is going to sing the songs because I can sing them." He put me on antibiotics and said, "Whatever you're doing, keep doing it. I can't see any [physical] harm, but I really wish you would rest." Not a chance. And I thought, "Well, that proves I'm singing properly. It just proves it to me."

What about the emotional impact? I mean, that's a lot to carry. Even if you leave it at the stage door, it's a lot.
Well, remember, I played Lear.

Yes, for a shorter time.
Well, doesn't matter.

You think? I've heard people say that your body doesn't know that you're acting, so the things that you feel—your body's reacting. In a long run like that, you're feeling it over time. That can be impactful to people.
Yeah, I guess. But it wasn't.

Michael Cerveris told me that you said the show made you drink.
I drank anyway.

Did you see other productions of it?
I saw his. *Silly Sweeney.*

Why do you call it that?
It was silly. The interpretation was that it was all through Toby's eyes. So if you're in an insane asylum, how does "Epiphany" happen? Every day? Get the fuck out of here.

You won the Tony for *Sweeney*.
Well, when I realized with *Night Music* what a crap shoot the Tony was, I said, "Maybe I'll be nominated [and not win] for the rest of my life. They're liable to give it to anybody." But at that point, I knew what it was, and I thought, "It doesn't really matter if I don't win the Tony Award."

Did it matter more when you did win?
Yeah, sure it did. I mean, I thought I was right, and they finally got it right. And I think in my acceptance speech I said, "This is a cutthroat business." But yeah, it was nice. And Angela won, and we got best musical . . .

That is a show that was a financial failure but has come to be revered as one of the all-time greats. Do you take pride in that?
Yeah, I do. You knew something right from the get-go. And it was very satisfying to know that we were right. This thing is a piece of genius. And I had a lot to do with it. John Logan

With Angela Lansbury. Setting a very high bar for all future Sweeneys and earning a Tony in *Sweeney Todd*. (Photofest)

wrote the screenplay [for the film]. He told me he was seventeen when he saw it from the last row of the Uris Theatre. He said, "You scared the shit out of me. I was absolutely scared shitless. I thought, 'My God, I got to be a part of this somehow.'" And he ends up writing the goddamn screenplay.

Do you like the film?
No.

Why?
No humor.

Angela Lansbury told me the same thing. Your next show looked, I am guessing, very attractive on paper. A Charles Strouse/Alan Jay Lerner score . . .
Dance a Little Closer? Yeah. It was based on *Idiot's Delight*. But Alan wanted to direct it because I guess he did not like the direction that people had done with his stuff. He shouldn't have directed because he wrote the book, too. He adapted the thing and I think he was overwhelmed by it somewhat. But Charlie wrote some really good music. And Liz Robertson was very good. It was just unfortunate, I think.

Charles Strouse said in his book that going in, he had some red flags which he chose to ignore. One was, as you've pointed out, that your director's also your book writer and your lyricist. And then, is also married to your leading lady. What made you sign on?
Well, it was him [Lerner]. And it's a good story. It just wasn't well told.

Tell me about Lerner.
He was a very romantic man. I enjoyed him very much. He had this terrible habit of biting his cuticles and his fingers would be bleeding. During rehearsals, he had white gloves that he would put on because everyone would say, "Stop biting your fucking cuticles!" But they would bleed and the blood would stick to the gloves and he would take them off. There would be these two blood stained gloves on the floor in front of wherever he had been sitting. He was pretty highly strung. He smoked like a chimney. He had a great, sharp mind, but he couldn't see the tree for the woods. He loved romance. [After the show had closed] I gave Heather an engagement ring on her birthday. She went to the Park Lane to show it to Alan and Liz. Alan was not feeling well. It was the start of the descent. He was in bed. Liz and Heather then went to lunch at the Oyster Bar. All of a sudden in comes a guy with a bouquet of roses for Heather. He was given the instruction to walk through the entire restaurant, calling her name, and he delivered these roses to her.

He really did love romance.
He had eight of them [wives], remember!

***Dance a Little Closer* was your first flop after three massively successful musicals in a row. We don't have one-performance flops any more. It doesn't happen. Do you remember it feeling like a shock to the system?**
Oh, yeah. It was a shock. And my wife, Heather, said to me, "Let's go to the dressing room and open the gifts." I hadn't opened them the night before. So we went, and I opened the letters and the gifts in my dressing room at the Minskoff, and then we went to see *Monty Python and the Holy Grail*.

Were you ready for those reviews? Did you know it wasn't working?

Yeah. Yeah. But I didn't think we'd open and close in one night. We get awakened with a phone call. The show is closing. We're not doing another performance.

That same year you did the off-Broadway musical *Up from Paradise*. An Arthur Miller musical!

And I got to play God. I did the song a la Tony Bennett.

That was your God? Tony Bennett is God?

Yeah. We did it at the Jewish Rep. And they were thrilled to have Miller. He was around a bit. Interesting man. Kind of like an old philosopher. If you were talking to him on a break, he might be waxing about the situation in the country or something like that. The show was fun but I don't remember it that well.

***Teddy & Alice* was next, a few years later.**

That was fun. The Shuberts shafted us there. They wanted to bring *Chess* in to the Imperial, so they wanted to move *Cabaret* to the Minskoff and kick us out. The producers just couldn't afford to move us. It's a quarter of a million dollars to do something like that. And the joke was that *Cabaret* ended up closing. We probably could have run quite a bit longer if it weren't for the theater thing. But I think *Teddy & Alice* was a good show. People loved it.

How about the experience of taking on Teddy Roosevelt?

I was up for that. I've also played FDR in the film *Into the Storm*. Somebody said the only one left for me to play is Eleanor. It was a very pleasant experience. Beth Fowler was wonderful in it.

That was the height of the mega-musical. *Phantom* had just opened. Both *Cats* and *Les Mis* were selling out. I wonder if a John Philip Sousa musical was not a good fit for the moment.

Probably. And Brantley was then the critic for *The Times*—and I know this because somebody who worked for *The Times* told me—he did not want to go and see it. He said so out loud. He had [practically] written his review already.

In his review he said, "If the show's creators had any respect for the dead, they would not give the defenseless Mr. Lerner partial artistic credit for such a bad show." [Alan Jay Lerner was credited for the idea but died before the show was written.] Those are some harsh words. Do you even read reviews?

No. I've made a practice of not reading them when I'm working. I read them after. Because if you believe the good ones, you got to believe the bad ones. Don't bother. You're the best judge of whether you did it right or you did it wrong. And having been around and having done the volume of work that I had done, you get to know. You just get to know what your chances are of it being a success. Even when you're doing Shakespeare, there's no guarantee. If you work with enough bad directors, you can learn to fend for yourself. And I had my share of that. I've had my share of the great ones, too.

You had another very big flop after *Teddy & Alice*: *Ziegfeld*.

You can only preview so long in London, and then you have to open. [We weren't ready.] It's the last thing [director] Joe Layton did. We were working on it and working on the book. And Harold Fielding, the producer, fired Joe. The plan was that while we were playing it [after opening], we'd be working on improving it, which you would have done anyway in previews. That is why virtually every show went out of town. And then Fielding fired me.

It's a very peculiar choice to fire your lead actor three weeks after you've opened.
Yeah. Well, he was not playing with all the marbles.

What was the experience like prior to the firing?
Well, it was pleasant enough. Really. Joe was a great guy. We had a great time in rehearsal. I had all those beautiful women around me. That was not hard to take. And then he fires me and says to the press something about me not understanding musicals. [Fielding said "The production was just bigger than the star."] After the evening show I gathered the cast around and told them.

You would think that the producer would take that on.
Yeah. Well, he didn't.

Did it sour you at all? Did it make you think, "I'm sticking with Shakespeare because this is a bummer?"
Yeah, I think maybe it did. It was sad.

You did take quite a hiatus from musicals for a while, but you did go out in '97 on the *Show Boat* tour opposite Cloris Leachman. Was that just another phone call from Hal Prince?
Yeah, pretty much. That was kind of fun, but she was—she has no discipline whatsoever. She would do anything. And I think had no clue as to what upstaging was. Didn't know. But kind of charming in her own way. But it was a good time. There were four *Show Boat* companies on the road at one time. [Producer] Garth Drabinsky was the go big or go home guy. You go, "How the fuck is this possible? How can he make any money?" But it was nice people. Except for Cloris.

In 2004 you were inducted into the Theater Hall of Fame. Did that give you a moment to consider your place, if you will, in the . . .
In the pantheon? Yeah, I think so. Yeah. And I thought, "I'm only half done here."

Still feel that way?
Yeah. Well, not really half done. Maybe three-quarters done by now. But it seemed a little premature. But a nice honor.

Well, when you say you're only three-quarters done, what else would you like to be doing? What do you want to do still?
Well, I'm doing a piece called *Broadway and the Bard*, which I did in 2016 off-Broadway, and then I toured it. I'm going to do it again.

Just because you want to?
Yeah. It was great, great fun to create. I had the original idea when we did *Applause* and *Henry V*. It takes some of the great soliloquies of roles that I've played and Broadway show tunes that either make a comment on or support the text. I thought, when we were creating it, that it would be a cabaret but it's a real theater piece. It's about eighty minutes long. We didn't print a program because I didn't want anybody looking at what I was going to do.

You have frequently said that you believe that actors atrophy when they're not working and that you have to keep at it, which I think may explain the amount of work that you do. And now you are a regular on a series. In the '70s you said that you would never do a series, and here you are doing one. Is that because you want to just keep working, or is it because the business has changed and . . .

Well, it's both. When I was in my twenties and thirties, I used to go to L.A. every spring for pilot season. I couldn't get arrested. So after about three or four years of that, I said, "I'm going to have a stage career and maybe when I'm seventy, I'll have a television series." And I was seventy [when I got one]. But you just have to exercise the muscle. And going into regional theaters, you're not making a hell of a lot of money, but you just have to work. I did that. I decided, "I can't sit here and not do anything, and I'm not going to be taking classes, and I'm not going to wait tables." I [was set to do *Death of a Salesman* in Dublin] and I came home one day, and Heather greeted me at the door and handed me this script. She said, "It's a television series called *Reagan's Law*. Tom Selleck is attached, and you're fucked because it's going to go, and you're going to have to say no to *Death of a Salesman*." "C'mon. What is the part?" "It's Tom Selleck's father." I said, "Well, fuck off. I'm about five years older than he is. Nobody's going to buy that in the first place." It was a three-line part. That was all they had written for this character. I go in for it, and then they call me for a second audition. I said, "Are they giving me another character?" No, they've rewritten the scene. Now it's five lines. Third time, I tell my manager to tell them to go fuck themselves. Two days later, I had the role.

And now it's been eight years! But do you hope to still do another musical?

Oh yeah. But whatever comes comes. I had a pretty good track record. *Sweeney* is the crown jewel of it for sure. But I just know that you got to keep going after it or you dry up. Theater is the actors' medium. So I am glad for *Broadway and the Bard*, which I am very proud of. I have always worked. Never had any down time of length at all. I like the action.

4

BEN VEREEN

November 2019

THE SWEEPING VIEW OF CENTRAL PARK from Ben Vereen's sixty-fourth floor apartment; the Tony Award on display in front of the six-foot subway poster from *Pippin* featuring an image of Vereen, fingers splayed, sparkling with magic to do; the glamor acquired over decades of stardom; all of it seems almost at odds with the small, soft-spoken man in an *Avenue Q* T-shirt ("Donald Trump is only for now"), with his leg up, recuperating from a knee surgery. I am not describing a diminished elder (I saw Vereen in concert weeks earlier and he delivered as much razzle-dazzle as one would hope for) but rather, a man of dichotomy. He is the guy who palled around with the likes of Sammy Davis Jr. and Liza Minnelli, who had his own variety show, who lived large and lavishly. But he is also the guy who has had a persistent cough ever since he spent weeks volunteering at Ground Zero in the immediate aftermath of the 9/11 attacks in 2001. He works hard at his spirituality and posts affirmations daily. His life is one of tremendous highs but also one that has had an outsized share of suffering. He smiles a great deal as he recounts his history and the people in it, but he is also easily brought to tears and moments of thoughtful, quiet reflection.

Ben Vereen grew up in Bedford-Stuyvesant and became a performer only because a teacher noticed talent and encouraged it at a time when raw talent alone was enough to propel a youngster forward. He went to the High School of Performing Arts and got work immediately following, first in an off-Broadway play, and then in the Las Vegas company (and then film version) of *Sweet Charity*, beginning his lifelong association with Bob Fosse. After a stint in the original production of *Hair*, that show's director, Tom O'Horgan, chose him to play Judas in the original Broadway production of *Jesus Christ Superstar*, netting him his first Tony nomination. But it was the following year when Fosse hired him as the sinewy Leading Player in *Pippin* that a star was born. As a handsome young man who could sing, dance, and act in the '70s, when club acts and variety shows were big, Vereen was a hot commodity. He spent the next decade on the road and in Hollywood, most notably with his indelible portrayal of Chicken George in the groundbreaking mini-series, *Roots*. He returned to Broadway in 1985 with the ill-fated *Grind*. And then things got very dark.

In 1987, his sixteen-year-old daughter, Naja, was killed in a freak car accident. Then in 1992, Vereen had his own car accident that led to a stroke (about which he remembers nothing). Late that night he apparently got out of bed and veered into the street while walking down the Malibu Highway. He was struck by a truck. His injuries were critical and numerous. He couldn't speak and was told he'd never dance again. It was only after a long, painful,

Pippin's "Manson Trio"—"Tah-dah!" (Photofest)

arduous rehabilitation that he returned to the stage, first in *Jelly's Last Jam* and then in *Chicago*, *Fosse*, and *Wicked*.

As I sit with Vereen, it's hard to know what he is really thinking. Like his dear friend, Chita Rivera, he is fiercely committed to positivity. He therefore says very little that one might call negative. The memories he shares are disproportionately good ones. Is that self-censorship? Is it for my benefit? Or does he truly manage always to find the positive and dismiss the negative wherever he can? I can't say. But the Vereen I met seems, despite having lived through incredible trauma, very much at peace.

What sparked your interest in going to the High School of Performing Arts?

My principal, Benjamin Raskin, saw me in a production of *The King and I* and he suggested that I go. I knew nothing of it. When I went to the audition, it was the strangest thing I think I'd ever seen. There were kids who were really into the arts. I had never been into the arts. I was into street dancing and hanging out with the kids on the block and church and things of that nature. I never thought about the performing arts. These kids were wearing tights and leotards. I wore a pair of Bermuda shorts and a T-shirt. I made up my dance to "Killer Joe." They made up their dances to Brahms and Beethoven. I didn't do well at the audition. I wasn't that good. I was lucky because that year they needed boys, and the next thing I know, we got a letter from the school saying that I was accepted. Now, once you're accepted to the school, you have to go out and get the dance clothes. I wasn't used to wearing tights and dance belts and ballet slippers. We went to a place called Capezio, and I got my dance belt, my tights, white T-shirt, and we went home. My mother gave me an attaché case and she said, "Put your clothes in here and take them to school." So I fold them up neatly in my attaché case. I put on my blue continental suit, which I wore with my tie and my Thom McAns, and I was off to school. The first day the class had to line up, and the teachers came out to welcome us. Norman Walker, David Woods, Malinka, Gertrude Scherr, and sitting at the table were George Balanchine, Jerome Robbins, Martha Graham. I didn't know who they were. It was a bunch of white people. They looked important, but I wasn't thinking about that too much. Important to me was the block. I wasn't thinking, "What's this?" So they asked us to go inside and put on our clothes and get ready for class. I'll never forget. I went inside, put on my clothes for dance, and I put my suit back on because I thought that was the proper thing to do. So I go back on line. Everybody's standing in their tights and leotards and I had a suit on. I thought they were wrong, I was right. I'm standing in line, and the dance principal, Dr. Yokum, says to me, "Are you taking class today?" "Yes, yes, yes, I am." "Well, where's your uniform?" "I have it on under here." "Get back in there and take that suit off." And then I met Gertrude Scherr, little lady. She was powerful. She had guys bend over. She'd stand on our backs. And I liked it. Something happened. It clicked. I just fell in love with it. We had to do a concert—a demonstration of modern dance. And David Woods, who was the architect of the dance of Martha Graham, he was very strict, and he said if you miss rehearsal, you're out. It was Winston Hemsley and Jerry Grimes and me. We're the only three boys left in class [of the original ten]. Then Winston got a job somewhere, and he missed rehearsal. He's out. So it was Jerry and me. And then Jerry was unable to make rehearsal, and I was the only boy in the group. They put me in the middle. I learned all this great stuff. And there was another teacher there who really taught me how to dance, Tony Catanzaro. Tony Catanzaro went on to head the Florida Ballet Company and now is retired and still teaching dancing. He started me out. He would work with me after school. Vinnette Carroll, who was the drama teacher, asked me to do an off-Broadway show, *The Prodigal Son*, after graduation. So that was my first show. She was wonderful. It was a small cast. One night I had this grievance with the cast, and I was storming out of the theater. There was a man standing there and he asked me, "Where's the men's dressing room?" I pointed to the men's dressing room. He says, "I'm looking for Benjamin Vereen." I said, "I am Benjamin Vereen. What do you want?" He says, "My name's Langston Hughes, and you look like you could use some dinner." So he took me to dinner. And we became good friends.

What was Langston Hughes doing looking for you?

He wrote the play. Good man. I went to Harlem for the first time with him. He gave me a few of his books. We talked for hours. He told me so many great stories. And from there, things got real thin as they do. [I did *West Side Story, Annie Get Your Gun*, and *Guys and Dolls* in summer stock.] And then I came back to Brooklyn.

Ben Vereen

Sweet Charity	Las Vegas, National Tour, 1967
Hair	Broadway, 1968; National Tour, 1969
Golden Boy	West End, 1968
Jesus Christ Superstar	Broadway, 1971
Pippin (Tony Award)	Broadway, 1972
Grind	Broadway, 1985
Jelly's Last Jam	Broadway, 1993
A Christmas Carol	Off-Broadway, 1995
Chicago	Las Vegas, National Tour, 1999
Fosse	Broadway, 2001
Wicked	Broadway, 2005

But it wasn't long before the audition for *Sweet Charity* came about.

I was living on Eastern Parkway right across from the Brooklyn Museum. I jumped the turnstile because I had no money and I went to New York. I stood on the corner reading "Backstage" and there was an audition for a show called *Sweet Charity*. I'd never been to a Broadway show, you know, because I couldn't afford it. I'd walk down the streets and look at the marquees. I wandered over to the Palace, and stood in line with thousands of people. That's when I met Bob Fosse. Bob Fosse came down the aisle as cool as he was, and Eddie Gasper was his assistant dance captain. I auditioned for the show, sang for the first time in a theater, and next thing you know Bob hired me, and I was on the way to rehearsals for *Sweet Charity* in Las Vegas.

You're at your first Broadway audition. You're on stage at the Palace Theatre. You just described thousands of people, and you've said before that it was like the opening scene of *All That Jazz* where the stage is just full of dancers. Did you feel intimidated?

I don't know if I felt ready for it. It's something I had to do. I needed a job. I didn't know who Bob Fosse was. I was just among the crowd. I was happy to be among the crowd. I didn't realize how important it was. I didn't realize how important Bob Fosse was and all the people in the house, Jeb Bernstein, Cy Coleman. These cats, I didn't know, I was just doing my thing.

And you booked it!

Yeah, yeah. It was exciting. You know what was exciting for me? Them sending me down to the costume shop and having them measure me for a costume. They were making me clothes, Man. That was like, "Wow! This is a kid from Brooklyn, and they were making clothes, they're making my shoes. I don't have to buy them?" When I got my costume, I was shocked.

Were your parents supportive? Did they get it?

Oh, yeah, my mother. My father did not. He didn't really get it until I was on TV in *Roots*. He loved TV. He never went to the theater. They were workers in factories, garment companies and things of that nature. And here I was—it was like I was going off to Mars. It's unknown territory. But my mom was saying, "You got to do this, do this." When I told her that I got in *Sweet Charity*, she said, "That's nice."

So leaving for Vegas . . . was it terrifying or exciting or both?

It was exciting. I'd never been on a plane. In my neighborhood in those days, Brooklyn was it. I had never heard of Las Vegas before. This beautiful woman, Juliet Prowse, was starring. Gorgeous. And there was another woman there named Paula Kelly. We were good friends.

***Sweet Charity* was the first Broadway show to play Vegas. What do you remember?**

I'm just finding my way. We got there, and I had to get a car and apartment.

You must have been with dancers who had worked with Fosse and already understood his style.

Yes. Bob was a very strict director. He was a perfectionist. He worked us hard and we were glad he did. It was amazing the work he'd get out of us. And we had a little connection. He really enjoyed the way I sang. He pulled me out to do some things for him, so it was nice. The thing about Bob that I found amazing was that he would take time to show you and explain things to you. But then he expected you not to have to ask him again. You should know it. And you did. Fine detail. That's what I think I learned, fine detail. Paying attention to the vibe and the pictures. He was great. We were there for six months, I believe, and everybody would hit the mark every time.

You were really a blank slate at that point. I imagine you were a sponge.
I was. I think I just made enough money to get my apartment back in Brooklyn because they had a padlock on my door. I had to climb up the fire escape and go through the window. Hadn't paid the rent.

Did you not have a survival job between *Prodigal Son* and *Charity*? You never waited tables?
No, I never—I don't knock that. I wish I had. I would teach every now and then and get a little money here and there. And I was hanging out at Bernice Johnson Studio in Jamaica with Jerry Grimes and Winston Hemsley. These cats . . . Michael Peters, Lester Wilson. I'd find myself going out there all the time, and we'd have these dance classes, man, we'd dance all night. All night! We'd come back, and we'd go off to school the next day.

So what I'm hearing is that at that time you were consumed with dance.
Oh, yes. That's all I had. I used to sing in church in a quartet group, but this was new, fresh. In those days I would go into a warehouse with nothing but a record player and just dance for hours, for hours.

Just for yourself.
Just for myself. I miss that.

Did you ever feel like you had made it, or was it putting one foot in front of the other?
Still is. Ours is not a career that is solid like that. It's audition to audition, paycheck to paycheck. You did what you had to do. I've been blessed. After Vegas, there was a lady named Elaine Dunn and she was doing *Sweet Charity* in the Circle in the Square in San Francisco. She asked me to do it with her. I was playing Daddy Brubeck. Bob Fosse came to see it and then all of a sudden I get a call: Bob Fosse wanted me to go join Chita Rivera on the tour. That was the first time I met her. I fell in love. . . . Excuse me. [Vereen's eyes well up with emotion]. She was wonderful. She's wonderful. Watch her work. Oh, man. Dance. Wow, wow. I didn't know people could do that. Rhythm. And she's so funny and just so loving. It was amazing. Wow. It's emotional. Her friendship, her devotion. She's a true person, and throughout my life she's very constant. She's a constant.

And watching her perform, do you feel like you learned . . .
It's a master class each time. I sat in the wings and watched her. It's a master class. The way she handles the audience and her consistency. No matter how she's feeling, her consistency. We were in Montreal and we get a telegram from Bob Fosse, asking us to come to Hollywood to do the film. We were off to Hollywood. And Paula Kelly met us there. And Shirley MacLaine. It was my first time on a studio lot. We stayed at the Yucca Hotel in Hollywood. And at that time, Watts was burning. I got in a cab and went to see the damage. I'll never forget it. It was devastating. And the next day was rehearsal. I walked through the Universal lot and was like "wow." All these stars were walking up and down the place. I was like, "I saw you on television! I saw you in the movies!" Like a little kid in a candy store. We go into rehearsal, and I was sure that I would get the part of Daddy Brubeck. Sammy Davis Jr. came in and I was brokenhearted. But watching the process of the way filming goes on was a whole new world for me. Different takes, separate takes.

How long did it take to shoot The Rich Man's Frug?

I think about a week. Maybe longer. And you had Bob Fosse as your director, so you know you got to hit the bar every time. You can't mark. There's no "I'm going to take it slow on this take." No. Nah. You don't do that with Fosse. You hit it every time.

And once you wrapped . . .

Sammy hired me to go to London. I told you I was interested in the riots. Sammy thought I was militant. So he asked me to dinner in Santa Monica. I get there at 7:00 and I am waiting and waiting. My cigarettes are stacking up. I should have left, but this is Sammy Davis Jr. Sammy walks in around 10:00. with about fifty of his closest friends. Sitting around the table with his agent, Dean Martin, Johnny Carson. He starts talking about this show called *Golden Boy*, how he says he wants to reflect what's going on in the street in the show, and he said, "I need someone who's militant, someone who gets it." His agent says to me, "Ask him for the role." So I say, "Mr. Davis . . ." "You got it." And the next thing you know I was hired for *Golden Boy* and off to London I went. First, we came back to New York and rehearsed, then we went to Chicago. The riots had just quieted. Martin Luther King got shot during that time and Sammy was just undone. I was in a room with him. He was holding court, and Liz Taylor, Richard Burton, and Peter Lawford were all in the room and talking, and laughing, and carrying on. A few of the cast members were there. Joe Grant, his bodyguard, came in and said, "They shot King." And a hush came over. I was, of course, this militant kid from Brooklyn. First thing I wanted was to go out and beat up some white people because I was so angry. And Sammy said, "Be cool, be cool." He went on the air and pleaded to America to not do anything that King would be upset about. He said we got to keep the peace. We flew to London, the London Palladium. And while we were there Bobby Kennedy got shot. Sammy knew all these people. He was going through it. Me, I was this kid who was angry that all this was going on in my country. But we got through it.

So at this time of incredible social unrest in the country, you found yourself alongside one of the most prominent black men who could actually help influence the national mood. Here you are, an angry kid, figuring out your place in the world, and you're having the example set for you of an entertainer who's making public statements and advocating for peace.

Well, you understand, I wasn't in a position to say anything or do anything. I was observing. And, of course, we were angry. Everyone was. We were livid. How dare they? How dare they shoot King? But then we had to be an example of keeping the peace. Every night, on stage, he'd say, "Keep the peace, keep the peace."

You were the understudy for the actor playing his brother.

When we go to Chicago, no understudy rehearsal. I'm in the wings watching and learning, watching everybody. And one night Sammy, after going around to all these gangs to keep the peace down in Chicago, was exhausted. He was wiped out. He said, "I can't go on" in the middle of the show. The stage manager turns to me and says, "You're on." I didn't even have a costume. Lonnie Satton [who was playing Davis's manager, Billy] went on for Sammy and I went on for Billy. That was my first standing ovation. Sammy's in the wings, watching this. I came off stage, and Sammy said to me, "I knew it," and he walked away.

After London . . .

I had met my second wife, and she knew an agent, Joanie Kovacs. Joanie looked at me and said, "You should be doing *Hair*." I didn't know anything about the show. So I go down to [audition at] the Biltmore Theatre, and it's packed of course. Once again, like *All That Jazz*. Everyone's here. When it was all over, I got a call that I'm going to Los Angeles with *Hair*. [Director] Tom O'Horgan was a genius.

Hair seems like it was almost the antithesis of Fosse's style. Fosse is all tight, tight specific, disciplined movement, and this appeared to be very free and loose.
Tom would give you the idea, then he'd let you go and meditate on it for a minute in your mind, and then come back [with your ideas.] He'd cut away what was not necessary. It was you or your expression of your character. It was quite a wonderful experience. It was about freedom. It was right up my alley. And we were talking about being against the war, we were for equal rights. We were way ahead of the game. That's what *Hair* was about. It was about us all being what God created us to be. Love. The idea was amazing. I like to believe we did make a bit of a difference. I hesitate to say it like that because in our determination to make a change . . . I tell young people . . . we didn't do the things we said we were going to do. Had that idea been really given a chance to ferment and be planted deep inside of our country and our minds . . . I'm a dreamer. I was hoping we could.

Well, it's not all or nothing. I think some number of people took that messaging of love and community and healing.
Oh, yes, but their voices are needed now more than ever. You're right. There are. You got to look for us though. [Anyway], when *Hair* started dying down in Los Angeles, they asked me to go up to San Francisco for a while. During that time, I started noticing people like Lou Rawls, Richard Pryor, Della Reese, and all these people playing little clubs. A friend of mine worked for Shirley MacLaine, as a drummer. He introduced me to a guy who played trombone, and he talked me into doing my first nightclub act. Also about that time, I get a telegraph from Tom O'Horgan, saying, "I'm directing a show called *Jesus Christ Superstar*. I'd like you to come and try out for Judas." They sent me a ticket. I go to New York to the Mark Hellinger Theatre and sing all day. And Robert Stigwood and a few other producers and Tom were in the audience. Andrew Lloyd Webber was in the audience, and I didn't know who he was. I had to sing "I Don't Know How to Love Him," and when I got up, I heard somebody say, "I'll play for him," and climbs up onstage. He starts playing the song, and he plays a different chord, and I turn to him, and I say, "Excuse me, sir, that's not the song." It was Andrew Lloyd Webber. He got really angry. He wouldn't speak to me for a long time.

You still got the part.
I got the part.

***Superstar* is such heavy singing. It seems you went from being primarily a dancer to a show where your dance skills were irrelevant. How was that for you?**
You throw yourself in. I did. I had never taken singing lessons so I didn't know about preserving the voice. I developed polyps. I was silent for about a month. I had surgery to remove the polyps, then I had to go on vocal rest for a while. I came back because I couldn't afford to not have that show. I was married with kids and I needed to work. About that time, we got nominated for the Tony, and I was nominated. Who's Tony? I didn't know! I really didn't. The stage doorman came and knocked on my door. He said, "You got an envelope." And I said, "OK, just leave it." He said, "No, no, you have an ENVELOPE." So I open the letter and it says "You have been nominated for a Tony Award." And I look at him, and I'm puzzled. I said, "Who's Tony?" But I got my suit and got myself together and went to my first Tony

Awards. Then when you're sitting in that audience . . . I'd never been to anything like that. People were so dressed up. I was excited. It was just a groovy thing to be involved in and be a part of. I went to the party afterwards, and some people from the Theater Wing came over and said, "You should have won." I said, "No, you don't understand. I did win. You invited me to the party."

Once you were on TV, performing on the Tonys, did you your dad finally understand what it is you were doing?

I did invite him to the show when I got *Jesus Christ Superstar*. There's a scene in the show where Judas goes to heaven. He comes back in a loincloth when he's singing the song "Jesus Christ Superstar." So my dad comes backstage and I said, "Dad, how'd you like it?" He thought about it for a minute, and he said, "Boy, you need to put some clothes on out there. You going to freeze." Only comment about my theater work. He didn't know what to say. It was cute.

Do you have memories of Webber and Rice?

Yes, yes, yes. They were around. Tim Rice was amazing. He gave me a staff. I wish I'd have kept it. But you're traveling all these years so things get lost. Yeah, Tim was wonderful. Andrew had a problem with me.

Everybody I know who talks about Andrew Lloyd Webber say that he's quite the peculiar bird.

He is a peculiar bird. He is a peculiar bird.

You were also in your fourth successive hit. Did it seem charmed?

If a show hits, it's great. It means you work for a long time. I get an opportunity to play, do what I like to do. But I don't go into a show thinking, "This one's going to be a hit. I can smell it." You go into it saying, "I got a job. I'm going to do the best job I can."

We talked about *Hair* and *Hair* being about love. Did you feel like ultimately the message in *Jesus Christ Superstar* . . .

Is about love. This was the ultimate sacrifice. I love you so much I'll die for you. Do you get it yet, people? Do you get it yet?

While you were doing *Superstar*, you auditioned for *Pippin*.

Yeah. I wore my blue suit. Gator shoes, white shirt, and blue tie. When I went to dinner with Sammy Davis, I didn't have the proper clothes. I was going to have dinner with Sammy Davis Jr., and this is the cat I'd idolized on television, so I went out and bought a suit and sat there for three hours waiting for him to come to dinner. I put the same suit on for Bob. And I sang some songs I had done in my act. He asked me to go downstairs and read the opening speech of the Leading Player. I read it, and Stephen Schwartz was in the audience. Roger Hirson and Stu Ostrow were there. Bob says, "Well, your reading isn't that good, but we will let you know." And so, I go back to *Superstar*. I get this telegram: Bob Fosse asks me to do *Pippin*. My agent says the show has a 20 percent chance of making it. "I wouldn't take it if I were you." I said, "Well, if Bob Fosse's doing it then I'm going to do it." And there really wasn't a part. There was no part in the beginning. I remember sitting across from Bob at the read-through, and Bob was chuckling. He [could see I was concerned]. He walked over to me and said, "Don't worry about it. I want you to go to the library to watch films of Bill Robinson, Jimmy Slyde, and Honi Coles. Look at those moves." So I went to the library and watched. And the next thing I knew, the Leading Player was developed. They wrote me "Simple Joys." They developed this character. It was an amazing experience.

We just got finished talking about how *Hair* **and** *Superstar* **were about love. This show . . .**
This guy, a manipulator. The way I approached it . . . there's a story about this Indian chief who tells his son, "My son, as you're going through the world, know there will be two wolves inside you fighting every day of your life. The wolf for good and the wolf for bad." And his son says, "Well, father, which one wins?" "The one you feed." That was me. I was the guy on his shoulder who was saying, "Try this, try this, try that." I played it for myself as a part of Pippin's consciousness. My troop of murderers were his consciousness showing the wonderful things in life just lead to death. So it became a wonderful script. And we talked about that, Bob and I. He said, "You're his closest and dearest friend. You're that part of him that he wants to be." It was wonderful finding this character. I find moments in the play where, if you watch me, I would actually . . . my eyes would go up, like receiving messages from the head station.

Fosse apparently was at odds with Schwartz and Hirson, fighting what he saw as the sentimentality of the text.
I didn't know really that Stephen and he were at odds with each other until later. I was in a work mode. I was in the land of finding this character, letting him express himself through me. I could feel the tension when we got to Broadway. But up until then, I didn't feel anything that was going on because I was into finding the character. How deep can I make this guy? How un-evil can I make him 'til the last moment? Pippin, to me, was a life force that my troupe needed. For him to die would be that sensation that we want.

What did the Manson Trio mean to you?
The dance of destruction. It was wonderful. So smooth.

I read that the troupe really did become a troupe, that you were all very tight.
Yeah, we were. We really were. We really loved each other, everyone.

So the show opens, and it's a major thing, and, of course . . .
Yeah, it opens, but it wasn't—we got good reviews, but it wasn't major. And Bob, in his genius, said, "We have got to do a TV commercial." [At that point, a Broadway show had never had a commercial]. So they put me in the studio singing "Simple Joys." Bob looked at it, and he said, "No, that's not going to work." He took myself, Candy Brown, and Pamela Sousa and we did the Manson Trio. I'll never forget. The cameraman got really upset with Bob. He didn't know who Bob Fosse was. So Bob came in the next day and he brought all of the trophies he'd won in a little wagon, and he said, "I think I can handle this." He directed it and cut it, and we put out the first TV commercial for the theater. The show was a smash, and the rest is history.

And, of course, you got your second invitation to the Tony Awards.
Yes, I did. And this time I was excited. I knew what it was now. I got a good suit for the Tonys this time. A green velvet suit, green little bowtie, brown platform shoes. They called my name, and I just flipped out. I flipped out. I was so happy because this time I knew what it was all about. I jumped up and down. I kissed Stephen Schwartz, I kissed Stu Ostrow on his bald head. I ran up on the stage, so excited. I'll never forget going into the park that night and standing in the middle of Central Park, looking at the city, I say, "You're mine." I don't even know what that meant but, "You're mine." After that . . . I had been wearing Benny Hill clothes. I thought I was cool. Polyester pants, loud shirts with colored flowers on them. My manager at

the time, Patti Falconer, wanted me to go to a party. I get there a little late. I am standing outside and this guy walks up, and he goes [in an exaggerated Italian accent], "You're a star." And of course, I had a brown, flowery, polyester shirt and brown pants, and brown and white platform shoes. He looks at me and goes, "[But] you don't know how to dress. Look at you. Brown on brown in brown." I was about to hit this guy, but at that time Patti walks up. She says. "Hey, Jack." He says, "No, no, no. I'm Jacques Bellini." She said, "No, you're Jack Bell." He said, "No, I'm Jacques Bellini, dresser to the stars. I'll take care of you." So the next day I go to 60th Street, Jacques Bellini clothier. I walk in, and within an hour and a half he transformed my entire look. I left there with satins and silks, gabardines, and sharp. I was sharp.

This period of your life was just represented on TV in *Fosse/Verdon.* **Did you watch at all?**
No, I did not, although the young man who played me [Ahmad Simmons] gave me the honor of coming and talking to me. But I couldn't watch it. I'm too close, and I didn't like what I was hearing about it. I did see a glimpse of it. I felt sorry for the gentleman who played Fosse because Fosse wasn't like that, and the way they wrote it made him look like . . . Please. It was the '60s and '70s. People were just like love, love, love. Everybody was making love to everybody. And for them to put all that stuff in there about Bob? Who cared? I want to hear about the genius of his work, not who he bedded. I'll watch it eventually. I want to see the young man's portrayal of me in it. I owe him that much.

You were a black performer on Broadway in the early '70s, just before *The Wiz* **and** *Raisin* **and just before the wave of black revues like** *Eubie!, Bubbling Brown Sugar, Ain't Misbehavin',* **and** *Sophisticated Ladies.* **Black people were being put in black shows, but there's not any real integration yet . . .**
There was a color line. There's a black show and a white show. It should be one show. I remember the Rockettes; you had to be very light to get into a show of that nature. I had faith that we would turn things around, and look, we turned them around.

People like you and Leslie Uggams were breaking out and doing club acts, and that put you in a whole other realm.
Understand I had just come out of two shows that were very controversial, groundbreaking. That mentality stayed with me. I went on to do an act where I made a statement about our time. When I was doing *Pippin,* a gentleman came over to me in a bar. He says, "I saw your show. Very good. You know, there was a time when a black person wasn't allowed onstage unless they blacked up [in blackface]." "Get out of here, man. We're already black. We don't have to black up." We had a matinee the next day. And there's a book waiting for me called *Bert Williams, Nobody.* I read the book. I didn't believe this happened. So when I was asked to do my act, I decided to do a tribute to Bert Williams, blackface and all. I was doing something to make a statement and tell you that this shall never happen again. That was my purpose in doing it. So I guess, in my way, I was trying to make things better, make people more aware.

When you left *Pippin* **ultimately was it hard to leave or were you ready to move on?**
I was ready to move on, but it's like leaving home. It was such a family.

You did your club act and spent a lot of time in Hollywood. *All That Jazz* **happened in that period.**
Yeah. We were doing our nightclub act. I'm in Vegas. I get a telegram or call that Bob's doing this movie and he wanted me to come in for a day and shoot this part. So I go in, come back to

New York, and we go up to Purchase and we shoot the TV scene where I'm the TV host. Bob wanted a Sammy Davis type of character. Gold chain, the whole thing. Sammy later said, "If they wanted me why didn't they call me?" So I'm doing this part, and I leave and go back out to Vegas. A couple of weeks later, I get another call. Fosse said, "Ben, I'm stuck for the finale. Could I have you for a week?" So I fly back out. Ended up taking three weeks. But we put together the finale of that movie.

Terrifying finale.

Yeah. He had a screening in New York. Paddy Chayefsky's there, Neil Simon, and some of his closest friends. We watch the movie, and at the end, he kills himself [Fosse wrote the death of the character based on him]. I was shocked. It was shocking. He turned to me, and he said, "What do you think?" I said, "I've got to go for a walk." I had to take it in. I was shocked. Everyone was shocked. This was a hard pill to swallow. He was eulogizing himself.

Grind, the show Harold Prince called his "most painful working experience." (Martha Swope, ©Billy Rose Theatre Division, New York Public Library for the Performing Arts)

You were away from Broadway for a long time until *Grind* in 1985.

Hal Prince asked me to do that show. But we had to go a lot of places and raise money. And we did the show. Good cast, good story, too. We open in Baltimore, and next thing I know Fosse's down there. They wanted him to choreograph the show. Lester Wilson was choreographing and they wanted Fosse to take it over. He wouldn't do it out of respect for Lester. So he says, "I'll do one number for Ben." "New Man." It was a wonderful number. It stopped the show. And he said to me in rehearsal, "If you learn how to dance like this, Ben, you'll dance forever."

What was different about that choreography than the other Fosse choreography that you had done already?

It was even smaller.

What was your experience of working with Hal Prince?

It was great. He is visionary. He was gracious. He's cool. He was easy to work with. He had all the right tools. He had the right people to call upon to make things happen. It's too bad the show didn't make it. I think the show was worthy, but it was very confusing at that time.

The show was very ambitious. Prince has said he did it as a comment on the violence that he saw in America. It's also been said that your being in it was problematic because it created the expectation of a star character with star numbers. Finding the balance between that and the intended messaging was very tricky. Did you experience that as it was happening?

Not while it was happening, but I realized that after the fact. You're busy working. I was working hard to make it a hit. You don't think about other things. But Bob asked me to do a show he was doing, *Big Deal*. I didn't want to overweigh his show.

Knowing that the show had an important message and pouring all that effort into it, how did you deal with it not working?

An interesting thing happened. Really opened my eyes. Opening night was a big huge stress on me. And the show got bad reviews. They called me in and said, "We're going to go up to Harlem and try and get the black audiences." I found that strange. So, we go into Harlem, and these journalists are sitting around, and they go, "You come to us now? Why weren't we invited to the opening night?" And that stuck with me. So every show I do now, I make sure that the black press is invited. It's very important. You must be inclusive of all people. It was the first time I really saw black and white.

During the two months that the show ran, did you feel like you were carrying it?

No, everyone was working real hard. Carol Woods, Leilani Jones, Stubby Kaye . . . Everybody was working hard for the show. You say, "Okay, let's buckle down and really get to work now." But now there's real desperation. What can we do to keep the show going?

And what do you do other than do the best show you can do and hope that word of mouth spreads?

That's all we can do. Tell people about it and do your show. And you want to get out there and tell the audience to tell their friends, tell their neighbors.

Were you devastated by the closing?
No, I think by that time we knew it was happening. It hurt. Nobody wants to see a show close. You spend two months preparing it, getting it ready, and it doesn't make the mark.

Prince said it became the most painful working experience of his life.
He tried. We did all we could. It wasn't the time. And also Broadway was going through some sort of dark change during that time. Everything was sort of off. It was a bad season. It was really off.

Only a couple of years later Fosse died.
I was in Los Angeles. When I got the news, I was floored. It was—took my breath away. You never think—you know we're all going to die, but that was so unnecessary. He was rehearsing *Sweet Charity*, had a heart attack just like he predicted. I came back for his memorial at Tavern on the Green.

I read that people were sitting at their tables, kind of somber, and that you got up and started dancing. That brought other people to their feet.
Yes. We were there to celebrate his life. Let's get up. Let's move. Let's—Fosse. Yeah, it's just the thing to do. And it was wonderful. I remember it now. Thank you. It was a wonderful moment seeing everybody dancing. The writers. Everybody trying to do Fosse. Neil Simon! [hums "Rich Man's Frug"].

You stayed in Hollywood for the next several years and then, of course, the accident.
I had a doctor say I'd never walk again. I was pretty beaten up. I had a trach and colostomy bag, stroke on the right side, broken femur. I was a mess. Prior to the accident, I had met a woman named Reverend Dr. Johnnie Coleman. I had been out of touch with a lot of what was going on in the church. I walked into her church and I see 5,000 black people meditating. I was blown away. And she's such an eloquent, gracious, statue of a woman, honoring God. She would take me to her home and teach me metaphysics about the mind. And so when the accident happened, I was lying in a hospital, couldn't speak . . . I didn't know what had happened. To this day, I can't tell you what happened. I can tell you what everybody else tells me. I woke up in the hospital and my belly was open, and I couldn't move my right side, and I couldn't talk, and my left side was in a machine going up and down. The doctor said you'll never walk again and as far as your career, you might as well get another occupation. Johnnie had taught me a precious thing about the mind. When negativity comes your way, cancel it. Use the mantra, "Cancel, cancel." So when the doctors are saying this to me I'd go, "Cancel, cancel." I'm thinking in my mind, "I got a show on Saturday. I know they're going to fix me to do my show on Saturday." [I later heard] the lobby of the hospital was packed. People were in prayer. I didn't know this. And boxes and boxes and boxes of letters were coming in from people all over. I come out [for rehab] to a place called the Kessler Institute in New Jersey. Bonnie Evans was the CEO, and they had a wonderful staff there. It was amazing. For my birthday that year I went to see *Jelly's Last Jam*. I'm on a cane because I had another operation. So I'm sitting there on canes and in a neck brace, and here comes Gregory Hines saying, "When can you be ready?" And I said, "What?" He said, "Well, Keith David is leaving the show. If you can be ready by April 3rd, you got the part." And that's all I needed to hear. I told Bonnie Evans, and she and my therapist go down to see the show, and they come back and say, "We can do this." And we went to work. One day I was working so hard and nothing was happening.

I called Chita [who herself had suffered a terrible accident and gone through a long recovery]; I said, "Will I ever dance again?" And she said, "You'll dance again. But you'll dance differently. And viva la difference." That's my Chita. I worked, and ten months later, we walked onstage in *Jelly's Last Jam*. I talk about the crew a lot because they knew that I couldn't do stairs. They built me a dressing room onstage so I didn't have to walk upstairs. I loved my crew. I love my crews. Love them. They're such special people. They make us who we are. They set the atmosphere for us to walk out and do our thing. They never get enough recognition. Bravo. Opening night was amazing. It was packed. Standing room. And Gregory was so gracious. The whole cast. Bonnie and all my therapists were in the audience. Thunderous applause. I was trying to hold back the tears, hold back the tears. Gregory was so beautiful. So happy for me. Such a gentleman. As we were taking our bows, Gregory just put me out in front: Here he is. And George Wolfe! They all were so cool. I remember that one year after the accident, I did my first pirouette onstage, and the cast cried, and I cried. Oh, my God. He did it, he did it, he did it.

I read the ovation went on for like five minutes when you entered.
It did, it did.

How do you even take that in?
You just do.

What do you think it means?
You're loved. And love in return. I had no idea how many people I'd touched until that day of the accident. All the mail, all the pouring out of good wishes and prayers. It was an amazing time.

It's a terrible thing to have to go through something like that to learn that you matter to people.
I wouldn't suggest it. But it was an outpouring of love. That's why to this day I dedicate my shows to my audiences. They deserve it. It's their show. They've been there for me. Times when I wasn't able myself, they stood with me.

I'm going to ask a really impossible question, but if you had to name the thing that it is that you think they get from you, why they're there for you, why that outpouring of love, why they show up, what do you think it is? What is it that you've provided for them that makes them love you that way?
I'm open. I'm vulnerable when I'm up there. And I give from my heart. I think that's what they identify with because we're the same. I'm just trying to be a reflection of what you are, what we are. Did I make you feel good? Then I've done my job. That's what I think it is. Spirit. It's the spirit.

And then *Chicago*.
Yeah, that was interesting. I was doing cruise ships, and I get a call from my manager at the time saying that Chita wanted me do *Chicago* with her. And I was having such a good time, had it not been Chita, I would have never come back. But they said the magic word, "Chita." I said, "I'm on the next plane." I flew into Canada. We warmed it up there, and then we took it to Las Vegas and opened the theater at the Mandalay Bay. And then Chita—I thought she was going to stay on so I up and committed for another few months,

and she said, "I'm not staying." Whaaaaat? She left me! She abandoned me! But I love this woman.

How did you feel about doing the show?
Oh, it was fun. The Weisslers [producers] were not fun, but it was fun. And we rocked it. Roz Ryan came out and the three of us smoked! It was great. I remember seeing *Chicago* when I was in *Pippin*. Chita and Gwen onstage at the 46th Street Theatre. I was at the Imperial. There was a door backstage to go from theater to theater. So I'd sneak over and watch them onstage. I'd come back and do my thing. I thought Ann Reinking did a very good job as far as keeping the tradition of Fosse's work.

Your next Broadway gig was *Fosse*, which she directed.
Ann wanted me to do it but I didn't know if I could physically cut it as a dancer. I hadn't danced. I had done *Jelly's Last Jam*, I'd done my show. But the movement for *Fosse* is a certain type of movement. I get to New York, I see the show, and I start rehearsal. We start working on the Manson Trio. I hurt. But I got through the number and tears are just streaming down my face. I heard Bob say, "Learn to dance like this, you'll dance forever." I lost it, lost it, lost, lost it. That was a moment for me. I turned my dressing room into my shrine, into my altar. I had my Buddha and the Dalai Lama and my incense burning. People were coming in to sit. It was beautiful. I would stand in the wings and cheer everybody on during the show. We had a good time. It was a good time doing *Fosse*.

I talked to Ann Reinking and Gwen Verdon when *Fosse* was in rehearsals, and they told me that there were those in the company who showed up really ready to embrace the Fosse and then there were those who didn't get it. They could handle the steps, of course, but they didn't quite get that what they were doing was carrying on a legacy. For them, it was just their next show.
I think that the spirit of Fosse was strong when I got there. Then Ann came in [to the show] and that backbone was there. I think everyone would step up to the plate. That's why I would stand in the wings and cheer them on. It was so wonderful to see those dancers every night doing Fosse movements and making it their own tradition. What a time we had. So my closing night, when I had to leave the show, I decided to throw a party for everybody. Most times you throw parties at a bar. I had it at a spa. I hired a bus and invited the musicians, the crew, the ushers, and the cast to this bash. They got on a bus and they go down to Wall Street where the spa was, and as they came off the bus, there was a woman standing there in white, giving them incense sticks, welcoming them to the cleanse. I had a numerologist, an astrologist, and I had three different masseuse people. I had Egyptian men standing around in Egyptian garb. I had a sitar player, vegan food. And there was a pool, a hot bath, a sauna, a cold dip. It was quite a night.

You already told me that Fosse talked to you about a way of dancing that could be done forever. But that show was famous for the number of injuries in the cast.
When you do it, and you do it right, you never get injured. But sometimes, you're not in the consciousness and so injuries happen. And the body sometimes doesn't listen so you hit a wall. You take care of it, get back up, and keep doing it. I didn't hear about all the injuries and things ['til later].

Well, you must have seen that people were out?
Yeah, I saw people out, but the show had to go on.

In *Pippin* and *Sweet Charity*, people got through those runs with similar choreography without calling out. Now, there's a lot of calling out.

It's different times. I'm not saying that their calling out's wrong, no. If you're sick, you're sick. But I came from that school that you don't miss a show. And the shows I've missed I could kick myself for.

Well, I'm not asking you to bash today's performers at all. But I'm also noticing a willingness to relax that standard of "I'm going to go on no matter what." That, I think, used to be symptomatic of what it meant to be a performer on Broadway. I will put some of the blame on producers who schedule five shows a weekend. And on creators who ask for crazy acrobatics or vocal gymnastics. It becomes impossible for people to maintain. But there's also a culture now that allows for calling out that didn't exist.

I think it's an individual thing. I can't talk for those other people. When it happens to me, I'm devastated.

Back on Broadway opposite Shoshana Bean, Megan Hilty, and Rue McClanahan in *Wicked*. (Joan Marcus)

I don't think it's an individual thing. I think cultural. Once Pandora's box is open, it gets normalized. Carol Channing going off the stage and puking in a bucket and walking back onstage . . . I think if you keep yourself to that standard that there's no choice, you'll deliver.

Maybe we need to embrace that more these days. Maybe that's been forgotten. But then again I went and saw *Hamilton* for the fifth time, and I must say they were tight. The choreography was tight, giving honor to the choreographer. That's dedication. Yeah. We got to get that back. When I teach classes, I talk about that commitment to yourself. What a quality you have. But you know something? As long as you and I are talking about it, somebody's listening. It's important. It's important not only for show biz, for your art and the honor of the art that you're doing it for; I feel a representation of that which is greater than ourselves so, therefore, we have a responsibility to show up to allow the greater self to express itself through us. Those sitting in the audience, we may never meet them in our lives, but their lives are changed because we showed up. If we hadn't shown up, that person's life wouldn't be changed. I hear that so often, "I saw you, and you changed my life. You don't know what you did for my family." This is what we do.

Your next show has changed many lives during its long run. You stepped into *Wicked*.

Stephen called me in to do *Wicked*. Shoshana Bean and Megan Hilty were amazing. The whole cast was amazing, but they were just unreal. Megan's dressing room was right across from mine so we joked a lot. And Rue McClanahan! We had a good time. I love *Wicked*. I learned to love it. And for me, it was hard at first to do one number and stop [the character is off stage for long stretches]. Wait. That's it? So I had to find out ways to preserve myself, to be ready to hit it again when I come back, to hit that energy point again. At first it was an adjustment for me, but I got it. We had a ball with it.

A name that has been a through line throughout your career is Liza Minelli.

Oh, yes, I was just thinking about Liza. I met Liza at *Jesus Christ Superstar*. My stage manager knocks on the door and says, "Mr. Vereen, Ms. Minnelli wants to say hello." I didn't know who Ms. Minnelli is. So in walks this little girl with the biggest eyes I think I've ever seen. Cute as could be. She slides in like this little shy girl, and with her is Desi Arnaz Jr. and his agent. She introduces herself and says how much she liked the show. Niceties. A couple of days later, she's back at the show. And a few days later, she was back. So we became friends. Very interesting. Very good friends, but she's a funny lady. When I had my accident, Liza was there. Liza showed up. She was right there in the hospital with me. I mean, here I was broken up, and Liza was sitting next to me. She loves doing show biz. And she taught me a lot. We used to go to clubs and sing—get up and sing.

So now what? You're touring with your club act but if another Broadway show came your way . . .

I'd jump right in. Injuries and things of that nature over time, we learn to work with them. I mean, I won't be doing cartwheels and splits, that's for sure, but I can do cartwheels and splits in the minds of people, and keep it alive that way. Yeah, I would love to do something.

5

MICHAEL RUPERT

March 2019

"ARE YOU SURE?" WERE THE first words out of Michael Rupert's mouth as he accepted his Tony Award for *Sweet Charity* in 1986. He was uncharacteristically gobsmacked. For Rupert, while totally appreciative of the life and career he's had, never describes himself as overcome. Aware, yes, but not pinching himself with disbelief. He relates his memories of legends (Fosse! Garland! Coleman! Kander and Ebb! Sondheim! Andrews!) with a nonchalance that, coming from someone else, might seem inconceivable. But Rupert, who is from California, grew up in the business, appearing on television shows like *The Partridge Family* and *My Three Sons*. He was on Broadway (and Tony nominated!) at sixteen, playing opposite Robert Goulet in *The Happy Time*. The world he describes isn't a world to which he struggled to attain admittance and then finally entered; it's simply what he always knew.

After *The Happy Time*, he played the title role in the original Broadway run of *Pippin* and then created the part of Marvin in William Finn's groundbreaking off-Broadway musical, *March of the Falsettos*. It's hard to appreciate now just how revolutionary and bold *March* was in 1981—a musical about a man leaving his wife and son for a male lover. It was the first of its kind with a truly unique sound and voice. It cemented the careers of Finn, Rupert, Chip Zien, Stephen Bogardus, and director James Lapine, all of whom reunited a decade later for a sequel, *Falsettoland*, and then, a year after that, for the pairing of the two shows, *Falsettos* (another Tony nomination). Marvin is not a nice guy; he's selfish, petty, immature, and controlling. But Rupert endowed him with a relatability and pathos (not to mention glorious vocals) that connected and reduced audiences to sobs—every—single—night. Other roles have included *City of Angels, Putting It Together, Sweet Charity, Ragtime, Legally Blonde*, and Rupert's own musical, *Mail*, but it is Marvin for which he will always be remembered and beloved.

Of late, Rupert spends the bulk of his professional time on college campuses, teaching and directing. His desire to perform nightly has waned. "I just have no desire to do that any longer," he says without bitterness. "I've done it. So when I work with students now, and I get to see who I was all those years ago, it's great because they have such enthusiasm to be in front of an audience. I don't." When he starts singing, though, as he did a few times in my company, one can't help but hope that maybe he'll change his mind and give us just one more show.

When did you start performing?
I got my Equity card when I was twelve years old—though I actually started in TV, long before I really got involved in theater. But the very first Equity production I ever did was a

With Stephen Bogardus in *Falsettoland*, nine years after they originated the characters in *March of the Falsettos*. (Photofest)

Michael Rupert	
The Happy Time	Broadway, 1968
Pippin	Broadway, 1974, National Tour, 1977
Shakespeare's Cabaret	Broadway, 1981
March of the Falsettos	Off-Broadway, 1981
Sweet Charity (Tony Award)	Broadway, 1986
Mail	Broadway, 1988
Falsettoland	Off-Broadway, 1990
City of Angels	Broadway, 1991
Falsettos	Broadway, 1992
Putting It Together	Off-Broadway, 1993
Ragtime	National tour, 1998; Broadway, 1999
Elegies	Off-Broadway, 2003
Baby	Milburn, NJ, 2004
Legally Blonde	Broadway, 2007; National Tour, 2010
The Full Monty	Milburn, NJ, 2009
On the Town	Broadway, 2014

production of *Peter Pan* at the Valley Music Theater in Woodland Hills, California. Vincent Price played Captain Hook.

You'd never get your Equity card today for being a Lost Boy.

Well, the business was very different when I was a kid. First of all, the competition was not nearly what it is today. Even by the time I graduated from high school there were not that many colleges or conservatories in the United States that even offered a BA in musical theater. Now there are literally hundreds. And certainly, musical theater has just skyrocketed over the last twenty years or so. So the fact that fifty-some years ago I was able to get my Equity card playing a Lost Boy in a local production of *Peter Pan* in Los Angeles was not unusual. When I work with students, sometimes I want to sit them down and tell them that what they are up against now is very different than what I was up against when I was a teenager. Many years ago, people would be very disappointed if an understudy was on because truly they were not going to see a performance that was as strong. Today you go to almost any show and you can see the second or third cover for someone, and nine times out of ten they're quite terrific because the depth of talent that's available to producers is much deeper than it was when I was a kid. I don't know if I was starting out today if I would last. Not because of talent but just because the competition today is so keen and so tough. I don't know if after a couple of years I would say, "Well, fuck this. I'm done. I'm going to go do something else with my life." I have, over the last twenty years, worked with students, and some of them are no longer in the business, and they tried. They just couldn't make a go of it. These were very talented kids. So anyway, the business has changed enormously since I started when I was young.

And I'm sure when you started, veterans you were working with like Robert Goulet and David Wayne would have told you that the business changed tremendously in their lives.

Absolutely.

You worked with them in *The Happy Time* in 1968 and made your Broadway debut.

It just happened. I had an agent in Los Angeles. My parents were very supportive of me doing all of this. They thought that I would just do this as an avocation as a kid, and then end up becoming a dentist or something, which is what my parents really wanted. But my agent sent me in for *The Happy Time*, by Kander and Ebb that Gower Champion was directing. I went in not really understanding the ramifications of my getting the gig. It meant moving to

New York. They already had a theater booked. They had all their money in place. Gower had this whole concept. He had been to Expo '67, up in Montreal, I think, and saw the projections and decided that's how he wanted to do *The Happy Time*, which didn't exactly make everybody happy. John and Fred had really written *The Happy Time* to be a very intimate, small story about a family. And Gower blew it up into this mammoth production using all of these photographs and all these projections. We're talking about the 1960s so the state of the art of projection design was in its infancy. They needed theaters as big as the Ahmanson in L.A. and the Broadway Theater because they needed a big amount of space between the scrim and the back wall to be able to mount a huge movie projector to do all of this. The Broadway Theater was literally the only house they could use on Broadway. It was the second show ever to play the Ahmanson Theater. David Merrick, the producer, had the money in place.

Did you have any concept of who Gower Champion or David Merrick or Kander and Ebb were?

No. I literally didn't. I had really started out in TV and film in L.A. I didn't have a real concept of Broadway. When my agent called me about this audition, he said, "Bring all your music because you don't know what they're going to ask you to sing." So I brought like twenty-five songs and that is what ended up helping me get the job. I was the second to last to audition. They asked me to sit over in the corner while they saw this last kid. The kid came in, and Gower said, "What are you going to sing for us?" And he said, "I don't know. I didn't really bring anything to sing." And there was an uncomfortable silence in the room. So fifteen-year-old Michael over in the corner piped up and said, "Well, maybe there's something in my music that he can sing," and I offered my sheet music. I think ultimately there wasn't anything in my music that he knew so he ended up just singing "Happy Birthday" or something, and he left. Then they told me to pull up a chair and talk with them for a while. I did, about my life and who I was, and all of that, and then I left. And a few days later I got the part. Sometime during rehearsal, a few months later, John Kander said to me, "Part of the reason that you got this part is what you did for that kid. That's who the character, Bibi, is. He would do that for a complete stranger, even though that complete stranger was his competition." I, of course, at the time didn't think in those terms. I didn't think anything about it. But I thought it was very sweet that John brought that up. So anyway, I got the gig, and suddenly I was in New York for a year doing a show.

You moved here with your mom who apparently was supportive enough to decide that it was worth uprooting you.

Well, they weren't really thrilled. I couldn't go by myself. I was only fifteen. That meant leaving her husband and my sister behind. We had to find a place to live. I had to be enrolled in professional children's school. It was a big upheaval in my parents' lives.

What made her decide to make that massive commitment given that they ultimately expected you to outgrow this theater thing? Was it your passion?

They knew I wanted to do it. I was very excited about being the juvenile lead in a Broadway musical. I was making money doing it, which my parents put into a college fund for me, thinking I was going to go to college.

Did you enjoy the rehearsal process and learning the discipline of Broadway?

Gower made it clear to me right from the get-go what he expected. "I'm going to be as hard on you as I am with Bob Goulet, or David Wayne, or Charlie Durning, or anybody else.

I'm going to expect you to pull your weight, okay, Michael?" He gave me a whole lesson in discipline in the theater. So I went into the experience with the attitude that I'm going to have to prove to them that I'm as hard a worker as Bob and David and everybody in the show. I'm going to do a great job for you.

Did you find it hard work or did it come fairly naturally to you or both?

It came very naturally. I still had an enormous amount of fun. We still goofed around a lot because it was a large cast, and there were other kids my age in the show. It was such a big show, there literally was no rehearsal space in Los Angeles that the show could fit in so Merrick ended up renting a soundstage.

John Kander and Fred Ebb said that they were kept out of rehearsals, that that was Gower's way, so that they didn't necessarily know what was going on. Jerry Herman had told John Kander, "It's okay. Trust it. You'll be happy with the result." It's interesting to consider that if they had been in the room, they might have pushed back at the size.

Well, certainly John and Fred were around because John taught me a lot of the songs. But I know for a fact, and I could even tell back then as a kid, that Gower was turning the show into something that they had not envisioned. Of course, Gower, at the time, was enormously successful. He had just done *I Do! I Do!* with Preston and Martin, and was a major force on Broadway. *Hello, Dolly!* was one of the biggest hits ever.

What do you remember about working with him?

I remember being him terrific to work with. He was a very hard worker and a really nice guy. I think I have stronger impressions of directors I worked with later only because I was more of an adult. I could start to be more aware of directors' personalities and idiosyncrasies and their work habits and everything else. I remember enjoying watching Gower because he was a dancer. I remember watching him demonstrate things when he was choreographing and working on the dances. I even said to him at one point after watching, "Boy, you really are a dancer, aren't you?" And he looked at me like I was crazy. I didn't know Gower's history. There was no Internet, there was no YouTube. I was very naïve about the history of Broadway.

What were your impressions of working with Robert Goulet?

I remember Goulet being very nervous initially. It was his show to carry, though he was co-billed above the title with David Wayne. I certainly knew who Bob Goulet was. I mean, he was a big recording star. But I was surprised that he seemed as nervous as he was initially. I'm just talking about in the first week or so. I remember the very first time we read through the script was at Gower's house in the Hollywood Hills. Goulet seemed very, very nervous during this read-through. After a week or so, all of that disappeared. Even a big star like Goulet had to find that place where he realized he was going to be able to carry this show. And he did end up winning the Tony for *The Happy Time*. Bob ended up being quite terrific in the role. I was always very impressed with him. He treated me like I was his little brother. He used to punch me and shove me around. No condescension at all. Some years ago, when he died, it was one of the first times in a long time that I actually cried a little. I don't know why because I hadn't seen Bob in some years, but when he passed away, I just found it very moving. I would go into his dressing room and talk with him like he was my older brother. He never said, "Kid, talk to somebody else." He would stop what he was doing and talk. He treated me like I was worth something. David Wayne was very different. He respected me, but David was very standoffish. Some months into the run, though, David pulled my mother aside and said how good he thought I was in the show, how special he thought my performance was. David had never complimented me at any point in the process. And, of course, as a kid, you're always looking for approval. Anyway. The other adults, June Squibb, and Charlie Durning, and Gene Arnold, and Julie Gregg, all of them, were always a delight to be around, and always treated me like an equal.

What do you remember of the New York theater scene in 1968?
I remember pretty much being a kid in a candy store. I had never been to New York before so I was running around Manhattan, and I immediately started seeing Broadway shows. First show I ever saw was *Cabaret*. I remember I wanted to see it because John and Fred—that was their last show, and I knew it was a big hit. I saw Angela in *Mame*. The fact that I was going to be playing one of the leads in a Broadway musical and joining all of these other professionals in the Broadway community didn't really hit me. I was a sixteen-year-old just having a great time. I was hanging out. I went to school with other actors and dancers, other people in the business. One of my good friends at the time was Lorna Luft. I hung out with Liza Minnelli. It was just all fun and games. It was actually my mother who started to understand the importance of all of it when we were at the Tony Awards. My mother suddenly called my dad back in Los Angeles and said, "I think we're in trouble. I don't think he's going to be a dentist." I was nominated for a Tony Award at sixteen years old, and my mother realized, "Oh, my God, I just hung out with Audrey Hepburn and Angela Lansbury and Peter Ustinov, and they're all treating Michael like he's one of the group. He's part of this world now." They weren't necessarily happy about it.

What about you? Were you realizing that, too?
No. It was just me having fun.

You weren't starstruck at all? Hanging with Audrey Hepburn or being friends with Judy Garland's daughters?
No. I remember meeting Judy. She was actually in a very bad way at the time. It was near the end of her life. I remember Liza inviting me to see her nightclub act in the Empire Room at the Waldorf Astoria. They sat me down at a table, and just a few minutes later, in comes Judy Garland, and they sit her with me. It's me and Judy sitting at a table to see Liza do her nightclub act. It still didn't occur to me that this was Judy Garland. This is like a big fucking deal. I mean, I knew who Judy Garland was but mostly just from *The Wizard of Oz*. At one point, the spotlight hit our table, and Liza sang "Mammie" to her mother. All of that energy coming at this table, the reverence you could feel that these people had for this woman who, by the way, was already drunk. She was pretty loaded. I just thought, "I am in this amazing moment right here, and I don't quite understand it, but this is a moment I'm not going to forget my entire life." It was just how people in the room were reacting to her. And then afterwards going up to Liza's hotel room in the Waldorf and seeing how all of these people were reacting to Judy Garland. A year later, she was dead.

I don't think that today, anybody of any age making their Broadway debut finds themselves at the epicenter of New York glamour as you did.
It's very different now. There is a lot more youth on Broadway, but that year I was one of three kids playing leads on Broadway: me, Scott Jacoby in *Golden Rainbow*, and Frankie Michaels in *Mame*. We became the Three Musketeers. We hung out together. At the time, there were the arcades on Broadway, where you could go and play all of these pinball machines

and games. We would meet between shows. Dinner was a slice of pizza and a Coke or it was a hot dog off a cart. We'd go to each other's theaters and hang out backstage between shows, play board games. It was just kids, having a good time. I'm very fortunate and very glad that I actually was able to be a part of the tail end of the Golden Age. To hang out with Steve Lawrence and Eydie Gormé, who were Bob Goulet's great friends. I don't know how this came about or why, but our schedules were a little different, and I remember Bob grabbing me after one performance and dragging me to his car and saying, "We're going to go see Steve and Eydie." We drove down from the Broadway to the Shubert Theatre [eight blocks], and Bob made a surprise cameo at the end of *Golden Rainbow*. He said, "Wait here in the wings. I'm going onstage, kid." And the audience, of course, went crazy. So just to be able to be a part of all of that world, I feel very lucky.

But never starstruck?

Oddly enough, the only person in my entire life that I was starstruck with was when I was doing *Sweet Charity*. Ann Reinking had taken over for Debbie Allen. Ann had a friend at the show one night and brought me to her dressing room saying, "He would like to meet you, and I think you'd like to meet him." It was Tom Brokaw. Tom Brokaw was the only person I ever met, and I almost didn't know what to say to him because I so respected him. Just like—wow! But Audrey Hepburn? I didn't think of her as a mammoth movie star. She was just nice. We talked and hung out.

Any memories of David Merrick?

I never even talked to him. He never talked to me. I remember seeing him literally three or four times during the entire experience. One incident that I remember was at the opening of *The Happy Time* in Los Angeles. David Merrick was throwing a party, and because David Merrick was a real cheap son of a bitch, he did not invite the crew or the orchestra to this party. He just invited the cast and the creative people. When Gower Champion got wind of what David was doing, he threw a party of his own at the Beverly Hills Hotel for everybody. Apparently hardly anyone from the show went to David Merrick's party.

What about Kander and Ebb?

John and Fred were terrific. I remember John pretty much teaching me all of my songs for *The Happy Time*. John was much quieter and much more serious. Fred was much more flamboyant and crazy. But I liked them both enormously.

After 286 performances, the show closed and it was back to California.

I had to finish high school. I went into my senior year. But I left New York deciding I really wanted to come back to Broadway. I had absolutely no plans to go to college, which pissed my parents off. I went back to doing TV and film. Once I graduated, I was working in L.A. all the time so I just decided I was going to keep working until I had enough money saved to move to New York. Gordon Hunt was the casting director for the Mark Taper Forum at the time and was also my acting coach. He knew that I wanted to get back to New York. At the end of class one night, he said, "I think I got your ticket back. Stuart Ostrow, the producer of *Pippin*, is going to be in Los Angeles looking for a replacement for John Rubinstein and I'm bringing in some people for him. I'm going to bring you in." So I auditioned for Stuart Ostrow. I went home and got a phone call from him saying, "Can you fly back to New York with me tomorrow? Bob Fosse has got to see you." So I got on a plane with Stuart the next day, and Stuart pretty much spent the flight giving me a whole history of Bob Fosse. The next day I auditioned on the stage of the Imperial Theater where *Pippin* was playing, and Bob was absolutely fantastic. It wasn't one of those clichéd things where he's a voice in the darkened theater and you're onstage. He was right there in the front row. He was very nice to me. A real gentleman. Two hours later I got the gig. I moved back to New York three months later as the lead in a Broadway show. Betty Buckley was playing Catherine in the show at the time, and she and I got on very well. I found her very odd and intense in a lot of ways, but I liked her a lot. Fosse put me in the show himself. It wasn't just the stage manager. He really liked what I did a lot. And he used to joke with me a lot, and Bob, as I'm sure you know, could be a terribly cynical and a very dark person. He was attracted to the dark side of things, and he loved telling me what *Pippin* really was about to him. It was about the Manson family, and Charles Manson, and about young men playing Pippin being murdered. But he loved his concept of *Pippin*, and he loved talking about it. He always thought of himself as a cheap entertainer. He said that to me one day. He said, "You're a cheap entertainer, aren't you, just like me." He even gave me a mug that had that printed on it.

What do you think that means?
I think that he knew that I knew how to go for the laughs, and he saw a lot of those laughs as being cheap laughs. He saw that I knew how to play an audience, I knew how to get a reaction. That didn't have to do with craft as an actor, that had to do with being a cheap entertainer. You had to entertain. To him it was razzle dazzle. It's cheap. "How can they see with sequins in their eyes?" The afternoon they gave me the job, they got me a ticket for the show that night. I loved the production. I thought, "This is great. It is so brilliantly staged, and it's so dark and creepy."

It's funny that you just quoted that line from *Chicago*, "How can you see with sequins in your eyes?" I think people don't realize that the text of *Pippin* is actually problematic because Fosse's production, and similarly Diane Paulus's for the revival, is so dazzling.
When he was putting me in the show, he actually gave me a copy of the original script of *Pippin* and said, "I want you to see why I did what I did. I want you to read this." It was awful. It was a terrible script. But he gave it an incredibly smart production. The original script was such a product of its time. It had this whole flower child aesthetic. Pippin was constantly talking to the constellation Orion for guidance. The whole sex ballet was nicknamed Gisella because in the original script that song was sung to a peasant girl named Gisella. Bob turned it into a sex ballet, which Schwartz just loathed. But had Bob not done what he did with *Pippin* it probably would have run about a month. There was nothing in that original script that was interesting at all. It was like an extension of *Godspell*. It was about this young guy who doesn't know what he wants to do with his life. Seriously? We give a shit about that? So Bob, being obsessed with the Manson family and the Manson murders in L.A., turned it into the leading player and the family of players around him who would get young men to play the role of Pippin and put them through a series of experiences, manipulating the experiences to the degree where each one was disappointing and the only thing that was going to bring true happiness was to kill himself at the end of the show. None of that was in the original script. I mean, none of it. But that production just dazzled the audiences and went on to have a seven-year run.

I never connected the fact that that trio is called the Manson Trio . . .
It's about Charles Manson. That's what the whole show's about to Bob.

John Rubinstein apparently told you that you'd enjoy it for the first month and then being at the core of all that darkness would wreck you?

Yeah. I actually ended up being in therapy because of *Pippin*. Not only—some months into the run, I started to miss Los Angeles a great deal. I missed home. I was also in a show where for two hours and twenty minutes there was constant negative energy coming at me. Psychologically that actually did some damage to me. I started missing shows. It started becoming a very dark experience for me. [Ultimately] it was suggested to me, after I told my therapist and our stage manager that I was very lonely and felt very isolated in the theater, "You don't have to be alone. Why do you need this dressing room?" I moved down into the boys' dressing room in the basement with the ensemble. All the guys looked at me like, "What are you doing? You're crazy. You're the star of the show." They all liked me. It's just that I never saw them offstage. I only saw them onstage. Things got better. They got to know me, not just as Pippin but as Michael. I got to know them, not as this ensemble that tried to kill me for two hours and twenty minutes, but as these guys. Between that and the therapy, I ended up being okay and doing two whole years in the show. *Pippin* was just not fun to do. It was a dark experience the entire time I was with the show.

You took it on tour.

I did. I actually did *Pippin* for three years altogether. I was already tired of doing *Pippin* but I thought, "Well, I'll get to see some different cities," and quite honestly, I was paid very well for the tour. This was back in the day when you really could make a lot of money on a national tour because you had per diem, which pretty much paid for everything, so your entire salary could just go in the bank. Tours don't work that way anymore. But there was a time when people really wanted to tour because it was a way to make money.

Were you happy on the road?

I had fun on the road. I really did enjoy going to some different cities. It was a good company. I was really terribly bored with the show, though. I had to continue to find a way to make the show fresh for myself. And in the original production it was done without an intermission. It was two hours and twenty minutes straight so even as a young person, it was really tiring to do. I was just tired a lot.

You came back and did *Shakespeare's Cabaret*.

Yeah, that was a fiasco. I came back from *Pippin* and there were several months where I didn't work at all. I auditioned for a few things, but I didn't book them. I did another job for Stu Ostrow in a show that closed out of town: *Swing* at the Kennedy Center. I did some regional theater. But the next thing I did on Broadway was this thing called *Shakespeare's Cabaret*, which was just a mess. It was a really interesting idea. There was some really good material in it, but the director didn't know what he was doing. And the producer ended up bouncing checks. It was just one of those awful experiences where Equity had to get involved. They started insisting that the producer pay us in cash or we wouldn't go on. It was still a fascinating work, but it was a mess.

Many actors work their way up to great directors. You started with two legends and then experienced the difference of a director without vision. Did you recognize that you were in trouble immediately?

Absolutely. Within a few days you start to realize that this person really doesn't know what they're doing. And it was the first time, whether in television or in theater, that I ever worked with a director that I didn't get along with. I've had the great fortune in my career to work with very few of those people. Most everyone I've worked with has been great.

You told me once that in the entirety of your career, there is only one person you would never work with again: Elaine Stritch.
She was the worst human being on the planet when I worked with her. I tried to get out of that show [*The Full Monty*]. I tried to have [director] Mark Hoebee fire me.

I would think the rehearsal process wasn't long enough for her to make it that miserable.
She made me feel like it was months in rehearsal. That's how awful she was. Just an awful human being. Evil. Evil. Mean-spirited, nasty evilness. I'm telling you it's true.

I am asking not just because it's Elaine Stritch but with any actor, how does evilness manifest? And to what end?
She would say things like, "You're not going to play it like that, are you?" I finally got to the point where I literally told her to go fuck herself. I said, "Yeah, actually I'm going to, and you can go fuck yourself, Elaine. I don't care if you're a fucking legend." Mark dragged me out of the room, and said, "Calm down, calm down." I said, "Fire me, Mark, because I'm going to hit her. I'm actually going to slug her." That's how awful she was. You have to really push me into a corner for me to push back like that. I've mostly only worked with great people. Anybody who understands the nature of theater knows that it only works if we're all in it together. Unlike film, where you can do great coverage and then walk off the set and be an asshole to everybody, and your work is still going to play. Elaine was miserable. She hated her life and she was going to make sure everybody else's lives around her were miserable, too. I think she was self-destructive and then even when she became a recovering alcoholic, she had not let go of this self-loathing that somehow was going to make her determined to make everybody else's lives around her as miserable as she felt her own life was. I could see her actively trying to make everybody miserable. I could see it. And because of that, I hated her.

After *Shakespeare's Cabaret* a life-changing show came your way.
March of the Falsettos happened, and who knew it was going to become what that show became? Bill Finn was out of his mind crazy at the time. I remember once we got into rehearsal, taking Chip Zien aside and saying, "What are we doing?" And then I went to Jim Lapine, and to Jim's credit, he kept saying, "Trust me. I'm not sure what it is either, but I think there's something here. Let's keep working on this and let's see what we have." And God love him, Jim was right. The first audience we had at Playwrights Horizons was going fucking crazy for this little show.

What do you think they're responding to?
I think they were responding to Bill Finn's voice. Certainly musically. He also was saying things with his words that I only later started to realize. I think Finn and his lyrics, certainly in *Falsettos*, had a way of saying rather profound things in very quirky, simple language. He would say things in very weird ways but there's nothing flowery or refined about his words. "What would I do if I had not met you? Who would I blame my life on?" That's something that someone who's lost a love really feels. Another writer would not say it that way. No one had ever seen anything like it before. Nobody had ever written a story like this. And in the way that Lapine directed it, the way the actors acted it, the way Bill wrote it, the entire enterprise had a rawness

to it, and a freshness. I think the audience totally was taken aback. I think one reason it worked as well as it did is because Jim kept saying, "This is not a gay play. This is a play about family."

How did telling this particular story resonate for you?

During *March of the Falsettos* certainly I didn't feel proud to be a gay man breaking ground in a theater piece. It wasn't about that. I just ended up finding what Bill had written and playing it as a piece of storytelling for an actor. None of us felt it was groundbreaking in that regard. I only mentioned my own personal experience because I was the gay guy in the show. Steve and Chip were not. So certainly from my perspective, it wasn't groundbreaking. We were telling a great story we ultimately figured out. Even though at first we had no idea what the fuck we were doing. It really was only some years later when we got into *Falsettoland* after the whole AIDS epidemic had begun, that we started to realize the power that we had in this storytelling. We realized that none of us will ever have an experience like *Falsettos,* ever in our lives, no matter what kind of work we do in the future. There is something about this moment in time and this experience, and this story that we are all telling together. There will never be anything like it. All of us have gotten to do other things we're very proud of, but . . .

When you say "there's nothing like it," I understand that it may not be something easy to articulate, but do you know what that means?

It is hard to say what that means because it's a mysterious, intangible thing.

When we did *Falsettos* on Broadway in 1992, I would have the most unlikely people come up to me at the stage door. The upper middle-class, middle-aged, Westchester, straight couple saying, "We just had to meet you. You don't know what this evening did for us." These were not people who necessarily had skin in the game. Do you know what I mean? Right before I would launch into "Father to Son" at the end of the first act, in my peripheral vision I could see the front row. I could see men who were sitting there looking like, "What the fuck did my wife bring me to?" By the end of the second act, I would see those same guys in tears, and I thought, "Oh my God, look what we just did. We took them on this journey." It was weird because of that. We would have people like Paul Newman and Joanne Woodward come backstage and sit in the little green room and just say, "We just want to sit with you for a minute." What? That's how powerful that show was. I only mention them because the celebs are the ones who can get backstage, but there were people who would just want to hang out with us afterwards in the alley there behind the stage door, just be with us for a minute. Also, the number of young men that I would meet that were in New York specifically because they were going to Sloan Kettering; they were ill, and they had to tell us how much the show meant to them as someone living with AIDS and struggling for their lives. There simply had never been any experience like that for me before *Falsettos*. To this day, that cast recognizes that we had that shared experience. That's special. When you talk about communal . . . the final part of that puzzle is the audience. It's a shared experience between the people who created it, and the people who were telling it on the stage, and the people who are calling those light cues, and the audience. There's nothing like it. You don't get that in a movie theater.

After *March of the Falsettos* you took an interesting turn, writing *Three Guys Naked from the Waist Down*.

Three Guys Naked happened because I just had some downtime. I always played the piano, and I had written music, just for fun. When I was working on *Swing* at the Kennedy Center, I was working with two guys, Jerry Colker, who I had actually done *Pippin* with, and Paul Schierhorn. Backstage at the Kennedy Center, we kept thinking in our arrogance, "This show's a mess. We could write something as good as this at least." We were just playing around with doing comedy sketches about three stand-up comics that just did these bizarre routines, and all of a sudden Jerry and I thought why don't we try writing something about these three stand-up comics? Paul became our sounding board. We just started coming up with this idea for some show about three stand-up comics. We didn't know what the hell it was going to be. *Three Guys* actually ended up opening in '85 off-Broadway. And all of a sudden, I thought, 'Gee, I'm a composer. I can write musical theater.' The show got very mixed reviews, but my work as a composer actually got quite good notices, and Jerry's book even went on to win a Drama Desk. It ran maybe about five months or something. Anyway, that's how *Three Guys* came about, because I had downtime, and I thought "I'm going to keep being creative."

A lot of actors find themselves happily surprised when they discover another creative outlet. Did you?

I found with *Three Guys* I got much more fulfillment than I ever got as an actor. Just because I had created something, and I really loved doing it. I loved sitting at the piano and just writing music. I found it much more satisfying than I had ever found acting in any way. I remember being interviewed when I was young, and saying that I felt more at home on the stage than I felt anywhere. I felt like I belonged there. With *Three Guys*, by then I didn't feel as at home on the stage. I didn't feel like I loved being there. In the '90s, I saw the revival of *Hello, Dolly!* with Carol Channing, and I got that feeling, even though she wasn't young, she would rather be here tonight doing this show than anywhere on the planet. You can feel it. And because of that, it was magic. Because of that, it was an amazing experience to watch her.

"Here was a man with no dream and no plan." With Debbie Allen in *Sweet Charity*. (Martha Swope, ©Billy Rose Theatre Division, New York Public Library for the Performing Arts)

Sweet Charity **came along shortly thereafter.**

Yeah, Bob, of course, knew me from *Pippin* and liked me a lot. It was great. It actually ended up being an enormous amount of fun, mostly because of Debbie Allen who was playing Charity. Debbie is truly one of the funniest people I've ever worked with in my life. The entire time we were together we just had an enormous amount of fun. We laughed a lot. Bob was a real taskmaster. He demanded real focus and was very hard on the dancers. He was much gentler with the actors in the acting scenes. But I remember him being incredibly strict with the dancers. If those movements weren't as sharp as they needed to be, he would yell at them.

Was he mean?

No. I don't remember him being ever mean. Bob had this thing that he did with actors where he would say, "It's not working. I'm going to go figure this out tonight and let's work on it again tomorrow." The way he said it to you made you feel like it's not just your fault. It was a psychological game that I think he was playing with the actors to work harder at this somehow, but he never would make it your fault. He would say, "It's me. It's not you." But he was saying it with this twinkle in his eye like, "You know it's you, too; don't you?" He was a really interesting man to work with, and I respected what he did so much. I always felt like Bob had a vision. He had a moral view, and this was his world, and whether you agreed with that or not, you always knew it was a Fosse show. I just loved what he did. And to have had the chance to work with the man was pretty swell.

You told me that you would hang out with him sometimes.

There were always a few of the Fosse dancers around. Ann Reinking was there a lot. You got to see a little bit more of what we then saw in the movie *All That Jazz* in terms of this insecure, neurotic person. He was a show business creature through and through. He would tell stories about his early days and when he went out to California to work at MGM and how they were going to try to make him a movie star, but his hair was already thinning, so he knew that wasn't going to happen. He knew he had to get more into choreography. He'd talk about Broadway in the 1950s and in the '60s. I remember all of us just eating it up. He drank champagne cocktails of all things.

Gwen Verdon was very present on that revival.

Yeah, Gwen really assisted Bob because most of that choreography wasn't even written down anywhere. It wasn't notated. So much of the choreography of *Sweet Charity* was only referenced by what they could see from the movie version and what Bob and Gwen remembered, and Gwen remembered more of it than Bob did. So Gwen was there a lot. She was a delight to be around. I mean, she was tough as nails, but she was great. One of the greatest memories I have of *Sweet Charity* is during tech in Los Angeles; Debbie couldn't be there and they're doing "Something Better Than This." All of a sudden Gwen is up there, doing Charity. It was like 'never forget this moment, Michael, because you're watching Gwen Verdon dancing with Allison Williams and Bebe Neuwirth.' Gwen was dancing like it's twenty years ago. It just blew me away.

Tell me about Cy Coleman.

Cy was great. He was a character of the theater. Again, it's so amazing having been able to work with people who worked in the Golden Age of Broadway. He was a consummate musician. He was a jazz pianist, which he used much more fully in *City of Angels* years later, those composing chops. He felt like a throwback to another era a little bit. He just knew his stuff. He was a delight to be around. I've always loved being around people that know what they're doing. I was so fortunate to work with people like Gower Champion, and Bob, and Gwen, and Cy. These were people that just knew what they were doing. Even when they would make a false step in their work, they almost immediately knew it, and they knew they had to go in another direction. The day after *Big Deal* opened and had gotten killed by the critics, we were still rehearsing *Sweet Charity*. I remember being at the Minskoff Rehearsal Studios and I got there a little early. Bob was there. Nobody else. Just me and Bob Fosse. And Bob looked terribly depressed. He just kind of looked at me and smiled a small smile, and he said, "They just didn't get it. They just didn't know what I was trying to do." So even in his failure, Bob still knew what he was and what he wanted to do and what his vision was. In an odd way it wasn't like he had failed; they had just failed to get what he had done.

You won the Tony Award.
Yeah, that was quite terrific. It's amazing to win a Tony Award but it doesn't really change your life except that whenever they write about you, they say "the Tony Award–winning actor." That night, as we're standing backstage after Bob winning for the *Big Deal* choreography, and me winning for *Sweet Charity*, he said, "The crazy thing is, Michael, tomorrow we're going to be last year's Tony winners." And he meant that in the nicest way. He was just saying "Don't think this is going to change your life, but love tonight. Have a great time. Go to the party."

You said you enjoyed doing the show for as long as Debbie was in it.
Ann Reinking took over for Debbie, and she danced the role brilliantly. I mean, much better than Debbie ever did. Debbie did a great job, but Ann was a Fosse dancer. She was built right. She has those legs. When she danced "Brass Band," it was mesmerizing. But Ann is not an instinctual actress. In a Neil Simon–written scene like the elevator scene, it's about timing. It's about doing exactly the same thing every time. The elevator scene never worked as well with Ann, and I even called Bob and said, "Can you work with Annie?" Bob said, "I don't want to talk to her. She likes you. You talk to her." So I talked to her and she said, "Okay, I'll try, I'll try." She's a wonderful human being, but she's not the actor that has the skill set to do the same thing eight times a week. I still liked working with Annie because she's such a wonderful person. The show itself never sold like it sold with Debbie. It ran maybe another five or six months, but it didn't continue on after that. I was fine with that because after a year and a half, a year with Debbie and six months with Ann, I was ready to move on.

You moved on to *Mail*. Starring in your own show.
Yeah, that was quite an experience. Jerry and I actually got the idea to write *Mail* before *Three Guys Naked* even opened. We brought on Andy Cadiff as the director, who was a friend of Jerry's from Harvard, who was moving into directing. He had been Hal Prince's assistant on *Sweeney Todd*. I had been talked into being in it by Andy, and Jerry, and the producers. Andy said, "I would cast you in the show even if you hadn't written it." So I just went along with it. We did *Mail* in Pasadena, and it was a huge hit. We got great reviews. It was supposed to run for six weeks but it just kept extending. All these New York producers decided they wanted to move it east, and we did, and it flopped. It got terrible reviews. I literally sat in my apartment, the entire next day, staring into space. I was numb. I didn't expect the show to get brilliant reviews in New York, but I didn't expect it to get pans across the board. I had spent a lot of energy writing the show, and then I was spending an enormous amount of physical energy just being in the show. It was exhausting. I was offstage for about a minute out of the entire show. I wanted the show to close immediately. The producers kept it open for like another three

weeks or something. The day after we opened I called the producers and I begged, "Please just close it. Let's take the money that's in the reserve and spend it on a recording. Then maybe there might be a future somewhere out there in regional theater." Jerry Colker was furious at me, feeling somehow maybe the show could build an audience. He talked the producers into keeping the show open for another three weeks. So we never made a recording because there was no money left. A few people like Steve Sondheim and Jim Lapine wrote me notes saying, "Don't try to figure out why the critics wrote what they wrote, just move on to your next project. We've all been there." But the whole experience put me off writing for a long time.

Mail brought Brian Stokes Mitchell to New York.
I can't say enough good just about that whole cast. Michele Pawk was in it. It was a wonderful group of people and all of them did a wonderful job. I look back on the people involved and I have nothing but great things.

***Falsettoland* was next for you. Even though that show is now paired with *March of the Falsettos* more often than not when it is staged, and it's true that there is power in seeing them together, I always find the two acts a little disparate. *Falsettoland* was written ten years later and it shows. The writing is far more mature and the story has an arc.**
Those are very correct observations. By the time *Falsettoland* came around, Bill already had Lapine guiding him more as a writer. Lapine was able to say to Bill, "We need an arc. Can you write within those parameters?" I think Lapine had a big influence on the maturity of the writing in *Falsettoland*. Bill even tries to address the fact that he has matured a little bit by having Marvin say [in the opening], "It's about time to grow up." Bill had matured certainly, and it was a different world. The reaction to it was tremendous. Some of Bill's writing is just dead on. His storytelling . . . Even in something like "Mister Choi and Madame G." in *Elegies* he's writing about a Korean restaurant that's closed now and what happened to these people. It's the death of a little part of his life, the death of his Korean restaurant. I found that moving.

You were working with Faith Prince right before she became huge.
I've just been so fortunate to work with wonderful people. Quirky, and she is as funny as her performances have been. Faith is a throwback to another era. Had she been born a little sooner, she would have had even a bigger career on Broadway than she had. She was terrific in *Falsettoland*. I think of her singing "Holding to the ground as the ground keeps shifting,"—the humanity that she brought.

You left *Falsettoland* to go into *City of Angels*.
Yeah. I left *Falsettoland* for the money. At the point when you have a mortgage and everything else . . . It was sad leaving *Falsettoland* because I really loved doing the show. And it took months for Finn to forgive me. I mean, he really was pissed off that I left the show. It felt like a family. Bogardus even gave a little speech at the curtain call. Steve Bogardus is one of the greatest people on the planet just in terms of his heart. He's a good man through and through. I watched Steve in the early parts of the AIDS epidemic take care of friends that he had worked with whose families had abandoned them, and he was there when they died. I watched him nurse people. He just has enormous humanity. At my last performance he said to the audience, "I just have to say that I am not a gay man. If I was, Michael would be my lover." That's how close we were, how much we loved each other. But I was offered *City of Angels* to replace Gregg Edelman, and they offered me a lot of money to be in the show. It was a big Broadway show. It had already won the Tony, and I got to sing some Cy Coleman stuff again, which

I loved. Michael Blakemore had directed a pretty dazzling production. And within six weeks, I immediately hated it. The role I played was completely thankless. Tom Wopat went into the show at the same time and his character got all the laughs, had all the fun. I had all the high notes to sing, all the serious stuff to play. It was not fun. Thank God for the crew because they realized that I was not happy doing that show, and they were determined to make it fun for me to come to that theater eight times a week. They'd do little things like, I would open a newspaper and they'd have cut out a big picture of some porn star with her legs wide open. The audience couldn't see it but I would smile. Vocally it was not an easy show to do. I had the terrible song, "Funny," in the second act, and dramatically it didn't even make sense. If I was vocally tired, there was a way to cut the song, and I could do that. I could actually go to stage management and say, Let's not do "Funny" tonight, and you could skip right over it and the story wouldn't be hurt at all. Later in my year's run, probably twice a week I said, "Let's not do 'Funny' tonight."

You went from that into *Falsettos* on Broadway.
I really thought *Falsettoland* was the end of the whole Marvin story for me, but then right after *City of Angels*, Graciela Daniele had done a production at Hartford Stage where she'd put the two shows together. Lincoln Center wanted to bring that production to New York, and Lapine called all of us and said, "We can't let this happen. This is our show." I mean, he's a great friend of Gracie, and I love Gracie. She's a great lady. [As it happened, she had staged it on a thrust stage and there was no appropriate theater available]. So then they looked for a proscenium stage, and Gracie said, "I don't have time or a desire to restage it for proscenium." So that's how *Falsettos* happened on Broadway.

Your next show was quite the Tiffany piece, *Putting It Together* at Manhattan Theatre Club, with Julie Andrews.
Yeah. That was great. I didn't audition for it. They just asked me to be a part of this little group of actors. Julie, Chris Durang, Rachel York, Stephen Collins. It was bringing Julie Andrews back to the stage for the first time in thirty years or thirty-five years. It was an enormous amount of fun to put together. It didn't really work in a lot of respects, but it also worked because this small group of actors were singing great Sondheim material and having a great time being onstage together. Cameron Mackintosh wanted to move it to Broadway but Julie didn't want to because she had already committed to doing *Victor/Victoria* on Broadway for Blake Edwards, her husband, and she didn't want to take any thunder away from that.

What was it like working with her?
She was—well, she was—it was odd, and it was great. She was absolutely terrific. She took care of all of us. She'd make us tea. She'd make sure we had our vitamins. She'd have throat lozenges for all of us at all times. We half-jokingly ended up calling her "Mom" because she really was like a mother to us. She worked like a dog. She was very aware that she was going to be onstage again in New York for the first time in a long time, and she knew that people were going to come see this because of her. But she always referred to it as our show—"our little show we're doing." She wanted us to not feel like she was the legend, Julie Andrews. She was just one of the gang. She loved being a part of the ensemble of that show. She loved it most when we were all in the same room rehearsing together. She liked that much more than when she was off by herself in another room. She was kind and generous and fun to be around. She was also a little weird because there was a time every day at rehearsal when she would have to go

away into another room because—and she was upfront with us about this—she had to call her therapist. Every day. You always had the feeling that she had her demons. She had her baggage, as sweet as she was. I think there was a part of her that was very scared about doing *Putting It Together*. She told me a wonderful story: [Before rehearsals began] she said, "Well, I'll have to get myself in shape." She was living in Gstaad, Switzerland, and she would jog through the lanes and hills, vocalizing at the top of her lungs. That rarified air, no oxygen, and she said, "One day I'm jogging up over a hill in Switzerland, vocalizing, and at the bottom of the hill is a busload of tourists looking up at me." She started laughing thinking "Oh, my God, they're thinking, 'Look, she still thinks she's Maria in *Sound of Music*.'"

What about Sondheim?

I enjoyed working with him. He was going through a bit of a creative crisis just as a writer. I remember one time sitting with him and out of the blue he says, "All of the really great writers did all their best work before age [sixty]." He didn't compliment you much. I even ran into Lapine in Shubert Alley at one point, and I said, "Steve never says he likes anything I'm doing." He said, "Steve is just like that. He's not going to praise you. If he didn't like you, you'd know it."

After *Putting It Together*, you weren't on stage for a few years.

[That's when I started thinking] "Do I really care about any of this any longer? Are there other things I could do?" I did do a few workshops of shows, readings of things that were sent to me during that time, but the things that appealed to me or the things that I liked ended up not going anywhere, so it shows you what I know. There was nothing that came along that I really cared about. I just thought, "Do I really want to do this eight times a week? Do I want to go to the theater? Do I want to just go through the entire process?" It was also just a physical thing. Eight shows a week, especially if it's a larger role, is just incredibly taxing on you physically. You wake up and the first thing in the morning you think is 'Is my voice okay today? Am I going to be able to do the show tonight?' Your entire world revolves around going to that theater that night. I had just gotten to the point where I just didn't want to work for a while. I did a musical written by Jimmy Buffet called *Don't Stop the Carnival* down at the Coconut Grove Playhouse, and I had an enormous amount of fun. The entire thing was just like a party. I had also gone to a couple of universities and done some directing, which is where I was when *Ragtime* happened. At that time I had no idea what I was going to do with the rest of my life and didn't really care. I just thought, 'Something's going to show itself. Something will happen. And if I go several years and nothing shows itself, then I will decide what I want to do next.'

***Ragtime* showed itself.**

Yeah. They were looking for someone to play Tateh in the first national tour. Garth Drabinsky had a reputation for paying his actors very well and I had not been out on a national tour in many, many years, so this sounded interesting to me. That tour only played five cities in a year, which meant we were going to sit in cities for chunks of time. I thought, "This could be an opportunity to see some other cities, and get away from New York, and maybe make some good money." So I ended up spending a year on the road with *Ragtime*. I was exhausted the entire time. It's a three-hour show, but also the journey that Tateh takes—it's emotionally exhausting. I loved doing it, though.

Since it was the first national tour, you were directed by Frank Galati and staged by Graciela Daniele?

There's so much musical staging in *Ragtime* because there's so much music. It was interesting to see how much Graciela Daniele really did. They had already staged the show, obviously, because it was playing on Broadway, and I don't know how they worked on the original production, but in the first national, I remember getting a lot more input from Gracie than from Frank. It was like Frank was the overseer and he would work with you obviously, but Graciela Daniele, who I'm sure you know is just this little spitfire Latina, was always right on the deck, getting her hands dirty, whereas Frank would sit in his chair in the back of the room and watch over everything. And it was the first time I had worked with this new concept of a resident director. Stafford Arima and a few others were going to go on the road with us and, rather than the stage manager, keep the show in shape. These resident directors were actually going to be in charge. I thought it was interesting to have these three other people always hanging around, and they were going to be the ones that were giving me notes. It was a real

Reunited with Betty Buckley, in *Elegies*, twenty-nine years after they costarred in *Pippin*. (Joan Marcus)

machine because it was such an enormous production. Frank and Gracie encouraged me to bring whatever I wanted to the role but I still felt I was being plugged into this *Ragtime* machine because 95 percent of the show was underscored, so oftentimes blocking was timed to the underscoring and you couldn't change it. It had been put together like clockwork. But they totally said, "Just make it your own." Fortunately, the three times I've taken over roles, I've had directors who don't want me to do what my predecessor did.

Elegies came after that. Did William Finn just call you for that?

Yeah, pretty much. I just jumped at the chance to do it. I mean, I knew it was going to be this very limited thing. There was no theater available for it at Lincoln Center so we just did it in the Mitzi Newhouse on Sunday and Monday nights when the theater was dark. And I knew Gracie and Betty Buckley, Christian Borle, Carolee Carmelo. So it just sounded like fun. I loved so much of what Bill had written. I thought it was really fascinating, and I loved singing some of those songs. We all got along famously. Betty very briefly started pulling her late-to-rehearsal shit, which she's notorious for, and Gracie immediately set her straight. She said, "Don't ever be late for my rehearsal again. If you are, I will fire your ass." She really respected Gracie. Graciela Daniele is one of those people that you want to be in the room with. You want to work with her because she's a good lady, and she's generous and smart. I'm glad we were able to record it because I finished up the month thinking, "I wish this had a longer life." The whole experience was a good one.

Shortly after that, you and Carolee played spouses in *Baby* out of Paper Mill.

Yeah, I saw it on Broadway and it was not one of my favorite shows. But there were good people involved. LaChanze, Norm Lewis, Chad Kimball, and Carolee. It was a good experience because of the people involved.

Did you enjoy working with Norm?

I had actually already worked with Norm once. I had directed a workshop of an absolutely terrible show called *Leopard's Leap*. It was just dreadful. I cast Norm Lewis as a drag queen and he was absolutely fabulous. It was the most bizarre show. And of course nothing ever happened with it. So during *Baby*, we just spent a lot of time laughing about *Leopard's Leap* and how awful it really was. Norm is just a sweetheart. He's one of the nicest guys around, and he was quite good in *Baby*.

***Legally Blonde* was next, in a role I wouldn't necessarily have thought of you for.**

Legally Blonde was the first time in my life where I felt old. It was an incredibly young group of people, which I thought was terrific, but we got into rehearsal, and by the end of the first week, I half-laughingly said to [director] Jerry Mitchell, "Jesus Christ, I'm so fucking old." I also noticed that there was very little discipline in the room. Kids were just goofing around a lot. They were just talking all the time. I had grown up working for directors that were very strict disciplinarians. By the end of the second week, I said to Jerry, "Are you going to start pulling all of this together? There's talent but no discipline in this room at all. You know that, right?" And he said, "Yeah, I know. I will eventually. But the reason I'm allowing that, Michael, is because I want the show to have this goofing around, fun energy." And Jerry did exactly what he said he was going to do. By the end of the third week, he had started to sneak discipline into the rehearsals so things were much more focused. I was seeing these kids be as free and as spontaneous as they had been, but now in a focused, more disciplined way. Jerry totally understood what that show needed to get the response from an audience that he needed to get. Being the old guy in the show, I could see where he was still finding his way as a director, but I respected him enormously working on that. He really learned a lot from Jack O'Brien. The audiences loved it. *Legally Blonde* was a lot of fun. The kids were great.

You obviously enjoyed it because you joined the tour.
Jerry asked me to go out on the last three months of the tour. The New York company had already been closed for almost a year. I ended up enjoying myself. The only thing I didn't like was it was a real traditional tour where we literally played most cities for a week. Every day off was really our travel day, so you end up not having much time off. The only time you have is once you land in the next city, you have that Monday night off, and then most of Tuesday until sound check in the new theater. So doing the last three months was plenty.

We talked about *The Full Monty*, and then you were out of New York for a while until *On the Town*.
During those years I spent more time at universities teaching and doing master classes, and then John Rando called me—not about *On the Town*, but like a year before that. He said, "I'm doing a workshop written by Harry Connick Jr. called *The Happy Elf*. I want you to play a curmudgeonly old elf who works for Santa Claus. Are you up for it?" Sure. So I went to Maryland and worked with John and Harry Connick Jr. on *The Happy Elf* in tights and pointy ears. When we left this thing, John said, "I promise I'm going to be calling you in the next year or so about playing a human being." And he did. He was doing a production of *On the Town* at Barrington Stage in Massachusetts. And he said, "I know you not interested in big roles. This is small but we're going to find a way to make it fun and funny, and it's a great way spend summer in the Berkshires for a couple of months." I played Judge Pitkin and had an enormous amount of fun. And then all of a sudden, there were New York producers coming to see it because it got a love letter from Ben Brantley, got brilliant reviews. We moved to New York and another good time was had by all.

It moved into a very big theater, which seemed like a big gamble.
Howard and Janet, the lead producers, just loved the show. And they are billionaires. They just wanted to produce it. I don't know if they ever felt it was going to make money. We could see right away that it just wasn't going to sell. We did pretty well the first six weeks. But none of us were stupid. We could read the grosses. We saw that the show was losing money. We were all shocked that the producers kept it open and kept pouring money into it as long as they did. I never saw the show suffering low morale, though. We all had such a great time putting that show together. John Rando is one of the greatest people in the business to work with. You love being in rehearsal with him. He's smart. He never gets upset. He's always nice. He's fun to be with. He jokes a lot. He looks like some guy who should be teaching English Lit in college somewhere. All of those young people in the show were just great. As the older guy, I felt swell and proud that I was working with these young people. It's so satisfying working with good people. It really was a pleasure.

So as I reflect on all that you've said, on the one hand, you say that you are not sure you want to keep performing. And on the other, your most recent credit you describe as a real joy and something you did as a bit of a lark. What do you think you want now?
I guess the difference between what I did earlier in my career and those later shows, it wasn't being onstage and the storytelling aspect of the experience that I enjoyed as much as just hanging out with these wonderful people. There was never once during either of those

experiences where I went to the theater thinking, "I can't wait to get onstage." I always went to the theater thinking, "I can't wait to come hang out with everybody again tonight, and have fun, and enjoy this experience." The only way I would do another show is for one of two things: Either it looks like it's going to be an enormous amount of fun and I'll look forward to going to the theater eight times a week, or it's a director that I want to work with. Those are really the only two reasons at this point. I mean, if John Rando called me tomorrow, I would say "yes." I would work with John anytime. I would work with Jerry again anytime. I would work with Jim Lapine again. There are certain people that I've worked with that I respect so much, I would do it again. But I fully expect at this point in my life that I'm done. I don't see myself doing another show. I mean, it can always happen. I've been offered some workshops and readings of things that don't fit those two parameters. I think, "Get someone who really wants to do this, not me who's just doing it because it'll keep me busy for a couple of weeks." I don't need to be busy for a couple of weeks. I get such a kick out of working with students and seeing these young people reminding me of what I felt when I was their age, seeing them at the beginning of their careers. This sounds so fucking corny but just being able to share ideas and stories and thoughts that I might have that might just turn on a light bulb as people did with me when I was young. . . Thoughts that might stick with them over the years. There are little things that I was taught when I was sixteen by Gower Champion that I've kept my entire life. And when I now get emails from students that I've worked with saying, "What you said made such sense" five years later, that's swell to me. I think that's great.

It sounds like what you're saying is that's enough.
It's absolutely enough. I'm more content now than I've ever been in my life.

6

TERRENCE MANN

May 2018

TERRENCE MANN IS WAITING FOR me on the stoop of the five-story, 1902 Harlem brownstone he shares with his wife, the actor Charlotte D'Amboise, and their two teenaged daughters. With his gray hair pulled back, his glasses perched at the tip of his nose, his torso casually leaning on a step, both hands around a mug of coffee, he looks totally at ease and calm. The house is warm, relaxed, and without pretense, like its inhabitants. There isn't much inside to suggest that a Broadway power couple reside within, except the twin Hirschfelds hanging side by side near the stairs (Javert, say hello to Anita).

That all makes sense given that Mann, though a Broadway stalwart, was never a Broadway baby. Born in Florida and trained in North Carolina, he had no exposure to musicals and no drive to explore them until he ended up in the original production of the 1980 smash *Barnum*, for which he auditioned only because he knew the director, Joe Layton. And despite a bio that includes originating leads in three landmark blockbusters (*Cats*, *Les Misérables*, and *Beauty and the Beast*) Mann is not rooted exclusively on Broadway, even now. Sure, the résumé boasts more than fifteen Broadway credits, but Mann keeps equally busy teaching at Western Carolina University in North Carolina and directing regionally. He is founding artistic director of the Carolina Arts Festival and served as artistic director of the North Carolina Theatre for fourteen years, directing more than twenty-five shows. He and D'Amboise co-founded Triple Arts, a series of musical theater training intensives that pull them south every summer. And then there's the film and TV work, which has included all four *Critters* movies and more recently the series *Sense8*. And there's the home! Mann and D'Amboise don't just live there; they created their space. Mann beams as he shows me the extensive work they've done themselves on the townhouse and the sparkling basement apartment, currently inhabited by Broadway dancer Mary Ann Lamb. He insists he's not handy but the rooms tell a different story. So how does a guy who never especially cared about Broadway end up a perennial? A step at a time.

What made you decide at twenty-eight to move to New York?

I was working with the North Carolina Shakespeare Festival, and on my break I would come to New York just to hang out with my girlfriend. I was looking through the trade papers one day, and there was an open call for *Barnum*.

So you hadn't even moved here. You were just hanging out here?

I was just hanging out. I didn't want to be here. It's—I love the vibe. I love being in the city. I love hanging around here. It reminded me of being at the county fair at nighttime all day long

"The Rum Tum Tugger is a curious cat." *Cats*. (Photofest)

because there was always something going on. I saw that Joe Layton was directing *Barnum*, and I had worked with Joe [regionally] on *The Lost Colony* for five years. He made sure that I made the cut each time.

At that point you were not a musicals guy.
Never did one. I literally thought, "I'll just go down and see." I had no expectations.

And you got it.
I was thrilled. Wow! But behind that feeling was—I don't mean this to sound pretentious but I was down in North Carolina wanting to be a classical actor. I was doing a lot of Shakespeare, a lot of contemporary theater, a lot of restoration plays. So what comes with that is a sense of confidence that can be egotistical as well. The only musical I had ever listened to before *Barnum* was *A Chorus Line*.

So you are in a room with Cy Coleman and have no appreciation for who he is?
No. I thought Cy Coleman looked like the hookah-smoking caterpillar in *Alice in Wonderland*. I was amazed at his musicianship. I mean, wow! He could play! All I knew was that getting *Barnum* meant I was going to make 600 bucks a week. It just wasn't anything I wanted to do. I was so naïve. I thought the St. James Theatre was an off-Broadway theater because it was not physically on Broadway.

How did you educate yourself?

What I did was I went to go see musical theater. The first two shows I saw were a matinee of *Chorus Line* and that evening I saw *Sweeney Todd*. And I went, "Huh. I'm never going to work in this business." I wasn't trying to grab any brass ring or anything. It was just like "I've got a gig making 600 bucks a week. It's in a really cool city that I like, and oh, yeah, it's this musical thing." But I was also serious about getting good at what I was doing.

But you weren't ambitious in that way that some people are dying to get to Broadway and . . .

No, no. I was lucky to have that on-the-job training. I will never forget the first moment—our very first performance of *Barnum*: I run out to take my position and I looked out into the St. James, and I thought, "I'm at the Mecca of this art form." That wasn't lost on me. It was profound and I was profoundly humbled by the notion of being a part of it and wanted to honor that as much as I could. I was twenty-eight. I'd lived a life already. I'd gone to college at Jacksonville University, and I went to School of the Arts. I did a bunch of theater there, then got into trouble. Got kicked out. Had to go home, had to work construction, and then started playing in rock bands around the area. Life got pretty scary down there. Ended up working as a car jockey in a Datsun dealership in St. Petersburg, and living at home by the time I was twenty-five. I was at a low. I bought a car and drove back up to North Carolina to Winston-Salem. I just wanted to be there. Got a job working as a busboy at a Radisson. I had done *The Lost Colony* in the early part of the '70s and fast-forward to '75. I wanted to go out to "The Colony," just to the beach, just to chill out, kind of decompress. So I went out there, and I'm standing at the back of the Waterside Theater, and I heard this voice go, "What are you doing here?" It was Mavis Ray, a dancer-choreographer and she worked for Joe Layton a lot. She offered me a job. I said sure. Went back to Winston-Salem, sold my car, hitchhiked from Winston-Salem out to the Outer Banks, and she cast me as a dancer. I was dancing in the company of *The Lost Colony*. Plus I got asked to understudy the lead, so everything from that moment on just started to finally come together at twenty-five, twenty-six. Things started to align in me so that I could start to really participate in what I now knew as something I wanted to do.

You stayed in *Barnum* for a good, long time. Did you, at that point, have ambitions to stay on Broadway?

I was first understudy for the Ringmaster and I was Jim Dale's second understudy. I didn't go on during the Broadway run, but on the national tour. Jim and Glenn Close came out to do

Terrence Mann

Barnum	Broadway, 1980
Cats	Broadway, 1982
Rags	Broadway, 1986
Les Misérables	Broadway, 1987, 2003
Jerome Robbins' Broadway	Broadway, 1989
Assassins	Off-Broadway, 1990
Beauty and the Beast	Broadway, 1994
Promises, Promises	Encores!, 1997
The Scarlet Pimpernel	Broadway, 1997
The Rocky Horror Show	Broadway, 2000
Lennon	Broadway, 2005
The Addams Family	Broadway, 2010
Pippin	Broadway, 2013
Finding Neverland	Broadway, 2015
Tuck Everlasting	Broadway, 2016
Jerry Springer, The Opera	Off-Broadway, 2018

the San Francisco/L.A. leg of it, and I was the Ringmaster, plus I went on for Jim on Sunday matinees. I was ascending. I was getting a hold of it. I was getting good at it. I was understanding. I was still young. I didn't really own who I was, but I was working at it. Dirk Lumbard was on the tour with me. He went on vacation to London. He came back and walked up to me in the dressing room when we were in San Francisco and said, "Terry, there's a show called *Cats* in London. You're perfect for this role. It's called Rum Tum Tugger. You ought to audition for it." I called my agent. He called me back twenty minutes later and said, "They don't want to see you. They're looking for John Travolta or Rex Smith." They wouldn't see me. I was married at the time to an English lady, Judith, who had friends in high places. Princess Miriam of Johor, who lived in London, was Judith's best friend. She called her and said, "Do you know anybody who's got money in *Cats*." She called back with a message from the general manager and said, "Yeah. If he can get over here, we'll talk about it when he gets here." I just flew over on my nickel to London. I saw it on April 5th and was like, "Oh, my God. This is so cool. This is my kind of shit." I go back the next morning to the stage manager's door, and I knock. Supposedly somebody told him I was coming. He says, "May I help you?" I said, "I'm Terrence Mann. I'm here to audition for *Cats*." He says, "What?" I walk in, and there they all are, sitting around on the stage. [Choreographer] Gillian Lynne's sitting over in the corner in the audience. I said, "I'm here to audition for *Cats*, Ms. Lynne. I'm sorry to bother you on your lunch hour." And she said, "Oh, darling. I think we have everybody we need." And I said, "No, for the American company." She said, "Oh, oh, oh, yes," remembering, I guess, what they had told her about me being there. I said, "If the pianist can come up, I'll give him the music." The piano was right there. "I'm sorry. He's gone around the corner for lunch to the pub. Not here." I said, - "Well, can I play for myself?" And she goes, "Darlings (clapping hands), darlings, we're going to be entertained by an American."

So you did your audition for the entire British company?

Correct. I sat down, and I played Elton John's "Take Me to the Pilot." At the end of it, she comes up and says, "Why didn't I see you at the auditions?" I said I couldn't get an audition. She said, "Fine. I'll see you at the callbacks." So callbacks are at the end of June in New York. There's three guys. There's me; there's this skinny, little ballet dancer; and this really handsome guy who's got this huge shock of blonde hair but couldn't sing. He could really dance, but he couldn't sing and act. I was an okay dancer. I could dance, and I could sing, and I was bigger than both of them. This is where the arrogant part comes out: I went, "I got this." We danced for like an hour. I walked out and over to the phone booth that used to be in Shubert Alley and called my agent. He goes, "They just called. You got the job. And by the way, happy birthday." It was my birthday.

Did that feel like a massive step forward?

Massive, yeah, massive. All of a sudden I knew that I was going to be working for at least two years. Knowing that I had that job security as an actor was the overriding experience and feeling. It wasn't like, "I'm on Broadway!" I mean, that's in there, but that wasn't the driving feeling.

That was the *Hamilton* of its time. THE sellout show, the cover of *Newsweek*. What was it like being within that whirlwind?

The reason that *Newsweek* photo featured the nine of us was because we were in the first van to arrive at the photography studio and they wanted to get started. And that's the one they used for the poster.

That is so random and . . .

So random. The whole thing is so random. I think the best lesson I learned is that you just kind of stay in the flow if you can, and be prepared. Just be ready for it.

Trevor Nunn was a very different kind of director than Joe Layton, I imagine.

Very different. I connected with him because of Shakespeare. He wanted to create that feeling of a repertory company—that vibe, that sense of ensemble that you have when you're in a regional repertory theater that's going through so many different plays. You've got to learn to trust one another real quickly. I felt very comfortable. Spoke the same language as him, but he was the smartest man in the room. And that's really nice when you're in the room with the smartest man.

Because you can trust.

Totally. That's all you want. And Gillian Lynne was just adorable and sexyand fun, and naughty, and I loved her and her energy, and her ability to act and do stuff was just—I was like a sponge. I was just soaking it all up. We'd play a lot of theater games. Everybody was crawling around like cats. We acted like we were litters of kittens. We're crawling around. And we would get up and try to do some storytelling. After [the gymnastics of] *Barnum*—and the floors were not as good as they are now, they were concrete, so crawling around on your knees so much—knees and hips were starting to feel it at the ripe old age of thirty-two. Harry Groener had shin splints and stuff so the two of us would just always be standing on two legs. So we would make the choice to stand. So in the original production if you noticed Munkustrap and Tugger . . .

Are always presiding—almost overseeing.

Literally just to preserve our legs. But it was just fun. I don't have a perspective on it because I was in it. I was just playing, just making it work.

It's a show that begs the performer to let go.

There was that whole section in the middle of the Tugger song where I run out into the audience. I remember one night early on in the previews, I ran down and saw this lady just looking [so happy] and I grabbed her and pulled her up, and we just started dancing, and so that became the thing to do. And then eventually we got from dancing in the aisle to dancing all the way up the ramp onto the stage and doing all that. When I was lying in the perch during the opening, I would start clocking the audience, because you can tell by the body language who's into it. Then I made the mistake of seeing Bob Fosse in the audience. I ran all the way across and stood in front of him. He says, "Don't touch me."

You were in it for two years. Was it fun the whole time or did it get to be a chore?

Fun the whole time. Too much fun the whole time. It was wonderful and exciting and always fun. Some days I was hungover. But being there, doing that, going there, putting on the makeup, the whole process of getting into the journey of that made it so much easier. You got your head into it. It's an applied science on how you have to get yourself up to perform, and nobody has to do it harder than people that work in musical theater, even more than plays. You're singing and you're dancing. People that have to do that—other than Olympic athletes—eight times a week for years? I dare anybody to try it.

You left *Cats* to do the movie of *A Chorus Line*?

Correct. My first movie ever. I know. So sorry.

But as an experience . . .
It was extraordinary. I had the best time. They shot me from the waist up a lot because I couldn't dance [like some of the others]. We stayed in the dressing rooms in the Mark Hellinger for six months.

Right at that time, that's when AIDS was hitting the theater community hard. This community you had just arrived in.
We lost so many people. For a time, every fourth friend was dying. Twenty-five percent of my friends had it and they knew they were going to die. It was like a war when all of a sudden the guy next to you is dead.

I would imagine that the atmosphere backstage was very fraught.
Yeah, yeah, yeah, because you depend on each other out there. And we didn't know how you could get it for a while. That it was only through blood transmission. So everybody's going, "Wow, I kiss people on the mouth all the time." You're rubbing up against them and sweating against them because you're working with them. The paranoia started to infiltrate all of us to a degree. If you weren't afraid for yourself you were afraid for everybody else. I really didn't know how to talk about it. I didn't understand and I didn't want to grieve. I just stopped. Kind of shut it down. I just stopped grieving. I didn't want to go there. I just denied it as it was happening. How many times can you say, "I'm sorry—I'm so sorry." It was selfish. Concentric circles of death keep coming closer and closer and closer, closer to you. You try to get away from it. I don't even know. I've never articulated it. I watched *And the Band Played On*, and I think that put it in perspective for me the most. I wept through the whole movie. It was the—maybe it was the catharsis.

After *Chorus Line* . . .
I went back into *Cats* for six more months, and then I met Charlotte, and we had a massive affair thing going on. But after that six months in *Cats* I got asked to do *Rags*. I didn't have to audition.

That probably felt like a moment of arrival.
Totally.

It's interesting that you were asked because the role of Saul was not like anything you'd done or shown yourself to be right for.
I don't know why I got asked to do that role. I don't. I mean, I loved doing it and working with Teresa Stratas and [director] Gene Saks for a little bit. And Judy Kuhn, Dick Latessa, and Marcia Lewis. All these incredible people.

When you are working on material that isn't working, can you feel it, or are you trusting the creative team to tell you what is and is not working?
You're listening to the creators, and you're trusting. You're also just trying to take care of yourself. I was so concerned with my performance because, to your point, why was I cast in this role? I mean, I loved it so I wanted to honor it as best as I could. I was consumed with trying to keep up with all these performers out there. I didn't really have a perspective on the show or on how much work it needed. All I knew was that the music was extraordinary. I just kept trying to get to the next moment.

And when you're getting daily changes or the director's getting fired, what's that doing to morale during the rehearsal process and the Boston tryout?

Well, [composers] Stephen Schwartz and Charlie Strouse were geniuses, and so you always felt in good hands when they were writing music for you. When they let [director] Joan Micklin Silver go, that was the right choice because we had all been in the room enough over that first week to realize that this was not her wheelhouse. She herself knew that. Graciela Daniele came in for a minute, which was great, and then she was gone. Then Gene Saks. He came up to Boston to see it and then left by the time we got to New York. We didn't have a director—it was Charlie and Stephen.

Do you think that a director could have saved the show or do you think the material's the material?

I really don't know. I wasn't outside of it looking at it enough to know.

***Rags* was a legendary flop. Four days. But by the time it closed you had already been cast in *Les Misérables*.**

Really, I'm the luckiest person in showbiz.

Patti LuPone said that the London rehearsals were very touchy, feely, arty, actory. Was it the same in New York?

It was touchy, feely theater games, improv games, environmental games. We did a lot of that stuff. I remember walking into one of the rehearsal rooms at one point and [co-director] John Caird was sitting in a chair and all the girls were just running in a circle around him. I couldn't believe I was there and with Trevor Nunn again. I'm not a great singer. I'm not a great dancer, and I'm a pretty good actor. But to land those roles for whatever reason . . .

Javert is the polar opposite of Rum Tum Tugger in terms of restraint and stillness. Everything's contained . . .

I mean, I was doing Oberon and *Henry IV* and *The Rivals*, all in the same season. I was stretching every acting muscle I had. Pretty lucky, pretty cool.

The show opens and like with *Cats*, it's this massive thing. What do you remember about the ride?

I mostly remember wishing I had more technique as a singer.

You didn't think you were consistent?

No. I wanted "Stars" to really land. I wanted to sound a certain way when I sang it, and I never really got there.

The overall experience . . .

I will never forget when we were in Washington, DC, at our last performance there, all the ushers came down the aisles and they threw out hundreds of roses onto the stage. We were all standing in ankle-deep roses at that last performance. That was one of the moments where I went, "This is iconic. A game changer of a show." We were experiencing something special from day one when we started rehearsal. It was the perfect confluence of theatrical genius and magic, and a way of doing musical theater that moved people. Really good theater is communication between the audience and what goes on up there on—but great theater is—it's communion. It gets spiritual. It gets lifted to another place that the collective shares. That's what the *Les Mis* experience was for me.

I could see this being much harder to do over a long run than *Cats* was, even though *Cats* was more physical.
Correct. I was pushing myself as a performer. And I wanted to be a better singer. Little did I know that everything that I went through with *Les Mis* vocally was going to be increased tenfold by the time I got to *Beauty and the Beast*. I left after ten months because I had done it and was ready to move on. I'd gotten two movies.

Before we move off of *Les Mis*, any standout memories?
There are two places in the show where Colm Wilkinson and I used to walk offstage together in the first act. We'd walk to his dressing room and we would stand there talking. We would be talking about stuff, life, his kids, Scotch whiskey, and stuff like that. The first time was just before Fantine's death. He would put her back in the bed, then I would come out, and we would do the confrontation [and then we'd go off together backstage]. The second time it happened each night, he would change into his next costume. One night after we'd been running for about four or five months, we [came to the first of those two backstage moments]. Colm went over and started changing his clothes [as he does in the second of the moments]. Leo Burmester was there and started to say, "Hey, Colm, it's not this time. You're early." And I went, "Shhh, don't say anything." He gets into his next costume, and he's talking about Scotch whiskey. His shirt is out and his pants are unbuttoned down to his knees, not off yet. And he hears Randy Graff, Fantine go [singing] "But I will sing you lullabies . . .," and then all of a sudden all you hear is like gibberish. And he goes, "Oh, you fucks!" And he's pulling up his pants. So what you see from the audience is Colm Wilkinson running onstage—Randy Graff has sung her thing in the bed and has crawled out of the bed because nobody's there. She is crawling to Bob Billing, the conductor, crawling down and laying right in front of him. Colm runs out pulling up his pants like he's been out in the alley fucking some whore. He gets her, picks her up, puts her back in the bed, and then I come in for the confrontation. He turns around and looks at me and says, "You fucker, you fucker"—onstage! And when he picks up that chair to smash it and get that leg, oh, my God, he was coming after me. We had a little run around the bed like two more times than we normally do. We were both kind of laughing about it, but I will never forget that look on his face. "Oh, you fucks, oh, you fucks!"

You're a terrible, terrible person.
I was. I am.

And then you got cast replacing Jason Alexander in *Jerome Robbins' Broadway*. What was it like working with Robbins?
He was at the audition, but I didn't work with Jerome Robbins at all. I worked with Cynthia Onrubia and with Jerry Mitchell and the production stage manager. I think Jerry came by one time during the rehearsal, but then he was gone. Then I did the show for two weeks, and Jerry came and saw it. I am in my dressing room and the stage manager comes in and says, "Jerry Robbins wants to work with you tomorrow, 10:00 in the morning." I meet him and he says, "We need to change everything. Jason is short and round. You're tall and thin. Some of the comedy doesn't work. Let's figure out what works for you." Then he started going through all the stuff that I do in the show. He did it, and I watched. Brilliant. Not only was he a choreographer, he embodied the character, nailed the timing. . . . I wish I had taped

it. Very, very specific. That is what I teach. Every moment has got to mean something and be specific. So we spent about four hours doing that. I still want to write a book about it if I can remember it.

Did you find him intimidating?
No. Loved actors. Loved—he was really, really kind and funny.

So you get to do that show . . .
Best experience of my life. It was awesome. I got to do all these great musical theater moments. Charlotte [who was in the show] and I were in love. I was literally put in the show in ten days, and then I think right after that ten days we moved in together, on July 25th, 1989. I got to watch her dance every night. Do Anita. I mean, it was heaven. Didn't get any better than that.

Your next show was *Assassins*. Debra Monk told me how on the first day of rehearsal, she felt like she was way out of her league, and she was relieved to learn that everybody felt like they were way out of their league.
Oh, everybody did. Everybody was scrambling. You're in the room with Stephen Sondheim and Jerry Zaks and [pianist] Paul Ford and [musical director] Paul Gemignani. With Paul Gemignani, you just knew you were going to be taken care of. He would get you to where you needed to get to, no matter what. Whatever Stephen wanted, he knew. He understood that language. Paul Ford could play anything. So you felt good. But with Stephen in the room . . . he would go, "Let me hear it again. Does that note not work for you?" He was so about making the melody marry with the emotionality of what you were bringing to it. He was never about the notes. And it was such a company. I mean, everybody wanted to just do the right thing and make it good. They wanted to be at their best and to really make it something special. I felt like I was in this rarified air, and I don't know why. I mean, thank you for letting me be here, but I'm not sure. I don't think I'm this good. But I'm here doing it, so I'm not going to question it. So I do it. Jerry Zaks wouldn't let me get away with shit. I would start to say my monologue, and he goes, "Stop, stop, stop. Just say the words." "No, stop." Until I wasn't doing anything but standing there just saying the words. So it got empty. Then after that, kind of saying the words so empty, I would say it again, but something else started to happen. A different point of view started to happen. More grounded. He did that for me.

The show said some pretty important things, but audiences were not biting.
It didn't bother me. I mean, if the product that you've got is brilliant, genius, timely, poignant, good storytelling—if it doesn't move to Broadway because people don't want to see it because of what's happening in the world, fuck them. Fine. That's okay. You move on. There are few shows that come along that change our perspective. Most of the time shows are succeeding because that's what we want at that moment. So it wasn't maddening. It was sad. Made me feel sad for society. This is smart stuff. It's speaking up to y'all, and you don't want it.

What do you remember about working with that company of actors?
I made great friends. Victor Garber, Deb Monk. I mean, and all of us when we see each other, it's special. We all still share that very, very special, deep, resonating moment of having done that show.

Being part of that group, were you starting to feel like you were someone in the business? I don't mean that egotistically.

As Leon Czolosz, with Victor Garber as John Wilkes Booth in *Assassins*. (Martha Swope, ©Billy Rose Theatre Division, New York Public Library for the Performing Arts)

No. I would say literally just now. After doing *Jerry Springer*, I started to feel like I'm in the community. I feel a part of it.

Why now?

Never felt like I was. I never went and did all those talk shows. I always felt like a fringe player. And after *Jerry Springer*—maybe it's not so much feeling like part of the community, but I'm just really comfortable in my skin.

Your next show was the opposite of *Assassins*; it was kind of the beginning of corporate theater, and I am not maligning it. I'm just saying it's a different animal. *Beauty and the Beast*.

At the end of the day, where's the gig? [Writer and director] Linda Woolverton and Robert Jess Roth—they were great caretakers of the whole thing. It meant so much to them. But you had [Disney executives] Jeffrey Katzenberg and Michael Eisner weighing in. Alan Menken and I were talking about it the other day. We did our last run-through at 890 Broadway. We had the mockup of some sets and levels, but it was just us dressed like we were doing the whole show. You could see it. And the show was great, it worked great, and everybody loved it. It was fantastic. Then we go down to Houston to do Theater Under the Stars, and now we have the prosthetics for everybody, for Gary Beach [Lumière], for Beth Fowler [Mrs. Potts], for Heath Lamberts [Cogsworth], all of us in that stuff, completely covered. The only thing that wasn't covered was our mouth. Everything covered. I had about twenty-five pounds on, a skeleton and a helmet with steel rods that went down my back. We did this run-through in the afternoon and all of the suits came to see it. Jeffrey was there. Michael was there. At the break, Jeffrey Katzenberg comes running backstage. "This is not working. We don't see you, we don't feel you. We have no sense of the humanity beneath all of this. It's all got to change." And between that last run-through and our first preview, they got all of these makeup artists and people from all over Houston to come over and start jerry-rigging all this stuff so that you could see my face. They put the fake teeth on. They took away all these appliances so that now I could move. I could express something. And they did it for everybody for the most part. And from then on they just refined it as we got closer to Broadway. That was pretty smart.

With this piece the audience had such strong expectations. There were boxes that needed to be checked in order to satisfy them. Did you feel constrained or creatively stifled by that, too?

I just remember treating it like a piece of Shakespeare. And the way I spoke had to be Shakespearean. That was the way to approach it externally so that I'd have a vocabulary and a technique. Shakespeare is big emotions with epic events. I just tried to make sure it was big emotion that was trying to be revealed, and I tried to make the words kind of match that. That was my point of view.

Did you feel successful doing it? Did you feel like you were getting the story through the way that you wanted to?

Yes, yes, yes. Except every time when I went to sing "If I Can't Love Her," I went through the same thing I went through with "Stars."

That you didn't feel like you had the technique.

Correct. Never tell a composer what your low note is and your high note is because they'll use them. And that's what he wrote. He wrote it from like an F to an F.

Right. Just because those are my lows and my highs, those aren't my eight-a-week lows and highs.

Yeah. Sometimes I would hit it and it would just soar. That's what I wanted every time and I only got there like 25 percent of the time. That's how I felt, which may have helped the struggle at that moment. "Please forgive me. I'm not going to sing this very well" translated to "Please make me a human again."

This being the first Disney on Broadway show, did it feel different than other shows?

I remember when we were at the Tonys, we went out and did our big numbers. It was a tepid response. They resented the shit out of us, I think, for coming in and making a cartoon a Broadway show. And, as you say, corporate. Disney had already announced that they were going to revamp 42nd Street. We were the poster child for what they resented about all of that, I think.

You mentioned Tonys. By now you'd been nominated a few times . . .

It was fun because I knew I wasn't going to win. I had a great time. Just along for the ride.

You did Sondheim's straight play, *Getting Away with Murder,* and then the TV movie with Angela Lansbury, *Mrs. Santa Claus.*

The best. I had the best time. Everything felt good. I loved being in L.A. I loved working out there. Makes me feel good thinking about it right now. Going in and singing that song, and I was really on my game. I was liking the way I was sounding as a singer actually.

Was it fun to play sinister?

Oh yeah. That's where I met Rob Marshall for the first time. He was choreographing but he really directed that more than Terry Hughes. It was fun. I had that one scene with Angela Lansbury in a barn and it was sweltering hot. They had lamps on us and she was in this Santa Claus outfit up to her neck with a muff, and we were in there for hours and hours. She was so dignified, so gracious, so sweet. Kept the whole temperature—pun intended, perhaps—down.

When you came back, three of the shows you starred in, *Cats*, *Les Mis*, and *Beauty and the Beast*, were all still playing. Did you ever revisit as an audience member?

No. It feels like the past. I'm just tired and ready to move on to the next thing. I rarely like to go to the theater. I've changed over the years because my wife makes me go to the theater. I keep trying to figure out why that is. I think it's just because I'm so competitive. I don't want to go, "Oh, I wish I was doing that."

Your next show was *The Scarlet Pimpernel*.

Yes. It was a romp. Peter Hunt directed and then Bobby Longbottom. I loved doing it, I loved that cast, and I loved seeing all the stuff they were doing with it. I think my singing on that album is probably my favorite. We really took time recording it.

Having fun seems to be a consistent theme with you. But your next one, you have said, was the most fun ever. *Rocky Horror*...

Most fun I've had legally or illegally. That was fun. That was me being able to do everything I know how to do: Sing rock 'n' roll, be that rock-y Rum Tum Tugger. Having all that feedback from the audience and reacting to it; being in a weird, out-there, fringe, crazy, wacky, musical thing.... When I went into the show, I just did my Tim Curry knockoff. Tim actually came and saw the show. I knew Tim because when I was doing *Barnum*, he was doing *Amadeus* [across the street]. I was so nervous. He came backstage. I swear to God he did this [kow-tows]. I kneeled and lay down in front of him, and I said, "No, no, my God, no, no, no, no." He was so lovely, so gracious. [It was] one of my favorite moments other than Leonard Bernstein running into my dressing room after *Rags* one night, kissing me on the mouth, and telling me how brilliant I was. And Carol Lawrence coming in with chicken soup. She just brought chicken soup to everybody.

Between *Cats* and *Les Mis*, I am sure everyone in the world has come to see you backstage.

Everybody in the world came. Michael Jackson came. Cary Grant came. All of them came. I wish I would have been more of a picture taker, but all of a sudden when you shift—"I'm going to take a picture of this," then you're not in the moment.

You got to do *Lennon* next and work directly with Yoko Ono.

That was strange. Kind of thrilling and exhilarating. Growing up, The Beatles were a huge influence. In rehearsals, we spent a lot of times watching movies, listening to music. Learning about something that you'd only felt, and now getting the history of what's attached to that fabulous feeling of what music does.... But that whole experience with Lennon was like—I don't want to say it was ill-fated, but even though the effort and what Don Scardino wanted to do came from such a great place of homage, you can't do the story of John Lennon and, in a ninety-page script, have Yoko Ono show up on page twenty and not be able to do any of the Beatles music. It was a very finite, limited approach.

And a very finite run. But then came *The Addams Family* . . .
I'm going to be on stage with Nathan Lane, Bebe Neuwirth, Carolee Carmello. That'll be fun. The guys who directed it, I felt for them. I loved them. I thought they were smart. What they wanted was not what ended up on the stage. I just sat back and watched it all happen, just trying to do my part and just be there because it was nice to be amidst all of those creative, smart people. And it still ran for a while. Being on stage with Nathan Lane is like being in the room with Jerry Robbins, like working with Trevor Nunn, or Joe Layton. That was worth every moment. Just to be out there with him and to be in his world as he does things. I was just a fan being there.

How is it to navigate the waters knowing that there was so much tension between him and Bebe?
The amazing thing about the chemistry between the two of them was that they were so incredibly professional. Onstage they gave it up to one another. And offstage, they lived in completely different worlds. Bebe keeps evolving, and every time I see her, there's something more fragile, and vulnerable, and humanistic about her philosophically. We honored her at a dinner recently and she was so nervous. She kept saying to me, "Terry, I'm fine if I have a character, but me, just to walk up as me . . ." She came up there to read a prepared speech, literally shaking the whole time. But the speech was so elegant and heartfelt. She's so deep, so private, and protected. Through the whole *Addams Family* process, she cared so much about the storytelling and the characters being really defined. I never fault anybody in rehearsal for taking their stand and demanding excellence.

Did you ever feel responsible for setting the tone backstage? In *Beauty and the Beast*, perhaps?
It was set by the director, and then the leads just kind of carry on that really inclusive, altruistic, "Thank you for all being here all the time." I did during *Les Mis*, too, actually. I used to hang out with the stagehands a lot, and on our last night I catered a whole dinner for them in their rooms downstairs. I wanted to thank them so much. I've never thought of it, but thank you for bringing that up because it's something that I try to do in every show I'm in. Everybody's the same. We're all here for the right reasons. Some shows really get it, some shows you have to work harder at.

After *Addams Family* you did *Pippin*.
There was a moment after *Lennon* where I started just saying "no" to everything. "No, I don't want to do this. No, I don't want this. No, no, no, no, no, no, no, no." I would go down and direct in North Carolina. I wanted to be offered shit. My ego was like, "Fuck it. I want to be offered shit. I don't want to have to go and audition. You don't know me now? I've got seven albums out of shows you put me in." I didn't want to do it anymore. I created this world of "no." So people stopped asking. I said, "Well, I've got to change that. I just got to start saying yes." Then I went in to audition for the workshop of *Addams Family*. I got that, and I just started saying "yes" to everything after that. I did a couple of workshops of *Tuck Everlasting*, and then *Pippin* comes along. "Will you come in and audition?" I said, "No, I'm not going to come in." I didn't want to go up to Boston. Char said, "You want to live in this world of yes? You got to." "Okay. You're right. I'll go in." I finished the audition, and Diane Paulus goes, "That was great. Charlotte busy?" Literally that's what she said. Fast forward. The rest is history. [Both Mann and D'Amboise were cast in the show, playing

"It's smarter to be lucky than it's lucky to be smart." With Matthew James Thomas in *Pippin*. (Joan Marcus)

husband and wife.] We ended up going. We took our kids out of school. We went up to Boston. I just knew the concept was spot on. And Diane was digging—she was just mining for gold every time. She had meetings with me and Charlotte. She said, "So you're the husband and wife in the circus. What act do you want to do?" And I said, "I want to throw knives at my wife, and I want to ride a unicycle." The whole process was just glorious—the best. It was effortless. It was creative. Made new friends. Constantly working on it and all we knew was that we loved being in it and doing it, all of us. Singing, dancing, acting, and circus in a concept that so wrapped around this notion of what *Pippin* was. But we did not know that it was going to get the reaction that it got. I was cleaning, taking hair out of the drain of the bathtub when I got the call letting me know that I'd been nominated for a Tony. I had a handful of hair in my hand. I loved going to work every day. First time I've ever loved going to work every day.

You told me that *Cats* was fun all the time, and you told me that *Rocky Horror* was the most fun you ever had. You like to have fun.

It was fun. but there were some tough times when I didn't want to do the show. I had to work myself into it. No matter what kind of mood I was in or what was going on, when I knew I had to go work I was joyful. For the whole year and a half, every night I was joyful. It was going back to *Barnum* in a way. It was everything I knew how to do. You're always working on it. Walking on the stage every night, you still get that nervousness, that good anxiety, that adrenaline rush of what's about to happen—but because I've done it for so long, once the curtain goes up, and you're in it, your world of possibilities is so much more colorful, animated, and the selection is greater. That is what makes it so like a drug practically.

For that particular show, while you may want to try new things and create, there's also a safety thing at every step because there's so much going on. I would think that would probably heighten the challenge.

It does heighten the challenge. What you're talking about was the exact same challenge in *Barnum*, too.

There's no phoning it in.

Absolutely not. There is no phoning that in. You have got to be present and going forward the whole time. Nothing like it: to be so involved and feel like you're wrapping your arms around the world. When I'm onstage it's the best part of me.

You went from there to *Finding Neverland*.

Oh. I loved it. Had a ball. Diane Paulus called me up, they rehearsed me in about a week. I took over for Anthony Warlow. Love him, love that voice. I knew a lot of people in the cast. It was just a love fest the whole time. Loved doing it. Here again, exercising everything I'd learned over the years and having a ball. Changing it up every night but keeping it within the box. Staying in the world of yes. Just saying "yes." Staying positive. "Yes, I'll come do that." It was a big deal to go from no to yes before *Addams Family*. So that was just beautiful. And then *Tuck*. I think it's a beautiful show. I love the sensibility of it. Beautiful music. It's a fable. I loved playing that character. I don't know that I fit into the fabric of the piece, but that's what I came in with, and I'm not—I mean, at the end of the day I'm not sure. Casey Nicholaw just let me do my thing. I don't know if the show worked on all levels. Probably not. But we all drank the Kool-Aid so we're believing in it. It was heartbreaking, and it was heartfelt, and everybody cared so much about it, and everybody wanted it to be brilliant, and sometimes it works, sometimes it doesn't.

But again, you've been around long enough now that its closing did not ruin your world?

No, no. When you get the gig, then you're validated for a minute. I'm working. I got the gig. Great. That means I'm a part of the world. When you're not in it, you're not in it. You're out of the world, and you've got to be okay with that.

Judy Kaye and Patti LuPone both talked to me about having won a Tony and having expectations that the phone's going to be ringing, and it wasn't. I could see how after *Cats, Les Mis, Beauty and the Beast*, it was reasonable to assume that you'd established yourself well enough that the phone should be ringing.

Correct. But to have no expectation is really where you've got to live. Say "yes" and have no expectation. I still get asked to audition for stuff. I don't have a problem with it. Nothing left to prove. I couldn't wait 'til I got to be older so I would get to play great character roles.

Well, you got a great character role. You got *Jerry Springer*.
Crazy. I had known about it because when I worked with Jerry in *Rocky Horror*, we went out to dinner and he told me, "Terry, they're doing an opera about me in London." This is back in 2001, so I'd always known about it. I get this email from Scott Elliott. "Will you come do *Jerry Springer*?" "No, thanks, Scott. I appreciate it, but I'm going to pass." I get another email. "Terry, I'm begging." "Well, if you're begging me . . ."

What made you pass?
I went and looked at the London version of it. I thought, "This is fucking weird. It's kind of a one-trick pony and then that second act—it was so bizarre." I get what's going on, but it's like quasi-good *Saturday Night Live* sketch comedy. That's when I said "no." And then he called me back and begged me. Nobody has ever done that. I'm going, "Wow, he really wants me to do it. I like Scott. I'll go do it for him." It was so fucking weird, but I loved the work. I love being in the trenches trying to make it happen. I loved going to work every day.

So what do you want now?
I would like a month off to do nothing. I'm doing what I want. I'm getting ready to go do *Sweeney Todd* at Connecticut Rep. And then Christopher, Charlotte's brother, is choreographing and directing *Jesus Christ Superstar* up there.

It sounds to me like you have enough creative outlets and homes that even not knowing what tomorrow or the next day or next year looks like doesn't especially matter. You know that there's going to be playing in the sandbox with the people you like to play with.
That's exactly right. I couldn't put it better myself. Can you say I said that? I mean, even back in the '90s, I was the artistic director in absentia at the North Carolina Theater, so whenever I was free I would go down there to direct. *Sound of Music, Camelot, Show Boat, Gypsy, Funny Girl, 1776*. I always loved being in the sandbox, and so I've created these sandboxes. When my agents and manager say, "You won't be available for film and TV!" I get heartburn. I want to throw up a little bit in my mouth. I really don't care! I just feel content with whatever happens next.

7

HOWARD MCGILLIN

March, April 2018

"EVERY ACTOR THAT CAME TO New York in the mid '80s wanted to be Howard McGillin," says Marc Kudisch. And why wouldn't they? Blessed with dashing good looks and a silky tenor, McGillin was the "it" guy of the mid-'80s careening from show to show within months of arriving in New York in 1984. *La Boheme* at The Public, *Sunday in the Park with George*, the starry *Follies in Concert* at Lincoln Center, and *The Mystery of Edwin Drood* (Tony nominated as the dastardly John Jasper) all happened within McGillin's first year. He followed up with *Anything Goes* opposite Patti LuPone on Broadway and Elaine Paige in London. Frank Rich said in the *New York Times*, "His full voice and Brooks Brothers looks are perfection." In an ironic twist, his steadiest gig literally masked those looks when McGillin took on Broadway's ugliest character, the Phantom of the Opera, playing it for 2,544 performances, a record yet to be broken.

Born in Los Angeles and raised in Santa Barbara, McGillin says of his upbringing, "My dad was an accountant, and my mom taught nursing and healthcare. Not a show biz bone in the body." He never even saw a musical until high school where as a freshman, playing the clarinet in the orchestra of *The Sound of Music*, he saw his brother as Captain Von Trapp. "I was in a theater for the first time, playing in the orchestra, looking up at the stage and thinking, 'That looks really fun.' I just loved the theatricality of it," he enthuses. But despite some summertime work at Sacramento Music Circus, McGillin was not initially chasing a life in musical theater. However, he lived in California after all, and his handsome headshot landed him a contract at Universal. They kept him employed for more than five years before he decided to hit New York at what appears (with hindsight) to have been the perfect time. At thirty, he was just the right age for the stream of work that followed. In the '90s, *The Secret Garden* and *Kiss of the Spider Woman* required him to dig deeper, and McGillin was up for the challenge, particularly in the latter. Director Hal Prince was impressed enough to offer him the Phantom, and then the highly anticipated and much-derided Prince/Sondheim disappointment, *Bounce*. More recent work has included revivals of *Peter Pan* and *Gigi*, along with concert tours and a few off-Broadway plays.

Sitting with McGillin in the warm and airy sunken living room of the pre-war, Upper West Side apartment he shares with his husband, Richard, and their dog, McGillin reflects on his career with both gratitude and wonder even as he acknowledges that roles are fewer these days. "I've always kind of hoped that I would just continue to work. There are less offers than there were in my prime. That's understandable. But I am so grateful when the phone rings, and somebody like Charles Busch says, 'How would you like to do my play with me in a 100-seat

Howard McGillin	
La Boheme	Off-Broadway, 1984
Sunday in the Park with George	Broadway, 1985
The Mystery of Edwin Drood	Off-Broadway, Broadway, 1985
Anything Goes	Broadway, 1987; West End, 1989
The Secret Garden	Broadway, 1991
She Loves Me	Broadway, 1993
Kiss of the Spider Woman	Broadway, 1994
Mack & Mabel	West End, 1995
As Thousands Cheer	Off-Broadway, 1998
Ziegfeld Follies of 1936	Encores!, 1999
The Phantom of the Opera	Broadway, 1999, 2008
Bounce	Chicago, Washington, 2003
Peter Pan	National Tour, 2004
Where's Charley?	Encores!, 2011
Damn Yankees!	Milburn, NJ, 2012
Gigi	Broadway, 2015

theater down on 1st Avenue?' Are you kidding? 100 seats or 1,000 seats, for Charles Busch? I am there! I love the work."

You did musicals in school but then, after college, you went to Universal Studios and TV guest roles. You didn't sing for ten years.

The reason I ended up in L.A. had mostly to do with my acting teacher, Bradford Dillman, He would come around and watch the kids in their local productions, and he would handpick a group of students every year to study with him. He rented out a space himself and donated his time. No one paid a cent. Every week we would have his great guidance, teaching, and experience. His influence was huge on me. He opened my eyes to a whole world beyond musicals. He brought me to Hollywood in a way. He said, "I'd love for you to meet my agent." So I went to Hollywood and met his agent who sent me over to Universal Studios because they had a talent program. I auditioned for them, and they signed me to a contract.It was insane. I mean, I'd been in L.A. maybe a month when I got this interview and suddenly I'm under contract to Universal Studios. It sounds very glamorous. The reality of it is there was no real contract system left in Hollywood.

But you had a home.

Exactly. I had a home. And I think in L.A. especially, if you're not working, it's pretty desolate. You had basically your own little agency within the studio. Universal was at its peak in television so I was always, always doing TV. I did *The Six Million Dollar Man*, *The Bionic Woman*, and *McMillan & Wife* with Rock Hudson. And then I played his son in a miniseries called *Wheels*. I worked with Raymond Burr on three different shows.

Were you happy?

I was, except I wasn't singing. I was not happy not singing, and so I started to study again. It was that as much as anything that finally flipped the switch in my head. [I realized] that I can beat my head against this Hollywood wall as long as I want, I'm not going to rise above this crowd. But I have this voice and I should be singing.

You were cast in *La Boheme* at The Public ten days after arriving in New York.

It was like falling into a barrel of honey. I'm at The Public Theater. It's wintertime. The snow is falling. My first snowfall. I'm looking out the window backstage on a view of

Heartbreaking as Molina in *Kiss of the Spider Woman*. (Martha Swope, ©Billy Rose Theatre Division, New York Public Library for the Performing Arts)

cobblestone streets. It was like something out of a movie. *La Bohème* is happening on stage, and I'm hearing this glorious Puccini score. Snow falling on the stage, too, by the way. I thought, "This is pretty great."

The show was not well received, though.

No. But I didn't care whether or not the critics loved it. We loved doing it. I was such a fan of Linda Ronstadt and now I'm singing with her? I can't begin to tell you how thrilling that experience was for me. Just imagine being picked up and plopped down in New York City and suddenly, you're really in it. John Kander and Fred Ebb came one night, and the next night I'm shaking hands with Jackie Onassis and John John, and Caroline. I thought, "Okay. I made the right decision here." [After] almost ten years in L.A. doing television and bad movies like *Where the Boys Are*, it was a kind of miraculous thing that this happened. I give my ex-wife credit; we were sitting watching the Tonys in L.A. and I'm thinking, "I should do that." She said, "Go. We'll figure it out." Even though we had a three-month-old baby. And within three months I had my first Broadway job.

***Sunday in the Park with George.* Right after *La Bohème*.**

I'm understudying George and playing the Soldier, and that was head-spinning. And I already knew I was going to be doing *Drood* in the park that summer. [Director Wilford Leach, who directed both *La Bohème* and *Edwin Drood*] gave me this role [in *Drood*] that changed my life—changed my sense of what I could do. I had been playing leading men in Hollywood and that's what I thought I'd do in New York. He saw something else in me. It was a huge gift. I miss him every day of my life. He was such an amazing, beautiful man. So giving. Just the sweetest soul you've ever met. I will never forget the day that he came into rehearsal for *Drood* at 890 Broadway in tears. He said, "Bill Elliott died." Bill Elliott had been the music director of *La Bohème* and he and Wilford had been lovers. I mean, of course we knew about [AIDS]. I was walking through Greenwich Village one day during *La Bohème* when I saw a newsstand headline that Rock Hudson had died of AIDS and I'll never forget it. Took my breath away. I had done that miniseries with him and worked with him for a couple of months. Again, one of the sweetest, most generous human beings ever alive. It was shocking. I was dealing with my own sexuality and coming out, and not at all ready at that point, but I knew this was a game-changer for the world.

But in the midst of that, career-wise, you were thriving. All the stories about how tough New York can be, and you leapt right in from job to job to job.

It was remarkable to say the least. When I was leaving *Sunday in the Park* to do *Drood*, I had a conversation with James Lapine backstage. I said, "By the way, James, I hear they're going to be doing *Follies* in concert." He said, "Oh, yeah. You'd be great for one of those guys." The next thing I know I'm offered *Follies*. So I'm doing *Drood* in the park knowing I'm doing *Follies*, and then *Drood* is going to go to Broadway. It's head-spinningly fast. But here's the crazy thing: At the time, it didn't seem—this is going to sound really selfish and stupid—it just seemed inevitably right. I don't mean that to sound like, "Oh, I deserve all of this." It wasn't that. It just was—it was my reality. But yes, I was aware that this was extraordinarily great. In Central Park, in rehearsals for *Edwin Drood*, thinking, "A year ago I was sitting on my couch in L.A. thinking I should give musical theater a try." But I think having spent ten years kind of knocking around Hollywood and trying to get traction and feeling so frustrated by it not happening, when it started to happen in New York, it just seemed like this is where I belong.

Let's get a little more specific on *Sunday in the Park with George*.

Mandy Patinkin had left and Bob Westenberg had taken over for a three-month contract, and he was leaving. They called me back and I walk out on the stage of the Booth Theatre, and out in the house are Stephen Sondheim, James Lapine, [producer] Jerry Schoenfeld, and Bernadette Peters. I sang "Finishing the Hat" and Sondheim came down to the edge of the stage and—I get goose bumps—I mean, I'm getting emotional just talking about it. He comes to the edge of the stage and he looks up at me, and he says, "Howard, that was great. Can we try this again? I just want to remind you that the phrase is finishing the *hat*, not finishing *the* hat." I'm standing on the stage of the Booth Theatre, and Stephen Sondheim is talking to me, and all I am hearing is, "Blah, blah, blah." It was like, "You're Stephen Sondheim!" He was giving me very important information and I didn't realize at that time. When I was cast as the understudy and I started to learn the whole thing, I realized there is a very Sondheimian kind of cadence to it, [sings] "finishing the hat." But I loved how my voice sounded on the word "the" because it's the highest note in the phrase. So I sang [singing] "finishing *the* hat. How you have to finish *the* hat." I heard later that it drove him crazy! I think that could have been what didn't get me the role. I don't know for sure, but they hired Harry Groener. At my callback for George, Bernadette came up on the stage, and we sang "Move On" together. That alone was worth the price of admission. I mean, I was so happy to have had the chance to stand on the stage and sing "Move On" with Bernadette. It was pretty fucking great.

The show closed but you went straight into *Drood* at the Delacorte, a theater you had been thrown out of?

That's absolutely true. I had jumped the fence when I first got to New York.

It's a free theater!

The season had ended and I wanted to see that stage. My friend and I jumped the fence and we got kicked out, but we got to see the stage! That was '84, and then I'm there doing *Drood* in the summer of '85. Pinch me. Wilford showed me an old advertisement for a perfume, Tabu or something. It was an old Victorian scene where a music teacher is teaching his student, and it was a very passionate kind of moment. He said "That's Jasper. That's who I want you to become." And so I seized on that image of the guy as this kind of over-the-top romantic villain and ran with it. I just knew what to do with it. I knew the size of it. It was pretty amazing. [But it was also] against the backdrop of my marriage coming to an end, although it took a few years. It was a lot, it was a lot.

Let's talk for a minute about your costars.

George Rose was such an amazing mentor and inspiration to me. He was a brilliant man and a brilliant talent who taught me so much about what it takes to perform on a Broadway stage. His energy was remarkable, and I realized that that's part of what you need to bring to this. You cannot walk through this—not that I ever did. I just learned so much watching him.

And Betty Buckley?

I remember standing next to Betty singing "Two Kinsmen" was somewhat akin to standing near a 747 jet engine. Literally every pore in my body vibrated from that. I'm serious. It was the most thrilling thing. I remember to this day the physical rush that I felt every night singing with her. I remember when Loretta Swit came in and took over for Cleo Laine, she wasn't being chosen [as the murderer. Nightly, audiences voted on the show's outcome], and so she spoke to Wilford about being in more scenes. She said, "There's a dinner scene where everybody's plotting against Edwin. I should be in that scene." "You're the Princess Puffer of an opium den. You wouldn't be invited to dinner." She said, "What if I'm seen looking in the window?" So Wilford came to me and said, "I just want to warn you, you may see Loretta looking in the window ominously. We're not changing the lighting and the windows aren't lit from the outside, so . . ." I saw her backstage, practicing in the mirror with a flashlight tucked under her arm to see if she could use her own light. She continued to peer in the window. I don't know what anybody saw.

Between the Central Park and Broadway runs of *Drood*, you got to do that landmark production of *Follies*, as you said.

I've never in my life experienced the audience reaction that I heard those couple of nights. The stomping of the feet of everyone in that house for the show to start!

***Follies* is such a part of the canon now, but that concert was the first production of it since the original. There was a hunger for it. What was it like rehearsing it?**

That documentary [*Follies in Concert*] shows it all. It was beyond thrilling, working with the crème de la crème of Broadway! I mean, Mandy Patinkin! Barbara Cook! George Hearn! Comden and Green! And having the opportunity to work with Lee Remick again. I had played her son years prior in *Wheels*, so that was really special. I will never forget Elaine Stritch coming in and dropping trou and changing into other clothes in front of everybody in the rehearsal room; hearing Barbara Cook singing "Buddy's Eyes" for the first time—I can't even begin to describe the thrill of it. *Follies* had been such an obsession of mine when I was a kid in high school. I remember when that album came out. A cast album was all you had of a Broadway show in Santa Barbara. I just wore it out. I thought it was the most exciting thing I'd ever heard. And there I was doing Young Ben at Lincoln Center, Avery Fischer Hall, standing in front of the fucking New York Philharmonic. And when they struck the first chords of the opening, I really thought I was going to die. I remember looking across the stage at Jim Walton and we exchanged a look of "can you believe where we are right now?" And the audience was seismic in their responses. I remember Stritch came off stage after singing "Broadway Baby" and I said, "Elaine, that was unbelievable." And she looked at me and said, "Who are you?" I don't know if that was a rhetorical question, or if she was doing a bit or maybe she didn't know who the hell I was! It was kind of classic Stritch. It was pretty thrilling. I thought, "There will never be something better. This is pretty great." I'll never forget [director] Herb Ross showing Lee Remick how to work a boa. It was kind of a brilliant moment. Lee was an amazing actress and an amazing star, but she didn't know how to play a vamp. He was working that boa like nobody's business.

And then after *Follies*, back to *Drood*, on Broadway. You got a Tony nomination.

I was in heaven, in heaven. I remember Angela Lansbury being one of the hosts. I remember really not feeling ready for it in a way. It just seemed the kind of ego stuff that starts to go haywire with being nominated for a Tony Award. Being brought to that kind of party as a full-fledged invitee felt undeserved somehow. I think I was terrified about it. I was thrilled and terrified at the same time.

This sounds like the first moment since you got to New York that you had any hesitation about your career.

I think in a way it probably was. Things kept happening so fast that there really wasn't time for me to take stock of how extraordinary all of it was. It was just that fast, that fast, that fast.

It continued that way, too. You were doing the workshop of *Into the Woods* while you were doing *Drood*, and then you had to choose between *Into the Woods* and *Anything Goes*. And you did a soap opera at the same time.

Oh, my God. I'd forgotten all about that! I played Julianne Moore's love interest on that soap. [The choice to do *Anything Goes*] was one of the toughest things I've ever done. I mean, a brand-new Sondheim musical versus a classic American musical for which I knew I was perfect . . . Sophie's Choice. And career-wise I thought that I—this is really weird; It's hard for me to be totally honest about this—I thought that it was going to be better for me to be seen as Billy Crocker in a romantic lead than to be a part of an ensemble.

What part of that is hard for you to be honest about?

I wrote Sondheim a letter saying that I thought that due to career considerations, I was going to be doing *Anything Goes*. He called me two days later and said, "Howard, I got your note. Thank you. I just want to suggest something: I would refrain from using expressions like 'career considerations.' You're in danger of becoming a cliché." I knew he was right. And I just laughed. And he said, "And the other reason I'm calling is I'd like you to do a backer's audition for us of *Into the Woods*." So he slapped my wrist and then asked me to do a favor and of course, I was thrilled to.

Tell me about *Anything Goes*.

Doing that show felt very much like home to me. I didn't regret not doing *Into the Woods* when I started rehearsals and saw the brilliant assemblage of people in the room and the Tony Walton sets and costumes. This was going to be a first-class experience, and it was, all the way. It was just great! I have to say that whenever anyone asks me what my favorite Broadway experience was, I always come back to *Anything Goes*. The joy of performing that show every night and the laughter coming from the audience—everyone should be so lucky. I had heard that Jimmy Stewart was in town and I got Bernie Gersten's help getting him an invitation to the show. I was singing "Easy to Love," and he had originated that in a movie called *Born to Dance*. I was such a huge Jimmy Stewart fan. And he came. He came backstage and I couldn't have been more thrilled. It was just like a dream come true. Lauren Bacall came backstage and she came into my dressing room, and took me in her arms and said, "Young man, you are a star." Head spinning. Every night there were people who would come back like that. Lucille Ball came back because she and Patti LuPone's mother had gone to high school together. It was a huge hit.

And working with Patti?

Adored her. Loved every minute of it. We laughed our off heads every day. Laughed and peed our pants. It was just so much fun. We worked together a year and a half, and we had dinner together between shows on each and every matinee day. She had her moments with other people in the cast that, you know, are legendary.

Patti told me that there are times when a company can go rancid and the entire energy will turn, and that happened during *Anything Goes*.

Long runs do bring out some really interesting behavior in people. I mean, the personalities of people who get bored and who are looking for ways to stay stimulated in the show can sometimes take on a very destructive bent. It can turn things bad. And there was a certain amount of that going on in that company. I would say that. It did not affect me. I was aware of it, but I tend to stay in my own lane. I try not to get involved in the petty stuff. I was also still dealing with a marriage that was crumbling and little kids. I had my hands full.

You got another Tony nomination. Were you more ready for it this time?
Yes, because it was a sure bet I wasn't going to win: Michael Crawford was nominated for *Phantom*. Patti and I went to the Tonys together. We shared a limo and went to the party and had a great ruckus the entire night. I had nothing to lose because I had already lost. So that was kind of great.

And you got to do the show in London with Elaine Paige.
It was what I needed emotionally. With the marriage really coming to a conclusion, I just needed the time away. I was the only American in the cast. It wasn't the American production because it's not the same when Brits do an American show. It's just not. But Elaine was just so great to me. She was my host, my best friend. She and Tim Rice were seeing each other at the time and they squired me around to the poshest of posh events; lunch with Princess Anne and Princess Margaret, Wimbledon finals, champagne and strawberries, it was fantastic. But it was a mixed time for me because I thought I needed the space to get away, but I missed my kids like crazy. I was in a foreign country. My heart was crying out to be with my boys. I was very much alone in London for that time. And this, in spite of Elaine who was just so magnanimous and wonderful. And it was agony going back into rehearsal. I'd been playing it on Broadway for almost two years and there I was back in a rehearsal room with tape on the floor and everyone's nose buried in their books. I thought I was going to go out of my mind. But then we played, and I was living in Mayfair, and I walked through Berkeley Square every day to get to the theater. But I was very much on my own most of the time.

How was working with Jerry Zaks?
Wow! I mean, his precision. I learned so much from him about comic timing, about how it's a rhythm, it's a music of its own. It was a great, great learning experience working with him, and I would work with him again. I felt very flattered that he wanted me to come over and play the part in London, and we had a great rehearsal period because the whole American team came over. We had the best time. We went to dinner every night, a gang of Americans sharing the experience of bringing this joyous show to London, then suddenly the show opens and the next morning they were all on airplanes on their way back to the States.

Even at this early stage in your career, you had worked with some amazing directors. Jerry Zaks, Herb Ross, James Lapine, Wilford Leach. . . . They each have very different styles. Were you learning from them how you like to be directed?
Huge differences, but I think their work method seemed to suit the style of work that they did. Certainly with Wilford—he was such a pussycat and such a kind of, "Oh, try this." Jerry Zaks has very specific ideas about things and will drill a scene with you. He doesn't give you line readings per se, but there is certainly a much more meticulous feel with Jerry that you don't have with other directors. But to me it worked so brilliantly on that particular piece. I've heard actors say that they felt that it was too controlling and that he wouldn't leave them alone.

I actually loved it and for this particular piece, I thought it was essential. I learned things about how to prepare a role that I've used in every role I've done ever since.

When you got back from London, you went to L.A. for almost a year.
And then I got a call—they'd offered me *The Secret Garden* out of the blue. Mandy Patinkin was leaving and I jumped at it. It was exactly—if you're lucky, the theatrical experience that you're involved in can teach you about your life and what you're going through. To me, it was like the perfect metaphor for me and who I was and who I wanted to become. The whole story of the garden having been buried and the gate locked and left to go fallow for so many years felt so much like what I had experienced personally in terms of not being able to be open about my sexuality or honest about the life I was living. It was a huge unlocking of that gate and allowing that garden to breathe again. That sounds so corny, but . . .

No, it doesn't. It doesn't . . .
I guess it's about life lessons, about forgiveness—forgiving yourself, letting go of all the ghosts, letting go of anger and confusion, and it was just fantastic for me. It's a beautiful show, and I was so grateful that I had the chance to be a part of it for so long. I think I was there nineteen months. So many actor friends scratch their heads and say, "How can you stand doing a show for that long?" I don't have an answer except to say that I love it. I'm the king of long runs. It's so fantastic that I have the stamina and the desire to stay with shows that run.

Were your agents telling you that you should be moving on while you were hot?
No question, no question. But, of course, they are happy for the steady commission. I like the routine of something. Am I someone who likes the safety of a show that's running? Yes. I certainly like the security of the paycheck, and with kids in private school, those were considerations as well.

What about creatively?
I find it endlessly satisfying to go out on a stage and to explore what I can do tonight that might be different. The business is tough and there is a lot of rejection. Even though I'm working constantly on Broadway, I'm also auditioning for things that I don't get. I was hoping that movies would start to open for me. It didn't happen.

But I don't sense regret . . .
None whatsoever. Curiosity and wondering what might have been, but no regrets at all, no.

How was the run of that show?
It was great. Daisy Egan was extraordinary. Open and wise beyond her years, and smart. Sharp as a tack, I was just blown over by her. I think she was just extraordinary in that role.

During this period, you were one of the go-to leading men on Broadway. Did you experience yourself that way? Or were you just going a step at a time?
A step at a time. Yes, I feel a part of the community. There's no question I feel like I've been accepted, and I am one of the team, but you're just going one step at a time, and you're just thinking, "Okay, this is really exciting. I'm really enjoying this. What can I learn from this?"

As a leading man, did you ever feel like there was a ticking clock?

I feel that now, certainly. At the time, no, I don't remember feeling that. I just felt "What's next?" I think I was always aware of trying to keep them guessing in a way. I've always been aware of how lucky I've been to be able to play many different kinds of leading men. I know I look how I look. Richard, my husband, is always joking about how I live in the world between 1890 and 1910, and it's so true. If you think about the shows that I've done, almost every one of them has lived in that era. That's part of how I look and what I bring to the table. But I've always been aware of the fact that I've been blessed with some range in that.

Well, your next one after *Secret Garden* was unexpected. You were the lothario in *She Loves Me*.

That was all [director] Scott Ellis because I really wanted to play Georg. He said, "I totally would not buy you as the guy who's sitting writing lonely hearts letters to a lonely hearts column. But you can play Kodaly and it will be so much fun." And he was dead right. It was so much fun to play, and again, a departure from the other stuff I had done. Boyd Gaines couldn't have been better [as Georg]. Nobody could have done that better. The whole cast was perfect. It was another joyous experience, except for the divorce that was occurring. I was hemorrhaging money on lawyers. That was a really rough time personally, but doing a show like *She Loves Me* was my lifesaver. It was a gift to be a part of that creativity every night.

Bock and Harnick were around a lot, weren't they?

That revival of *She Loves Me* was the first time that they had been together in a while. I think there was some kind of break between them after *The Rothchilds*. So now skip forward to 1993 and they were in the room, but they were kind of sitting on opposite sides of the theater for many of the rehearsals. I don't know for sure, but I think seeing the show remounted finally broke the ice for them, which was really nice to see. And the generosity from both of them toward the cast and the production itself was so wonderful and warm. Jerry Bock was such a lovely man. It's such a loss to the theater that he's gone. And Sheldon Harnick is such a sweetheart and one of the all-time greats. It was so neat to look out in the house and see them sitting there, knowing that we were part of something that was deemed special enough to them to be present for. I had played Georg in high school, so to now be in this revival, with this company, and them as part of the process—there aren't words.

Did you see the recent revivals of *She Loves Me* and *Edwin Drood* with Gavin Creel and Will Chase in the roles you had played?

Yes, I did. It was out of body. Gavin and Will were both great but please don't ask me to have any objectivity. I'd lived with those shows for so long. Both of them were long, healthy runs. I guess there's a part of me that feels like we did it a little bit better, but I think that that's just—you feel a little bit territorial about a show.

And then *Kiss of the Spider Woman*.

I left *She Loves Me* a couple weeks before it closed. I'm not sure if Scott Ellis ever forgave me for that. He was not happy that I left, but I couldn't resist. I had wanted to play that part as soon as I heard they were adapting the book for the stage. I had tried to get seen by Hal Prince for Molina, and he said "Absolutely not. He's totally wrong for this." And then [years later] I went in for the audition for the replacement on Broadway. Rob Marshall was in the room with everybody sitting at the table and later told me that when they said, "Howard McGillin is next,"

Hal said, "Why is he coming in? He's totally wrong for this." But when I finished my audition, he turned to the table and said, "That's our Molina." That was pretty thrilling to hear.

How much work had you done to get prepared?

A lot of work. I really, really wanted that part, and I spent a lot of time working on it. But I just knew I could do it. I knew who he was. It was challenging. Brian Stokes Mitchell and I didn't always get along. Let me just say that replacing in a Broadway show is very difficult—not just for the person coming in, but for the other actors whose own role interpretations may now have to adjust in ways that they are not necessarily comfortable with. At least at first. I think that he was used to another style of player in the role. I think that I saw Molina as a much stronger adversary to Valentin, and I think that Stokes—I know he was not happy at times with me. There was tension.

So how does that manifest?

A lot of silence. We didn't communicate very well. It was difficult at times. We get along very well now so—but it's always delicate. It's a long time ago, so I don't have clarity about it, but I do remember that it got tense for a while, and then it changed. That's part of a long run. When you're doing a long run, you hit walls, personally or creatively, and then you somehow get over that wall. And then you're in new territory and a new place to play. That certainly happened with us. That run was hugely rewarding and overall a fantastic experience. I will always be grateful for it. We played a long time. Nineteen months, I think, through three spider women. Chita was my first, and thank God I got to play her last three weeks, but I was hit by a car on my bike over Chita's final weekend. It was the day of Vanessa Williams's put-in, and I was riding my bike in Prospect Park in Brooklyn. A car turned and stopped dead in the bike path, and I had been coming down the hill at around thirty miles an hour. I slammed on my brakes, but I flew over the handlebar and I separated my shoulder, broke three ribs. I got to the emergency room but I am thinking, "It's Vanessa's put-in and I've got to get there." They put me on some serious pain killers. I get there, arm in a sling, bruised, and I say to the stage manager, "I'm fine. I'm going to be fine." That was the pain killer talking. But halfway through he came to me and said, "You're turning green. You are going home." I was back on stage in three weeks, but in such pain because of the broken ribs. That takes months to heal.

Did Hal Prince work with you?

He came after I was in. He lets you find it and then comes in. He was very, very attentive. I got lots of notes, but he seemed very happy with what I did. He said, "My wife said she loved what you do in this show. She doesn't say things like that very often." Thank you, Judy Prince!

And Chita?

Chita was fantastic. I was still doing *She Loves Me* while I was rehearsing. Rob Marshall said to me, "I just want to warn you, Chita can be really tough so you better know your shit." Not that I didn't know that, but he was just saying, "Make sure you're confident and know what you're doing." I get to my rehearsal with her, terrified. I mean . . . it's Chita fucking Rivera and I have to do a tango with her. One of the greatest dancers of all time. She looked in my eyes and without saying a word said to me, "You're going to be great. You're going to be all right." I just knew—her communication to me was, "I'm in this with you, and we're going to make this work." It was such a huge relief that she was so completely generous with me. I'm sure everybody was waiting for her verdict, but she couldn't have been more generous and more supportive.

How did you feel about playing a gay character just as you were coming out?

I remember one night my son, Brian, who was maybe seven or eight years old? The boys hung out with me backstage in all of my shows. They were theater babies all throughout their lives and they came to see every show I was in. I was reading Brian a bedtime story one night, and he said to me, "Daddy, why do you have to play a character like that?" The boys were going through their own preadolescence. That just came to me when you just mentioned coming out. Molina is somebody who wears his sexuality and his essence, his spirit, and his defiance on his sleeve, and that was hugely liberating for me. I loved it so much.

Do you remember what you responded to Brian?

I think I tried to explain to him that some people are born a certain way and they behave a certain way because that's who they are. I can't remember but I think it was awfully sage and smart of me!

I think that for a person who lived in the closet for a good number of years to then be able to let go as much as you did is extraordinary. Did it feel scary?

It remarkably didn't. It felt exactly right. Again, I think that there's something that I said earlier about *Secret Garden*: The universe and the gods of theater all kind of conspire to bring something to you that teaches, on a daily basis, about who you are and what it can be to be alive in this world and fully open to what's being sent to you. That felt like a huge gift to me. It was joyful, it was stressful . . .

I don't think you can chalk this up to the universe. You manifested this one. You went after it . . .

That's true. I remember the great disappointment that I felt when my agent said Hal would not see me when they were first doing it. And then to have it come back and for it to be such a huge turning point in my life, a moment that seems so right in so many ways. It was extraordinary.

John Kander and Fred Ebb were fairly hands-on, I understand.

They were, they were. I remember sessions with John at his house. He is such a gorgeous man and so fantastic. To be singing his music and having him help me to understand the character and why, musically, it's written as it is? That was an extraordinary time.

After *Spider Woman* you were lured back to London.

Yes, indeed. I was doing *Spider Woman*, and my agent called and said they're interested in you doing *Mack & Mabel* in London, but Jerry Herman wants to meet with you to talk about this. So on my day off I flew to Jerry's in Beverly Hills and I stayed at his house. Paul Kerryson, the British director, flew in as well, and we ate together and talked. It was so beautiful. The butler brings us the lunch in the dining room. . . . It was something out of a movie. Not a role for which I would normally be considered: this kind of gruff, ball-busting, knock-them-down-before-they-get-you attitude. John Wilner, the producer of the show, saw me in *Kiss* and said, "This guy should play Mack." And Jerry was totally onboard with it. After dinner he said, "Just sing 'I Won't Send Roses,'" and he sat at the keyboard in his living room! And that was it. I got on the plane the next day and flew back and my agent said, "You're playing Mack Sennett." *Kiss* closes and I'm off to London to do *Mack & Mabel*, and again, with reluctance because I knew I was going to be the only American in a British cast. And my kids . . . I had huge reservations about leaving them again. But John Wilner was extremely generous. He said, "I will make this promise: If you come to London, I will fly your kids over every weekend. As many times as you want them to be there, they will be there." And he said, "I'll fly your boyfriend over." And that was Richard. I think maybe our relationship today exists because John Wilner said that. Richard came over multiple times during the time I was there. But even so, almost from the minute I got there, I felt like I had made a big mistake, an ocean away from my kids. I loved the work but I was unhappy. The show was a mixed bag. Caroline O'Connor and I had some problems personally and there was tension there. I left earlier than I probably would have if things had been better.

That's two in a row of costars where the relationship was not harmonious. How do you handle that?

Well, you either figure out how to make it work or you get out. It is a shame. It happens. I think that there was also tension in trying to make the show work. I don't know if *Mack & Mabel* is ever going to work. It is Jerry Herman's best score. He's often said that he felt that this was the baby that he loved the most and it got the least amount of attention. But when the book writer is dead, it's almost impossible to fix a situation like that. I don't know how you do it. So the show was fraught with those issues. So I kind of knew it was time for me to come home. We have a great cast album. I think that cast album is pretty super, but I feel disappointed that the production wasn't everything Jerry wanted it to be.

You've worked directly with five legendary composers: Sondheim, Kander, Herman, Bock, and Lloyd Webber.

Oh, my God. I mean, I think no one makes me more terrified in the room than Sondheim because you know how exacting he is, and you know how smart he is. I always felt like I was trying to prove myself to him in some way, which is maybe a good thing. And maybe not because you can't help but feel like you've given up some of yourself. Jerry Herman wants to hug you. It's a very different experience with Jerry and given his sentimental streak, I think that *Mack & Mabel* will always be a difficult puzzle to solve, even if he had Michael Stewart still with us. I think maybe he has a little trouble seeing the forest for the trees because it's a baby that he feels so protective of. That's armchair psychology; I certainly don't know. Andrew tends to be a little bit like the Phantom: He's in and out of the theater before you know it. And John can be so wonderfully emotional. Sometimes he weeps. They all weep. Well, not Andrew.

How incredible to be able to have performed their music for each of them.

At the Kennedy Center Honors honoring Comden and Green, Patti and I did a whole medley of Comden and Green stuff for them. Talk about a wild weekend. Your head's exploding all the time by the people . . . I mean, Lauren Bacall introduced me to Audrey Hepburn. One minute you're chatting with Walter Cronkite and, "Oh, hi, Gene Kelly." That gives you a sense. You try to take it in, but there's so much pressure because you're doing this live event on television. The lights are up in the house so you are looking dead in the eyes of Audrey Hepburn, Gregory Peck, Senator Kennedy. Oh, my God! And Betty and Adolph, of course. It was pretty great. Fantastic.

Kristin Chenoweth told me she's still just a fan-girl at heart and she geeks out when she meets those kinds of people. Do you think it ever stops? Do you think Lauren Bacall was geeking out?

I'm lucky enough to have been invited to Hal Prince's Christmas party, and when I'm there, I'm thinking, "My God, I cannot believe I'm here." But Charles Busch told me he was there standing in the corner and Barbara Cook was singing "In Buddy's Eyes." Joan Rivers was Charles's date for the party, and she said to him, "Can you believe we're here?" I don't think it changes for anybody. I remember at the Kennedy Center, Bacall wanting to hang with Patti and me during the rehearsal, and we're sitting there on the steps of the stage, and she's just like a pal. That night after the broadcast she said, "Who's your date for the ball?" I said, "I don't have one." She said, "You do now. I'm your date." So I'm on the dance floor with Betty Bacall. This is my life. How did this happen?

So somewhere within all of that, do you think you felt like you'd "made it?"

The business is so hard, and it is constantly throwing curves at you. You're constantly being rejected. You're met with frustration in the business no matter who you are. The theater is an elusive, shimmery, gauzy thing that kind of permeates our lives. We love it. It's like the air we breathe, but you're constantly wanting more oxygen.

So you never felt secure?

Oh, no! God, no. Every time the show I was in closed, there was that sense of "God, now what do I do?" I know I have some things lined up but who knows? I am plenty insecure. And I'm getting older. I'm not being called that often so, you know, there's a reality to this that is not just my own insecurity. It's reality. I don't know that I've made a peace with it. I don't think you can because I love to work. I love the work itself. And it's that never-ending need to find approval on stage. It is definitely a part of my makeup.

Things did indeed slow down for a bit after *Mack & Mabel* . . .

I did several workshops of *Time and Again* over a five-year period. We were really trying to make that show work, and I was lucky to be a part of it for so long, but it also felt like, "Okay, enough. I have given all of my blood." Because when you're in a show that's not working, there's nothing harder in the world. You're on a stage trying desperately to push the rock up the hill, and it's not moving, and you can feel the audience—you just know it's not working, and you keep trying valiantly, like actors do, to make the story come to life. It was really hard to see that thing crash and burn because I really thought it could possibly work. It shows how wrong I could be.

After investing so much time, moving on without the satisfaction of a production must be so hard.

You've got to move on. There were a couple years where I was doing TV stuff here and there, trying to advance the career in any way that I could. Work. Feed the family. Do what you need to do. Then *Phantom* came along. A friend of ours was with Hal in Europe, sitting on a boat when he got the fax saying that Hugh Panaro was leaving *The Phantom* to do *Martin Guerre*. Yes, on a boat. It's like hilarious, right? And he said, "What about Howard?" Next thing I know I get a call to go sing "Music of the Night" for David Caddick, who was Andrew Lloyd Webber's music guy. So I did, and they said, "Well, when do you want to start?" Luckily, I had the experience with Hal, and he felt he could trust me in the role.

So you step into *Phantom* . . .

When I went in, I didn't watch the show. I had seen it originally with Michael Crawford, but I purposely thought, 'Okay, let's just see if I can find a way to at least fool myself into

Undergoing his nightly, arduous metamorphosis to haunt *The Phantom of the Opera*. (Bruce Glikas for Broadway.com)

thinking that I'm opening this show.' It's not ego. It's just that I wanted it to feel like it was mine. I think I had three weeks of rehearsal, and Hal doesn't come anywhere near the theater until you've actually been in the role for a couple weeks. He knows that for the actor, it's [getting used to] the climbing of ladders in a cape, a hat, and a mask; it's dropping through trap doors—that got cut when I left, by the way. People were injuring themselves. It was very dangerous.

You're talking about at the end of "Masquerade"?
Yeah. Suddenly there's a huge puff of flames and smoke, and he's gone. There is a trap door the size of a postage stamp that you stood on. You had to put your toes exactly in the right place. The signal was lifting your arm, but you had to lift your arm straight up because if it was out, you would break it. There were no hydraulics involved. A shock absorber in the basement that broke your fall. Pins came out and that thing dropped with the weight and velocity, and the physics of a human being's weight. You had to really be careful. Anyway, that's the process that the Phantom learns while you're on your feet because when you're in the rehearsal hall, you don't get to use any of that stuff. You don't get to climb all the ladders. You don't get that until you're put in the day of your first performance. It's just too much to absorb, so Hal waits until the third week, once you've had a chance to work out all that stuff. He wants to see a performance that's going to be somewhat your performance as opposed to "Where do I go next and how do I keep breathing?" That's really the learning curve for *Phantom*. "How am I going to have a voice by the end of the first performance?" It's just so intense. The emotional pitch of that character is so huge that even though he's only on stage for like thirty-five minutes, it's an intense time out there. It was exhausting.

You did it for so long. Did you feel like you were in your best shape because . . .
Oh, absolutely, absolutely. Especially physically and vocally. No question. How can you not be? You have to do it, and you find your stride. Having experienced many long runs, I know how to pace myself so that I'm not burning myself out. I certainly know a lot of actors who say, "I could never do a show for more than a couple of months." Obviously if you're in musicals, you learn to do that.

Did you stay for so long because it continued to be artistically satisfying, or because it was an annuity, or because . . .
You know, I would be lying if I said it wasn't partly for the financial security of it. The business is so rough, and I'd gone through a period of not working as much as I had been. So when you have a job like that and you know that they are happy with what you are doing, it's pretty great. And I loved playing the role. I loved working out all that dark stuff. I don't know what that says about me. I'm not asked to play roles like that very often. There's something very fun about playing a role with that kind of heightened emotion, even though you feel wrung out at the end of the night. It's a great feeling, and they just don't write many roles like that. Three and a half years went by and that's how it happens in a show. That was the longest time I'd ever done anything. And Hal sent me the script of *Bounce*. I had done readings of that show from the very first reading. It was a juicy role. The guy is just such a snake oil salesman. Smooth as glass and, as Sondheim described him, Jack of all trades, master of none. What a gift! We did a reading of it. It was called *Gold!* Cast changes ensued, but I stayed on. Hal said, "We're going to do this at the Goodman, and I hope you're excited about it. We'll have to replace you at *Phantom*." Thrilled. So I left but three and a half years seemed like a decent run for a show. Never in a million years did I think I'd be going back to it. And *Bounce* didn't work out.

As I understand it, Hal Prince left Chicago after you opened and was not around to continue to work, so you went to Washington with essentially the same show.

Hal's schedule was set. He wasn't going to be there after opening. But even though we knew in advance, we all felt very frustrated by the lack of work that we could do on it minus a director after we opened. Steve and John Weidman continued to work but there was no work being done in the theater. We had two weeks in New York before we went to Washington and we worked on new pieces of it and then we got down there and put the whole thing together. But musicals are beasts to mend. So many ingredients have to come together. I think that the opportunities to work on it in Chicago were unfulfilled.

You described the *Time and Again* experiences as pushing a boulder up a hill. Did you feel that way during *Bounce*?

Enormously so. First of all, it's such a big, sprawling musical with a huge cast. It spans decades in the lives of two unlikeable leading characters. You feel the audience sitting there saying, "What's the story trying to be told here? What are they trying to tell? How do we follow this? Who are we supposed to care about?" It's really tough with this piece because you've got two shady characters who are the leads. That was part of why Hal thought there should be a love interest. There should be sex involved, which is always a smart thing on paper. It was just an enormous puzzle whose pieces never quite fit. Steve and John came back frequently and were very supportive. When we got to Washington we thought, "Okay, we've got a second shot at this," but it never really took off. But it was great to be in the room working on *Bounce* even though we didn't know what it was when we first got to Chicago. Richard Kind said to me, "It's like Mt. Rushmore, looking across the table at the creative team." You're always aware of the fact that even though the child itself may be having trouble developing, you're still working with these geniuses, and you're very, very lucky to be in the room with them.

Do you think you come out different as an artist?

You can't help but feel that you've grown and learned as an artist just being there with them and seeing how they work. If you're smart, or even half smart, you're listening with all ears and trying to soak up as much as you can. These are people who have shaped the American musical, and you're very lucky if a little of that rubs off on you.

And then you went on tour.

I went off to do *Peter Pan* with Cathy Rigby shortly after *Bounce* finished. I had never been on the road doing a touring show in my life. We were in a different town every week. I had a license to chew scenery and be outrageous as Captain Hook. I loved every second of it. I think I'd been out about ten months and got a call to come back to *Phantom*. You reach a certain point where you just want to be in your own bed. So back I came, happily, thinking, "I'll do that for a year maybe," but I was there another three and a half years. But why not? It was great.

It's so rare that actors stay for that long in one show. I think it's a combination of getting restless and/or they think they have other opportunities that they must grab or their careers will go down the tubes.

I will say that there is a sense when you do a show like *Phantom* ten years into its run, you feel like you have, in some ways, dropped off the face of the earth because no one [in the industry] is coming to see *Phantom* anymore, so you might as well be in cold storage. I could have sat around for a year not doing anything. Instead I was doing the leading role in an iconic

At the Kennedy Center's pre-Broadway run of *Gigi*, with Victoria Clark. (Joan Marcus)

musical. It's much better to be working. There were other offers that came along to do shows that I turned down. You do a quick assessment: Is there a chance for that? And if you don't think there is . . . I had college tuitions I was paying. Mortgages. Did I sacrifice anything? Probably. I don't know.

Is it rewarding being the record holder?

It's great. I will be singing "Music of the Night" in Tokyo in June. I've sung it all over the world. What a great gift. It's been a calling card for me. I don't mind it at all. I never tired of it. Never tired of it. It's like an old pair of gloves that you slip into and you say, "Oh, yeah, I know why this feels so good." I remember when I first went into the show, there were people who were clearly bored doing what they were doing. Nothing makes me crazier than to see that. I don't care how long you've been doing something; there is an audience sitting out there for the first time. It sounds cliché but it's true. They're out there seeing a show for the first time and many of them have never seen a Broadway show. They're thrilled, and if you can't find some connection to that and want to give them a great experience, go home. Don't take your paycheck. That's death.

Let's talk about *Gigi*.

When *Gigi* knocked on my door, I told Richard and he said, "You'd be perfect for that." But I thought they wanted to see me for Gaston [the Louis Jordan role]. But then the look on Richard's face when I said they wanted to see me for Honoré [the Maurice Chevalier role]. He said, "Well, what did you think? You are not forty years old anymore." I was happy to be a part of it, trying to make it work. It's a show that never really worked, and again, you're aware of the thing not working, and there you are once again trying to make it work back at the Eisenhower Theater in Washington, DC. It's just a big old flawed piece, and I don't know how you fix it. Everybody was in the rowboat paddling as hard as they could. And it just never made it. Vanessa Hudgens worked very hard. She was delightful.

So now, at this stage in your career, you seem pretty relaxed about whatever is coming. The phone will ring or it won't, and things are going to happen.

I'd say that's a pretty good description. I don't feel the kind of burning desire to tear up the Broadway stage. I would love to have something come along that really challenged me, that I felt would be worth investing my time and energy in. I'm not dead, and I hope that there will be lots more along the way. I'm just in a place now where I feel fairly content with who I am and the journey that I've come on thus far. I'll see what's next. I am so blessed to have had the crazy journey that I had personally. I have these two grown sons who are blessings and loves of my life, and now to have a grandson! I am still having a little trouble actually getting over the fact that I am old enough to have a grandson. The joy that I feel about it is something that is hugely leavening in terms of the business. It certainly puts things in perspective. I still want to do as well as I possibly can every time I'm out there. The stakes are still as high, but there's just a more-rounded sense of what it all means. I used to be so hard on myself after a performance. "Why didn't that work for me? What was it that didn't get the laughs that I got the night before?" To be able to let go of some of that stuff and just say, "So that's the way it was tonight," I think that that reflects some maturing on my part. I love the challenge of doing something new and different. I'm most alive when I feel challenged or scared that something might be a risky endeavor and that's what's always fueled my love for the theater and, I hope, will always be there.

8

BRIAN STOKES MITCHELL

February 2018

IN A 2004 *NEW YORK TIMES* article entitled "The Last Leading Man?," Bruce Weber opined, "It is no exaggeration to say that Brian Stokes Mitchell is right now in a class by himself as a Broadway leading man. No other actor can match his singing voice. No other singer can claim his acting range or experience. No other man—at least, no one who works in the theater regularly—can say, 'I want to play Don Quixote in *Man of La Mancha*' and bring it about. Mr. Mitchell has reached a rare perch in the American theater: He can make his dreams come true with other people's money." Indeed, not since the likes of Alfred Drake, John Raitt, John Cullum, and the original man of La Mancha, Richard Kiley, had the Broadway musical had an above-the-title male star, minted in the theater. Yet Stokes, as he likes to be called, first came to national attention on television in *Trapper John, M.D.* from 1979 to 1986, but he is that rare animal whose musical theater work made him a bankable star.

Born in Seattle, Stokes grew up in Guam and the Philippines, part of a civilian family living on military bases (his father was an engineer). When he was fourteen, they settled in San Diego, and Stokes, who had always been fascinated by music, discovered theater. It quickly became his obsession, leading him to Los Angeles which led to *Trapper John* by the time he was twenty. His first post-series job was the musical *Mail* at the Pasadena Playhouse. It moved to Broadway in 1988, taking Stokes with it and beginning a Broadway career that included lead roles in *Oh, Kay!*, *Jelly's Last Jam*, and *Kiss of the Spider Woman*. Then in 1998, his searing portrayal of Coalhouse Walker Jr. in *Ragtime* cemented his stardom. The smash revival of *Kiss Me, Kate* followed, winning him a Tony, and then *La Mancha*.

Stokes was the go-to baritone in the decade that followed, and he found satisfaction touring the country in concerts and symphony halls and recording solo albums. He became chairman of the board of The Actors Fund, "which is not just for actors," he tells me proudly. "We help anybody who's made their living in show business or performing arts." He returned to Broadway in 2010 in the short-lived *Women on the Verge of a Nervous Breakdown* and again in 2016's *Shuffle Along*.

Stokes is an easygoing, disarmingly friendly presence. But he still manages to command attention when he walks into a room. Partly that's his height (six foot one), partly that's his seemingly ageless good looks, partly that's his charisma, and partly that's his grace. He is genteel in a world that seems increasingly ill-mannered, a throwback of sorts, easier to imagine in a tuxedo than in sweatpants. He claims that his Brooks Brothers brio is a bit of a show for the staff at The Actors Fund where we are meeting, but I am not buying it; this is a man wearing his blue blazer effortlessly.

When did you start performing?

I was singing from a very early age. I've been doing that longer than I remember talking. My brother, John, who passed away a number of years ago, was a brilliant, brilliant kid. Starting in his early years and in adulthood, he could sing, he could write music, he made electronic instruments, he could sculpt, he could paint. If it involved artistry, he could do it. He taught me how to sing duets and harmony. I was maybe three or four years old at the time. We'd call ourselves the Charlton Brothers. I don't know why, but my brother named us that, and we would sing for the family. And then later on, when we moved overseas, I started studying. When I was about six years old I asked for an organ. I was just fascinated with it from the very beginning. I realized that I could play different note combinations and it made me feel different

Making his Broadway debut in Michael Rupert's musical, *Mail*. (Photofest)

Brian Stokes Mitchell	
Mail	Broadway, 1988
Oh, Kay!	Broadway, 1988
Jelly's Last Jam	Broadway, 1992
Kiss of the Spider Woman	Broadway, 1993
Ragtime	Los Angeles, 1997; Broadway, 1998
Do Re Mi	Encores!, 1999
Kiss Me, Kate (Tony Award)	Broadway, 1999
Carnival	Encores!, 2002
Sweeney Todd	Kennedy Center, 2002
Man of La Mancha	Broadway, 2002
Kismet	Encores!, 2006
Women on the Verge of a Nervous Breakdown	Broadway, 2010
The Band Wagon	Encores!, 2014
Shuffle Along	Broadway, 2016
The Light in the Piazza	Los Angeles, 2019

things: scary, happy, a little sad. I was intrigued by the feeling of the notes when I put them together. So, when I started learning to play actual songs, I would make up my own arrangements without even knowing what I was doing. I learned to read music but I preferred playing by ear. When I was in junior high school, I started playing the trombone. I realized I could pick up an instrument and understand it pretty quickly. I'd check out a French horn, a clarinet, a trumpet, I learned to play the timpani. I was curious and I loved it. My brother, George, was the thespian in the family, and I was the pit pianist in some of the shows that he would do. When we moved back to the United States, I was always in chorus and in band, and in junior high I finally took drama. Some people in the class were involved with an organization called San Diego Junior Theater. I joined it and the first show I auditioned for was *Bye Bye Birdie*. I played Conrad Birdie, and I remember hearing and feeling the response of the audience. I felt an energy moving between me and the audience, and I thought, "Oh!" Up until that point I hadn't thought much about being an actor.

So when did that change?

It discovered me more than anything. I got out of high school and immediately got a call from a gentleman named Larry Carpenter, with whom I had done *Godspell* at the Old Globe Theater when I was sixteen, and he had been asked to be the artistic director of the Twelfth Night Repertory Company in San Diego. I ended up being a resident actor and composer there.

Were your parents encouraging?

I don't remember them saying, "You should become an actor for a living," but they were supportive. We were a very middle-class family. We didn't have everything we wanted, but we had everything we needed. My dad made good money but he also had four kids. He always said, "If there's ever anything you want to study, anything you want to learn, let us know, we'll do our best to get you classes."

And you went to the library . . .

I discovered the listening rooms where there was a huge selection of scores and cast albums. I would put on the albums and that's where I started learning and stealing from the likes of Richard Kiley and John Cullum and Alfred Drake. "I can do that. That sounds like my voice. Oh, I gotta learn how to do that." That's part of what I was doing, I think, when I was doing shows at San Diego Junior Theater: learning to steal from people and learning what works in my voice and what doesn't. I was just talking to a bunch of a students and I told them, "Steal! Just steal from everybody." That's how I learned. You just steal, steal, steal—tone, vibrato, phrasing. . . . Because once you've stolen from enough people, after a while people stop saying, "You sound like so and so," because you start coming up with your own ideas and that's how you get your own style. And I stole from a lot of jazz artists. I think that's what makes me different as a Broadway performer. I don't have the usual Broadway respect for the eighth note or the bar line. I tend to sing in a little freer way. The note's not important. It's the spaces between the notes. Anybody can play a note. It takes an artist to play the spaces. Anyone can paint a stroke. It takes an artist to know where to put the spaces. And without really knowing it at the time, what I really wanted to be was an artist.

At some point, after all this youthful exploration . . .
And theft—thievery . . .

And grand larceny, you decided to make it a career.
When I was offered the job with the Twelfth Night Repertory Company, I saw a chance to learn a lot, get my Equity card, and move to Los Angeles. I'd performed in every theater that I could perform in in San Diego. There was nothing else there left for me. And Los Angeles had film.

I am surprised you were drawn to that because everything up till that point was music-driven.
I'd already read books by Boleslavsky and Stanislavski and Uta Hagen and a bunch of other theater teachers on my own to see what I could learn from them as well. I also studied film and TV acting with Sal Dano who taught method. I would study with him three times a week probably six hours a day. We'd start sometimes at 4:00 PM and sometimes go as late as 4:00 in the morning. Then I would get up at 6:00 in the morning and do shows with the Twelfth Night Repertory Company, and then I would come home and go to sleep, and then I would go back to Sal's class, rinse and repeat, and that was my life.

Did you experience yourself as an usual teenager because it sounds like your social life was . . .
Nil. Except for in class and on set.

That kind of dedication and passion is unusual in a teenager.
Yeah, I guess. I didn't realize until my twenties that everybody wasn't a passionate autodidact. I didn't realize people approach life differently and people have different ways of learning. And I'm glad my parents never said to me, "Wow, you're really special." I just felt like a normal kid, just like the rest of the family. But I was raised with a family doing unusual things. My sister was involved in music, my brother was acting, and they were very dedicated. The kind of music we had in the house—that was unusual, I realize now. I didn't want to be with other kids. By the time I was in the eleventh, twelfth grade, I couldn't wait to get out of high school. I had no interest in the prom. I had little interest in hanging with those kids. I wanted to move on. I knew what I wanted to do. I knew where the interesting people were. It made teenagers incredibly dull to me. My fellow actors and artists had a focus, a passion, a love, a joy to learn, to perform, and to give something to an audience. I had found my tribe.

When you decided to move to Los Angeles, were you thinking about it as a career move?

At that point, yes. I started to get a feeling about my direction—an inner compass. I have a little thing—I actually call it "my little thing that goes off." I first became aware of it at fourteen with *Bye Bye Birdie*. I knew that show was incredibly important to do. Never done a show before, but I knew I had to get that role. I knew it was very, very important. My "little thing" went off. It's an energy, a feeling of excitement, a vibration, a knowing. When I auditioned for *Trapper John*, even when I first saw it in the trades, that "little thing" went off. When I first saw an audition for *Roots: The Next Generations* in *Drama-Logue*, out of all the hundreds of other listings that I'd seen, my "little thing" went off. I don't know—when the Twelfth Night Repertory came, I thought, "This is where I'm supposed to be." When something's supposed to happen, it feels like the universe gives it to you on a plate. And when the universe gives it to you on a plate, you eat. When you're *supposed* to be doing something, it comes easily. If you're continually knocking your head against walls, and nothing's happening, you're probably not supposed to be doing that. If you're working hard, focused, devoted, and prepared, then the universe opens—you feel it happen. I was watching this really fascinating interview with Oprah Winfrey and the guy that runs LinkedIn. They were talking about when preparation meets passion, that's when things start opening up for you. That is such a concise, brilliant way to put it. When preparation meets passion. You have to have both. The passion is natural and easy, the preparation is the hard part.

So you get to L.A. and in short order you land a lead role in *Roots: The Next Generations*, and then you book a seven-year series!

My first audition for a TV series ever.

People must hate you for that.

But you know how I got that role? I was doing a show called *Festival*, and the producer, Don Brinkley, and his wife, Marge, came to see the show's star, Gregory Harrison, because Don was considering him for the role of Gonzo. In the middle of the show, I was later told, Marge leaned over to Don and said, "How about that guy for Jackpot?" And something like a hundred auditions later, I was cast in *Trapper John, M.D.* You know, something I teach is that luck favors the prepared. I like to believe that everybody gets their shot. I don't know that that's true, and if it is, we probably only get one. If you're not prepared for it, bye! Next! Gazillion other actors in the line waiting for their shot. I always liked to work. I enjoy the process. For me it was never about "stardom." I just loved doing shows. I love learning new things. I love working with new people. Because of that, I always said "yes" to things. "You want to do this?" "Sure." Because I knew it might lead to something else or, at the very least, I'd learn something. Sometimes I did some really terrible, terrible, awful shows, and probably some very terrible, terrible, awful performances as well, but I learned something from them. "Don't do *that* next time." The constant doing of it—I think that's what's kept my career going for so long. My motto is "I reserve the right to be full of shit." I have my own way of doing things, and if people are reading this book, and they say, "Oh, I can use that!" Great! Steal it. Use it. And if you can't, if you think I'm full of shit, great. Walk your own path. Make the goal the work, just doing great work. There's never an end to that. If you make the reason curiosity, the search never ends. I remember people asking me after I won a Tony Award, "What's it like winning a Tony Award?" I didn't want to seem ungrateful because I'm incredibly grateful. But—I just put my Tony Award out for the first time two months ago. It's been sitting in a box in the corner. When I first got it, I sent it to people who supported and taught me. My parents, and siblings, and teachers. And then when it came back to me, I put it in a corner and I only recently took it out of the box. I'm deeply grateful for it, but the bottom line is that I've still got to pay my rent. The Tony Award doesn't pay the rent. The work pays the rent. Practice pays the rent. Learning lines pays the rent. Learning a new song pays the rent. Knowing how to do a new role well and not suck is what pays the rent. I'm not unappreciative of it, but that was never my goal, and I think that's a problem when I talk to a lot of young kids: They want to be a star. There's lots of stars. While doing *Trapper John*, I'd look around at everybody, and you go, "Where are these people going to be ten years from now? And where are the people from television shows from ten years ago?" It seems that most people are one-hit wonders. Most people have one big show. That's certainly the nature of television. By the way—one of the best things I learned on that show was to keep my mouth shut. Just watch. Watch what happens. Observe people. We had constant Broadway guests—Joel Grey, Rita Moreno, people that I had listened to on my albums were coming to *me* and onto *my* set. I could talk to them and interact with them. I was able to learn. I thought, "Just keep your mouth shut. This is the time to listen and learn." And I was also watching people around me being assholes, and I thought, "OK, don't do *that*. Don't *ever* do that."

Again, that's unusual. You were in your twenties, and I think watching assholes when you're young gives a lot of people permission to be an asshole. You chose something else.

I couldn't get arrested after *Trapper John*. It was really hard. And I decided, "Now's the time to get back into the theater." *Trapper John* allowed me to go into the theater on a different level because now I had TV cred. When I got a call for a new theatrical production, my "little thing" went off again.

That show was Michael Rupert's musical, *Mail*, at the Pasadena Playhouse, and it moved to Broadway.

It went to the Kennedy Center first, and then it came to Broadway. It was really exciting. I remember standing on my first Broadway stage. It was the Music Box, Irving Berlin's theater. His piano was still there. And there's a speakeasy in his old office! Just to be a part now of that community—I had listened to all those Broadway albums in San Diego and now, here I was! And then the show ran for two months. So I ended up going back to Los Angeles and while doing voice-overs for animation, I got called to audition for David Merrick for *Oh, Kay!* in New York. The studio where I auditioned was rundown, which wasn't unusual back then. I remember waiting, and waiting, and waiting, and nobody seemed to be coming out of the room. Finally, the door opens, and out walks this guy, old and stooped forward, almost like Tim Conway's character on *The Carol Burnett Show*. He's walking really slowly, and kind of points to me and he says, "Next, Mitchell, next, next. Bathroom, bathroom." I could barely understand him. So he goes down to the bathroom, and about forty minutes later, he slowly and feebly comes back. "Next, next, next, next." And I remember thinking, "This is David Merrick?" I didn't know about the stroke. He was still producing. Anyway, he loved what I did, and I got the role. It was fascinating. Just an amazing experience. David Merrick couldn't speak. He could get maybe one good sentence out and then it would turn into a garble. But he had a lady who was helping him, Natalie Lloyd, who, incidentally, later became his wife. She kind of interpreted for him and spoke for him. On the first day of rehearsals, she said, "Mr. Merrick has asked that you don't wear jeans or tennis shoes, that you dress up for rehearsals because you're the lead in the show." Very old school. He was there at every rehearsal. He was there at every show. I realized he still had quite a spark and he had an amazing eye. He knew what he wanted, and he knew what needed to be done. That was the last show that he produced on his own. And then, due to some legal issue, we had to close the show. But I got to know some fiercely talented people including my future wife, Allyson.

That was your second Broadway flop and this time as a leading man. Did it sour you on Broadway at all?

No. I felt—"Well, if they keep calling me, I'll keep coming back," And I still had work and a house in Los Angeles. A place to go back to. Whether my show hits or not is out of my control. All the stars have to align just so.

That doesn't mean you don't have anxieties about it.

I don't. I just don't. What good is that going to do? I have a good deal of control over the quality of my performance—but the rest of it? If I'm supposed to do this, and I am still searching and working and curious, I have faith that the universe will send it to me. I'll get that "little thing" that'll go off in me, and the plate will be there for me to eat from. I've learned from having that repeated over and over to trust. One of the things I try to teach students is to listen to their inner voice. First, learn to hear it, and then know when it is your inner voice and when it's your anxiety speaking. When you find your inner voice and trust it, it will always lead you right. At that point, I had learned to do that.

They called you to replace Gregory Hines in *Jelly's Last Jam*.

I worked my ass off. The hardest show I've ever done. I lost about five pounds a show in water weight. Physically, it's the most difficult show that I've ever done, and I'm so glad that I did it. Every day I would go in before the show and I'd just tap my feet and work through the solos and go through everything that I needed to do. Another amazing group and amazing dancers. What an amazing place to learn. Man, just watching these folks dance! That show is very underrated, I think.

It was the first of your darker characters.

Yes. And I've always liked dark characters, frankly. I've always been very attracted to people like that. I did that show for eight months.

And you went back to Los Angeles again, and it was not long before they called you to replace in *Kiss of the Spider Woman*. What do you remember about that show?

Chita Rivera is what I most remember! I had seen her perform on TV and in *The Rink*, but I had never met her. On my first day at the theater, she happened to come by and she was so warm and wonderful. She asked to see my ass 'cuz she loves a good dancer's ass. And who doesn't! When I showed her mine, I could sense her slight and not-so-well-disguised disappointment. She laughed when I apologized for having a singer's ass. It was the best welcome. I just fell in love with her right then, and that continues. My wife calls her my girlfriend. She is a consummate performer, and tireless perfectionist. Everything she did—I can still see her in that white suit, kicking the cigarette—she had such style, grace. I watched her work an audience. She knew how to work the spaces as well as the lines. She knew how to be dynamically still. She was just amazing. And what I learned from her wasn't just watching her on stage. She knew the crew by name. She knew who the musicians were, the doormen. She would always say "hi" to people. She was incredibly friendly. If somebody did something wrong, which was not often, she would say something about it, but she just led by example. She never missed a show and she never phoned it in. She was always at her absolute peak. She performed with such professionalism, but she was also nice about it, she was always kind. I thought to myself, "If I'm ever the lead in a show, that's what I'm going to do." I learned that from Chita. I think that's part of who I would be anyway, but watching somebody actually do it and do it on such a high level and do it effectively, and see how it affects a cast . . . That's Broadway. That's the

Broadway that I want to do. That's the kind of person I want to be. And then Vanessa Williams came in, and we're all thinking "Vanessa Williams? Miss America? Really? Following Chita?" And she just knocked it out of the park. She made it her own! She was also just a lovely, lovely human being.

This was your first long run.

It was great being in a long run. Finally I was in a hit! This is what it feels like! I learned the craft of keeping it fresh and making that very last audience think they're watching you do your performance for the very first time. There's a whole lot that you need to do to make that happen. You can see it when somebody's just kind of doing it by rote and phoning it in. I started a habit I continue to this day: I'd get an acting book, Michael Shurtleff's, or Uta Hagen's, and I would read the book while doing the show, and I'd look at their exercises and think "Let me try that tonight. I never thought of that." That helped keep it fresh. And watching Chita, you just don't phone it in. You keep exploring. Just be excellent no matter how you feel, no matter what's going on, always be excellent.

You had the opportunity to record the show's second cast album. That almost never happens with a replacement cast.

I was really, really happy because it was my first cast album. At that point, I'd been doing the show for months so it was totally comfortable. I remember listening to other cast albums and sometimes thinking, "That person doesn't sound so good. They sound kind of tired." And now I understand why: They usually record cast albums during the opening week of the show—the most exhausting period with rehearsals, performances, and extra press. Plus, it takes me three weeks to know a role, performing it in front of an audience, and three months to own it, so I don't feel I really know what I'm doing until three months into the run. I have come to learn that other performers feel the same. You rarely get the luxury of recording well into the run, except with *Kiss of the Spider Woman*. And John Kander was at the session. After I did "Marta," he came out of the recording booth with tears in his eyes and gave me a hug. He said, "Oh, that was so beautiful, that was so beautiful." John-freakin'-Kander loved the way I sang his song! That is one of those moments forever etched in my memory.

It was during the run of *Spider Woman* that [producer] Garth Drabinsky kept telling you that he had a show for you, which turned out to be *Ragtime*.

We went to Canada and we did a bunch of workshops for it and then we did the production up there. We were all sitting around the table during that first reading, and I remember the piano started, that little piano riff that starts the show. A massive energy descended on the room and never left. I usually have to work on a character really hard for a long time, and then at some point the character just blows into me, but this character blew into me right away. I knew what to do with this guy, how he walks, how he sings. I just knew him. And that feeling never left that show for me. I knew that this was the show that I'd been waiting for, that it was going to be something very special. And that's when I changed my name. I was going to change it totally because Brian Mitchell is kind of a crappy stage name. This was the beginning of a new career, a new chapter in my life. *Trapper John* was totally behind me, I'd just done my training period on Broadway. Now, it felt like something new. I put in my middle name. It's a verb in the middle of two words. Brian Stokes Mitchell. You stoke a fire, you know? It's got positive word value. *Ragtime* was an amazing show. You could feel the effect it had on people. I'd never felt that kind of energy. It was profoundly deep. It felt different than the usual applause. It felt like something special happening to them, too.

In *Ragtime*, the show that cemented his stardom and christened his new name. (© Catherine Ashmore)

It was very unusual that the show had its American premiere with another cast in Los Angeles.

That was a blow to the original cast who'd worked and created the show and done all the workshops. They thought they were going to be the ones premiering the show in the United States. That had been the plan. And then Garth invited all the leads to a lunch in his office—it has been referred to as the F.U. lunch—and he says, "I'm going to do the show in Los Angeles, and you guys are going to stay up here for the year." Everybody was devastated by that because that meant some other cast was going to premiere *Ragtime* in the states. Meanwhile the cast that had created the show was going to be stuck in Canada. Nobody wanted to be in Canada for a year. I knew my contract had right of first refusal for Los Angeles, London, and New York, so I left that lunch and immediately called my agent David Kalodner. Then Garth wanted to meet with me. He said, "I hope you stay in Toronto. I'd like to keep this cast together." But I knew even then that I was going to Los Angeles. I had lived there for years. I had a house there. I wanted to do the American premiere—like everybody else in the original cast. So that's what I did. It was the right decision for me. And when I rejoined them in New York, I could feel how much Garth's decision had demoralized them—not that they didn't still turn out amazing work—but it was heartbreaking. It took a while to heal.

Well, let's go back a bit to the run of the show in Toronto. I think there are not a lot of opportunities when people get to feel like the thing that they're working on really, really matters. Did you know?

That was "that thing" that descended on the room, I think everybody could feel that. It stayed all through the rehearsals. Magical things kept happening during rehearsals. It was this incredibly creative, positive, wonderful, thing. And warm because of director Frank Galati, and choreographer Graciela Daniele, and Lynn Ahrens and Stephen Flaherty and Terrence McNally. They were all coming from the same place and the whole cast became part of the conversation. It morphed into something even greater. I could speak about *Ragtime* for hours. During the run up to the Tony Awards—everybody's saying, "*Ragtime, Ragtime!*" Then *Lion King* opened, and all of a sudden it became the battle of those two shows. The majority of the awards went to *The Lion King*, which was disheartening to us. But you still have to do the show after you lose the Tony. We were still getting an incredible response from the audience, but we were bummed. And then, a few days later there was a news story about James Byrd, an African American man living in Texas, who got chained to a truck and dragged by some racists until he was dead. We had a cast meeting and we talked about it and it kind of invigorated the show again. I remember feeling so ashamed. Like, "Oh, man, I can't believe I'm bummed out about not getting a Tony Award." Some shows get a Tony Award and some shows are much more important than that. Some shows are making another kind of statement. It's not about awards. The fact that that's still going on in the country—that's what this show's about. It was a stark reminder about the real reason we were doing this. It gave us this really deep sense of purpose. It was a kick in the butt. And then, maybe two weeks after that, I get this long letter. It's maybe six pages, single-spaced and very neatly written. This person starts describing his life: "I'm Caucasian, twenty years old . . ." It's this long, rambling letter about his very ordinary life, living in the suburbs where he was raised and all of this. And then I get to the last paragraph: "The reason I'm writing this letter is because a couple of weeks ago I saw *Ragtime*, and when I left the theater, I realized that I'd been a racist all my life and didn't even know it." And for me it was like, "Oh, shit, there it is again! There it is again." Those signs that kept happening [at this point, Stokes is fighting tears]. That's why I do this. Sometimes you get lucky. You get to do *Kiss of the Spider Woman*, and you get to do *Ragtime*. You get to do a show that speaks out about inequities, problems in our society, and calls attention to things that happened 100 years ago and are still happening. The ability that art has to change somebody's life in a second—I can't think of anything else that does that except for a traumatic experience like a war. It changes people immediately. Art that has the ability—for somebody to look at a picture, to leave a show, and never think the same way again. I feel so lucky to do what I do. How did I get to be that guy? That I got to be a part of that? It's mindboggling to me. I get to do something for a living that is not only fun, I'm making a good living at it, and it's putting good food into the world. It's doing good things for people. It's enlightening people. It's making people more empathetic. It's making people care about each other. It's making people understand cooperation. It's making people want to hug somebody else. It's making people want to learn to be like somebody else. It's making people want to be a better person, you know? One of my mottos is "ride the wave." Sometimes the wave's big, and it takes you someplace wonderful. Sometimes it's a little thing, and you just grab and ride as best as you can. Take it where you can. You ride the wave. The wave has taken me to some incredible places and continues to, and it doesn't seem like it's going to stop, and it's great, and I'm thankful for that. I'm just so incredibly grateful for my life and doing what I do. I just can't believe it. And then to be a part of this community and the theater? It's a very elite group. And I don't mean that in a snobby way. I mean it's rare. It's rarified air that I'm getting an opportunity to breathe. I'm an astronaut. I went to the moon. Whoa. Amazing.

When I asked Audra McDonald about *Ragtime* she went [sighing deeply], "Oooooh, *Ragtime*." I said, "You're exhausted already by my just mentioning it." To take nothing away from any of the gratitude that you just expressed, or any of the awareness of the impact, did it take its toll?

It did. And especially on that cast that stayed in Canada, which included Audra. I had a different experience than they did. I think it was still special for everybody else, but man, they put in the grunt time in the trenches. They were not treated well. I would have felt the same way if I were there. And I missed them terribly when I was doing the show. It doesn't take anything away from the Los Angeles cast when I'm saying that, but there's something about creating a show. You have the shared history of those rehearsals where people get to sit around a table and discuss things. There is something special about an original cast that creates, and the bond that is forged. When I was doing *Shuffle Along*, man, that was the most fun rehearsal—one of the best rehearsal periods I've ever had on a show because it was George C. Wolfe directing, who's just brilliant. I just love him in a million different ways. Sitting around a table getting the most interesting conversations happening, all having to do with the characters in the show. George was like an Australian shepherd, nipping everybody in the ass so that they come closer and closer together in the particular direction that he wants them to go.

You said that you knew *Ragtime* was taking you to someplace else, career-wise.

Mm-hmm. I got more offers. I didn't have to audition anymore. I remember talking to Michael Blakemore when I was trying to decide whether or not to do *Kiss Me, Kate*. He said to me, "Don't think about it too long and too much. When you have a big hit show, and you've had a great part, you can get so stuck on what to do next that you don't make a decision at all." But the other thing is, it can mess with your head, too. Now you're the *star*. Now you're supposed to know everything. Now it's on *you* to carry a show. That messes with people because sometimes you just want to explore and work and discover. You lose that freedom.

Did having Marin Mazzie along for the ride on *Kiss Me, Kate* help?

Oh, it was great. She was immensely talented, and I just loved her to pieces. She was a force on the stage. In *Ragtime*, our two characters are like passing ships in the night. We hardly see each other. Both of our roles were so hard, we didn't hang out a lot after the show. Before *Kate* started, we actually went to lunch and talked about the whole *Ragtime* experience and how challenging it was. We made a pact: "Let's have the most fun ever." And we did! We wanted to simply do good work and have a good time. No drama, no high maintenance. That was a fun show. I had never done a show with that kind of humor—farcical, over-the-top. Somebody asked me once, "You play instruments and you write and you compose and you orchestrate and you conduct and you act and you sing and you dance and you do TV and you do film. What do you think you do best?" I thought, "I'm a student. That's what I do best." I love learning new things. And that's what I was at *Kiss Me, Kate*. I was a student and I let Michael Blakemore teach me.

And you had a massive hit.

People were ravenously excited about *Kiss Me, Kate*. I didn't get it really. Audiences just loved the show. I finally realized that sometimes people just want to forget their lives. They just want to laugh. I knew that on an instinctual level, but I didn't know it on an intellectual level. I realized, 'Oh, you idiot, *that's* why people love silly shows. It's about escaping. It's about getting away from the humdrum of your life, the horror of your life, the outrage of your life, the terror of your life, whatever it is.'

I think revivals like *Kiss Me, Kate* are hugely important. As we get further and further away from the Golden Age of musical theater, we forget the structure of a well-produced, incredibly

"Where is the life that late I led?" *Kiss Me, Kate*. (Photofest)

scored musical. But when we experience one, it's thrilling and you realize what that art form has the power to be. The success of this came as a surprise to you?

A bit of a surprise. I did it for a year and I was exhausted. It was so physical. There was not very much time I was off stage. And I knew while I was doing the show that I wasn't going to miss getting slapped in the face five times a show!

Did you see the 2019 revival?

I did and it's always a weird experience. When I saw the revival of *Ragtime*—I had an out-of-body experience. Once I finish a show, that show's gone from my head. It's gone. I give it up. I can't remember the lines. But during that show I was reliving the entire thing. I knew what was coming up, I knew where I was when I wasn't in the scene. "Oh, I'm down in my dressing room now. I'm coming up the stairs getting ready to do this cross . . ." If you asked me if I remembered anything like that, the answer would have been "absolutely not," but while I was watching that show, I had a really hard time paying attention because I was having this weird experience in my mind. I am seeing myself walking up the stairs. I'm seeing myself making a quick change. I'm *seeing* that. Bizarre that I would have this weird kind of psychological chamber that I went into that I didn't even know was there.

You won your first Tony for *Kiss Me, Kate*.

Yes, and it's a pretty exciting thing to have happen to you. But I have always realized that awards are a commercial endeavor. They're about promotion. Nothing wrong with that. But frankly, everybody that's nominated for a Tony Award deserves to win. It's not fair, you know. And whether you win or lose, you still have to keep plugging away.

Between *Ragtime* and *Kiss Me, Kate*, you did your first Encores!, *Do Re Mi*.

Those were fun. I mean, you're shot out of a cannon. But working with that cast was a joy. Heather Headley understudied Audra in *Ragtime* in Toronto and left to do *Lion King* and I always loved her. And Nathan Lane is a master comedian. It was another great learning experience.

You did *Carnival* at Encores!, too.

Carnival freaked me out a little bit because it was right after *King Hedley II*. *Hedley* had like ten monologues, and the last one at the end of the first act was a twelve-page rant. The character was very angry, and yelled a lot. Normally when you have a month or two months to rehearse a show, part of the process is you learn how to yell and scream in a safe way. I didn't have the time to do that with *Hedley*. I had two weeks to rehearse. I was doing these scenes balls out and my voice started doing weird things. By the time that show ended, I had blisters on my vocal cords. The next show I did was *Sweeney Todd* [during the Sondheim Celebration at the Kennedy Center]. That was another amazing experience. But I was having problems singing. I got through the run. We were only doing two shows a week because there were other shows in repertoire. So I had just enough time to rest and then I'd do the show and it would kind of knock me down again. And then from the first day of *Carnival* I was having problems. I ended up having bilateral vocal surgery because both my cords were screwed up. After the operation I had to be totally silent for two weeks. I couldn't say *anything*. I would go to Riverside Park and I would sit and watch fireflies and wonder if my voice was going to return to its former glory.

Was this the first time that you had to be protective of your voice? *Ragtime* also has you singing some stratospheric notes. Were you that monk who's silent after shows?

Oh, totally. Singers are delicate flowers. As a matter of fact, I literally call it my monk mode. There would be weeks I wouldn't speak outside of the show. I wouldn't say anything to anybody. I didn't answer the phone, I would barely talk to Allyson. Voices gets tired for all kinds of different reasons, especially around opening nights. You're recording the album and doing all those other things we talked about [promotions, TV appearances]. And you start very quickly down a road of no return. It's really, really hard to rebound because you're doing eight shows a week. You don't have time to rest. I ended up, bringing it back slowly, and it finally returned. But I remember sitting in on the auditions for *Man of La Mancha*. I couldn't really talk very much. I still didn't know if my voice was going to come back all the way or not.

That seems panic-inducing.
By the time the rehearsals started, I knew I was going be OK.

Let's go back to *Sweeney* for a moment.
That's a role I'd always wanted to do. When I first heard that album, it blew the top of my head off. Len Cariou singing those songs! I think that's Sondheim's masterwork. The complexity of it, the way he weaves themes in and out—Jonathan Tunick's orchestrations, the construction of the show. I just love that show. But doing only fourteen performances was a little like getting a taste of the most delicious meal you'll ever eat, and that's it. That's all you can have.

What was your direct experience with Sondheim like?
He sat in during the sitzprobe [the actors' first rehearsal with the full orchestra] and he didn't say too much. He was really respectful of the director, Chris Ashley. And he was respectful of the actors' process, as well. I think he knew that there wasn't enough time to do a deep dive. He was incredibly relaxed. He was incredibly charming. We had dinner with him and he was really talkative. People have said he's not very talkative, but he talked, and told stories. He was open and funny. It was great to hear about his process. One of the reasons his songs are so easy to do is because he's writing like an actor. He puts spaces in the songs for you. You don't really have to do too much. There are other things you can also add—obviously, but he does so much of that work for you, whereas Cole Porter's writing a charming song, and it's up to you to add the character to it.

And what about your experience of being part of the overall festival?
Oh, that was a blast. There were so many exciting things going on at once. I wish that somebody had done a documentary on that from the very beginning, from its first conception. Seeing all those shows rehearsing and hearing all these different Sondheim scores coming from different rooms. Sets from one show hung three stories above sets from another show. I mean, the festival was a recipe for total disaster and the fact that it was executed so brilliantly was extraordinary. We were calling it "Camp Sondheim" because it was like being at summer camp—getting together with all your friends and putting on a show. Everybody loved to watch each other work. It was amazing.

Your next show was *Man of La Mancha*. At this stage, you were a bankable Broadway star who got to choose his next piece. And you said, "I want to do this" and they built it around you.
I called my agent and he called Mitch Leigh and set up a meeting. David Stone jumped on board. That was the first show that David produced by himself. Good news and bad news about starring in *Man of La Mancha*: the good news? You get to sing "The Impossible Dream." It's a song that everybody knows and loves and has been covered a million times. The bad news?

You have to sing "The Impossible Dream," a song everybody knows and loves and has been covered a million times. The challenge is finding a fresh approach. Whenever I sing a song, I deeply analyze it. I take the words apart, I take the music apart, dissect the rhyme scheme, the choice of words, the inner rhyme scheme, and understand how it's all connected. As I was exploring it, it occurred to me that there was some space to put in the song. There's kind of an implied question in it—To dream . . . What? The impossible dream. To fight . . . Who? The unbeatable foe. To bear . . . What? With unbearable sorrow. To run . . . Where? Where the brave dare not go. There's a question, and it's answered. And the song, by the way is not titled "The Impossible Dream," it's called "The Quest." I knew I wanted to make it my own. As I was working on it, I started thinking, "This song's too short and a key change would be useful. What if we go back to 'this is my quest' again, and take it up a half a step?" I could even see, "This is where I move downstage." When Mitch Leigh heard my changes at a rehearsal, he liked the key change but not the high note at the end. He said, "The song is called 'The Quest.' It's about trying to get somewhere. It's about working at something, and when you hit the high note at the end, it feels like you've arrived." I understood. But I thought, "Well, I'm going to sing the high note anyway," because I wanted to put my stamp on it. We opened the show and recorded the album that same week. But about two weeks later, I realized Mitch was totally right. That song is about climbing Everest. People climbing Everest go very slowly. And some don't reach the top. But they try. And that's what the song is about—trying. So I went back to singing the lower note—the correct note. The note he wrote. And I do have regrets—slightly—about showing off on the album to this day.

Given that the show was essentially built around you, did it do what you wanted it to do for yourself?

Yes. When I sang "The Impossible Dream," I felt the same powerful connection with the audience that I felt during *Ragtime*. I could feel something coming through me that touched people deeply. That was the reason to do that show.

After *Man of La Mancha*, you decided to work less so that you could be at home with your son.

If something came along that was a spectacular show, I would not have said no because I've still got to buy diapers, still got to pay the rent. I still have to work. I just changed how I work. That's why I focused on concerts. It was still a lot of work, and I had no idea if it was going to be a viable option. But it worked out, and I realized, "Oh, I don't have to do eight shows a week. I can just do concerts." And I can constantly change up the repertoire. I don't really listen to that much musical theater for pleasure. I studied it when I was young and I know the pantheon quite well, but if I put on an album, it's usually jazz, world music, Bobby McFerrin, Jacob Collier, pop, gospel, country, bluegrass. So doing those concerts allowed me to spread my vocal wings. I could sing what I want and say what I want. They are musical theater-centric, but I get to introduce other musical languages.

But the impetus to work that way and to choose to not do eight a week was . . .

Lazy.

Was it? I thought it was influenced by fatherhood.

Yes, it was. I joke about lazy because, man, doing eight shows a week is really, really hard! Doing *Shuffle Along*—loved the process, loved the people, loved everything. Didn't like eight shows a week so much. It was hard. I'm gone so much. My son gets home from school, and then I'm off to the theater. I never see him unless I get up very early in the morning. I was one of these people that always loved kids but never had a strong desire to have them. I had a career that I was focusing on. Knowing how fragile and important childhood is, I didn't want to have a kid and not be around. When we decided to have a child, it changed our lives in the best way—our son is a fantastic, beautiful gift, and I love being a father. Doing concerts allowed me not only to raise him and make good money, but it allows me to perform for an audience, sing the songs that I love, talk, create. It's my show, and if it's great, it's wonderful. And if it sucks, it's my fault. It's like a high wire and I enjoy that responsibility and risk. Now I have the best of both worlds: a terrific family and terrific career.

In 2010 you did another book show, *Women on the Verge*.

Yes, and that was a limited run. I always wanted to work with Bartlett Sher. I love his direction. And it was a great cast. The movie was crazy fun. It's [composer] David Yazbek, and I love Yazbek. It was just a great team. My "thing" wasn't going off, but I thought, "Let me see what it feels like to do eight shows a week again, and this is a limited run." It's not a show that I enjoyed doing so much actually. There was just not enough time to refine it.

And there was animosity among your costars. That's really interesting terrain to have to navigate.

Yeah. And, you know, sometimes it's best to just stay out of it. That theater is an unusual theater, too, the Belasco. Theaters are like people. Each of them has a very, very different personality. Some are very happy and friendly. Some are kind of big and cavernous and impersonal. Some are imperious. Some are beautifully dark and mysterious, like the Belasco. I think it makes a lot of sense to put the right show in the right theater. *Sweeney Todd* feels like the Belasco, as does *Follies*. It could be that the Belasco wasn't the best match for *Women on the Verge*. But most probably it's that the show just didn't work. What's amazing to me is how everything has to be right. If any one person messes up their job, the lighting person, the person that's calling the cues, the curtain puller, any of the actors, the conductor, things can go terribly, horribly wrong. It's kind of miraculous when you get a huge group of people—designers, craftspeople, actors, musicians, technical people, producers—all with different abilities, sensibilities, talents, and somehow it works. So it's not so surprising when it actually doesn't work. It's more surprising, I think, when it does. There are just so many things that can go wrong. A set piece doesn't work, and it can throw everything off. You still have to open the show.

When you are in a show that isn't working, can you tell?

Oh, yeah. Sometimes you're so in it, you're just focused on getting the job done. You can tell if an audience response is tepid, but in terms of whether or not the thing actually works? I could feel the audience coming in on this big high—they were so excited to see this cast in this show with these creators. And as the show went along, you could just feel them getting a little bit more and more disappointed, wanting to be with the show, but you could just feel the balloon deflate. You could feel the energy wane. That's why I love when Chita says, "When a show's not working, sometimes you want to just stop and say to the audience, 'Hey, we're not doing this on purpose.'" You want to say that, but you can't. You just have to go on. But it's obvious when you're in a hit and in a show that people—you can feel—it's an energetic thing. And that manifests as applause, as laughter. When it's not working, it manifests as people coughing. There's a lot of coughing. There's a lot of rustling. There's not very much laughter. There's a certain energetic arc that is just not there. . . . You just can feel when it's not right. And a lot of times you know that before the rehearsal process is over, but ultimately the audience is the judge of what you're doing. They will tell you if they like it or not. You'll know. There's no mystery when a show's going to close or when your show's floundering or you're having problems. You're listening. You can feel it. You know.

This was you getting your toe back in the water of eight shows a week and seeing how it felt. And?
And I thought, "Meh." I'll go back to concerts and television.

So then it took *Shuffle Along* to get you excited enough again to sign on for another show?
Well, it was George Wolfe. I'm nuts about George. I love him. He's brilliant on so many different levels. [Unfortunately, during rehearsals] we were running long, and a lot of the things that I really loved doing in the show ended up getting cut. It was a great experience, though. Amazing. And I wouldn't change anything, but it wasn't a role that I loved doing eight times a week. I loved the ensemble aspect of it, but I also like being able to have a number, a monologue, or a whole energy that I can sustain and work throughout the show, and this wasn't that kind of show. I was very sorry to see it close because I really love the show and I think it was an incredibly important piece. The original show [the original 1921 *Shuffle Along*, the creation of which is the plot of the 2016 *Shuffle Along*] changed Broadway and musical entertainment forever. It introduced syncopation to a white audience. In a sense, it brought races together. As George used to say, "It brought uptown downtown and downtown uptown." I think all of us looked forward to resurrecting those people and telling their story. It felt really, really great to be doing that. It was a great company. And low maintenance. Everybody just showed up to work and for months after, we would still call each other. "What are you doing? Let's go out to dinner." We couldn't get enough of each other because it was such an incredible group of people. And man, that dancing ensemble! Savion Glover has taken choreography to another level. It's a show that should still be running and that everybody should see.

It closed quickly due to a lot of factors: *Hamilton* winning all of the awards, Audra McDonald's unexpected pregnancy . . .
There are always things that we're not even aware of that factor into shows closing. My brother, George, became a really wonderful costume designer. He designs for a theater in the Midwest sometimes and he was asked to be at the replacement audition for one of the characters. So he sat there and he's wondering, "Why am I here?" All these incredible performers coming in, singing and dancing. After they would leave, [the producers] would turn to him and say, "Can she fit the costume?" He felt terrible because all these women were coming in, singing their faces off, doing their best, and they never realized they weren't getting cast because they didn't fit the costume. Sometimes you just don't fit the costume. After he told me that story I thought how many of those actresses went home and beat themselves up. "Oh, I didn't nail that scene like I usually do." "Oh, I should have really pushed that phrase." "Oh, I didn't get a good spin on the high note." "I knew I should have worn heels." But they didn't fit the costume, and that's the same thing with the show closing. So what are the reasons? I don't know. Maybe it didn't fit the costume. We don't really know all of the reasons. You just can't spend that much time with that stuff. I have lots of theories on why I thought the show closed, but the truth is, I don't know.

Having gone back to the grind of eight shows a week and having two disappointments doesn't bode well for having you back on Broadway anytime soon.

Yeah, but, you know, I'm riding the wave. If the wave takes me back to eight a week, you know, I'd be doing it if the right show came along. But my field of vision is getting narrower to the kinds of shows that I want to do. Every year I am asked to do a new show, but sometimes it means I would have to go on the road. They may mean going out of town for six months. I can't go out of town for six months. I have a kid who just started in a new school and needs me around. When we were younger, I didn't have a close relationship with my dad. I always felt my dad was there. He was always supportive as he could be, but like a 1950s dad. We'd sit down, have dinner. "How was school today? That's good." And then he'd go, and sit, and read his paper. Not really want to be disturbed. If we did disturb him, he wouldn't make us feel awful about it, but you could tell he really didn't want to be disturbed. Then he would go up to his room. I found out much later what he was doing up there: He was studying some manual so he could get a promotion to better take care of the family's needs. To put his kids through college. It was always about the family. His job was to go make money, and raise the kids, and make sure everybody was fed, the mortgage was paid. But I remember coming back home for the first time when I was working with the Twelfth Night Repertory Company. I had a really early morning and I was heading back to Los Angeles, and my dad kept saying, "You sure? Do you have to leave now? Can you go back tomorrow morning? I'll wake up with you at 4 in the morning, and get you up so you can drive." I said, "Dad, I'm sorry, I have to go." He walked me out to the street and I remember driving away and seeing my dad in the rearview mirror, just standing staring at me, totally still. I think he realized he'd missed a lot of my life. I watched him the entire way until I had to make a right turn, and he stood there for the two and a half blocks. Didn't move.

So you decided to do it differently as a father.

I have that luxury. For one, I don't have four kids! I can do concerts and voice-overs and television and films and recordings. Because I have many choices, I have the luxury of choosing a show that's going to fill me up, that I feel enthusiastic about doing eight times a week. If my "little thing" doesn't go off, I'm not doing it. My "little thing" has to go off. But even when my "little thing" doesn't go off, there are still things to learn: to be able to celebrate the people in *Shuffle Along*, to work with the people I worked with on *Women on the Verge*, even though the show didn't work. Sometimes they work, and sometimes they—you know, it's not for lack of trying. There's no shame in that. It's all about the journey. It's all about the doing. It's all about "The Quest." That song's kind of become my song because that really is kind of my life. It's about that. It's not about summiting. It's about getting pushed back and picking yourself up and going up again, or blazing a new trail. It's about marching to the beat of your own drummer. That's what *everybody's* life is about, I think. Living through it all, and recognizing and loving and acknowledging the great moments, the moments you're able to touch another person, or share something with another person, or open another person's mind, and enjoying the journey. There's going to be more crap coming your way, you know. I tell students, "You don't have to search out the dark. It will find you." It's about getting through that. That's part of the journey, too, and the longer I live, the more I appreciate that. That is what acting is about, what art is about. That, I think, is what's inspiring about the theater. When I do my own concerts, I want the audience to leave with a sense of hope and joy and empowerment, and empathy and understanding. Perhaps a newfound excitement about life and a sense of appreciation of the miracle that we are all here together.

9

MARC KUDISCH

February, March 2018

MARC KUDISCH IS A CONVERSATIONALIST's dream. That's not just to say that he's talkative (which he is) or that he's got strong convictions (which he does) or that he's analytical (which he relishes); he attacks topics with gusto. Loudly. Passionately. Assertively. He leaves no doubt about what he's trying to convey and no notion that he's holding back. Like a ricocheting bullet, he's all over the place in a flash. He's the first to tell you that he speaks his opinions as if they are fact but also the first to reverse himself if he's wrong. He's been accused of having an ego, but that's a misunderstanding of what makes him tick. Kudisch isn't driven by self-aggrandizement but by confidence in his beliefs and his need to express them. And he's not restrained by manners. He may come off as a bit of a bull but one who trusts the durability of the china.

Given that and knowing his credits, one might expect that Kudisch came to New York ready and determined to conquer musicals. He didn't. He was born in Hackensack, New Jersey, and reared in Plantation, Florida, and theater wasn't even on his radar until high school, and he didn't consider musicals until he landed the role of Conrad Birdie in the 1990 Tommy Tune/Ann Reinking national tour of *Bye Bye Birdie*. But after that, his musical career exploded: *Beauty and the Beast*, *The Wild Party*, *Thoroughly Modern Millie*, *Chitty Chitty Bang Bang*, *9 to 5*, and fourteen other musicals fill his résumé, netting him three Tony and four Drama Desk nominations. If his roles have anything in common other than his rich baritone and his imposing physicality, it's supreme confidence (or occasionally the appearance of it to mask insecurity). The only time, in fact, that critics were dismissive of Kudisch was in *Bells Are Ringing*, when he played a man unsure of himself and teetering on the edge. That's not to say that Kudisch usually plays himself, but he sure knows how to harness his own essence.

In person, there is no pretense to Kudisch. He arrives on a motorcycle, in jeans and flannel, and greets me with a bear hug. He isn't especially interested in being liked, which makes him instantly likable. But he is unapologetically himself.

When did the theater bug bite?

Theater was never a part of my family. I didn't know what I really wanted to do. I knew I loved Houdini. I loved Carl Sagan. I had books on cosmology and black holes. I loved the theory of relativity. I was very much the black sheep in my family, and because I got grounded a lot . . .

One of Kudisch's lesser known triumphs, *The Glorious Ones*. (Joan Marcus)

What were you getting grounded for?
Oh, anything.

Were your parents especially strong disciplinarians or were you acting out especially?
I would say my parents were strong disciplinarians, but my parents weren't strict. They had their rules, and you followed them. Mark Twain has a wonderful quote: "When I was fourteen I thought my father was an idiot. It was amazing how much smarter he was seven years later." I rebelled against my parents, I think, because I didn't understand their relationship. Look, I loved them. Don't get me wrong. But I also grew up in a period of time where if I did something really stupid, I was grounded, or I'd get it over the butt. My father was strict that way because he was brought up strict that way. Today we would call it child abuse. I know in my heart that my father's one of the best people I ever knew in my life, truly. The nicest, kindest, most generous, funny, loving . . . couldn't have asked for a better dad. So when I got disciplined, I deserved it. Believe me, I deserved it. And when he disciplined me, it was so calm and cool and collected. I'd come home, I'd walk in my bedroom, if my father was sitting on my bed I knew what was coming. And I also knew if that if he got to that place, I deserved it.

So what happened in high school in your senior year?
My brother, who was two years ahead of me, was very popular. He was the president of his class. So when I got to be a junior, and I finally wasn't just "little Kudisch," I kind of wanted to figure out who I was. In my senior year, I decided I needed to do something so that my high school career wasn't a total bomb. I tried out to be a male cheerleader, and I became one. I'm not even sure how it all happened. The guys, most of them, were footballers that either had shitty grades or had an injury so they couldn't play and they still wanted to do something

Marc Kudisch	
Bye Bye Birdie	National Tour, 1990
Joseph and the Amazing Technicolor Dreamcoat	Broadway, 1993
Beauty and the Beast	Broadway, 1995
High Society	Broadway, 1998
The Scarlet Pimpernel	Broadway, 1999
The Wild Party	Broadway, 2000
Bells Are Ringing	Broadway, 2001
Thoroughly Modern Millie	Broadway, 2002
No Strings	Encores!, 2003
The Thing About Men	Off-Broadway, 2003
Assassins	Broadway, 2004
Chitty Chitty Bang Bang	Broadway, 2005
See What I Wanna See	Off-Broadway, 2005
The Apple Tree	Broadway, 2006
The Witches of Eastwick	Washington, DC, 2007
The Glorious Ones	Off-Broadway, 2007
9 to 5	Broadway, 2009
Girl Crazy	Encores!, 2009
The Blue Flower	Off-Broadway, 2011
A Minister's Wife	Off-Broadway, 2013
Finding Neverland	Broadway, 2016
Hey, Look Me Over	Encores!, 2017
Girl from the North Country	Off-Broadway, 2018; Broadway, 2020

athletic, so they were cheerleaders. But they were popular. So just the fact that I was around them sort of . . .

Upped your stock?

It did. And then, from there I remember we did some kind of a homecoming show and the drama teacher, Pat Cook, came up to me and said, "I want you to audition for the school musical this year." *My Fair Lady*. And I got the role of Freddy Eynsford-Hill. I'd never done anything like it before. It was never anything I thought of before. And I found that I liked it. So after I graduated high school I auditioned for community theater, and I got cast as the head waiter, Rudy, in *Hello, Dolly!* Then I did the play *Ordinary People*, and then when I went to college—I was at Florida Atlantic University—I was a poli-sci major and I took theater courses to just lighten the load. I knew I enjoyed it. I was spending more time in the theater department than I was in poli-sci, and my professor said to me, "Look, you do great on the exams, but I know you're spending more time there. You really need to explore that." So I listened to that and I decided to change my major to theater. And also, I put myself through college so there was this wonderful sense of ownership. When I told my parents, they were like, "Well, don't you think maybe you should minor in it?" Nope. I felt pretty solid about it. The good news was I had no pipe dreams about it.

Right. It's not like you spent all this time idolizing it or dreaming about it or . . .

No. I was lucky: I had classes with Edward Albee and Josh Logan and Zoe Caldwell and Hume Cronyn. All of the teachers down at FAU were lions of the theater in the '50s and '60s, and they all retired together. So my training—and mind you, I didn't sing a note. There was no music. It was just theater. But I got a real old-school education. We had a 1,000-seat theater. No microphones. I didn't know what a microphone was until I actually got to New York. That's how I was trained. I worked my ass off. When I graduated, I was already working professionally, and I decided that I was going to work [locally] until I got my union card. Then I moved to New York. I literally got in a U-Haul and drove to New York. Rachel Bay Jones and I grew up in the same area, and we moved to New York together. What finally got my ass here—I was lucky. My friend, Pat Hoag, who is married to [late theater critic] John Simon, was doing her graduate work when I was doing my undergraduate work. One day she called me out of the blue [from New York]. She was working for a casting agency in New York and called because there was a role on a soap opera that she thought I'd be right for. I knew I wanted to move to New York but I hadn't really actually thought about doing it yet, so that was the thing that nailed it. I flew up and within twenty-four hours I did the audition. I remember that there was this big fundraiser in Times Square for Walter Mondale. Mandy Patinkin and Bernadette Peters were up on the stage. I was standing right below the stage and Mandy was standing up there. That's heroin for anyone that's thinking about moving to New York. I flew back to south Florida and was like, "I'm getting the hell out of here as fast as I can." So I did. Four and a half months later I got my first play.

What were you doing for those four and a half months? Did you have a job?
Waiting tables. I mean, that's the thing you do, right? And four and a half months after I moved to New York, I never had a regular job again.

You did plays for your first couple of years. What made your agents submit you for the national tour of *Bye Bye Birdie*?
Me. I wanted to go in. I was working off-Broadway. I was doing recurring roles on soap operas. But I had friends that were doing musicals and you're young, you have ego. I always felt like musicals were for people who couldn't act so they just sang and danced a lot to cover that fact. I'm like, "I could do that. Lord knows I can act my way around those people. I just need to learn how to sing and move a little bit." Now, again, when I moved to the city, Broadway was never a goal. We were in the heat of off-Broadway. Shows could run for years off-Broadway and be huge hits. That's what I wanted. *Bye Bye Birdie* was the first musical that I really wanted to do. I just liked it. And, you know, the whole audition story in itself was crazy. I had agents, but I had no musical experience. I couldn't get an audition. So I went to the open call. You know what the cattle calls were like, but I liked them. I went to the open call for *Bye Bye Birdie*. I did my thing. And because I'd grown up listening to Elvis—I wasn't a singer, but I could mimic it—I got a callback. I auditioned again, and they liked me, but they told my agents, "This is as far as it goes. He doesn't have the experience they're looking for." Then three months later, I got invited to the final call because they had scraped the bottom of the barrel, and they weren't finding what they were looking for. Everything I'm about to tell you is absolutely true. So I get to the final call. I believe it was at the Broadhurst Theatre. I had my leather jacket and my boots on. It's 1990 so I had the silver spurs and the tips and all that crap. I was ready to go. The holding pen for the actors was in the balcony so everybody was watching each other's auditions. Walter Bobbie and I were buddies. We went to the same gym back then. He was auditioning for Mr. MacAfee, and we were both hanging out waiting to go in for our final call. They call my name. I'm about to walk down when [casting director] Stuart Howard stops me and says, "Whatever you do, don't sing 'Sincere.'" And I was like, "But that's what I prepared!" He's like, "Don't do it. Don't sing it. Everybody's been singing it. They don't want to hear it anymore. Sing something else." So I'm walking down the aisle of this Broadway house. I've never been on a Broadway stage. I've barely seen Broadway shows 'cuz I can't afford it. I'm walking by [producers] the Weisslers, Tommy Tune, [director] Gene Saks. I'm walking across to the accompanist, Brad Garside. Brad looked at me and he went, "Dude, are you okay?" And I said, "They told me not to sing my song. It's the only thing I have. I don't know what to do." He said, "Whose audition is this?" I said, "It's mine." He said, "Yeah, it's your audition. You prepared. Go sing your damn song, man." I got out there. I stood in front of everybody and the

minute he hit that first chord I saw Stuart Howard throw his hands up and walk out. Then I sang it. I thought to myself, "This is the first and last time I'm ever going to sing this music, and sure as hell, it's the first and last time I'm ever going to sing it on a Broadway stage, so if I don't enjoy the moment, why show up?" And I really had a good time doing it. It went over and I got applause from all over the place. They had me read and then I talked to Gene a little bit on the way out, and then I tried running out of there as fast as I could because it was like, "Don't do anything to fuck it up." And then right before I got out, Stuart stopped me and said, "Thank you for not listening to me." So, you know, that was a huge lesson.

As an actor at his first musical audition it is highly unusual for somebody to behave with that kind of chutzpah.

That's why I do what I do. I always just saw things and committed to whatever the choice was going to be, come hell or high water. Sometimes it doesn't work out that way. I had two auditions on the same day once. One was for Maine State for their season and right after that, I had an audition for the workshop of a new Kander and Ebb musical called *Steel Pier*. I figured I might as well use the same music for both of them. I had Maine State first so I thought, "Great, this will be a warm-up." I used to sing this wonderful standard, "I Feel a Song Coming On," but I sang it like I had to take a crap, so to feel a song coming on was actually quite painful and uncomfortable. The music was all up and bouncy, but the action was the complete opposite. It made me look good. So I went into the Maine State audition with it, and I sang the song. And I remember I was like, "Would you like to hear anything else?" And he said, "God no." Next up, Paul Gemignani, Scott Ellis, Susan Stroman, John Kander, and Fred Ebb. We're doing the same song. I had Fred and Paul rolling with laughter. They loved it. You make decisions. Not everybody is going to go a roll with your decision. If you're fortunate, you've synched up with the people you really want to work with, and if not, that tells you something, too. I am not everybody's taste.

Let's get back to *Birdie*.

I still didn't know how to sing. They hired me because of the way that I acted the role. I was losing my voice at the end of every week. My friend, Susan Egan was like, "You need to learn how to sing, Marc." She wasn't wrong. But again, I learned on the fly all the time. When I was doing *Beauty and the Beast*, my dresser, Eric, was an ex-opera singer. I sang okay. I mean, I was better by this time, right? But I remember when he was dressing me one night, he said, "You have a beautiful voice, Marc. Too bad you only use 25 percent of it." There is nothing to a performer more sensitive than his or her voice. Nothing strikes a chord more. But instead of saying, "Fuck you," I said—because I knew he was right—"So what do I do?" He introduced me to my voice teacher, Alan Seal, who was an operatic teacher. For eight years, I busted my ass while I was on the job.

Wow. But during the *Birdie* tour, you were obviously able to wing it well enough. What else do you remember?

I remember a lot. I had never toured. I never made that kind of money. I spent frivolously. I had to buy a duffle bag to just be able to haul my boots with me. It was so stupid. But it was a great experience. It's very hard touring, even on a good tour, because it becomes very insular, right? It's a bubble. So having any kind of relationship is incredibly hard. Everyone knows your business. Obviously I learned a lot. Tommy taught me how to tap. I would help him break in his tap shoes because I had the biggest feet in the company next to him. And I learned a lot from Annie Reinking. And Gene Saks, who's like a grandfather to me, reminded me of my dad in so many ways. It was just a really nice group of people, and it was also really hard, especially when you're young and you're still not sure who you are. It was fourteen months. I found myself on my own a lot.

That's not what I would have guessed only because younger people on a tour gravitate toward each other.
But there were different cliques. Remember, I wasn't really one of the cool kids in high school. I spent a lot of time on my own. I had a relationship with someone in the company. It didn't go well, so that was a part of it.

Did you make a conscious decision during that show to do more musicals?
Well, the conscious decision, especially when I got home, was to learn how to sing. I had taken a lot for granted. And, of course, now I'm learning about what it is to actually do music theater. And in my opinion, it's one of the hardest things to do. Just physically, it's so demanding. Eight shows a week is already demanding. But to have your body available to dance and sing, and to have it all there all the time, it's a really hard thing and it will wear you down. You need to know what you're doing. It is a discipline and a talent and it takes practice. So when I got back, I was like, "I've got to learn." And then I got my first Broadway gig, *Joseph and the Amazing Technicolor Dreamcoat*, which was great. But again, we went out of town. We were in L.A. for a long time. I did better in that environment and with that company because there were older people in that show. The cast of *Birdie* was great but I just didn't fit. But in *Joseph* there was this ensemble of really wonderful people that I felt more at home with. That was, in many ways, a great situation. But when we were doing *Birdie*, I blew my knee out. I did dumb shit. I've always done dumb shit. I've always done physical stunts and stuff like that. I blew my knee out badly on *Birdie*, but I kept performing because I was young and frankly, no one was really looking out for me. It's something that I have to deal with for the rest of my life. I blew out my ACL [anterior cruciate ligament] altogether. When I was doing *Joseph*, I ended up blowing out my knee again and this time there was a complex tear. That's when I discovered what was really going on. So I had to be out for three months. I learned the hard way. Pretty quickly you learn to take care of yourself doing musical theater eight shows a week. You can get hurt and no one's going to look out for you better than you. *Joseph* was wonderful though.

How did you end up in *Joseph*? You came back from *Birdie* and decided that musicals were a focus?
Yeah. I wanted to do them. I wanted to do *Forever Plaid* really bad, and I got in right after *Birdie*. They offered me an opportunity to go into the New York company or open a new company in Kansas City. [The latter] paid twice as much money, and it was an original company so I wanted to do that more than replace someone else. That was a great job. *Forever Plaid* was awesome. I loved that show. I was singing harmonies and really having to work hard.

***Forever Plaid* is not that kind of show that somebody who's not well-versed in music takes to so easily.**
Nope. You work hard. And then I got *Joseph*, doing the country western brother and I'm covering Bob Torti who's playing Pharaoh. I loved Bob and I loved Bob as Pharaoh. He was so much fun. It was more fun to watch him do it than it was for me [to do it].

Were you always very opinionated?

I really don't give a shit what people think about me. On a personal level, I really don't give a shit. My job is to do my job, right? I think that I can intimidate people because I'm just going to tell you how I feel. It's not about you, it's not about me, it's about the audience. They're the ones paying the money to come and see whatever the idea is tonight, and it's not theater without them. And the only way to engage them—I'm not interested in entertaining. I am interested in engaging. And if I know there's an easy laugh I will avoid it like the plague. I've played big, heightened characters . . .

You were Gaston and they direct you for easy laughs!

I bucked every easy laugh they wanted me to do. Anyone can walk across the stage, scratch their ass and get a laugh. The best humor is three-dimensional. And my favorite humor is release of tension. I like to make an audience uncomfortable. Sure you think you know the character, but on the flip of a dime, what's really funny can be really not really fast. An audience needs to be kept off their center. You've got to engage them. And I like relevance. I want to talk about where we are and what's going on. I love humor. That's why I loved doing *Hand to God* so much. It was just weird and uncomfortable. I remember I would hear half the audience laugh and the other half shush them for laughing. There's nothing better than that because that's when people are in it. I don't care about laughs. I don't care about people liking me. I don't care about applause. I just want to engage. I don't even know how much I like performing. I love process.

So are you somebody who is happiest in rehearsal?

My happy place is sitzprobe [the actors' first rehearsal with the full orchestra]. Huge discovery. So much energy. So much information. First preview leading all the way up to opening night and a couple weeks after that. That's my happy place. After that, what's next? You have to know what drives you, what focuses you. Why are you doing it? I was never doing this to be famous. I know the kind of a dialogue that I like to engage in with an audience. I'm a talker. You want to have a talk about religion, I'm happy to have it. Politics? I'm happy. Where other people want to avoid, I'm like, "Let's talk about this shit." That's the problem with politics and religion: No one wants to talk about it. But if you do have a respectful argument in the classic sense of an argument, we can actually gain more respect for each other's points of view. I like directing very much because there's so much more humility to it. As an actor, I have to drive forward because I'm the one that's out there eight shows a week, along with my fellow castmates. I feel this mega responsibility to do it right for the people who are paying. Everyone else [involved in creating a show] gets to go away. I've got to stick around with everyone else and make sense of this. The director gets this great humility of assisting everyone. I'm an assistant. I'm not going to tell you how to do your job. I know you know how to do your job. But I'm going to be as specific with the bigger picture as I can so that I can best assist you in your work. I love it because it's about the product.

Have you ever done a job where you felt it wasn't the conversation you wanted to be having?

I chose not to do *Steel Pier* because I saw where it was going. I saw on the third day of an eight-week workshop where it was going, and I saw that it wasn't going to happen the way I thought it could. Even back then I was like, "I know how I would do this and I don't see that happening, and I don't know when it's going to come together because I don't think that the decisions are the right decisions. Maybe I'm wrong but to me this is not the show I think it can be."

That is crazy talk.
Everybody told me it was crazy talk. I love [director] Scott Ellis and I know I pissed him off. And I don't blame him for being pissed off. Who the fuck am I to have that kind of an opinion? But I remember saying, "These supporting characters have to be developed or it's not going to work." I also began to realize I wasn't going to be helpful in this environment if I couldn't get on board with it.

I continue to be amazed by you. Not that it's illogical, but as a young actor who's decided musical theater is his course, here's an opportunity to do a new Kander and Ebb show and to work with greats . . .
There was no doubt in my mind. I was engaged to Kristin Chenoweth at the time. I remember turning to her on day three saying, "I've got to get out of here." I just got a sense of where it was, and I knew myself well enough. It's really hard for me to stop myself when it comes to certain things. People say, "Pick your fights, Kudisch, pick your fights." And I always say, "I do, I do. I pick all of them." You know, that doesn't mean I'm right.

Right, right. But you are clear?
For me, I know it's the right choice. Live or die by it, and that's the thing. Live or die by it. I was also working on *High Society* at the time, and the role I had in *High Society* was much clearer. Did I want to work with John Kander, and Fred Ebb, and Scott Ellis, and Susan Stroman? Of course I did. Was I going to be happy doing that show? No way, and I knew it. And I would be angry every day, and I would be wanting to fix, questioning, every day, and that's not helping anyone else. I had to withdraw—for the production, for myself, for Kristin. She was having a very different experience than I was. Am I going to make it all about me? I chose *High Society*, and that was a whole other nightmare. I'm a pain. I mean, I just am. I'm a pain. I'm a bit of a battering ram. I think I come from a place where it is about the work. But sometimes I need to shut up.

Well, you did that in *Steel Pier*. You left. But not always?
I've learned—listen. Sometimes I need to shut up in a moment, and things will reveal themselves better. That was a situation where I knew I just needed to not be there.

I can imagine feeling the way that you're feeling and also thinking, 'These are masters! They're going to pull it together, and they know more than I do so I just have to be patient.'
I have been wrong plenty of times. Not everybody is always right no matter how smart you are. But I will say this: When I was wrong, I wasn't angry about it. I'm like, "I know why I made the choice, and I was clearly wrong here." But it's not like, "Oh, I wish I had a second chance."

Let's go back to *Beauty and the Beast*. After everything that you just said, stepping into something that is such a product and where the opportunity for discovery would seem to be a challenge . . .
But what I love about *Beauty* is that it was a real satire in so many ways. Gaston was a very satirical take on an archetype. I was not that type growing up. I know what people see but that is not who I am. I was the kid picked on. So I can satirize that. And Burke Moses [the show's

original Gaston] set the mold for that. There's no Gaston without Burke. He physicalized it. He embodied it. He took the animated character and he made a person. He heightened it, stylized it, and it was beautiful. It was easy to build on that. But I think what I brought to it was a darkness, was the psychology of it. I remember [notes saying], "We love your second act, you've got to lighten up that first act, Marc." And I understood. But I also wanted to satirize. I would do things like—I would love to smell my own armpits. "Marc, you can't do that." "Why not"? And then I did this thing where I'd go into a full split at the end of "Me." I would just be stuck and the silly girls would have to help me up, which is very embarrassing for him. Then I would sort of shake out the [genitals] and they were like, "You can't do that." "Why not?" It took them awhile, but eventually they appreciated it. So the product went beyond just being a product. They saw that the show could be interpreted in many ways. I had a really good relationship with them, and because I was so confident and committed, I think they just trusted my confidence. And I get Disney. I get they're very conscious about their brand, and there's no reason for them not to be. I had a really good time on *Beauty* and I had a great relationship with them. They let me take many leaves of absence and come back. That show established me in New York City. [But] If I see someone that's very confident about a choice . . . go with it. Let's see where it takes us. In theater, it's the engagement that's important. Do it well. Do it right. Have a point of view. Don't apologize for your point of view. Hit it.

You've had the experience of performing in things that were not necessarily living up to that.

Because not everything's going to be perfect. You're going to try to create as collaborative an environment as you can. Everyone has the opportunity to organically invest and apply themselves within the story, so that we're all on the same page together and we're all playing the same play. We're all offering the same point of view and message to the audience. I've been involved in shows where that hasn't happened. Bottom line gets in the way a lot.

That was your complaint about *High Society* [a musical based on Phillip Barry's *The Philadelphia Story*].

No one had faith in the story, or at least in the telling of it the way that it should be told. You'd think it would be easy to just put on a good show, but there are so many outlying challenges and political moods. [Director] Chris Renshaw had just had this revival of *The King and I* and it was a huge success. But the emperor wasn't wearing clothes. I love Chris. He's a sweet man, but when you actually have to create the show and build it . . . I don't know that he understood the sensibility of the play. It's a very American play [Renshaw is British] with a very American sensibility, and it was a social satire. It is about a day in the life of the idle rich. It's all about the language. What is active in the play is the dialogue, not the activity. That is very important when you're talking about Philip Barry. When we were in San Francisco with the show, it was a big hit and we got good reviews. There's a lot of old money in San Fran, and we were very close to the Philip Barry play. Back in New York, Randy Graff and I were walking down the street in Midtown, and we heard the marquee went up so we went to go see it. [It featured an illustration of three kittens in suits]. The two of us just stared at it, and then Randy said, "Oh, we're fucked." One of the most important things about a show is your imagery. When we were in San Francisco, it was beautiful, elegant. It looked like a wedding invitation. Bubbles and champagne. Effervescent. Perfect. And then we get back and it's a bunch of cats in a boat. I remember our first day of rehearsal, we're all sitting there, and they're doing the big intro and everything. Randy Graff, hand up: "What the fuck is with the cats?" And I'm not even going to tell you what the explanation was. We all get it. Fat cats of Philadelphia. What does that say about the play? Nothing. That poster could be for anything. We knew we were in trouble. And then of course they did bring in a show doctor. Des McAnuff. And I like Des. I have a lot of respect for Des. That was not a play for Des. He didn't understand the play, either. I remember [producer] Michael David saying, "He's making it better, he's making it better." No, he's making it shorter. You think a running time is going to be the success of your play? Look, I'm all for editing. Let's get to the meat. Let's tell our story. That said, you've got to have enough meat on the bone, otherwise all you have is style with no substance. Making it shorter so that an audience doesn't get as bored? That's your goal? C'mon! What's the story? What are we saying? What are we delivering to the audience tonight? You do your best to fill it and you have to work overtime to compensate for the lack of other things. There's a responsibility we have to the audience that is paying to see this thing, and they're paying a lot of money. With *High Society*, it felt like every choice was being made outside of the right choices for the play. A lot of the same problems that I felt on *Steel Pier* I felt in *High Society*. Randy was like my big sister. I learned a lot about the business and about integrity from how Randy carried herself. But I also enjoyed it. I am naturally a neurotic, Jewish person, okay? That's genetically what I am. It was rough, and there were a lot of things I didn't like about it, but I was in it. Creativity is a volatile thing. I was also developing my sense of awareness in what I really wanted to do. It's taken a long time. I don't know that I've ever loved acting. Not the way that other people love acting. I don't know. To me, there are more important—I'm not saying it's not important or it doesn't have its importance. I think it does. But I was learning more and more as I was doing this. I was really focused on wanting to tell the story and wanting to hit them in the gut a little bit. And I was becoming more and more aware of the business of the craft of what we do. And I was beginning to understand what was important to me as a person in the industry. I don't want to say as an artist anymore. I'm sorry. I just—I don't—an artist? I think we all do art in one form or the other. A person in this industry—because we're also business people, and too often we forget that. Especially actors. There's a bottom line to everything and I was learning that decisions were being made on a bottom line. A lot of times when decisions are made on bottom line, those decisions are out of fear. And I can understand that because stakes are high. And shows went from having an individual producer to multiple producers to the corporations to the film companies, more and more and more and more and more and more money, and in many ways, more money meant more people involved. More people meant more people who didn't actually know. So now you've got a whole bunch of people throwing all kinds of money with no experience in execution. And I was just watching decisions being made and beginning to understand how real choices are made. Any idealistic view of how a show gets put together was getting smashed to pieces. I wasn't going, "How do I fit in this?" I was going, "How can I get my work done now, understanding how this all works?"

That's a nice segue into talking about *The Scarlet Pimpernel*.
I did version 3.0. [in a very unusual move, the show closed, went into rehearsals with a new cast, new staging and some rewrites, and re-opened]. We rehearsed in New York, went out, did a mini tour for six weeks, and came back into town. When it came to the song "Where's the Girl?" I asked Frank Wildhorn to take all the percussion out of the orchestra. "I'll be what's percussive. Let it be romantic. You don't need to do anything." He's like, "But the whole point of this song is that you're seducing her." And I said, "Frank, I actually don't think I have to. I think the song is seductive. There's a difference. If I'm seducing, I'm working too hard. It indicates where we're going. If it's seductive, she'll come to me." And so that's what we did. All the percussion went out of the song, and suddenly there was this lush, beautiful, beautiful

song. I love Frank and his music can be great, but a lot of times he writes just to show off. We got rid of the staging of it, too. It was great. I never moved. She came to me. So *Pimpernel* was a fun exploration and re-working of that show. It was Carolee Carmello, who I adore and have worked with many times since, and Ron Bohmer who is the sweetest guy on the face of the planet

You said Frank Wildhorn sometimes writes to show off.

He was absolutely a product of the '90s on Broadway. That was his time. This is what I call "the nouveau bel canto aria" period of time, when the writing was just an exploration of how high can we go, how far can we go. It was just this big explosion of spectacle. That's what the audience wanted at that time. And I think he's not had the greatest of collaborators. But I also know with Frank, Frank's in charge. Frank needs someone to butt up against him, to argue him. He needs that because he's actually a really good writer.

After *Pimpernel*, you went right into *The Wild Party*.

The only reason that I got in to audition for that was because I happened to bump into [composer] Michael John LaChiusa in the subway. I went into the room to audition and it was one of the best auditions I've ever had. They were so direct. They knew what they wanted. [Director] George C. Wolfe is one of the clearest people when it comes to giving direction. He would always give you enough information that you'd go, "Oh!" and the minute he saw you got it, he'd say, "Yeah, that's it, Honey, now go." I loved it. I always say, "You audition for them, they audition for you in return." You've got to be able to communicate. Sometimes you'll walk in, and you will just be it. Like in *Millie*, I just walked in and did it. There was nothing for them to say because I just did exactly what they were hoping for. But that was serendipitous. Sometimes you walk in a room, and you get absolutely nothing. And so no one leaves satisfied. And then if you're lucky, you walk in and you start to have a conversation, and then you are already understanding what the working relationship is going to be like. I got the gig, and I loved it because it was a real character role, and they were really interested in getting the play right. No one had ever given me the opportunity to play against everyone else's idea of me. Bisexual, hedonistic, drug-abusing playboy. I loved it.

There was well-documented tension between the costars of that show. How did you navigate those waters?

You check in with everyone else around you, and you see where they are and what they may or may not need. You let everybody know that you are there and that you can be trusted. So when people are self-indulging, there's a whole bunch of other people out there that are taking care of each other, and that's how we moved through it. And there was always Eartha Kitt. She was always a beacon of how to be, setting the right example all the time. If anyone could have been misbehaving, it could have been Eartha. Nope. She was the epitome of what it was to be an ensemble member. Every day she showed up, she was there, ready, on. She never complained. Her dressing room was open to everybody. I was very friendly with Eartha. She loved to hang. She liked to be around the company. Eartha was brilliant. Onstage, she would do nothing and do everything at the same time. None of us ever left the stage and Eartha could turn it off and turn it on on a dime. So when she turned it back on, not only were you aware that she was there, but you were also aware she had never left, and that in itself was powerful. And you were so impressed at the fact that she was able to hide in plain sight. She was in amazing shape. So no matter what other behavior was happening, there was always Eartha.

So morale...

It was tough. Our morale in that show was challenging, but the show itself was challenging. For me personally, I lost my dad. I lost my fiancée. We just went our separate ways. It all happened right up to the opening of *The Wild Party*. I'm playing a completely destructive, incredibly flawed character, and my life feels, in many ways, in a shambles. When we got near closing, I even said to George, "I've got to be honest with you: There's a bit of relief because I can't feel like a complete failure twenty-four hours a day anymore." It was rough. But I love that show. I'm proud of it. I'm proud of all of us for what we accomplished with it. That show is magnificent.

***Millie* in La Jolla was next. What a difference!**

I needed that break. To play Trevor was just such a wonderful breath of fresh air. It just gave me the opportunity to feel good about myself, even though he doesn't end up with the girl. It's not like I live my life through my art, but I do believe that you have to hook into your genuine emotions on a nightly basis, so it just felt good to be that good person after I had just played a very flawed fatal person. And I have to say, the lyrics that Dick Scanlan wrote for "The Speed Test"—from the minute I auditioned for that show I did it as fast as I've always done it. I was the first person to audition for Graydon. I got those lyrics. I got the music, and it was so easy for me because it was such a clear story that had an A to B to C to D to E. I can't remember list songs to save my soul. I would constantly go up on my lines and my lyrics in *Chitty Chitty Bang Bang* because it was just a bunch of nonsense. I mean, I loved it, but it was a bunch of nonsense. But in *Millie*, it all makes total sense. I walked in and I just did it. It's in the writing. Genius writing. Those lyrics, forget about it.

Between the La Jolla run and Broadway, you did *Bells Are Ringing*.

I'm thrilled that I did *Bells Are Ringing*. To work with Betty Comden and Adolph Green? I mean, c'mon, man. They built the bricks. And I'm a history guy. I always say that to know where you're going, you have to know where you are and to know where you are, you have to know where you've been. Betty and Adolph never stopped working. That was so amazing to see. We beat the crap out of that show. When we went out to Stamford, Betty and Adolph wanted to see it on its feet again in its original inception. The show runs like three hours long. It was written in 1956. The style of writing was very different. So to honor that, we rehearsed the original show. We went to Stamford for one week. We performed it seven times, then we came back to New York, and we went into a full rehearsal process to then do edits and cuts. Mitch Maxwell was a very interesting producer. He was very passionate about the piece. He was always positive and Lord knows where the hell the money was coming from. Every time we needed to do a new orchestration, he'd find another investor. Mitch was dicey as hell as a producer. Checks would bounce, but he was also so damn passionate and a real supporter of the play. I liked Mitch but I don't know that I trusted him. The work was actually really good, and it was a really good cast of people. I love Faith Prince. We had a great time together. But it's a challenging show. It's a show very much of its time. And for the first time in my career—I was above the title and my name was in lights, which was really embarrassing. I thought, "People are looking up there, seeing my name, going, 'Why is that asshole's name above the title?'" I've never been a self-promoter and the goal has never been to have my name up in lights like that. I think it sends a signal that is not the right signal for a play. It exposed me in a way that was uncomfortable. It's different than being exposed on a stage when you are the character. I got terrible reviews. People ask me if I read reviews and I'm like, "Yeah, I read the reviews because *Bells Are Ringing* now makes me read the reviews." On my answering machine,

I had sixteen calls or something like that at 8:40 in the morning. Everyone was like, "I don't care what they say, Marc, you be proud of what you did." Just one after the other. It was a little shell-shocking. But we kept doing the show and audiences were really liking it. And that's when I began to realize for the first time that with criticism and critique, it's only one person's point of view. In every situation, it's just one person's point of view. At the end of the day, I'm talking to an audience, not one critic. I actually started to feel a lot better about what I was doing and I began to understand that I don't have to take the reviews personally. I'll read them because it's going to inform me about how the audience is coming in. It's not going to inform my performance. I like good criticism. I think good criticism is healthy, and necessary.

You fared much better with *Millie*.
Trevor Graydon was one of the easiest characters I've ever played because he's just so straightforward and honest and open. Trevor is quite simple. He's an operatic character trapped in a modern musical so the rules that usually work for him just do not apply, which is where he gets off kilter. That's the joy of Trevor. I can explain Trevor, but I can't really explain how he comes out. He just does. His voice was always there for me.

He is sort of a hybrid between a leading man and a character part.
I always say I am Nathan Detroit in the body of Sky Masterson. That's just it, and that's always been my life, and that's fine because I've never looked at roles going, "When am I going to be Billy Bigelow." I never had interest in being Billy Bigelow. I was just having this conversation last night with Rachel Jones. We were talking about people that we grew up with that were in the industry, people that I was inspired by before I even knew I wanted to be an actor. I said to her, "I don't know why I'm the one that we know that had success consistently for the longest period of time." How did it all end up this way for us?

You know the answer to that.
I don't. I genuinely don't. I know my skills. I know my focus. I know my abilities, and I know the intensity with which I approach things that can drive something forward. But I know other people that are intense, and brilliant, and wonderful, and like . . .

Right. So all of that will take you to a certain point and then the rest of it is

happenstance.
I could have made a dozen other choices in my life that would have put me in a very different place. Through the years I figured out more and more of what I do want. For me, sometimes that means you do something out of love and passion, and you don't know what the outcome's going to be. It's not winning the Tony. It's getting into the game. That's the accomplishment. After that, it's all a rat race, or the politics, or the moment, or the way that things line up.

It's Plinko . . .
It's literally Plinko. If you happen to be in the show that's the show of the season or you just happen to be in the right place at the right time, and it just happens to be the way that the water went this year . . . This is the way the wave went. That's just how it goes. But to be in the game at all . . . When I think about the amount of stuff that I've gotten to do . . . When they were like, "You can't have a career in the theater anymore. It doesn't exist." Yes, it fucking does. Or at least it did for me.

After *Millie*, you did your first *A Little Night Music*.

I've done *Night Music* three times: City Opera, Ravinia, Los Angeles Opera. And then we did a benefit at the Roundabout. It was so great, and that was actually supposed to happen on Broadway. Natasha Richardson as Desiree, Vanessa Redgrave as Madame Armfeldt, Victor Garber, Christine Baranski. And then two weeks after we did it, Natasha died. She was fabulous. But I mean, I loved doing *Night Music*, and I loved playing that character. I never get tired of that show. The thing about Steve Sondheim is that he's willing to play and he's willing to experiment. I do not think a writer should ever direct their own material but I do think Steve should because he's the most insightful when it comes to his material. People get scared shitless when Steve's in a room. I remember when we were doing *See What I Wanna See* one night, and in the middle of "Morito," I saw Idina Menzel almost freak out in the middle of the song because she saw Steve in the audience. He just wants to have a good time as much as everyone else. He wants to be engaged as much as everyone else.

Your next Sondheim followed immediately; you did *Assassins* in 2004.

Starting with *The Wild Party*, something happened to me. I became acutely aware of the reasons I wanted to be an actor. I wanted to have a dialogue with the audience. Less than entertain, I wanted to engage. I found that I was excited by the idea of making an audience uncomfortable and putting them off their center, offering them an event that left them with more questions than answers. That's one of the gifts of theater. I learned the power of ensemble in *The Wild Party*. It was an incredible company of people who were wildly talented and equal in their ability to hold court. I was more prepared to go into a show like *Assassins* after that. And it was the kind of work that I love; it was dark, it was weird, it was not shying away from its point of view and what it was talking about. We were all in it for the same reasons—we all wanted to communicate this message. Throw me a steak like that and I am going to chew that shit to shreds. I have never experienced on stage, before or after, anything like what we experienced that first performance in front of an audience of *Assassins*. You could cut the air with a knife. It was so charged. We could feel the audience. It was after 9/11 and there was a deep innocence that we had lost. People were ready for *Assassins* and that message. The opening lyrics, "Hey, Pal, feeling blue/don't know what to do? Hey, Pal, I mean you/ You want to kill a president?" I mean, could you be more direct? "Everybody's got the right to be happy/ Don't be mad, life's not as bad as it seems/ If you keep your goal in sight/ you can climb to any height/ Everybody's got the right to their dreams." When you put those words out there it sounds kind of heroic and all-American until you attach it to, "You want to kill a president?" I loved doing that show. I loved talkbacks with the audience. They barely talked to us, they were yelling at each other. That's why we're here, that's what we're doing. That's the only reason to do it; to bring hard ideas and hard conversations to the table in a socially acceptable way. We have to talk about these things or we are shit out of luck. When we talked about "Another National Anthem" in 2004 it was still something that people didn't quite understand, but it was a warning. If we don't wake up, this is coming. Well guess what? It came. And we missed it. Those dissonant people are now the people running the government.

Since the first production did not do well, did you feel like with this production you were giving the piece redemption for Sondheim and Weidman?

Of course. We all could see it all over Stephen's face. He was really proud of it. It was finally getting its due. It meant a huge amount to him and all of us. We were proud every night. It's a singular theatrical event. There has never been and there will never be anything else like it. It is singular in what it is attempting to do and what it achieves. The work that I am most

"You're my little chu-chi face." Fiercely committed with Jan Maxwell in *Chitty Chitty Bang Bang*. (Joan Marcus)

proud of has not been the work that I have been nominated for. Those were not the shows that really tested me as an actor or tested the company as an ensemble or tested the audience as a community. It was a moment that continued to define me as a person and an actor. I am really proud of it.

***Chitty Chitty Bang Bang* was next for you.**
It should have run for five years. And with that cast? Some of the finest actors you could possibly cast. Phil Bosco. Raúl Esparza, Jan Maxwell, Chip Zien, Robbie Sella, and Erin Dilly. I was so excited! But again, why are you doing it? What is the point of what you're doing? Jan and I were incredibly different than [the characters in] the film, because why else do it? And I know that was Raúl's stress with the show. They hired him, and then they didn't want him to do anything he auditioned with, and he's like, "Why did you hire me? You hired a really, good, interesting, dark actor to offer something new. Let it be dark. Let it be interesting." And hence, where it ultimately broke down, I literally said to the producers, "The car doesn't fly if the cast doesn't fly first. Otherwise, ten bucks a ride and save a shit ton of money." There is a certain expectation that you want to fulfill and you can't go too far away from it because the audience has the expectation coming in. But take them on a journey unexpected through the story, if you can.

A lot of what you're touching on reminds me of what Christian Borle had to say about *Charlie and the Chocolate Factory* and the complications of putting that on stage. It's true of *Frozen*, too. We watch those movies again and again, and the touchstones that we're looking for become sacrosanct. Producers, and maybe audiences, are going to require you to check certain boxes but at the same time what you're doing is not the movie. So satisfying those two animals is a very, very tricky balancing act.

I think it's not as tricky as everyone makes it out to be. There are two ways to make choices: out of fear or out of passion for the project. If choices are being made out of fear, you're already off the rails. I've done roles like that twice. *Chitty Chitty Bang Bang* and *Beauty and the Beast*. With *Beauty*, I had a ball. I always say it: Meet expectation as quickly as you can, and then fuck with it like crazy the rest of the night. What do you have to add to the story? Just do it. Go there and figure it out. That's why *Millie* was as big a success. There was more to say than what the film was.

So when you're rehearsing *Chitty Chitty Bang Bang*, and you're seeing where it's going . . .
You do your best. I mean, look, I was fortunate to have Jan Maxwell as a partner in that show because the two of us were on the same page with really wanting to push the boundaries. In this childlike, family show, we really wanted to see how far we could go with this relationship. They kept giving us crap about the sexuality of it. They had a problem with that, but not with the fact that at the end of the show they shoot and kill this creature that is not like them. That's okay. They literally pull a gun and blow the Child Catcher into smithereens. But a married couple having their own relationship sexually was a huge problem. I think because she and I pushed the boundaries, we were very successful in the show.

You were both Tony nominated for it.
But that doesn't qualify in my opinion. We had a specific idea of those characters and how they fit in the play. You had Phil Bosco, the finest actor in that play, and they just didn't listen. They didn't allow for that expression. Confidence is about having everyone be in the pool, finding the best idea, letting everyone organically be a part of it. Who cares where the idea comes from, right? And so I felt like Jan and I were very successful at the end we came out with pretty damn good reviews. I thought we were going to get our asses kicked. We didn't. I'm thankful that I was out there with Jan.

Your Tony experience in general . . .
It's tough. The first time you get nominated, it's thrilling. And then, of course, you worry that it will never happen again. The second time you get nominated you realize it wasn't a mistake. The third time you get nominated, you know the politics, the rat race, how all this works. It doesn't in any way, shape, or form, define any kind of quality whatsoever. The third time I got nominated was *9 to 5* and that was really hard because a lot of the show did not.

You took a leave from *Chitty* to do *See What I Want to See* at The Public.
It was like taking a good, hot, bath because I didn't have to overwork to make something work. It just worked. The first act is all about tension, and the second act is all about release. "Central Park" is one of my proudest achievements, this crystallized moment in a play. Michael John and I worked so hard on "Central Park," and it took a while to get there together. So much of the music in that show is just spectacular. "There Will Be a Miracle?" I cried every time I heard that. And with Michael John, it was the first time that I heard a certain spirituality to him as opposed to an esotericism. There was so much heart. That second act was all about faith. [When I went back to *Chitty*] did I look at my script at all? No, I did not. I'm getting back into my costume and everything. Did I even think to look at the first scene? No, I did not. I get out there, haven't done it in two months, and I'm jittery. I'm never jittery. I don't understand why I'm jittery. I get out there. I start the scene. I do the whole Baron thing, I laugh maniacally, and then I just look at Jan. I don't have a fucking clue what to say. Not a clue. And then I looked at Ken Kantor who was on for me for the last two months, and I said in full character, "So what

happens next?" Literally. And then I look back at Jan. No help at all. I hear Kristin, our maestro, cackling, cackling. No help either. Thank you. Ken feeds me the line: "Ah Baron, perhaps we should . . ." I'm like, "Ya, ya, let's do that." And then I just grabbed him, and I said, "Tell me what else you think we should do." I made him say every line in the scene to get me to the song. When the lights go out on us, I run up the stairs, and I rip open my script and shove my head in that thing. I just was like, "You are an asshole, Asshole." Literally the actor's nightmare.

Was it a relief of sorts when it closed?

I loved *Chitty*. But I think maybe I had done it long enough. There was a pretty good run, so I was satiated in terms of exploring a character. You're always sad to see the paycheck go, but you don't want it to just be about the money. I was sad to see it go. But I've never been one to get emotional at the end of a run of something.

You got a bit of a palette cleanser with *The Glorious Ones*.

Oh, it was great. Beautiful. The kind of work that really drives me. I was the leading man, but thank God that leading man is an absolute character. Ahrens and Flaherty are just wonderful people, and such beautiful writers. And again, I love collaborating. I loved being able to get in there and have a real conversation about stuff. And, of course, [director] Graciela Daniele! I mean, she's just a wonderful human being in general. I've been really, really lucky. I've worked with some really good people, even when I didn't know what the hell I was doing. I remember the first time an understudy went on in the show. She said, "This is the actor in the show tonight, which means it is about her tonight, which means you will not do what you usually do tonight. You will listen to the new energy that this person is offering tonight." She was so clear that this was not someone who is going to just fill in a hole. I so appreciated that she was giving that much respect.

Your next show was *9 to 5* . . .

I'm going to say this right off the bat. Everyone should have five minutes with Dolly Parton in their lives. I love Dolly Parton. I love working with her. I love her as a human being. I love her energy, her commitment. Here's the difference between Dolly Parton and every other pop writer that I've ever worked with in musicals: That woman showed up every day at rehearsals. She took it seriously. This is a woman who has never collaborated, has never had to. And I think she wrote beautiful music for the show.

Oh, it's incredible music. It's just not great theater music.

I agree, I agree, but she's a really good storyteller, and more to the point, when Dolly writes, there's a very specific point of view behind what she writes. It's got activity behind it as opposed to just waxing poetic. It's also the first time she's ever been asked to write for a man. She said to me one day, "This collaboration stuff is hard. I've always just written for myself or for another soloist. I've never had so many people having an opinion on my work. But I have to say I really do like it." She was open. Like, for instance, the second act song that I had started as a song called "Mundania." It was essentially a list song of how mundane his life is [in captivity]. It didn't really go anywhere. I said to [director] Joe Mantello, "The challenge is that if the song isn't active, I must be active." We got all the way to Los Angeles, first preview, and I was still asking questions about it. He said, "Can you live with it out here in L.A.?" And I'm like, "Well, of course, I'll do everything I can, but I'm having to work overtime to keep it active." Immediately following the run in Los Angeles, I got a call from Joe, and he was like, "So what do you think the song is about?" I said, "You need the danger. It's a revenge play. The women think they're safe but actually the pressure cooker is on high. The time to stew on those fucking women makes him even more dangerous." That's where the song, "Always a Woman" came from. I got back together with Joe and [choreographer] Andy Blankenbuehler, [musical director] Steve Oremus—I mean, it was a pretty damn good team. Steve was playing through Dolly's new song. It was a little more like a cowboy song, if you will, and it didn't have the bite or tension that we wanted, so he added some funk. I was ecstatic because now I have this James Brown thing, and I'm in chains, and now I'm physical. Andy didn't want to choreograph it until he saw me move. He just watched me and started to play with it. And then he began to choreograph. It was fucking good. So unapologetic. So nasty. Just right for the character. We presented it for Dolly, and she went, "Well, that is not what I intended at all, but Lord have mercy is that sexy!" I remember doing that number and having the audience go apeshit nuts for the worst behavior in the world.

As sexist, egotistical, lying, hypocritical, bigot, Franklin Hart in *9 to 5*. (Joan Marcus)

It sounds like Dolly really respected the process.

She would come in my dressing room. I'd be in the shower and she would stand outside the bathroom door and just talk to me while I'm in the shower. And she'd make moon pies and lemon squares for us. She had her big-ass trailer sitting on 45th Street. That's where she lived because it was like home for her. So she would be up early in the morning making moon pies and lemon squares in the trailer. And let's talk about that cast, okay? Allison Janney? Crush. Major crush on Allison Janney. Such a good person. So talented but such a sweetie. Stephanie Block's great. And Megan Hilty? And I had to treat them really badly. I really had to be a dick to those women. So I'm thankful that it was those three women because the only way to do that show was to have that kind of trust, which I believe we did. And, of course, Kathy Fitzgerald, who I bloody adore.

But the show was not well received.

I believe that our show was not marketed or produced as well as it could have been. I think that the image that was being put out about the show did not match the experience that the audience was actually having. I did all the voice-over work for all the commercials, and I remember saying to the ad guys "What is this stuff? I sound like I'm promoting a Lifetime movie, not a revenge play." It felt like it was girl power/friends/fun. And they were so busy selling Dolly, they weren't selling the show. You don't need to rely on Dolly, sell *9 to 5*. There are always extenuating circumstances as to why a show does or does not run. But I'm in it. I didn't see it so I don't know how it looked from the outside. I loved playing Franklin Hart. One day I said to Joe, "Do you mind if I chew gum?" I know they wouldn't chew gum in the office, but he's the president, and he can do whatever the fuck he wants. Then, "I want a football. Can I have a football? And a hand thingy?" So they got me all this stuff and Dolly came up to me, and she went, "Honey, you're doing Burt Reynolds, aren't you? He would be really honored by that." It was my homage to Burt because he was the iconic male at this point in time. I don't get starstruck but there are two men—Paul Newman and Burt Reynolds—who I actually wouldn't meet. Dolly really wanted me to meet him on opening night and I just couldn't do it. I actually did meet Newman when I was doing *Summer in Smoke* at Hartford Stage. I was in my dressing room, and there was a knock. I literally had my towel on. I opened the door and there was Newman. "What's up?" That was all I could say, standing there in a towel. He was incredibly complimentary.

After *9 to 5*, you did *Hand to God*, and then went into *Finding Neverland*.

I was actually the original Hook. While we were working on *9 to 5*. I did the first reading. And then after *Hand to God* I got a call saying that Kelsey Grammer was leaving and Harvey wants to know if you want to do the role. I don't like to replace, I like to create. That's what I've always said I'd do. But I cannot tell you how much fun I had. I went into the show in like eight days on the backs of other people's talents. I get the payoff in eight days instead of eight years [of workshops and rehearsals, etc.]. It was an amazing cast. That ensemble made that show. Do I think it's a completely successful show? No, I don't. Do I think it's better than what it got credit for? Yeah, I do. It could have been executed in different ways, but I mean, I never felt like I was selling out. The audiences loved it.

You went from Dolly to Dylan with *Girl from the North Country*.

Opening night of *Girl from the North Country* . . . When you can be a part of theater that affects your peers in ways that are surprising and cathartic, that is genuinely wonderful. It took an Irishman from Dublin [Conor McPherson] to write the most American piece of theater

I have seen in I don't know how long! But why is that surprising? The more we embrace the diversity of what created us, the more we come together and understand who we are. He was given carte blanche by Bob Dylan's people, who contacted him to say, "Dylan's a big fan. He would love for you to do a piece around his music." Dylan never got involved, never said, "Boo" to anything. He just let Conor do what he wanted to do. He directed the damned thing. I would usually say that's a conflict, for a playwright to direct his own work. This was one of those times. No one else should have directed this because it was all in Conor's head. His whole thing is that the play is all tension and the release comes in the music. That's why there is music. "Do not release in the scenes, drive it, drive it, drive it." This piece is its own unique creature. It goes out there every night and offers thoughts and ideas about who we are in times of survival. It's tough. Life is fucking hard and there are very few answers. But there is huge catharsis in watching other people go through hard times like that. It gives you great faith in the human condition and in who we are as a people. There are lessons to be learned. There is a song at the end called "Pressing On." We all press on, we continue to as we reach to the higher calling. That's the human condition, to press on.

So now here you sit. You're very clear about the things you want to do, the things that you can tolerate, the things that feed you. Are you thinking that maybe you'll keep doing musicals, but maybe not?

I am in a place that's maybe, maybe not. But I will say this: I got shit to talk about, and it's not small, and I like to engage in conversation. I don't know if music theater is the place for me to do that right now. I've done so much work in this industry, I feel quite satisfied. I don't need to be on the stage anymore. I don't know how much I've ever loved being an actor. I do know I love the process, and I love the theater. I know that I love putting together great stories. I do know I love watching my friends and my peers who love doing it. It's the most exciting thing. I think the reason that people retire is not because they're necessarily tired but because they've completed whatever the task was they set out for. I don't think there's anything wrong in our business with transitioning to do something else. It doesn't even have to be in the theater. I've done this for thirty years professionally in New York City alone. How long do you do something? I would love to be the artistic director of a theater. I think it would be great. I love teaching. As I said from the start, I don't know how this even happened. I don't know how I got in here. The gift has been being in the game. I never expected to be on Broadway. So how I ended up there thirteen, fourteen shows later—seriously—I really don't know how that all happened. And at this point now, I just feel like there's nothing else I'm really searching for. Now, of course, there'll always that thing that comes along, and I'll see it, and I'll go "No, I have to do it." Or maybe not.

10

MICHAEL CERVERIS

March, May 2017; March 2018

MICHAEL CERVERIS DOES NOT BELIEVE in the unexamined life. There isn't an opportunity he's had or a show he's done that hasn't been deeply considered. He's keenly aware of what he brings to any equation and how what he brings fits into an overall whole. He is seemingly unencumbered by fear or ego. He's just present (not to mention smart as hell). And motivated only by a desire to be stimulated. "I just always pursued things that were challenging or of idiosyncratic interest to me," he says. "I didn't bother myself too much about whether it was the right thing to do."

Cerveris was born in Bethesda, Maryland, and grew up in West Virginia. While theater was important to him, musical theater was not especially on his radar. "When I graduated from Yale I thought my ambition was to work in regional theater and do Shakespeare in the Park," he says. "I was a serious actor. I got a job on the series *Fame* and I was really not certain I wanted to do that at all. But I told myself I should go because maybe if I did a TV show I could work at Shakespeare in the Park." *Fame*, on which he played a British rocker/student in the final season, took him out to California, where he stayed, working in regional theaters. That led to the La Jolla Playhouse and the title role in world premier of *The Who's Tommy*. The show was a smash and moved to Broadway with most of the La Jolla cast intact and Cerveris found himself a Tony-nominated star. He defied type-casting, however, with his next show, *Titanic*, and then boomeranged back to rock with *Hedwig and the Angry Inch*. If his subsequent roles have anything in common, it's a specialty for dark (and mostly real-life) characters in shows that brood more than they buoy. John Wilkes Booth in *Assassins* (for which he won the Tony), *Sweeney Todd*, Juan Perón in *Evita*, Kurt Weil in *LoveMusik*, Wilson Mizner in *Road Show*, and, of course, his searing portrayal of the closeted Bruce Bechdel, in *Fun Home*, which netted him his second Tony Award.

Cerveris's Chelsea living room is comfy but also filled from floor to ceiling with cherished personal items. Shelves of record albums line one wall while another holds musical instruments. There is a well-stocked bar, and art from New Orleans, where Cerveris has a second home. Above a large chair, which is clearly the province of his dog, Evie, an out-of-the-way shelf displays his Tonys. But the least decorative and perhaps most interesting item on display is a framed 2016 essay Cerveris wrote for *The New York Times*, detailing the experience of the *Fun Home* cast when they volunteered, on their day off, to perform a concert version of their show in Orlando to benefit the victims of the Pulse nightclub shootings.

Every time I meet with Cerveris he is thoughtful, calm, and unassuming. The hours fly by as Evie patiently waits in her chair or ambles over to the couch for a little attention. We're in no hurry. There's a lot to be said, the couch is comfortable, and a venti coffee can be nursed for quite a while.

"See me, hear me . . ." Making his Broadway debut as the eponymous *Tommy*. (Photofest)

Tell me about your early years.

My dad was a piano student at Juilliard and my mom was a modern dancer. They decided early on not to have performing careers. He went into academia, and she taught dance for a while but mostly had her hands full with my sister and me and later, my brother. I grew up in a house full of music and art. My dad would practice piano when we were going to sleep, so that was the sound of my going to sleep for years. He would direct university productions or community theater things and so I would be the little kid, third from the left, or in the chorus of his shows. When I was doing *Caucasian Chalk Circle*, we basically just played in the green room and then we'd come out, do our little scene, which is basically just running around and playing some game. At some point the kid who was playing the little prince left and they asked me if I wanted to take over. I said "no" because I would then have had to learn lines and be responsible. I was having too much fun just hanging out and being a kid. I think that does point to something that's always been true of me—for all the opportunities and things I've gotten to do in the business, I've never felt like a very ambitious person. I even had a teacher

Michael Cerveris	
The Who's Tommy	Broadway, 1993
Titanic	Broadway, 1997
Hedwig and the Angry Inch	Off-Broadway, 1998; West End, 2000
Passion	Kennedy Center, 2002
Assassins (Tony Award)	Broadway, 2004
The Apple Tree	Encores!, 2005
Sweeney Todd	Broadway, 2005
LoveMusik	Broadway, 2007
Road Show	Off-Broadway, 2008
Evita	Broadway, 2012
Fun Home (Tony Award)	Off-Broadway, 2013; Broadway, 2015

once tell me that I would never make it as an actor because I lacked ambition, I wasn't hungry enough for it, and I thought that they were probably right.

Do you ever have guilt about that, given that there are so many actors who would absolutely kill for opportunities?

I do sometimes. I was raised Catholic, so it kind of comes with the territory. I have worked incredibly hard; I just haven't worked hard to get things. I've worked hard because I wanted to be better or I wanted to overcome some obstacle, but I wasn't working to achieve the things that I've gotten. I found myself at the Tony Awards never having intended to do that. So I have sometimes felt a bit of guilt that I've had these opportunities that other equally or more-talented people never had. [So I try] to make sure that I appreciate the things that I get because there are other people who would love to have them.

You went to Yale, but not as a theater major.

I went to college thinking, "Well, I want to continue studying as an actor, but I want to also see if there's anything else that I want to do more." And it turned out there wasn't. But again, it wasn't like, "I'm going to go to New York and make it and be a star!" It was like, "I'm going to New York, see how it goes." I got enough encouragement enough times to not leave, basically. I kind of used every chance I got to do stuff [to learn]. I ate hamburgers in the background of every soap opera in New York, doing extra work. That was a lot of my on-camera education. You don't have a lot of responsibilities when you're an extra so if you're smart, you can watch how things happen, and that was how I learned. And I would get small parts in Shakespeare plays where I had a line or two and I would go sit in the back of rehearsals and watch. I went to fight calls when I wasn't in the fights.

But none of this would seem to prepare you for a career in musical theater.

No, that came about because I always enjoyed singing. In junior high school, I was in the Glee Club, and I had this fantastic teacher, Ervine Parsons. She's why I had a rock band and why I sang, really. One day, she said, "I want you to see me after class," and I was terrified. I figured I was in trouble. She said, "I want you to sing a solo at the spring show." That was the first time anybody had singled me out in any way for anything artistic.

But again, it happened as opposed to your going for it. No ambition.

I wasn't trying to get a solo, no. And then, she thought that the school should offer a rock band class, and so she talked the principal into funneling money into buying instruments. We became the band for the rest of the year. We'd play at dances and we never knew enough songs to play a whole dance, so we would play them three or four times. Without that, I may not have ever been in *Tommy*.

Even so, to audition for a musical where you'll sing solo, not having trained, and expect to be taken seriously . . . that takes either . . .
Arrogance.

Chutzpah was the word I was going to use . . .
I did prepare for it though, but not intentionally. I actually prepared myself for all of these things to happen; otherwise, it's just a complete fluke. With singing in particular—I love singing. When I got to Yale, there was no voice and speech program. I thought, "Well, I want to do Shakespeare, and there's no speech work here, but if I study voice, I'll at least be training my vocal instrument and it will be interesting to learn classical repertoire." So I studied with a guy from the music school who mostly taught graduate music students to be opera singers. He said, "I know you're not going to be an opera singer, but I'm going to train you the same way I would train an opera singer because that will give you all the tools you need to do whatever you choose to do with it." He had me do solo recitals every year because that's part of it. I guess I was always telling myself that I wasn't doing this for a specific purpose, but there was some other voice in me that was telling me to learn this stuff and anything I did, I did fully. When I got to New York, I was mostly selling myself as a dramatic actor, and all my early stuff in New York was non-singing. [I auditioned a lot.] I sort of felt, "If I'm going to do this, I'm going to do it my way, and if they aren't interested in that, that's fine, but the way that I would do it would be this." Plenty of times that turned out not to be the way they wanted somebody to do it, but when they did, it was the right thing. I don't mean to say that I haven't tried desperately to be what people wanted in auditions. Most of the time that is what I'm doing. But I do remember being really influenced by David Hyde Pierce. He was a year or two ahead of me at Yale undergrad and I remember him coming back one time, and we were all like, "What's it like?" He said, "You know, the one thing I've started to figure out is that if you go in and you try to be what you think they want, it's really just a roll of the dice because you're guessing what they're looking for in the first place. Say they want it to be a stereotypical kind of character and you're not interested in doing that, and you try to make yourself into that [for the audition]. If you get the job, you're going to be miserable because you're going to have to be maintaining something that you don't believe in the whole time. Or you may have gotten away with it in an audition but not able to maintain that. That's going to be really hard. If instead, you go in and you do it the way you think it should be done, if they don't hire you, that's too bad, but if they do, then you'll probably have a good work experience because you're working for people who see the role similarly. You'll be working with people who are hiring you to use your judgment and contribute something the way you see it, and you'll probably be a lot happier." That really made a lot of sense to me. That's how I had started to approach things. It was really a valuable lesson.

So when you got *Tommy*, it was different from everything you expected to be doing. I don't just mean the material, I mean, the size of the show, the success of the show . . .
I think that's all very true, I think if you were writing the TV movie of getting your first Broadway show, you would write this story. It was deliriously fun from beginning to end. Incredibly hard work putting it together. It took me into a whole new world. Almost all of us went from La Jolla to Broadway. They added a few more people, but it was almost all the people

who put it together in the first place, which doesn't happen all that much. We always felt like this little band of outsiders who kind of snuck in the back door of Broadway through this rock 'n' roll thing. I think that helped me not get so overwhelmed by being on Broadway in a big musical. If I'd been plopped into *Kiss of the Spider Woman* I would have felt more like a fish out of water. But because *Tommy* was built around a world that I got . . . And Pete Townshend was there with us. The progress and the groundbreaking we were doing on Broadway was kind of in soft focus compared to getting to hang out with Pete Townshend. I mean, that was kind of dizzying and disorienting, but that somehow gave me an easier way to orient myself. So when things like the Tonys happened, it was exciting and really, really cool, but I felt like I was able to be myself through it.

Were you tuned in to some of the business aspects of it? Were you paying attention to reviews? Were you aware of Broadway with a capital B?

I was definitely paying attention to reviews. I mean, I can quote you my earliest bad reviews when I first got to town and in shows that people bothered to review. Over the years I started to realize that they were just affecting me too much, and so I tried various steps along the way to minimize that. For a while I would have somebody read them to me because hearing them read to me seemed to have a little less of an impact. That worked for a while and then I realized it still was upsetting me too much if they weren't good or weren't good in the way that I wanted them to be good. Then I would have somebody read it and give me a synopsis. But I still would be annoyed with myself because something would get in my ear and I would carry it around with me. Finally I'd . . . I still do this . . . I get all the papers and then after the show was over, I would read them. I forget to read them sometimes. I still haven't read the *Fun Home* reviews. But still, you always hear. Here's the other thing: People think that they can say lousy things about the show that you're in as long as they say nice things about you. No—these people are my friends and my family right now, and this show is what I'm knocking myself out to do. It may not be the best thing in the world but I don't need to hear it, and you telling me that you thought I was good and everybody else sucked or the play sucked is not actually helpful or welcome news.

***Tommy*, ran for over 1,400 performances and you stayed.**

Yeah, I think this is where my lack of ambition served me really well. And the really odd choice was to go do it in Germany, because that would seem like a career stopper after you've just arrived on Broadway. I really had to be talked into it at first, actually, because while I wasn't looking for my next career thing, I wasn't looking to move to Germany either. But I went and did that, and then I was enjoying it so much. I wasn't making any progress in my career but I was putting money away. And I was living and having experiences and thank God I did. When would you take a year and a half off to go explore? And this experience of life made me able to do *Hedwig*. I came back planning to go back to my original idea of doing straight plays. I just didn't get those jobs. The first job I got was *Titanic*, and it seemed different enough musically and intriguing because it was being directed by a European director, Richard Jones—this opera director. It seemed like a new and different challenge to me. [Getting *Titanic* was very lucky because] even just the visuals of putting a picture of me in *Tommy* up against a picture of me in *Titanic* forces you to go, "Whatever we thought of this guy, we're going to have to recalibrate." Again—not a conscious decision. It was just this was the job that I got and so that's what I did. But doing *Titanic* really made clear that you are not going to be able to think of me as one kind of actor. And then, as if to underline that, I left it to tour with Bob Mould, and *Hedwig*.

***Titanic* was undergoing so many changes as it progressed . . .**

I will always be so happy that I had that experience. I don't think people get that experience much anymore because things are workshopped to death before they ever get to [production]. Not that shows don't change a lot in previews. . . . If they hadn't had to dig out the basement of that theater to put the hydraulics in, we probably would have had out-of-town runs. But that wasn't possible so we did all of our growing pains in public. Michael Riedel essentially used his articles about *Titanic* to make his name in New York so, sadly, I'm afraid we were responsible for that. With *Tommy*, the script we had on the first day of rehearsal at La Jolla looked very similar to the final script for Broadway. *Titanic* could not have changed more. And watching Richard Jones, who had never seen a Broadway show before—when he got to town, they took him around to other Broadway shows to say, "See, this is how Broadway is." To watch him try to merge his aesthetic—his very non-American musical theater aesthetic—with two dyed-in-the-wool, American musical theater writers [Peter Stone and Maurey Yeston] was fascinating, and kind of perfect for me because I had sort of adopted a European aesthetic myself, having lived there. I was finding it disorienting the way you do when you come back home to America. And then seeing him actually addressing all of us in a meeting and saying, "I've brought this as far as I know how to and I feel that my task here is not simply to put on stage the version that I would do. I've been hired to deliver a show that can survive on Broadway and hopefully have a life beyond that and I owe that to these producers and writers, so I'm yielding to them. I'm going to need to learn and change a lot, and I'm asking you all to do that with me. In some cases, this is going to mean radical changes to what you were hired to do . . ." and in particular with Judy Blazer and Don Stephenson. They were leading characters and their parts were whittled away to next to nothing, and along the way Bill Buell's and Vicki Clark's characters, which were kind of incidental in the beginning, became showstopping set pieces. They told Judy and Don, "We know this is not the gig that you signed up for, and if you want to leave we totally get it." To their eternal credit, [they stayed]. That had such a profound effect on how I think of an actor's responsibility and commitment to the production. They said, "We signed on to do the show and we'll put our talents to the use of the production however you think we should." They never complained. I'm sure they had moments with their friends over drinks but we never heard it, never saw it. I admire them so much for that. I had that Broadway experience of being given an entirely new number in the afternoon [and performing it that night]. Really using the previews for the process. You could see it five times in a week and see five different shows. It was thrilling and terrifying but really bonded us as a company.

Did you think you were going to make it? Did you ever think, "This is doomed. We're going through the machinations of all of this work, but this is not going to come together. There's no way."

If I'd known more, I probably would have thought that. I was mercifully still young enough in the business that I just didn't know enough to think that. And there wasn't time to think! It was just, "We can do this." There had begun to be a defeatist kind of sense. People were starting to get demoralized, and Richard's speech to us, letting us in on the process, I think that was a really important thing. It's something that many directors would not have done. Maurey and Peter were not going home; they were going to a hotel room and sitting up all night, writing stuff. Instead of treating the actors like children, which is what so often happens—"either they'll start having ideas and contributing things, and God knows we don't want that, or we'll shake their confidence if we let them know that we're concerned . . ." Now we were going to try to figure this out together. We don't know if it's going to work, but we know that we don't have to pretend that we don't know that there are problems. So now that we know that everybody knows there are problems, we can just go back to doing our job, which is to try to make it better. We were rehearsing it up until the dinner break, and people were wandering around with sheet music in the wings during the show, trying to make sure they knew what they were doing. When we did the [new] ending for the first time the audience just erupted. We could feel while we were doing it that this is where it was headed all along. It was one of the most thrilling things. The beauty of creating in the theater—where you just keeping chipping away until the form finally reveals itself. I'm so happy that I got to have that experience. *Tommy* was thrilling in so many ways, too, but that was a different feeling from going from "We don't know if we're ever even going to get to do this" to "Now we found it! We solved this problem finally!" Then, being the underdogs going into Tony season, Rosie O'Donnell almost singlehandedly reoriented people's thinking about it by going on her show every day and saying, "I love this show" and having us on several times. The reviews were not terribly good, and the producers brought us in the next day and said, "That didn't go how we hoped, but we have a plan." So we just kept doing our job, and they did theirs.

And, of course, the show won the Tony for Best Musical. This was your second Broadway musical and your second time at the Tony Awards. Do you remember starting to feel like you were part of the business at that point?

Yeah, I think I did a little more. I wasn't nominated myself, but none of us were. I think I was feeling a little bit more a part of the establishment, proving that it wasn't a total fluke that I could get hired on Broadway. And I had shown that I could sing something besides rock 'n' roll in this world.

And then you left the show to go sing rock 'n' roll.

And then I left to sing rock 'n' roll! John Cameron Mitchell asked me if I wanted to do four weeks [of *Hedwig and the Angry Inch*]. He was just exhausted and needed to take some time off. He and I had known each other for a long time, you know, just kicking around as a couple actors doing weird stuff in our spare time. We had run into each other on auditions and we were in a workshop of what became *We Will Rock You*. He had this notebook with stuff for *Hedwig*, and he was telling me about it, and one day on lunch we went over and looked at the Jane Street space that was being renovated to do the show. And then I went to see it and I loved it. I saw it another three times over the next few months and I told John how much I'd loved it. So he just called me out of the blue and said, "Look, I need to take a month off. What do you think about playing Hedwig?" My initial reaction was nausea. I'd never even thought about anybody but John doing it. But if you put something terrifying in front of me, I go, "Well, okay, that's what I'm going to try to do." So I said "yes," and we discovered—and when I say "we" I mean everybody including John and Peter Askin, the director, and Stephen Trask, the composer—that they had actually created something incredibly well-constructed that can be done by all kinds of people. That was an enormous relief to John, who now knew that he'd created something that he wasn't going to have to do every night to keep it alive, And it was such a game-changing thing for me in my own development as a performer. I never would have thought I could do that until I did it. I don't know what the right word is to describe *Hedwig*, but it was a kind of extroverted performance that I wasn't used to doing and wouldn't have necessarily thought that I could do. It gave me a lot of confidence in training new muscles. I want to say confidence, but I don't know that that's exactly the right word. Probably fearlessness more than confidence. The lesson of Hedwig, the character, is kind of a really radical acceptance of yourself in all of your frailty and vulnerability and flawed mess. I think that's what I started to acquire as an actor, too. I felt like this was the most "me" I'd ever been in something. This was the most completely open, not hiding myself. Drag is just a full-body mask basically, and there's something about being behind the protection of that façade, you can reveal so much of your vulnerability and your essence. I understand drag in general now and why I think it's such a compelling and fascinating thing. I don't know that every drag performer feels that way. I think I've been able to be more honest as an actor because of the things I learned in *Hedwig*. I did that month and then I went out on the road with a band across the U.S. and England and disappeared [from theater] again for a while. I came back and John was ready to stop doing it altogether, so I took over and did it for a long time here, and then L.A. and then London. By this point I had been doing *Hedwig* on and off for a couple of years. I was dating this girl, Charlotte, who was the guitar player in this band called Ash that were hugely popular in London. When *Hedwig* ended in London, I should have gone back to New York to pick up my acting career, but I had no interest in doing that. Charlotte lived in London, and I put a band together while I was there. My agents were calling me with auditions and things, and I kept not being interested enough to come back for any of them.

[Cerveris was ultimately cast in an American television show shot in London]
When we wrapped I came back to New York to get stuff together because we all assumed that we were going back to shoot the rest of the series. Within the span of a few weeks, the show aired, it did really poorly, they pulled it, my girlfriend dumped me, and suddenly I was back here with no jobs, no prospects, no nothing, and the audition for *Passion* at the Kennedy Center came up. I was a mess then. I was really torn up about this relationship, and I gave this emotionally raw audition. It was perfect, and when I got the call from my agents that they were offering it to me, I was like, "I hope they know that I plan to not be in this state by the time we do the show! I can't guarantee I'm going to be like that every night." As it turns out, I could be. That heartache's never that far away. I hadn't even heard that they were doing this Sondheim Celebration [six Sondheim shows in repertory] because I'd been in England, but this really set me on a path of all this Sondheim stuff. I would have struggled to get an audition for *Assassins*, I think. That led to a Tony Award and that experience working with Steve absolutely had a lot to do with *Sweeney* and all the rest of it. That was a turning point, but again, it just kind of came out of the blue.

Before we talk *Passion*, I am curious about one thing; all of the choices you describe making seem to have been made without a lot of concern for making money.
It worried me all the time, but I never make work decisions based on it. That's not to say that I shouldn't have. I made the young actor mistake of thinking that it's all a ladder that goes up, no backward turns. I've never been an extravagant person. More often than not, the first months of a new job, I'm paying off the debt I've accrued since the last one. That's happening right now. I'm smart enough to save money when I'm making it and not just squander it all so I've got a cushion for a while. But I've turned down screen tests for things when I had nothing, and I was juggling bills. I also recognize that there may come a time where I will do jobs that I don't necessarily want to do because I have to eat. [I might not] find a Broadway musical that I want to do that also wants me to do it. But I do think, partly because I learned to be scrappy and survive, I will do what I need to do. If I have to go get a job at Starbucks for a while, I'll do that. I would rather do that than do something I don't believe in. And I don't say that in a superior way at all. I think it's almost more of a failing that I just—I find it really hard to do the work that I do. I do these characters where you sort of disembowel yourself for the audience's (hopefully) enjoyment. Maybe if I did more pleasant things, it would be a little easier? I sometimes think that despite the fact that I work so hard so much of the time, I kind of don't have

a good work ethic because I can't just say, "This is a job, just do it." I have to care about it. I get very prickly when friends have said, "It's easy for you because you can decide what you want to do," and it's like, "No, the reason I can decide what I want to do is because I decided that I would decide what to do." Nobody gave me that. The advantage that I have is that I lack that thing that would make that impossible: I lack that drive for a particular kind of notoriety. Even though I do consciously feel and get panicked about the idea that I don't know what's going to happen next, and the longer a stretch of not working goes the more I think, "This could be it." But something has always come up eventually, and often not from an expected place. And often not presenting an answer to how I'm going to make ends meet.

Like *Passion* at the Kennedy Center.
Going to do *Passion* at the Kennedy Center was like, "I'm going to be in the most overgrown, overachieving summer camp in history, surrounded by Sondheim. I want the experience of doing that. How much does it pay? Oh, it is enough for the months that I'm there? That's great." If it had been less, I would have worked it out. I guess there is a confidence in my resourcefulness, to think "I will figure it out."

So let's talk about that particular experience.
It was thrilling from beginning to end. I adored Judy Kuhn and Rebecca Luker whom I didn't know personally before that. When Steve finally came and watched our first run-through, afterwards he came up with tears in his eyes and gave us all a hug. It was when I began to learn that getting Stephen Sondheim to cry is not always the most difficult thing. He's primed to be a puddle if you give him a chance. But the first thing he said to us was, "Thank you so much for working so hard to get everything right. Now forget about it and just do it." I had heard that after that first run-through [of another Sondheim Celebration show] he immediately took the actors away to another room and drilled them on stuff that he was less than pleased about. We had heard that, so we were determined to not have that happen. I think he appreciated that we were being so reverential and now wanted us not to be so reverential. That's the approach I've taken ever since.

Audra McDonald says that she could sit at his feet and listen to stories for hours and hours.
Yeah, and he loves young artists. He devotes time and energy to young composers and does charity things for educational institutions. He was that kid at Oscar Hammerstein's feet. For us it's access to a vanished world. I think this in every aspect of life but especially the arts: "Is it dying with us or are there young people who know enough to care about it? Or is it just a kind of quirky museum piece?" I totally understand you wanting to talk to people like Barbara Cook for your last book because she was in the room where it happened. I'm at one of those ninety-seven Sondheim birthday things, and the thing I'm thrilled about is to be in the room with John McMartin, listening to him talk. Anything he has to say—like, I don't want to say anything, I just want to listen to everything that is being said. I know the value of listening. And I don't always sense that this is a global thing. I am often around younger artists and I'm thinking, "Do you have any idea who is in front of you? I know whatever you think is important right now seems important, but you're missing the chance to learn something from this person. If you knew and valued who they were, you would be paying attention." I wonder if so much gets lost from generation to generation in the pursuit of doing something new and different. And I think respect is a very important part of that equation. I used to feel that in *Tommy*. I was on the older end of the spectrum—I was older than anybody who ever played my

parents in that show—but I had always approached every job as a chance to learn from the people who knew more than I did, whatever their age. People who have done it more than me know more than I do, so I'm going to assume that I have a lot to learn from them before I start imposing my ideas on anybody. As we would get successive casts and replacements and the average age started to go down and down (because producers love to get people right out of school since they're cheap), we started having people who were actually saying, "I'm just here doing this ensemble thing to get my first Broadway credit so I can get on to my next leading role." And if they weren't saying it out loud, they were saying it in their approach. I would sometimes get really pissed off at the lack of respect for yourself, your craft, for the knowledge of people around you, for the piece itself, for the audience. I think that has something to do with whether you think you have things to learn from the past. What has brought all of us to this point? *Tommy* didn't arrive out of nowhere. [Director] Des McAnuff is a well-educated man of the theater. Jeanine Tesori, who I first met as the assistant conductor on *Tommy*, didn't write *Fun Home* as though musicals had never existed; Jeanine is a total student and master of the craft. She knows the history of theater, a variety of styles. What she made looks like something that you've never seen on Broadway before, but it's made with the elements of the craft, the form.

Back to Washington; how did it feel to be immersed in the Sondheim Celebration?
That might have been the first time that I really felt like I belonged in this Broadway community. And it was a particular subset of the Broadway community. For me, Stephen Sondheim was what musical theater is in its highest form, so to be on a footing with everybody else there, from Stokes to Barbara Cook, all there in the service of a singular vision . . . That summer, more so than going to the Tonys during *Tommy* or *Titanic*, I had a sense that I'd begun to achieve some things. I'd arrived some place.

As you said earlier, that really started the Sondheim trajectory for you. Coming from that you had the opportunity to do *Passion* in Ravinia . . .
Entirely thanks to [director] Lonny Price. Those things are thrown together so quickly and to be standing toe to toe with Patti LuPone and Audra McDonald—Audra makes you feel loved from the first time you talk to her. But because I had done it recently, I had done a lot of the nuts and bolts work; I'd played the part so I wasn't going to need a lot of help in rehearsal, discovering that stuff. I could therefore be a help and a support for Patti who was taking it on for the first time. That laid a really great foundation for getting to know each other because I didn't need to take any time in rehearsal; she recognized that and appreciated it right away. Early on she started calling me her rock, and I was like, "I will take that." She's a very professional, hard-working colleague. And then, over the next several summers, we became this little Sondheim Family Players with her, Audra, Lonny, and me.

You guys did *Anyone Can Whistle*, *Sunday in the Park*, *Passion* over three consecutive summers. And you did *Assassins* within that period? I think, when the history books are written, they will say that that production redeemed the show. Not that there was anything that needed fixing in the original production, just timing . . .
I think you're absolutely right; it was a question of timing. Which is also why I'm absolutely certain someone's going to do a production of *Road Show* [that's better received]. I don't think there was anything wrong with our production other than it arrived at the wrong time, at the beginning of the financial collapse. People didn't want to look at greed and the idea that

ambition as a society is responsible for our own problems. I'm sure someone is going to do a production that is going to land at the right time and it's going to be rediscovered and put in the canon someday. But anyway, I think *Assassins* this time landed at the right time. There certainly was never the thought that "We're going to fix what went wrong" or, "We're going to really do better."

It's a dark piece to do every night.

It's a really dark, dark questioning place that that play leaves you in. And it was probably my first experience with having something that heavy to take home. And then I just double-downed on it as the years went by! But with *Sweeney*, you get to work through it in rage. It leaves you, in a kind of dreadful place, but you've at least purged something along the way. With [playing] John Wilkes Booth it just feels like festering energy. He's just angry and he sits there and stews until he has a chance to get somebody else to do what he couldn't. In a weird way, the way the scene works is in a really positive, affirmative way. The group's task becomes getting this thing [Kennedy's assassination] to happen, and then you actually manage to make it happen, so you have the illusion that you've done something positive, you've bonded together. But the thing you made happen is horrific. It's exhilarating but horrifying at the same time.

How was winning the Tony for *Assassins*?

Oh, well, it wasn't bad! It had been just a bit more than ten years since my first nomination. I still remembered the whole experience from the first time through, which didn't end the way people hoped it would but it didn't devastate me in any way. And it probably made life easier in some ways to, you know, just go back to normality. If you've never gone through it before, it's extremely hard to find your way. I tried to guide Emily Skeggs through it [during *Fun Home*] because I saw me in her. And it's gotten so much worse since when I was first involved. There are so many more outlets and events. If you're the kind of person who is comfortable in a swirling kind of social environment you'll thrive and you'll have fun. If you're not somebody who's instinctively able to navigate those things—and not so many of us are; that's why we ended up actors in the first place, because we don't really fit in well with society—it can be really disorienting. And even if you have been through it before a number of times, you can find it just excruciatingly exhausting and life sucking. You can't jump in the pool and not expect to get wet. I find it impossible despite how consciously I try to put as little as possible on the eventual outcome of this whole thing. As you go to all these things it's impossible not to start to invest something in what the outcome's going to be. I don't like competition in that way and I don't enjoy it or celebrate it. I used to run cross-country/track. I loved running. I hated racing. That's kind of the way I am about all of this stuff, too. You know, I try really hard to not care. I've succeeded fairly well. I think if your ambition is to win a Tony Award or to be a movie star, I think you may find yourself making decisions that seem to make sense in order to accomplish that but are not going to serve you well in terms of your own personal growth and experience. And you may pass up opportunities that might actually be affording you those opportunities, but you don't realize it. I mean, if I looked at my circuitous route to the Tony Awards, there are a lot of choices that I made that were not the logical choices to end up having that kind of success. It was a very roundabout kind of path that, in hindsight, has a narrative sense to it, but at the time didn't look like I was making the choices to get to a Tony someday. I can recognize it when people are so anxiety-stricken by the whole process, like deer in the headlights. And I'll see some people who like just working it like this is their job. I guess, at that moment, it is.

I would imagine that for some people, whether or not they win, these events and luncheons are career moments on which they feel the need to capitalize.

That's absolutely right, and the number of people that put that fear into you that this is it—your one chance, and it's possible to blow it, and you may at any moment. Poor Beth Malone. I also tried to talk her through some of this. She had a friend who got into her head exactly that; win or lose doesn't matter. You were nominated. This is your moment. You've got to seize this. Her friend was telling her, "You've got to contact this person to get a dress, and you've got to get this person to do your hair, and you've got to make yourself up to look [different from your character]. You have to show the other side of things." And she just got so wound up. It was really making her miserable. She came down to my dressing room and said, "Am I blowing this? Is this my one chance to have something happen and I'm not doing it, right?" I tried to impress upon her that she'd already done it. She was doing this part and people were seeing the work, which is always the main thing. [The nomination] meant that more people were going to see that. Beyond that, nobody knows what any of it means or what the result is going to be, and the last thing you should do is feel like your moment is slipping through your hands. My first year, the *Tommy* year, I didn't think this was going to be the first of six nominations. I think every job is going to be my last job so I didn't expect to come back to the party. Thank God Kelli O'Hara won last year. I ran into her at one of these events and she was just trying to tell herself, "This doesn't matter." She's been through it a number of times, but you could see how incredibly important it was and how much she wanted to be there doing this but didn't want to be there doing this. She'd been there five times before and yet didn't know whether she would ever be back again so as far as she was concerned, this was her one and only chance. Again.

I have heard others say that, too. That "this could be my last show."
The reality of the business.

But it's not been your reality thus far, so why would you assume it's even in the cards?
Well, maybe because at some level you're not sure you ever deserved it in the first place. Or you have watched the way business goes. You've seen other people who were equally or more deserving of work, recognition, whatever, not get it. For some people a Tony immediately validates them and makes them convinced what they always knew, which was that they were born for this. For others like myself, it just kind of adds to this sneaking suspicion that somehow you've just gotten away with it, and there's going to come a day when they're going to figure it out. They're going to realize that you've just been making it up all this time. "Who let him in?" You're still working for your next job all the time and there are people coming up behind you. You're getting older. When the tipping point happens that the people you're auditioning for are younger than you, it starts to get more unnerving. As time goes on the people with the keys to those doors are younger and seem to have shorter memories or value of history.

Back to the *Assassins* Tony . . .
Being nominated in a Sondheim show was totally the win for me already. It was Puff Daddy and Phylicia Rashad presenting and all I could think of was just how hilarious it was that P. Diddy and Mrs. Cosby read my name from an envelope. I remember really clearly the overwhelming feeling was not like, "Yes! I won!" It was the incredible joy of being acknowledged and recognized by this vague cloud of colleagues. I just thought everybody should feel

like this in whatever line of work they are in. Wouldn't it be a nice world if that was what happened? I wanted to make sure that I acknowledged the other guys in the category. For five or six weeks you've all been equals in having your work celebrated, and then suddenly one person is picked out and it's as though nobody else ever was this close to it. I hate that, and I hate when I see speeches that seem to imply that people got themselves there somehow, which is never true. The rest of it was kind of a whirl. The orchestra of doom starts playing very quickly, and then they sweep you offstage. Walking offstage, immediately Puff Daddy's massive security detail all surrounded us. When Phylicia Rashad is one of the people giving you an award, you feel like the queen has given you the award because that's how she carries herself. I'd never been in a press room like that before and that was overwhelming and fun. I eventually came back and was able to enjoy the rest of the ceremony. The *Assassins* party was at Bryant Park where the rest of the company had been watching the awards, so we all got back there eventually and just had a great, great night. And then the next morning, Monday morning, we convened in the recording studio to record the cast album. You can hear in the recording all of the really ragged voices! Then it was just back to work. I got food poisoning the night before opening night of *Assassins* and spent the day of opening in the hospital getting four liters of saline solution put in my body. My cords were like dog meat from the stomach acids and stuff. It was funny watching all of this hubbub about Andy Karl [Karl was injured during opening week of *Groundhog Day*]. I mean, yes, that, I'm sure, was terrifying, and he was a real trouper to go on, but that happens every day all over town. Half the time it's some chorus member that you never hear about. But I already felt like I could retire because I had opened a Stephen Sondheim show on Broadway. That's it in musical theater if you grew up the way I did. So it was really wonderful, and it also just made me relax because I'd crossed a finish line that I hadn't ever been intentionally aiming for. Now I would never be somebody who had never won a Tony, and whatever that meant, it meant I could at least relax and know that.

Your next New York musical was *The Apple Tree* at Encores!

That was really fun. I mean, Encores! is terrifying. It's white-knuckling through the whole thing. They tell you it's book in hand, and it's casual. It's not at all, and, of course, Kristin Chenoweth came to rehearsal off-book. The rest of us had to try to catch up. I had a great time working with her. I don't usually get to do broader kind of comedy stuff like that, so that was really fun for me, too. Also getting to know Sheldon Harnick through that process was a real honor and treat. But I was also just panic-stricken the whole time, trying to remember everything.

You went back to more Sondheim: *Sweeney Todd*.

I think *Sweeney* was the first job that I was just offered [without auditioning]. [Director] John Doyle just wants to find the people that he wants to be in the room with, and then he'll make the piece with those people. Patti and Audra and I were at Ravinia the summer before we started rehearsals for *Sweeney* doing *Anyone Can Whistle*, and John came up to see it and to hang out with us [knowing that he'd be directing them in *Sweeney Todd*]. Patti brought her tuba to Ravinia, and there was a night in the hotel when she was demonstrating her tuba prowess at like, midnight. Security came up to ask Ms. LuPone please to refrain from tuba solos after 10. Anyway, John came and I think he figured out a lot just from that evening he came to the show. He's one of these directors who is so insightful about people and how to work with them. I thought we were having a social gathering but he was also doing his homework.

"Swing your razor high, Sweeney!" In *Sweeney Todd*. (Paul Kolnik)

You played guitar in *Sweeney*.
Patti's and my musical contributions were minimal compared to everybody else's. I was busy killing people a lot of the time. You only have so many hands. I knew that original production inside out. I'd seen it seven times. I'd worn the vinyl record out. I knew everything about it and it was still very vivid. As I sat down and read the libretto for the first time in years, I could hear Len Cariou's voice on every word I was reading. So if it had been a traditional remounting of Hal Prince's production, I would have been just terrible. I would have been trying and failing to be like Cariou all the time. We were just doing this play that we'd been handed, the way you would do Shakespeare if it was handed to you.

My own sense of Patti LuPone is that she cares fiercely about the work and that sometimes she's not aware how sharp her teeth are. She doesn't know that she can be terrifying.
I don't think she's concerned with whether she's terrifying. I was on a panel once with Liev Schreiber and a couple of other actors. It was a conversation about leading men on Broadway

and they asked what responsibilities we feel as the leader of a company. Liev was saying that he felt like everybody's there to do their job and it's not his responsibility to take care of anybody else. He's working, trying to give the best performance he can. His idea is that everybody fights in their character's corner exclusively, and if everybody's doing that, there are going to be times when the needs of those two characters/actors are in conflict. You work that out and you compromise but you don't go into it making sure that you're taking care of everybody else. You go into it making sure that you get the time you need to do your best job. And I think Patti is somewhat of that mindset, at least in these situations. So I think you're right that if she's getting upset about something, it is because she perceives it to be standing between her and her giving her best performance. That doesn't necessarily endear you to everybody when you're doing it.

But when you're doing a musical, there is so much more company energy required. Liev . . .

I think Liev's comments were in reaction to mine. I said I felt a real responsibility for the feeling in the room and I feel like it's an ensemble thing regardless of what your status is. And certainly there are things where you need to step in and set an example or set a tone, but sometimes that's by giving focus to somebody else or giving somebody else the time [in rehearsal] when you could justifiably take that for yourself. The last thing that I like is having strife in a rehearsal room or backstage. I really, really dislike working in that kind of situation if it can be avoided, and I believe nine times out of ten it can be avoided. There are other people who thrive on that kind of tension and bring it into their work in a positive way. But then everybody else now has to take that onboard or has to navigate it. I think Patti cares emphatically about what she feels she needs to do.

Those fights aren't always for herself. Sometimes it's on behalf of another actor or the company.

Yes! And there are always going to be multiple sides to these kinds of things. I'm sure that I have said or done things—I was told once by a PR person that I have a reputation of being kind of demanding. I was flabbergasted. She was saying that people sometimes feel like I take everything too seriously. And I thought, "Well, okay, I'll take that." Because I do take it all seriously. Even the fun stuff. And if something's not right I'll say something about it. I try to say it respectfully and nicely, but if I need to, I'll say it pretty firmly. But I've learned that if you are too accommodating you get walked on. When I was doing *Total Eclipse*, my first off-Broadway show with Peter Evans, he made a big fuss [about his dressing space] and it was so out of character. Later, he said to me, "I saw that you seemed a little concerned about what was going on. I learned a while ago that if you make a big fuss about something minor early on, then you don't have to fight for everything later. They'll actually consider what they're doing and think about you, not to give you preferential treatment, but just to give you what you need so you don't have to spend the whole time asking for what you need." It was the only time I ever saw him raise his voice about anything. From then on, they were like, "You know, Peter, is it okay if . . ." I sort of told myself, "That's what I'm going to be when I grow up." Of course, I don't find myself able to do it most of the time, but I do recognize it. Were I Patti LuPone, people would have checked with me first before doing a lot of things—setting schedules, doing planning and things, just informing me of stuff. They don't because I don't make them. And then I have to become a more strident voice later. It's protecting the work and your ability to do it well. In our business, respect is earned absolutely, but it needs to be insisted upon often because there are so many people juggling so many things.

Anything else you want to say about *Sweeney*?

I'm sorry we didn't get to do it longer. We ran a year. I had felt from the beginning that if it closed after the first performance, it would have been the most satisfying experience of my life to that point. We had no conductor so we had to listen so intently to each other. The cues were all connected to things that other people were doing so you were constantly connected to other people, listening to each other like I've never—listening to everything that's going on onstage in a way that you seldom do. That it was embraced by *Sweeney* fans was really gratifying. Critics resoundingly embraced it. So by the time it ended, all we could have done was enjoy that experience longer, and I would happily have done that, but we didn't get to.

Well, having racked up a tremendous amount of experience working with formidable leading ladies, you move on to *LoveMusik* with Donna Murphy.

Exactly. This was the stretch where I started to refer to myself as Broadway's premiere diva escort service. It was sort of like, "We've got a formidable leading actress. Call Cerveris because he gets along with all of them." I did joke about that, but I was also proud of it because I admire all of them enormously.

Donna told me she drove Hal Prince crazy with her exactitude.

I will tell you a story that exemplifies that. She had a different shade of lipstick for every costume change, every period in Lenya's life. There were scenes where various people and I would be onstage just trying to kill a little time because we can't start the scene until Donna gets out here, and we can see her in the wings, and—okay—she's in the outfit now, but she's stopping to put the lipstick on. She won't come out until it's done. She was sick for a little while, and her understudy went on and was onstage in half the time, which showed all of us that the costume change can be completed in the allotted time as Hal had been saying all along. I don't know whether she did the lipstick every time or not, but I guarantee nobody knew or cared. She knew. In rehearsals when a scene would kind of grind to a halt because Donna needed to discuss everything, I would rather just do some Zen breathing, and let Donna do that because she clearly needed to.

And you probably knew that allowing her to do that was going to breed genius.

Yeah, exactly. I know myself to be a pretty flexible person. I mean, I certainly have strongly held opinions and things, but I try not to assume that my idea's the best one in the room. I think that flexibility has stood me in good stead sometime.

And leaves you open to learn the most.

I think that's because my fundamental assumption is that I have more to learn from everybody around me than I have to teach them. I know for a fact that I have learned so much from everybody I've been around. I didn't close the door on different ways of working. The downside of it is a desire to please and to not ruffle feathers. Sometimes that has put me at a disadvantage. You know, the feeling that "we can get to me later" sometimes means we never get to me. Maybe this is why I feel like it's sometime after opening that I'm ready to start working.

Anything else you want to share about *LoveMusik*?

I met Hal Prince backstage at one of the 800 Sondheim birthday celebrations. The next day I got a call from my agent saying Hal wants to meet you about this new thing he's working on. It was like, "This is the way it's supposed to work!" like in the old days. And you go into his office, and it's like the living, breathing heart of Broadway. Photos all over the walls of him and various people. He sits down and we start talking, and he's really complimentary and really nice, and all I can think of is "This is really Broadway." And he's telling me about this book of letters between Lenya and Weill, and it very slowly dawns on me that he's pitching me the idea. I wonder when the audition's going to be and he's basically selling me on it. He had me at "come to my office." That whole experience was so thrilling, just to be around him, to hear the stories, to work with him, and to be treated like a colleague by a titan like him. He comes from the school where you're the producer and you make it happen. He just makes what he wants to make. They knew [with *LoveMusik*] that what they were doing was not like anything else on Broadway, and it was not serving the current tastes. They just didn't choose to care because they knew what they were making and they were proud of it. I felt so proud to be part of it and proud of realizing this vision for them. Not being universally embraced was disappointing and frustrating and when we came in the next day after the reviews, Hal said, "Look, I've been through this a few more times than even the most-experienced of you. It would have been nice if they had reacted differently but we were never doing it for them. We're doing what we set out to do. I couldn't be more proud of it and I wouldn't have done any of it any differently." I loved that whole experience, and I thought it was beautiful. To be able to say I have Hal Prince on my résumé—I can't put a value on that experience.

So when you are actually doing the work with a Hal Prince or a Stephen Sondheim, as you were on your next show, *Road Show*, these pinch-me moments, how do you stay sane in the room? Does the work just take over?

I'm constantly trying to close the door and hope that nobody else is hearing the sounds while I'm literally screaming. [With *Road Show*] I was getting to do that in a room with John Doyle and if there's anybody who's going to make you feel like the fact that you're doing a new Stephen Sondheim musical in New York is irrelevant, it's John Doyle, who will just daily remind you that your only job is to show up, be who you are, and do this thing. Alex Gemignani and I had worked with John before. In the early rehearsals, the rest of the cast would be coming up to us like, "You guys seem to be okay with this." And we were like, "We were there once, too. It's going to be fine." Because on the first day, we did six versions of the opening two minutes at the end of which he said, "Well, good. I think we have six good starts. We may do one of them. We probably won't do any of them. Let's move on to the next two minutes." Steve and John were rewriting stuff and that was thrilling. The coolest thing was the day [musical director] Mary-Mitchell Campbell came over to us to say, "Steve's writing a new song. After rehearsal tomorrow, the three of us will go in a room and learn it and then we'll do it for Steve the next day and see what he thinks." We go into this little room, and we get handed this handwritten sheet with music that's never been seen and it's a tiny, little song, but it's really sweet, and it's written with Alex and me in mind. It's simple as can be but intricate as hell. You just have chills through the whole thing. And then the next day we do it for Steve, and you realize this is the first time he's hearing anybody but himself do it. And he says, "Yeah, that's great. I think that's good." I loved that whole experience.

You did several straight plays after that. Was that by design or was that just what showed up?

A little of both. I think I passed on opportunities to do other musicals because, as has often been my preference, I like to do something very different from the thing I've just done. So between *Sweeney* and *LoveMusik* I did *King Lear* down at The Public.

You did *Hedda Gabler*, and *Cymbeline*, and *In the Next Room*. Your next foray into musicals was *Evita*, so it took a while.

Yeah, which, I guess, is why so many people were like, "It's so great to have you back." I hadn't really gone anywhere. And I was not looking to do a musical necessarily. I certainly was not looking to do an Andrew Lloyd Webber musical. But I loved [director] Michael Grandage and I had seen a couple of other things that he directed, so it was purely the chance to meet him that got me to go to the meeting. My meeting with him was everything I hoped it would be. We talked for an hour about the show. He made a pretty good case for it, and I left the meeting feeling like, "Well, I guess it actually does sound like something interesting." And then the offer came in and it didn't in any way reflect anything that he had been saying about the importance of the role in the production. My agents felt strongly that we could infer from that that maybe not everybody involved sees Perón's importance in the same way, so if it wasn't really something I was dying to do, maybe this wasn't the next thing to do. I let go of it completely. A month or more went by and then I got a call out of the blue from Grandage saying, "Since we met, I've been thinking about you as Perón and I can't let go of the idea. Would you mind if I talked to the producers?" It had nothing to do with money really. I would have worked for him for $400 a week at The Public if that's the world that we're working in. I have no problem working for nothing. But this was a huge commercial thing with an international pop star [Ricky Martin] in it, so if that's the arena . . . They [ultimately] offered everything that I had initially wanted. Thank God I did it because I really loved that production, and everything that he said about the way he wanted to work on it was true. I loved working with him. I loved working with Ricky. He's like one of the most generous people I've ever been around. And I loved working with Elena Roger. I really liked the three of us together and that whole company. I was really proud of that production in general and my contribution to it. I learned a great deal about Perón. He was a very complicated but fascinating person. I went to the Perón archives and met this guy who brought out all kinds of original documents for me. I was really proud when people would come up to me and say that they had never really realized how good a part it was until they saw this production. I think it's because of the way Grandage thought of it. I really loved all of it, as much as it was annoying. . . . I ultimately started delaying my exit from the theater until after Ricky had gone because of the madness. There were 3,000 people out there and the theater only holds like 1,500. It was mayhem. I was in the production that at any other time I would have been bitching about—fucking pop star comes and they have a several-million-dollar advance before they even open. But it's not bad to be in a show that is impervious to reviews. I still feel the objection to star casting and stuff, but now I know that person might be really nice and might be—it was fascinating because Ricky's alternates [would go on sometimes], both of whom gave better, more nuanced acting performances than Ricky, but Ricky would take up so much space just . . .

Energetically?
Energetically. Like sheer radiance-wise. A lot of that is what we endow him with, but a lot of it is that charisma.

You counter that "star presence" with an Argentinian playing Eva. Authentic.
Yeah. And poor Elena just suffered so much from people's comparisons to Patti's version of it. If you actually look at documentary footage of Eva, she looks and sounds like Elena. I thought it was thrilling to have a different kind of voice on Broadway, and my philosophy about revivals is if you don't have something new to bring to it, why do it? I loved her performance. I remember watching her in those last critics performances before the reviews came out thinking, "She's just going to be on the cover of everything." When that, so decisively, was not the reaction, I think you have two choices: you either double down and try to instruct

people and try to give a context, or you cut the rope and just go to your strengths. I think people read our Tony performance as our having no confidence in our Eva; we're going to put her on a stage and say nothing while the pop star runs around and sings. I think they could have tried to change the narrative and might have had some success in that. They just seemed to think, "Well, there's nothing we can do with this so let's focus on the things that we have." I think if that show were being done now, [as a white man] I probably couldn't play Perón anymore. And on balance, that's a good thing. But it's a very delicate thing because when you are growing up as an actor, all you're told is that you should be able to play anything, which, of course, isn't true. You have to figure out where you draw the line about who can play what because if you get too specific and say you can only play something if you actually are that thing, you start to cross lines that you don't want to cross. I had some people—very few but a couple—complain about having a straight man play Bruce Bechdel in *Fun Home*. You want to be careful saying something like that because that can quickly turn into, "Well, then you can't have a gay man play a straight character," which you certainly don't want to say. It gets very complicated very quickly. If you've never killed anybody, you can't play a murderer? So it's a fascinating moment in our history, and I think, as with any kind of big, important social changes, often the pendulum has to swing a little too far in one direction so that it can settle back where it ought to be. I have absolutely benefited from the privileges that came for such a long time with being male, with being white.

Did you see male white privilege in musical theater?

I'm not sure. I would have to think a lot about that. I mean, when you think about it, it's not strange that your first book was about women because the female side of Broadway is so much more prevalent and more what you think of when you think of musical theater. When you start to add up the names of the guys, you're like oh, yeah, yeah, yeah, but I don't think any of us really quite rise to the levels of the Pattis and the Bernadettes in terms of audiences' devotion and affection, and I think that's great. I don't have a problem being in whatever position that leaves us in. I'm finding myself in this interesting place now, in the early late period of my career, where I'm finding that the competition for roles is different. Actors of color didn't have the access to compete with me for certain roles. Now I'm finding the opposite's true, and I'm being told that, "Yeah, they like you, but they've got three white male actors in this thing, and so they've decided that the director of this law firm or something could be male, could be female, could be white, could be non-white, could be anything." So suddenly I'm competing with a much bigger pool and actually have to give them more reason to hire me than just being the best actor for it. There are other agendas and balances that are at work. And I'm kind of okay [with that], I guess, because I've been really fortunate, and I've gotten to do a lot of really fantastic things. So if I have to step to the side a little bit and let other people have a seat at the table, I'm okay with that. But I mean, I loved my experience in *Evita*, and I worked really hard. I brushed up my Spanish a lot. I really immersed myself in it as I do with any character I play. I learned far more than I think people [typically] do about Perón. I really wanted to be faithful to the character—more faithful than the show actually demands, and in some ways more seriously than Elena and Ricky did because they didn't have to work to be authentic. When you're aware of your outsider status, just by virtue of your accent or your birth or whatever, you can work far harder than somebody who's actually from the place "to care about it," in quotation marks.

In a way that can seem embarrassingly overcompensating.

Yeah, exactly. In hindsight. And sometimes in the middle of it! It was a bit easier with *Fun Home*. I didn't have to have a different accent or anything, but one of the things that was very important about that show was the place it had for a lot of people who were gay or trans or figuring it all out. We did a lot of talks to groups. It was always really important to me, and I felt like it was really part of our responsibility doing the show to stand up and to be present. That's why we went to South Carolina when the College of Charleston banned the book. We took everybody down there and did these lecture/demo performances and discussions. And that's why I led the charge to take us all down to Orlando [for the benefit staging of *Fun Home*] after the Pulse shooting. But I was always really careful to make sure that when it came to talking about people's actual personal experiences, I tried to never make the mistake of speaking before other people who actually were facing being discriminated against or treated differently. It's that weird thing of trying to be a really strong and sincere ally without forgetting that these problems are not your problems entirely. You care about them, and you care about your friends and loved ones, but if you want to, you can walk away from it in a way that people who actually are gay, lesbian, trans, whatever, can't. It's just not about you.

I am guessing that when you come through the stage door and there are people so eager to connect . . .

Yes, yes, that was an extraordinary part of doing the show every night for me, and I think for the whole cast. I was really proud of everybody for caring a great deal about the audience that we had just put through this experience. We used to call it "the second act" since we didn't have a second act. The second part of our show was to connect with the people who wanted to stay, and there were hundreds often. A certain amount of it is selfies and stuff, but a very high percentage of the people who stayed were people who needed to tell you how it had affected them. A jaw-dropping number of people would tell you that their father had just committed suicide or that they lost their mother. People saying, "I brought my parents to see the show.

Stealing a clandestine moment with Joel Perez in *Fun Home*. (Joan Marcus)

They're standing right behind me. I'm going to come out to them at dinner." Every single show, even two-show days, I felt like it was really important to be there for anybody that needed to see us afterwards. I don't think I ever got out of there in under a half an hour, and sometimes it was an hour. The rest of the company would do similar things. But it really felt important because the show was having a profound effect on people, way beyond anything else that I had done. I mean, we had tons of fans after *Tommy* and after *Sweeney*, but it was really very different.

Let's go back to the beginnings of *Fun Home*.
I read it, and I loved a lot of things about it, but I wasn't certain about Bruce in this draft. Bruce was still a little two-dimensional. He was just a mean father. I said I would do the two-week workshop but without saying necessarily that I would do the run of the show. Because people say, "We really want your input" all the time but then they don't listen to anything that I say. Well, by noon of the first day of rehearsal, I was in. It was astounding to me that they [director Sam Gold, writer Lisa Kron, and composer Jeanine Tesori] would cut stuff that others would give their eyeteeth to have made. They could do another show or two with the songs that we cut! And they knew that it was good; it just wasn't the right kind of good for that moment in the play. They were ruthless with themselves and would keep working until they came up with something else. That kind of work went on big time throughout the workshop. [At The Public] we were getting new pages all the time. We worked to refine the show at every performance, and in some ways that never changed. It felt like a story that we had to tell every night. I think that is why I could have done it for ages longer than we did, because as exhausting as it was, and it really weighed on me, it was so exhilarating to do every night. I didn't have to psych myself up before the show or get ready to do it. [I'd go on and] it was Bruce's time. The membrane between quote, unquote, "real life" and "stage life" was super thin and permeable in that show.

You mentioned that playing Bruce was exhausting. Obviously there's reward in that, but does the weight of the character seep into your life? Even though you said you could have kept playing him, was it also a relief to stop?
There was a plan for me to do the tour, actually, and I really was excited about taking this story around the country, but I decided I just was so invested in my Broadway family that I couldn't . . .

Imagine doing it with other people?
Yeah. Part of me looked forward to the idea of reinventing it. But in the end, I just couldn't. I just couldn't let go of the family that we had here, so I ended up deciding not to do it. I think I was kind of saved from myself in a way, because I don't know how healthy it would have been to continue to do it for another year. It's not like I am unable to discern between my characters and my actual life. I'm not some sort of method person. But I think you create this reservoir in yourself. That is the place where you go—the well that you go to for the performance that night. Keeping the access to that well clear and available to you at a moment's notice means that you keep those doors in you open that you would otherwise keep closed for daily maintenance sake. You keep them propped open.

Your defenses are down, and you've exposed yourself to all kinds of different things?
Yeah, yeah. And stuff can seep out that you wouldn't otherwise want wandering around in your head. I think I was—and this would be confirmed by people around me—I think I was

more short-tempered. One of the things I remember really struggling with was developing this emotional gymnastic ability. Because of the way the play is constructed, jumping back and forth in time—you may have a hugely dramatic, angry scene, and then jump immediately into something years before that, complete calmness. You put one set of feelings completely behind you and pick up another one and then abandon those immediately because you're jumping back and forth. It took us a long time to do that. But I think when you do that over and over again—I mean, as my shrink has explained to me, you actually program your brain and electrical impulses to access things that you feel frequently. So when you break up with somebody, part of the process of getting over that is literally reprogramming the electrical impulses in your brain to not have the same reactions that it had all the time when you see the face of that person. Going down the path of being able to get very angry very quickly, you actually are training your brain to get good at doing that, and so it's not surprising that it can happen at other times, too. I think I was more quick-tempered in life. I was also carrying around this sadness, this feeling of inability to connect with people, feeling outside of things. It didn't just go away at the end of the night. I'd had a similar experience in different ways with *Sweeney*.

You've played your share of tormented characters.
I don't know what it says about me—or I do. I remember somebody teaching me during *Sweeney* to do a little cleansing ritual thing at the end of the night, after I'd taken makeup off, just to consciously and mindfully wash my hands and think about letting go of all of those things that I'd had to pick up and carry with me for the performance. You trust that it'll all be there tomorrow when you need it, but for now, let it go and watch it go down the sink in a mindful kind of way. I had dinner with Len Cariou after he came to see *Sweeney*, and he said, "Oh, yeah, *Sweeney* sent me first to drink and then into therapy." *Fun Home* was carrying Bruce's story, and all the more because of coming to know Alison Bechdel. Unlike all the other real-life people I had played, I was actually playing somebody in living memory of the person who created the whole thing. Allison and her brothers came to the see the show at a preview at The Public. Alison had been living with the story—had told the story and written the story and lectured about it—but her brothers had not. They all watched the show together and apparently it was a hugely important thing for all them. They never got to grieve as siblings. They never really talked about it. This was the first time they got to sit together and actually cry for their parents, for both of them really. Being a part of giving somebody their parents back is beautiful but also a really heavy thing.

You talked before about the desire to tell this story and to connect to a community. I can't think of another show in recent memory that has had that much power to affect in that way. That is a lot of responsibility to carry for a long time. And a privilege.
That's what I think I felt most of the time. Whenever I felt like there was a burden, it was pretty easy to remind myself how lucky I was to have that burden. I hope I will have other experiences in my career that are meaningful and satisfying and exciting and all those things. I don't know that I'll ever have something that will be like *Fun Home*. You tell yourself as an actor you want to believe that what you're doing makes a difference in the world, but you kind of suspect that you're just bullshitting yourself, and that it's really just entertaining.

It's always hard not to think that you've peaked after a peak experience.
I think even Sondheim struggles with it now. I went over to see him just a month or two ago and he was talking about how he finds it so difficult to write anymore. He doesn't enjoy it the way he used to. He said, "When I'm in it, I still do, but up until that moment and

immediately after, I hate everything else about it." And part of it is that he's struggling with his own legacy. Which he's entirely disinterested in confronting.

You won another Tony for *Fun Home.*

The first time felt like a real gift. It could just as easily have been Denis O'Hare, except that he had won the year before. Raúl Esparza was up for *Taboo* that year—it really could have gone any way. It just went my way, and I felt really fortunate and lucky. I really felt like I had worked hard to earn the second one, not just in *Fun Home* but in the years since *Assassins*, and again, it was an insanely competitive category and year. What each of us was doing was so different. What Brian d'Arcy James was doing in *Something Rotten!* was a million miles away from what I was doing, and from what Robbie Fairchild was doing in *An American in Paris*. Each of us was doing things that were kind of our particular best skill—we were all in the perfect shows for ourselves. It was just kind of a toss-up. But I felt like I left everything on the field that season. But you can do that and it still doesn't happen. I mean, during *Sweeney* I felt like "if I can't win a Tony Award in this production . . ." So I was very prepared to have that experience again. So prepared, in fact, that I was entirely unprepared to actually win in the end. I proved that with my rambling speech. But it felt especially gratifying to get that acknowledgment for that show. *Fun Home* was so satisfying in every way that matters to me as an artist and craftsperson and then just human being and citizen. Since that time, I haven't done any plays. There have been a couple of things I was offered that just weren't—at other times I would have jumped on them, but I think I knew that I would be constantly comparing and find them wanting. So I've been either not pursuing or turning down things. And then coincidentally somehow this whole world of television work has suddenly opened up, and it's been perfect because there's no temptation to compare that to *Fun Home*. It's such a completely different thing. So that's where things have been in the aftermath of that. It took a long time, years after the show was over for me, to disconnect from parts of the experience that were still holding me close to it. I found out from Twitter that I wasn't going to be in the London production. That was painful at the time, but ultimately a kind of tearing the Band-Aid off of the last bit of me that was still kind of holding on to the show.

I want to read you two quotes just to hear your response to them. On the first I'm quoting you to you.

I don't believe a word of it.

You said, "Ever since I was a little kid I felt like I'd rather sacrifice sleep or meals than miss out on something good."

I remember when I was little, I was a big fan of monster movies. Friday nights were Chiller Theater Night, and I could stay up to watch TV late and see the monster movies, and, of course, they always put the best ones on latest, so I'd have to stay awake through one or two earlier ones. The rest of the house was all quiet, and during commercial breaks I would run upstairs and throw cold water on my face to keep myself awake so that I could see the rest of the movie. We didn't have VCRs or anything. I was either going to see it or I wasn't going to see it. And I kind of feel like I've done a version of that through the rest of my life. I will stay up 'til all hours. I'll skip meals. I'll do whatever because I have some feeling that I don't want to miss something. It would manifest in me doing double duty, rehearsing one thing during the day and doing another show at night a number of times because I didn't want to say no to either. I didn't want to leave the thing I was in, and I didn't want to miss the chance to do the next thing, and if other people were willing to work around the schedule and make it possible, it didn't matter to me that it meant I wasn't going to have a second to myself for months at a time. Plus, I think every actor's fear is that at any moment they're going to figure it out and realize that it was a mistake when they called your name in the first place. I better get it before they notice. Yeah, that's absolutely true of me.

Two other quotes. Stephen Sondheim said of you that you "can do anything." Oskar Eustis called you both "a true star of musical theater" and "an actor able to inhabit the classics with a spirit as big as anyone on the New York stage." So when you're getting the stamp of approval from titans in the business, how does that resonate?

I mean, I would trade everything on that shelf [indicating his awards] for those words. And it's not because they are from titans in the business. It's because I admire those men so much. There's literally nothing more valuable to me than approval from men like that and my dad. And from the kids that I talked to after *Fun Home*, who told me, in a way that I could actually hear, that the thing that I had spent years working on left them with things that would change their lives. Those are the only reasons to do any of it and to put up with all the other shit that you have to to get to do it. It's surreal and bizarre to have people like Stephen Sondheim say things like that. And I do find myself having to take a minute every once in a while and go, "You do know that that was Stephen Sondheim saying that about you."

You mentioned before that you went to see him . . .

I went to his house. He said, "Was there something you wanted to talk about in particular?" I was like, "No. I just wanted to come visit." He was like, "Great. Okay." I'm trying to make more time for things like that because it all goes by. It's such a blur when you're working, and it's exciting and it's thrilling, and it's wonderful, but . . . It's part of me disconnecting from social media, too. It's like all that stuff just takes you away from yourself and from the ability to be clear about what matters or what you think or what you care about. I'm finding more and more that I really love just sitting down with people and having conversations. It's such a rare thing now. This conversation is great fun because it's spending time with somebody in a situation where you actually are spending time with them. I'm trying to do more quality over quantity kind of experiences. But the fact that I can write to Stephen Sondheim and get a positive answer and invitation back is kind of weird. I still am just a dorky fan kid really. At the Sondheim eightieth birthday celebrations, I wish they'd had cameras all over backstage because a lot of the show was back there. From Mandy and Bernadette and Patti on down to Laura Osnes and the youngsters in the group, all of us were kind of pinching ourselves and going "Can you believe we're here?" Recognizing that the people that you looked up to as light years ahead of you, because that's how you've always thought of them, were all peers for the night. We had this shared sense of gratitude for being alive in a moment where we could be here and celebrate this man with him still here. And to celebrate it with each other, being fans of each other, it really was like the most overachieving high school musical class ever. Watching everybody in the wings, watching each other in as nonjudgmental a way as it is possible for musical theater actors to be. I was in the room with other people who still understood what all of this meant. And it's things like your books that are going to give the best chance for other generations to discover this later. I'm not somebody who thinks that musical theater is going to disappear because I think it serves a purpose in the world and in our culture that nothing else really can. I think when theater tries to compete with movies, and TV, and pop media, it kind of shows its underwear in a weird way. When it instead focuses on the things that it does that no other thing can do, that's usually when it's most successful. When it emphasizes that live human connection and that experience in the moment—theater's able to do that in a way that nothing else does.

11

NORM LEWIS

March 2016; August 2018; June 2019

IT IS IMPOSSIBLE TO WALK through the streets of New York City with Norm Lewis without bumping into someone he knows. Usually it happens multiple times. Without fail he greets them warmly, genuinely, taking the time to truly connect. He is, in fact, sometimes called "the Mayor of Broadway." He's the guy everyone knows they will get along with in a rehearsal room. He's the one least likely to create any drama. He's the actor who will almost never say no to a benefit if his schedule allows. Ask anyone about him and watch their face immediately soften into a smile. He's Broadway's favorite nice guy. It's a lovely reputation. And also a lot of work to maintain.

Born in Tallahassee and raised in Eatonville, Florida, Lewis had no connection to theater, but like so many other Broadway names, he sang in church. It wasn't until his high school years that he got involved in theater and even then, it was just a lark, never anything he considered professionally. Once he determined to head to New York, though, his career took off, with featured roles in *Tommy* and *Miss Saigon*, before he really made his mark in the short-lived *Side Show*. He made notable contributions to other notorious flops (*The Wild Party*, *Amour*) before he was cast against type as the stern, uncompromising Javert in the first revival of *Les Misérables* (a role he repeated in London and in the show's starry twenty-fifth anniversary O2 Arena concert). *The Little Mermaid* and *Sondheim on Sondheim* followed, but it was starring opposite Audra McDonald in *Porgy and Bess* that put him into the category of above-the-title star and Tony nominee. When he took over the title role in *The Phantom of the Opera* the following year, he was the first (and still only) black man to play the role on Broadway.

Lewis once told me that he wanted to be the black Michael Bublé, and while he has since modified that dream, his calendar is full of concert dates all over the world. He has also dipped his toe into both the TV and film worlds. He is always working, always on the go, always excitedly looking forward. Pinning him down is no easy task, but when I do, he's always fully present and engaged. When there are other people in the room, he works hard at shifting the focus off of himself, making sure everyone's included. Occasionally I have found it embarrassing having him recite my résumé to strangers, but Lewis, without fail, wants to make sure that everyone in the room knows the ways in which each person is impressive, not just him. How many actors think to do that?

Do you have an early memory of being aware of the size or the quality of your voice, or were you just somebody singing in church like everybody else?

Someone singing in church. I played tennis. I didn't do any theater until my senior year. It was in a theater called Theater on Park, in Winter Park, Florida. It wasn't a dinner

"If I had known from the beginning that I was going to have to be naked, I'd have negotiated with them to get me a trainer!" As Triton in *The Little Mermaid*. (Joan Marcus)

theater, but you could order food, like soup and sandwiches. And my first show there was *Purlie!*.

How did that happen?
They needed black people. I saw that there was an audition in the paper, and I think I heard it on the radio, too. I had been listening to the *The Wiz*. I had no sheet music or anything. I just went down there to see what I could do, and my favorite song on the album was "Soon as I Get Home." That's what I sang and they were like, "We've got to have this kid in our show." And I was in the chorus.

So never having performed, what made you decide, "This is for me"?
So let's go back a little bit further. Tennis was my passion. I had pictures of Bjorn Borg and Arthur Ashe and Jimmy Connors and Guillermo Vilas, and all these people who I just

admired. I wanted to be a professional tennis player. I ate, drank, slept tennis. I loved it. And I was good, but I wasn't great. And I don't know, it was frustrating to try to get great. I loved practicing, and when I was practicing, I was fucking awesome, but when it came to actually doing it, in a tournament, I didn't have that fighting spirit. I played from age nine to about eighteen, and I just knew by eighteen—plus it's a very expensive sport. I was very lucky those nine years to have had the tennis lessons for free. This amazing man, Denton Johnson, just decided to dedicate his life to teaching the kids in my town. All African American. He saw a way for people to get scholarships. . . . We used to call him "Pop" Johnson. He was an old and wise man, but he loved teaching kids tennis. Then, when I was sixteen going on seventeen, we had to have so many electives to graduate. I'm thinking, "I sing in church. Let me try the choir because it'll be fun. I'm sure it'll be easy. I'll meet some girls and have a good time." The first day I show up, and there's a folder for me and all this music. I just sat there, and I listened. And all of a sudden this wall of sound . . . like . . . "What the hell is this? It's beautiful!" It was a Latin song. I couldn't read music—still can't—but I just listened to their sound and I picked it up. It just fascinated me. Then weeks go by, and I'm learning the music. They were singing stuff that was from Broadway shows. I had no idea what Broadway was. That sparked an interest for me to go the library and just start looking at some Broadway albums, and what stuck out was *The Wiz*. There was a theater training program that you got paid for at Theater on Park, and luckily, the summer after graduation, it worked out. We trained all day and at night we performed *The Wiz*. I would get there at 8:00 AM, and I didn't come home 'til 11:30 PM or something. I was there all day and I was in heaven. And guess who was the Scarecrow? Wesley Snipes!

Norm Lewis

The Who's Tommy	Broadway, 1993
Miss Saigon	Broadway, 1995
Side Show	Broadway, 1997
A New Brain	Off-Broadway, 1998
Captains Courageous	Off-Broadway, 1999
Sweeney Todd	Washington, DC, 1999
The Wild Party	Broadway, 2000
Amour	Broadway, 2002
Golden Boy	Encores!, 2002
Baby	Milburn, NJ, 2004
Chicago	Broadway, 2004
Dessa Rose	Off-Broadway, 2005
Two Gentlemen of Verona	Off-Broadway, 2005
Les Misérables	Broadway, 2006; West End, 2010
The Little Mermaid	Broadway, 2007
Sondheim on Sondheim	Broadway, 2010
Porgy and Bess	Broadway, 2011
A Bed and a Chair	Off-Broadway, 2013
The Phantom of the Opera	Broadway, 2014
Cabin in the Sky	Encores!, 2015
Sweeney Todd	Off-Broadway, 2017
Once on This Island	Broadway, 2018
The Music Man	Kennedy Center, 2019

But you walked away from all that? You did two shows there, and then you didn't pursue theater . . .

Yeah, it was just fun. I was a practical kid. I went away to school—Lake City Community College—and I majored in business. But they gave me a scholarship to sing in the choir, even though I didn't have to take any music classes. I didn't even have a thought of me going into this business. I genuinely like business. I like the business world. Singing was a hobby. And I didn't consciously think I was good enough. I just thought I had a nice voice and people kept giving me all these nice accolades. But again, it just didn't penetrate. My sophomore year, they were doing *Grease* so I decided, "Okay, I'm going to get a little bit more involved in the theater department." I ended up getting Doody and Teen Angel. That was the first time my parents had heard me sing solo. They were in the last row of a 500-seat house. I start singing and my dad stands up and says, "That's my boy!" My mom had to pull him down. That was a beautiful moment for me.

But you still didn't pursue it.
Yeah. The director of the theater department offered to introduce me to someone at the Neighborhood Playhouse and he was sure I'd get in, but when we found out how much money it was going to cost—I just didn't want to burden my parents with the money. So I kind of let it go. When I graduated I decided to go to Florida State University. But before that fall, my dad, who owned a construction company, was in a major accident on site. He was seriously injured. I stayed home to help him with his company. I applied to a liberal arts school in town, Rollins College, and I luckily got in. I got a job at the *Orlando Sentinel* in the production department. [Eventually I moved to advertising.] I thought advertising was going to be my career. I worked there for four or five years. I started wanting to sing again when I had more freedom to sing. People knew that I sang and they started asking me to sing at their weddings or some event. I sang at pageants. While I was working at the *Sentinel*, there was an audition for Opryland, summer of '85. They gave me a leave of absence for like three months to work the summer at Opryland. And that was my intro to real theater people—professional, determined-to-get-on-Broadway people. These are career people, not the community theater people that I worked with before. That was intoxicating. When I came back, I auditioned for Disney about seven times over a two-year period. I always got called back but never got the job.

You ended up working on a cruise ship right around then . . .
Yeah, for four and a half months. I was going to go back to school, study theater, and in maybe two years go to New York. I had decided to make this my career choice, or at least try it. I remember being at the midnight buffet, and there was a guy, Michael O'Carroll. He intimidated the hell out of me when I first got there. I just didn't know what to say to him. But one night I told him my plans to go back to school and maybe in two years try New York. He was like, "Okay. But, if you ask me that's some bullshit." I'm already nervous being by myself with this guy, and then that comes at me, but that was one of the most significant nights of my life. He said, "Let me tell you something: You got talent. You're good. What better place to study than in New York?" I said, "What about those people who went to the Royal Academy of Faa Faa Faa?" He looked at me and said, "Fuck 'em. When I go into an audition room and I see those people behind the desk, I realize they have a problem. I'm going to solve your problem." I said, "What if you don't." He said, "Go solve everybody else's problem. That's what you do as an actor. You try to solve these directors' and producers' problems." That was the light bulb that went off, and from that moment . . . I went home after the contract was over, I packed my bags, and I moved to New York. [I was only there for a month before my dad fell ill. I went home to take care of him.] I did that for about seven months. Mom didn't want me to work or anything. She needed me at home. I would probably watch him twelve-plus hours a day. After he died, I stayed home to help her dissolve his company for another nine months. I wanted to have a job that was convenient so that I could be with her most of the day. I got a job as a bellman at the Sheraton. When I got my nametag, it said "Norm."

So you became Norm instead of Norman. And eventually you made it to New York?

September 28, 1989. [I shared] a tiny, one-bedroom apartment. I had the front. I slept on a futon. It was enough. I started temping, and that sustains me. I go to every audition trying to "solve everyone's problems." I got a job two weeks after I got here, working for Candlewood Playhouse—$150 a week. Woo-hoo! I was in the chorus of *Joseph and the Amazing Technicolor Dreamcoat*. Seth Rudetsky was our musical director. I auditioned for Nipsey Russell—like, for Nipsey—he was in the audition room—for *A Funny Thing Happened on the Way to the Forum* at Harrah's Marina in Atlantic City. I got that job. That was a five-month gig. That first year I did a lot of non-union work.

Were you meeting other actors at auditions?

Absolutely. But I didn't feel part of the community yet. I got my Equity card working for ArtsPower, doing children's theater. I started temping again, catering some, and I get a show called *Abyssinia*, which takes me to the Cleveland Playhouse. I met people who were so embracing and so supportive. For the first time I wasn't the token black guy in a show. And then I met LaChanze, and we started dating. That's when I met the negro theater elite.

I've never heard that expression.

People say it all the time.

Given that there are so few opportunities for black actors, were you each other's competition?

Absolutely. I mean up until *Abyssinia*, there was the one or two or three blacks in a show. These amazingly talented people who just don't get a chance to be in a show unless it's a black show. You know what I mean?

Your first production contract was for the national tour of *Once on This Island*.

I did two and a half months as a swing. That was a major breakthrough.

And right after that you booked *Tommy* and *Miss Saigon* in the same week.

Yeah. I ended up taking *Tommy* because it was a new show and I was going to be on an album and get a chance to work with Pete Townshend. It was creative, it was going to be something new. I was really green when it comes to this stuff. In fact, I got picked on a little bit by some of the cast members. But I was still just bouncing off the walls. I'm like that goofy guy that people love to make fun of, which I didn't mind. I was so excited about my new show and willing to do whatever you need me to do.

That show was a huge hit.

It was a big deal. I invited my mom to opening along with my brother and my sister, and that's when my mom gave me her blessing. Up until then she was still very worried about me. Unfortunately, she passed away the next year. But I was so grateful that she got to see her son on Broadway.

What do you remember about that time, doing *Tommy*?

Well, God, where do I start? I mean, the high of being hired, the high of being in a hit show was overwhelming, and satisfying, and all that stuff. The high of doing an album and hearing yourself for the first time was really cool. People coming to visit, that was really cool. Ann-Margret, Liza Minnelli—I'm meeting Liza Minnelli! I'm meeting Janet Jackson! Whoa!

And you got to perform at the Tony Awards.
I remember crying. "Listening to You" is kind of an emotional song. But I also remember meeting Diahann Carroll and I'm like. "Fuck, that's Julia!" It was like "Damn, yeah, here I am on a Broadway stage at the Tony Awards. Small town boy who didn't know jack shit about theater. It's really cool."

Damned *Kiss of the Spider Woman*, winning the Tony!
We loved them actually. Our associate choreography was Lisa Mordente, Chita Rivera's daughter. One night, during our intermission, we ran across the street in our costumes to hang out in Chita's dressing room. We ran back over for Act II. We got into so much trouble!

You left *Tommy* to do *Miss Saigon* in Toronto. You were John, a lead role!
Yes! I felt ready. I didn't know what to expect. I had no idea. I just knew I loved to sing. I didn't realize that I needed to have vocal technique by then. You would think I would have figured it out by age thirty. I didn't realize the range of that song ["Bui Doi"]. When I finally got my dream of doing it, it's like, "Oh, shit. I got to do this eight times a week!" And I remember in one of my auditions [casting director] Vinny Liff, God rest his soul, asked, "How's your B-flat?" And I said, "Well, you know, it's okay. Sometimes, it's there, sometimes it's not." He told me, "Don't come back 'til you get it." And I loved him for that. I was in the back of a cab in Toronto, thinking about taking some vocal lessons. All of a sudden there was this card in the television section on the little screen for an opera coach. So I called the guy and I started taking lessons from him. After my six months up there, knowing I'm coming back to New York, he recommends another teacher. I started taking lessons from him.

What about the acting? This is the first time you were really called on to act.
I guess I relied on whatever natural thing I had. Fred Hanson was our resident director, One of the things he taught me was to simply speak my words for like two days. He said, "Let's just speak them. No singing. And I want you to really focus on what you're saying."

That's still an exercise you use now, isn't it?
Yeah, yeah. Because you hear it differently. That helped a lot.

You stayed in *Miss Saigon* for a long time.
Six months in Toronto, two years and two months in New York. I was the longest John on Broadway. I kind of knew after that two years that I was done, so that's when I got my real estate license. They didn't renew me. I'm sure they wanted some fresh meat, and I understood why they did that.

You would have stayed?
Hell yeah.

And how much time did you spend in real estate?
I stayed in it for a few years, but I was really heavy into it for about six months, while I still was auditioning. I was making good money. I didn't really work that hard. I didn't want to work that hard because that wasn't my goal. I wanted just a supplementary income so I could go on to the next gig. I would always wear a suit, no matter what. Because I wanted people to take me seriously. But right after that six-month period, that's when I auditioned for *Side Show*.

Side Show was a breakthrough. Your first time originating a lead.

I remember it being the perfect scenario for me in my career because it wasn't the lead, but it was significant enough to be noticed. And it was a show that people really gravitated towards, even though not enough of them gravitated. I had auditioned for the workshop the year before and they told me that I was too "leading man." A year later they had me audition for it again. I had booked a Wendy's commercial and had to go down to Miami [but went to the audition on the way]. For two hours, they had me learning some choreography, they had me learn a couple of songs, they had me sing with Alice Ripley. And at the end of that two hours, I was kind of emotionally high. They whispered in each other's ears. And [director] Bobby Longbottom just turns to me and says, "How would you like to be part of our family? You got the role." I said, "Can you give me a moment?" I go by a window and I just start bawling. I was just so overwhelmed. The scene itself was really emotional and then getting the part. . . . Who gets a job right there? And I leave there with my bags going to the airport having booked a Broadway show. And I'm still crying in my seat. The flight attendant is like, "Are you okay?" I didn't tell her why. I was just so happy.

That show's an interesting one . . .

It was the same season as *Scarlet Pimpernel*, *Ragtime*, and *Lion King*. And I think we may have gotten the best reviews out of everybody. We opened in October of '97 and we could have picked from any review to put on the theater's wall. It took them two and a half months to put a tiny sandwich board up in front of the theater with our reviews, and it was so small no one could read them. *Scarlet Pimpernel* down the block had an entire wall of review quotes. Our producers were so cheap. They had no budget for marketing. There was no signage. There was nothing. [We had] the dumbest poster. And I remember that was my first time knowing that marketing was very significant in the world of Broadway. There was a lot of—one of the things I hate on Broadway is all of the fourth quarter quarterbacking. "Oh, Broadway just wasn't ready for a show about conjoined twins." That's bullshit. I don't think that had anything to do with it. It isn't a typical show but so what? Market it! We had really terrible houses but we were fighting. We were going out to TKTS and saying, "Come see our show. It's great!"

You personally?

Yeah. All of us were. And we sent messages out—we were in the early stages of Internet. So we're fighting for this show. Fighting, fighting, fighting, fighting. During that time [producer] Garth Drabinsky calls my agent and says "We want to see him for the national tour of *Ragtime*." And my agent says, "He's got a year's contract with *Side Show*." Garth said, "We'll wait." Two weeks later we got a closing notice. I get the job and we start negotiating. At the closing party, the producers of *Side Show* come to me and they say, "We just want you to know that we're going to fight to bring the show back." I said, "If you get it, you can count on me." My agents and I were very transparent with Garth. "If the show raises the money, I'm going to stop negotiating, and I'm not going to do *Ragtime*. I'm just letting you know." They were offering a lot, and a lot of perks, but then I get a phone call saying that we're going to reopen *Side Show*. I stop negotiations with Garth and he lays into my agent, gives him a new asshole. "Who the fuck does Norm Lewis think he is? Doesn't he know that I'm the most significant producer on Broadway? Doesn't he know that he would be meeting the president of the United States?" But the final thing that really made me know I did the right thing: Garth said, "Doesn't he know what I've done for blacks?" I'm done, I'm done. That's what he said to my agent. "Doesn't he know what I've done for blacks?" I go to L.A., vacationing, and I get a phone call; *Side Show*'s not coming back. The director pulled out. That hurt [composer] Henry Kreiger so badly. They thought that this could have been major publicity. It'd be the first show in history to ever come back in the same season. But I get a call saying that it's not coming back. Garth Drabinsky finds out and they offer me half of what we had previously negotiated. It was nothing to sneeze at, more than I had been making, but the perks were gone. And they had to know immediately because they made an offer to someone else and they were going to have to rescind that offer. I called my sister, called another couple of friends. I just sat and meditated on it. And all of a sudden I realized, "You can't do that. Someone already has the job, and I know who it is." I mean, I didn't know who it was specifically, but there's only a few of us out there. So I'm sure I know [the person]. So I turned it down. And I had no job. What did I do? I went back to real estate. Then I got another show [*A New Brain*] but I turned it down because that same week I ended up getting *All My Children*.

But you ended up on the *A New Brain* recording because Chris Innvar was having vocal difficulty after they opened.

Something happened to his voice. He'd been trying to make it through since the beginning and was having trouble. So they asked me to do the recording. I got the music, learned it in two days, and went into the recording studio with the cast. A week later, Chris had decided to leave and they offered me the role. I said, "Well, I'm the low guy on the totem pole over here at *All My Children*. I don't know if they'll need me or not on any given night." They were like, "This is what we'll do: If by 6:00 they do need you, call us, and we will put the understudy on." It was two blocks away. So that's what they did and I only had to call out once. I remember loving that summer.

You worked with an amazing cast: Malcolm Gets, Mary Testa, Kristin Chenoweth, Liz Larsen, Chip Zien, and Penny Fuller. Graciela Daniele taught you the show?

She was so passionate! I had to learn the show in a week. She was teaching me about the tango that they did in the show. That was when I learned that tango originated with men. It was a competition between guys. That was their way of showing their masculinity. I just loved her teaching and her passion in trying to get me into the show and understanding who this character was. I couldn't wait to work with her again.

Working with people of that caliber, did you ever feel out of your league or did you feel like you were up to it?

I felt I was up to it. You know, when I was doing *Porgy and Bess* with Audra, I felt like I was playing a tennis match and if I did not keep up, that ball was just going to keep flying right by me. If you're not there, you're going to look like shit. That's basically it. She's there so you've got to be there. And I also felt that way with LaChanze when we did *Baby*. I felt that way with Sierra Boggess when we were doing *Phantom*.

After *A New Brain* you continued on *All My Children*.

Yes. And I was still doing real estate. I was my broker's assistant. I was the one that would go do an open house while she did another open house or something like that. I didn't really get into the meat and potatoes of what a real estate agent really does. It would have taken up too much of my time. Then three shows back to back: *Captains Courageous* off- Broadway, Bobby in *Company* in Nyack, and then immediately I got to play Sweeney Todd at Signature Theater.

Those two Sondheim roles were the most emotionally meaty parts you'd done to date at that point?

Yes. Bobby was me. Bobby was very charming, and, in fact, they just wanted me to be me, and then I had to dig deep down at the end of the show. I was actually the right age for it. Donna McKechnie was in the show.

Was she imparting wisdom from her experience in the original?

She did bring in a lot of what she went through in the original and tried to help the director. We had a really good group of people. And right after that, I went down and did *Sweeney Todd*. Now, *Sweeney Todd* was more of a challenge because that is not my personality. [Director] Eric Schaefer was like, "You're doing all the right things. I'm just not getting it. You're not giving me enough." And I just didn't know what to do. Luckily that night the universe God, Jesus, Buddha, Hindu, Moses, whatever, came into my apartment; there was some television program about racism and civil rights, and I got to see people being hosed—you know, I've seen this image before, but for some reason it came into my house that night—people being knocked down and beat up by the police, and it just made me angry. I used that the next day in rehearsal, and Eric said, "I don't know what you went through last night, but that's exactly what I need."

Rage doesn't come so easily to you. Have you found other ways that help you get to where you need to get emotionally?

Yeah. I tap into injustices. If someone were to come at me, I can take a lot. But when I see someone else being wronged, that's when I step up immediately. And so I use that. And what I've learned along the way—I did start training and I use the techniques that I've learned, and also watching other people. In *The Wild Party*, I watched Toni Collette in her process.

***The Wild Party* was another one with high, high expectations. There was a lot of press swirling around that show and the drama between Toni Collette and Mandy Patinkin. You have the star presence of Eartha Kitt in there. You have George C. Wolfe as the director. Were you tuned into all of that? Or doing your best to filter it out?**

I remember it brought us closer. Like you said, the swirling around, some negative, some positive, some high expectations—we just bonded as a group and we tried to be true to the story. That was all we could do. I remember realizing how genius Michael John was. His music was very smart. I remember loving the challenge of it. And also being with the legend of Eartha. I mean, she was seventy-four at the time. When she was offstage, she would be doing sit-ups or pushups. She was very strong, very fit. I used to call her Eartha Mae. We got invited to her house a lot. She really loved us. It was great being in that show. We kind of knew it was going to go down and not necessarily be critics' darling.

So when you know that, is performing it every night any different for you?

I'm just doing my thing. I enjoyed it. And what was so great for me was the challenge of communicating this difficult music and making it true. The challenge of it as an artist was so fulfilling. I was hoping and praying that it could translate and people would like it. I just wanted to make sure that I did what I was supposed to do.

I'm going to throw out some *Wild Party* names. Let's free associate. Mandy Patinkin.

Talented. It was amazing to watch his process. It was amazing to be on a stage with someone that I had admired for so long and to learn a lot about him. He's very intense. He does do things differently every night. I admire that.

Eartha strikes me as the opposite. Eartha strikes me as somebody who's very consistent. Does her show.

Does her show. She is. You're very right. She was very, very consistent. I don't think she ever missed a show. And everything was the same. I remember people loving her. She got thunderous ovations several times.

Tonya Pinkins.

Tonya is another one who is consistently inconsistent but not in a bad way. She goes with you. In fact, Mandy and Tonya had a couple of scenes together and it was great watching that. It was like a tennis match.

I loved talking to her for *Nothing Like a Dame*, and one of the things that she makes no apologies about is that that's the way that she works, and hopefully she's with actors who are on it enough to play the game, but during rehearsals, it can be maddening to some actors because they're trying to set a show, and they don't know what they're setting it against. She's aware that for some actors, she can be a difficult partner.

I like it. As I mentioned, when I have worked with my favorite actresses, Audra, Sierra, and LaChanze, we all trusted one another and I felt so comfortable being with all three of them because I could do anything. In *Baby*, we did every fucking thing. Said the same lines, sang the same songs, but it was brilliant. I loved it. I loved going to work. *Porgy and Bess* you just kind of—you never knew. I mean, it was consistent, but yet not, which was great. In *Miss Saigon* when understudies would go on, even though they were told to do the same thing [as the permanent actors] it was always different and I loved it because it helped me keep it fresh.

George C. Wolfe.

George Wolfe was great. He's a genius. I saw an interview the other day with Audra and George and she was explaining that you have to be with George for a while to understand his language. I knew exactly what she was talking about. He says things and you go, "Huh?" And then once you understand what he's trying to say, you're like, "Ohhhhh, okay, okay, got it!" It's like learning Spanish. It really is. He is so quick and his brain works faster than his mouth and he's trying to get things out. So you just wait and you put pieces together. But he's such a genius. I hope I get another chance to work with him again sometime.

After *Wild Party*, your next show on Broadway was only one night, but what an amazing night! September 24, 2001. The *Dreamgirls* concert.

Yeah, that was—I can't even describe how that was because it was hitting all kinds of emotions. People had been wanting to see the show and hadn't seen it in forever. You had three Tony Award winners [Audra McDonald, Lillias White, and Heather Headley] playing those roles. I was lucky enough to be asked to be a part of it. It was right after 9/11. We needed it. We just needed that. It was a great night.

It was your first time working with Audra . . .

Well, I've always had a crush on her. And I'd known Lillias for years, but we'd never really worked together. Heather—it was just great to be in the presence of these people who had done so well and had gotten to a certain level that I was hoping to get to.

Tonya Pinkins calls it "the club."

I felt like I was just being initiated. I got a lot of attention for *Side Show* and that was great. But it was such a short run, and people's memories are kind of short. *Wild Party* didn't last that long either, so not many people saw that. I started meeting people in the club, if you will.

Your next show was Encores! *Golden Boy*.

It was great! I got to work with [choreographer] Wayne Cilento again. And I also got to work with [director] Walter Bobbie. It was great to work with Walter. It was definitely a major initiation to that world of learning shit quickly. I knew how to learn the lines from doing the soap opera, but it was still very difficult. But it was fun. It was a great group of people and we all just kind of pulled together and did it. And who knew that music was so amazing?

That summer, you played Curtis in *Dreamgirls* again, this time opposite Jennifer Holliday.

That was huge. To be starring opposite the woman who was iconic in that show, who I had seen on the Tony Awards? I had not seen her on Broadway, but I heard people rhapsodize about that performance for years. I didn't even really think about it until we were in rehearsals and she started to sing "And I Am Telling You." She wasn't even singing full out. But just hearing that voice on those notes, it all came whooshing out. It was really exciting. That show changed the face of Broadway for a lot of African American actors and inhabiting that role with her just felt huge.

And that same year, you did *Amour*.

I had done the workshop of that show. It was called *Le Passe-Muraille*. It was a really big hit in Paris and they just translated it verbatim. I remember watching [director] James Lapine—because we didn't have much time—wheels spinning in his head. He knew something just wasn't right, and when we revisited it a year later [for Broadway] he just kind of dissected it. He knew that there was a Parisian sensibility that was not going to work in the United States, so he moved songs around and moved the wording around. It was like a little gem. That was another flop in my line of flops, but I enjoyed the show. I thought it was too small for a Broadway show. Off-Broadway would have been fine. But I liked what it ended up being. Michel Legrand's music was—someone said it perfectly—it was very effervescent. It was a very bubbly-type show. It didn't have any big power ballads or anything like that, but it just was a sweet, sweet story. It was really cool to be a part of the process, watching James Lapine put a book together because that's his strength. He knows how to put a book together.

How is he with actors?

You have to get to know him. He's got a very dry humor and if you don't know that, you could be really intimidated by it. But once you get to know him he's very down to earth. He's really good at casting a show, and he's also really good at putting a book together.

You stepped into *Chicago* for a bit.

I got asked to do that role. No audition. That was nice. It was so much fun because you can bring whatever you want to that role. I loved being with all those great, sexy dancers. I got to do it with Charlotte D'Amboise who is one of the most giving people I have ever shared a stage with. My time there was too short. I'd love to go back again.

And then came *Dessa Rose*.

I have to say, it's a really tricky thing for black actors; every time I am offered a role as a slave or a subservient character, I have to really think about it. But this show was saying something pretty special and had things to say I had never heard said before. And this particular slave was in control. And this is fact-based, by the way: He was cunning. He won his own freedom. And he was having a love affair with the white heroine. He was as far away from stereotype as you could get. And it was a chance to work, once again, with LaChanze and some other great people: Ahrens and Flaherty, Rachel York, Kecia Lewis, Michael Hayden. And of course, the amazing Graciela Daniele. It's hard to pass up an opportunity to create in a room with that kind of talent. I was nominated for a Drama Desk for that. That was my first-ever nomination, and I won an Audelco award, so that was pretty great.

You spent some time in L.A. after that and then came back to New York with *Two Gentlemen of Verona* in Central Park directed by Kathleen Marshall.
She was great! It was fun to work with her and to see what she wanted to do with this show. I mean, we did cartwheels on stage. It was a great summer. It was a hot summer, but it was a great summer to be outside. It just was so cool. And yeah, there's a prestige doing Shakespeare in the Park.

But you went back to L.A. after that.
I went out there, and I stayed a year and got very little work. Some bites but nothing much. I was offered some stuff back in New York and I decided to turn it down just because I wanted to stay in L.A. for other reasons, but definitely to try to make the TV thing work, and it just was not fulfilling artistically. I love L.A. a lot but you have to have a reason to be out there. When the offer came to do *Les Misérables* on Broadway, I said, "I've got to take this." I always wanted to be in that show. It was one of the first shows I ever saw on Broadway, even before I got into this business. I got to work with John Caird, who, with Trevor Nunn, was the original director. It was amazing. I didn't know this, but I was the first African American to play it on Broadway. We were in this iconic show and I'm playing a lead role. It was one of the first times I'd ever worn a wig in a show. And it was one of the first times I actually had to worry about makeup. I had to think about an extra routine instead of just jumping in clothes and running out on stage. I worked with my acting coach, Alan Savage. We broke down all the lines. I wanted to try be as specific with the text as I possibly could, and not just sing it well. I was looking for subtext everywhere. It was only supposed to be six months. I felt great to be doing the show, but I still felt like I was trying to make it my own, you know? Then I got *Little Mermaid*. Triton was not written to be black, and I love the fact that they did that. I didn't know the song that well and the director, Francesca Zambello, said, "I want you to relearn this song. Come back in a couple hours. Here, take my iPod. Go study it." She was very insistent. I went away to learn the song, came back, knew it verbatim, and did it. A couple days later, I found out I got it. I finished *Les Mis*, took a couple of weeks off, and then went straight into rehearsal in Denver. We did a costume parade and my costume of mesh looked horrible. They said, "Would you mind going topless?" So I went topless and they used makeup to make me look underwater-ish, and then glitter. If I had known from the beginning that I was going to have to be naked, I'd have negotiated with them to get me a trainer! They wanted me to be hairless so they had to take care of all that monthly. Anyway, cut to—that's where I met Sierra Boggess. It was her Broadway debut. She was fucking phenomenal. Tituss Burgess—amazing. Sean Palmer—perfect Prince Eric. Sherie Rene Scott—incredibly funny. We had a pretty interesting run out there. I'd never worked for Disney before, and to see how everything was put together—they were such a corporation. They want to make sure everything is meticulous and on point. And

also, Francesca was from the opera world so her directing was a different style. It was a little bit more visual.

Could you tell that it wasn't working?

No, no, I thought it was. Because during an out-of-town tryout you try different things. I was okay with the process. I just knew it was Disney and Disney had a lot of money. I figured that they would figure it out. They had been pretty successful in their approach to Broadway by that point. The whole Heelys idea [so the actors could glide on stage to approximate swimming] was interesting at first and questionable. I didn't have to do it but I chose to do it. I said, "I think I need to understand the language of it. Let me learn it." After seeing the rehearsal of the girls singing "Daughters of Triton," and then moving around [on the Heelys], I'm like, "Oh, my God, that's kind of cool!" Did I think it was not working? No. I just trusted the process.

Was it a happy experience?

I had a good time. It was not necessarily artistically fulfilling, but that time allowed me to make enough money to fund my CD. And I got to do other things. So I took advantage of that time.

You said *Les Mis* was your first time having to do makeup. Now . . .

I had to learn how to do the makeup on my face and on my body. I put glitter on my body, which I still find in my house.

After *Mermaid*, you played Sweeney again regionally, and then you did *Sondheim on Sondheim*.

I did a reading/workshop of it like a year before and it was fine, but I just didn't see myself doing it on Broadway. And all of a sudden the offer comes. Then I realized it was this master class/documentary/revue/concert. It became this amalgam of different things, and people loved it. And seeing this iconic woman, Barbara Cook, on Broadway after such a long time, and then Vanessa Williams, and Tom Wopat . . . It was a very interesting six months for me and I'm glad that I did it, even though the money was not necessarily the best. I wasn't sure how bills were going to be paid. But luckily, I got this huge check from a commercial I had done the year before. It's so interesting how the universe works. The fact that I did it introduced me to a whole new audience. I had done nine Broadway shows at that point but still, people were coming to me at the stage door saying that this show had introduced me to them.

How was it working with Sondheim on something so personal to him?

He was there at least once or twice a week. To see him coaching each individual person on different sections of their standout performances . . . I got a chance to sing "Being Alive" in an actual production of *Company* at thirty-seven and it meant something to me at that time, but then ten years later at age forty-seven to sing "Being Alive," it meant something completely different. And then to be coached by him—I would always sing [singing] "somebody hold me too close/ somebody hurt me too deep," and he was like, "Nope, it's [singing] someBODy hold me too close/ someBODy hurt me too deep." He wrote it specifically to emphasize "body." It was amazing to be coached by the guy who wrote the song, giving me the original meaning, the way he wanted it.

In *Sondheim on Sondheim*, alongside Barbara Cook and Vanessa Williams. (Joan Marcus)

Was it ever intimidating?
No, because I'm never that way. I mean, it was trying to make someone proud like you want to make your parents proud. You're doing something that that person wrote, but I never felt that pressure, no.

And what about working with Barbara Cook?
Barbara was this person who I'd seen and listened to throughout the years. All of a sudden being on stage with her, and her voice at age eighty-two, still sounding so healthy, it was wonderful. To hear her experiences, and listen to her speak backstage, and talk about her life, but then, also, at age eighty-two she's still this young lady who's scared, and vulnerable, and wants to get it right. It never ends, which is perfect for me. I believe if you're finally satisfied, then you're dead. She worked so hard. It was fun just hanging out and talking with her. Sometimes between shows I would go and get my food and come back and hang out in her dressing room. She

wanted to be there, you know what I mean? She wanted to be part of a company. She wanted to play with us. And Vanessa Williams, that was beyond. She was always there, always present, always knowing her music. Tom Wopat—just a dude, just regular "frat guy." That's what I love about him. What really would get me every night was Sondheim saying [on video, as part of the show] that he was sixty before he fell in love for the first time. I came to a conclusion personally—I could be totally wrong, but I think he's a great observer of life, and it's hard for him to participate, but later—he later became a participant. But he was just someone that would sit back and watch people, and that's why he was so masterful at putting stories together.

You went directly from *Sondheim on Sondheim* to *Les Mis* in London.
I only did Javert for six months on Broadway so it was nice to have the opportunity to go back and revisit. And to work in the West End? Fuck! The universe gave me a gift by taking me away from this environment because I was going through a major breakup at the time. It was awesome to have a different focus, and to help me try not to think about it. The *Hair* cast was there—mostly Americans from Broadway. Their theater was right next door so I hung out with them when I could. They gave me the lowdown of what England was all about, and they gave me great advice. They said do as much traveling as you can on your day off, so I committed myself to going somewhere every Sunday. Sierra Boggess was there doing *Love Never Dies* and we became closer there. But for the most part, it was a lonely time for me. They are more official over there, more formal. There was a mandatory warm-up before half hour. And there was always an announcement of when you were supposed to go on, on the intercom. "Mr. Lewis, your entrance is within the next five minutes." We don't do that here. I met some new friends that were not in the business and cultivated some really good relationships that I still have today.

You did *Porgy and Bess* immediately after.
Cameron Mackintosh gave me three weeks off to do the workshop. It turned out to be amazing. I went back to London, finished up my contract, and as soon as I got back, I went straight into rehearsal for *Porgy and Bess* at A.R.T. We went through different incarnations of it because we had the permission of the Gershwin Estate, and then Stephen Sondheim wrote a letter to *The New York Times* that almost killed the show. He was trying to figure out why we needed to touch it. He said that it's a beautifully written show and doesn't need to be touched. And I think he was upset because Diane Paulus, Suzan-Lori Parks, and Audra McDonald all said that these characters were not fully fleshed out, and it would be nice to see if we could do something about that in this production. He was really upset about that and how it messes with the composers' original ideas. A lot of people jumped on the bandwagon who had never seen the show. We hadn't even done our first preview. We were just trying things out. But Sondheim's letter really scared a lot of our investors, and some of them pulled out, which meant that we were not going to go to Broadway. [Lead producer] Jeffrey Richards reassured us. He said, "Just stay quiet. Don't say anything. Don't go on social media. Don't do anything." Audra felt like she had to respond, and I thought she did something brilliant. She tweeted, "As the master himself said, 'Art isn't easy.'"

It's interesting to me, though; we don't rewrite music as if we think we can do better. But we can be very casual about the book. It's a bit of hubris, I think, to assume "we got this better than Oscar Hammerstein did" or "than DuBose Heyward did" or whoever . . . Even if you can look at those characters and think, "Oh, that's not how I would write them if I was writing this today," you're not. Somebody else wrote it, and it's their piece, not yours, to rewrite. That's an argument to be made.

As Javert in *Les Misérables* on the West End, a role he'd played on Broadway and would repeat in the starry 25th anniversary concert staging. (Catherine Ashmore©, Cameron Mackintosh, Ltd.)

But we got permission from the Gershwin estates to do that. George Gershwin only got to see the original production in his lifetime, whereas Sondheim has had the opportunity to revisit his shows many times over the years. We don't know what Gershwin might have done had he lived. But when we did it, the show was only being performed in opera houses. Musical theater audiences were not going to see the show. A lot of people are not into recitative for fifteen minutes. Ninety-five percent of the people who came to see it had never seen it. They knew the greatest hits, but they didn't know anything about the story. And quite frankly, when you go see it at the opera, it's not about the story. It's about the music.

What did that whole thing make the working environment like?
Brought us closer together. We wanted to fucking prove a point. We had a successful run at A.R.T. People were blown away, wanted to come back and see it, couldn't get a ticket. Had some time off and they reworked some things, and we came back to rehearsal on Broadway. We were all very excited. It was a lot of our cast's debuts.

The show put you in a different place career-wise.
I did feel like it was a fantastic opportunity. I was happy and overwhelmed by who I was working with. I was just happy and blessed to be in the cast. The nominations were amazing. I really didn't expect anything from it, but it felt good to be recognized and celebrated. I was happy for Audra. It wasn't a show that I'd ever dreamt of doing. To get that role and to have the accolades I got was fantastic. It was a great time. I really enjoyed going to work every day.

You said being onstage with Audra McDonald kept you on your toes.
I can't be slacking. I'm going to work, I am not going to play. I'm going to look like shit if I'm not matching her. There was a trust there and a play. But also it gave me confidence, knowing that I could play with someone who I admired with that much skill . . . Confidence, trust, and playfulness; those three things, those three words. One night, Shonda Rimes's people came to see her because she had done *Private Practice*. That's how I ended up on their radar and how I got *Scandal*. For six weeks or so, I was flying back and forth. I would leave on a Sunday after the matinee, go to L.A., stay as long as they needed me, and then come back and do the show. It was awesome because here I am on a hit TV show and still starring on Broadway, thanks to the generosity of the *Porgy* producers.

You did *Bed and Chair* next.
Bed and Chair was weird. I always wanted to work with John Doyle. And it was a chance to work with Bernadette Peters. Fuck, to kiss on her, be her lover. Yeah! Sign me up! And Jeremy Jordan, that powerhouse of a singer and great guy. And then to have those great dancers, Tyler Haines and Elizabeth Parkinson. Bernadette is such a superstar. Another giving person as well, but she also knows she's a superstar, and holds that. She knows that people are coming to see her and wants to be the best that she can be each time, and she sells it. It was a lesson to just watch her command that stage. My crush became a reality.

And then you got the call for *Phantom*.
I got called in. I remember dressing up, trying to be as Phantom-esque as I could, with a black turtleneck and a blazer and some black pants. We had to sing onstage. I remember waiting in the wings, and closing my eyes, and I saw Paul Robeson, Sidney Poitier, Andre DeShields—I saw people alive and dead all saying, "Go for it, go get this." It was almost like it was audible. And I got it!

And how was the actual experience?

It was great. Sierra called me to congratulate me. She knew because Andrew called her and said, "How would you like to play Christine when he comes in?" Thank God she was there. If she had not been there, it wouldn't have been as much of an artistic experience as it was. I did what they told me to do, but she put in my head some textual stuff that I did not get from them. She says her DNA comes from Hal, Andrew, and Gillian Lynne [from when Boggess starred in the Vegas production]. So because of that, I learned a lot more about who Eric, the Phantom, was.

You said that it was the hardest role you've ever played.

You asked me about the experience. The experience was wonderful. But there's an expectation of a certain sound and a certain way of being that was nerve-racking. It had been ingrained in people's heads for so long, there's no messing up. In *Porgy and Bess*, if I hit a note in a gravelly way, it kind of fit the character, and I could work around that. And I was hitting the same notes or higher in *Porgy and Bess* than I was in *Phantom*, but there's a pureness that people are expecting because the Phantom is so pristine. And it's all about the music. It's all about him teaching her this way of life. That's why he wears the mask and always touches himself—to make sure everything is in place. Even though I was not onstage as much, I never had down time. I had the person putting my face on. I had someone helping me put my clothes on, my shoes on. I never had time alone to really get Eric in my body before I went onstage. And sometimes it was a little challenging because the makeup person was talking to me the whole time, and I'm thinking, "Please just get it done so I can warm up," but I'd have to sit in the chair. I needed that time to get into the character, so it was just very challenging. And going up and down those stairs and sitting on the cross—I was really scrunched in. I'm probably the biggest guy they ever had. I'm not the tallest but I'm the biggest. In the angel, there was only one little hole in which you could stretch your leg out, and I had to be in there for a long time. And you're squatting. You can't make that thing move, so it was that pressure.

You chose not to renew with *Phantom*.

Yeah. I felt like I had done what I wanted to do. Some people stayed there for years. I didn't want to stay there for years. I will say that I got out of it exactly what I wanted, and that was to play that role. I didn't go into it wanting to be the first black Phantom on Broadway, but I wanted the opportunity to do it because I just knew I could do it.

After that, you did a lot more concert work. And then *Sweeney Todd* came about off-Broadway.

The concert world is fantastic; you go in, you do your own show, you have fun with the audience, you make some good money, and it's not eight times a week. The fact that I had done *Phantom* and the twenty-fifth anniversary of *Les Mis* actually helped boost that. Then the opportunity of *Sweeney* came about in September of 2016. I had a meeting with the director and the producer, and that's all it was. It wasn't an audition. It was just a meeting. Because I had done the role twice before, I knew about it. We talked about what I could contribute to the role, and I was eager to see their concept of it. It was a love-fest. Then we start rehearsals, and we only had like ten days of rehearsal. We had a very limited amount of time, six hours a day, and then maybe two hours on the weekend, because we were on the actual set [while the show was performed with its original cast at night]. They had not gotten a studio for us. They were trying to fill in for what the Brits had done and we didn't want to do that. They wanted me to do it a certain way. They were more concerned about the lighting of me bringing the razor up and trying to hit a light so it could reflect onto the audience as opposed to the truth of who Sweeney was, which was pissing me off. And, in fact, I was going to quit the show because I just was not happy. I'm like, "I'm making $2.50 a week, and you're asking me to do something I didn't sign up for. You promised me one thing, and then you're making me do something else." For instance, there was a moment where Mrs. Lovett finds out who I am, and she calls my name out, Benjamin Barker. I ask, "Where's my wife?" and she tells me she poisoned herself at the apothecary, right? To me, what does that sound like? She's dead. But they wanted me to ask about my daughter right away. No time to react to the information. I had just sung "Barber and His Wife," You think I'm going to go, "Where's my daughter?" He was like, "No, mate, we need you to move forward." I was pissed. They wanted me to come in mad, be mad in the middle, and be mad at the end. For a couple of weeks, I was pissed, and I wanted to quit. I even talked to Chuck Cooper. Chuck told me to stay in there. The producers were not getting what they wanted either, and I had to argue with them. "You promised me I could bring my shit." And, in fact, there was a threat of them saying, "Well, maybe we made a mistake." Maybe you did. Do you want to fire me or do you want me to quit? Like I was that close. And luckily, I hung in there. I eventually brought my shit and put it in there, but I couldn't wait to leave. I love the role, but it just was not satisfactory. I got to meet some great, interesting people.

That is the first time I ever knew you to be really at odds with a director. I wonder if your friendliness and collegiality has given people the impression that you are always a "yes" person.
Well, maybe so. Sometimes I think people take your kindness as weakness. It's an interesting rep because if you come across as being difficult and being an angry, black man, that's in front of you. I felt like Barack Obama, like you had to be careful what you said and how you said it, and step in power but step lightly.

So is it always a conscious thing for you then?
Yeah.

I just always assumed that your constant optimism was a personality trait.
It is, but I also know that you have to feel out your environment. I'm genuinely interested in people, and I try to find a common ground in what interests you, and that comes from back when I was working in advertising. It was always making it about that other person. My reputation is important to me. Like out of everything else, my rep is important. One of my best friends told me, "Your gift is not your singing and your acting. Your gift is getting along with people, and making people feel comfortable," and so I've always tried to embrace that. It gets tiring, of course.

You got to come full circle, with a return to *Once on This Island*.
I get a call in December of 2017 about *Once on This Island* from [composers] Lynn and Steve, and they said, "Quentin Earl Darrington's going to be out for a couple of months. We thought it'd be fun to have you come do the role again." So I went to see it, and I was like, "Oh, my God, this is amazing." Twenty-five years later I got to play Agwe again, and it was such a beautiful experience. I loved it. I loved going to work. It felt really good to be a part of a major ensemble. I didn't have to worry so much about my voice since I wasn't carrying the show. I didn't have to worry about—just so many things. It was a great chance to look at the story from a different perspective. And then immediately after, I went into rehearsal for NBC's *Jesus Christ Superstar*. There are probably so many people in the background I need to thank for that

opportunity because they could have chosen anybody, but I think my name was thrown around by friends of friends, which put that in people's heads.

And then *The Music Man* in Washington.
I've always loved that role. It had not been on Broadway in nineteen years, and I went into this with the hope that we could get some traction. I knew that Scott Rudin had the rights and that he wanted Hugh Jackman, but it had not happened yet so maybe I could change the conversation. We had to find the right person to be Marian, and Jessie Mueller was beyond my wildest dreams. I knew that she had a beautiful legit voice, but when you're up there with her, it's something else. I love her. And Rosie O'Donnell, Mark Linn-Baker, John Cariani, Veanne Cox. It was just the perfect cast. We got great reviews, from what I heard. I don't read reviews. And guess what? Two weeks later, they made the announcement that Hugh Jackman was doing it on Broadway.

How much was Barbara Cook in your head?
Oh, the whole time. And, in fact, there were moments that Jessie sounded just like her, and it brought back so many memories of me listening to Barbara doing that, but also memories of Barbara's personality and our friendship. Her spirit was around. I had no idea that I would ever become friends or that close to someone who is so iconic.

At this stage of your career, what do you want?
I've played a lot of the dream roles that were in my head: Curtis in *Dreamgirls*, Bobby in *Company*, Sweeney Todd. I'm waiting for some new stuff. My passion right now is to help younger people in this industry, and it's in a different way than what people think. I'm not looking to teach anybody how to sing, dance, or anything like that, but how to survive in this industry. Kids tell me that they listen to my stuff, that they want to sound like me and that's . . . when people reflect on your career, you go, "Wow. I guess I accomplished something."

12

WILL CHASE

August 2018; March 2019

WILL CHASE WALKS INTO A room ready for action. He's all playfulness and smiles, confidence and mischief, presence and charisma. He speaks rapidly with ideas and stories seemingly ricocheting off the walls and each other, but he also exudes an aw-shucks charm, the product of his Kentucky upbringing. He is neither guarded nor nervous that anything he says might be misunderstood or misconstrued. He is just unabashedly, unashamedly himself, comfortable in his tattooed skin and cowboy boots. That's not to say that he's cocky, but he is assured. And when he leans forward, locking eyes and putting his hand on my knee to emphasize a point, his bouncy energy is suddenly a focused beam and it's electric.

Don't count on his résumé to give any of that away, however. His debut in *Miss Saigon* as the oh-so-serious Chris paved the way for more brooding (Roger in *Rent*, Radames in *Aida*), frustrated anger (Tony in *Billy Elliot*), and narcissism (Rob in *High Fidelity*, Jerry in *The Full Monty*). Only recently has he had the opportunity to show his playful side in shows including *Something Rotten!*, *The Mystery of Edwin Drood*, and *Kiss Me, Kate*.

Since appearing on the TV series *Smash* and then *Nashville*, he's been a fixture on television, often shooting by day while performing on stage at night. He loves the variety. He also loves the money. Money, in fact, is a topic that comes up with Chase a lot. That may be because he didn't have a lot of it growing up, or perhaps because he is a dedicated father with responsibilities. But Chase is unusually blunt about the business of show business. While it's a recurrent theme others have mentioned, Chase does not demur on the topic, admitting freely (proclaiming, even) that he follows the most attractive paycheck, and right now, that's in television. It's a reality that no theater devotee wants to hear, but it is indeed reality. And Chase is quite happy about it. He likes bouncing from project to project, from soundstage to rehearsal room. He likes the challenge and the pace. And fortunately, the business likes him back. We may not see him quite as regularly on Broadway as we used to, but according to Chase, he will always be back as long as they keep inviting him.

When did you start performing?
I was very lucky to grow up in a very musical family with my dad and mom both musicians and teachers. I grew up in the church [musically], but Dad had a degree in music and math and a master's in divinity. My mother played piano and organ and worked in state government. Music was always part of my trip. I happened to go to a high school with a great band, great band director, great choral director that taught me theory. I fell in love with being

Flanked by John Pankow and Lance Coadie Williams in *Kiss Me, Kate*. (Joan Marcus)

excellent at music. I didn't grow up listening to country. My dad was very much a classical music person, and having two older brothers that were awesome at it, having to sing a lot in church, the singing thing was like—what you do. I was good, but I wasn't good enough to be a singer. I knew early on that I wanted to get out of Frankfort, Kentucky. I love Frankfort. I love going back. But I knew that I needed to get out of there. I don't know why I knew that. But trying to be excellent at music added to it. It was very important to me at an early age. I became this really great percussionist and I thought drums were [my path] at first but then as I started to be a conductor, I knew I had some kind of—I hate the phrase—God-given talent, but . . . I watched my dad wave his arms in front of the church choir and knew, just knew, he was excellent. Everybody thinks their family or parents are good, or parents think their kid is the most amazing dancer in the world when they're not. But I knew we were good musicians. I knew I was going to go to school for percussion.

But you did some high school theater. *Bye Bye Birdie* . . .

I knew I was a good singer, and I knew that I enjoyed the acting, but at that point, I wasn't interested. I wanted to use my percussion skills, my conducting skills, to become F. William Chase, not Will Chase. Pretentious, long-haired . . .

Is there some part of you that still wants to be that guy?

That still turns me on. I would love to do it. I think I will. I don't know where and how. I keep revisiting this classical part of me.

So how did you detour into theater?

At Oberlin I became friendly with a theater guy. They were doing *Sweeney Todd* and he said, "I think you should audition for Anthony." So I did [and got it]. Listen, when *Miss Saigon*

Will Chase	
Miss Saigon	National Tour, 1996; Broadway, 1998, 2000
The Full Monty	Broadway, 2001
Aida	Broadway, 2003
Lennon	Broadway, 2005
Rent	Broadway, 2005, 2008
High Fidelity	Broadway, 2006
The Story of My Life	Broadway, 2009
Billy Elliot	Broadway, 2009
Bells Are Ringing	Encores!, 2010
Pipe Dream	Encores!, 2012
Nice Work if You Can Get It	Broadway, 2012
The Mystery of Edwin Drood	Broadway, 2012
Something Rotten!	Broadway, 2016
Kiss Me, Kate	Broadway, 2019

came out I thought it was the biggest piece of crap. I was a total snob. Ponytail and Birkenstocks, just a conductor and a drummer. But I was obsessed with *Sunday in the Park with George.*

You were already a total elitist.

At Oberlin the pretentious thing kicked in and I was all about classical music. But Sondheim made it through. And then enough people—even the opera teachers—said, "You should think about doing this." So I start taking some singing lessons—very few. I wanted to see what they were talking about. Just technique stuff. I learned a lot. My junior and senior years, I took every acting class I could. So, I'm doing percussion, I'm doing conducting. I was spreading myself way too thin. I knew at an early age that I didn't like to do that. I knew that if I'm doing something, I want to do it really well. I didn't like to be concentrating on ten different things. I still don't. But I was doing everything at Oberlin my junior and senior years. And I did summer stock in Cape Cod. Nine shows in nine weeks. I thought, "Okay, if I enjoy this, after this summer, I'm going to be an actor." I did *No, No, Nanette, Annie Get Your Gun, 42nd Street*—I can't tap to save my life. *New Moon. Cinderella.* I loved it, and I knew I was good. Now what am I going to do my senior year? I'm conducting, I'm playing in every ensemble, and I want to take every acting class I can, which I did. I hated my senior year because I was spreading myself so thin. But I still wasn't thinking, "I could do this." And then they couldn't find the lead in this original Jack the Ripper musical in Chicago. It was one of those situations that you read about as a young actor: Ten guys on stage. You all do the same eight-bar phrase from the hardest part in the show. High A. I nailed it. I walked out of the room, and they're like, "Would you like to play this role?"

Were you ready, do you think? Had you learned enough in school?

Something I'm trying to introduce to my nineteen-year-old who wants to be an actor—the craft constantly changes. My craft is constantly changing. I have a method that I use, but it definitely changes. It changes with each show. But I was just so enamored with acting. And I knew that I was a good conductor, but I was only an okay pianist, not great. [Other students in my classes] were better.

So summer stock was a real blessing for you. It allowed you to see over nine shows how you measure up in this arena.

It did. And it taught me about having to shed fears. I teach a bit, and one of the things I teach is to go and try something even though you're going to fail. That's still the hardest thing for all actors. They're lying if they say anything different. In every rehearsal room, we're still up against our own insecurity and our own fear of failure. If you fail you can try again and try again and try again. On TV, the reason you got hired is because of what you did [in the audition]. What you are is what they want, so don't stray too far from that. In the theater, when you experiment and find things, those are the best. My favorite thing is being in a rehearsal room with Broadway people that I like. The worst thing is being in a room for five weeks with people who wear their insecurities on their sleeves. We all have bad days but when it's constant bad days, you're sucking all the oxygen and air out of the fucking room. There's nothing worse. On TV it doesn't matter to me. I don't like being on a set with an asshole but we shoot the scene, great. I might not see you for two weeks. Theater is another thing. I've turned down jobs because I don't want to be in the room with someone for five weeks. I don't mind if you're a pain in the balls artistically. I mind if you're a pain in the balls because of your own insecurities. At this level, c'mon, we're grown people. Let's go have fun.

You are fortunate that you are in a position to make those choices. Back to Chicago, before that was the case. Why did you choose Chicago over New York?
Chicago was a place to find real theater. It still is. I was lucky, lucky, lucky. Got an agent with my first show right away.

The Jack the Ripper show? Where your parents saw you kissing a guy?
Young Lovers. I was fortunate enough to grow up in a very conservative, southern Baptist family that wasn't terribly judgmental. To this day my parents are my biggest fans in the world. They'll come to everything. But yeah, at my first professional show ever, I'm kissing a guy and my parents are in the audience. I'm almost fifty and I still think, "What's Mom going to think of this?" "Mom, you can't watch *The Deuce*. I'm fucking Maggie Gyllenhaal. You're not allowed to watch it. The ladies at church can't talk about this. They can talk about *Nashville*." Anyway, after the show, my dad was like, "It was one of the most beautiful things I've ever seen." My parents are awesome. I don't tell my parents I'm doing readings because they'd fly up and come. I'm like, "Guys, it's just a reading." But they would come.

So life in Chicago as an actor . . .
Was great. I did everything. I did the regional premiere of *Assassins*. I met [my ex-wife] Lori and she was like, "We've got to get you to New York. Let's go." So we moved to New York. The *Les Mis* folks came through Chicago before we left. I go in like every other fucking time [I'd auditioned for them before]. I sang and Richard Jay-Alexander was like, "Do you know the Chris stuff from *Miss Saigon*? I want you to look at it. I'm going to fly you to New York. We're having a tour go out." They asked me to understudy Chris and play one of the soldiers. We moved to New York, and I dove right into four weeks of rehearsing *Miss Saigon*. I went on the road for two and a half years. I eventually took over the role on the road. I was making a shitload of fucking money (for me, then.) It was one of the biggest learning experiences I ever had: experiencing different Kims; taking over the role; what it means to take over the role; how you star in a show; how you sing this shit; fresh-minting something every night. I ended up doing over 1,600 performances. That requires a different discipline that you can't know until you do it. You can't know that. And some people aren't good at it. I'm not saying I was always good at it, but I was good. And I loved it. This will sound cheesy and clichéd, but I still think about it all the time—this audience—they're seeing it for the first time. Even if they're seeing it for twentieth time, they're seeing it for the first time.

This goes back to you being someone who strives for excellence.

Perfection [on stage] can't be doing the same thing every night and expecting this other actor to do the same thing. Perfection comes from paying attention and always adapting. You deal differently every time you're acting, literally every day, especially on television sets. Sometimes I need to do the exact same thing regardless of what another actor is giving me because it's my coverage, and I'm no dummy. It's quick, and it's my coverage, and sometimes this other actor can't or isn't giving you what you need. On stage it changes. So "perfect" for me was feeling this night out, feeling the conductor's tempo differently. We slow down here, we speed up here. I started to realize that my musicianship is what has gotten me through—I mean, it's everything that I am. It's how I hear things. It's how I technically can do things.

But in something like *Saigon* you're fitting into a template . . .

I have to be a certain way, but I'm also trying to bring my own thing. It was eye-opening, but it was great. I was a different human by the time I closed *Saigon*. It taught me how to be on stage every night.

I think that it takes a rare kind of person to be out there on the road for two years and stay conscious as you are describing. You were constantly recalibrating. Many people can, I think reflect on something after the fact. It's harder to be learning and changing as it's happening.

I wish more people had that because, look, teaching acting, you don't want students to be objective at all. You want them to be completely subjective when they're learning and putting together something. The doing of something would have to be completely subjective. You cannot be objective. But I think playing by myself as a child, and I played a lot by myself as a child, taught me—I think that I eventually got good at being objective and then still being able to go on stage and be in the moment. It's the conductor part of me. The way I listen, the way I hear things. And thank God for Peter Lawrence. Peter Lawrence came in [to refresh the show] around the time I got on Broadway with it. "You guys that did the ensemble for ten years? We're going to revisit every moment, every scene." At the end of the day, it still looked like *Miss Saigon*, it was the same show. But what was happening on stage was different. And it was kind of like, "If you're not digging this, there are ten guys around the block who we can call."

Cameron MacIntosh . . .

Cameron was still into it. Cameron wants actors to know their value and that they're being taken care of. Our costume scraps were Donna Karan scraps. You're valuable, even in a twenty-second cross. You're in Donna Karan.

That's interesting because a minute ago you described the notion that "if you're not interested in being here, there are ten other guys" . . . being completely expendable. But at the same time, it seems, while you're here, you are valued.

For some producers. Not everybody. But even on television and film, you make everybody feel like a million bucks on a television set, from top down. Connie Britton, for example, is the coolest fucking lady in the world when you walk on the set. Doesn't mean she's in a great mood every day. Doesn't matter. When she walks in, she is ribbing the crew guys. Everybody feels like a million bucks. When you feel that, that stuff does matter. I understand that it can't be like that every time, and sometimes you're going, "We've got to shoot this fucking thing right now because we're losing the light and I don't care if you're comfortable." I get that. I've heard of Broadway producers who are not like that; they can't all afford to put you in Donna Karan scraps. They make their Will Chases and Stephanie Blocks feel great and they make the ensemble feel like crap. And as I've gone through my career, in *Saigon* and *Aida* I'd show up at work, do my gig really well, and not get into the politics of what's going on in the show and with the cast. That changed in *The Full Monty* years and a little bit after. I was like, "We're all doing this show." I'm an alpha male. Listen, everybody's got their own trips and stuff, but if you're on a trip of deliberately making someone—belittling for belittling's sake . . . No, sorry. Don't talk to me like that. Or don't talk to that person like that. We're all in the room. I've become that kind of guy. Or on a television set, I don't give a fuck. I would have been arrested if I had worked with Jerome Robbins, for example. Probably wouldn't be working. I understand directors having to do things to get to the emotion of a scene. I'm not talking about that. I'm talking about when it's belittling for belittling's sake. I don't have time for that. I really don't. We're family, and we're doing this thing right now. Let's do this. If we should have gotten a break twenty-five minutes ago, I'll be the first person to speak up—you know what I mean? I don't have a problem. I used to shy away from that.

So what changed?
Comfortable in my own skin. People looking to you. And I'm not saying that everybody that looks to you becomes your responsibility.

Let's get back to the end of the *Saigon* tour. You come off of the road from *Saigon* . . .
With no job. It was the end of '97. I auditioned for *Phantom*. Nailed it. Getting told, "Yeah, you're just not right for it." And then right before the holidays of '98, *Rent* was looking for a Roger/Mark understudy.

What were you doing for money? Living off of *Saigon* savings?
Correct. Got a job opening at the Powerhouse Gym in Hoboken, 5:00 AM shift. I got *Rent* on Broadway and I was rehearsing and still doing my side job. I remember my opening night, January 30, 1998. I couldn't believe it. It was exhilarating. I'm in *Rent* on fucking Broadway. It was unbelievable. Lori in the back with a Chanel bag, cutout with a video camera. You had to fit the whole camera in there! So there is footage somewhere of me singing "Will I lose my dignity . . .". Just nervous. So I did Roger/Mark cover. Went on a lot for Mark. Peter Lawrence shows up at a time that I'm on for Roger. After the show he goes, "You want to play Chris in *Saigon* on Broadway?" I asked the producers, "Is there any chance I'm up for Roger [down the line?]" "We just don't know." "Bye." I don't know where I got the balls. Six months—that's all I did, six months. At that point, that was not that long doing that show.

Well, you know where you got the balls. You were getting an offer for another Broadway show.
Yeah but *Saigon* had been around for a while and this was the hot-shit new show. The pay was like $2,000. $2,000? Yeah, I'll do it. Peter Lawrence is really responsible for a lot of moments in my life. When I was on the road with *Miss Saigon*, they were like "They'd like you to come in for Enjolras on Broadway for *Les Mis*." *Les Mis* is one of my favorite shows. I was unprepared. I mean, I flew in, was tired and all that stuff, but totally unprepared. Playing Chris on the road . . . big for my britches . . . Not one of the worst auditions I've ever given, but in my brain at that time. . . . And Peter was like, "What's going on? What are you doing? This is a big chance." It was one of those moments that was like, "Oh, yeah, well, this isn't just going to fucking happen for you. You've got to continue to work this." From that moment on, it was like—it's about getting that next job and auditioning well and being reputable in the industry.

Your next succession of roles were Broadway replacements.

So *Saigon* happened, then I got to do it in the Philippines. It was great. Came back, closed the show on Broadway. Then I go into *Aida*. I stood by for Adam Pascal. Heather Headley loved me. That helped. *Full Monty*, replacing Patrick Wilson, was the first time that I really learned how to star in a show. It was also the first time that I had to carry a show. And it is the first time I allowed myself to be ugly and not be likable. I mean, [the character of] Jerry has a great redeeming moment with his child, which I love, but he was ugly. It opened up everything for me acting-wise. Then 9/11 happened. We're going to close the show. We got our closing notice every week, then they'd take it down, for two months. So you think on Tuesday you're closing Saturday. At that point, Lori's in the show. She was understudying two of the female roles so it was an awesome time. Then I was back at *Aida* for my second go-round. "Do you want to do it with all the pop stars we're going to bring?" Deborah Cox, Toni Braxton . . . "Great." I knew the role. Some of the most fun I've ever had on stage. I loved learning that show. I loved the Elton John. I loved doing it. I loved being in rehearsal. The associate director, Keith Batten, was awesome. We went back to rehearse the scenes the way that [director] Bob Falls wanted them done. The care that existed back in those long-running shows was for the most part really great.

Have you found that in replacing you have sometimes been denied the latitude to find your own character?

On *Billy Elliot*, the associate director was [married to the original actor's interpretation] and then Stephen Daldry came in and goes, "Will, just fucking do what you want to." He's like, "We have him in this role now. Let him discover." But with some of these long-running shows, you feel sorry for some of these associate directors. "He steps left on count three, then turns." I understand some of that.

I understand it because you're trying to give the same show, but at the same time, it's counter to the notion of what theater is.

Right. And the actors who are still doing the show, I have found, really like it when someone new comes in with something different.

So, during the succession of replacement roles, how are you feeling about yourself in the business?

I'm thinking I got to stop replacing.

Separate from that, are you thinking, "I've made it."

Aida was great in that it was Disney money. Back in those days, you could still work for your quote. You still had a quote. Those days are kind of gone. For a role like Radames in *Aida*, making that kind of money doesn't exist anymore. In a show like that, they are either going to get somebody really famous and pay them a lot of money, or they will get an unknown [and pay scale]. There's no way Drew Gehling in *Waitress* is making what I made in *Aida*. There's no way. It's wrong. He should be. But producers don't want to necessarily do that, and most actors are okay with that. That's fine. Theater—unless I am doing it for love, and I think I only do it for love now . . But if I'm doing it because you want me in your show, you better pay me what I am worth, what the market value says. Because to do it, I'm turning down television for the next year? No, I'm not turning down potential television work that will change my life financially. And to be clear, we're not talking about an exorbitant amount of money. Anyway, after *Aida*, I knew that I had to do something original.

You did *Lennon*. That was a conscious decision? You turned down replacement work?

Yes. I wasn't financially stable, but I wasn't in the poorhouse. I knew that I was going to get offered things, and I gave myself a year to turn things down until I was offered something new. With *Lennon* of course it was a huge failure. But it was great being in a show with Terry Mann and Chuck Cooper, guys who'd done a million fucking shows. Terry was in his early fifties, and I'm becoming that now. I look back at the things Terry would say to me. He gave me great advice about learning to pour yourself into something whole-heartedly, but not so much that you lose yourself when you're not performing. Balance, I think, was his point. And that's really what I think, with age, I've gotten really good at. Doesn't mean I don't pour myself into roles, but when I'm not at work I really let it go. Doesn't mean I don't work at home, learn lines, read, contemplate. But I really try to carve out what should be work time and what should be home time. And it's made my life a lot more fun and relaxing in the past several years, trying to adhere to that advice. Also, he told me all you can do is show up and do great work. But you can't control anyone else and their process—including producers, creators, etc. That, of course, was on the heels of realizing *Lennon* wasn't going to be a hit. You can only do your part and control your input. And that has definitely been useful advice over my years of hits and misses in the theater! Anyway, it closed within a month.

Could you tell it wasn't working?

When I got the first script, it was this downtown, kind of dark—we're playing our own instruments! Then it started spinning into this Broadway show. There's a band on the stage.

Rocking out in the "last real record store on earth" with Jay Klaitz (*left*) and Christian Anderson (*right*) in *High Fidelity*. (Joan Marcus)

You're not playing your own instrument, you're pretending. If I'm playing something on stage, I want to be playing. The Boston run got cancelled so we could go back to the studio and fix things. You knew. But I got to be in the room with Yoko Ono, so that was all dreams-come-true for me. I was bummed, but I'm no dummy. We knew.

High Fidelity was next. Another big disappointment.

I was going through the thick of a divorce, my girls were six and four, I was in a new relationship. Out of town in Boston—I remember thinking, "Okay, the show needs work but . . ." There are two shows where I still don't understand what happened: that one and *The Story of My Life*. I know there have been other incarnations of *High Fidelity*; a buddy of mine did a production of it in Chicago. I wonder if it would work now. I love the antihero. I love the guy that we don't want to love. But with these shows, one thing I learned: It's not about me. It's not, "Will Chase sucks." I know when I don't fit something, and it's usually well before I'm auditioning for it. I can read a TV piece right now and know I don't fit or I don't like the material enough to figure it out. I knew that I worked, and I knew it wasn't about me not working in it. That show opens and closes in a week and a half. I was devastated. Not like I was in *The Story of My Life*, but I was devastated. *The Story of My Life* was like, "Are you fucking kidding me?" I mean, Malcolm Gets and I gave up offers for other things because of this little chamber piece we wanted to do. You [the producers] didn't know what this was when we did it out of town? We didn't think it was going to run for more than three months, but why have you made us all put our lives on hold if you were only going to run it for four days? With *High Fidelity*, it was like, "Oh, we really missed the mark." The show closes. Newly divorced. This is all December of 2006. New agent. So I immerse myself in pilot season. I have fifty-five pilot offers that year. I tested for six of them. That's when I realized this TV game really is a game. And I was like, "Oh, I have to be part of this game to succeed." I had done little bits of television. I was in my mid-thirties and starting to feel like a dad. I fit in the lawyer/dad/policeman type of television. And then I started auditioning and getting roles: 2007 is the year that I did not set foot in a theater. Then *American Idiot* shows up on the radar. "They really would love to see you." I love Green Day with passion. So I auditioned for *American Idiot*. I immersed myself. It's one of the best auditions I've ever given. Poured my soul into it. Get the call maybe a week later. Didn't get it. I've learned to let things go. But I was bummed. I get a call, "They would like to offer you *Billy Elliot*." I literally just found out I'm not doing the other thing. I was like "I'm not going to replace, but let me see the show." Eat those fucking words. I was over the moon. I loved it. I couldn't believe it. So I'm replacing, I'm making good money, but I was having my contract TV outs. I can go do whatever I want to television-wise, and I did. Performing *Billy Elliot* every night was one of the most wonderful things I've ever done. Rehearsing it was a pain in the balls. We rehearsed constantly. But thank God I had the release of TV. I started doing recurring roles, and I started getting offers on jobs that would take me away for a week. It was awesome because I could come back to my Broadway show. I was living the dream.

Let's back up. You said that after *High Fidelity*, you didn't set foot in a theater for a year. Is that because you were so burnt out from the experience?

Sad. Was burned out. How dare they not like my piece. Why isn't there room for this? There's room for all kinds of crap. Why isn't there room for this? I know it's not the best piece ever, but . . . So yeah, I was just disenchanted. I didn't want to go to the theater. Walking up 8th Avenue, you don't look down 45th Street. I never once got mad. I never thought it was because of me. But it was heartbreaking.

Sutton Foster told me that when *Thoroughly Modern Millie* opened and it got disappointing reviews, she went through several months of real depression because she thought, "I'm carrying the show, and if it's disappointing, it's me."

I've never thought that. My ego was too big. In rehearsals, however, I had heard about Walter Bobbie being that old-school kind of bossy, picking the person that they're going to pick on for no reason or whatever it is. I mean, on the third day he got rid of the musical director. So I knew that that was a game. If I'd been younger, I think I would have been scared. I knew that [scare tactics] was a thing. That would never motivate me, ever. He was just the wrong director. Walter can direct some musicals. This was not the one he should have directed. [Composer] Tom Kitt and I talked about it. A year later, he's winning the Pulitzer [for *Next to Normal*], but first he's written the worst musical ever? They were changing it literally moment by moment. In New York previews I was learning a new monologue virtually every night. It's like, "You're not letting me figure this out. Let the actor figure this out before determining that it doesn't work." You [the creators] are good. We can all be good. But you can't just change it willy-nilly so I'm a nervous wreck. Jen Colella talked me off a couple of intermission ledges.

It sounds like *Billy Elliot* was redemptive.
It was redemptive in a lot of ways. I ate those words, "I'm not going to replace," but I knew it was a hot-shit show. I knew it was a dark role. I knew that I loved the artistry of it. The boys were amazing. The staging was beautiful. And I needed the money. It was like the perfect setup for where I was in my career, starting this TV adventure. Doing the show every night was one of the most rewarding experiences of my life. But [when we weren't performing] it was toxic. The way they ran the show . . .They treated the boys poorly. They rehearsed it nonstop, like it was a ballet company. We're not a ballet company, we're a Broadway company and we have to do the show at 8:00 every night. You can't have us all rehearsing all day. You just can't. The energy level required by this show, down to the last ensemble person, is insane. It was toxic.

Is that the first time that you felt like it was a toxic environment backstage?
Yeah.

And so how did you cope?
I drank. I drank a lot. I drank during the show. I coped also by getting to do television. But Greg Jbara was just like, "This is awesome. Stop drinking. Don't do it in here right now. Will, you're not digging ditches. You're on Broadway. I'm not saying that's easy. You've worked hard. But calm the fuck down." It was moments like that . . . But that also doesn't excuse how that show—it was the management. I understand that ballet is part of the show but it's not a ballet for everybody. And these kids . . . Like enough. They're going to fucking crack and so are we. So I look back at that and go, 'That was both rewarding and toxic for me.' That was when I really started becoming a TV actor. I was thinking, 'I would like to make money, and I love the challenge of TV.' When you make an inroad in television, you want to keep that. I love the television pace. Films I've worked on are slow, slow, slow. I love the TV challenge of "right now you have to have this emotion. NOW!" And it's only fed my theater. I love theater, but I'm also getting older. I love television. I love the challenge of the acting on television. I love the pay. I love the pace. Would love to get a television show and in my hiatus do a play next and do that every year for the rest of my life? Yeah. I love theater that much. But I don't love that as much as I love television right now.

But you used to.

I used to because it was the only thing I knew. And unless the piece really speaks to me . . . like *Moulin Rouge*: I was ready to do it. I was ready to put things on hold. I was ready to go to Boston. Wait around. Come to New York. Wait around. But not for that money. I can't live my life like that. So no. Not for the love of it for a long-running show. Will I do *Kiss Me, Kate!* for no money for six months? Yeah. And I love [director] Scott Ellis. I love Kelli O'Hara. I love [Roundabout artistic director] Todd Haimes. I love everybody there. I love it. When a new piece comes along, it really has to move me on the page. Like with *Story of My Life*; when *Story of My Life* happened, I did a reading of it. I knew what that piece was. I knew it was storytelling theater, hour and a half. There was no, "Man, I hope it gets bigger when we have a budget." This is what we're doing. And I wanted to tell that story of these two friends. Totally unsexy, totally not all these things that we want Broadway to do. But if tickets cost $100, it becomes about other things. I can't worry about that.

Well, you have to worry about it though, right? Even though you can only focus on the work, the business element is certainly your concern.

I have to like the piece and then do that piece. I'll show up for my interviews, and I'll do everything I can within reason to promote your show, but it's got to speak for itself. And while I never thought *The Story of My Life* was going to run for more than two or three months, I never in my wildest fucking dreams thought they were going to give up on it in a day. We're having a company meeting at 7:00 the night after opening. Why didn't they tell us at 3:00 in the afternoon so we had time to digest it? They're telling us just before curtain? What did you think the reviews were going to be? I literally heard him say the words "We're closing," and I was out in the alley on the phone with my ex going, "I'm fucking coming home." She's like, "You have to stay and do the show." I was beyond livid. I wasn't upset at the world; I was upset at these people. I'm in my dressing room with all my opening night gifts still unopened with my manager and my dad. One of the few times I've sworn around my dad. And now I don't trust anyone. I don't believe I've gotten a television job until I'm on set shooting. I've got this protective bubble around me now.

Between *Billy Elliot* and *Story of My Life*, you actually had an unexpected sojourn. You did *Kiss of the Spider Woman* in Washington.

Oh, God, yes, of course. Oh, my God, I forgot. That was one of those great, little nuggets in my life. Hunter Foster is—and he's a director now, but if that had come to Broadway that would've changed his fucking career. He was beautiful. He was amazing. It was great. It was one of those nuggets before I went back into *Rent* that was so grounding. [It reminded me] oh, yeah, I love acting. I love character. Remember when I used to pretend that I could play any character. Well, for the last ten years I've pigeonholed myself as a leading man. What does that mean? That means you worked out. That means you look a certain way. I forgot that I play characters. We pigeonhole ourselves like everybody else pigeonholes. And we do it just as badly as the casting director does it. I did *Spider Woman* and then when I went back in to play Roger in *Rent* the last time, it was like night and day.

You said at one point that being in the closing cast of *Rent* you thought, "Oh, my God, I was part of that." Do you still feel that way?

Oh, yeah. I don't know that I'll ever understand the phenomenon that was. It's changed so many people—it's changed people's lives. When people say, "That piece got me through," you're like, "Oh, fuck yeah." And it changed theater.

After *Billy Elliot*, you did *Smash*.

After *Billy Elliot*, I was doing a shitload on TV, and then I did *Smash*. That was my first foray into being on set every day. They kept trying to get it right but the rules kept changing. The pilot, which I thought was phenomenal . . . "Let Me Be Your Star" is really a book number in the show. We're singing. It's breathtaking. Well, no. Once we started shooting Episode 2, the rules now are we're only singing practically, when it's the show within the show. "What do you mean? I thought our characters sing." Then the rules would change again. It was frustrating to say the least. Either my character can sing or he can't, not he only sings in rehearsals. It just missed the boat. They had this amazing cast. We wanted it to be great. Amazing. Listen, I had a great time shooting it. Fell in love with Debra Messing. I got to hang out with Christian Borle all the fucking time. We became besties. I made money, and it boosted my career. In the second season, they got rid of many of the guys. It was a bummer but it freed me up to do some other things. That next year with *Drood* and then *Nashville*. My life changed. When I got the call for *Drood*. I'm like "*Drood?* Be still my heart." I loved Howard McGillin [in the original]. Loved this character. If I could do that show for two years, the fun we had, I would do that show. We had so much fun I can't even tell you. Everybody across the board was just so much fun. That's a hard show to direct. Scott Ellis was learning, too, and it was the first time that I realized that directors don't always have all the answers. They're not supposed to. We're all learning. Everybody's allowed to be open and themselves and fail. I knew we were doing something good.

Any particular recollections of Chita Rivera?

Well, she's a notorious prankster! She would always be in the wings with something. It could be a big face of you on a stick. Everybody in the wings would have a big face of you on a stick. Or she'd have a pizza box you open up, and it would say something cheeky.

Trying to make you break?

Absolutely about making you break. Very rarely onstage. Sometimes she'd say stuff under her breath, and she has that low laugh that I always loved. And the thing about Chita is—I mean, it's probably just because she's done so many shows, and she's been onstage so many times—she doesn't always know her lines. That's age and memorization. She didn't give a fuck. It wasn't like she was in the wings going, "What's my next part????" which I've been known to do, even if it's my 300th performance of the thing. But she's just fucking around with people, saying things under her breath, and she's just dear. I remember when Warren Carlyle, who choreographed *Drood*, was staging the Act I finale and he's like, "Will, you're going to come through the line here, and you are going to be with Chita center stage." And I thought, "I'm going to be dancing, step, touch, kick, with Chita Rivera center stage. Oh, my God! Like who am I?" I texted my mom that night, just proud as you could be. I can't believe I'm dancing center stage with the quintessential dancer, do you know? Who can still kick a leg up high at eighty! I wanted *Drood to* run for three years. It was the most fun I've ever had onstage in my life. And then to be with Stephanie Block? We got our Tony nominations. The show had closed and we had no chance of winning. No chance. It was almost liberating. I could get drunk at all the Tony parties and not care. I didn't have to go do a show. But we talked about how this felt right. We finally got this recognition from the community. If I ever win a Tony, it'll be fucking amazing. But I'm honest when I say I could care less if I ever win. I really could. I'd love to get nominated for everything I ever do, but I really don't

"There You Are" with Eric Sciotto, Shannon Lewis, Kyle Coffman, Nicholas Barash, and Chita Rivera in *The Mystery of Edwin Drood*. (Joan Marcus)

care if I win. Would I love to win it someday? That would be amazing. But it really was nice to just be nominated.

So you did *Nashville* . . .

And literally the day that ABC cancelled *Nashville*, Kevin McCollum texted me and was like, "Hey, want to come do *Something Rotten!*?" I was like, "No, I don't." And of course he knew that I knew that he knew I was out of work. I said, "I'll be auditioning a lot now and I'd rather not be tied down." "Come do it for six months." "No way." "Four months." "Nope." "Three months, and you can shoot whatever you want whenever you want to." "Let's talk money." I had done all the original workshop stuff. Basically, I created the role with Danny Burstein who was playing the Brian d'Arcy James role. We both had commitments so we knew that if the show went forward neither of us would be available. But at this industry reading in the back row was fucking Christian Borle and Brian d'Arcy James! [who ultimately assumed the roles]. Christian was laughing. He would laugh at anything I do, even if it's not funny, which is why he's one of my dear friends. But he was dying. Anyway, cut to him winning his Tony. Anyway, I knew this piece and loved it and was bummed, but I was on *Nashville* making a shitload of money and starting my television career. So, to get to come back and do it was great. I'm in rehearsals the week before I'm supposed to go on for *Something Rotten!* And I booked *The Deuce*. So I opened my show and then I missed the next two shows because I was shooting. Then I booked a series regular on a show that lasted just a year called *Time After Time*. Throughout the run I was shooting during the days. It was one of those moments—one of those arrival moments. I know it sounds weird. I am tired as fuck but living my dream. I'm in a Broadway show and shooting two television shows. One as a series regular. And at night, I get to have fun doing this thing I always wanted to do. I'm living my dream.

Were you able to take that in? Or were you overwhelmed?

I loved every second of it. And I realized this wasn't one of the accolade moments, winning the Tony where you're the hot shit for a little while. This was the actual footwork. At the end of the fucking day I felt awesome. I'm doing a Broadway show, and I'm having fun doing television and making a lot of money. I'm doing all the things that I want to do. It wasn't about high profile. It was working. I don't care at the end of my career, whenever that is; I hope I die onstage or in front of a camera—that'd be weird. I could give a fuck at the end of all this if I'm the guy whose name no one can remember. I want them to go, "Oh, he's the guy from the thing. He was awesome." I want to do a lot of work. I want to be known as a chameleon. I watch someone like Bryan Cranston, who I admire so much, become this fucking amazing thing in his forties and fifties. When the Broadway show was over, *Time After Time* didn't get renewed, and you're back out there auditioning. You're expecting a little bit more heat. You have cachet, especially in the television world, but you're not quite at the place where everybody's offering you everything. It slowed down. I mean, I was guesting on a lot, but that's slowing down for me after having some high-profile series regulars and things. I did *Madam Secretary*, *Versace*, and *Sharp Objects*.

Did you enjoy the actual work in *Something Rotten!*?

Oh, my God, it was so fun. Rob McClure was fucking phenomenal. Christian has great mischief about him that I love, that I try to steal sometimes for a lot of different things. I'm mischievous but not in the same way he can look mischievous. Look at any picture of him smiling for a red carpet, and it's like he's up to something. I love that. It's a quality that I try to infuse sometimes in characters. I couldn't get my arms nearly as big as his for the role. It was funny mimicking him mimicking me-ish. Do you know? Once I got past the tap dancing, it was a lot of fun. I'm terrified about tap dancing, but it was fun.

And now you're doing *Kiss Me, Kate* with Kelli O'Hara, with whom you did *Bells Are Ringing* at Encores! and *Nice Work if You Can Get It*, and *Oklahoma!*

We did *Oklahoma!* In Oklahoma! *Bells* was a lot of fun. That was when I first got to hang out with her and realize what a goofball she is in rehearsals. Like "Oh, my God, you're really funny." [*Kate* was] a year and a half in the making. I've been working on *Kate* in some form for that long. I watched every fucking *Taming of the Shrew* I could. I read every edition of *Taming of the Shrew*. I started learning Shakespeare. I watched every *Kiss Me, Kate*. Not to mimic performances but to see tone, and understand why, and how. That kind of stuff. On television, you can't do any of that kind of work because they haven't written the script, but for theater you have to do that kind of work.

You told me this is the first time you've felt that you had to live differently to protect your voice. Is that because you find that this show is that much more taxing or because you are older?

All of the above. I have to sound clear and big and pretty. It takes more of that big sound. That, in turn, means I have to rest more. As you get older, it's just harder to do. You're more tired.

Does that make it harder to do the stage door, especially now that so many more people seem to wait?

I've never ever, ever felt an obligation to that. That said, I'm flattered. I love it. I will spend however much time. I will sign autographs and talk 97 percent of the time. I waited at stage doors for Rebecca Luker, Bob Westenberg, Mandy Patinkin, Howard McGillin . . . I know what that theater experience is like, and you want to say to this person, "You were amazing!" Sometimes after the matinees I don't go out. I stay in. I have already ordered food. I turn on basketball or whatever I happen to be watching, I eat and sleep. Then there are times that something has happened in my personal life, or I'm in a bad mood, or the show didn't go well. It's very rare that the show didn't go well that I go "I can't" but I have, in the past, been that guy that had a horrible show vocally and I can't have them go, "What a great job you did."

Are you sorry that this is a limited run and that you can't continue?
We were talking about *Kiss Me, Kate* maybe extending, but Kelli has commitments. I never want to be in a long-running show ever again. I don't need that fix anymore. I don't need to show that I can do that anymore. *Saigon* for three years, *Full Monty* for a year. *Billy Elliot* for a couple years. I liked the security of that. But artistically, for me, there's not enough payoff in finding something new two years into a run of a show. Talk to me after I've been on a TV show for six years or something. But also, the payoff for that is the payday. I would love to make a lot of money to where I can do whatever the fuck I want: television, theater, whatever. I want to work because I love it, and I want to dig my teeth in. I want to be challenged. I think I'm challenged by Fred in *Kiss Me, Kate*. I don't ever want to lose that.

You told me that you don't think of yourself as one of the actors who is beloved by the community.
I think that there are actors—I'm going to name a few: Laura Osnes, Santino Fontana, Norm Lewis—and I'm not trying to self-deprecate either, but those names that I mentioned are beloved theater people. That doesn't mean everybody loves them—but they are beloved in the theater community by certain critics, by certain voters, by the people that pay attention to theater. They are the ones who always say "yes" to the benefits and the ones who are asked to do tributes and such.

And you perceive yourself on the periphery?
Yeah. Well, I mean, when I hear you say it like that, that sounds stupid. Maybe it's because I haven't had that big moment. And it's funny, doing this show and being part of the community again is probably why I'm vocalizing it the way I am. When I am not in a fucking show, I could give a fuck. Isn't that weird? It doesn't define me. But I want to be invited to the party. I don't even know what that party is and what that even means. Of course, I want people to love my performance in *Kiss Me, Kate*, but I don't care to the point where it's like if I don't get a Tony nomination . . . that's not why I'm doing this show. I love Kelli. I love Scott. And now I love all these people in this show. But for years—I'm not kidding—my big things were before Sondheim dies, I need to be in a Sondheim show or do something with Steve. I don't even know what I'm searching for in that, other than validation from a group of people I don't even know exists. I love my body of work. I can easily say I don't love how it happened. I mean, sometimes it was absolutely horrible, and check to check, and all those things. Or being in a Broadway show that closed in three days. I mean, those moments kill you. Those moments kill your soul. Why do I do this? Fuck everybody. You know what I mean? I can look back at those now, and they only inform my wanting to do something like *Kate* just to do *Kiss Me, Kate*.

You've got nothing to prove.
Nothing. Well . . . a little bit. The good part about my whole journey . . . I've had a hodgepodge, but that allows me to not—I feel like now especially I don't get pigeonholed. People that have only seen me do *Kiss Me, Kate* go, "Wait, he was Roger in *Rent*?" I get that a lot. I mean,

for me, it's Sondheim. If I can do one of those fucking Sondheim tributes . . . but I never get asked, and I don't think it's because people don't think I can sing it. I just don't think I'm in the world of these beloved Broadway actors. I don't know where I'm going with this beloved thing other than it's something I say. It's "Oh, God, fuck that, I don't need that. But can I get invited, please?"

13

CHRISTOPHER SIEBER

February 2018

IN MUSICAL THEATER, THERE ARE many people who do comedy brilliantly. But there are very few leading man clowns. We're not talking people who can land a joke; we're talking about a take-no-prisoners style that throughout his career became Christopher Sieber's most valuable asset: an adventurous fearlessness in go-for-broke comedy wherein he seemingly lives by the mantra "more is more." Sure, he was handsome as a Ken doll and could sing like a dream, but his comedy was that of a daredevil and it nabbed him a pair of Tony nominations for *Spamalot* and *Shrek*.

Sieber describes himself as the elementary school class cutup from his hometown of Wyoming, Minnesota (population: 642. There was literally a man who changed the population sign after a new birth). It took until the seventh grade for Sieber to get his first taste of performing a solo, when he sang Neil Diamond's "Love on the Rocks." "You hear the crazy applause. I need more of this drug, please. I need more of this fix." He got it by joining the high school speech team, eventually winning first place at nationals, performing a cut from *Torch Song Trilogy* by Harvey Fierstein with whom he would share a Broadway stage thirty years later. *Torch Song* was forbidden by his devoutly religious mother, but Sieber was undaunted; he just didn't reveal his material to his parents until after he'd returned from Washington and won the punchbowl. That same bucking of control took over when his parents refused to help him move to New York. Instead, he paid his own way at eighteen years old.

Almost as soon as he got to Broadway, Sieber was one of its stars with a résumé that included original works (*Triumph of Love*, *The Kid*, *The Prom*), replacement parts in established hits (*Beauty and the Beast*, *Chicago*, *La Cage aux Folles*, *Pippin*, *Matilda*), and the aforementioned big shows for which he was most celebrated (*Spamalot*, *Shrek*). Even with a dozen Broadway shows on his résumé, however, he is probably best known for his time on television in the series *Two of a Kind* (in which he played father to the Olsen twins) and *It's All Relative*, each of which ran a year. Of course, in New York, it's another matter. "I always call it 'The Eight Block Radius Famous,'" he laughs. "You can't go anywhere without saying hello to somebody, or a theater fan saying hello to you, which is perfect and wonderful. You see everybody you've worked with. We were all the nerds and we grew up and now we're on Broadway—the community that I love more than anything. We know how hard we've worked to get here, so everyone is grateful and respectful of each other. It took everything we got."

Sporting one of Broadway's more memorable manes in *Spamalot*. (Photofest)

Christopher Sieber

Paper Moon	Milburn, NJ, 1993
Triumph of Love	Broadway, 1997
Beauty and the Beast	Broadway, 1998
Into the Woods	Broadway, 2002
Thoroughly Modern Millie	Broadway, 2003
Chicago	Broadway, 2004, 2011, 2013, 2016
Spamalot	Broadway, 2005; West End, 2006
Shrek the Musical	Broadway, 2006
La Cage aux Folles (as Georges)	Broadway, 2010
The Kid	Off-Broadway, 2010
La Cage aux Folles (as Albin)	National Tour, 2011
Pippin	Broadway, 2013
Matilda	Broadway, 2014
Big River	Encores!, 2017
Annie	Milburn, NJ, 2017
The Prom	Broadway, 2018
Cinderella	Milburn, NJ, 2019
Company	Broadway, 2020

You put yourself through school.

[When I told my parents I wanted to go to the American Musical and Dramatic Academy in New York] they were like, "We're not going to help you with that." I was like, "Okay." That frustrated them to no end because they did not want me to leave. They offered their furniture to me if I stayed. My parents are awesome right now, but I'm just saying . . . I worked my ass off. I did every job that I possibly could. I worked at a carwash in Forest Lake, Minnesota. I worked my way up from towel kid to sprayer to assistant manager to head of detail. I would get there at 6:00 in the morning and would leave at 9:00 at night every single day for about a year. I saved up a lot of money. I bought my own airline ticket, I put my own down payment on school, I paid for my rent in New York City all by myself. And then I pretty much put myself through school. [I arrived] October 3rd, 1988, scared out of my goddamn mind. Landing at LaGuardia, and taking a cab, and just being dropped off at 73rd and Broadway. The cab takes off and . . . it's all you. Our apartment was really a flophouse. Even then I knew it was pretty awful. It was a studio apartment, and the closet could hold about a jacket. We did have a bathroom, a hotplate and a refrigerator. No microwave. I shared it with Dirk Etchison from Indiana and I thought, "This is living." I didn't leave the apartment the first day I arrived because I was scared out of my mind. But Deb Bendix [my speech coach from home] said, "Be afraid. Always be afraid. But never let fear stop you. Just go forward with the fear." And so I went out. I worked for this toy store on 73rd and Columbus, The Last Wound-Up. One of the students at school was working for this guy named Barry Hendrickson, a [Broadway] wig designer. This kid was his dog walker and kind of personal assistant and he was leaving [and offered me his job]. He introduced me to Barry, the most outrageous homosexual I had ever met in my life. This flamboyant, crazy, fabulous, wig designer, and we hit it off. I walked his dogs, I went grocery shopping for him, I cleaned his kitchen every now and then. He was one of the reasons that I knew it was okay to be gay. I wasn't necessarily out at that point. Coming from this small town in Minnesota, it was just intoxicating. Look at these people just living their lives like no one's watching. I love it!

Were you attempting to audition at all?

There was this new ship in New York Harbor that just started hiring actors, The Spirit of New York. I auditioned for it and got the job. You're auditioning for a waiter job, but then you get to sing so it's great. The show was horrible. But you're in New York Harbor. You're in the beast. You're pretty much on Broadway! Andrea Burns and Idina Menzel were with us. We had vests that were black during dinner and then when it was show time, we would turn them inside out and they were shimmery red. The whole show was about fifteen minutes, and the last three minutes were, of course, an America tribute. That's how I put myself through school. There was a rumor that the mafia was laundering money through the ship, but it put me through school. [And then I was] hitting the boards, waiting in line [at auditions] just like everybody else. Getting there at the crack of dawn. I auditioned for the Troika Organization and got *Anything Goes* at Harrods Casino in Atlantic City. Troika had a bunch of people that they always kept around, and they called us the "affiliated artists." They paid $1,000 a week whether you're working or not, but you are signed to only work with them. I worked for them for about two years. That was a great place to learn skills. I was scared of being Equity actually. I was like, "I am not ready to play in the big boy sandbox yet." So I was grateful for the experience because I was making really good money for a twenty-two-year-old and learning. It became clear to me that you can communicate with an audience. You can feel them with you or not with you. You can rehearse and rehearse but the audience is going to tell you right away if you're on the right track or not. I paid attention to that all the time. And I also learned that the people you work with are going to become your best teachers, good and bad.

So your first Equity gig . . .

Paper Moon at the Paper Mill Playhouse with Christine Ebersole, Greg Harrison. Linda Hart, Chandra Wilson, Johnny Bolton, Brooks Ashmanskas, John Dossett. God, it was like an insane cast! I considered that my very first Broadway show because we did indeed sign our Broadway contracts, and we did get paid two weeks. I had one line. "There you are. I thought you rode off. Where's your pa?" I'm like, "Oh my God, I'm going to be on Broadway, I'm going to be on Broadway!" I thought, "I could get a Tony nomination." So silly. I took myself very seriously then, too. I don't anymore, but—I thought the show was quite good. I thought the performances were terrific. We had a problem when the creatives started fighting out of town. We didn't know what was going on. We just knew that we would get new pages and new lyrics every day, and we were like, "Okay, fine. I can do it." And then we had a company meeting about a week before we were going to move to Broadway. [Producer] Roger Berlind gave everyone their Broadway contracts and he wanted us all to sign them before he had anything else to say. "Make sure you sign them and hand them back to me. Is everybody's contract signed? Okay. Great. We're not going to Broadway." He did that because he wanted to make sure that we got paid our Broadway salary. Two weeks' notice. Only a gentleman producer would do that. They would normally just close you. But Roger did a very generous thing by making sure that we all signed our contracts and got paid two weeks of Broadway salary. The show closed about a week later. Our marquis was up at the Marriott Marquis and it stayed up for months.

You got your Equity card doing *Paper Moon*?

Actually, [when I did *Some Like It Hot* for Troika] the director of that was directing *Oliver!* at the Kansas City Starlight, and he asked me if I wanted to do it. So I got my Equity card by doing *Oliver!* with Davey Jones and Donna Murphy. No one knew who Donna Murphy was but she was awesome. She played Nancy, and Davey Jones was Fagin and an absolute nightmare. Remember how nice he was on *The Monkees*? He was acting. He was so mean to the kids. We were staying at this terrible motel in downtown Kansas City, just rat infested and horrible. They had a karaoke bar. Davey did try to kind of redeem himself because he realized he was being a real jerk to people. So he shows up at the bar. Now we're not the only people in this bar. Davey Jones walks in and you could see like Carl and Marge at the bar going, "Hey, is that Davey Jones?" He has a couple drinks and gets up there and he sings "Daydream Believer," and it was magic and horrible all at the same time.

Horrible as that sounds, with that as your first professional gig back to back with *Paper Moon* **. . .**

It felt magical. The anticipation of getting to do the thing that you always wanted . . . to be on Broadway. You're in it, you feel part of it. Your dream has come true. [In *Paper Moon*] the changes are coming fast and furious, even minutes before you go on stage. That's how we lived. We didn't really know we were in horrible trouble.

Do you have a memory of watching the leads?

Oh, God, watching Christine Ebersole just kill it every night? Absolutely! And watching Greg Harrison! It didn't deserve what it got. I think it would have run. I don't think it was a disaster by any means. It was sad to see. And, you know, us youngsters felt blindsided by it. It wasn't that disastrous. They just needed to get over themselves.

You had a healthy off-Broadway run in *Boys in the Band* **after that.**

And that's where [director] Michael Mayer and [author] James Magruder saw me [and eventually cast me in *Triumph of Love*.] We went out of town to Baltimore with Susan Egan, Robert LuPone, Mary Beth Peil—an unbelievable group of people. We came back and we did it at Yale for another three months and then we were going to Broadway. Susan Egan and I were the only ones that survived from out of town to Broadway. I kept a diary of this thing because I was so excited about it. I still have it. It's hilarious. It's like, "Just signed my contracts at Abrams." "First day of rehearsal so excited. I hope Betty Buckley likes me. Smiley face." You know, very optimistic. And then a few pages later I'm so frustrated and angry and the writing—it looks like it might have been written by somebody who had epilepsy. Like the pen is going through the paper.

So what happened?

There were a lot of problems. At the first read-through, I was feeling great about everything. F. Murray Abraham was wonderful. Just a doll. And Betty Buckley just terrific. The next day we had a press day, and I get the flu. We took pictures and I left. I was back about two days later and Elayne Boosler's gone. She quit. She just up and left. Her name was up on the marquis so they put packing tape over her name. At night, when the lights came on, you see "Elayne Boosler" coming through green tape! And then they let Patrick Breen go. They brought in Roger Bart. Roger's wonderful always [and we got] Nancy Opel but we only had five weeks to put this whole show together. Betty did not show up sometimes to rehearsals. She was very insecure. I think she was afraid. [Her character] has to be undone by love and Betty was afraid to look like a fool. But that is the point of the part. The part is hilarious if you just let yourself go. She finally understood that if she did just let herself go and be the fool, people loved her more, but it took her a long time to understand that. Michael Mayer tried for the longest time to convince her to trust him. She resisted. And then she finally got it, and then we closed.

Did the rehearsal process hurt morale?

Very much so. It was frustrating. I remember I cried a lot going home. I already knew what the show was [having done it out of town] and I was waiting for other people to catch up. Just let go. Everyone has to do that in this particular show and it pays off. And yes, the characters in the show get disappointed at the end. A few are triumphant. Some are disappointed. But in the end, everyone triumphs, and that is *Triumph of Love*.

"Maybe we'll meet someone at the wedding." [The show's final line]

Do you know who wrote that? Our lighting designer. They were like, "How do we end the show?" He said it and they're like, "It's in the show!" I thought by the time we had opened, we

With Susan Egan as Leonide, making good on her promise to "do anything for love" in *Triumph of Love*. (Photofest)

were good. And then we didn't get the *Times* review. I don't look at it as a failure. I just think of it as a missed chance. In the long run, it was a great experience. It was such a sweet show, and the score is great. Back to the grindstone.

Was that devastating?

Here's the deal: There are times in actors' lives where you always think you're never ever going to work again. After *Triumph*, I thought I'd never work again because I had a Broadway failure. Then I audition for *Hunchback of Notre Dame* with James Lapine directing. This was the second time I had worked with James Lapine.

The first being?

The first was a workshop right after *Paper Moon* called *Muscle*. Everybody that has ever done this famous, disastrous reading—Norm Lewis, Karen Ziemba, Kevin Chamberlin, Dee Hoty, Harry Groener—we're like veterans and/or war heroes together. Totally bonded.

Actually, you're bringing up something I was going to ask you about a little later on. You've done a ton of readings or workshops . . .

Always.

You're expected to work for virtually nothing to help writers explore whether or not a piece is feasible, and you do it because you want to be part of something at the ground level?

Mostly. In the beginning I was just happy to create, and I still am. I love helping out and I also like to see what they come up with. Sometimes it's inconvenient, but I always end up doing it. By the time I'm done with it, I'm so fulfilled. It's great. Even if it's not good. I like doing the thing that's not good. It's okay that it's not good. That's why we're here: to see what it is. It's a billion dollar industry we're in. You better make sure your product is good before you put it out there to sell. And the people that I get to work with are so much fun. It should be fun, and it should be collaborative. The room is safe and you can make the biggest, grossest mistakes ever. Just fail. I love that. I'm so invested when I do these things because I really do want to understand what they're going for. I ask a lot of questions. But sometimes they just need to see it and hear it out loud. Some things are just awful but hey, at least you put it up and found out it was awful. And some things are not quite there, but there's something there.

Back to post-*Triumph of Love* when you thought you'd never work again. You booked a starring role on a TV show with the Olsen twins.
Two of a Kind. That was a crazy experience, but it was cancelled after a year. I didn't necessarily want to be on TV. Of course, everyone wants to be on TV, but I was content and happy to just do my theater thing. I came crawling back to Broadway

Is that how you felt?
No. It was disappointing. The one thing from the TV show that I did learn is not to spend so much money when they give it to you. Put it in your bank account. [I did another play, *Avow*] and then I went into *Beauty and the Beast.* I went in [to audition] and I did everything I possibly could that was gross and hetero and disgusting and it worked. Rob Roth, the director, was there, and told me in the room, "You've got the job." That never happened to me before. *Beauty* is where I met my husband, Kevin Burrows.

Was there any part of you that felt like coming into a show three years into its run was a step down after having a lead on TV?
I've never been that person. If something comes up, I want to do it. My trajectory is just keep working. I just like to do stuff. I was there about a year and a half. The last six months of it I had a hematomic cyst in my spinal cord that developed over the course of the show because of the movements of Gaston during the fight scene. I'd be doing the show and I'd be like, "Oh, that hurt" and just continue. Then, over the course of months, this little blood bubble just started getting bigger and bigger. I didn't know what it was but it was exquisite pain and then my legs started numbing. I went to a neurologist and he [put me into surgery] that day. It was so fast that I couldn't call my stage manager. I had Kevin call. I had to learn how to walk on my right leg again because it was basically just gone.

How long were you out of commission?
Eight weeks. I suspect there were moments [before the surgery, when I missed shows] where the stage manager was like, "Well, he just doesn't want to do the show tonight." I always want to do the show. I don't like being out. But if I can't fucking move, I'm not going to do the show, and I couldn't. My stage manager was apparently very upset with me that I didn't call him personally.

You also broke your finger during that show.
My left pinky. On stage. During a bit with Le Fou my finger goes into the track [in the floor] and it snaps right on the second knuckle from the fingernail. It's dangling like a wet piece of meat. My arm goes numb. I go blank. I'm stunned silent. But because I've been doing the show for a year, my body takes over. The body just does it. Now, if you know *Beauty and the Beast*, you know there's the clink line of the heavy metal pewter mugs. Each person has two in their hands, and they clink with each other. Imagine doing that with a broken pinky that's

exposed on the outside of that mug and getting hit over and over and over and over again with a heavy, metal mug. I finish the number, and I walk to Roosevelt Hospital. I came back two weeks later but it wouldn't bend. So every time I went to punch Le Fou, I had this like little pinky that came out like a pointer! Lot of accidents on Broadway.

After that you went right into *Into the Woods*.

I left *Beauty and the Beast* to do *Into the Woods*. That was great. I left a fairy tale to go do another fairy tale. *Into the Woods* was one of the reasons I wanted to do what I do. I'm there with Gregg Edelman, who's another idol of mine. He's such a sweetheart, and he's so great to work with. First day of rehearsal, Gregg and I just clicked. We were brothers right away. We worked on "Agony" together [with Stephen Sondheim] and he told us the story of what it is—it's blue balls, of course, but it's Steve that's telling us this, and I'm just—"Am I really here? Am I really doing this? Oh, my God!" It's blowing my mind. I understudied Gregg. I played Rapunzel's Prince, he played Cinderella's Prince. We were in previews and I hadn't had an understudy rehearsal, but I'm one who pays attention so I knew everything he did. And when I wasn't on stage, I was watching him. "Hello, Little Girl" was done by both of us. And when we both went [howling], he twisted his back. He had to crawl offstage. I'm getting out of the Wolf mask and getting into my Prince garb. It's a pretty quick costume change including prosthetics. Beverly Randolph, our stage manager, comes running downstairs and says, "Gregg hurt his back really bad. You're on as Cinderella's Prince right now." And I was like, "No problem." She said, "You're really calm." I was like, "This is my favorite show. I know every lyric. It's fine. I've been watching. I've been paying attention." I was so cool about the whole thing that she was like, "You're freaking me out." I will say I was quite good. I thought I was killing it. At the end of Act I, though, there's the blood bag; when the Evil Stepsisters cut their heel and their toes off, and there's blood in the shoe—that's the only thing I didn't rehearse. It's a simple stage trick. There's a bag of blood on your back with a hose that runs down your arm underneath your jacket and then there's a little pump. You just squeeze this thing and a little blood comes out and spurts into the shoe, then you pour out the blood, and it's a funny stage trick. No one told me how to work this thing. So when it came up, I squeezed it like twenty-five times. I didn't know how to work it. The air pressure builds and this thing sprays out into the audience and it won't stop. I'm spraying Paul Gemignani [the conductor]. It's getting on the cast, it's getting on the floor, it's getting everywhere. I'm like holding my hand over my wrist, and it's not stopping. Everybody got blood on them. Laura Benanti comes on and has no idea because she was off stage. I put the shoe on her and it's filled with blood. She kind of looks around and there's just spatter of blood everywhere. And then I have to lift her up on the horse—this plastic, fiberglass, white horse, and it just smears with blood. Darkest fairy tale ever.

Anything you want to say about Sondheim?

Vanessa Williams would throw a party every now and then and she'd invite everybody and Steve and James Lapine would show up. It was cool just being able to talk to Steve Sondheim—just to talk to him. After a while, you know, he's just—he's Steve. And you can just talk to him like a human being. It was really neat to sit down with him and just talk about stuff. He's just a brilliant guy that happens to be Steve Sondheim. "Agony" was the song that he wanted to cut. Can you believe that? He said, "I kept trying to cut it. Every time we did a reading or a workshop of it, that song never worked for me. I know. It's stupid." That show was just the magical . . .

But a disappointment, though.

It was. We thought we were going to run a lot longer. They decided they didn't want to run it any longer when Vanessa Williams's contract was up. So we were closing, and we were all like, "Now what?" It was insane. So I get a phone call from my agent. They want to see me for *Thoroughly Modern Millie*. Marc Kudisch was leaving for three months. We closed *Into the Woods* on a Sunday and I started rehearsals for *Millie* on Monday. I was in the show the following Tuesday. Really fast! Trevor Graydon is a great part, and it's very memorable, but it's not that huge so it was okay. I went into the show with the original Broadway cast, except for Marc, and I got to play that wonderful, fantastic role opposite Sutton Foster and Gavin Creel. It was such a fun show to do. Another injury happened! Oh, my God, I'm so accident-prone. There's the elevator in Act II and it's a caper so we're running around. Graydon opens this safety gate—this big, iron safety gate, and Millie gets in, Jimmy gets in, Trevor Graydon gets in, and I close this gate. There's a safety latch that makes sure that we're safe. The elevator won't move unless this safety latch is down, and it works every time unless your hand is right in the place of this meat cleaver of a safety latch that cuts your hand—You can still see the scar from here to here—cuts it wide open, and . . .

Again, blood squirting into the audience . . .

Again, blood everywhere. This one was real blood. Left hand broken, spurting blood. Blood is just spattering and at that point, Graydon does not leave the stage until the end of the show. I wrap my hand in this handkerchief and I'm holding it. I'm wearing this navy blue jacket, and the blood is turning the jacket black. I'm desperately trying not to bleed on people. Five, six stitches in my hand.

Amazing that anyone insures you. Christian Borle came into the show while you were doing it.

He's just amazing. When I've worked with him, I can't even believe I'm on stage with him. He makes everyone better. So does Sutton. Because you have to rise to it. I was so happy to be a part of it. It was a nice, brief, wonderful experience.

And then you went off and did a series with Harriet Harris from *Millie*. *It's All Relative*.

I put my money away this time.

And after a year you crawl back to Broadway, like you do.

I come crawling back to Broadway. That was the first time I did *Chicago*. Now I've done it five times in the same theater. I love doing that. Every time they call me and say, "Hey, you want to do *Chicago*?" I say, "Yeah, absolutely." I love it there. It's a great company always. It's a fantastically marvelous show. What's so brilliant about the story is it changes with the things that are going on in the world. People start identifying with the scandal du jour. The show is exactly the same but it plays differently based on the stuff that's going around. It's so fun playing. They keep that show bubbling because they rotate people out so much. New energy, good or bad energy, whatever, it's always bubbling.

Your next show was *Spamalot*. It's interesting to me because even though you were well established by then, that show kind of set your reputation for a willingness to be completely committed to total silliness.

I was a very lucky person with that. I was doing *Cinderella* at City Opera, and Bob Boyett who produced *Two of a Kind*, my first sitcom, had left Los Angeles. He had had enough of television and wanted to produce theater. He had more money than God. So he started putting money into shows and for the first or second season that he did, if you just looked down 45th Street, every single one of those shows was his. I get a call from Bob, and he says, "Hey, I need a favor from you. I need you to tell your agent to call [casting director] Tara Rubin tomorrow. I need you for *Spamalot*. Do not say a word." They were already like four or five weeks into rehearsal. I get a call from Tara Rubin at 7:00 in the morning, asking me to be in front of Mike Nichols and Eric Idle at 11:00 AM. I'm freaking out because it's Eric Idle and Mike Nichols. [They hired me in the room.] I'm like, "What just fucking happened?" They were five days away from tech in Chicago. [I went right from the audition] to rehearsals, a block away. Doug Sills decided he didn't want to do it anymore so—And then the next thing I knew I was whisked into the studio and measured for costumes. Next moment, I met Sara Ramirez, and we were learning "The Song That Goes Like This." I'm very fast at learning things and I learned the song probably within ten minutes. I'm holding music but I got it. Fine. And so Sara and I started working on the song, and we ended up creating what the song became. We started making up things and that ended up being "The Song That Goes Like This." I mean, it was written, but it was never extended to the point where you're yelling at the conductor, and then there are key changes. That wasn't in there originally. On day two Sara and I did "The Song That Goes Like This," for the company and it killed, it killed. From that point on, I would go home and cry every night because, number one, I can't believe this happened to me, and number two, it was such extreme pressure. Everyone in that show was just extraordinary, and to have to come up to that level in days . . . David Hyde Pierce was very sweet. He walked me through some stuff on day three. And thank God he did because I just didn't have time. Mike Nichols, I will say, at first he did not like me. He seemed to tolerate what I was doing. It wasn't until previews in Chicago that he actually started liking me, and then later on, he adored me.

How did his not liking you manifest?

He was very—he would just move on [in rehearsal]. He wouldn't give me attention. I think he was frustrated at the time lost from the four weeks that I could have had. By the time I had two to three weeks, I was ready to go. We were all on the same page. And then he started really liking me and he would talk to me all the time and give me hugs and ask me for cigarettes. He was the only guy I knew that could smoke in the theater and no one would say anything. The greatest gift ever was working with that man because he taught you so much about comedy and so much about just being with your fellow actors. He would never say anything about your performance. It was just, "I want you to do this and go there with that and do this with that, and emphasize that word." And he always said, "Kill your babies." Babies were things that you created that get laughs but don't necessarily have anything to do with the story. Bits. He said, "Darlings, I love your babies. I do. But I want you to kill them now." And he would say, "Please make babies, make babies! Always make babies. But then kill your babies." And he was correct. He'd come to your dressing room [during the run]. "Oh, how are you? I love you. You know I do. Yes, my boy. I would like you to do me a favor." Of course. Anything. "I want you to have a massive abortion. I love what you're doing—I do, I do, I do. I just know you can do more. So I want you to have a massive abortion. And just remember, sometimes trying to get a laugh from that audience is like trying to make a whore come: It's just not going to happen." He was right. We loved it. You know, a lot of times you'd have a director come back to your show and everybody's freaking out because things just kind of evolve. Some directors get really upset that you aren't doing what they told you to do. It's just some things—they can evolve. We couldn't wait for Mike to come and see us. We were so happy for him to see us. We hung on every word he said. The other thing I learned from him—surprise your fellow actors just by doing something—just the slightest thing might be different. The way you inflect a word—constantly changing. That will make everybody alive. After he told me to have the massive abortion, I did. I didn't do any of my bits, and it forced me to find new ones and/or just be there. I remember giggling through the entire show. I giggled because I was discovering all these new things. You get so attached to the things that you've created because they're surefire. Just let it go and find something else. That whole show was never work. It was fun. It went like a bullet. We would get to the theater early—sometimes an hour and a half, just to hang out with each other. There's a scene called "At the Feet of God" and we're sitting there, bowing before God, and we're just laughing. I kind of turned to David Hyde Pierce and under my breath I said, "It's been a year and a half. Should we stop giggling?" And he said, "Hell, no! Never. Don't stop giggling." And we loved getting Hank Azaria to laugh. Christian Borle and I called him "the wounded antelope on the prairie" because he could break like that [snaps fingers]. We didn't have to do much, we learned. It was the most insane thing. John Cleese was always hanging around. Again, one of my comedy heroes. He was like, "Christopher, do you mind if I just hang out in your hallway?" And Michael Palin, hanging around. Terry Gilliam. After the show, Eric Idle and Mike Nichols would ask me if I wanted to join them and we'd go to Angus McIndoe and/or Joe Allen's and hang out. You'd sit at a table with Robin Williams, or Billy Crystal. I didn't even know what to say. And then one night I'm there with Eric and sitting next to Salman Rushdie. It's crazy.

You got a Tony nomination.
My very first. That was unexpected. It's so cool being nominated because you really do feel respect from your peers. And then the next five weeks or so are exhausting. You're trotted out for absolutely everything. And, of course, it's my first time around so I'm just like, "Yes!" and then you realize "I got to sleep." A lot of the parties happen at like 10:00 AM and/or between shows.

But you were sharing the experience with practically your whole company?
Pretty much. So we were all there together. We went en masse. Laura Linney started this Tony Award brunch, like the Oscars have, where it's just the nominees. No agents, no press, and all that. You are all the same and you can go talk to the biggest stars or the people you've never heard of. It's great! I mean, to go to Radio City and see that you're sitting across from Angela Lansbury and then there's Darth Vader [James Earl Jones].

You also got to do the show in London.
That was a cool thing. Mike Nichols and Eric Idle asked me. But it was a very lonely time in the West End. They don't have a community like they do here in New York. It's so expensive in the West End, you can't live there, so everyone takes the train home and the last train is usually around 11:30. Everyone just bolts to the train after the show. So I walked home over the Thames every night [to the apartment they provided], and I was just there watching their five channels of TV, and listening to CDs, and reading books. It was rough. I did seven months in London and then I did four months back in New York.

So it was a full two-and-a-half years of your life?
Almost three. And then during that time, I was doing the workshops for *Shrek*.

And that happened because Jason Moore called you?
Jason Moore called me while I was in London doing *Spamalot*. We've done a lot of projects, a lot of readings, a lot of workshops of things that just never came about. But every time

that we've done stuff together it's been a hoot. He likes me and I like him a lot, and we work really well together. He said, "I've got this weird project, and I want you to do it. Can you help me out?" Yes, yes, fine, Jason. If you ask me, I'll do it. I always say yes to Jason. I got back from London, and we dive into this thing. It's only one act, and they have four songs. But for some reason this part connects with me so much. This is funny. And it turned into another reading, and another reading and another reading and then a twenty-nine-hour workshop and another twenty-nine-hour and then a lab, and then another lab and then the Seattle production and then Broadway. It was one of the most collaborative things that I've ever been part of. It was completely rewarding and also very damaging to my body. I was the one that came in one day and said, "Why don't I do it on my knees?" I brought in these little sticks with these little shoes. It was like Charlie Chaplin in the movie *The Kid* where he dances with little feet on the table. It's my fault that I ended up doing the whole show on my knees.

Were you doing a lot of physical therapy?
Three to four times a week. It actually felt better, after a while, to be in the costume than it felt to be out of it. I called out about six times because I'd wake up and I couldn't walk. All the weight goes into your hips for that. So I would roll out of bed, and I'd be like, "I can't walk. I'm so swelled up." I developed weird muscles on my quads. I gained all this weight 'cuz I couldn't move. I couldn't do a treadmill or an elliptical. I could only do a bike. So I gained like sixty pounds.

Were you happy doing the role?
No. It was so much fun at first. It was absolutely a blast. What happened was the audience—people think *Shrek* is a kids' show. It's written for adults. That was the whole idea. But I guess people think "bring my kids," which is great, but kids—I love that they're seeing Broadway—but they don't respond. They sit with their mouths open and their eyes wide. They don't respond because they don't necessarily understand it. So towards the end, it was really a little deadening and soul-crushing because you're doing some of the funniest stuff that you've ever done in your life and it's silent. There were times when we—it would be Sutton Foster and Brian d'Arcy James and Johnny Tartaglia and Danny Breaker, and me. [Our dressing rooms] were all in the same hallway and we're just like, "We're here for each other, let's do it for us." It was weird. I guess it was a letdown. I mean, we had a blast when the audience was theater-going people. We knew how good it was, but the audiences just weren't responding to it [later in the run] because of the demographic of the audience. People still talk about it to this day. I was very proud of the show.

You got another Tony nomination for it. Did it feel different that time?
Well, I learned all the things from the first one. I was thrilled. [The other nominees] were all my friends, so whoever won, I was going to be happy. [For the broadcast] they were doing my number, "What's Up, Duloc?" They decided the set that they built for the Tony Awards was a little unstable, so they built a little lip on the edge of the opening of the elevator doors without telling me. I'm already freaking out because it's my number. I have live cameras on me and 6,000 people in this place. The elevator comes down, they open the door, and I trip [on the new lip] and everything slows down. Slow motion. My mind went blank. I don't remember any of it. But my body's taking over and I do it. I finished the number. But I don't remember any of it. I was worried about fucking up on the live TV, and fucking up in front of 6,000 people that know me, and most importantly, I would never be able to go to Musical Mondays at a gay bar across the country ever again because they would point out that Christopher Sieber was the guy who fell on the Tony Awards and forgot all his words live on TV. It was a terrible experience

until they called my category. If they could bottle that moment they open your envelope—that feeling of hope, and surprise, and joy, and then split seconds later it's despair, and self-hatred. It's a terrible feeling. But when Greg Jbara won, I was so happy for him. He's a friend of mine, and I honestly was truly happy. I unconsciously stood up.

Your next show was off-Broadway, *The Kid*.
Based on Dan Savage's book. That was terrific. It was such a good story. We had a great cast: Lucas Steele, Susan Blackwell, Ann Harada, Justin Patterson, Tyler Maynard, Jill Eickenberry, and Michael Wartella. During the tail end of *Shrek* I got an offer to do a reading. Sounds interesting. Let's do it. And I happen to have read that book. It was so good. And then we did it at the New Group, and Dan Savage got very involved. He was at many performances, and gave notes about the story. It was a wonderful, wonderful experience. It was a wonderful story. Lucas and I made a point of being together more than we had to. We would hang out before rehearsals, and just talk, talk, talk, talk, talk. To get our chemistry. That worked so well and he was so wonderful to play with. On the subway we'd always take the local home because it took longer. It never got the run I think it should have. But apparently we didn't get the kiss from *The New York Times*.

When you take a show like that, is money a concern?
Always—money's always a concern, always, always. There's savings. But there are things that you really want to do. And I look at most everything that I do as an investment. That's why I do every reading and every workshop. I do it because it's an investment. It may turn into something later on, but also just for your performing soul. You can create something and make something.

After *The Kid*, you got a singular opportunity, to step into *La Cage aux Folles*.
That story is hilarious. I get a call to go back into *Chicago*. I'm not doing anything. Fine. So I would like to go see *Chicago* again because it's been seven years since the last time I did it. So I go to the Ambassador Theatre box office to pick up my ticket and my phone rang. It's Robert Adderman, my agent, saying, "They don't want you to see *Chicago* today. They want you to see *La Cage aux Folles*, which is two blocks away." But they didn't say why. I thought, "What a strange way to go into *Chicago*, by seeing *La Cage*, but whatever. It's the Weisslers [the producers of both shows]. I'll do it." So I see the show and I'm just loving it because I've never actually seen the show. Harvey Fierstein's in it and I go backstage [afterwards] and I go up to Harvey's room. He grabs me, throws me onto his couch, closes the door, and says, [doing a perfect Fierstein impersonation] "Are you going to do the show with me?" It's like, "What show?" He says, "Jeffrey Tambor up and left me. He's got problems. He just left. I've had one-night stands lasted longer." The producers were there and they swarmed. I said "yes" and I go right down to costume fitting, that night. I start rehearsals the next day and then seven days later, I'm opposite Harvey. The first week was a little rough because I didn't quite know the script. I knew the words, but I didn't know the cues. I just knew where not to get killed by a set piece, and when somebody stopped talking, I figured that was my turn to talk. I did that the first couple days, and then I was into it. Ten days from my first performance, the reviewers came. Like, why would you do that? Harvey called me at home, and he said, "They love us." He read a review and it was so nice. But we closed two months later. But we had such great chemistry that Barry Weissler came to us and said, "What do you think about you guys going on tour together?" Harvey was working on *Newsies* and then *Kinky Boots* so he wasn't available. Barry Weissler came back to me. He says, "Do you still want to go on tour? I think we have George

Hamilton." I was like, "George is going to look weird in a dress." He said, "No, no, no. You play Albin. He would play Georges." Interesting. So I went on tour with George Hamilton. He was the best. So sweet, so generous, so lovely. Not a theater actor. And I say that with absolute love, and he'll be the first one to admit it. He doesn't trust himself to know his lines. He worked like nobody I ever saw before. If he wasn't on stage, back to a music stand with a light on, going over his script to make sure that he remembered his lines. He just wouldn't trust himself. I would tell him, "George, you have this. You have to just enjoy yourself." But he was so much fun to be with. We did a year and three months out on the road together.

How was the experience of touring?

It was like prison. It was very lonely. You cannot go out at night. It's so vocally and physically demanding you cannot—plus there's no time to recover. Every week or every other week, you're traveling and going to the next place, so there's no real downtime. I understand that's how it works. It's just so exhausting. The Cagelles would go out every night and have a blast. I could not do any of that. I would go home to my hotel room and have seltzer and celery and room service and go to bed.

When you came back from the *La Cage* tour, you went back to *Chicago*.

I was exhausted. Went back to *Chicago* one more time and then Barry Weissler called me and says, "Have you seen *Pippin* yet? Why don't you come see *Pippin*." Now, after the previous experience, when I hear, "Why don't you come see . . ." I think, "Why don't you just ask me what you want?" He says, "I can't get you a seat, you're going to be in the standing room." So [director] Diane Paulus is standing next to me. Barry Weissler's next to her. I'm just blown away by *Pippin*. At intermission, he says, "So what do you think? Could you do what Terry [Terrence Mann] does?" Terry had concert dates and teaching gigs, all this stuff that was contractual [and was taking a leave]. And they're like, "We'll see you on Monday." Again, it was the Barry Weissler experience: you got five days, you'll be fine. I was there for nine weeks and then I went off to A.R.T. to do a play called *The Heart of Robin Hood*, and it was wonderful. [While I was there] I get a call to audition for *Matilda* as Agatha Trunchbull. I went to London about two years prior specifically [to see that show] because I knew it was coming. The audition was on a Tuesday, and I had a show that night so I got up at 4:00 in the morning and took the first train out from Boston, went to New York, and had to be on the train back by 11:00 AM. I did the audition, kicked it out of the ballpark, and went back to Cambridge. I get an email from [director] Matthew Warchus, and he wants to speak with me by Skype.

He wasn't at the audition?

He was in London, but they videotaped the whole thing. It was this forty-five-minute conversation where he did most of the talking just describing the character and the show, and I'm listening. And then he says, "So have fun with it, and have a great time. I'll see you soon." I'm like, "Wait, whoa, whoa, whoa, whoa, whoa, Matthew. Do I have the part?" "What, no one told you?" I went back to New York and started rehearsals. They put me through boot camp. Six weeks of rehearsal for this show. You're doing exercises and doing this, and doing that. They want you to get your stamina up. I was kind of, "That's my responsibility, not yours," but the way they work, that's what they did. I was standing up on a block, for three minutes, then jumping rope for three minutes, doing all these exercises. It was insane. I went to Pilates. They had me doing yoga. The last week of my training, I broke my hand [in rehearsal]. It was going to be six weeks to heal. So Barry Weissler, who has money in *Matilda*, calls. "C'mon and do *Pippin* again for us." I said, "I have a cast on." He says, "We'll put something over it. It'll be

All malevolence and padding in *Matilda*. (Joan Marcus)

fine." So I did *Pippin*, and I was still under contract from *Matilda*. I was doing performances of *Pippin* at night and rehearsing *Matilda* during the day. I went from theater to theater, back and forth. And then finally my hand healed and I went into *Matilda*.

And then you did two and a half years there?
And then I did two and a half years of *Matilda*. It was very fun at first. That was a tough show because the morale there was really low. The communication wasn't very good, and the rehearsals that they called every single day all the time—we rehearsed so much for that show even though we were up and running. They had rehearsals every single week up until the time I left. I did my best to raise morale, which is very important to me. I did everything I could to make happiness and joy. I would do a Saturday night on Broadway speech over the monitor every Saturday and make a little jokey radio play for everybody; I'd have pizza parties, whatever I could do to raise the morale. It helped a little bit and then it would just go back down to despair. They were so adamant about constantly rehearsing. Even stage managers were like,

"This is insane!" It was hard, it was hard. And then I kind of succumbed to the misery of it. I decided to leave with nothing on the horizon. The show is a brilliant show, and I loved it. I actually loved it. And then you just succumb because of the relentless rehearsals that I thought were unnecessary. And then I went to Atlanta to do *The Prom*, and that was great.

When you walked in today, you mentioned that you did *Annie* at Paper Mill in 2017 because you needed your Equity weeks [actors must work a certain number of union weeks per year in order to maintain their insurance benefits]. Do you feel at this stage in your career like, "Oh my God, I have to take work just to get my Equity weeks!" Does that worry you?

You always worry. You always worry. There are ebbs and flows in this business, and the ebbs are sometimes just unbearable. There are times when you just got a streak that keeps going, and then there are times when . . . you can only do so much planning because in show business, you never know. Money is always nice but health insurance is always better for me.

Well, if you keep breaking your hand.

I've injured my hand five times! But when there's ebb, you just do what you have to do. There's no shame in that. It's never comfortable. I wish it were. When it's bad, it's bad but when it's good, it's good! Just keep going. That's what I always say. Just keep going.

14

NORBERT LEO BUTZ

December 2018

ON THE DAY I MEET NORBERT LEO BUTZ backstage at the Vivian Beaumont Theatre during the final weeks of his Tony-nominated performance in *My Fair Lady*, he arrives schlepping pastry boxes: apology gifts for the cast. Butz had missed the prior night's performance because he had forgotten that that particular night during a holiday week, curtain had been at 7:00, not 8:00, and he found himself stuck on the PATH train as the lights were dimming. It was, of course, an honest mistake, but the fact that Butz's shame translated to the sheepish delivery of cast donuts says a lot about the man.

Perhaps his thoughtfulness can be attributed to the fact that he was born in St. Louis, the seventh of eleven kids, and had to learn cooperation and sharing pretty early in life. Perhaps it's a perspective on responsibility that comes with being the son of a Marine and the father of two teenaged girls. Or perhaps it's just a graciousness learned on the job after more than twenty years on and off Broadway in over a dozen shows including smash hit musicals (*Wicked, Rent*), demanding straight plays (*Speed the Plow, Fifty Words*), and painful belly flops (*Thou Shalt Not, The Last Five Years, Big Fish*).

During that twenty years, Butz picked up a pair of Tony awards for *Catch Me if You Can* and *Dirty Rotten Scoundrels*. The former was another disappointment despite a tour de force performance from Butz, but the latter was that rare Broadway experience in which the cast seemed as happy as the audience. And it allowed Butz his first real opportunity to show just how fiercely committed he could be. *The New York Times* called him "criminally talented."

It was only after we'd completed our conversations that Butz shared with me how much he dislikes talking about himself. "It is my firm belief the less we know about the personal lives, even work lives, of our actors, the more we as audiences are able to surrender our disbelief and accept the actor as the character they have been hired to play," he told me in an email. "You are tasked to do exactly the thing I tend to resist most!!" I was thrown. Because even though Butz went on to say that he enjoyed our time, I hadn't realized that he had been at all uncomfortable. And the seemingly unvarnished candor of his answers suggests that he managed to resist his resistance. Once we were in it, he committed fully. And that, of course, is the very trait that makes his work on stage so very compelling.

You applied to the Conservatory of Theater Arts at Webster University on the sly. Why so secretive?

Well, I was afraid of how my parents would react, specifically my dad, to my coming out of the acting closet as it were. I adored him but my dad was a really complicated guy. He was

As the dreamy Fiyero, with Idina Menzel in *Wicked*. (Joan Marcus)

an ex-Marine. He disciplined with a lot of fearsomeness. So I was afraid. His family were German immigrants and very, very poor. The idea was that you go and you study something practical and respectable and work your way up to financial security. So even when I started doing theater in high school I had to lie often. I lied a lot.

Do you remember what got you hooked?

My oldest brother—he could do anything; he was smart, athletic, and musical. He got the leads in the plays, and when he was a senior in high school, he was cast as Emile De Becque in *South Pacific*. And then another brother of mine played Anna's son in *The King and I*. I remember going to see those high school productions, and I remember the cast—there's no backstage—they just came out into the gym where they set up the stage. Seeing all the powdered heads and the Polynesian eyes and the greasepaint, I was really, really fascinated by it. But my parents were very strict Catholics. Catholic education all the way through, confirmed, altar boys. Pretty much every morning we would serve a mass.

That's where you first sang, right?

Yes. But I always say that was the first theater that I did. I remember taking that very seriously, the ritual of it, what I was supposed to be, the props. I was enchanted with all of that. Still am. Ritualistic storytelling. The church is similar to a theater in that way. I think that the leap into acting from church actually made a kind of sense to me. So then I just started doing all the plays in high school. My parents eventually came around and became huge fans of mine. My dad saw everything I did like four times and was incredibly proud. St. Louis is a very Catholic city, and there were all these all-girl Catholic high schools, and they always need guys for their musicals. If you could walk and talk at the same time, you got a part. It was like seventy girls and six guys. And if you could actually sing and move, you were the lead. I played

Norbert Leo Butz	
Rent	Broadway, 1997
Cabaret	National Tour, 1999
Thou Shalt Not	Broadway, 2001
The Last Five Years	Off-Broadway, 2002
Wicked	Broadway, 2003
Dirty Rotten Scoundrels (Tony Award)	Broadway, 2005; National Tour, 2006
Catch Me if You Can (Tony Award)	Broadway, 2011
Big Fish	Broadway, 2013
My Fair Lady	Broadway, 2018

Harold Hill in *The Music Man,* Luther Billis in *South Pacific,* Pappy Yokum in *Lil' Abner,* Rooster in *Annie.* I got to do all these great musical theater parts. I always had girlfriends in all of the casts. Not like I was a dog or anything, but I liked being around that many girls, and I found my place in a way that I don't think I did at home. When you're from a big, chaotic, noisy, sometimes scary (also really loving) family . . .

Was theater a way to differentiate you?

Absolutely. It was that. And I was real shy, actually. I was real quiet at school. But when you get distinguished for something . . . I should also say that a defining moment for me was when I got to see some theater that came through St. Louis. My dad was a gospel music lover. We had records by Mahalia Jackson, Leontyne Price, Sister Rosetta . . . it was a strange record collection. And there was this show that came through St. Louis called *Your Arms Too Short to Box with God* starring Patti LaBelle. My dad bought tickets for me and like eight of my siblings, all these tow-headed kids in a sea of the whole St. Louis black community. I remember seeing that show, and I remember Patti LaBelle singing with that gospel choir and that level of dance, and something really clicked with me there. I've never forgotten that performance. I became obsessed with black musicals. I went to the library and I got cast albums for *The Wiz, Purlie!* . . . I wanted to be in musicals, but I wanted to be black. Probably my strongest memory of being utterly transported and seduced by a piece of acting was at a regional production of *A Christmas Carol.* While the audience was being seated, Scrooge came out onto the stage and stayed in character, and counted his money. I remember being riveted by this man, and I kept telling everyone, "Shhhh!!!!" I was in a panic. I was like, "That man is on stage. He's working on something. Shh!" I tried to keep the audience quiet. I watched this guy for like twenty minutes just behaving. It was astonishing to me. So I don't know—somewhere in the mix of all of those experiences . . . By the time I was a senior in high school, I had won some singing competitions. My choir teacher was really urging me to study music. I was starting to study privately and my parents were starting to support that. I was learning, doing some of the classical canon, some of the arias. I thought I'd go to the University of Missouri, but I just couldn't let go of this acting thing, and so at the last possible moment, I auditioned for Webster. I remember I told my parents out in the backyard and my dad was very angry, but we weathered through it. In the first year of the program at Webster you can't perform. You're in the studio all day and you do backstage and tech work at night. The first play I got cast in in my sophomore year, we were the first non-professional production of *The Normal Heart.* I don't know how they managed to do it. I got the role of Felix, the young man who dies. It was the first time that I knew that something was way, way bigger than me, and that I had something to fulfill. I didn't know how to tell my parents. And I remember going to an acting teacher of mine, Michael Pierce, and I was just sobbing. I'm like, "I have to tell my parents I'm in this." News crews were starting to come, and it was a really stressful time. He said to bring a copy of the play to them, sit them both down, and say, "This is the play that I'm doing at school. It opens next weekend. You can read it, and then you choose." And that's what I did. My mom came, and at the closing performance I saw my dad in the parking lot. We hashed it out a little bit. It was a leap for him.

Wasn't it a leap for you?
No, nothing could have stopped me from the chance to act in that. I was scared, but I was also really ready. I didn't find those kinds of scripts in musical theater. So I stayed in the acting program.

So when you came to New York, did you not initially intend to be doing musicals?
I wanted to do work that challenged me. I wanted to do work that allowed me to transform into a part. I knew early on what a good part was. I wanted to do good parts. By a "good part," I mean, a part where there's a real journey to go on, but also something where there's something to figure out. That part of it appeals to me. A right brain sensibility. I didn't have to work at singing. I was just something as I did as a kid. Once I got to studying when I was twelve, thirteen, fourteen, and I started learning the exercises and scales, it could be a challenge, but music came naturally to me. I could play piano naturally. I could play guitar instinctually. I could harmonize instinctually. When I got to college, I felt confident as a musician, but as an actor I didn't know my head from my ass. I didn't know how that actor playing Scrooge got to literally make me think somebody just walked in off the street and sat down counting money. And by the time I got to college, I had discovered some of my acting heroes: Robert Duvall in *Tender Mercies*, Pacino in *Dog Day Afternoon*, Gene Hackman. So as soon as I got to college I wanted to focus on acting. My twenties were an odd time. It took me five years to graduate from college because I dropped out in my sophomore year and I went to London for a year and a half. I really fell in love with British actors and British theater. Came back. I finished my BFA. I was in love. I followed a girl to Omaha, Nebraska. I did some non-Equity touring out there. We broke up. I applied for a graduate program down at the University of Alabama in Montgomery. Did that MFA program for two years. Spun my wheels. I got married quite young. I was twenty-six. Right after I finished graduate school. Married. Living in Montgomery. Adjunct teaching at Auburn and doing roles at night at the Alabama Shakespeare Festival for three years. And then at twenty-nine . . . I think it was just maybe thirty coming down the pike, I was like, "I have to try New York." So just before my twenty-ninth birthday, moved to New York with my now ex-wife. We had like five grand and thought, "If we're starving we'll leave." And in that first six weeks I booked *Rent*. I had a friend who was having a benefit to raise money for a small theater company, and I had my guitar. I came and sang a song. A publicist was there and said, "You'd be really good for this musical that just opened." The swing had been fired. But even though he [recommended] me, I lost his number. I couldn't get that guy, so I went to the open call down at The Public and waited nine hours in line like everybody else. But at the first screening, [the monitor] saw my name, and was like, "Norbert, Norbert, that name. They told me to listen for you." She took me out of the line and put me right into the callback room with Bernie Telsey. I had four auditions and then I did *Rent* for the next year and ten months.

You weren't freaked out at your first Broadway audition?
I could do the things I was asked to do when I auditioned with great confidence. I don't have a lot of confidence. I have bombed musical auditions when I have gone in with sheet music from a traditional musical. [Once] they told me to bring my book to an audition and I brought a novel. I didn't know they meant a book of music. I thought I was just going to have time to kill. But I came up with my brothers singing folk and rock 'n' roll songs with a guitar on my body. In college we'd go down to bars and play for tips in pubs and clubs. So for me to

put a guitar on and sing a Cheap Trick song—it would be like asking Gavin Lee to tap for us for a minute. Do you know what I mean? So in the wheelhouse. I could do it and not have to put anything on. I could just do it.

Let's back up for a second. You decided to come to New York. Was that just because that's what actors do?

I think so. I think through a lot of my life, I had this balance of wanting to take risks, but then also wanting to follow propriety. I did a BFA and then an MFA so that I could teach college and have something to fall back on. That was the German work ethic, practical side of my dad. I was a professional actor doing Equity shows at night, but I got to learn how to be a teacher. All these things that I felt I should do were the smart things to do, they were the adult things to do. But I missed that stage where I went to a big city, lived with five people, did readings, and starved. It was like "now or never." I waited 'til the last possible moment. But by the time I came to New York, I was already Equity, doing professional roles in good regional theaters. It was different than coming when you're twenty or twenty-one years old.

***Rent* was already explosive by the time you got here.**

It was a strange time for sure. It was a really strange time. I can't overestimate how my life transformed utterly in that couple of years. I literally don't even have the words to talk about it. So much happened. I became a father. Here I'm singing Roger in *Rent* every Sunday night and playing Mark often. Adam Pascal had to go down to a seven-show week because that score just tore those guys up. I went from having no money to making more money than my dad. I had to do *Rent* the second year as a new dad. It put a strain on that marriage. It was a lot. Had health issues. I tore my ACL [anterior cruciate ligament] eight months into the show. I had to have surgery. Had vocal swellings. And it was an amazing experience. I had so many great experiences in that show. And I had one moment that made any hardship all worth it; my dad loved *Rent*. My homophobe dad. By that time he'd seen me take my clothes off several times, and make out with dudes, and have to perform violent acts on stage. I did a lot of edgy plays. It all became old hat to him. He loved *Rent* and he saw it every time he'd come to New York City. He was standing in the back of the theater while we were singing "Seasons of Love," and he became friends with Al Larson, Jonathan Larson's dad. I saw them just holding each other, these two men, and I'll never forget that moment. I could barely get through the song. And *Rent* was—look, the show is a very naïve show. It's very, very sentimental. The dramaturgy is a mess. But watching that original cast, the sense of purpose that they had every night with that show was palpable. It was kinetic. It was such a gift to have a reason, a real purpose. Like you're doing a service. And it was odd, too, because I turned thirty when I was doing *Rent* and like I said, I had a newborn and I was married. My life was actually starting to become one of real bourgeois, suburban, regularity. But on stage you're playing these people living on the very edge of counterculture, survival. I was the only parent in the cast. I was the only married person, I think. They're still going out, going to clubs, going to premieres, and partying. I remember a real sense that my stage life can be really different from my home life, and that's okay. It took me awhile to learn how to bridge those two things. So yeah, *Rent*, huge. After that it gets really boring.

Boring?

Every job has just come from a job. You just build on that. It just all flowed really organically.

So you went from classical training into a rock musical, and then to a classic musical.

I left *Rent*. I would have stayed because I had a mortgage and a baby, but Rob Marshall had come to see it and asked me to come in for the Emcee in the first national tour of *Cabaret*. So I left *Rent* and went straight to that. That role really, really kicked my butt. That was a tough year. But it came from Rob seeing me in *Rent*, and the fact that I speak some German so I had the dialect. I had all this classical training so I could fulfill the dramatic parts of the show, and I had the musical chops. Just the right place at the right time.

Still, he took a leap.

I do think it was a leap. And that stuff is tough. When we rehearsed, I was on cloud nine. I'd seen Alan Cumming, but I was getting excited by this different thing that I could do. The rehearsals were just so thrilling. Sam Mendes came in, too. Then we got to L.A. [and they kept changing my makeup and hair color]. "If we go too blond, we've missed the Jewish thing." They suddenly starting losing confidence. Every night, "No, no, it's not working." I'll never forget that opening night in L.A. I mean, there were famous people that came to see *Rent*, but we couldn't see them. In *Cabaret*, as the Emcee, you [mingle in the audience.] It was fucking nuts. Shirley MacLaine, Tom Hanks, Sarah Jessica Parker, Betty White—I mean, there was no one who wasn't famous. I can be confident, but I just didn't—I developed terrible stage fright. Terrible. And then reviews came out, and I did the thing you're absolutely not supposed to do: I read them. I did. I got off pretty well but it was definitely unfavorable compared to Alan, and I remember that fucked me up for a good couple of weeks. It took me three or four cities of that tour to relax. As it went on, I found, I think, a really interesting character there and started having the kind of freedom that that part needs. But that's a hard role. Really, really hard. I'm a language person so I really want text. His [character] is all done through song. And also the pressure of just knowing you're the guy that the audience is going to latch onto to bring them through this nightmare. So it needs a tremendous amount of power and seduction and danger and mystery and humor. It takes everything you have to get them to come with you. Maybe I was too young. And I'll be totally honest with you; one of the biggest struggles was my body. The androgyny of the part was really important for that production. I'm a yoga person. I'm a swimmer. I'm pretty physically active, and I was really buff at the time. I remembered feeling way too butch. It was like, how do I shed the muscle on my body? I remember being really stressed out about that. I'd go on these crash diets and then be starving. But as I leaned out, and my body was more malleable and could take on a rock 'n' roll star, and also a concentration camp victim, and also a woman in a 1930s flapper dress—that shape-shifting quality that the Emcee has to have. I didn't have a lot of time to prepare. I left *Rent*, and we started rehearsal on *Cabaret* the next week.

Was it just the discovery that was rough for you, or the whole run?

I had a one-year-old. I was in a marriage that was complicated. We got pregnant on the tour with our second, and for her, having two small babies, accepting the realities of my not being home every night and sleeping in the days really started to make her unhappy. It was a strange year.

You came back and booked *Thou Shalt Not*, which was yet another step in showcasing your versatility and range.

I just always say "yes" to work. I've really never had the luxury—financially or in any other way—to say "no." Sometimes the quality is just not there or there's something offensive in it, but [overall]—I say yes to everything. It was a deep, deep, deep desire to work, I think. Workaholism is a word that's been used by my loved ones to describe me.

Do you see that as a necessary reality of the business, or does it feed you because you get to keep exploring, or both?

It is. On my bad days when I'm feeling sorry for myself . . . "Why am I not further along than this? and yada, yada, ya . . ." But mostly . . .

What would further look like?

Have what the next guy has. It's not logical. "Why don't I have a film career like Ethan Hawke?" Or you're watching *The Greatest Showman*. "Gosh darn it, I can dance." Those are the bad days. But most of the time, I do feel truly, truly, truly blessed and really, really lucky. [But I don't have a goal.] I don't think like that. It's just, "What's the next job?" It has always, always, always been about "what's the next job."

Thou Shalt Not **was the next job.**

The critics just ripped it apart, but [for me?] I'm being offered this wonderful role with music that Harry Connick Jr. is writing for me, choreography by Susan Stroman. . . . I really loved that script. I loved that story. They asked me to audition for Craig Bierko's role, and I said, "No, but I'll come in for the other guy."

That was ballsy at that stage in your career.

I know, I know. But I was never going to be a leading man. This guy [the character] has got consumption and is kind of an asshole and then gets murdered, and then comes back as a ghost. I mean, that's so interesting! I had a ball in that show. Our first day of tech was 9/11. It was a really complicated time. I learned the greatest lesson. You can be in the biggest bomb in town, and it *was* the biggest bomb in town, and still love it. You couldn't write worse reviews than we got for that show. But you can be in a terrible show and have the most wonderful time if you are able to create, if you've done the work. A strong bond is there among the cast members and that's a safety net for you. When the audiences don't come or fall asleep or . . . incredible dancers on that show. Amazing people. I had the greatest time. Deb Monk! She is somebody who is clearly in it to be in front of a dressing table and communicating with actors. Her love is palpable.

What was you experience of Susan Stroman?

She had tremendous confidence in me and she instilled a lot of confidence in me. The second act wasn't working in that show. They cut a huge number and Harry wrote a new song that became this big, swinging, Sinatra song and I did this dance on the bed. That was written on a Thursday in the afternoon. I got sent a disc of it that night, sat with the music, the next day I learned it with Harry. She choreographed it, we teched it, and I did it that night. A six-minute song and dance number. Brand-new song, all new choreography. Only Susan Stroman could lead you through that and have it lift the entire show. I would go, "You're fucking crazy." She's like, "You can do this." She had this real quiet strength. Utter confidence in herself, and in me. I was super grateful to her. She saved my ass on that. But after 9/11, the absolute worst thing you could offer an audience in trauma was that show. Our subject matter was as dark as you can get. Two awful people murder the woman's husband. There was a scene that took place in a morgue! The best thing you could offer an audience in trauma was *Mamma Mia!* Opened the same week. I guess that was also the beginning of the time where you start to have a real long talk with yourself and your shrink and your spouse and get very, very real about the business, the whimsy of it. How quickly your fortune can change. It becomes really, really clear. There's just not a lot of security, and so much is out of your control. You have to get really, really right with that at some point.

You think that's when it became real for you?
I think so, because then it was bombs for me. I went from *Thou Shalt Not* to *The Last Five Years*, which couldn't have been a bigger bomb. We didn't know that regional theaters were going to be performing it, and a movie was going to be made, and a whole bunch of college musical theater majors were going to sing those songs for years and years. No. We were just in a bomb show. But again, an amazing time. It was really emotional. Jason Robert Brown asked if I'd come over to his apartment to do a work session on the music before my audition, and he played me two songs from the show. I asked him where the bathroom was and I excused myself, and I started crying, and crying, and crying. Right away.

It's to your credit that you took the show, knowing how emotionally raw it was going to be for you. Or did you just feel like you needed the job?
No. I took it as a good sign. If I had such a visceral reaction to just two songs . . .

It was a bad time for you.
Yeah, it was. My marriage was really dissolving while I was doing this play. It was just super weird. I had a three-year-old and a one-year-old. I was broke when I took *The Last Five Years* and really hoping that it would run or transfer. Brantley's review was just a big dismissal. But Sondheim came, Audra McDonald came, Carol Burnett came, Idina Menzel and Taye Diggs. Masters of the form came and for the first month we had full houses. There was a buzz with that score and word had gotten out. It didn't appeal to theater critics as a piece of theater. But gorgeous music. "Really noble effort, but it doesn't work," was the general tone of the reviews. So then I was fucked when that show closed [in two months]. And I didn't work. I got nominated for a Tony the day after *The Last Five Years* closed off-Broadway. *Thou Shalt Not* had closed like six months before and we only ran like a month. I mean, they shut that thing down. I couldn't believe anybody remembered. I didn't even remember that I did it. I got this Tony nomination. Oh, my God! I was so thrilled. I remember, before the awards ceremony, my ex-wife and I had some friends over at a hotel room and we're all having champagne and toasting, having fun and getting ready, and I remembered—I was like, "Oh, my God, I forgot to call unemployment! Shut up everybody, I've got to call for my fucking $209 this week!"

What was the Tony experience like?
My agents called the hotel room, and they're like, "Don't forget to walk the red carpet. Somebody will greet you there from the Tony Awards. You've got to get the press." We were staying on the East Side and I'd never been to Radio City Music Hall before. We're walking down 49th Street and there's a red carpet that goes into the kitchen with a rope around it. I'm like, "Honey, this is it." The two of us get into a hallway that leads into the ass of Radio City Music Hall and get lost in there for twenty minutes. We missed the entire red carpet and I didn't get one fucking photo of myself from the first time I got nominated. Mary Louise Parker announced my category, and when she said my name in the mic, and I heard "Norbert Leo Butz" for the first time in a big sound system, I had a panic attack. I thought, "That's the

worst fucking name. Why didn't I change it? Everybody on TV heard that." It sounded so bad to my ears in a great big room like that. "You're an idiot, and now you can't do anything about it. What are you going to do now?"

Before we leave *The Last Five Years*, Sherie Rene Scott . . .

Sherie and I had done *Rent* together so we were chums and had great shorthand. I still adore her. We've done three shows together and we got really close during that process. We'd rehearse and sing our hearts out and then we'd go to the Minetta Lane Tavern down the street and have therapy sessions and open our hearts. You have that thing in the theater. I call it a "fast-track intimacy" where people that you know a little bit or total strangers, suddenly you start working, and then you're divulging huge secrets. If you're not saying it, you're showing it in the work. It's an odd thing. But Sherie was fantastic. And I loved working with [director] Daisy Prince. That was a joy. I guess I've always been an intuitively correct singer. I've been able to sing a lot, a lot, a lot before I get tired in a show. [But this], more than *Rent*, really drove me to the edge. Jason writes right up there at the top and stays there for the whole fucking show. It was the first time I had to get a proper coach. Studying really saved my butt, and that's something I still really, really fall back on. So it was a show that really pushed me to the very edge. It was a great, great time for me to really get to know my voice well. By the time I finished it, I was like, "There's nothing I can't sing." I felt like Superman. But it closed early. And I still get asked about it all the time. It's probably what I get asked about the most.

That surprises me, given that your next show was *Wicked*.

I got the script to *Wicked* while I was doing *The Last Five Years*. I was talking to Sherie about it through the curtain separating our dressing rooms. I had read the novel years before. I'm a big reader but it's dense. I remembered being absolutely blown away by that novel so I had a really strong image in my mind about *Wicked*. When I got the script, it was not nearly done, and the part was not fleshed out. So I passed on the audition. I said I rarely turn things down, but *Wicked* was an audition I turned down. And then *The Last Five Years* closed and I had the longest period of unemployment [I've had]. My wife had decided she wanted out of our marriage, so it was a really, really crazy time for me, and financially it was bad. And they came back around and I needed a job. I don't think that team wanted me. They needed a younger, typical leading man for that part. But [director] Joe Mantello really rooted for me, and I think Idina Menzel rooted for me because we'd been friends from *Rent*. And frankly, I think I got it because Kristin is so tiny and I'm only five seven. It would be hard to cast somebody who's six foot two next to Kristin. So I did it. And that was a really good lesson because I wasn't entirely happy in *Wicked*. Personally, obviously, I was going through hell. But in the process I was really unhappy. They had such a difficult time trying to figure out what the play was and what it was about. The supporting roles got lost in the shuffle. I remember feeling hamstrung and like it wasn't good enough material to work on. I was wanting more and I was wanting to make more of an impression on the play and to make it deeper. One of the producers joked to me, "Who cares? It's all about the girls," but I realized he was right. And the creative team had some differences of opinion about the way that it should go. So as an actor, it wasn't completely fulfilling. But I was so grateful to have a paycheck. It just saved my butt. I kept thinking I was going to be fired any week. People were getting fired left and right from [the tryout in] San Francisco. I was so grateful when they kept me for New York.

Idina and Kristin both spoke to me about the fact that they work very differently. Was navigating that a challenge?

I just knew that the best way for me to get through *Wicked* the best I could was really to—and I learned—I really stayed quiet. I did the best I could with what I had to work with. I did the best I could to fulfill what was there. And the other thing that was happening during *Wicked*—I had met Michelle Federer ten years before doing a reading, and we were acquaintances, and then we got into *Wicked* and became super, super close friends at first, and then fell wildly in love somewhere between San Francisco and New York [they married in 2007]. And then I broke my neck. Unbeknownst to me at the time, I had a herniated disc in my neck, and there was this move in "Dancing Through Life" that was really, really hurting it. I ruptured two discs in my neck a week after we opened. It had been bothering me through previews, but because of the size of the show and all of the problems, understudies were not prepared to go on, so I kept performing on this injury until I finally ruptured it. I had to have an emergency spinal fusion. I was out of *Wicked* for two months on a medical leave. I felt great after two weeks and wanted to come back to work, but they had replaced me with Taye Diggs for a [contracted] period, so that's when I did the workshop for *Dirty Rotten Scoundrels*. *Wicked* is this strange thing; it's by far and away the most famous thing I've ever been a part of, and yet, I've always felt like a post, post, postscript on it. I'm like the forgotten *Wicked* member, and that seems to make sense to me because I went straight into this other thing that I think I became more well known for.

Were you at least happy being in something that had job security?

No. Well, yes but I was so unhappy in the role and with my performance. What I thought I could uniquely bring to the part wasn't supported by the script. "It's all about the girls." So creatively I just felt so hamstrung. I would have been desperately unhappy there if I had stayed any longer. I have such fond memories about *Wicked*. My little girls were three and five years old and they grew up backstage at the Gershwin. They'd be in the wings waving to Idina as she's going [sings final notes of "Defying Gravity"]. She'd look down at them. It was a magical time for them. And then I met this woman [Federer]. The process of putting the show together was a tough, tough process. Very traumatic on a lot of levels. I had met this woman who was just so delightful, and we created our own little cocoon, and stayed away from all of the dramas and the press and the Tony Awards. We didn't have to be a part of any of that. We didn't have to show up at the press events or all that kind of thing. We got to have our own little intoxicating love affair. My memory of *Wicked* really is Michelle. I'll forever be grateful. Even as hard as the process was, I will forever be grateful.

And you roll right into *Dirty Rotten Scoundrels*.

The reading of that really was the audition. And that's a lovely way to audition because you could spend a whole week in the room, trying new things. Something just clicked. I did it first with Brian Stokes Mitchell. I remember just going for it in the workshop. It was funny, funny writing. Our first day of rehearsal in San Diego—we started on a Tuesday. My divorce was legal on Saturday. So I had to go to the courthouse in Newark, New Jersey, stand in front of a judge. My marriage was dissolved and I was at a really, really, really low point. Sherie had just given birth to her son, Eli, and it was an emergency C-section like a week before we started. And John Lithgow had been diagnosed with prostate cancer and had had his surgery only a few weeks prior. So our first day of rehearsal, I'm uncontrollably sobbing in the bathroom all the time. Sherie can barely move. John literally can't move. I called us "The Walking Wounded of Comedy." And we started laughing from the beginning and became such great friends, so that was a lesson in the transformative power of laugher. Underneath all the show's craziness and silliness were some really damaged people physically, emotionally, and mentally. We just jumped onto the train. That was my first time working with Jack O'Brien, who I now consider my mentor. I learned so much from him.

Like what?

I guess one of the most important things I learned from Jack—and it's about comedy but it works for everything as well—he would say over and over, "You're not funny. The play is funny." Jack would really kick your ass if you were gilding the lily. If you were someone who needed that laugh, he would really come down hard. In the silliest of comedies, the most dramatic of plays, Jack understands the central driving through-line. It's like a rope; the plot of a play has to keep a tension. You can let it go at certain points, and then it's got to ratchet up. But laughter actually is a release, and if you're mugging too much, if you become a laugh whore, you're just letting go of the overall arch of the piece. You have to be disciplined. I was just throwing everything out there. He became an incredible editor to me. And sometimes he was very hard about it. Look, any actor who does comedy will tell you, I mean, that shit can be like crack. Just pure heroin. It affects something in your brain. That thing with the audience. And then when you can get a laugh from a laugh, and then when you can get a third laugh, and you haven't even said the next line yet . . . And I have an addictive personality. Jack was the person to say, "I'm going to kill your darlings here . . ."

That's a Mike Nichols expression.

That's right. Jack was a mentee of Mike Nichols. Mike Nichols came to *Dirty Rotten*. Did notes. Gave them to Jack. Those are guys who take their comedy very, very, very seriously. The characters aren't funny, they are desperate, insecure, greedy, enraged—the active things that make you pursue such ridiculous ends have to be firmly in place. No matter how crazy comedic situations get, the integrity you have to have for the logic of the storytelling has to be crystal clear. Jack taught me that. The other thing with Jack coming from such a strong classical background—there's a way of delivering text on stage. You have to do it in Shakespeare, but you also have to do it in comedy. You have to keep on going to the end of the line so that you get the thing on the "boom." There's a rhythm and a drive and an energy in the text when you're speaking it. Jack was the person to constantly be reminding you of what the target words were, what the thought under the thought was going to be. He's just a genius at language. I couldn't get enough of it. I found it all so fascinating. It was a huge period of growth for me.

Was it hard to maintain that discipline?

Jack's a director who comes [back to a show during the run] a lot. He's rare in that way. And he has excellent assistants. Those guys are super disciplined about keeping their shows tight. And so yes, you're given notes a lot of times. Jack said, "I want the characters to feel like they have found themselves in the wrong play." So Joanna Gleason, playing her extremely vain, ditsy, deadpan, rich lady, Muriel, was supposed to be playing *Summer and Smoke* but she ended up in *Dirty Rotten Scoundrels*. That's fucking funny, right? And it keeps you on this really honest track of trying to figure out where I am and what's going on because I think I'm in the wrong play. He had this ability to create these metaphors that made it just so creative and so fun. I'd never worked with someone as smart and as joyful as him, and as tough. I will work with him anytime he asks me. Because when you have someone who pays so much respect to the intelligence of the audience, that's a director that you want to work with over, and over, and over again.

As Ruprechet, who "likes to save up all his farts in a Mason jar." On the lap of John Lithgow while Sara Gettelfinger looks on in horror in *Dirty Rotten Scoundrels*. (Craig Schwartz)

You won the Tony for *Dirty Rotten*.

I think I'm just a neurotic person. I won the Tony Award. My girlfriend and I went to the parties. We went back to the hotel room. She fell asleep and I think I cried for three straight hours. It wasn't misery; it was just a release. I had been working really hard to that point. We opened in the fall so I'd been doing the show for ten months, tons of press. At the Tonys you're shot out of a cannon. You're on the stage, on a TV camera, thanking people, you shake a thousand hands, you take eight million pictures, it's so, so, so much sensory overload that it's very difficult to stay present. I have to watch footage of it to even have any memory of it at all. My memory of winning the Tony was weeping in the bathroom. I'll tell you one thing, though: it is terrifying to accept an award. It's terrifying to get up onstage. I don't care if people make fun of me for saying this. I have awful, awful stage fright. If I have a score and a good script and six weeks of rehearsal and my costumes and my makeup, I still don't want to get out there. Once I'm out there, I'm in my happy place. But you asked me [to be myself]?! Why am I sweating this much talking to you? I get very, very, very self-conscious and nervous, and I look at myself, and I stammer. I'm not naturally somebody who . . .

Opens up as yourself?

No, I'm not an exhibitionist in that way at all. I save it all, I guess, for being onstage. And so it was scary. It produced a lot of anxiety. And obviously I'm extremely proud of it. It was wonderful for our show. And all of the benefits of it are wonderful. And that was a fun experience because we were all nominated: the score, and the show, and the choreography, and Jack, and all of the other actors, and that's a joy. You go through the whole thing as a big unit. I've been on the other end where you're like the only one nominated and that's a very lonely experience.

You stayed with *Dirty Rotten* . . .

It was just an embarrassment of riches! I got to work with John Lithgow, and then Jonathan Pryce came in. And then I got to go on the tour and do it with Tom Hewitt, who I fell in love with and is like the greatest kept secret in New York. It was one of those things that I will spend the rest of my career just being grateful for.

After *Dirty Rotten*, you did a series of plays. *Is He Dead? Fifty Words. Speed the Plow. Enron.* But your next musical was back with Jack O'Brien.

Catch Me If You Can. Jack asked me to come and be part of a reading again. My dad, who has since passed, struggled the last dozen years of his life with congestive heart failure. He had had a surgery the morning that I got script. He was in the hospital in St. Louis, and I was waiting for word. So I took the script to a diner and I had this beautiful breakfast. I open the script, and I start reading. *Catch Me If You Can* is really the story of a son in search of a father and father in search of a son. I had to go to the bathroom and start bawling. And that's kind of how I choose jobs. I mean, honestly, when it's that little fast gut punch, you're so lucky when you get that. You get arm hairs up. The intellectualism is taken out of it. I've had certain experiences in my life where that initial reaction carries you through the whole process. The trick is to not get too in your head, to just follow that. I've seen people intellectualize themselves out of roles. That show was also a tricky one to get together structurally. It was hard. I watched the creative team really struggle with the tone and rewriting. It was a hard, hard, hard process. And it's all out of your control. When you're in those big, Broadway musicals, it's like being in a major studio film. You realize you're really limited in terms of those bigger aesthetic decisions. You've got your part and what you think you can contribute to it. You work like hell on it. I knew exactly who this guy was. He reminded me of my dad. He reminded me of my grandpa and several uncles. He was a pre–World War II, greatest generation of America, Tom Brokaw, square, straight-edged, don't-break-the-rules type of guy. The whole role was just an homage to my dad, and when my brothers and sisters came to see it, they cried. I tried to look as much like my dad—that's why I padded myself, and I grew this mustache. [He starts to tear up.] I'll get upset if I think about it too much. I just loved it. And Aaron Tveit—is there a more effortless, smarter singer working in musicals? And the Tony was such a surprise. I really didn't expect that. It's more of a supporting role, really. The reviews were not good. It was a mess of a show. I knew that. Looking back, I think there were three or four really separate and strong opinions [among the creators] about what it could be, and in order to try to give everybody a little bit of appeasement, it turned the show into something, at least from what the critics had to say, not nearly cohesive enough. The show had problems, but I loved my guy. I loved my guy.

And what about the physicality of it, because you were dancing up a storm?

That was lucky. I had asked them to pad me, for my pants to be too short, for my shoes to be too big. I'd asked them for the dorky glasses. When you start to add that with Jerry Mitchell's leggy choreography, it made for this ridiculous marriage that worked really, really well. I was thinking, "How would a guy like that do Jerry Mitchell choreography? How do I get the choreography wrong but still really right for him?" It was a blast. But we needed that review, and it didn't come. It's just a matter of time before you close.

You told me you don't read them . . .

My manager calls me every opening night. She's basically like, "We're good!" or "It's not going our way." I always want to know if I have to start having other irons in the fire.

I had this conversation with Bebe Neuwirth and she said of reviews, "It's none of my business." I would think it's exactly your business in the truest sense of the word.

You're so, so right. I say that, too. I always say other people's opinions of me are none of my business, but are we going to have a run or not? That's your business.

And then after reviews come in, you can feel the house change?
Absolutely.

Is it a bummer to come to work?
It can be. Yeah, it's a bummer. It's a huge fucking bummer. You're like, "Now we have to work three [times as hard to get their attention]." But the beautiful thing that does happen if the group of people is right—that was a great, great ensemble. People did really, really come together. If it's not going to be coming from the audience—and the reviewers tell the audience how to react . . . They know that they're sitting in a hit show that the *Times* loved and they have to be as smart as that critic at *The New York Times* so they are laughing and clapping. I'm not saying that they're not enjoying it, but there's a psychological thing that happens. They know that they should be laughing and clapping at a hit. And when something's gotten bad reviews, it's very much of a "Show me" attitude. You're battling that. And the only thing to do is put a big, big wall up between you and the audience and pretend and do it for your other actors.

Big Fish was next for you.
Big Fish, which I don't really want to talk about, was the biggest disappointment in my career. That's the most unhappy I've ever been in a show. It's the show that really, really, really kicked my ass in every way. I was really unhappy with the process, with the run, with how it was received. We were just not able to get that story onstage in a way that satisfied audiences or critics. And that's the time when I really did say I need a break from this. I was broke. I had two Tony Awards and it was my ninth or tenth Broadway show and I couldn't make any fucking money. I read an article that a producer of *Big Fish* actually wrote for *Variety* when the show didn't get any Tony nominations. The article said, "I wouldn't change anything about *Big Fish*. We had a beautiful show. It was perfect. Norbert Butz is a super, super-talented guy. But Hugh Jackman did our first readings and he wasn't available. Norbert was brilliant but Norbert doesn't sell any tickets." He wasn't throwing me under the bus. He was saying—and I'm not angry about it—a truism. Now, having said that, the way *Big Fish* was produced and directed—I did the math on this with a couple of guys backstage—*Big Fish* would have needed to run for two and a half years with every single seat sold to recoup its investment. That's how expensive it was. So you could take the argument I'm not famous enough to sell seats or you could say production costs and design got way, way, way out of balance with the realities of Broadway financials. That's when I was like, "I'm out." And it wasn't with any kind of sadness—there might have been some bitterness—it was more acceptance. I was like, "I'm this musical theater guy, and there's no place for me on Broadway." You work a year and a half, two years on these things. You do the regional production for little money. You go and do another workshop. You pass on other jobs. You open and close in two months. You make Broadway salary for two or three months for a year and a half, two years of investment. *Catch Me If You Can* was five years from start to finish. You only run five months. Five months of pay spread out over five years of your investment time. It just didn't add up for me. Here I am [on Broadway, now] contradicting myself, but I said, "I have to find another career." I was always onstage and so I couldn't do any TV and film of any length, I just had to say "no" all the time. Plus I didn't want to travel a lot. I'm raising my girls right here in Jersey. That was the first time I was like, "I've

got to find a new way." So I started auditioning for film and booked a television show that took me to Florida for three years and then another one took me to Virginia for two years, and here we are. I spent five years not on stage at all (except in a limited-run off-Broadway play), and then *My Fair Lady* was the thing that came up. I had told my manager, "No more new musicals. I'll only do a revival, and only if the writers are dead and have been dead for half a century." I couldn't do another project where the writers are still writing it and developing for so, so, so long. I'm not putting down writers. I'm putting down the process. It's so difficult to do a Broadway show. It's so collaborative. There are so many moving parts. It's so hard to get everybody together. You've got to take it out of town to try to have some space and privacy, but that all comes at a huge financial cost. Gone are the days when people would be put on retainers and told, "Here's a hundred grand. Don't take any work for the next year." That doesn't happen anymore. If you're going to continue with the show to Broadway, there are going to be big, big periods where you're giving up your time. You have to be an actor and a dramaturge when

"I'm willing to tell you. I'm wanting to tell you. I'm waiting to tell you." As Alfred P. Doolittle in *My Fair Lady*. (Joan Marcus)

you're working on a new piece. You're actually trying to help them find out what the part is, find out what the structure of the thing is. I just like being the actor. All the other stuff, while it can be really fun and exciting and scary, it doesn't work for my life as much right now. While my kids are still young I have to still be earning. And a Broadway show, especially a musical, just takes everything. It takes your whole body, your whole mind, your whole heart; it takes your health, it takes you away for months and months at a time, and it takes away your money. It makes living your life really, really difficult. I said I'd do a revival because I thought, "Well, even if it's a bomb, I will only have invested four or five weeks of rehearsal. I won't have invested the year and a half to two of workshop, workshop out of town, workshop" . . .

With a show like *My Fair Lady* . . .

The piece works. What do I want artistically? I want to do scripts that work. I want to do pieces of writing or scores that are dramaturgically solid. This job has been a joy from beginning to end. I have loved every second of it. The Shaw! I'm not going to get better words in a musical. The numbers are so, so much fun. The piece is just so deep and so rich. I've been in creative teams where there are a bunch of different points of view. With Bart Sher, there's no ambiguity about who is absolutely at the helm of the show. It's Bart all the way. It's so fantastic when you have a guy with a vision who's so confident in that vision. I got to do the thing this time that I don't ever get to do—just work on a part and get lost in it. I've had a ball. I was doing an interview with somebody who said, "Aren't you a little bit young to move into the one-scene, one-song guy?" I don't see it like that. If what I'm looking for is quality of writing, great storytelling, designers, and the director who are the best in New York City . . . I've just loved it. I mean, it is time to go because I'm breaking down. I am fifty-one, and even that might be too old for Alfie Doolittle.

How does it feel to be leaving?

I've been feeling kind of a low-grade, kind of depressive thing. You've just done a ton of work. You've thought, and thought, and thought about it, and walked with it, and lived with it, and then there's just a real vacuum. There's a real bereft feeling when it's all over. I'm better at it [than I used to be]. And it's also why I think I always try to have the wheels going for the next thing, so I don't really have to deal with it. But I'm sore. I've torn a hamstring that's just not healing, so I've been living in a lot of pain for several months. And I haven't seen my daughters for dinner in many, many months so it's really, really time. I do have to admit it is difficult for me to sign up for the long runs now. I really like to switch things up on stage. Not intentionally, but you just have to stay open. You have to keep trying new things. You have to keep making new choices. You have to go deeper, and there's just a point where you've done everything. You've had so much fun. And when it starts to feel like you're trying to recreate last night's performance, it's time to get off the train.

15

CHRISTIAN BORLE

February, April 2016; February 2018

JUST INSIDE THE DOOR OF Christian Borle's stylish midtown apartment is a bust of William Shakespeare that looks remarkably like the one on Bruce Wayne's desk in the *Batman* TV series. "Does the head lift off when you want to flick the switch for the Batcave," I kid? Borle lifts the head, which is hinged at the neck, to reveal the room's light switches. Perfect. It wasn't until later that I realized that this one home furnishing also represents the meeting of Borle's two childhood loves: the theater and comics.

Borle was a shy comic book artist throughout his youth in Pennsylvania. His guidance counselor was disappointed that he didn't audition for *Guys and Dolls* because she hoped it might get him out of his shell. "And then my friend basically peer-pressured me into auditioning for *Oklahoma!*," he says. "I got cast as the tiniest Will Parker in history. I was as raw a talent in drawing comics as I was in acting, and I had to choose between those two."

He chose, going off to Carnegie Mellon and then hitting New York where he made a name for himself in *Footloose*, *Jesus Christ Superstar*, *Amour*, and *Thoroughly Modern Millie* before landing the gig that showcased his particular talent for zaniness, *Spamalot*. While other shows followed (*Legally Blonde*, *Mary Poppins*, *Angels in America*, and the TV series *Smash*), Borle was most indelible in roles that allowed him to cut loose (*Little Me* at Encores!, *Little Shop of Horrors*, and especially *Peter and the Starcatcher* and *Something Rotten!*, both of which won him Tony awards). In his *New York Times* review of the latter, Ben Brantley called Borle "a master of carefully stylized excesses." In the 2016–17 season, Borle did double duty, top-lining both the intimate revival of *Falsettos* and the oversized *Charlie and the Chocolate Factory*.

Borle himself, I imagined, would have some of the kinetic energy he so frequently displays on stage. He isn't that guy. He's warm and welcoming but also grounded. He's introspective, thoughtful, disciplined, and very bright. He's serious, which isn't to say humorless. Not at all. But he makes no effort to entertain me. He has shelves of books, but also, on my third visit, an in-progress, massive Lego sculpture of the Millennium Falcon dominating the kitchen table. (The apartment, incidentally, had seen its share of Tony Awards long before Borle moved in; previous inhabitants included Michael Bennett and Tommy Tune. Thank goodness for the mantel.)

You went to Carnegie Mellon . . .
They had a fantastic dance program. We took dance every day. By the time we left, I could do a quadruple pirouette, the right side. And yeah, I started getting hired as a dancer in all the

In *Falsettos*, the same season Borle did a total 180 and played Willy Wonka. (Joan Marcus)

shows. I was a bit of a natural. I still have the worst flexed sickled feet, so it's all about distracting with the arms. To this day.

Were you fitting in with all of those die-hard theater kids?
Yes, our class was really strong. The ten musical theater students completely gelled. We were a force to be reckoned with. I was really young for it. It took me a couple of years to understand how to take it seriously. I do think the school served me well and I did it proud, but it took a while. I'm a late bloomer on all fronts. Even in this crazy business, I feel like I'm just now hitting a particular stride, even though I've been able to work.

Do you feel like what you've done up until now only taps a part of what you want to offer?
I guess I just now feel confident in my adult skin. I was successful at thirty-three by any measure. But I look back at that person, and I still feel like I was a kid on some level. And you have that seven-year thing where all of your cells shed, you have a different physiological

Christian Borle	
Footloose	National Tour, Broadway, 1998
Jesus Christ Superstar	Broadway, 2000
Amour	Broadway, 2002
Prodigal	Off-Broadway, 2002
Elegies	Off-Broadway, 2003
Thoroughly Modern Millie	Broadway, 2003
Spamalot	Broadway, 2005
Legally Blonde	Broadway, 2007
On the Town	Encores!, 2008
Mary Poppins	Broadway, 2009
Sweeney Todd	Lincoln Center, 2014
Little Me	Encores!, 2014
Something Rotten! (Tony Award)	Broadway, 2015
Falsettos	Broadway, 2016
Charlie and the Chocolate Factory	Broadway, 2017
Me and My Girl	Encores!, 2018
Little Shop of Horrors	Off-Broadway, 2019

makeup. I think that's true emotionally. I think every so many years you look back at the person that you were and think, "God, what a nincompoop."

After Carnegie Mellon you came straight to New York and in not a lot of time you booked *Tommy* in Germany.

That's right. It was incredible. *Tommy* was one of the first shows that I saw when I was thinking about moving here. I think it was the summer of '95. I sat in the top-most row and just fell love. I remember the paratroopers jumping through the hole in the floor and I so desperately wanted to do that. I ended up [doing it] for about five months in Offenbach, which was glorious. And I got to jump through that trapdoor. It was amazing.

Next you were cast in *Footloose*.

I did the tour in 1999. It ended up being not-the-happiest touring experience. As much as I enjoyed that show and the people involved in creating it, there was something about the dynamic. Touring can be tricky because you're on top of each other at the theater, at the hotel, on travel days, and if the dynamic is a little off or a little dramatic, then it can just be a nightmare for a year. And it was a lot of very young people and a lot of [older] character people who seemed to me to be disenchanted to be doing the tour *Footloose*. I spent a lot of time off by myself, trying to extricate myself from drama. I left the tour—Looking back, I had not figured out how to be quite as gracious and as much of a team player as I think I am now. I left with a month left so they had to rehearse my replacement and go through the last month without me, but such was my yearning to get the fuck out of there. I did the ill-fated *Jesus Christ Superstar* on Broadway and I left that early because Tom Plotnick was leaving *Footloose*. I thought, "Well, it'd be foolish of me not to play the role on Broadway." So I went back to *Footloose*, and it actually redeemed my entire *Footloose* experience. I was too young to appreciate that I was bouncing from job to job. One week after I was in, they got their two-week notice. I had a three-week tenure in *Footloose* on Broadway.

That's a good little résumé builder.

Yes, it was. I actually do think that that was how I felt at the time. I loved having the *Footloose* experience end on a positive, happy note. And then yeah, it was enough. Three weeks was great actually.

Was the theater scene different then, in 2000?

I think the major difference was not having social media at all. The connections at that point had everything to do with parsimony and neighborhood and socializing after the show, so the people that you got to meet, you actually genuinely got to meet. I am absolutely, vehemently anti social media. It is causing the corrosion of not only society in a macro way, but particularly Broadway, too. I just can't get on board with it. Relationships seem less genuine to me and less based in time and actually getting to know someone.

What you're describing are the liabilities of social media in general, but for Broadway specifically, are you talking about social media relationships with other cast members? Or are you talking about fan relationships? Or are you talking about Broadway gossip? Or all of it?

I guess less about Broadway gossip because I'm not in the know in that way. I'm not tapped in. The fan relationship has certainly changed. That's become its own hydra. I think it's changed the stage door. It's the selfies. On some level, it's obviously flattering that people would want to brag [about meeting you], but when everyone's taking selfies of everything it dilutes the entire thing. So it's not like I feel special in any way. I recognize where I am; it's a high-class problem without a doubt, but the stage door has now become an assembly line. And if what you're looking for is a genuine moment with somebody who you positively enjoyed on stage, or even respect or admire . . . [The show] is what I consider to be my job. This is not what you pay the money for, and this is not my job. If you don't do it, you seem ungrateful, understandably. It's a small price to pay for the lovely success.

You either don't do it and allow yourself to be vilified, or you give into it and dutifully pose every night.

You do have to pick your moments. I have allowed myself, for example, to not come out after matinees because I immediately fall asleep. I need to nap between shows. Then I can wake up at 5:10 and have dinner and coffee. I can't do it the other way around, which is the usual traditional thing to do. That means I miss the matinee stage door. I get notes saying, "I came all this way, and you didn't come out" and that type of thing. And people say that to you in person, too. And it's like, "Well, we just had our moment, and you chose to use it to chastise me." And I also understand; there was a sweet girl that flew all the way in from Ireland and saw the matinee yesterday and was disappointed. I understand that. My best friend, Jen Colella, has the best take on it; she says, "What other job can you think of where when you're done with your job people are waiting for you as you leave to say 'you're amazing?'" Brian d'Arcy James and I have both had to find our stage door demeanors in order to kind of survive with our souls intact. So the people who meet me at the stage door are meeting my stage door version, which is just kind of quiet, seeming to be like, "I've just done—I've given my all to my craft." So I just say "hello" and "thank you," of course.

After *Footloose*, you did the musical *Amour*.

I really loved that experience. I was the standby for Malcolm Gets and Norm Lewis and Chris Fitzgerald, and they were lovely to watch. My task was to sit in that rehearsal room and just watch them and watch the changes, and then to sit in the audience and watch the show. I thought that show was beautiful. It was an all-around positive, great experience and short-lived, but I got to be in the historic Music Box Theater, which was wonderful. I actually only went on once in that show, and it was during a preview. Malcolm Gets gave me the heads-up because there were so many changes, and he was carrying that show. He was in every single scene. He basically said, "I'm really thinking about taking a Sunday matinee off. Are you ready to go?" It was whirlwind. I got up to his dressing room and he left me a bottle of Veuve Clicquot and a note that said, "This is what I used to drink when I loved to drink, and I hope you enjoy it. Break a leg." He was so gracious and lovely. And it went well. I think there's a bootleg somewhere, which I'd like to get my hands on just for curiosity's sake.

Your next show was *Elegies*.

It was the first time in my career that I was asked to do something without auditioning. I loved [composer] Bill Finn so much. It ended up being this enchanted, magical gift. [Director] Graciela Daniele was just unbelievable. Warm, patient. And she was one of those directors that doesn't make acting seem like a mystery. I've gotten direction from some really, really big, major, fantastic, award-winning directors that have left me thinking, "I actually don't know what you're talking about. I don't know what you want from me." But with her, [she'll just say] "Maybe come in from over there."

So she trusts her casting?

Yes, yes. That was the first time I felt trusted in that way. And it was also a good fit material-wise. Everybody had [music that] was perfect for them. There was one glorious, gracious moment—Carolee Carmello originally sang "When the Earth Stopped Turning." That was her song for many years, actually, during developmental productions. One day Graciela thought that it would help the balance if that song went to me. Carolee could not have been more gracious and perfect, lovely, generous, and supportive. That's what the whole experience was like. I'm in awe of Betty Buckley. All I saw from her was intense focus, presence, warmth, and generosity, with me in particular. She took a shine to me and it was a magical, wonderful thing. And to watch her, too—when you're creating with a writer and a director, and you're molding material, being able to make a suggestion at the right time in the right way is a skill that you develop over time. I feel like I've gotten pretty good at it. I learned a lot from her—when is the right time and when is not the right time. I could see the moments that she chose to ask certain questions or make certain changes that worked. It's all about timing. It's like talking to my mother. It's strategy.

And then shortly after that, you did *Thoroughly Modern Millie*.

That was such a long, beautiful journey. Sutton Foster and I started dating [they later married] in between the La Jolla run and rehearsals for Broadway [before Borle was involved with the show]. We went to school together for a year. She was a freshman when I was a junior at Carnegie Mellon. She immediately knew that she wanted to work rather than go to school, which seems to have worked out. We met [again] doing *The Three Musketeers* in San Jose. That was during my idiot squire years. We started dating, and I went off to do *Just So*. And I remember sitting on my little screened-in porch listening on my discman to the three-song demo of *Thoroughly Modern Millie*, listening to Sutton, knowing this is about to happen for her, then coming back to New York, and experiencing it from her point of view, the beginning of this epic rise. Moving in with her during rehearsals and—so I experienced *Millie* from that perspective . . .

She told me that period was really harrowing for her. They had to keep taking in her costumes because she was losing so much weight from the stress. She says she was a basket case.

I can confirm that she was. That was one of the first shows in this modern era of musicals where the leading lady is called upon to do everything—to sing to the rafters and also be in every scene. A whole new paradigm was built, which continues today. Leading ladies are forced to carry the whole show, be a diva star. It is now required of every leading lady to sing her face off. Watching her come home every night . . . and she had to necessarily be a monk and recluse. And again, the stage door, she had to sneak out the back because she couldn't add that on to everything that she had to do. I saw the show so many times. I loved it and I loved her in it. And I loved Gavin Creel in it. And when the time came for his replacement, I didn't know if I could sing it. I certainly wanted to do it . . .

Who put your name in the hat?
I don't remember, but I do remember there being a lot of frank conversations with [composer] Jeanine Tesori, [librettist] Dick Scanlan, [director] Michael Mayer, and [producer] Hal Luftig basically saying, "Before we even consider seeing him, Sutton, is this realistically something that is going to be good for you? For him?" We were in a great place, and it did seem reasonable. And then the next conversation was, "Well, okay, but just so you know we're only going to cast him if he's right. We're not going to do it as a favor." And it worked out very well. It was a freaking joy to do. It was just an easy, breezy run. We would get to the theater. She would do her thing, I would do my thing. We'd mostly go home together at the end of the night. And I loved doing that show. Singing that show eight shows a week taught me how to sing. Almost every show that I've done starting with *Millie* has taught me a new way to sing. Even *Something Rotten!*—after doing it for a year, I've discovered a new, different part of my voice.

Have you had vocal training or have you been learning on the job?
It's really just the eight shows a week, having to sing and stretch in different ways. I got a high mix in *Thoroughly Modern Millie*. In *Spamalot*, I really built my falsetto. *Legally Blonde* opened up my A. And *Something Rotten!* is opening up a different rock sound for me. The only time I ever studied was when I was doing Pirelli [in *Sweeney Todd*] at Lincoln Center. I don't have a C, and I studied for a short time with sweet, dear, patient Joan Lader. Through no fault of hers, I never got there outside of the shower. Stephen Sondheim came to see the show, which of course is scary as hell but yet thrilling. He was very kind about the way I acted it. And he said to me, "It's not supposed to sound good. It's supposed to be funny." It was very generous. I said, "I can never do it in front of people, but I always had it in the shower." And he said very quickly, "Did you ever consider showering in front of people?" That's the only time I've studied vocally, and you can't just do a crash course in vocal study. It takes a lifetime obviously.

At this point in your career did you think, "I'm not going to have to wait tables anymore. I've made it?" Or did you still have insecurity about that?
I did have insecurity. It was between *Amour* and *Millie* that I had to have a survival job, so that didn't feel secure. And New York is fricking expensive. It felt good that I was working obviously, but it felt very much at that point, like every show could be the last one. Only now do I feel okay—and obviously those two baubles [indicates his Tony Awards] help. But all through the first decade I never had that feeling.

There were a couple of years between *Millie* and your next show, *Spamalot*. Were you off doing something elsewhere someplace or were you . . .
Panicking. Thinking this is it. It's over. I did a workshop of *Take Flight* by Maltby and Shire, which was beautiful. I played one of the Wright brothers. I did a few iterations of that over the years, and it never really . . . took flight, pun intended, but it wasn't for want of being beautiful. And that was with the luminous Kelli O'Hara as Amelia Earhart. That was my first run-in with her. Glorious. And then *Spamalot*. I auditioned for it three times and didn't get it, and each time [the character of] Herbert was, at that time, a pink [chorus] contract, and it was being offered to great, funny, fantastic guys. I don't think they'll care if I reveal them because they're doing fine: Jesse Tyler Ferguson, Chris Fitzgerald, and Steven Rosen, who ended up

playing Bedevere. It didn't seem right that it was on an ensemble contract. But that worked in my favor because the role kept getting turned down by other people [because of the contract], and I kept going in and kept not getting it, and not getting it, and not getting it. I almost didn't go in for the last time. I was like, "This is ridiculous. They've seen me." And my friend said, "You're an idiot. Go in. You never know." I auditioned in the basement of Lincoln Center, and when I was done I said to Mike Nichols, "Is there anything that I'm not doing that you'd like to see?" He kind of stopped for a moment, and then he went, "Yes." And he gave me a little adjustment with the Historian, and I did it, I guess, to his liking, and then that was it. And thus began one of the most magical experiences of my life. Working with him, Hank Azaria, David Hyde Pierce, Tim Curry, the whole cast—and Eric Idle who is an idol of mine. Monty Python was huge for me growing up. All of those heavy hitters actually live up to what you hope they would be. Every single one. It was heaven. And that's where I learned—truly learned—because I was always funny or funny-ish—but it was from Mike Nichols and Hank and David that I learned the craft of stage comedy and the art of taking your time and making every single joke land. Because at that point what I had been taught is to kind of drive it.

Faster, funnier . . .
Yeah, yeah. But it's actually the opposite of that. I learned that you have to let the audience finish laughing so that they can hear your line. That's where the magic happens. There was also a confidence that they had that I did not have. They felt ownership of themselves and their comedy and the show. They could just stand there, and it's what I stole to do Shakespeare [in *Something Rotten!*]. You fake it until you feel it, and I feel it now. I think it's absolutely fair to say that that was like school—the next school. Carnegie Mellon taught me how to learn, and then at *Spamalot*, I actually learned. We were all contributing ideas. It was a very open room. And because everyone was so successful and so confident it really was the first example I'd seen of "the funniest idea wins," and it doesn't matter at all where it comes from. So you have Casey Nicholaw choreographing, and Mike Nichols who was just a god walking among us in terms of the economy with which he could make an idea clear. His graciousness and his sense of comedy and truth . . . But it was the first experience that I had with contributing ideas and having those ideas heard and implemented into a show. I went to see *Spamalot* in Pittsburgh, and there were moments where I was like, "That was mine, that was mine."

That was your first time creating a role in a bona fide smash hit. How did that feel?
Heading into Chicago, until the first preview, we didn't know. We genuinely didn't know if it was going to go over. And from the first moment when they started going crazy—they never stopped going crazy the whole run that we were there. And so it was like a fantastic roller coaster ride, and it was peppered with these incredibly generous moments. It's where I learned to be generous with your company and how good that is for morale.

You mean on stage?
And off stage. And socially. David Hyde Pierce is the king of generosity; everybody knows that. It's a way of life for him. I think it's how he shows his gratitude for the enormous success that he's had. It's what makes him, I think, able to live with that success—by making everybody else feel taken care of and special. He does it wherever he goes. Sutton and I were having our anniversary dinner, and we asked him if he knew how to get a table at Per Se. It had just opened, and we really wanted to go, just for fun. We ended up finding a way to get in and we got to the end of our dinner and the bill was empty. David was the only person who knew that we were going so we knew it must have been him. The next morning were the Tony

nominations, and he was the only major player in *Spamalot* to not get nominated. I wrote him a card that had nothing to do with the Tonys but basically said, "An incredibly generous, amazing gesture was made last night. I have a feeling that it was you. If it was you, thank you from the bottom of our hearts. It was amazing. If it wasn't you, then fuck off." He came in, and he put a Post-it next to his sign-in on the call board that said, "I came in anyway." And then he walked up to me and said, "I normally wouldn't take credit, but on a day like today, I do have to say, 'yes, it was me.'" And it was the most beautiful, the sweetest—which is just who he is. So the whole experience was full of that type of stuff. We all loved and supported each other, and everybody was firing on all cylinders. You could rely on everybody to knock every single joke out of the park. And so, yeah, it was like the best ensemble I'd worked with at that point.

Patti LuPone describes ensembles where there's that lovely, fantastic energy, and then ensembles where it goes south and how quickly it can get rancid backstage.

It starts at the top. I've been lucky going from Mike Nichols and Casey Nicholaw to Jerry Mitchell [on *Legally Blonde*], who is so gracious and collaborative and full of positive energy, and then hitting Roger Rees and Rick Elice [*Peter and the Starcatcher*], and Casey [*Something Rotten!*] again. You set a tone. And I think it's a thing to be conscious of when you are the first, second, third, fourth, or fifth lead in a show: You have to actively contribute to making that dynamic happen. It takes work. It's another part of the job. It's the David Hyde Pierce syndrome. You have to actively show and demonstrate generosity, which is challenging sometimes because I'm ultimately a pretty private person who likes to keep everyone a little bit at arm's length just for the sake of professionalism. But making little gestures here and there is good for morale. Also being impeccable with your work ethic. Casey also will tolerate no assholes. He will tolerate no attitude. He has the power to do that. I think the same is true for Jerry.

You left *Spamalot* . . .

Sweet Jerry Mitchell asked me to do the first reading of *Legally Blonde* in the stairwell of the Shubert when I was in the middle of my *Spamalot* run, and I thought he wanted me to play the idiot weird guy that she stands up for. Happy to do it. That he wanted me to play Emmett was like, "Wait, what do you mean?" I saw an opportunity to play someone who was actually close to myself. And I indeed was able to just kind of walk out on stage and basically play myself in a corduroy jacket. It was liberating in that way. After all the makeup and the voices and the posture of *Spamalot*, to play a guy close to me was exciting. It was a lot about figuring out the reality and the groundedness of the love story because there was so much pink happening, which was the stuff that was firing on all cylinders. And at that point, Laura Bell Bundy and I were collaborating in a way and kind of falling for each other. We wanted to bring a little bit more of our actual dynamic into the thing. It just seemed like the obvious thing to do. And so we'd have moments of, "Well, I wouldn't say that, I would say this. I actually have said this." And they actually listened to little moments or inside jokes that we had found. There was one epic hotel room night with [the creators] and me and Laura, which is very delicate because you are obviously there because something isn't working and it's in the writing. To gently figure out together how to crack it took weeks in San Francisco. A lot of politicking and a lot of gently talking, gently finding a moment, going out for drinks with producers to figure out what's wrong and how to make it right. It's obviously not the first time that's ever happened. But it was the first time I felt genuinely heard, like they trusted me that I knew in my bones what was working and what wasn't. I think we got pretty close, and I think one of the things that surprised people about *Legally Blonde* was that it actually did have moments of heart and soul and a sweetness to it. A genuine love story. It was really fun and gratifying in that way to—it was the first time that I felt like I molded a role.

You were nominated for your first Tony . . .
That was the first time that I started to understand the politics of the Tony Awards. It's this dream thing. Everyone wants a Tony because . . . why wouldn't you? But it was the first time that I started to understand having the discussion with the producers about which category to position [myself] in. And it was the first time that I started to understand how much narrative has to do with the Tonys.

The narrative being?
You can feel momentum happening behind a show, and you can feel momentum happening behind shows that aren't going to get the big prize so you know that there's probably going to be some—what's the positive version of collateral damage? Like, *Peter and the Starcatcher* ultimately was not going to win Best Play, so they wanted to reward as many categories as they could. That seemed feasible. And I fell into one of those categories. And same with *Something Rotten!*, I think.

That's diminishing your accomplishment.
No. I think I deserved to be invited to the dance, and I don't think I didn't deserve the award, but to say that any one person deserves the award more than anybody . . . I just don't think that's true.

So you're talking about the narrative of the overall show and the way it fits into the season. But in terms of the politics of it, during *Legally Blonde*, did you find yourself politicking or . . .
No. For the sake of representing the show I felt compelled to go to all the events and still do. But it's my least favorite part of the whole thing. I am kind of a private person and I don't ever want to be perceived as campaigning. But showing up and being grateful is not the same thing as campaigning.

What about the community part of it, where you are at events with tables full of your peers. Is that fun?
[The producers have to campaign] but everyone else relaxes, and there's not a lot of competition. It's so out of your hands. The narrative is out of your hands. The voting is out of your hands. You all kind of get together, and you meet people that you hadn't met before, and everyone's obviously so excited and floating on air, and somebody gets to go home with the bauble—but in general, there's not a lot of competition at that point, which is lovely. It speaks to the community.

And what about the experience?
The experience of going? It's business actually. It's a great business night. The parties are not fun. The parties are probably more fun when you don't win, but when I have, happily, twice, then it just becomes about representing and showing your face and talking to certain people. Not networking. It's just showing up and saying thank you, which is easy to do because there's so much to be grateful for. But on those nights, I didn't really ever get to hang out with my friends. I got to our party too late and it was kind of winding down—which is totally fine. The task is to look halfway decent, prepare a speech, and try to sit there as calmly as you can.

Did you find yourself courted in terms of stylists, the way women are?
No, what a rip-off! It was just like, "I'm going to go treat myself to a Tony suit." I have a sweet person who comes in, who's very calm and Zen, and gives me a little makeup for the cameras. The prep of it all is more fun than the evening. I like sitting here and putting on music, having a couple of friends over and having a bottle of champagne. The calm before the storm is very sweet.

During *Legally Blonde* you decided to end your marriage. Career-wise did it change anything for you?
It made me paranoid for a little while, in a personal way, because in any community gossips have an opinion. Do you know what I mean? But I think there are enough people that have been around and lived long enough to know that you can't really know what goes on in anyone's relationship. And I think Sutton and I ultimately handled the whole thing in a private, respectful way, that it was ultimately nobody's business, and it certainly didn't feel like it had any effect on my career. On some level, I was able to ride that out through *Legally Blonde*. I was there for like two years, and at the end of *Legally Blonde*, everything seemed to have calmed down. Again, one of those high-class problems: "You have an opinion about my life? I must be someone." But the most important thing is that Sutton and I are family.

Did it change you in a way that's connected to your work?
After being married, I had to figure out who I was at that point in my life. There was something about getting married and having it dissolve so quickly that was indicative of the fact that neither of us were really looking at where we were in our lives—or I wasn't. I can only speak for myself. And so I had to really look at who I was as a man at that point. Sutton and I started dating when I was twenty-seven years old, so I'm really looking back at the twenty-seven-year-old kid and having to examine who I was heading into it, how I changed as a person within that relationship, and now being outside of that relationship, figuring out who I was as a person. And then how that person now navigates being an actor and having a career.

And you were both on the rise in terms of career.
And that was part of the really sweet fun for both of us. We were kind of a Broadway super couple, and so being on the other side of that took some reexamination. Therapy helps. And after *Legally Blonde*, after Laura moved down to Nashville, and after I had to put up with the country music scene for a few months, we went our separate ways. So then I really truly found myself as an individual moving through life. And on some level ever since then—it's such a cliché—but I have been married to work and my career. And it's worked to the degree that you can kind of chart it with baubles [he indicates his Tonys again] and jobs, you know. And my work ethic totally changed.

You already described yourself as somebody who back in *Spamalot* was working within a group of people where discipline was really important . . .
It was just kind of kicking it into another gear. On some level, in *Spamalot* and even *Legally Blonde*, I was still coasting a little bit on charm and a little bit of talent. After that . . . part of it was *Angels in America*, which requires having to commit to every ellipsis and every—I actually got myself sick, because I felt unworthy of the material. I felt like I had to pay for it on some level. [I decided then that] I will always be the most prepared person in any given room. I will never ever go into an audition not completely memorized or without having worked on it for

days. Pacing back and forth in my kitchen has yielded dividends. All of the jobs that I've gotten I got because I just worked and worked and worked and worked and memorized and paced and—I confess, there's maybe a little holier-than-thou part of it. I know my shit. You know what I mean?

I think that is example-setting. If you show up totally prepared you are almost daring or shaming other people to match you.
It happened with *Little Me*, and on some level I still feel a little bit guilty about it because Encores! is now this ridiculous thing [as the series evolved the shows have gone from semi-stage concert to fully staged production]. I knew that I couldn't have my script [in hand], I came in on day-one totally memorized, completely off book, and it did set a tone. It was great.

Your next show after *Legally Blonde* was your first Encores!, *On the Town*. That's such a dance-heavy show. Did it strike you as a departure?
Yeah. I've never had to dance like that here in New York. It's all been kind of character dance-y stuff, but that was intense. It felt good. It was dynamic and exciting. The cast was spectacular. I had a huge crush on Jennifer Laura Thompson. I've admired her for so long. Encores! shows are a whirlwind. They come and go. I have like two memories of it and the rest is just a blur. But what a great, fun show. Warren Carlyle pulled me aside for a day before rehearsals started and was basically like, "I think you've got this. But let's have a full day of just you. I want to get it in your bones before we start rehearsals." I still brought sickled flexed feet to it. Look up here! Look at the pretty hat, pretty hat.

"When you're with a sweep you're in glad company." With Laura Michelle Kelly in *Mary Poppins*. (Joan Marcus)

And you went from that to another dancer part, Bert in *Mary Poppins*.
It was so nice. I was going into the show with Laura Michelle Kelly, who originated the role in London. We fell in love with each other—this time in an appropriate way. The surprise for me was that they let us create our own stuff. The blocking was very fluid. They even adjusted some lights to accommodate some changes that we made in the blocking, which on a Disney show seems like . . .

You would think it's a machine.
It was not a machine. It was really lovely in that way. And they let me put my own spin on it. I never got the tap dancing to my own satisfaction. And Gavin Lee is just a fucking glorious tap dancer. It was built on him. But I fudged my way through and did the upside down thing [tap dancing while hanging upside down], which was crazy and scary. The whole thing was a blast, and I love that theater. Laura Michelle Kelly and I got in trouble more than a handful of times because part of the Bert and Mary dynamic was that I would try to get her to laugh and warm her up a little bit, which I actually think is appropriate for the show. But sometimes we got a little carried away.

Was that your first time being on a set that could kill you?
Yeah. And I'm not great with heights, but I got through it. Sweaty palms right now just thinking about it. But obviously they had so many safety mechanisms in place that it was fine. That house—when you're acting underneath that house that comes in—you've got to forget about it.

You talked about the tap dancing never being what you wanted it to be.
I just try my damnedest every time. And there were certain sounds that I knew I was never going to get because I literally didn't understand how to do it. That "Step in Time" number is so physical—jumping off the chimneys. There was shin pain and knee pain, the whole thing was pain. Back pain. Hanging upside down, I had sinus pain. I thought my eyeball was going to burst at one point.

So that was your first time really experiencing physical trauma in a show?
Yes. I suppose that's true. Although I did a major fall in *Millie*, which herniated a disc years later. And then in *Spamalot* falling flat as "Not Dead Fred" exacerbated that so I spent a lot of years with a pinched nerve and herniated disc pain but acupuncture—miraculous. Then I left *Mary Poppins*. I took a left turn into *Angels in America*.

You're not what I automatically would have thought of for the role of Prior.
You're not alone.

I'm not saying it didn't work but not what I would have thought.
I'm saying it didn't work, but that's okay.

Why do you think that?
I don't know. The weight of it. There was a part of me that shut down a lot on it. My father was dying at the time. So there was an unwillingness to bring any of that into it because I was packing all of that down. One of my biggest fears as an actor in school was having to cry on cue. And Prior, in every scene, either it says he weeps or somebody tells him to stop crying. It was this constant conjuring up of having to kind of fake getting there, or sometimes getting

there. The hit and miss aspect of that. I wanted to look emaciated and so I wasn't really eating, which was stupid, and I got genuinely sick.

That sounds aspirational.
That's a nice way of putting it. I guess it was that. I really wanted to see what I could do in that way, to see how I could transform. You think of movie actors as being transformational, but you don't think necessarily of stage actors being that. I do think that there was some merit to it. I just didn't do it in the smartest way. Then you have the weight of the material, you have the first New York revival of it, the expectation, the limitations of that particular space. I wouldn't trade it for the world. I was so grateful that [director] Michael Greif trusted me to do it, which was such a delightful surprise. I was just as surprised as everybody else that I got it. But again, I worked my ass off and auditioned and was really ready for it.

Were you consciously seeking something dramatic or did this just happen?
It did occur to me that after *Mary Poppins* this would be a great—no one would know what to expect at any given moment [from me] and there's still an element of that as we head into the future after *Something Rotten!* I'm trying to surprise people. I want to be in this for the long game, basically forever. And I also realized over the last year or so that as fun and as lucrative as television is, the network series regular paradigm is not for me. You just get lost. Basically what you're doing is making money. That's all that is. You can do it and be creatively satisfied on some levels but that's a gamble. But what I figured out this year is that I know, I know that I am happy and gratified living in New York City, walking to work, eight shows a week. I've gotten myself to a place where people accept me, hire me, trust me. That's it. The rest is just like fluky, crazy stuff, which is great and fun and potentially lovely, but this is the heart and soul of it.

Doing *Angels in America* as you describe it, feeling like you didn't quite rise to the occasion in the way that you wanted to, did that make going to work tough, or was it an opportunity to aspire to the level you wanted?
The thing I think helped me sleep at night was that I was tearing into it in the way that I knew how at the time. I was committed to it. I never gave up on it or myself. And you have no choice with that material. It was so daunting before every show, honestly, and being depleted of energy and putting myself in a place where I wanted to actually be depleted so that at least I didn't have to act that part of it—you know what I mean? It's one of the shows that you just have to start, and then you just go and go and go, and then at some point you're soaking wet and having to create this kind of sickness and desperation and fear and anxiety and terror eight times a week. It's another one of those experiences that's almost a blur. I have like five memories of it—five pictures in my head. It just seems like so long ago and almost out-of-body.

Why do you suppose that it's such a blur? Is it because it was so intense?
It was intense. Again, so much of it—my father was dying. I left the show at Christmas to go home to him basically to see him for the last time. I brought him a DVD of the production. As he's wasting away at home, he's watching my performance of somebody who's wasting away at home.

Are you someone who uses your life experience in your work?
I've actually never really worked that way. I've gotten more mileage on some level out of the actual empathy that I feel for the character than digging up my own shit. We'll see what happens.

You talked about realizing that television is not for you. *Smash* **was your next gig. Was doing television, at that point, part of an overall strategy?**

I've always wanted to try it all. I did want to try TV and see what that was all about, but it just happened as a crazy surprise. It was fun to be privy to network television—all the clichés about how many cooks there are in the kitchen, and the rewrites. But it was a blast. It was a gift. It was hard work and everyone worked hard. Kat McPhee and Megan Hilty set the tone; there is nobody that worked harder than those two did. They were so sweet with the show. It was really astonishing.

You could have been signing up for ten years.

The advice that I would give a friend who was in my position, and I guess this is what I said to myself, is you don't not do that when it's handed to you. You just get on that ride and see what happens. I do wish it had lasted longer. It was fun work and just stupidly lucrative. TV is—what it has shown me is that anyone who works in TV or has worked in TV who complains about anything at all has lost their fucking mind. Period. I don't care how miserable it is, how long the hours are. You're paid for that. Paid for weekends off, holidays off. Like what are you talking about? Food, not only at lunchtime but throughout the day. I think some people are just hard-wired to have a hard time with things.

As somebody of the theater, to be in a show that purported to be about theater and had absolutely nothing to do with what happened in theater—how was that?

So bizarre. It was so bizarre. We tried. But again, it was a machine that was beyond my control, and there were so many decisions that had been made at different levels before we got a script. I think they were worried about needing to make the subject matter somehow more universal. But in doing that, they made it accessible to no one. We tried in our little ways every day to bring a touch of verisimilitude to it. I remember I drove one of the props people crazy on one of our first days; we were shooting a scene backstage, and there was a quick-change area, and there was a shoe caddy that people keep their water bottles in, and it was full of Poland Springs bottled water. I'm like, "So sorry, but we use refillable." That was obviously like the least important detail, but I was very surprised that they didn't bring in those of us who were of the theater and say, "Tell us your stories." They never did. It was so bizarre.

After *Smash,* **you had back-to-back theater/TV hybrid experiences with NBC live shows of** *The Sound of Music* **and** *Peter Pan.*

It was almost two different things. There was the doing of it, and then there was the product itself.

That's always true in every show, isn't it?

Well, in theater, the doing of it is an ongoing thing. What people saw in *Sound of Music* and *Peter Pan* was like our first preview. Really. Writ large. So we've been through this whole rehearsal thing, which on both shows was joyous. It truly felt like doing theater plus, like, the added zing—it was the opposite of what I was saying about people who complain about television. You had this merry band of theater troupers who were working their asses off in a rehearsal room, and then all of a sudden we were out at Grumman Studios, and everyone was in trailers, and everyone was getting lunch, and everyone was just like, "What is this magical place?" and having a blast, and being taken care of in ways that they've never experienced before. So the sense of camaraderie and the sense of optimism was off the charts. But I remember seeing some of the rehearsal footage and thinking, "Why does this look like a soap opera?"

But that's just the nature of this particular type of live television. It looks like video. But my bigger takeaway is that everybody's trying to figure this form out, and I think there's a step forward every time.

Did you feel like *Smash* and these two shows changed your marketability?

I don't think it hurt. But my theater stuff has helped me more than the TV stuff did in terms of actually having a footprint. But I also genuinely don't care. I really just want the job and the next job and the next job, and I'm fortunate enough to have two things in the pipeline. It's not because of any kind of celebrity or fame or notoriety. I think it's just because of people that I worked with and, for them, it doesn't seem like a terrible idea to have me do [their show]. I don't think I'm a box office draw in any way, shape, or form. And that's fine. I actually don't want that responsibility. I feel the same way, too, about the new responsibility that people feel and the pressure that is sometimes put on us to market the shows that we're in through social media. There are whole swaths of people whose job it is to market the show, and I am not one of those people.

You did two other shows for very limited runs. *Sweeney Todd* . . .

Sweet [director] Lonny Price who gave me one of my first jobs in New York City—it was a reading of that old TV movie *The Girl Most Likely To*. At that time he was holding auditions for *A Class Act*, and they were looking for someone to play Marvin Hamlisch. I was so young, but he brought me in for the team. I didn't get it. And later, he said, "I knew you weren't going to get that; you were way too young for it. But I just wanted to start introducing you to people. People need to start seeing you." He's so glorious and generous. And then he called me [about *Sweeney*] and I had to do it. I know the show so well, but to be inside of it was so different, and there were so many different little plot points that I discovered. I'm sure everybody has realized this except me—but the moment at the end of the show where Johanna is in the trunk, and he catches the Beggar Woman? There's a moment where the family is reunited in that room again. I just never clocked that that beat happens. It's heartbreaking. Such good melodrama. I fell in love with Emma Thompson because who wouldn't? She was so down to earth, so hard-working, and delightfully and appropriately a flirt, which is so great. And I ultimately was happy with what I laid down there.

And then *Little Me* at Encores! That was another one of your signature go-for-broke performances. Nothing left on the table.

The adage that I cling to most fervently is always to leave them wanting more. Now I understand sometimes in individual performances I might not do that, but career-wise, that is kind of what I think about. I think consciously about making sure that I take left turns and do unexpected things. *Falsettos* couldn't come at a better time because it will cleanse my career palate after all of the histrionic, bigger, kookier, funnier roles. . . . *Little Me* obviously is a cartoon. I went back and I watched some Sid Caesar clips. It's very clear what the show was, how it was built. He wasn't losing himself in these characters. They were just excuses for these vaudeville bits. They built this part around this bit that they used to do, and that around another. . . . It just seemed to me like an opportunity to be a chameleon and create ridiculously distinctive characters. There was no time to do anything but just be crazy and find characters as fast as I could. And [director] John Rando is amazing. He's so funny and endlessly inventive. The stuff that he came up with and the stuff that he allowed me to come up with . . . I loved each of those characters. They're so stupid. There was no one moment of that show that I didn't love doing.

Tony-winning as William Shakespeare, the likes of which had never been seen, in *Something Rotten!* (Joan Marcus)

You went from that into *Something Rotten!*, which you described as a "moderate hit."
Nobody sets out to have a medium-sized hit. With *Something Rotten!*, for example, we all wanted to be in that *Book of Mormon* bracket.

So when it becomes clear that you're not *Book of Mormon* and nobody's buying $450 premium seats, does that energy trickle down to the actors or are you just doing your show? Obviously you know when you're in a huge hit. You know if your show is dying and if your show is going to run. How much attention do you pay?
Well, I pay a lot of attention to it because I'm fascinated by the business part of things.

Do you think that's common or do you think you're an anomaly?
I don't know that it's common. It's somewhere between common and anomaly. I will say that I'm always flabbergasted by friends of mine who do not read the theater news of what's coming in, what's going out, who's doing what. It's very important to be in the know as a businessman. I like having my finger on the pulse. [When negotiating], what's the landscape that's out there? What is an unrealistic, shoot-for-the-moon ask? What is realistic? When is it time to accept the parameters, the reality of the business? You do want to be a team player, but you also have to kind of fight for every little thing. You have to have a nest egg so that when the sweet, artistic choices come along, you can say, "God, yes, please. Let's do it [for low pay]." But it can't only be that; otherwise you don't get to pay your rent.

What was it like working with Casey Nicholaw again?

It's been a long journey with me and Casey. We became friends through *Spamalot*, and we vacationed together. He was with Tripp and I was with Sutton at the time. We were friends before we worked together. As he made his transition into being a director—it's a really tricky transition that I think he navigated incredibly well. You suddenly find yourself in a place of extraordinary power after being part of a business where you are maybe the most powerless. So to see him take his friends with him . . . Now he has the power to grant people work for the rest of their lives, people that he's cared about for more than three decades. It's a responsibility that he takes incredibly seriously. I was surprised to get [this show], but I did a lab and it seemed to fit. I find it to be sweet and hilarious and good-natured and clever and silly, and then it just becomes ridiculous. But it is not for everybody. I'm enormously proud of how hard we worked and how smart Casey was about just how much goofy works, how much you need to take out, how much heart you need. I think it's an incredibly well-calibrated show. But when people don't like it, they really don't like it. Brian d'Arcy James is carrying the show on his back like a fucking champ. To get to know him slowly over the course of a year has been a treat. He is so open and available to little barometric changes, and he works so hard. When he gets tickled, even in the smallest way, it is one of the happiest times that I've ever had on stage. He is one of those people that you can have meta fun with while still trying to tell the story. And you get into trouble sometimes, but that's also fun.

In the course of a long run, I don't think a stage manager, whose job it is to keep the actors in line with the director's original intent, can be objective about what opening night looked like versus what you have right now. Theater grows, it breathes, it does what it does.

It morphs. I think that almost probably beat for beat we would all be surprised to look back on opening night and see what we were doing because it changes, it evolves. You find things. You let things go. A year later, it may all be different. The energy may have shifted with new cast members, departures, the whole thing, but they're still laughing in all the right places. It's a very smart group of actors.

Was winning the Tony for *Something Rotten!* any different than the first one?

It felt different. It was loaded in many ways because I wanted the show to do better, and it looked like the tide had turned against us. There were other stories being told that did not involve us. I felt a little bit guilty as the lone representative from the show [to win]. I wanted so much more for everybody else, too. It did feel like being granted membership into a very special club of multiple wins. It was surreal. And also again, just helpful, very helpful for the long game—for longevity, for career.

Do you read reviews?

I typically don't right out of the gate. I give it some time. Bad reviews don't bother me the way they used to; everyone's entitled to their opinion. How can you expect everyone to love what you do? I just think it's rarified, privileged air to be in the game at this level, to even be written about in *The New York Times*. I still can't believe I'm even mentioned in *The New York Times*, you know what I mean? It's all gold.

Did you find it hard to maintain your energy and focus a year in?

In that particular role, and it's not because of the material, it's the nature of the character, I actually got a little sick of myself on stage as Shakespeare, a little soul-weary of playing a douche.

You went straight from the *Something Rotten!* into *Falsettos*.

It exceeded all of my expectations in terms of working with William Finn and James Lapine again and being with the group that Lapine assembled. We bonded so quickly and became this family, which is what happened in the original cast as well. We got to talk to Michael Rupert and Stephen Bogardus about their dynamic, and they are still all in communication. We achieved a very similar dynamic. We dove in together so thoroughly and took such good care of each other. There were days when it was daunting. We balanced out the heaviness of the material by getting to the theater about an hour before half hour to get together in my dressing room and cuddle and giggle and catch up and laugh, to balance out where we were gonna end up at the end of the night. James Lapine's major edict to us was that he didn't want any acting. He said, "It's okay to be on stage and do nothing for a moment. Like people."

Was it hard shifting gears after a year of such freneticism in *Something Rotten!*?

By the end of *Something Rotten!*, the challenge I had set for myself was that I didn't want to exert any effort; that Shakespeare should be so fabulous that he only has to lift an eyebrow and people go crazy. I wanted to do it without sweating. I also wanted to do Willy Wonka without sweating, and that didn't work out so well. Marvin was certainly more of a grounded, real man than I have played recently. So I started there, as myself, and then you just do the play, as written. And I decided to put on a bit of a dad bod. Being able to eat anything I wanted was kind of fun. Andrew Rannells and I knew each other a bit. I was so excited to hear that he was cast because I am such a fan and he's so damned nice. We decided early on in the process to be incredibly affectionate with other. In the original production there was not a lot of touching. We very much wanted to go the other way. Andrew and I were very physical just to establish that comfort and bond. Stephanie Block and Brandon Uranowitz also bonded quickly and they had their own love-fest.

In 2017 you could tell this story with a physicality that was much harder to do in the '90s.

During "The Thrill of First Love" dance break, they would cut out our mics and we would basically say whatever we wanted to say to each other. Sometimes it got filthy. If you listen to [that song during the] PBS broadcast, they didn't take my mic all the way down and at one point you can hear me say to Andrew, "I'm gonna fuck you over camera two." One of the gifts of the staging of that production—no actor wants to be sitting on the side of the stage watching the whole time, but in this case I have to say it was a gift to watch everybody work every night, doing that material. It's still my favorite material. I can't believe I got to do it. Because it was so personal to all of us and we cared so much about it, I stopped doing the stage door. At the end of the show it was so fresh for us and for the audience, everyone needed to go to their separate corners and digest it. I couldn't deal with . . . Very early on I got, "When are you going back to doing comedy?" and that was it. I even stopped receiving friends and family backstage. I couldn't do it. Because we were dealing with that emotional material for [only] a finite amount of time, that allowed us to commit fully for the entire time. If it had been more than a limited engagement . . . My sweet dresser Meredith also felt the effects. Coming back to the dressing room and having a bourbon at the end of *Something Rotten!* was very different than coming back to the dressing room at the end of *Falsettos*. You're living in that dark place for quite a chunk of time. It was hard to shake it off. At the end of the run, I was really excited to not cry anymore. Your body doesn't know that you are faking it, so you feel the effects of it for months.

January 2017, *Falsettos* ends and . . .

I whisk off to Hawaii, get some rest, and on February 2nd I start with Charlie and that chocolate factory. It was an enormous challenge and, on a lot of levels, a gratifying challenge. Working with [director] Jack O'Brien was everything that I hoped it would be and working with [composers] Marc Shaiman and Scott Wittman was an absolute joy. I still wake up with some of those songs stuck in my head—happily. The reception was disappointing, obviously. The reviews were pretty universally bad.

As you were rehearsing, did you know it wasn't working?

There was a tension . . . as there is always going to be, inherently in the property itself. Part of the problem is that it's "property" and that we use the word "property." How do you meet people's expectations? How do you subvert expectations? How do you give them what they want while also giving them something new? What's the point of doing the musical *Charlie and the Chocolate Factory*? Why not just put the movie on? Can you hang the first act just on Charlie Bucket and four grandparents stuck in a bed? How do you surprise people when you introduce them to four awful children, knowing that they are going to be knocked off one by one? There are inherent story issues in trying to put it on stage that you can't do anything about. We tried at every turn to make it fresh, while also trying to honor what people loved. By the end of the run, the weight of expectation, of having to meet Gene Wilder's performance, totally went away. They really gave me carte blanche to be Bugs Bunny and go crazy, which I think I did responsibly. The show itself was this strange Frankenstein monster, and I think it had a Frankenstein gait because of it. I had a major revelation with this show—if you don't give the ensemble something gratifying to do, their own story to tell and their own joyous moments that win, that play to their strengths, there's like a rotten core in the show. And then, if you make them get on their knees to play Oompa Loompas with twenty-pound puppets hanging around their necks for a whole act, I think that energy reads in the audience. The ensemble didn't have a joyous opening number to do. They didn't have "It's a Musical" [from *Something Rotten!*] that they knew through their sheer hard work was going to bring down the house every night. I don't think the ensemble's talent was used in the best way. And I really think that reads.

We talked about what happens when a company turns and how that's a seeping thing.

It's corrosive. I felt a great responsibility coming into it, given my experience and given that I was playing Willy Wonka, to follow David Hyde Pierce's lead and to be a generous leader. I try to lead by example. Rob McClure, in *Something Rotten!* would go around and visit everybody in their dressing rooms because he was going to be so isolated on stage. I tried to do that. I threw a party. When things started to get a little rocky, I felt a great responsibility. On some level I thought it was my fault, that I wasn't enough of a cheerleader or that I wasn't doing enough to keep everybody happy. That goes back to the textbook analytical people-pleaser that I have been since I was three years old. But there's a new thing, which is a piece of everything else that's happening in the world: social media. It is changing the backstage environment for the worse.

How so?

I am going to sound like a curmudgeon. Millennials have a totally different way of working and I don't like it. There is a greater sense of entitlement in this generation. Already wanting to be on top, deserving to be in front, deserving to be in a big hit show. We were not the big hit of the season but you're still working on Broadway. You still got that paycheck. Okay, so this one may have missed a little bit, but there's always the next one and you know how you get the next one? By being pleasant and hardworking and good, against all odds. I *see* you on your knees. How are there [other] people on their knees, every single night, bright and having fun through the pain? How is that possible? It *is* possible and those are the people I want to work with again. But the other end of the scale was so shocking to see. And the entitlement also to be heard, to have your opinion known, whatever the cost. Because I think that's what people are used to now. You *will* hear me. No matter what the cost.

Cost being?
Morale. Reputation. Decency. Kindness. Privacy. Gone, it seems, is the notion of playing the long game. Instant gratification: You *will* know what I have to say and how I feel about this. And on some level it's a gift. Thank you for showing me who you are.

In some places I think that's a good trait. But making your Broadway debut seems like the time to shut up, listen, and learn.
That's right. Quite literally. Do your job and mind your own business. Backstage, instead of engagement, I witnessed heads down in phones. I saw someone watching the live feed of *Project Runway* during a quick change in the back hallway, as you are putting on your costume. It's stunning to me. And that was that person's Broadway debut.

As you are feeling this contempt, it's still your job to cheerlead . . .
It didn't go well.

So was the majority of the run a slog?
No, no. It was a challenge. The thing that kept it grounded was working with those sponges, those sweet boys [who alternated in the role of Charlie], Ryan, Ryan, and Jake. That was the highlight of the whole experience—working with those kids. At the core of the show was people rallying around those kids in their Broadway debuts and the fun that we would have. They had a wipey board outside their room and you could actually chart the morale of the building by that wipey board. In previews, coming out of the gate, people were all in it together and putting up uplifting quotes and silliness. And slowly, slowly, slowly, the wipey board would . . . The darkest, right before we got our notice, someone wrote, "Let's all try to be loving toward each other." And someone else wrote, "Really?" First of all, that's in front of the kids' room, so, well done. But things did flip back around once we realized that we only had two months left together. The happy people really made the most of the last two months and the miserable people didn't and started counting down to when unemployment would happen. As frustrating as it was, in my calmer, more empathetic moments, I felt bad for people tromping up the stairs chanting "thirty-five left." Until unemployment! But it must be so bad and so dark up in there for you if you'd rather be unemployed. That's tough. And I'm sensitive. So putting on the top hat and velvet and having to put a spin on things and then getting hit with a negativity bomb made it harder. But I do have to say that the last two months were a celebration. The show got better. Our last show was the best show we ever had. Once the yoke of expectation was thrown off, there was something that was liberated and allowed people to have fun and enjoy each other.

There's a real sadness in you as you talk about it. Did this sour you at all?
No, no. As Yoda said, "Failure is a great teacher." Not to say that the show is a failure, but I had moments of failure in it. We all had moments of failure. I am very good at finding my

own joy within a situation. We all learned something from each other, but as one of the senior members of that show, of the community, with a certain amount of experience and some stories to tell, there were people who were paying attention to both my good moments and my clumsy moments. But what I can't abide, and what I am still sensitive about and get hurt by and perhaps inordinately affected by, is meanness. I just can't. We're all insecure, and whatever the justification, bad behavior is bad behavior.

Does any of it change your feeling about what you want to do or the way you want to do it?
It has put me in the mindset of wanting to control, as much as I can, my surroundings and who I work with. That means getting into writing, getting into directing. If something comes my way, being in control of who I am playing with.

How did it feel to be over the title?
It was positively thrilling. I worked my ass off and I kept trying to make it better every day, and did. I really am proud of the vocal stamina that I was able to maintain over the year. It's one of the most vocally challenging things I have ever done. I had to choreograph my swallowing. I was very proud of the work that I did technically. And it was never awful to take that last bow next to John Rubinstein, who is just a prince.

Do you have a vice?
Drinking. Pot. So that's two.

Do you drink after shows every night? In the dressing room?
Mm-hmm. That to me is a big part of the fun.

16

RAÚL ESPARZA

February, March 2019

"YOU WERE REALLY GOOD," SAID a stagehand to Raúl Esparza early in his career. "I mean, you're a fucking diva prick, but you're really good." Really good Esparza is. And if Tony nominations are an indicator, he's got the proof: he's one of only two male actors (along with Boyd Gaines) ever to be nominated in all four of the acting categories. As far as the diva prick? Esparza knows that he has not always been the easiest person to work with. He's hyper-intellectual and while that can produce some great results, it's not a stylistic match with everyone. Some people prefer to just dive in and work on their feet. Esparza is an analyzer. He thinks, re-thinks, second-guesses, doubles back, and thinks some more. It's all in the service of the work, of course, but it can be a challenge to collaborators. It can be intimidating, intense. But it's also fierce commitment.

That commitment, that intensity was immediately evident in Esparza's Broadway debut in 2000. As Riff Raff in *The Rocky Horror Show*, he was an appropriately unnerving presence with an insistent, angry gaze and a rock belt/wail that made people sit up in their seats. *tick, tick . . . BOOM!* followed, less anger, just as intense. *Cabaret,* back on Broadway. Unnerving/intense. George in *Sunday in the Park with George* at the Kennedy Center. Intense. *Taboo.* Super unnerving/super intense. The opportunity to finally play something light was what led Esparza to *Chitty Chitty Bang Bang*. It didn't work (through no fault of Esparza's). But then the perfect marriage: an unusually intense portrayal in the quintessential cerebral musical, *Company*. In his *New York Times* review, Ben Brantley said of Esparza, "He is in a steady state of thaw. Given the subliminal intensity that hums through [his] deadpan presence, you sense that flood warnings should probably be posted." After two well-received (and intense) turns in straight plays (*The Homecoming* and *Speed the Plow*), Esparza crashed hard in the ill-conceived *Leap of Faith*. The experience was so devasting, it led to a six-year detour from the stage and onto TV screens as Assistant District Attorney Barba on *Law & Order SVU*. Only now, having left the show after feeling he had learned what he could learn, is Esparza feeling ready to return to the stage, where he has done limited runs off-Broadway and at the Kennedy Center.

Though Esparza and I had met several times, he didn't want to have this conversation. Or rather, he did, and he agreed to it, but then avoided actually sitting down with me for months. Only after he got a thumbs up from Norbert Leo Butz, with whom he shares a manager, did he finally schedule time. It turns out that Esparza is still pained by a 2006 *New York Times* profile that left him very cautious about interviews. "When you decide to make this into a career," he told me, "you suddenly become someone who is on the line all the time. You have to develop a really thick skin and that thick skin is actually going to keep you from being a really good actor. But if you don't have it, you won't be able to be an actor. It's this big circle." It doesn't take long to understand his reluctance, because once Esparza starts talking, he is an open book. He allows himself to be vulnerable, to reveal the ongoing battle between his absolute self-confidence and his raw insecurity.

When did you start performing?

I got bitten by the bug of getting up on stage in second grade in Fort Lauderdale, Florida. I can't remember if it was *The Wizard of Oz* first, and I was a bunny rabbit, or if it was a Christmas pageant, and I was a tin soldier. All I know is with *The Wizard of Oz* I was obsessed about the play. I wanted to be the Scarecrow so badly, but I was too little, so I would play *The Wizard of Oz* at home, like it was a game. I also read the book cover to cover again and again and again and again. If you mention *The Wizard of Oz* to my mom, her eye twitches slightly. And then right around the third grade, I started writing stories

Making his Broadway debut in the wig his grandmother hated, as Riff Raff in *The Rocky Horror Show*. (Carol Rosegg)

and then plays for my friends to act out. In fifth grade I wanted to write a short story about an actress who goes crazy, and I asked the teacher what part would she play. She said, "Lady Macbeth." Didn't know what that was. So I went to the school librarian and said, "You probably never heard of this, but I'm looking for Lady Macbeth." She brought me the play. It took like a month or so to get through it. I remember obsessing over *Macbeth*. And when I got through it, that same librarian gave me a full copy of all the Shakespeare plays in a bound edition that had been in her family forever. Wrapped in tape, leather binding, and paper that will tear in your hands if you're not careful. I read it cover to cover. I would act them out. I'd get friends to be in them, and I would build sets in my bedroom. And I would act out the plays with my *Star Wars* action figures. If you turn to *Macbeth*, it's covered in ketchup.

Raúl Esparza	
Evita	National Tour, 1999
The Rocky Horror Show	Broadway, 2000
tick, tick . . . BOOM!	Off-Broadway, 2001
Sunday in the Park with George	Kennedy Center, 2002
Merrily We Roll Along	Kennedy Center, 2002
Cabaret	Broadway, 2002
Taboo	Broadway, 2004
Chitty Chitty Bang Bang	Broadway, 2005
Company	Broadway, 2007
Anyone Can Whistle	Encores!, 2010
Leap of Faith	Broadway, 2012
Chess	Kennedy Center, 2018
Road Show	Encores!, 2019

Because of the blood that you were using?

Uh-huh. Han Solo was definitely Macbeth because I liked him better than Luke. Luke was Banquo. Obi Wan was a perfect Duncan. Lots of ketchup. I had an erector set and made the stage out of it. I had a curtain that I made out of a Dracula cape that my grandmother had made for me. Going to the library in that same period of time, I would get cast albums. I would also check out the plays themselves or opera librettos. They were stories to tell. Play after play. There was a compilation of Neil Simon plays that I remember obsessing over. I use that word on purpose. Very one-track-minded. Crazy. Like the only thing I can think about when I'm not dealing with school.

Is that still true?

Yeah. Hard to get me started, but once I go . . . Just now with *Arturo Ui* you would think I was a young Nazi in training. If you look at my search history, people would be like "this guy's trouble."

It sounds inevitable that theater was going to be your path, but apparently you had all kinds of thoughts about maybe being a lawyer?

I resisted it a lot because I was afraid of not working.

Teenagers are usually not afraid of not working.

I'm the son of Cuban immigrants. First generation. There's a practicality to how you're supposed to live your life that definitely did not include acting. I was mildly ashamed of the concept of becoming an actor. It wasn't a real job. People would think I wasn't a serious person or I wasn't an intelligent person. Some part of me thought, "Oh, I'm not using all my capabilities." There was also the feeling that my parents went through hell and they left behind paradise, and there is absolutely nothing you will ever accomplish that will be as great as what they lost. The Cuban story was the most important story of my childhood. How they lived in this paradise and how it was taken from them by an unexpected communist revolution. How they suffered and how they overcame that. All the heroic ways they figured to get out. That isn't the whole story. I know that now but at the time it was very romantic and maybe a little bit of my personal fairy tale. It kept us apart. We felt very special. I realize I wanted so badly to fit inside that narrative, and I don't know that I thought theater was a way to live up to that. I didn't.

But something gave you permission to let go of that.
My parents absolutely encouraged me to try, which was surprising. They said, "Life's too short, and there's no guarantees with anything so why don't you do the things you love."

So something shifted?
Well, the biggest influences on me theatrically throughout my middle school and high school years were actually at Belen Jesuit Preparatory School. I had a Spanish teacher named Beatrice Jimenez who has continued to be a massive influence in my life and is a friend. She believed that we should have some theater program at the school. There was nothing. So she would stage these Noches de Teatro, Nights of Theater, and do these little tiny very experimental pieces. She had me do a play called *Mañana de Sol*, which means a sunny morning. It's a two-hander. Myself and another boy in school, Jorge Santa Marina. I played an old lady and he played an old man, and they meet in a park in Madrid and come to realize throughout the short half hour they spend together on this park bench that they used to be lovers. They tell the audience but they don't tell each other. It's very funny and then it has a real sad kicker at the end. I had some horrible wig and glasses. The parents and teachers and even other students, instead of laughing at us, they were laughing with us and then crying. It was really surprising. The vice president wrote me a letter to say that I had done something very extraordinary and that I had a major talent. I shouldn't be ashamed that I was playing an old woman, that people like Alec Guinness had done this—my Obi Wan! Something about being able to tell those stories that way and affect people . . . I don't know where it came from. So that was the real through-line that went through my teenager years, aside from playing at home. And it was dangerously close to that age where I should not have been doing this at all. I remember my grandmother coming in the room once when I was playing *Deathtrap*. I had taken all the knives from the kitchen and hung them on the walls. I was acting it out by myself. That play and that experience told me there was something deeper and even more dangerous about what you could do on stage to make people laugh and then make people cry. I don't know where it came from. Something was happening to me. I will often close every door so that I only have one choice left, but I'm not doing it consciously. I will back myself into a decision. I find it very hard to make decisions—period. Some subconscious part of me knows exactly what I want to decide. I will slowly work it out so that I only have that choice. And so, with deciding to go study theater, it ended up becoming that. This is a long-winded way of saying that nothing really changed. All these things were bubbling . . .

You just kept closing other doors.
I did. I closed all the doors until there was only one left. And it was "I have to do this."

So you go off to Tisch School of the Arts at NYU.

I was working at the Coconut Grove Playhouse in the box office. There were some kids there who got accepted to Tisch from the Coconut Grove Playhouse theater school, and I thought, "Fuck that! If they can get in, I can get in."

You have gone on record as saying that acting school was not especially the best way to learn acting for you, and that doing was far more informative than anything you got out of the school.

I found New York very challenging. It was very hard for me to be here. I wasn't comfortable with myself. Too much of the city felt like forbidden territory. I wanted to explore but was afraid to as a college student. That sense of judgment that I applied to myself as an actor, I spread like butter. Tisch was a challenge for me because I met people who were just as talented as I am, and that was a first. I was always the best. And people were a lot more comfortable in their skin, in their sense of self, in their sense of identity, both sexually and personally, and in their intellectual curiosity. And also confident in their knowledge of so much that I didn't know about. Half the writers they were mentioning in dramaturgy class I had never heard of. So, I got angry at it privately. I'd be like, "If I don't already know, I don't want to know." Thank God I stopped doing that, but there was a lot of fear during those first few semesters at Tisch for me. Eventually you come to grow into yourself in a school like Tisch, but my biggest problem was there were so many of us in the class, and some of the students were clearly going through something. People would get up to act and then sob for ten minutes while they would get critiques. I couldn't understand that. But I realize now how much I actually did learn in spite of myself.

After you graduated, you went to Chicago where you spent almost a decade doing straight plays, and then, randomly, *Evita*. A massive singing role.

They were doing the twentieth anniversary tour. I don't know what to say about that tour except that it was really hard. I went through like seven auditions for it. And then when I actually got the role, it was not a comfortable fit. They had this creaky, old stage manager's book [from the original production] and so we would do everything that they did. I think that's the death of any kind of art—trying to recreate what somebody did. I actually got a note one time: walk upstage and throw your hands in the air with your back to us on stage right. Why? That's what Mandy Patinkin did. I said, "Why?" "You're summoning the set." I called Elin, my manager, and said, "I don't think I'm the right fit for this. I can't do what somebody else did. I'm not the actor for this." Along with my lack of confidence and fear of being judged, I clearly have a great big set of balls. I wonder where I got the guts. It wasn't until Judy Prince [wife of director, Hal Prince] came and watched a run-through and said, "That young man is something, and he's struggling." Then Hal came in and watched the run and said, "What Raúl is doing is excellent. He needs to do what he needs to do. Let him do it. Let him be himself." I tried to do more with Che because . . . My grandfather knew Che Guevara. My father had met Che Guevara. He circles our lives as Cubans. I couldn't play him as a hero. I also responded to this idea of an untrustworthy narrator, like Tom in *The Glass Menagerie*. Because Che is our narrator, we assume he's telling us the truth. And I thought, "What if he's not? What if he's just as bad as she is?" I don't know that *Evita* can handle that without some rewrites, but it is what I was trying to play around with. The play is about image and manipulation of image. She is a dangerous woman. You've got a narrator here who's like, "Look at her. I hate her, and I'm speaking for you." What if he's not? Somebody else had already done Mandy's version of the role: Mandy. I can't be Mandy Patinkin. Not in a million years. Don't sound like him, look like him, feel like him.

It didn't take long before you got *Rocky Horror*?

It didn't. It felt like it did, but it didn't. Six months. Every day felt like a year. I had no furniture. I was sleeping on an air mattress. *Rocky Horror* was such a great introduction to Broadway. Tom Hewitt: the grace with which he led the company. Alice Ripley and Jarrod Emick. Jarrod once said to me that if I really wanted to keep myself level, walk through Shubert Alley every day on your way to work. You'll never forget where you are. See all those show posters. Think about what you're part of. Every day. It was great advice. You walk past those crowds, and you're like, "Oh, everybody's going into these theaters. I am, too." Look at that wall of things that are happening on Broadway. You're a part of that. Because it's hard to do eight shows a week and that reminder was really important. Daphne Ruben-Vega: She was life-changing for me later with *tick, tick . . . BOOM!* When Lea DeLaria and I did "Time Warp" and "Hot Patootie" at Broadway on Broadway, I had just been cast in the show. I was terrified. Lea's the one who pushed me up there. "You got this." She just decided to support me and she didn't need to do that. That was amazing. At the first read-through of the show, right before "Time Warp" was about to start, Lea says "Wait 'til you hear this," to the whole cast of big-ass stars. They all got up and cheered for me like it was a rock concert. It was amazing. They were so good to me. I thought that's what Broadway was. Broadway is not always like that.

You've said that the makeup and the hair in *Rocky Horror* was freeing because it was so not you and that you could, therefore, do anything.

That's been true in a number of roles I ended up playing. *Taboo*. *Cabaret*. I always felt like those guys were playing me. In *Taboo*, I would sometimes ad-lib things that I'd be like, "Where the fuck did that come from?" It's obviously me, but it's not me. It's Philip, and Philip has a way with words that I don't easily have access to.

You said the same thing about *Comedians*, too.

Yes, in *Comedians*, he's a skinhead. He's in a total rage. Anger seems to be a real key for me. And I don't know because I had a really good childhood so I don't know what the fuck I'm so angry about, but anger and hostility . . . . Lenny in *The Homecoming* is all about hostility towards the other characters and to the audience. And yet I think of myself as a pretty nice guy. Riff Raff is furious. He wants to go home. That ended up being a really extraordinary experience. I remember our first preview so vividly. It was like a rock concert. I thought that's what Broadway was. Maybe it always is when you make your Broadway debut. I guess this is what that feeling is of being lifted up above something, or finally arriving somewhere you always wanted to be.

Did you start to feel like you were "making it?"

No, not at all.

Do you ever feel that?

No.

Not now?

No, not at all. Every day I wonder what the hell I'm doing with my time. I think about Audra. Every day she'll come into my mind. How is she doing? Would she be sitting and playing her piano by herself for two hours? Should I find something more useful to do with my day? What's Lin up to right now? Is he in Puerto Rico? What's going on with Lin? You wonder how other people get through the day. I'll spend my day structuring it around whatever the next project is, which makes it very difficult when I don't have the next project to go to. Part of the reason that I ended up leaving *SVU* [*Law & Order: Special Victims Unit*] is because it became a job that I knew exactly how to do and could look at the lines five minutes before I walked on set and not challenge myself. Nobody needs that. And my days were completely empty. I couldn't do anything except show up for filming, and it was not feeding me in any real way. They feed financially, of course. The television money's great. It can be very creative, but it can also be, in a show like *SVU*, a series of tasks to accomplish. They shove cameras around, make sure that's done, how many hours do we have left, moving on because there's no room for anything else. It's just how the machine works. You learn a great deal, but when you stop learning, when it's become just the job you show up for, I don't know if you're always the best actor. This is true as well being in a long run. I wonder whether I made the right decision [to leave the show] at least once or twice a week. You got a regular gig starring on a series for NBC. There is nothing as definite in show business as *Law and Order*. Nothing will happen like that ever again. So, if there's a steady paycheck in this business, that's it, but did I become an actor in order to play the lawyer on *Law and Order* for the rest of my life? No, I didn't. Was I happy going to work every day? Well, when I was in the room with Mariska, yes, 100 percent, but otherwise, no. Does the theater have any guarantees? No. Was it really hard to do *Arturo Ui* just now? Yes. Sometimes it was packed, sometimes it was empty, sometimes people liked it, sometimes people were angry at you. Sometimes the show just spun away from you because people were on their phones or reading the program or whatever. Theater is really hard. And theater has changed. But I've had an incredibly creative year.

Well, on the subject of walking away and into the next thing, you did walk out of a happy time at *Rocky Horror* and into *tick, tick . . . BOOM!*

Yes and no. *Rocky Horror* was very good creatively and a very happy place to work, but *Rocky Horror* was also a job where they were paying me less than some of the other members of the cast who had lesser roles. They would not advertise me. They did not put my name on any billing because I wasn't anybody. But I felt taken advantage of. I felt like I worked very hard, and the part is what the part is, and I wanted some credit for it. I see now that there was a lot of credit coming. It just wasn't financial, or in the billing. So, part of the decision to leave there was knowing that I had to kind of make a name for myself; *tick, tick . . . BOOM!* came up, and I did not know what it was. They gave me the material and I was kind of overwhelmed by it. I was pretty sure I shouldn't take it because I was on Broadway. Why would I leave Broadway to go do an off-Broadway show in a small theater? Two things happened: Daphne was like, "You have my blessing. Go play my friend [Jonathan Larson]. Go do this. I can't think of anybody better to take care of Jon." And going through the script, Michele [ex and best friend] was in Miami, and I was reading the end of *tick, tick . . . BOOM!* out loud to her over the phone. I just started weeping and she was like, "You need to do this." Jon Larson wrote a piece about moving forward as an artist even when you're not sure it was the right thing to do. I wanted to tell that story. It was scary. I remember the first day of rehearsals, I had auditioned for *Assassins*, and I was getting on the subway at 44th and 8th. I thought, "What have I done? I'm going to rehearse off-Broadway. This is crazy. They were paying me fine." When I left *Rocky Horror* they turned around and offered me the billing and the money. That's business, but you can't help but take it personally as an actor. It's very hard. Coincidentally when I got off the subway down in the Village, Elin called to say "You just got *Assassins*." So it was like, "Woo-hoo! I have a new show on Broadway." Unforgettable audition, that one. For the callback, I went in for Sondheim. When I finished, he says, "Hey, Raúl, you're fucking terrific, kid." I said, "Thank you, sir," and I walked out and burst into tears and cried the whole way home, just weeping and sobbing, a complete wreck. I'm drooling, just a mess.

If you had to articulate what those tears were about, what would you say?
Stephen Sondheim is probably the most important influence in my life professionally. Until then, I thought I couldn't do his work. I thought I wasn't good enough. And he said I was. To me, he's our Shakespeare, our Chekhov, and our Gershwin rolled into one. We have a lot of good playwrights. He's unparalleled, unmatched, and I always appreciated that. So it was a blessing from someone that I admired and respected beyond my ability to describe. I was overwhelmed that he believed in me enough.

You got *Assassins* the day that you're starting rehearsals for *tick, tick . . . BOOM!* I know you say you don't believe that you were making it, but something had to be clicking like, "Wow, this is actually working?"
I often feel a sense of blessing. I am very grateful. The biggest thing that I take from what Jarrod said about walking through Shubert Alley is that you have to remind yourself where you are. I do that all the time. It's important to touch base. I call it roses and thorns. What are the roses? Every day. I'm not always completely able to do it, but with major events, yes. And my grandmother had died at the beginning of 2001. My grandmother raised me. My parents both worked, and Abuela . . . I played guitar for her, and I sang songs for her, I acted out plays for her. I spent every minute with her from five years old 'til I finally left home. She came to see *Rocky Horror* on her ninety-third birthday. One of the last things she said to me was what a terrible wig I was wearing as Riff Raff. Her going away was a big deal and I was haunted by that absence. So, as I was going to *tick, tick . . . BOOM!* every day I was both mourning her and also celebrating simultaneously. There was a great deal of gratitude that belonged to this experience. I wouldn't say, "Oh, I feel like I made it." It was just like, "I wish you could see this. Things are going well. This is an accomplishment. What an amazing thing." I mean, the Jane Street Theatre is this tiny rat hole, you know? None of us felt like this was going to be a big deal. The show was overwhelming to work on. It was like a direct plug into an emotional circuit for us. It just spoke. And then when 9/11 happened, this show took on a whole other weight that was larger than us. Jon's lyrics felt sort of prophetic all of a sudden. We were singing about what it takes to wake up a generation. *tick, tick . . . BOOM!* is a play about [the idea that it's great when they say an artist is good] but what if they say you suck? Do you still keep at it? Jon does. The song "Why" is his definition of "I'm going to do this. This is why I live."

I'm sure you understood all that perfectly.
I really did. It was massive conveying that. Every night, I would look up and say thank you to him but also maybe my grandmother. Papa Larson sat in rehearsals every day and would watch us, and he would just hurt. You could see him hurting. And we'd be like, "You don't need to be here every day." He would have to. "It's Jonny's play, it's Jonny's stuff. This is his journal. This is him." That show just kills me. It just taps into something. Who do I want to be when I grow up and can I do this? What am I proud of? What do I want to say? What do I want to leave behind? Am I worth it? That show really taps into something very universal that goes beyond composing for the theater. And that was a play in which I began to learn to get out of my way. I didn't have to do anything.

You said it was one of your proudest experiences on stage.

9/11 really influenced what was happening in the theater. Here we were, faced with a situation where it was feeling really silly to do a show. We were so close to the towers at the Jane Street Theater you could smell it. And I had been volunteering that week, translating. It all felt very stupid to then go to a play. The first night back, I began to sing this song "I make a vow right here and now. I'm going to spend my life this way." And these kids were looking up at me—not like I had answers, but just like, "We need to hear this." And even on September 11th, I went to go light a candle at St. Patrick's because you feel so ineffective. One of the cops stopped me on the stairs heading up to St. Patrick's and said, "We saw you in *tick, tick . . . BOOM!* You need to keep doing that. We need to hear that stuff." That was a little pat from the hand of God. So, the show felt important to do. I might not be rescuing people from the rubble downtown, but this is what I can do. I know that it sounds slightly deranged to say this, but some of my favorite times in New York City were around 9/11 because the city seemed to just go out of its way to become a huge, small town in a way. Everybody did everything they could to support each other here.

And because of 9/11, *Assassins* was canceled, but Roundabout offered you *Cabaret*.

It was only supposed to be for two months. And then we got reviewed, and the show was selling really wonderfully. I came in with Brooke Shields as Sally [for her final five shows]. There had been issues with other Emcees and Sallys where there was a lot of drama. Brooke had changed that for the cast, and the cast was really, really having a hard time imagining her going away. I was told that if I could be the kind of leader she was, it'll go a long way. So I went out of my way to do that. The show had already been set. The real growth there happened when Rob Marshall and Sam Mendes would come visit and give notes. They treated me like I was creating the role and gave me the freedom to do my version of it, and that was very freeing. Rob came in and said something that I still hang onto. He said, "You need to understand, Raúl, that you doing almost nothing is as powerful as ten actors doing everything they can. So when you pull out all the stops, it's too much. Just trust that you standing still is as powerful as ten actors giving everything they've got." It was a great note. Sam came in later and we had a note session at Joe Allen's that went on into the night. He gave Molly Ringwald one of the greatest notes I've ever heard ever, ever, ever. [In the song, "Cabaret"] when you sing, "I think of Elsie to this very day. I remember how she'd turn to me and say . . ." What's turning to you? There's a rotting corpse. That's what you see. It's a dead thing in its coffin turning to you to say "Come to the Cabaret." And I was like, "Oh, fuck. I could play that every night." That's an amazing note.

You won the Obie that year, too.

When I was twelve, I went to the Kennedy Center in DC with my parents. There was nothing going on in the Opera House and I asked an usher [if we could look inside]. "No." And I turned to my mom and said, "I'm going to work here one day." The first day of rehearsals for *Sunday in the Park with George*, the Sondheim Celebration, we were rehearsing in the Opera House, and my manager calls me to say I had just won an Obie and was nominated for a Drama Desk. I got very emotional. I walked out in the hall like, "Oh, my God, look where I am. This is crazy."

Let's talk about the Sondheim Celebration.

It was a truly a magical experience. They offered me both George in *Sunday* and Charley in *Merrily*. So yeah, of course, you feel like it's all happening. "This is extraordinary. Oh, my God, look what I'm part of." I do believe that I'm good at being present and grateful for what is happening, but I also worry that the other shoe's going to drop at all times. I do have a tendency, which I wish I didn't have, to try to find all the things that are negative first, so that hopefully I can get ahead of the bad stuff. Whatever you say about me, I've already said it or I've already thought it. Whatever horrible things you think, you don't know how bad I really am because I already know it. It's a way to protect myself. It doesn't work at all. It just makes me very unhappy. I did a thing for PBS last week, *Poetry in America*, discussing "Finishing the Hat." I sang it and then talked about it. I said that the thing Steve is really trying to name in that song is that . . . "you're always turning back too late from the grass or the stick or the dog or the light"—the moment where you are creating something, and you're in that flow, you realize there's something else pulling you. Life itself is pulling you. The thing you are making is not life. He's always just missing it. And he's okay with that. Maybe he is, maybe he's not. In the end, he's like "I made this thing." He's still a lonely man. There's extraordinary loneliness in that song. And I realized that I really relate to that because the things that make me a good actor, if I can say that about myself, and even that makes me feel weird, are not great for getting through life. They make me not the easiest person in the world to deal with. And they also make me—I wish I could take the kinds of risks in my life that I take onstage. The fearlessness with which I approach my work, and the absolute confidence I have in it . . . You put me in a rehearsal room, or now, on a film or TV set, I fucking know what I'm doing. I wish I could have that in my day-to-day and I just don't. And so it would never be useful as an actor to try to get ahead of an experience by thinking of all the bad things that are going to happen. It would be a bad way to perform actually. But I do that in life. That is something I'm very in tune with. And I think I always feel like I just haven't quite measured up.

In life?

Yeah. Or even as an actor, too. I haven't quite measured up. I always wondered what do I have to say that hasn't been said before. I wondered that a lot at Tisch, too. What do I have to contribute? I think about legacy a lot. What do you leave behind? What do you create when you're an interpretative artist? Brando had something to say. Look at the roles he created. Are you that kind of actor? No. Don't kid yourself. But we're not necessarily the best judges of what our talent is. My manager says it's really not up to you to make yourself a star. It's the others who make decisions about what you are, so it's the others who make decisions about your work, or what your legacy is, or what your work is worth. We don't ultimately control that. And I do try very hard to control it. It's like an extended case of existential FOMO. I used to believe that we had to create out of chaos, that every rehearsal room was really a battlefield. You had to see how many prisoners you could take, and that most directors were thoroughly inept. Most directors are thoroughly inept. Most directors have no idea what they're doing. But every now and then you'll find the one that can be life- changing. I feel a fundamental insecurity even now that drives me back to the drawing board on every role I play, and that's part of my process. I will go back to Uta Hagen's books as though I have no idea how to do this. I think, "Oh, maybe I should read Stanislavski again," and I do start a few chapters in, and I go, "What are you doing? Stop this." But I need to go through that at least the first week of rehearsals. It's not the best way to create. I put myself through at least a week of thinking I don't know what I'm doing. "I missed something," is always my assumption. There must be an answer I don't have that will make it better this time. There is nothing you're missing. You're missing the thing you don't know about yet.

The Sondheim Celebration . . .

When the Sondheim Celebration came up, I remember thinking "I hope I get tickets. I'd like to see it." I didn't think I'd be in it. And what was interesting about that summer is

In *Sunday in the Park with George*, his first foray into the work of Stephen Sondheim, the man who Esparza says most influenced his career. At the Kennedy Center's Sondheim Celebration. (Joan Marcus)

that Steve made himself available to talk about the shows before we started. I was very nervous going over to see him. I felt like a pilgrim at the shrine, and I didn't want to come off like a fool. I wanted to know what the show was about. That's really all I talked to him about. What is the part of George about? And he gave an answer that I think is the key to the piece: It's about creation. It's about something we make, and it's about someone who makes something that never existed before, whether it's a work of art or a child. And it's the most important thing you have. In the first half he makes the painting, and in the second half she makes life, and their relationship is mapped out over a hundred and some years in four or five songs. That's it. And obviously it's about many other things, but that was such a clear way of beginning to talk about the play. He would come to rehearsals every week. It was a lot of fun. It was fun to learn the music. It was fun to be at the Kennedy Center, surrounded by so many artists you admire. They were rehearsing the song "Sunday," which George doesn't really sing in, so I went for a walk. I opened the door to that hall and standing outside was Christine Baranski, who was leaning in listening. "Oh, I'm sorry," she said, "I was in that show at Playwright's. It's so beautiful." I walked down the hall to the next room, and Alice Ripley is coming around the corner, singing, and then you turn another corner, and I'm in the big, giant Opera Hall, and Stokes is singing "Joanna Part 2." Holy shit, this is amazing! This is what we're part of. And then on the weekends Steve would show up and work with you and rip you a new one. From what I understand, we got him as a kind of pussycat, but he is a serious collaborator and a serious taskmaster with actors. At first I found it very hard because I thought I was disappointing him. "I don't belong here. I can't sing this. I'm not good enough." No matter how much I could see that people were happy with what I was doing, I felt like a fraud, and he kept kind of riding me about things to the point that it almost felt like I was in a straitjacket. There were some happy days where I would sing something, and I'd see his face light up, where [director] Eric seemed pretty pleased, but it's a very tough show, *Sunday*, and trying to figure out what you're going to do with it, and how you play it, and what the concept was . . . We weren't getting a lot of questions answered, and Melissa Errico and I both felt inadequate. And then we did a rehearsal in the theater itself and Steve was not pleased. We went to work with him that night in the Eisenhower—just Melissa, myself, Linda Stevens, and Steve, over and over and over again on songs. We particularly worked on "Beautiful," and "Sunday in the Park with George," and "Color and Light." It was really hard. He was so specific with his notes and nothing seemed to be right. But I began to realize that everything he was working on with us was like opening a series of doors into the play. One idea after another after another was being released by tiny things, like, "When these two notes happen in the orchestra, you're changing brushes. It's a new color." "When this diminuendo occurs between them, it's their whole relationship in one breath. They begin to sing loudly to each other and then they fade away. It's not finished yet." "The second time you say the word 'look' it means something different and beautiful because you're talking about change, and you're talking about the passage of time." Each one of these things was a window. And I began to understand with him that it's never finished. There is no perfect way to do this. The biggest thing I learned from Steve was that you can never get it right, and that sounds depressing, but the corollary is what's interesting, which is if you can't get it right, you can never get it wrong. He's not interested in a finished product. He's interested in what the work is. This attention to detail, having worked with him often, only happens if he believes that you've got what it takes. It is a kind of respect that is immeasurable, and it's priceless. He has said that the biggest thing that Oscar Hammerstein gave him was treating him like an equal. His way of showing respect is to say, "I will take you seriously. I will assume you can deliver, and I will honor you by giving you what I give myself."

It's hard to learn for someone like me that all that criticism doesn't mean you're a terrible human being. And at a certain point I started to laugh it off. When we got to *Merrily Roll Along*, we worked on "Franklin Shephard" for over two hours. [Director] Chris Ashley said, "I think he gave you 700 notes." They were fascinating, and it was like tuning an instrument. But that was also thrilling. Every night the cast would get together during the overture and stand onstage waiting for the curtain to go up, and everybody would start dancing, just jumping around. A couple of times Steve would stand in the wings and watch, and then one night he was very emotional about it. He's like, "They're dancing to my music. Nobody dances to my music." The little boy joy of all of that was—you felt very lucky to be part of it.

You came back to Broadway with *Taboo* . . .

That was a really fraught experience. Great score. I still feel like it's one of the best scores I've ever sung. It was not a happy play. I see now that Rosie O'Donnell was going through real hell with her magazine and having left her show and come out. Rosie's generosity is pretty extraordinary, but in this case it was almost destructive. She was trying to control everything, and she couldn't, and it led to a really, dysfunctional experience. There's a funny book to write about it, but at the time, it was fucking bonkers. We had seven different directors at one point. There was a day where seven different people came up to give us notes. Rosie's assistant, Bobby, had designed these loofah sponge costumes: giant, orange, loofah sponges that went on the ensemble's feet, hands, and head, which I guess was based on a Leigh Bowery thing. And if you don't know what Leigh Bowery's stuff was just look at Lady Gaga, because she just copies everything. I had to stand downstage and sing "Touched by the Hand of Cool." The first time we're onstage [in these costumes], the company began to slip and slide all over the stage, and no one could see where they were. They started falling into lighting towers, trying to hang on for dear life to the proscenium. Just a complete catastrophe. So Rosie just cut the number. She was like, "That's out" on the God mic. That's $50,000 wasted. The producer on the God mic! Never heard of that before. So now we didn't have an ending for Act I. Already in the rehearsal hall, she had decided she didn't like the opening of the show, which she decided she was going to stage herself. And she wanted to figure out the ending of the show. She wanted *Longtime Companion* meets *Rent* meets *Pippin*. So, notice how we now have no opening number, no closing for Act I, and no ending for the show. These are the most important moments in your whole story, and now we don't have any of them. These wholesale decisions were being made. In the rehearsal hall I thought that we actually had a hit on our hands because the score was so good. Never in my wildest dreams did I think it was going to go down the way it did.

Do you think the whole thing was undone by Rosie?

Yes. There was a battle about who was in charge of the show, about who was the director, who wasn't. There was a battle with [Boy] George and the rumor mill fueled by Michael Reidel. And also, a real sense of "who the fuck do you think you are, Rosie?" It just surprised me because she had been such a champion for Broadway. And I was very angry because I kept seeing things taken away and changed and nothing being solved. She never took it out on me until the day she did. The day that she came for me, I quit. Polly Bergen and Charles Busch were the ones who talked me back to work. Charles came to find me after I stomped out of rehearsals in my full makeup, eyelashes, and glitter. "Fuck yourself. Take this show and shove it up your ass, Lady." I was wearing balloon pants and tights, floppy slippers, and a cape. She and I made up within a few hours, but it was a mess, and I just had to stand up for myself.

Once the show opened, did it feel like it let up? Did you feel like you ever got to live in the show for the 100 performances that it ran?

Not for one second. I hated it. I hated everything about it. I used to make deals with myself that I would come to work and that I'd only do Act I, and I would sit backstage and say, "I could leave. I don't have to do Act II." And then Act II would roll around, and I'd say, "Fine, I can do Act II but I'll give myself something. I'll buy myself something."

Was that just anger at the whole process?

Yeah. The empty houses. You could go moose hunting in the balcony. The constant gossip. The sense that something had been squandered. Just the waste. Shuffling deck chairs on the Titanic was what it felt like.

And yet you got a Tony nomination.

I was doing *Normal Heart*, which is one of the greatest experiences I had in New York. The cast album came out, and I put on my headphones and listened to "Petrified" in this dingy little gay bar in the East Village. I cried so hard in that bar. I remember just snot running down my face . . .

What was that about?

Because I missed it. Because I was so angry the whole time, and then it was like, "Oh, my God, this is so good."

Did you question whether or not you had missed the opportunity to live through the show differently?

I know I did. Later on towards the end of the run of *Normal Heart*, I went out to London to meet with Barb Broccoli and Adrian Noble about *Chitty Chitty Bang Bang*, and there I was in London again. I had spent ten days in London preparing for *Taboo* with Philip Sallon, whom I played. So being back in London, walking some of the same streets in Soho, it really hit me that I had missed it. I was so busy holding grudges and being mad that I missed it. I missed the whole thing. Whoops.

The Tony experience . . .

That was a big deal. There's only one first time you get nominated, right? I was nominated with friends that year, Denis O'Hare and Michael Cerveris, people that I loved and respected in the same category, which was pretty cool.

For *Assassins*, a show that you were supposed to be in.

Isn't that wild? I remember when Michael won, Denis, sitting right behind me, hugged me, and he said "Well, that's over, but at least it was one of us." I had won the Drama Desk so I certainly hoped that maybe I'd get the Tony. Jim Dale always said to me that the funny thing about those award shows is that even if they don't call your name, you still hear it. No matter what name they say, you think you heard your name. I mentioned that in an interview with John Doyle a few months ago, and he said, "Well, you would know." I felt pretty insecure on the red carpet because who the hell am I? I remember Kristin and Idina across the aisle looking like a gazillion dollars. I remember Hugh Jackman winning. I didn't win, and I was feeling my usual, "I'm not really a success, I guess." There was a commercial break, and I look down the aisle, and Beatrice [Esparza's schoolteacher] has come down from where she was sitting. She doesn't say anything. She looks at me, and then she looks up, around Radio City, and turns her head, and then she looks back at me, and she just shrugs and smiles and walks away, and it was like a weight came off. I just went, "Oh, right. Wow." We had a theater in our high school where we would nail flood lights to two by fours to do plays, and there we were at the Tonys. Her glance changed everything. I enjoyed the rest of the night so completely. That glance just reminded me to be where I was. I've really hung onto it. So that's really the biggest thing I remember about that night.

You went into *Chitty Chitty Bang Bang* and at the time you said that it appealed to you to do something light.

Barbara Broccoli really believed that I would be good for the part, and I fell in love with her. She is probably one of the greatest people I know in this business. She's such a lovely human being and such a wonderful person to spend time with. Now, falling in love with your producer is not the greatest thing because she's not the one who's going to be in the room. Gillian Lynne taught me so much. I had danced in shows, but I never considered myself someone who could really dance. Gillian made me a dancer. I would show up for rehearsals an hour and a half early, and we would fucking drill shit. I was suddenly doing split leaps and pirouettes and flips and God knows what else. She was like, "You will do this. I believe you can dance." I never had the training. It wasn't something I thought I'd ever really be doing, and so every musical that I've danced in, I always felt out of my league. I had a hard time learning it, but I'm Cuban so we have to dance. I ended up being okay. Gillian's choreography was really hard on that raked stage. I got such bad shin splints. People had pinched nerves and cracked ribs and broken arms. Her choreography was seriously intense. Interestingly enough though, no matter how hard we danced and how hard we worked, the audience would have almost no reaction to what we were doing. They were just, "Where's the car?" So the show was discouraging because we believed that we'd be able to reinvent it in an American vaudeville vernacular. They had hired such amazing people like Chip Zien, Robbie Sella, Marc Kudisch, Jan Maxwell, Phil Bosco, and Erin Dilly, and the feeling was that we would be creating something new. They had done well in England but we were going to do some powerhouse American vaudeville version of *Chitty*. That is not what happened. We ended up basically just doing what they had done and so everybody was frustrated because everybody felt like they had been sold a bill of goods. And even though I guess the show got some nice attention, and it ran the year, I think it probably should have run much longer. That car was certainly spectacular except it broke down every couple of shows. You had to wait because it's floating over the audience. They would have to go out to find the programmer who was working on *The Woman in White* while we were suspended over the audience. It would happen often, and we'd just be suspended up there, and then the orchestra would have to go around in a loop playing "Chitty Chitty Bang Bang." Or maybe it wouldn't fly so we'd talk to the audience for forty-five minutes while they fixed it. There were a lot of shows where people were out. People were just finding reasons not to show up because they were generally discouraged. Nobody felt like they were essential. I'll tell you one of the finest Broadway shows that I've been in was *Cabaret* because the ensemble felt utterly essential. Everybody knew that if they were not there, this show is not going to go on. And that makes a difference. When the company feels like what they have to offer eight shows a week is really appreciated and needed, spectacular. We made the best of it. We played games. There were kids. You couldn't be a miserable bastard around those kids. They were fantastic. The hard part is when the kids grow out of the roles, and then they're screaming their heads off and weeping because they have to say goodbye. We used to play with a Nerf football in the wings, and we got into water-gun fights with the orchestra. We would exit through the trap doors and we would put water guns in our pockets, and shoot the trumpet players. We thought that was very funny because they couldn't do anything about it. And then one day they all had super soakers. They drenched us. Wardrobe was like, "What the fuck is happening in the pit?" That was joyful.

The next season . . .

In the middle of all that . . . I went to see John Doyle's *Sweeney Todd*. Hated it. But then I couldn't stop thinking about it so I went back again just to be sure, and then I loved it. I saw it like three times and Patti LuPone demolished me. I weep watching her. Sounds like I'm a crybaby, but I am a crybaby about great performances. In the sequence when Mrs. Lovett realizes she's about to get killed, the desperation in her and the clawing and both anger and vulnerability that she was playing simultaneously—unmatchable, just unmatchable. I kept going back to see her. What is she doing? How is she doing that? What is happening up there? Completely different and emotionally stunning, and clearly the villain in the piece in a way that Sweeney usually is. And yet she was making you hurt for her. So when Bernie Telsey said, "John Doyle is doing *Company* in Cincinnati and I'd really like to get you in a room with John." I said, "I'd love to meet him." Especially because in *Chitty* I felt like I was spinning my wheels. Pun intended. The way John Doyle does auditions—you just talk. You sit and talk across from each other. We began talking about ourselves, our lives. I remember the two of us saying that *Company*'s really about Bobby finally learning to walk on his own. If those people are his friends, they're also parents, and they have a version of him that they imagine, so he needs to walk away. Then the trick is earning "Being Alive." I will not make excuses anymore. I will live. I will take the good with the bad. I am not perfect, and that's all right. Is that what it means to grow up? He's finally a grownup. Is he going to run off and get married? I don't know. So, we had that conversation. It was just a conversation. And a couple of days later, it was like, "Yeah, he wants you to do it." And I knew that I wanted to press a reset and get back to basics with theater. Going out to a regional house, Cincinnati Playhouse in the Park, [felt right]. And also getting to work with Steve again was really important to me. When you're working on his work, the world is different. When you work on the writing of a great composer or playwright, you see the world through their lens, and it changes. I have never been more of an artist than I was when I was playing George because I saw through George's eyes. That's what happens when you come into contact with great works of art, great artists, and you try to embody their visions as an interpretative artist. You take all that in and then try to get out of the way so that the piece can speak for itself. I knew that I wanted to live in that mind again. And also, he was a friend. We spent time socially. A bunch of us would go to game nights at his house or we'd grab dinners. Now I love his exactitude and his difficulty and his irascibility. And now all those things that were terrifying, I think are endearing. The other thing that was really instrumental for me was that Patti and Michael both said to me, "Raúl, this is a great director." And Michael said, "Go in, make no plans. Just go in completely blank. Don't do your usual. Don't make any decisions. Just walk in the room. Trust him. See what he does."

That's a massive thing for you to do.

Huge. And so I really did walk into rehearsals for *Company*, having done nothing but read the script once at home, on my thirty-fifth birthday actually [the play is set on the character's thirty-fifth birthday]. On the first day, John talked about T. S. Eliot's four quartets in "My End Is My Beginning," partly in order to say that he did not know what the show would be until he knew what the show would be. He didn't talk about a set. He didn't talk about anything. We didn't do a read-through. We started staging the first number. The way that John works is he'll rehearse scenes in the morning, the orchestra rehearses in the next room, and then he puts everything together in the afternoon. The afternoon rehearsals become the most creative thing you've ever been part of ever, ever. He is the best director I've ever worked with and I have worked with some real greats. This man is a genius, and he has a way of working—remember how I said I always felt like I had to create out of chaos? There's no chaos with John. He has a way of working that is straightforward and uncomplicated. You repeat a lot. You might do a scene thirty, forty, fifty times in a row, and the repetition becomes a way of learning it that you didn't even realize you were doing. You're not going back and working on the script at home. You're just doing it in the room because you have made no plans. You're responding to everything that's happening around you. He wants you to constantly change what you're doing in rehearsals so that each repetition is an opportunity to try another variation. It's like finger painting in that you use all the colors and now you have a big, black paste. With John, you get past the big, black paste so that you start taking colors away, and you end up with yellow or whatever. It's a reductive way of talking about it, but it is a tremendous process for me. To do it so much that you stop trying to be clever and you stop inventing, and you just are, it's frustrating. It can be tedious when you've done the same thing forty times in a row. It's indescribable. At first, I challenged him a lot. I remember we were working on the opening number, and I was running around, doing this, and climbing here, and singing that, doing all the musical theater things. I did it again, again, again, again until I finally ended up just standing at the crook of the piano. I was like, "What do you want me to do, just stand here?" And he didn't say anything, he just raised his eyebrows. So I just stood there. I'll show you. And it was fantastic. But we had already done forty versions of that number. Stephen said he'd let me do "Marry Me a Little" as long as I didn't make it bigger than "Being Alive," and that if I so much as tried to turn it into a big deal or showstopper, he would cut it. I did it in the rehearsal hall, and John said something like, "Wow, that was really impressive and thoroughly self-indulgent. Never do that again." [Once we opened] people just started pouring in from New York. Steve asked, "Why are you giving such a good performance in this show? You, and Michael, and Patti [in *Sweeney Todd*], you're just—John's bringing out something in you guys that is so great. What is he doing?" I gave him the same long-winded thing I just told you. And he's like, "Nope. I don't know what it is, but that's not it. You don't know what it is. You can't name it." So I don't know what gift John has, but I just experienced it again on *Arturo Ui*. This sense of I will do anything. I'll put on the blindfold, walk to the end of the cliff, and push me. I know I'll be able to fly. Seeing my name go up on a Broadway marquee was overwhelming. I actually wish my name hadn't been over the title. It puts something on you where you feel very responsible. The pressure of being a star in a commercial theater venture is intense, and you feel like it all sits on your shoulders. It doesn't. There are many factors that make a show a success or don't, and I think it's probably better in the end for the show to just be selling itself. I was really overwhelmed about having my name up there, but then I felt the extra responsibility of feeling very much alone, and like it was all sitting on me. If people didn't come, it was because they didn't like me. I thought if I'd won the Tony, then maybe it would stay open. These are things you can't—they really don't have anything to do with you, but all of those factors of loneliness bubble under what it is to be a star on Broadway.

You said that losing the Tony was a blow.
Yeah. I didn't notice that I had gotten on the treadmill. I was winning everything: the New York Critics, the Outer Critics, the Drama Desk. I haven't read reviews since *Evita*. They damage me. Even if they're good, they damage me. They get in my head. But you do become aware of what's being said about you. And I thought, "This is going to happen and it'd be foolish to pretend that it doesn't matter. It's the Tony Award." Frank Langella sat down behind

me [at the awards] and said, "I want to be here with you when you win it." I didn't notice the treadmill obviously. I didn't notice that I had bought into the hype. The whole thing just felt like this strange out-of-body experience, but it was also matched by the joy of the show winning the Tony. We went to the Ball afterwards, just kind of try to stumble through it as best you can. I was standing with John Doyle and Steve, and I said, "What can you do?" and John goes, "I'm really sorry." And I said, "I'll get over it." And Steve goes, "No you won't. I'm still not over *West Side Story* losing to *The Music Man* in 1957." I wish that I could be above it. The night after, though, I'll never forget. That's one of the greatest moments in my career—the audience response to me. A three-minute standing ovation at the end of "Being Alive." It was overwhelming. It went on, and on, and on, and on, and on, and the cast couldn't even speak, and I couldn't move. The outpouring of love from that audience. Shame on me for ever doubting stuff sometimes. You've got to remember things like that because . . . holy shit. Most people don't get that in their lives.

Your next show was more Sondheim. *Anyone Can Whistle* at Encores! with Donna Murphy and Sutton Foster.

Donna and I had done a workshop of *Dessa Rose*. I think Donna is really one of our greatest performers. I was doing something—working on a moment, and I'm walking back and forth pacing. Graciela Daniele is like, "What are you doing?" "I'm just not doing this right. I haven't figured out this moment." I look over and Donna's got her script in front of her, and she goes, "I know you." She turned her script over, and she had written on it, "Donna, are you usually much better than this?" Gracie goes, "Okay, you two, opposite sides of the room."

For two actors as analytical as you and Donna, having only two weeks of rehearsal must have been hell.

I actually loved working on that. I thought Casey Nicholaw did a tremendous job on it. Staged the hell out of it. And it was crazy that we were able to put that together the way we did. Steve was very supportive, and I thought Donna was thrilling. Steve always said that they were smart alecks showing off [when they wrote that show]. But he praised Sutton and myself by saying that we were particularly great at that kind of writing, that satire, comedy. I would go anywhere or do anything with her. I think she is special beyond all measure. I want to see her play Lady Macbeth. I really do. I know it sounds nuts. I think she's got it in her. We did a reading of a musical based on Virginia Wolfe's novel, *Waves*. She read Rhoda, the Wolfe character who kills herself. The depths that she plummeted to were overwhelming. She was attached to *Leap of Faith* for a little while. I dreamt that that would happen because she had so many good ideas about how to develop the story, in a simple but rewarding way. Casey was joyful to work with and the show was fun to put together, and it was great to have a completely sold-out crowd losing their minds. Angela Lansbury came backstage in tears and said, "I'm having a very strong reaction to this because this was my first musical and it changed my life." She's so good and kind. We were seated backstage during a Sondheim birthday event at City Center, and the night began with the *Follies* overture. Angela leans over, and she's like, "Raúl, he does not write happy music. We are in for a very sad night." There's a thing where you're like, "I want to be part of that Broadway someday" and then I look at these amazing people I know, to be sitting backstage with Angela Lansbury or talking to Len Cariou, and then to walk out onstage and to be treated as their peer, that's never really sunk in. And that's okay. I don't ever really have to take that for granted.

Let's talk about *Leap of Faith*.

That was a disappointment. It's a serious disappointment, and it required a lot of time away from theater to appreciate the good parts of *Leap of Faith* because I really had high hopes for it. When it came into my life, I was doing *Company*, and something about the material moved me really, really deeply. What's most interesting to me is the gesture that the main character, Jonas Nightingale, makes at the end. Two very small things happen that were lost by the time we got to Broadway. He heals the boy. And he then prays for the first time. In his confrontation with God, which is a truly great song that Alan Menken wrote, he realizes maybe he was used. Maybe there is a God, and instead of continuing with his ministry, he divests himself of everything, and walks away. That was a very interesting take on the story for me. In divesting himself and walking away, he is redeemed by the town, and he does not deserve this redemption. An act of grace functions in his life, and he doesn't deserve it. I even get chills talking about it. It makes me want to weep when I think about how moving the idea is. He was fucking the people, the faith healer's stealing people's money, ready to get out of town, selling miracle cures. This guy is dangerous. He was an ugly man with ugly tendencies, who is, by the end of the show, redeemed. And so the last thirty minutes of the play were so unbelievably moving to me. I thought there was something interesting to say there about faith. And over the five years of development, that got obscured. I have a lot of theories about why. One theory is fear on the part of our producers that the material that they were looking at wasn't going to speak to everyone and therefore not sell tickets. A lot of the big changes for Broadway had to do with taking out any sense that he was bad, taking away all the curse words, taking away all the bad behavior. Really softening him. Another thing that happened was they never quite cracked the town's people. In Los Angeles, we had a town. By the time we got to New York, they were village idiots. If the ensemble doesn't have something specific to do and contribute, you're fucked. And so we ended up with that. That removed so much of the actual beauty from the show. There's a moment in L.A., I always think about where one of the ensemble members, a beautiful young dancer, he would look at me every night during the song, "Leap of Faith," at the very end as Jonas begins to hand everything over to people. He would just look at me and nod, and not a nod of like "you're forgiven" or anything. It was just a nod, and it was so honest that it would floor me. It was like a key right in my heart. There was no pretense to it. Something about that moment made sense to him, and he just looked in my eyes and as simple as—just that glance was enough to knock the whole rest of the play into the right emotional place for me. And that was taken away by the time we got to Broadway.

So as you are watching things that you think matter get whittled away, you're not somebody who's going to be silent . . .

And I wasn't. It was a big struggle. I wasn't silent, but then, this is the other side, which I wonder about all the time: At what point does my intelligence become a liability as an actor? And for the show, too? As the lead, I have a great deal of power. But I'm certainly not going to exercise it. There are destructive ways to use that, and then there are ways that I think are contributing to the story, contributing to what's happening in the room, being collaborative. But at what point is collaboration damage? I think what they wanted was a much simpler show than what I imagined when I responded to it. Maybe I hurt the show somehow. Maybe in pushing constantly against their softening and against their sitcom version of the story, I was hurting it. What if I had just said, "Okay, we're just going to do a musical comedy. That's what you're doing. Even if it reminds me of *Music Man* and *Elmer Gantry* and all these better shows." Kendra Kassebaum and I clicked in a huge way. That also told me something about the material. In the film that part was played by Debra Winger. That's the interesting role. The relationship [that matters] is between the brother and the sister, not the love story. But everybody was like, "We need a bigger love story, you got make the leading lady's part bigger." But what they did instead was cut the sister's material to make the romance. Then we went to Los Angeles and Brooke Shields worked harder than any actor I've ever met, but nobody met her halfway. That's another really smart woman who says, "I can't do what you're asking me to do, but I can do other things." She's a great comedienne. Maybe you shouldn't ever put your leading lady, who's internationally famous, in a position where she can't deliver to the very best of her ability. Don't do that.

Alan Menken certainly knows better than that.
But this was not Alan's call. That's not how it works. What does Alan want? Alan wants someone who can nail his music, but Alan's not making the decision about who is going to sell tickets.

No, but once he has Brooke Shields he's deciding if the music needs to change.
Yeah, except there were so many other problems that needed to be dealt with. Out of town, the musical is nothing but a series of constant changes. Alan is almost obscenely prolific with his talent. He can write a song, and you're like, "That's the most beautiful thing I have ever heard," and then it doesn't quite work for what we need. "Okay. I'll write you another gorgeous thing for tomorrow." And you're like, "Oh, *that's* the most beautiful song I've ever heard." No? This doesn't work? All right, I'll write you something else. All his cuts in *Leap of Faith* were equally as good as everything that stayed.

So when you're leading the company, and you're watching some things being really right and some things being really wrong . . .
I'm not the easiest actor to work with. I know that. I'm opinionated, and I always speak up, and that's part of the deal with me. I don't believe that good actors are not intelligent people, and I feel like it's part of our job to contribute. But often we are told to shut the fuck up. I wrestled with *Leap of Faith* over and over because it came to the point where I thought, "Should I walk away?" One of the reasons I didn't maybe has to do with ego because I'm always worried about—I think about legacy a lot. I think about what I leave behind? What am I worth? What contribution have I made to this field? I thought that there would be something that would live beyond me. Now I look back, and I think oh, *tick, tick . . . BOOM!* certainly will live beyond me. And maybe my performance in *Company* may live beyond me. I don't know. We filmed it. I don't really know what my legacy is, and is that all ego or is that a real consideration? I don't know. So part of me wanted to just create something new for Broadway because the last new thing I created was what, *Taboo*? Boy, that was a mess. Plus, it's a great role. I mean, a great, great, great role, and I thought that could be something that people could do all over the world. There was so much to play with; how exciting! When we did the first reading the entire room was on its feet cheering. That never happens. And then in L.A., I'm sure the show wasn't perfect, but Rob Ashford was struggling with ways to tell the story through dance, and he hadn't cracked it, but he was working on it. Was it perfect? No, but that's why you're out of town. I think Rob has serious talent. And very jaded showbiz types would come backstage and sit in my dressing room and begin to sob. So you're like, "Something's hitting hard." That didn't happen once we started previews in New York. I went, "Something's wrong. The show isn't connecting." But you can't tell because you're in it. What went? Where did the change happen? Was it in softening him? Was it in changing the love story? Was it in trying to suddenly make this an immersive theater thing? Was it playing the St. James and being in too big a house? Was it switching the director, the writer, the choreographer, the set design? Should I walk

Doing a lot of heavy lifting in the ill-fated *Leap of Faith*. (Joan Marcus)

away? It just seemed to me like there were so many good reasons to stay. And I really believed after Los Angeles that we could find a good version of the show, but I didn't believe we were ready to come straight to Broadway. That's about finance though. There was a lot of money involved. It was $15 million. [Replacement director] Chris Ashley, a beautiful man who I love, was essentially trying to do his very best as quickly as possible.

Do you think there's a lot of blindness when all of this is going on? Because everything that you're describing feels like a lot of people potentially saw what was what. But maybe they are all thinking, "I hope I'm wrong about this. I hope it'll work."

Yeah, I think there's a lot of blindness in putting together a musical. Later on, when I worked on *Fun Home* at Sundance, they were also really struggling with how best to tell the story, and they took their time over a series of years. They really wrestled with it. *Leap of Faith* did not go through that kind of process.

It's strange, though, when you consider that there was a time when creators put together very good musicals in far less time. None of the musicals before 2000 used to take years to develop.

I've wondered about the AIDS crisis and whether we lost that entire generation of artists who might have been able to carry something forward that just stopped in the '80s into the '90s and only now are things beginning to pick themselves up a bit. I don't know. That seems facile, but I wonder, how many artists did we lose? How many people did not carry forth the things that they learned from other people? How much experience was lost, how many great choreographers, and directors, and actors, and singers, and composers, and writers did we lose?

There's also real estate. New York real estate in the '70s, '60s, and '50s versus now changes everything in terms of the business of the theater.

Ticket prices are too high. There are not as many theaters to work in. The competition is ferocious for those spaces that you're going to inhabit. The expectation has become different though. After those mega musicals in the '80s, suddenly a musical has to be this thing that runs for years or it's not a success.

And that ushered the *American Idol*-ization of Broadway where everyone has to sing their face off or we're not happy.

I remember doing *Taboo*, and I would sing the B flat in "Petrified." I would get applause in the middle of the note. The audience is screaming like I'm competing for something.

It makes me insane because you're in the middle of expressing. The song's not over. You're still working.

And especially a song like that where the reason you do a note like that is because [of the feeling]. But it was an athletic feat. I get it. But it also means they're outside the story.

And now you can't compose a musical where at least every second song, if not every song, features . . .

Some kind of show-stopping, wailing. This is a little bit of my problem with *Dear Evan Hansen*. I thought the music was really good, and I thought it was a lot of fun, and I also thought that Ben Platt's emotional accessibility was astonishing. But he was going a hundred miles an hour the whole show, and also singing these songs that were just showstoppers, and wow, what he can do, but at a certain point, I thought, "Does he have to do it every two minutes? Would it have been a more-balanced experience of that story if he got to save it up for later? When would it be the best storytelling to let this thoroughbred loose?" He gave you everything he had and bled on stage for you. But what would happen if you didn't feel like you'd seen that all night? What if it happened later? What if it happened when he's caught? But from the first number, this kid who's supposedly not socially adept is extraordinarily adept at speaking to the audience and magnificent in the way he encompasses the stage. That says nothing about this great talent that you're watching and these great songs that you're hearing. But is it the best way to tell the story?

I want to finish on *Leap of Faith*. So the show closes after twenty performances after twenty-two previews . . .

I was shattered. It broke me. I felt responsible. I felt, it's my name over the title. It's $15 million down the drain. That's a hundred-plus people who've lost their jobs. I knew that a lot of the energy behind the show was about me and about my performance, and I felt that I'd let everybody down. It costs [actors] so much to do this: You're living through a part every night, and you're experiencing what that part is experiencing, and you are trying to think like that person, and when that person is suddenly gone, it's a life that's gone. I know that sounds crazy, but I don't know how else to do it. And if you're good at it, it can hurt really bad. It's real grief. It sounds absurd to some people. And musicals are so hard. You have to give so much of yourself, and then it's gone. There's nothing. Just empty. And you can't comfort yourself with "Well, I made a lot of money on that." It's fine. Financially Broadway can be great. It doesn't compare to what you're making on television, though, and there's some sort of sense that if you're not a star in film and TV, then you're not really a star, are you? That comes from every angle so you think, "Well, no, it's got to be enough. This is enough." Being a star on Broadway isn't a small accomplishment. This is a big deal. You comfort yourself with that. I starred in the show. We tried to do this work. It mattered enough that all of us put our energy behind this one. Yeah, but what do you have to show for it? It hurts when you try your very best, and you're told you're not good enough and bye. And you can't do anything about it. So I just kind of shut down and I was pretty sure that I didn't want to set foot on a stage again. It was a conscious decision to be like, "I'm going to step away." Look, it is an amazing career. It is great work, and it has rewards that are extraordinary. It has blessings in the ways that you see the world. So there are other rewards, but you've lost perspective when you're angry about finance, and audience sizes, and structural issues. You're suddenly running in place, and you've lost all perspective about why you wanted to become an actor in the first place. I thought at the time "I just hate acting. I don't want to do this. I'm done." There's a certain amount of shame. When you're the child of Cuban American immigrants, conservative, Republican types, growing up in the '70s in Florida, kind of an intellectual goofball, interested in in things that the other kids aren't interested in, gay or bisexual or whatever, just not fitting in, there's so much shame that starts to become attached to you, and you don't want to be seen. You just don't want to be seen as anything other than flawless, or at least that was true for me. I didn't want to be seen as anything other than someone who can be extraordinary at all times. And so when you're not, the shame is massive. Now, they know the truth though, right, which is that you really do suck. I shouldn't even be here. I'm a complete fraud. You feel that at every read-through. You sit down to read the play on the first read-through, and you're like "Oh, my God, they're going to figure out that I don't know what I'm doing." Well, guess what? On *Leap of Faith*, they figured I didn't know what I was doing. It is a deep, deep-seated shame and embarrassment that you're tapping into, which goes all the way back to being a little kid. But it's probably what makes you a good actor. It's probably what puts you on stage in the first place. I think all human beings all experience this to some degree or another, but the public side of it is massive for an actor. But you ask for it in a way because you're putting yourself out there. None of us are trying to be famous if we're trying to have careers in the theater. The actors that I admire, they're not pursuing fame. They're pursuing some revelation of human experience and putting themselves on the line. It's very easy to be famous on YouTube for ten minutes. That's just fame for its own sake. I always say that trying to become a star is like trying to get struck by lightning. You're just running around in a rainstorm hoping to get hit. And it can also be that destructive, I suppose. So I'm rambling around the central issue. I can't quite name it, but it has something to do with feeling like—there was like a great thaw after *Leap of Faith* fell apart. I needed to take a break to appreciate what I did have and not get hung up on the things I don't have.

You spent six years on *Law & Order SVU*. But now you're ready to be on stage again?
Yeah, I really missed it. I longed to be in the conversation again with an audience and to be challenged. Filming can be very lonely because it's just you and the camera, and even though the company creates something—there are a lot of people working—you don't really see what that thing is until many months later. You're often alone in your dressing room waiting to be called, so you don't get the sense that you've created something put together with the other people. Everybody stays in their own lane. There's never that sense of family. And you have no idea what the audience is experiencing. You're never talking to the audience. I started to really miss the conversation because what I love about theater is that it does change every night, and the audience makes the performance as much as I do, and that's great. And I have become soppy with awe at the talent of the ensemble of a show. Like in tears, watching these people do their thing. They start singing, and I'm just like, "Jesus Christ. Look how hard that is. Look at the talent." I felt it on *Chess*. Karen Olivo and I were watching the ensemble doing

these incredible numbers. These people are so talented, and I find it so moving, and I don't know. Maybe it's my current dementia, but I really like it. I'm really grateful for being able to appreciate that and feel like I want to be part of that again.

So *Chess* was your return to musicals.
It was just a week at the Kennedy Center, but we're still revisiting it. Every night after "Pity the Child," I would sob in the wings. I don't know why. Just completely collapse in tears. I can't figure that out. Maybe it's the song and the character, but it's not.

Don't you think it connects to what you were talking about in feeling "less than" as a kid?
When I think about my own childhood though, I don't think of an unhappy childhood.

I'm not saying Freddie is you, but I am saying . . .
You're probably right. There's a lot of me that plays into Freddie, and that surprised me. It surprised me what a good part there is here. The themes in the song definitely pain me, and this concept of a genius who's really excellent and troubled, and he's a severely damaged, sick man, which is fun to play.

You used the word "legacy," earlier. What does it mean to you?
Something that goes on beyond you, which is harder when you're an interpretive artist. Something that lasts when you're not here. Why did it matter you were here? I've wondered this since I was a kid. It's not like oh, as I get older, I'm suddenly really aware of it, but I'm more and more aware of it. There's a Leonardo da Vinci—I'm paraphrasing—"Do a work that is meaningful, do a work that fills you, do a work that is worthy of what you are, which is a grandchild of God." I've always thought about that phrase. You just do your work. Do something you're proud of. Do something that you want to get up in the morning and do. At a certain point with filming, I began to feel like I just didn't want to go to work. I've never felt that in theater, not ever. No matter how hard it is, you still want to go do it. So what does it mean to you personally to get up and do this thing? Legacy. . . I guess I can't really do anything about what is left behind. So why do you this? Is it for money? Is it for fame? Is it even for the audiences? Is it for a claim? You do this because you have to because it is the meaning of your life, and you get to do it. Accept that. Accept yourself. You would do it anyway. Once you even did it just for yourself, which is true. I would just do plays by myself in my backyard. Even if you didn't pay me, I'd still show up. It's very seductive as an actor to be like, "I'm retiring." Like a great diva. And, of course, I have that in me. Is that realistic? No, it's not. I want them to be like, "But come back. Where have you been?" You do this because you have to. Stop being such a drama queen and just accept it.

17

GAVIN CREEL

August, December 2018; January, March 2019

GAVIN CREEL'S DRESSING ROOM AT the Shubert Theater is looking . . . sparse. *Hello, Dolly!*, the show for which he won a Tony Award but also sidelined him for ten weeks while he underwent back surgery, is closing the next day. And the usually ebullient Creel, who has stocked the shelves just outside his door with jars of treats for the cast to enjoy, seems a little melancholy, experiencing both relief and sadness. But he's ready. Because after more than fifteen years of leading musicals in both New York and London, Creel is excited, giddy even, for the next step. He's principally eager about *Loud Night*, a show he's creating and for which he's been writing songs. But also about teaching, about concert work, about collaboration. The theme that comes up again and again in speaking with Creel is his aching desire to genuinely connect, whatever the form may be.

Creel, the youngest of three, comes from Ohio. He made his professional debut in the tour of *Fame* in 1998, and understudied in the off-Broadway cult hit, *Bat Boy*, before he rocketed to prominence opposite Sutton Foster in *Thoroughly Modern Millie*. Creel's long limbs, effortless charm, and soaring tenor were a perfect match for Foster's pluck and gumption. Lead roles in *Bounce*, *La Cage aux Folles*, and *Mary Poppins* in the West End followed before the show he calls the highlight of his career (thus far), Diane Paulus's smash revival of *Hair*. He originated the role of Elder Price in the West End company of *The Book of Mormon* before taking that show on tour and then joining the Broadway cast. *She Loves Me* followed, and then *Dolly!*, a show that, like *Millie*, was an ideal fit for Creel's gangly charisma. Short stints in *Waitress*, both in New York and London, both opposite Sara Bareilles, followed and were ideal for Creel; not only did he enjoy the role, his limited time on stage gave him time to work on *Loud Night* from his dressing room, where he set up a keyboard.

"In that movie, *Into the Wild*, Emil Hirsch writes in the margins of a book, 'Happiness is only real when shared.' I personally believe that," Creel effuses. "I can feel happiness but for me, it's just not really real until I pass it to someone else and we share it. I think that's why I love theater so much." And in turn, that may be why theater loves Creel. Is there another star working today whose sheer exuberance and desire to spread joy match Creel's? When he's on stage, it's infectious. And when you're in a room with him, his eyes sparkling, his thoughts tumbling out of him in rapid bursts, it's inspiring.

With Will Swenson in what Creel calls the show that changed his life, *Hair*. (Joan Marcus)

It's your second to last day in *Dolly!* at the end of a long run . . .

I'm ready. I usually am at the end of a run. I start packing up my dressing room about six weeks before we're going to close. That way I'm already letting it go early. I hate being at a closing night party and then you're like the bag lady, dumping all your stuff in the corner. And then when you get a car late at night, and you're drunk, and you've got eighteen bags, and you get home, it's depressing having to clean it all up. So I like to do it slowly. I'm ready technically, but I guess I always get a little depressed the week after. Last night David Hyde Pierce and I threw a little party to use up the booze that we had left over. We had a five-gallon thing of margaritas. David brought in a bunch of champagne. The thing about show business, that I really realized when we did *Hair*, is that we engage in these relationships, we basically meet someone, the show, the people in it, the director, we fall in love, and then we break our hearts; we break up with each other. It happens over and over again, and after a while you sort of have to become numb to it or else it's like the biggest mind fuck ever. Your brain and heart can't take it. In the second hour of the first day we're making out with somebody we've never met before. It's just this false sense of intimacy that becomes deep intimacy and goes past regular relationships. And then you go. It's the day before our final show. But I think I'm—yeah, I'm ready. Yeah.

You left for an extended period for back surgery and then came back. You got to take some time away to reflect on it and then return. Bette Midler said that after her own leaving and returning she was newly appreciative.

Me, too. My initial return was a little bit fearful because I had this injury, and I had done it doing the show, so I was a little nervous to do it again. I herniated my L4—my S1 and the disc between my S1 and L5 joint vertebrae. It slowly got worse over four and a half months until I couldn't walk. I think it was just lifting that steel door over and over again. With bad form probably. Bette Midler was the one who said to me, "Don't believe anybody who says their doctor's the best. But my doctor's the best." When it said "referring physician" [on the form], I just wrote "Bette Midler" because I had no other answer. Pretty great.

How do you feel?

I feel good. Knock wood. I'm in a place of realizing that I'm aging.

I've heard you say multiple times over the last decade that you're old. In your thirties.

I certainly felt older than I was when I was in my twenties. I have had a lot of—*She Loves Me*: I mess up my foot. My ankle was *Hair*. *Millie*: surgery. *Mormon*: surgery. And that's not me being irresponsible—I was working out three times a week when I herniated my back. I was training. I was tight. I asked Charlie Stemp the other day—Charlie's twenty-four—I said, "Is the eight-show-a-week thing hard?" "No, it's a breeze." I remember saying that. I remember hearing Marc Kudisch talk about his back or his knees or whatever. I remember saying, "Oh, those poor guys! Those poor old people." They were like six years younger than I am now, you know? It's hard. And I don't intend to stop. I'm proud of it. I'm going to start training again, slower weightlifting and—glamour muscles are done. Fuck that. I don't need to be lifting weights. That's stupid. Why? Pilates and core strength are what I need to do now.

Let's go back to the beginning in Ohio. You're the youngest of three.

Two older sisters. I had the most white-bread, normal life. Very conservative and small-town feel, Flag City, USA. Very American. Church every Sunday. Bringing straight A's home. That was the goal: get all A's, go to church on Sunday, be a good person. My parents were amazing—still are amazing people. I was on the basketball team, which is hilarious. I swam. I was in church choirs. I just sort of followed the path that was laid out for me. My grandmother used to play piano and I would sing with her. I started taking piano lessons in second grade. I went to choir, glee club. I learned how to sing three-part harmony. It was just a very normal upbringing. Americana. Like almost in the '50s.

Very white, yeah?

Oh, my God. No diversity. There were no Jews. There were very few blacks. It was just like a very mayonnaise-y, white upbringing.

Gavin Creel	
Fame	National Tour, 1999
Bat Boy	Off-Broadway, 2001
Hair	Encores!, 2001
Thoroughly Modern Millie	Broadway, 2002
Bounce	Chicago, Washington, 2003
La Cage aux Folles	Broadway, 2004
Mary Poppins	West End, 2006
Hair	Broadway, 2009; West End, 2010
The Book of Mormon	National Tour, 2012; West End, 2013; Broadway, 2015
She Loves Me	Broadway, 2016
Hello, Dolly! (Tony Award)	Broadway, 2017
Waitress	Broadway, 2019; West End, 2020

Was it then or later that you learned an appreciation for technique? Because you're quite conscious of what you're doing vocally.

I went to the University of Michigan, and I found a voice teacher who I work with now still. She's like my second mother, best friend. Her name's Melody Racine. She brought a joy to singing by being healthy, understanding breath, understanding line, understanding the parts of your voice. I'm just going to keep learning, especially as my voice changes as I get older. Nobody can teach you how to do eight shows a week. It's insane. And especially like *Book of Mormon*, I loved playing the part but it was the most stressful and the hardest job I've ever done because it was just so loud and so high. I did it for three and a half years. I did it longer than almost anybody who's played the part. Nic Rouleau did it for like seven years. He's twelve years younger than I am. That's how that goes. But he started when he was twenty-four. And Andrew—I remember Andrew Rannells pissed me off [laughs]. He goes, "Sorry, I just kept raising the keys [during rehearsals] because I didn't want to get fired." They actually lowered it a half step for me, and I felt so shamed and embarrassed. And then when I sang it, I was like, "Oh, yeah, this is my key." So you can either do it in Andrew's key or you can do it in Gavin's key. But what asshole would do it in Andrew's key? Do it in my key. I just knew I was going to be sunk if I didn't have a solid knowledge about what my voice could and couldn't do.

What made you decide to pursue it professionally?

In college, deciding to major in musical theater. I was sort of making a declaration to the world—to my parents. The world didn't give a shit.

So what was your context for musical theater at that point? You played Sir Sagramore in *Camelot* in college.

That was the awakening for me to theater. I had like an inch of Ben Nye makeup and rented costumes from some non-Equity tour, and I'm thinking we're just superstars. We were taking the set apart and everyone's crying listening to Vanessa Williams's "Save the Best for Last" on cassette on repeat. We're all going to go to Dietz's and get ice cream afterwards and cry.

So this was the first taste of that instant intimacy that you were talking about? Having your heart broken, and you decided that you loved it?

I was like, "I want this twisted, fucked-up life. I want to fall deep in love, and I want to get my heart broken again and again." It's the seismic shifts of theater. But then you come to the professional world, and the space between when you're actually employed could be years.

But it's never been that for you.

I had a good stretch here and there.

You've never had a professional flop unless you count *Bounce*.

A flop, yeah. *Bounce* was a flop. *La Cage* was a flop. I've been lucky. I also think I'm a bit of a snob. I read things and I'm like, "I don't want to be in that." And there was a time when I was younger when my agent would say, "I'm sorry?" And I'd say, "I'd rather wait." The thing that saved me was my songwriting. I started writing kind of early on. The first thing I wrote was when I was like twenty years old. I was at Pittsburgh Civic Light Opera getting my Equity card, and during breaks I would sit in the practice room and write my feelings, and schmaltzy, sentimental stuff. I had this epiphany when I was thirty-six when I was doing the tour of *Mormon* in L.A. For ten years prior, this guy in me was whispering—well, not whispering—he was obnoxiously saying to the world, "I do musical theater, but I grow my hair out and bleach it blonde. I don't really want to be in musical theater. What I really want to do is pop music." I was obsessed with pop music as a kid. I loved Top 40 radio. I didn't really become obsessed with musicals 'til freshman year of college when I really studied it. But from twenty-six-ish to thirty-six, I had this ten-year love affair with the idea of being able to write music and play stadiums—it's that hubris of youth that I think we all have. We think we want to conquer. "I'm going to be a big deal." I didn't really accept my lane until the tour of *Mormon*. It wasn't until I was thirty-six. I'll never forget it. I was peeing after the show, and I thought, "I'm making more money than I've ever made. I'm on tour. It's not what I thought it was going to be. I'm originating the role on the tour. Slow down. Stop. You've never bowed last in your life. This is everything you could possibly want and per diem, and really cool." It was "the" show. The iconic, big, international hit, and I was in it. And I just went, "You need to accept this. This is where you're strong. This world, this lane."

Did you feel yourself rejecting the lane prior?
Yep. Hundred percent. I think it was just me being a snob, being a dick. Kind of thinking I was better than something. I wasn't. It's owning what you're good at.

Just to play devil's advocate with you; if you were looking at material that didn't speak to you and you knew you'd be unhappy doing, does that make you a snob?
I was afraid. It was more my fear.

You weren't ready?
Yeah. It's what you're ready for.

Speaking of your growth, I saw the *Thoroughly Modern Millie* reunion concert. I loved you in the original production but you were even better now.
I was better—I was way better. You know why? I wasn't afraid. I was afraid the whole year the first time. At twenty-five. It was not an easy rehearsal process for me. I did not feel safe. I was not coming to work with ideas. I wasn't confident. It was my first Broadway show, and—I don't take big bites out of things. I nibble when everybody else has had a bite. I don't come to a rehearsal process with a million ideas. I come with a good couple. And then I kind of read the room, and if the room is toxic, I disappear. That room wasn't toxic, but a lot of people in that room were up to bat for the first time, and I think there was an energy in there that was scary for me. And I didn't step up in the way I did fifteen years later. The minute I walked out onstage at the reunion was a tipping point for me in my career. I was like, "This is going to be fun. I'll go out there, and I'll do my thing, and I'll sing my two songs, and that'll be that." And I walked out onstage [to massive applause], and I almost started to cry because I hadn't realized that the community had accepted—had decided something of me or about me. I had not realized that until that moment. I know it's sad to say. I didn't know it. And it was moving to me.

It sounds like you didn't really have a sense of yourself as somebody who's appreciated in the business or who people want to see.
Yeah, I didn't realize that. And I think if I had to objectively step out and look at myself and where I fit in, as compared to where I would like to fit in, I don't think they're too far apart now. Because I've kind of accepted where I'm at. But what I learned from that concert was that I belong here. People want me to be here. And that was really wonderful. They did a fiftieth anniversary concert of *Hair*, and they brought the entire cast [of the revival] back, and I couldn't do it. I was devastated that I couldn't be there, but Scott Rudin wouldn't let me out [of *Dolly*].

He was like, "Gavin, you've got to think about this"—and he was right—"1,500 people came. They paid money. You won a Tony Award." I couldn't be objective about that. I was like, "They're not here to see me." And he's like, "They are. They may not all be here to see you. They're here to see Bette, yes. But if the Tony Award winner isn't in the show, and they hear that he's down the street doing something else, that's not fair to them." I was upset, but he was right.

I think people are happy to see you and it goes beyond the work. There's an energy and an affability that you bring and I think that you're somebody people are rooting for and want to see around.

I felt that last year at the Tonys. I worked just as hard in *She Loves Me* as I did in *Dolly*. I got no recognition for anything I did for *She Loves Me*, and then I won almost everything for *Dolly*. They were a year apart. I dreaded the award season just like I dreaded it in *She Loves Me*. It was really fun that it all worked out nicely and that I had a nice time.

[We are interrupted by a quick visit by the actor, Michael McCormick]

He's the greatest. Having him in the company changes the company in the same way that having David Hyde Pierce changes everything. David's the greatest human being alive. He's selfless, egoless, generous, quiet, astute, exemplary. He is—he's everything I want to be as a company leader, only I have more hyperactivity. He's quiet leadership. Always has the ear of the company from the producers all the way to the dressers.

When you say "leadership," in what ways does that manifest?

I learned it when I was doing *Mary Poppins* in London. I was thirty. And I realized, "Oh, I think if I don't do it, nobody will. Mary is too busy." It's looking out for the company in a way that the stage management can't, you know? It's morale. It's—he puts a bottle of Veuve Clicquot on your station if it's your birthday. Veuve. Like, he buys a case, and on your birthday: "Love you, DHP." That's just a tiny example of what he does. I'm stealing that. He had all of us out to his house on the beach—and when I say all of us, all of us from front of house to wardrobe to cast to the band with a plus one. Hosted basically at his beach house in Amagansett. Buses from here. Lobster and a piece of chicken for anybody who wanted it on white tablecloths. It was like a life-changing day for all of us to be together at his unbelievably modest but unbelievable house on the beach in Amagansett. Those are two examples—little and big. But also if there's something going on, I'll go down and I'll ask him. He goes, "Leave it with me. I'll take care of that." Or "You don't need to worry about that. That's not your concern. And I understand why you're upset." I want to be that for every company I'm in from here on out. People need a home base within the company that isn't the deputy and isn't the person who's looking after them. And you need a place to go and have fun. Sutton used to buy bagels for everybody on Saturday. I bought donuts once a week when I was in *Mary Poppins*. But the only place you could get them was if you came in my dressing room. So the crew and all the cast would come down and grab their donut and say hi. And you start to build a community within the building. And then it just becomes a fun place to go to work because people are kind, and nice, and smiley, and who doesn't love free shit? I'm paid well. I'm going to take a slice of that money, and I'm going to just say I don't make that money. That money is going towards this. It's hard doing a show over, and over, and over again. So in any way that I can make the space around me fun, it makes it easier to come to work. If the stuff offstage sucks, it's like trying to navigate through a thorny brush to get to that little clearing where there's a beautiful beach. The beach has no value if I am all cut up by that thorny brush.

You talked about being in a toxic company . . .
Yeah. I tend to go, "What do I have control over? How can I make this better? There's something good in here right now." If I just breathe a couple times, I can find it. It's so easy to become one of those Toxic Tessies and Negative Nancys just because you're bored and you want something to complain about. That's what we do. We just complain. "Oh, can you believe the producers?" You're here because the producers give you a check on Thursday. You're not here because you love art. We love art, but if you don't get paid, you can't afford to live. The producers are the ones that are taking the ultimate risk. The fact that they didn't throw you a good party—maybe you need to organize an outing and get the morale up yourself. I threw a taco party a couple weeks ago, at which David Hyde Pierce dressed as a human bottle of tequila and got everybody wasted on margaritas and tacos. I'm doing it for joy. That's good for us. And I make more money than you do so I'll pay for that. This isn't about show business at all. It is about how you survive in a long run.

Let's go back to Ohio. You're doing stuff in high school. With very little context for musical theater you decide you want to pursue it. Is that a correct assessment?
Yes. I was really looking at Carnegie Mellon but I chose Michigan. I don't know why, but I knew it's got to be Michigan. And it was fucking mind-blowing, amazing. It was the people I met there. It's always the people. Every decision I make—if it's about connection, it's always better than stuff. And you've got to make decisions for stuff sometimes, too. And it's okay. I made the decision to be in *Book of Mormon* on the tour strictly—it was an impossible financial decision to walk away from. I thought, "If I do it for a year, I might be able to have a really nice down payment for an apartment in New York." And then I did it for three and a half years. It turned out to be a master class in comedy and understanding that I can do funny.

You didn't know you could do funny?
No. God no. No. I thought it was a business decision. The show blew my fucking mind. Getting to meet the people, getting to go to London again and do it for a year and a half and have that whole experience. Just growing up, turning forty playing a nineteen-year-old on Broadway the last year.

Did you come to New York right after you graduated?
Mm-hmm. I never thought about going to L.A. or being on TV. When I came to the city in 1998, I looked a lot like what the business wanted at the time. They were interested in young, white leading men. They were not really taking the risks, and I was fortunate in that regard. It's time to have every color, every size, every shape, every gender identity acting on stage, and forcing the audience to expand their minds. I'm not quite sure how I become more of a help with that, but I hope to as I get older in the business. If I keep acting, it would be a dream to be able to be the lead in something and therefore influence that.

If you keep acting?
I think I will, I think I will. But I love to teach. I'm loving writing. I might enjoy doing that. I want to do something new and contemporary. I'd like to be a messenger. My friend, Jenn Gambatese said, "There's the message and then there's the messenger." And I'm lucky enough to be able to attempt to do both. I never wanted to be the message. I wanted to be the messenger.

I think that changes all the time. A lot of actors become creators because after having been the messenger for a while, they decide that they no longer just want to be a conduit.

I want to collaborate. My friend Robbie Roth wrote the new music for *Flashdance*. I did four workshops. I was about to take *Flashdance* instead of the *Book of Mormon* tour, and Scott Rudin wrote to me. He's like, "I will have you committed if you take that job for what I'm offering you in this show." And I was like, "Okay, I'm going to do it," but I wanted to be in the room with Sergio Trujillo. I care less about what's great, what's fancy, what's important. I care more about collaborating, and I loved being in the room with Sergio. I just loved being in that room and creating and going back with Robbie when he was writing the songs. I want to do more of that. I went and taught a six-week course at Michigan which I called "The Process Project," to see if we could exist in a process-based environment—no expectations of a final product. Because I think young actors are watching YouTube videos and emulating what they see. They're not spending the time going, "What's proper technique vocally? What's proper line? What is using your consonants? What's an over the bar? What's an ad-lib verse?" They're just going, "I need to be fierce and belt high. People clap when I belt." Yeah. Dumb people clap. People cry when you communicate. People experience magic in the theater when you're doing more than just screaming in their face. When you're actually committed to those basic things—what do you want and what are you going to do to get it— that's the stuff that we love. The same six stories Shakespeare's told over and over again, and we're telling now. We did that course and it was successful some of the time and not successful some of the time, but ultimately transformative for me and for those students.

When you got to New York, were you holding down survival jobs?

I made a fake résumé based on all my food service. I had been a delivery boy, a busboy, and a singing waiter, a bagel maker, a cashier, and a fast-food guy, all through school. I got [a restaurant job] and I trained one day, and that night I got the phone call that I got the tour of *Fame*. I worked a day in New York City and then I haven't worked a day since. *Fame* was a life changer because I was being paid so much money: like $800 a week. I was like, "Oh, my God, I'm a millionaire." It's not the greatest musical in the world, but I met some of the most talented people, and the producers were great. We went all over the country. I had my first unrequited love and I found songwriting, so I wrote all about my feelings. It was great.

I love that you call unrequited love "great."

Oh, my God, I was in so much pain and so sad, and I was sitting at the piano every place we went and I would write. [When I got back, I moved in to an apartment] in the Lower East Side when the Lower East Side was still the Lower East Side. It was so funky and dirty and cool. The apartment was immaculately decorated with stuff my roommate found on the street. I was there for almost three years. My roommate moved out and Celia Keenan-Bolger moved in. It was just heaven—totally heaven. You know that movie, *Beaches*? It was almost exactly like [CC's] apartment. She would walk underneath my loft bed to the bathroom. The shower was in a closet in the kitchen. Every room was a different color. The floors were slanted. We spray painted the bathroom silver. We put up string lights. I had this little keyboard that my parents got me, and we would sit in our cramped, little bedroom and I would play the piano. We would sing and drink wine. We didn't have heat so we'd have the oven open to heat the kitchen.

You describe it with such a patina of romance. Do you think that is because you were so young, or is it your personality to look at things at their most positive?

It's my personality. I was a singing waiter on the *Spirit of Chicago* after my freshman year. Anybody could have justifiably been like, "This fucking sucks. The bathroom smells like sewage, the band's doing coke in the bathroom . . ." I was in heaven. Even jobs now. I get really annoyed with actors who complain, who bitch. Don't get me wrong; I love a good vent. Sometimes I get angry, I get frustrated. But toxicity breeds. Some of the best shows in the world have the most miserable buildings. And some of the biggest flops have the tightest casts because if something outside of us is negative, we bond together. But I can hear myself when I start to bitch and I think, "You can change." Every job I've had I could have complained. There were things in every job that annoyed me. But I was like, "I'm in control of this." It was my parents, I think. My mother's an optimist at heart. Whenever I am in a line and have to wait, it's like, "Look around. There's something awesome here. There's something to see." And there always is. It's healthy, I think. I think it's helped me in this business.

You made your New York debut as replacement in *Bat Boy* **and then you got** *Thoroughly Modern Millie.*

I did a lot of readings: *Hairspray, Wicked, Spring Awakening.* [Director] Michael Mayer said, "I've got this show that I think you should come audition for." Jim Stanek [who played the role in the tryout] is super talented but he was shorter than Sutton Foster. I think that's the only reason I was called in. He was cast with Erin Dilly, who left the production in La Jolla. Sutton came on and never has my bean-pole-ness been such a benefit! Sutton's so tall and lanky so we're like the female/male counterpart of each other. And then in previews, I blew my knee out and was out of the show for two and a half weeks and had surgery. It was insane. And the whole time I thought I was getting fired. But I loved playing Jimmy. Oh, it was just so great. Terrifying but great.

You were nominated for a Tony . . .

Insane. I didn't get nominated for anything before that [the awards earlier in the season]. I remember being behind the set with Marc Kudisch, and he was like, "What's going on?" And I said, "I'm just a little embarrassed. I feel like I'm letting the team down." He put his hand on my shoulder and he goes, "You're really good in this show. Fuck all that stuff. Believe me and believe that you're good in this." It was exactly what I needed to hear. The morning of the Tony Award nominations, my phone rang at like 8:35, and [on my answering machine] I hear my agent going, "Congratulations!" I had a little loft bed and I jumped up and smashed my head into the ceiling. The night of the Tonys, I made margaritas before because I wanted to be drunk for the red carpet because I was so nervous about that. During the fall of that run I got a call that Sondheim was doing *Bounce.* It was for a workshop they were going to do in December. I auditioned and I got it. The dates of the workshop were the week that I was going on vacation to St. Maarten with my [then] boyfriend. We weren't in a great place at the time.

So he went to St. Maarten without you?

No. I turned the workshop down. I wrote to Hal and Steve. I said, "My relationship will not recover from this if I do it. This is more important than my career." They each wrote me back, and they totally understood. "If it comes back around, we hope to be in touch." And it came back around, and they asked me to do the production. And then [my boyfriend and I] broke up and I was miserable during all of *Bounce.* The music of *Bounce* became the soundtrack to my heartbreak. I did not break up with him responsibly or gracefully. He basically had to break up with me. It was bad. But I was learning.

You left *Millie* **to take this gig?**

Yeah. And that was a shitshow in itself because I didn't know how to do that, and I didn't do it appropriately, and properly.

What does that mean?

Well, they offered me to re-sign, and I thought, "The deal isn't done until you sign pen to paper." That's not the case. We were negotiating so I thought, "Well, we're still negotiating. We don't have a deal. It's not done." And I was wondering if *Bounce* was going to happen. But I didn't tell [*Millie*'s producers] that that was a possibility and they were pissed. So I went and did *Bounce* in Chicago. Cried most of the time.

You told me that doing a new Sondheim had been your life's dream, so to end up miserable in the midst of living your dream . . .

It was the best lesson ever. Imagine saying to the universe, "Give me this and I will be happy." And the universe gives it to you, and you're not happy. Imagine how I had to grow, how I had to learn. Not only was I not happy offstage, onstage it was a troubled piece and it was still finding its feet. Stephen Sondheim, Hal Prince—I was like, "These are the best of the best. This will be perfection. This will be the greatest musical ever written." I remember calling my agent and being like, "If this thing comes to Broadway, I can't do it." [The breakup pain] was deep and I could not get past it. He said, "We're not going to make the same mistake we did with *Millie*. We're going to let the producers know." So we called Roger Berlind, legend of the theater. I just told him the truth. He said "I'm sorry you're going through this. We want you to play the part. But if we go to DC and we get panned, we're not coming in. So I'm going to keep this from Hal and Steve until we open." They were never the wiser. I have him to thank for them not hating me.

The personal stuff aside, as the optimist you are, were you able to find any joy?

Yes and no. It was hard. It was meeting your idols and seeing their humanity. Watching Hal Prince just get discouraged as he couldn't figure a moment out. Or thinking, "Why is Steve in New York and not in Chicago writing with us?" But then getting to sit and have drinks with him, and hear him say, "I think that no great composer has ever written a great score past the age of sixty-five." Being in *Bounce* helped me learn that they're human and not infallible. That's when I started working out and writing music seriously. Writing song after song. Misery loves a piano. I can look back and go, "Oh my God, it all led to [good things.] Something beautiful is here." And in the midst of my breakup, or breakups, or deaths, or whatever bad news, maybe I'm lucky because I'm chemically predisposed to this or because my parents put it in me, but there's something awesome here. There's awesome around here. I remember when I was in *La Cage*, putting up a Post-it note that said, "Happiness is right now." I would make myself look at that.

Why were you having to buck yourself up during *La Cage*?

I had a lovely time in *La Cage*. I just wanted more to do.

So why did you take it?

I was poor. It was the money talking. I was humbled because Jerry Zaks was willing to entertain me, and he's a legend. It worked out. I ended up having a really amazing time. I just didn't go into it with the same joie de vivre that I—I think it's still a little naïve that I want to feel fired up about every job I take. I want something about it to fire me up.

Why is that naïve?

Because I think in the beginning, it's just work that begets work. It's not a luxury I think we should have when we're young.

You said at one point that you didn't feel like you were very good in it.
I don't think I was special. I did a fine job.

Do you think it's a role that affords you the opportunity to be special?
I don't know. I'd like to think that there's always something you can do. Maybe there's a way to make yourself feel like you're doing special work. And it's also me being mature enough to see—and I think I see it more now, but to see my part in a piece. Even if I'm the lead with the last bow and I'm above the title, I'm still a part in a piece. Bette Midler was obsessed with making sure that she was playing Dolly Levi, and she was part of the story even though we all were there to see her and to be with her and to experience her Dolly. So yeah. I enjoyed what *La Cage* afforded me, and it was a really good job, my second Broadway show. That year—2004—was an election year, and the hot button topic was gay marriage. It was really cool to be a part of a piece that [challenged conservative notions on marriage].

Did you have a working experience with Harvey Fierstein? Jerry Herman?
Jerry was around. Lovely, kind, warm, smiley is Jerry. And Harvey is one of those people that, when you're talking to him, you're the most important person in the world. He has a way of making a person feel like he has been waiting to hear everything you have to say, and he means it. I really think he does.

So that show closes and your next theater gig was *Mary Poppins.*
In 2006. Yes. I went to L.A. for pilot season, which was really short and basically just me working out at the gym all the time, not loving L.A., and auditioning occasionally. I knew that *Mary Poppins* was coming around so I really campaigned. I said to my agents, "I really want to get this job. I think I'm right for this." I auditioned in 2006 and I didn't get it. I auditioned for four days straight at the little Shubert Theater. They kept calling me back. On the last day it was me, and the director, and stage management, and associate directors, and Ashley Brown, just the two of us, doing scenes in the lobby while the ensemble is auditioning on stage. And then I found out two days later that I didn't get [the show]. She did. And I was bummed because I was out of money again. They told me on a Friday, and then my agent called me Monday morning and says, "How about London?" I'd never considered working there. [The show was opening on Broadway while continuing in London and they brought New York's changes to London.] It was really neat to see them continue to tweak and work it. It was really neat to be a part of something still morphing and changing.

What was your experience doing it?
Amazing. It revitalized my love for musical theater. I was burned out when I went. I had gone to L.A., I was running out of money. It was like, "I think I'm going to take the time and try to figure out what I want to do next with my life because I don't think it's this." I was thirty and I didn't love going from money, no money, money, no money. I just got my joy brought back. I said yes to everything: invitations to go to people's houses and parties, exploring and taking day trips, exploring Europe. I just had such a good time in life and, therefore, in the show. And that was the first time I ever became a company leader. The company was so incredible. I had the best time with them.

Did that make the decision to do *Mormon* over there easier?
Yeah. I spent just five months shy of four years over there. I came back from *Mary Poppins* hungry. I auditioned for *Catch Me If You Can* and *Godspell*. I was dead set on

"And dang it, a Mormon just believes!" In *The Book of Mormon*. (Joan Marcus)

getting *Catch Me If You Can*. "Oh, this is going to be it. I'm ready. I'm hungry. It's a brand-new show. I love [composers] Marc and Scott. I think their stuff is amazing. I want to play this part. I know I can do it." And *Godspell* was like, "Okay, I'll audition for it. I don't really want to do *Godspell*, but it's a good show." I obviously didn't get *Catch Me If You Can* and I got *Godspell*. We did a workshop in the summer and I sat around and waited. They called and said, "We're going to fit you for the crucifixion lift. And then you'll pick out your dressing room at the Barrymore." I was thirty feet in the air and I'm like, "This is happening! I'm going to be Jesus in *Godspell*. Cool." And the day I went and picked out my dressing room I was on my first date with this guy and I got this urgent email from the director: "I'm so sorry. We have to postpone the show." One of the big $5 million investors pulled their money and they were scrambling to find somebody rich enough to do it and they couldn't. And then I decided to get a dog because I was just taking charge of my life. I auditioned for a couple things, and I was trying to find my way. Then I heard from Patina Miller that Jonathan Groff wasn't going to reprise his role on Broadway in *Hair* so I called my agent, and I was like, "Can I get in for this?" So I went in and I was nervous. I was like, "I need this job. I want this job. This is something I know I can do." And I got it. *Hair* changed my life—100 percent best thing I've done. I doubt that I'll have something that matches it and I've done awesome things. But *Hair* was visceral. *Hair* was my blood, it was my breath, it was my dreams, it was pushing my boundaries. *Hair* changed my life offstage because I came out of the closet professionally in that experience. I fought for marriage equality offstage with that experience. And also accepting myself, truly going, "I'm gay. Thank you for that." Like thank God I'm gay.

So your life totally changed from an experience you never saw coming.

It just reminds me that whatever happens . . . I have to look at the track record. I can't be a person who is perpetually anxious about money or jobs when I've been given the proof I'm going to work again. It's going to be fine. And in the meantime, be creative! Do something with your life that is proactive. Don't just sit there and go, "Why aren't they calling?" Are you practicing? Are you writing songs? Are you being a student of the theater? Are you being a businessman? I could probably be more famous, or richer, more successful. . . . It's just not what I want to spend my life on. Those are not my goals. It's not what I'm most hungry for. What I'm most hungry for right now is writing a piece of theater that blows people away.

You got to take *Hair* to London.

And had it fail. And the show itself, I thought, was almost a tighter, more powerful production. I was going through horrible heartbreak at the time so I had other things that were happening in my life. It was this amazing opportunity for me to harness that in my writing. I was collaborating with new writers through this amazing manager who I was working with at the time. I was expanding my writing and my music. I was experiencing life, and stage, and also it made me realize the differences between the American and the British audiences. How can you have an identical show—the identical cast, and yet these two cultures are so different? . . . There's no equation that always equals X. You can do the exact same things and believe in it and make it tighter and more beautiful and have amazing producers like Cameron Mackintosh and publicize it, and still . . . you never know. I was sad to see it go, but I needed to set it down. I needed to let *Hair* go. And then, right after that, I got a call from Diane Paulus saying, "We're doing this reading of *Pippin*. I want you to play Pippin." And I did it, and it was really awesome. Fran and Barry Weissler were producing. Diane said, "I'm still waiting to hear about *Pippin*, but I got this piece *Prometheus Bound* at the ART. It's brand new. It's really weird. Will you come and let me talk to you about it?" It was experimental and weird and loud and really, really exciting to do and not without its problems and challenges, but I was really proud to be a part of it. And to do something that was so outside the box. I did a bunch of workshops and meetings of *Flashdance, The Musical*, and then *Mormon* happened. Three weeks later, Diane called and was like, "Tell me it's not too late. We got the green light for *Pippin*." I'm sad I didn't get to do *Pippin*, but *Mormon* was a no-brainer, and *Pippin* would have been another hippy-ish musical like *Godspell* and *Hair*. I did *Mormon* for three and a half years—tour, London, tour, Broadway. That was the hardest thing I've ever done. I still had PTSD from it.

PTSD? Really?

It was so joyful, unbelievable. To do something 1,300 or more times is traumatic to your brain and your spirit. As joyful and amazing as it is, I worked really fucking hard for them and I broke a lot of my body for that show. I had knee surgery and I got viral laryngitis and was out of the show for like five weeks. I thought I might quit the business because I could not figure my voice out, and I know how to sing and how to take care of myself. It was just hard. It's really hard music to sing. It's hard work. Other Prices would call me and they'd go, "I don't know what's going on." "Talk to me."

At least you got to take home an Olivier Award.

I did, I did. Working in London—now, it's part of my life, but I think if you had told me before my thirtieth birthday that "you're going to go spend almost four years of your life in London in the next eight," I would have been like, "What?????" So to get recognized by their community, that was a very big honor. I felt the same way I did about winning the Tony here: you put your time in, yes; you're good, yes; we loved what you did; but you're also committed to this community, and we see you. It was a really nice acceptance. I dream about going back, but I want to go over there as a writer. Their work ethic is a little different, and it's a little more around the table for a lot longer there. It feels slightly less product-based. Their auditions are very different. There's a lot of like, "Come in, and sit down. Talk to me." And then you perform whereas in America, (snapping fingers) it's just like "Let's go, let's go."

Do you have a particular memory of winning the award?

Yes. I had damaged my knee that afternoon. It popped, and I couldn't put weight on it. I remember saying to Scarlett Strallen who was my date, "I kind of hope that I don't win because I don't know how I'm going to get up those stairs." I was in so much pain. And then they call my name. I was like bouncing up the stairs. Adrenaline is a beautiful thing.

After all those years in *Mormon,* *She Loves Me* **came along.**

It was nice to be playing a part that is not something like I've played before. I can't say I totally enjoy playing a villain. It's not really my thing. I like joy. I think somebody else could have done it better.

Did you feel like you shouldn't have gotten the role?

I think the more I did it, the less I felt that way. But in the beginning, I think I just felt a little seedy. I was really glad to have done it, and it was fun, it was good work, but there are other parts where I've locked in. I guess that's an important lesson, too. I gave it everything I had. I'm learning that the part doesn't necessarily have to be the perfect match. Ideally you want it to be, because you want to feel like it's like a glove, like a costume you put on. But sometimes they're not like you, and they're malicious and double dealing. The next year Cornelius Hackl was like putting on a suit of joy. I'm really glad I did it.

Dragging Jane Krakowski across the floor in *She Loves Me.* (Joan Marcus)

Tell me about working with Laura Benanti and Jane Krakowski.

Laura is fastidious. Laura is staring right at [the work], constantly looking at it, analyzing it. I've known her for a long time, and I think there's now an awareness of, like, "This doesn't need to be everything in my life." She was pregnant through the whole thing so she's like barfing her way through most of that production. It was rough. But she has perspective now. Jane is constantly mining for comedy. In every single thing, she's like, "What can this be? What can that be?" It's a level of comic mastery that I don't have, and I don't care to have. My comedy and my humor come from a more-random and a more flawed sense that's not as mathematical as she or Jerry Zaks or Bette Midler. Jane is a master of understanding: "There's something here, and I can find it." Chris Fitzgerald, Christian Borle . . . people who never stop tweaking. Sometimes I think it drove Jane crazy. She's like a dog after a bone. She's also responsible for one of the most iconic moments in that production. "I feel like he just needs to be dragging me across the floor on a split." I'll never forget, she slammed down to the floor in a split, put her arm in the air, and goes, "Forty-seven, still got it!" And I dragged her across the floor. Figuring out how to do that was really complicated, and she hurt herself. It was really hard on her body, but she was committed.

You admire that approach but you don't want to utilize it? It's just not the way I want to think, yet I want to be able to achieve the effects that they do. I think comedy takes a lot of head, and I just know who I am. I'm not as good when I get up there. When I'm preparing for an audition, I don't know what to do, but when I'm in the room, and the person's reading with me, I know what to do because they're living and breathing and I can talk to them. That's magic to me. I can plan it all out in my head a million different ways, but the magic [is in the exchange]. I need a great director for comedy. [Rehearsing the song "Dancing" in *Hello, Dolly!*], I'd say, "What should I do here? I feel like a phony. Am I supposed to do something funny to make the audience laugh? It feels like the audience should be laughing now." And Jerry Zaks is like, "No. You just walk forward and try to get it right. They will laugh or they won't, but you have to play what's real." And then once they would start to laugh, I would get excited about it, and the next thing I know, I'm doing too much. He'd come back, and go, "Just walk. Trust me." And then it would be funny. I'm getting better at that.

So for you, preparing . . .

I hate rehearsals. Notes, and going back and working little things, I then become a people pleaser, and it's less about the moment I'm playing and more about my showing you that I can do [what is asked]. I'm becoming more confident. I've just recently been able to own that I'm a good actor. Like, recently own it. I'm always feeling like I could be better, I should be better, and I don't ever want to lose that, but I'm starting to accept. I accept [my ability] more as a teacher. If you wanted to be a better actor, I think I can help you get there. I don't know if directing—I always wanted to be a director, but now that I see what directing is like, babysitting so many of our stupid egos as actors . . .

You described yourself as a pleaser. Are you somebody then that doesn't demand time during rehearsals?

No, I don't. And I'm trying to find a space where it's authentic to me to do that. I am the guy who will try to not get the director to say anything to him, and I need the director to say things to me. I will look away from the director's gaze. I will try not to bother the person. It's not a good thing. I don't want to disappoint them so therefore I don't want to go scratching where there's no trouble. In so doing, I think I sell myself short in a lot of ways. I'm not able to find whatever that is until there's the danger of the audience in front of me. I'm not good at calling things up again and again in a rehearsal room. Usually I don't have it until I have the danger of the audience Then I come to life. I come to life when—I hate that I have to say this—but when it matters. When I have to do it.

Hello, Dolly! was next. Bette Midler . . .
It was intimidating at first and—intimidating throughout. But she's amazing. I love her. For somebody as funny, and as zany, and as effervescent, and life of the party as she seems, she's maybe one of the most serious people I've ever met. Asking the questions, furrowed brow. "Why? Why do you like that? Oh." Like a genuine curiosity about things. And dry, and caustic. I just loved her. I loved everything she did. Even when she'd be tough in rehearsal or finicky about a moment, or maybe even giving me a note, which she did not do very often, but once in a while. "We can make this better." Tweaking always. There was a moment when we were in workshop: She's like, "You just stepped off the stage," because I had stepped over the tape on the floor. I said, "Oh, Bette, I don't pay attention to any of that stuff down there." "Really?" "Nah, not until we get on the stage, and then I won't step off it because I'll see the ledge." "Oh, okay." But to her, those are your marks. You don't step off your marks in film. That was one of the first moments where I realized, "I'll just talk to her." [But on stage] it was like—it was not a musical, it was an event. She appears, and there's a roar that goes on for thirty seconds. They stand up in the middle of the show like three or four times, and you realize the audience is largely made up of people who don't go to the theater all the time and they're not necessarily there for the scenes when Bette's not on the stage. But I was like, "I'm on this train and I will ride it." And when Bernadette or Donna came in, those were theater audiences. All of a sudden I'm getting entrance applause, which is bizarre. They're laughing louder at stuff I'm doing because I'm one of theirs. But all the people that don't come to the theater, don't know not to yell out "You go, Bette!"

Did people do that?
All the time. I'd get so angry. And she never acknowledged them, she never blinked.

Jerry Zaks is an old-school director . . .
He's got everything worked out before you get in there in that old-school way. I'm an actor who needs a good director like that. I love Jerry Zaks. A lot of people call him, and I have called him, micromanaging, because he will craft the tiniest moments. I found that just to fall face first into his specificity, I'll be taken care of. When I showed him that I'm willing to try anything, then I gained his trust, and then he allowed me to try things. Then he'll explain to me why it does or doesn't work. I think some actors who don't want to be told every little moment don't enjoy that. And Jerry's the first to realize "then you're not the actor for me, and I'm not the director for you." But I think I tread the line, and I see his immense value and beauty.

How was it working with the three Dollys?
Bette was bawdy and brassy. Donna was ballsy and beautiful. And Bernadette was. . . beatific. And heartbreaking. She was slightly mysterious but also she was wicked. She giggled a lot. She really had fun. They're all so different.

You won the Tony . . .
I mean, Sutton Foster handed me a Tony Award! And I'd like to say it changed anything but nothing really changed. Maybe people's view of me, a little. I think it codifies a place for me

in a way. It's really, really nice to be introduced as a Tony winner, and it helps with selling concerts. But I can't really be objective about how it might have changed my career. In the center of it, it just feels like I have a little piece of stone and metal in my house. That's about it.

Is that fun, having stone and metal in your house?
Yeah. I like teasing people with it. When I have guests that come over, sometimes I'll set up the airbed in the living room when they're going to sleep, and I just put it right by their headboard. "Just in case you get scared at night, you can spin this a couple times." Sometimes I'll hide it in people's bed.

What do you remember about the night?
I remember my outfit. I remember feeling like a million bucks. I was like, "Let's take a risk." I wore a navy-blue boot-cut bell bottom. Beautiful ice blue velvet, handmade tuxedo top. I had $20,000 worth of diamond studs, vintage Cartier. I just felt special. And I was really proud of my speech. I wanted to make a speech about the arts and my education. That was very special for me. I was very happy. That was the only reason I really, really wanted to win. Of course, it would be nice to win a Tony, but I'd lost twice before. "Lost"—It's so stupid. "Win/lose." It's not a loss. The night was awesome, the parties were awesome, and I'm honored, and I never need to be honored again. If it happens, I'll take it, but . . .

What do you think you want now?
I'm excited about TV and film in a way that I never have been. I don't want to stop acting in theater at all, but I also see the value, having worked alongside people like Bette, and David, and Sara Bareilles, and I see the value of being able to reach into people's homes and hearts. I want to make a lot of money. I want to make a piece of theater, and I'm going to. I want to believe that there's a really great part in TV or film that I can step up and play. I think I want to take that challenge on. And I want to do something new on stage that doesn't kill my body or voice. I really enjoyed playing Dr. Pomatter in *Waitress* because it was contemporary, it was new. I guess I got what I asked for. I want to create something that I'm proud of, that I'm excited about, and hopefully people are moved by. Talking about something that matters to me through music and all the things I've learned, telling a story through song, whether it's a musical or a concert, whatever it ends up being, but that it affects people in positive, powerful ways. The way that I feel when I'm teaching. The way that I feel when I'm in the sweet spot on stage. The way that I feel when I'm able to stand up in a crowd when my voice is tired, and take a microphone and tell a story with music. Oh, my God, that is the greatest job ever. I'm excited about the music I'm making. Shit. Now I've got work to do. For some people it's scary because people are expecting a certain thing from them. I'm not that guy. I'm the guy who—somebody says I look nice and I'll go mess up my hair. I'll get a compliment about something onstage and I'll deliberately sabotage that moment the next day because I want to keep off balance.

You don't want to rest on laurels.
I don't even know if I have any laurels to rest on.

18

CHEYENNE JACKSON

January, November 2019

THE POOL DECK OF CHEYENNE JACKSON's tranquil, Hollywood Hills house with its sweeping, cinematic views of the city and the imposing mountains beyond is striking, not just for its own beauty, but as a representation of the man's third act. It's worlds away from the rural Idaho home in which he grew up without an indoor bathroom. And worlds, too, from the bustle of Broadway where, despite never starring in a bona fide smash show, Jackson managed to become Broadway's It-boy. He didn't burst onto the scene with a star-making role, just an imposing physique, an aw-shucks charm, impossibly good looks, and the voice of an angel. The house belongs to the Jackson of today, a family man, working where the work has taken him.

Jackson spent his early years learning the ropes in Seattle. He came to New York relatively late, at twenty-seven, but defying all probability and convention, booked a job instantly. Within weeks of his arrival, he landed his Broadway debut, as the understudy to Marc Kudisch and Gavin Creel in *Thoroughly Modern Millie*. Then came *Aida* and *Altar Boyz* before the flop that improbably made him a star. In *All Shook Up*, the Elvis jukebox, Jackson's gifts found their niche. He was indeed a hunka hunka burning love and the theater world noticed. Jackson was suddenly everywhere, appearing at benefits and concerts, on magazine covers, and at the top of casting directors' lists for seemingly every workshop that came around. One of those was *Xanadu*, a show Jackson turned down when it was headed to Broadway. But when leading man James Carpinello was injured during previews, Jackson roller-skated in and stayed. A memorable turn in *Damn Yankees* followed, as did two sell-out shows at Carnegie Hall and symphonic concerts all over the country. *Finian's Rainbow* in 2009 marks Jackson's most recent Broadway musical.

He says he is very much on the lookout for the next one (and indeed, on the first day we met, he was weighing the merits of the then developing *Magic Mike*), but from up on the pool deck of the house he shares with his husband, Jason, and their two kids, his reluctance was unsurprising. Like Will Chase, Norbert Leo Butz, Jonathan Groff, and others in this book, Jackson has found the rewards of television too good to eschew. For him to make himself unavailable for TV work, the show has to be just right. And there's the family; "I don't know," he confessed, "if [*Magic Mike*'s merits are] enough to schlep my family to New York for ten months." So for now, his musical forays are bite-sized (*Into the Woods* at the Hollywood Bowl and *The Most Happy Fella* at Encores!, in which Ben Brantley called him "perfect"). Jackson seems at peace with that. He seems, in fact, more at ease and comfortable in his skin these days than at any time in the years I've known him. He's happy.

In *Xanadu* as Sonny, the epitome of Jackson's dim but lovable hunk roles. (Photofest)

You were raised in Idaho, forty miles from the Erie Nation Compound, no running water, an outhouse. How did Broadway enter your world?

I was thirteen, and the French teacher of our little school, Mrs. Henry—she was known as the culture lady because she'd been to Seattle—she came to class one day and was like, "There's this show called *Les Misérables* in Spokane and you're all coming. It's direct from Broadway." I had never heard the word "Broadway" before. I didn't know what it was. I'd seen it on records, like the Broadway cast album of *Annie*, but I didn't have a concept for what it was. But we were so excited to see *Les Misérables* because we had to sign parent/teacher consent forms since there were prostitutes in it. We all just felt super naughty and fun. We got to go on a bus for an hour and go to the city of Spokane. I remember sitting in the Spokane Opera House and I just—it's just one of those visceral experiences that I can still remember. The opening chords played and the hair on my arms—I just couldn't—I couldn't believe what I was seeing. I couldn't believe that this was their job, that they got to be in this show and travel around and have cool rags and smudges on their cheeks and climb

Cheyenne Jackson	
Thoroughly Modern Millie	Broadway, 2002
Aida	Broadway, 2003
Altar Boyz	Off-Broadway, 2004
All Shook Up	Broadway, 2004
Xanadu	Broadway, 2007
Damn Yankees	Encores!, 2008
Finian's Rainbow	Encores!, Broadway, 2010
The Most Happy Fella	Encores!, 2014
Into the Woods	Los Angeles, 2019

up the barricade and sing. It just blew up my mind and I could never get it out of my brain after that. I just thought, "That's what I want for myself." I didn't know how it was going to happen coming from the little town that I come from, sixty people in my class. Most people stayed in the town, had a bunch of kids, worked at the mill. It's what you did. So I didn't know. I just knew that had to be the end goal because the feeling I had in the audience . . . incredible.

Ultimately you moved to Seattle to pursue it, but what happened between *Les Mis* and your move?

As soon as I saw *Les Misérables*, it was definitely game on. I had a lot of work to do. I had a lot of back work to do. I went to yard sales and I would find cast albums for everything I could find. I would listen to them on heavy rotation and mimic all the voices. I think that is why my voice is the way it is; I can sing really low and really high in a lot of different styles. I didn't have any formal training, but I just tried to sound like everyone I heard, whether it was a high soprano or a crazy Patti LuPone recording of *Baker's Wife* or whatever. I wanted to make those sounds and see if I could do it. So yeah, I had a lot of work and a lot of catching up to do. I would just spend hours and hours and hours in my room, listening and mimicking and dreaming.

As the only person you knew into theater, did you feel isolated?

It was definitely a little bit of a secret of mine. I knew that the other thirteen-year-old boys didn't know who Billie Holiday, Lena Horne, Sarah Vaughan, and Ella Fitzgerald were. But I had a tape, "The Best of Billie, Lena, Ella, and Sarah." So I knew that my worldview and my artistic tastes were different than everyone else's. But I didn't feel ostracized or separate. It was almost like my little secret, my little prize, my little treasure. My safe place. I wasn't lonely, and I wasn't tortured over it. It was exciting. It was my thing. Then I had a mentor in high school, thank God, Mr. Mark Caldwell. He knew that I had something, and from eighth grade he just fostered it and he respected it. He would give me material to listen to and work on. In my high school [I played Albert in] *Bye Bye Birdie*. We had lavalier microphones and it was so exciting. I got a laugh on one of my first lines and . . . it's the oldest story in the book; I just thought, "Oh, yes! This is my jam." And then on top of it, I got to sing!

Did you perform out of school at all?

Right out of high school I did *Cinderella* at the Lake City Playhouse in Coeur d'Alene, and then I did *Anything Goes*, which was my Spokane debut. I did a few shows there, and then I got cast in the Coeur d'Alene Summer Theater, which was the first time I ever got money for doing a show, and we did rep. It was great. And I came out at nineteen and then had sex with all of the [brothers in] *Seven Brides for Seven Brothers*, as you do when you're nineteen. It was a great time.

All seven?

Well, four maybe. Then I met a boy and I ended up following him to Seattle. They had a big theater world, and I started working at the Civic Light Opera in Seattle. I did *Children of Eden*. I played Cain and that was my first big thing in Seattle. Everyone's like who is this guy? My life [has had] many moments where I'm the new guy in town and I have a lot to prove yet nothing to prove. Those are the instances where I feel like I thrive. I did Seattle for four or five years and really made a name for myself. I got my Equity card. I got some good training. I did a bunch of character roles and a lot of different things.

So by the time you got to New York at age twenty-seven, you felt ready.

And I knew that I had a natural gift. I had enough of the tools. What I didn't have was the training. I didn't have voice lessons and I'd never taken a dance class or acting class in my life, so those things were mentally weighing me down. I was famous in Seattle and living a great life, but I knew there was something more. But I couldn't get over the fact that I was going to have to compete with people that had been to Carnegie Mellon, Juilliard. I felt like I hadn't paid my dues. I felt like I just couldn't really compete, and I definitely couldn't be in the chorus of something because I couldn't dance.

But September 11th happened . . .

September 11th happened. Also a death in our family. My brother's daughter. And both of those events made me realize how short life is and how much I need to take risks. We just don't know how much time there is. I did this production of *The Prince and the Pauper* with big Broadway people and they were going to fill the chorus with the stars of Seattle and possibly go to Broadway. I was cast as Marc Kudisch's understudy. We started a friendship. A lot of people thought him to be so over the top and bombastic, and he is, but that's just him. He is so wonderful and lovely, and has a heart of gold. He really took me under his wing, and he said, "If you're ever in New York, I'll hook you up with my agents." I had heard that before, but there was something about him. I thought, "He doesn't want anything from me. He's a straight man. He has his own career. He just sees something in me."

Was that a thing already? Were you feeling like there were people who were objectifying you and trying to get into your pants?

Yeah. Of course. All of the creepy, older, gay dudes. I didn't get the vibe from everybody, but yeah, you definitely know when somebody wants something that they're not saying. I came from a little town, but I wasn't born yesterday. One of the things I used to do is play dumb really well. I would act like I didn't know what people were talking about. I think that's probably why my biggest roles have been dumb guys. It was a safe way for me to navigate tricky situations when I was twenty-one and twenty-two. But Marc . . . six months after 9/11, I thought, "I'm just going to do this." So I did it. I moved to New York and I stayed at a little hotel in Midtown and I called Marc. The very next day he hooked me up with a meeting/audition and I went in, sang for them, read a scene, and they signed me right then. The first big audition they sent me on was two days later for *Thoroughly Modern Millie*. It had just won the Tony. I had two days to learn this show and to get up to speed. They needed somebody who could cover Gavin Creel and Marc. Marc didn't know that I was going in for his understudy, by the way. I had to be able to sing that high, high stuff like Gavin, but also do the fastest patter song in the world, and also sing low baritone [like Marc], and also tap dance, which I did not do. I didn't have headshots yet. I had a busted Seattle résumé. But I had so much confidence.

I knew that I could do it. I knew that I was the only person that could do it. I was really worried about the dancing, but I thought if I just nail the scenes and I nail this music, and I charm the pants off of them, I will find a way to make the dance work. I remember [director] Michael Mayer was like, "Cheyenne Jackson?" He thought my name was fake. And I told him the origin of my name: It was a TV show in the '50s that my dad loved. And I sang the song, and I could tell all of them were like, "Who is this person?" And that was exciting. I wish that I had that confidence now. Fifteen years ago, where I don't have anything to prove, I have all of this confidence. And then you get a modicum of success, and . . .

Sure. Because now there are expectations of you and then there weren't.

Right, right. But it was down to me and two other guys, and then it came to the dance call. I said I had left my tap shoes in Seattle. That was my story. I didn't even own any. Rob Ashford, says, "We're just going to do a simple time step one by one." First kid does it. Second guy. Comes to me and I didn't even try. And Rob comes to me really close, and he's like, "You don't tap, do you?" And I said, "I don't, but if you cast me in this, I will learn. I will take tap day and night. You will not be sorry. I can do it." And he believed me. And I did. I took tap day and night. I went down to the Broadway Dance Center and it was me and a bunch of ten-year-old girls. They put me in the back and as long as I didn't pull focus from Noah Racey and all the great tappers, then I was good to go. [Before I was cast] I had one final thing. I had to go down to the theater and sing "I Turned the Corner" one more time. It was call time and the actors were showing up, and Marc comes down the hall. He's like, "What are you doing here?" "I'm maybe going to be your understudy. I don't know." He was so excited, so sweet. They take me into a little room and I sing. I guess Gavin was warming up, and he hears through the wall some dude singing his song. Gavin is just such a dream. He has my favorite voice of all time. He is the kindest, most amazing—he was so generous with me, and he was so wonderful. I was a bull in a china shop. I was aggressively enthusiastic. I actually got in trouble. A few weeks into being there, my agent called me and said, "The producers have had a complaint that you have been making fun of Marc Kudisch." When we'd all be in the green room and Marc would be onstage, I would mimic his voice [Jackson does a flawless Kudisch impersonation] and people thought I was mocking him. Here are these Broadway dancers who've been in twelve Broadway shows, and here's this shit who comes in, and he's like making fun of their—I totally get it. I was just enthusiastic and excited and it all came from a fun place, but I was like, "Oh, I really need to cool it and relax a little bit." I was just bouncing off the walls. And then Marc got a gig with the opera, and so very soon after, I was playing Trevor Graydon. I didn't have anybody in the house for my Broadway debut. I didn't have any family, and my boyfriend at the time wasn't there yet. I remember I had my feet up on the desk, and I was ready. In a minute, I'm going to turn around, I'm going to scream, "John!" and Sutton Foster is going to come out, and we're going to have a scene, and I'm on Broadway. This is real. Just be in it. That whole year was just a dream come true. Being in that company and learning from all those people . . . And then Gavin got a TV movie, and I went on for him.

Was there any sense, as you got this gig minutes after getting to New York, that you were the luckiest person alive, or did you think, "This is how it works. You come in, you're prepared, and off you go?"

It took me a couple years after the fact to realize that that just doesn't happen. I didn't believe that it wasn't going to happen, and so that's why I believe that it did happen. I didn't ever doubt myself. I knew that I could do it. I was manifesting it before I even knew what that was. I just thought, "You know what? I don't have four years at Carnegie Mellon, but I'm twenty-seven. I'm not eighteen. I've done a lot of shows and I have a lot of work behind me. I paid my dues in other ways. I've worked shitty jobs. I have been poor as shit. I have been in a teeny little white town, 'fag' written on my locker. I've been through it." Inside I knew I had enough emotional capacity to fake it. I'm just going to fake it until I can figure out how to do it for real.

And you did study once you got to New York; you didn't just coast.

I am a sponge. I am a student. I love knowledge. I love learning and training and I love the research. I remember even in my little community theater productions of *Babes in Arms* or *Evita*, when I wasn't onstage, I was in the wings watching the people that were the leads. I wanted to learn by watching the best people do it. Since I didn't go to school, I thought, "I need to just be near the people that did and watch them." I would watch the dancers roll out their legs and so I'm like, "Oh, I'll do that, too." Gavin had a vocal warm up and a warm down. I'd never heard of that. So I thought, "Well, I should warm down, too, because I want to make sure that I have the flexibility in those high notes." So training, I knew that was something that I had to do immediately. I didn't ever want to coast. [When Gavin was leaving] I didn't get a formal offer to play Jimmy, but the production team had said, "You're next," and then when I heard it was going to go to Christian Borle, who I thought was great, I peaced out. I gave my notice. My neighbor was Jerry Orbach, who was my mentor of all mentors. He said, "You're crazy to leave a Broadway hit. A long running show doesn't happen very often." And I just said, "Emotionally I just don't think it's healthy for me to be there. I have to push myself and see what else there is for me." So I gave my notice without having another job, but I knew that I would find one.

We're going to come back to that in a second. I want to ask about working with Sutton.

Sutton was—I was so in awe of her, like everyone was. She was so good and such a star, and so wacky and so beautiful. I remember seeing the pressure that she was under. I would watch her from the wings, and—it was just an incredible amount of pressure vocally. She had just won the Tony so everyone was there to see her so she had to be in every show, and she was having some vocal issues at one time. I had my eyes on her. I wanted to see how she navigated this, and she was amazing. And she was generous with me. I remember me being too forward with her and too buddy-buddy too soon. She doesn't remember it like that. I've asked her over the years. I remember when it all really hit me. I was on for Gavin once, and there's a scene where Jimmy and Millie are in that box. They're in a crate, and they pop out. Gavin's a tall guy, and I'm even taller. I weigh about fifty pounds more than he does, so I was crammed in there. Sutton's five ten and all legs, so we were just like nose to nose, and I just said, "I cannot believe I'm here. I can't believe this is my job. I can't believe I get to kiss you." She was chewing on a Ricola, and she gave it a chomp, and she's like, "I know, it's crazy, right?" I was so verbal with my "I can't believe this is real." Calm down and do your job! She was great. She was generous and great. I learned so much from those people and had great friendships. It was incredible.

So, given that, it's that much more surprising that your decision to leave was so definitive.

I was following my heart. I just had a sense, and I knew myself. I had also done a couple of readings of *Altar Boyz* at the time, and Matt Morrison was supposed to do it, but then he got bumped up to the lead in *Hairspray*, and so I was the guy. I thought, "I can create a musical where I can use my weird comedic sensibility." Doing scenes with Tyler Maynard, who was the funniest person I'd ever met in my entire life, he made my guts ache because I would laugh so hard. I just knew there was something else out there for me, whether it was *Altar Boyz* or something else. And then I was brought in for *Aida* to be Will Chase's standby. And Will was hysterical, and funny, and irreverent, and would drink a triple espresso before the show. He had tons of eyeliner, and he was just such a bro. He was great. That was a different kind of role for me. It wasn't funny, and it was a way of singing that I really liked. I loved that kind of pop/rock, Elton Johnny-type thing. I didn't get to do that in *Millie*. That was a great experience as well. I got to go on a lot. And then Adam Pascal came in for the last six months, and I got to go on a lot for him, too, and I learned so much. It was a different style of acting.

Were you feeling part of the Broadway community?

I jumped fully head first into the scene. You couldn't stop me from going out at night. I mean, you're so hyped up after a show, how can you possibly just go to bed afterwards? My first few years on Broadway, I can't believe that my voice survived, and that physically I survived. I was drinking so much and I started doing drugs. I started hanging out with people that did ecstasy, and then I started doing cocaine. I always kept it to just at night and just when I didn't have to work. I never was drunk or high at work. That was a hard, fast line that I never crossed, but I could never be as good as I could be, because I was always recovering. I definitely just jumped right in and met people, and then got jobs from being at parties.

Did you ever have survival jobs?

No, I never—I only acted in New York.

Tell me about being Jerry Orbach's neighbor.

Jerry and Elaine immediately took me under their wing when I got to our little building on 53rd and 8th. They loved that I was like an old-school Broadway guy. He used to say that I was like a John Raitt: a big guy with a big voice. He was just kind and wonderful. I'd see him all the time, and honestly, I didn't even know what a huge Broadway vet he was until I got to New York. That's how uneducated I was. I knew him as Lumière from *Beauty and the Beast*. And then I was quickly schooled. I would run things by him all the time, and he was so dear. And then when he passed, we went and sat with Elaine at her house, and I sat in his chair. We all just kind of had a moment.

After *Aida* . . .

Altar Boyz at the New York Musical Theatre Festival, and it was quite the hot ticket. I got to create so much of it on my own. [Director] Stafford Arima just kind of let us play, and I felt free, and silly, and sexy. It was just a great experience. We were all going to go off-Broadway, and that's when *All Shook Up* came into my life. Jarrod Emick had been doing that for a long time, and then he was no longer with the project and all of a sudden they needed somebody new. I grew up listening to Elvis music. My dad was the biggest Elvis fan. I saw *Blue Hawaii* and *Viva Las Vegas* more times than I can remember. So I went in. They brought me in five or six times to sing all of the different songs. Jenn Gambatese was continuing [with the show], and they wanted to see chemistry stuff with her. I just thought this was what I was supposed to do. My first lead of a big musical. I think there was some convincing people needed just because I was an unknown. Up until that point, I'd only been an understudy. But then I got it, and that was a whole new world. They wanted me to be [the character of] Chad, but they wanted me to sing all of Elvis's songs and basically play Elvis in every movie that he ever played. They thought I looked too similar to him so they made me blonde. I'm like, "You guys, it's a bad idea. I look crazy as a blonde. I've had a couple of drunk summers where we bleached our hair after too much Sun-In, and my face looks green." But they're like, "Well, try it." So we did. I had blonde hair. There's a YouTube video of the only time I ever had blonde hair as Chad, and I look like a crazy cyborg android murderer. It's horrible.

That's what previews are for. Where was your brain? Pressure? Excitement? Fear? All of it?

All of the above because now I felt like I'm the Sutton. I knew that I was the guy whose face was five stories high in Times Square, which was wild. My parents got to New York, and I was on taxis. I remember thinking, "Everybody has one huge, big break in their career, and this is yours right now. You don't want to look back and be like, 'I was so nuts I barely knew it was happening.'" I definitely was like, "Please just experience this and be in this because this is fleeting." And it was. The show only lasted like seven months. And it was hardcore. It was a heavy, heavy singing show. I sang seventeen songs. They were really high, and it was super energetic. I remember just wanting to keep it going, wanting each show to be great. Unfortunately, there were so many jukebox musicals that came around at the same time. People had had it. I truly believe that we got an unfair shake because there was a saturation level. If you look at the book, and you look at what we did with the story and *Twelfth Night*, it was really clever and great. It was just the wrong timing. No one can ever take it away from us, and it goes on and lives forever in community theaters. At the opening night party, Priscilla Presley and Lisa Marie were there, and they told me that Elvis would have been proud. They gave me a guitar [of Elvis's]. It was nuts. I remember getting word that the show was getting mixed reviews, but that I was getting good reviews. That's a hard thing to hear because you want the show to continue and to do great. But I was so proud of myself and the work that I had done. In between Chicago and New York, I started working with an incredible acting teacher. Larry Moss. I wanted this character to not be a cartoon. And I also got a trainer and lost like fifteen or twenty pounds.

You grew up husky.

Yes. It's always something that I have to keep on top of because I'm just naturally a big guy. Sometimes the part you play shouldn't be that way. I mean, I can't tell you how many sad, long callbacks for Roger in *Rent* I went to. They were like, "You just don't look like Roger. You sound like him, and your acting is great." But I looked big and healthy and Roger is not. Anyway, so yeah, I just did a lot of work in between Chicago and Broadway. I worked with Larry Moss, and I created a persona. He had made me do this exercise where—I'm always afraid of hurting people physically because I'm a huge person. I'm six three, and I'm always about 210, give or take. I remember walking down the sidewalk of New York, always bobbing and weaving, "Sorry, sorry." I'm just one big apology. He's like, "This guy is not that. People will move for you. I want you to walk down the street and not move [out of people's way]." It was so difficult to even just walk on 9th Avenue but I did it and people would move. And I got a couple people like, "Asshole!" and a shoulder here and there, but it was definitely important work for me. It really helped me plant my feet, and own everything that this guy was. I really wanted to create something that was nuanced and funny. I loved what we ended up doing. And that's because I put in a lot of work.

Then the reviews happened . . .

Yeah. But I got huge agents and huge people to be in my life out of it. All of a sudden I was in the conversation more than I ever was before. It opened my world up.

As Chad in *All Shook Up*, the portrayal that inspired fans to scream, grope, and even bite. (Joan Marcus)

It's pretty extraordinary to do what you achieved with this show, which is to become a star from a flop.

Right. But it hurt. We knew that the writing was on the wall. They kept saying, "We have a few more weeks, we have a few more weeks." And then the inevitable meeting, and everybody cries. Oh, it was terrible. I didn't take it personally because I knew that I did everything I needed to do. But it would have been nice [to run]. It was a big paycheck, and it was stability. But I just had faith that the next thing would happen, and it would happen when it was supposed to.

You won a Theatre World Award.

I won a Theatre World Award. And a lot of people were saying that I was going to get nominated for a Tony, and it didn't happen, and that hurt really bad. But I had seen that world. In the four or five years that I'd been there, I'd seen what it had done to my friends. Working your way up and then possibly getting a nomination and then even winning, but then the next year you can't even get hired in anything, so does it really make a difference? Does it matter? I had to really justify this for myself so I could still have confidence. Some of the most talented people I know have four Tony nominations and they're looking for their next job, so I couldn't hang everything on that. I just—I wanted that validation. I wanted not just the audiences and not just a couple of powerful critics; I wanted everybody to go, "What he's doing is great, and we should all agree collectively." At that time I also got into reading the chat boards and the message boards. *All Shook Up* is when it started, and then it was like an epidemic around *Xanadu*. Me and Kerry Butler were like, "No! We're done. We can't anymore." It's such a horrible, masochistic thing to do, but I always think it's important to take the temperature of people out there and see how things are coming across. But yeah, of course, I wanted the Tony nomination for that, and I really wanted one for *Xanadu*. Within the Broadway world, it's the ultimate. It's validation not just from your peers and from the committee, but it's from the community at large. But I'm finally at peace with all of that, and I'm sure I'll win a Tony one day.

After *All Shook Up*, your next Broadway musical was *Xanadu*.

I did the workshops. The first time I heard the music, and the first time I saw Douglas Carter Beane's book, I'm like "Oh, here we go! This is it. I know how to do this. This is in my wheelhouse. This is somebody who is just gleefully clueless, and childlike, and passionate, and it's very clear how it needs to be played." I love it when I'm reading a script, if I start to do the voice or speak the lines out loud, I just know that I have to do it. It's very fast. I don't have to be like, "Oh, I don't know. Should I?" I just know. Yes. Done. I have very strong intuition and I trust it. I knew that I was going to do that, and I loved it. I loved working with Jane Krakowski. She was so funny. But she had just done the pilot for *30 Rock* so we didn't know what was going to end up happening. We did a few different workshops. I remember in one of them, I put a nail through my hand. I got mad playing one scene, and it looked like I had a ball of hamburger in my hand. Theater scars. But I remember that it was really important to me that the chemistry between the two of them was on fire. You just had to—the story was so thin. And it was eighty-nine minutes long. Unless you really cared about them . . . And then when *30 Rock* got picked up I said I didn't want to do it without her. It was a sad decision, but I thought, "I can't. I don't want to do it with anyone else." So I just let it go. That's what you do with workshops sometimes.

Workshops, I have been told, are a mixed bag. You are in something from the beginning but on the flip side, you are helping create the piece and not always getting the payoff.

I was replaced for *Book of Mormon* right before Broadway. But I did love that experience of doing something new. I liked to be the first person to do it and put my stamp on it, sing it my way, have the freedom to do a vocal improvisation here, find a funny joke there. I loved that process. I did lots and lots of them. I worked on this one piece with Kelli O'Hara called *The Red Eye of Love*, which we tried—I tried it with Kelli. I tried it with Elizabeth Stanley. Kristin Chenoweth flirted with it for a while. It was just way too weird. It wasn't linear enough. And I did *Tale of Two Cities*. I did a bunch of those before that came to Broadway. I didn't end up going with it. It wasn't a great fit for me. My first workshop I ever did was a revival of *Little Mary Sunshine* with Kristin Chenoweth. And then I did the workshops with Kelli O'Hara for *Nice Work If You Can Get It*. I did the first workshops of *Little Mermaid*.

When you put in all that effort and don't end up in the show, is that hard?

Sometimes. Sometimes you want to continue. I mean, *Nice Work If You Can Get It* wasn't what it ended up being. I never saw how it ended up, but it was really fun. I had a great time, and I loved working with Kelli. And sometimes you're like, "That's enough for me." But sometimes it's like, "Oh, my God, I can't believe I don't get to do that anymore." And sometimes, some of the things that you create end up on stage: lines, bits, vocal improvisations. That's happened to me lots of times. That's the biz. I'm putting it out there in the world and that's my art and I'm not getting credit for it, but there it is. Whatever.

Well, I would also think that how one feels about that has everything to do with where one is in one's career, too.

Yes. I remember [musical director] Michael Rafter got mad at me once during *Thoroughly Modern Millie* understudy rehearsal. I was marking because I was heavy workshopping. I'm telling you—this is my first six months of *Millie*. I was a bull in a china shop. This is a perfect example. I was marking Jimmy's songs that day because I had major *Altar Boyz* work, and he's like, "Are you marking?" I was like, "Yeah, I'm doing *Altar Boyz* right now. I just really need to make sure I'm healthy for everything." He's like, "You're singing two songs. Sing them." And I was like, "Oh, my God. You're right. I'm sorry. This is my main job. This is my priority. I fully apologize."

You were new to the business . . .
Totally. But can you imagine?

So you walked away from *Xanadu* . . .

I did a couple other little things here and there. They were moving to Broadway. I wished them well. I was happy for all of them. I wasn't super heartbroken because it didn't feel right. And then I got a call late at night from [director] Chris Ashley, who I loved, who also directed *All Shook Up*. I don't remember how he put it, but he was basically saying "We're fucked, and we need your help." James Carpinello broke his leg in a few places, and they asked me to come in and just help get the show up and open and then they would find someone to permanently replace me. Would I do it? And of course. I mean, of course. All those people had worked so hard, and I love Kerry, and . . . I have to backtrack a little bit. It actually wasn't that quick of a "yes" now that I think about it. That's so funny how we—time goes by . . . When I really think about it, I said, "I don't know" because the main thing that made me walk away from it was that Jane and I had created this relationship, and I couldn't see Kerry in the part. I loved Kerry in other things. I thought she was brilliant in *Hairspray* and a million other quirky things. I didn't see her as Kira and I told Chris that. He's like, "Do me a favor and just come see the show. She's totally different from Jane, but she's totally insanely brilliant." So I went and watched it, and from the very first moment, it was so crazy amazing. It's so different. Jane was sexy and was basically born on skates because of *Starlight Express*. Kerry was a horrible skater and was clumsy and adorable, and it busted my brain open. I thought, "I've never thought of it like that. Absolutely. Yes, I'll do this." And I did. I went in, in maybe a week and a half or something. It was in me enough to where we actually moved up the opening a couple days, and I went on a couple of days early just to get it going. It felt great. James was supposed to come back within—I don't know exactly what happened. I had a very awkward encounter with James at the theater one day, and he was like, "So you're staying?" He was on his crutches. And I was like, "I don't know. Are you coming back?" I honestly didn't know what the deal was. I think we were both being told different things by people. Producers. Can you imagine? It was a tough situation. And then they asked me to stay, and I said "Yeah," and it was just a blast, a total blast. Mary Testa and Jackie Hoffman were bonkers. It was just a great group of people, and Anika Larsen and—yeah, it was a great group. We were gearing up towards Tonys, and we were just the little show that could. But the Tony thing [Jackson not getting nominated] happened, and I had to come to terms with that. I realized that's not why I'm in New York. I'm not in New York to win a Tony. I'm in New York to share my art, and to live my dream, and to sing my heart out, and to create wonderful scenes with people, and take people's minds and imaginations in places they didn't know possible. So I had to do work on myself to make all of that okay because it was tough. It was really tough. And then *The New York Times* comes out, and they say who should have been nominated and I made that list, I'm like, "That doesn't help. It kind of feels good, but it hurts."

You're damned if you're on that list and you're damned if you're not.
Right, exactly. But I remember the night of the Tonys, we were asked to sing, and they decided to do my big number. It was a running joke—my shorts would get shorter and shorter as the run went on. As I got in better shape and felt more comfortable, I'm like yeah, I'll show off more. I had longer ones, and I had really short ones, and the producers asked me to do the longer ones for the Tony telecast. You mother fuckers have been using my legs and my body on posters and stuff, and now you want me to [back away from that?] I say that with love because I love the producers. But I chose my tightest, shortest ones. I thought, "You know what? This is my moment. I get to sing on the Tony Awards. I get to sing my big song. I got a big high note. I got a big emotional, fun thing, and let's just go for it." I remember backstage my heart was beating so hard out of my chest. I could see my pec moving. Me and Curtis Holbrook would always do pushups backstage, so I was doing pushups, and my heart was beating, and I was like, "This is another moment. Just be here. Just breathe." I wanted to feel like a matador. I wanted to be fully in control and just blow the roof off the house. I wanted to sing like I've never sung before and I believe I did. Lily Tomlin announced us, and we did it, and it was incredible. It was an incredible night. I felt like "Oh, this was my Tony nom, and I'm good with it." Yeah.

During *All Shook Up* and *Xanadu*, you had some pretty passionate fans.
The Cheyennetologists.

The stage door . . .
Man, it's crazy. There's a lot expected of you. My going out to sign autographs is not part of your ticket. It's a nice thing, and it's fun. And you have people all across the spectrum. You have Hugh Jackman who signed everything for everyone at every show always. That's the way he wanted to be. And that's great for him. And then there's people that are like no, my job is done when the curtain goes down. That's it. So you need to respect that. And then everyone in between. I was always of the mindset that if I was healthy, and it wasn't too crazy, then I would always sign. I think it's important because those people are the reason that I'm on the stage. But the fervor of the fans, especially the Elvis fans of *All Shook Up*, was nuts. I remember a lady taking a bite of my leg. And handsy, handsy, handsy, handsy, handsy. There were times when I felt very uncomfortable and felt very much like a slab of beef, but I also understand what the part that I just played represents to the older demographic group of women. I represented Elvis to them, and in their view, he was a certain thing. I have been pinched and grabbed everywhere. I have had tongues in ears. It's crazy that people think that they can just do that. And

I'm not good at boundaries. I am now, especially with kids. Until you've experienced it, it's hard to explain.

I imagine there are some days it's fine and some days it's exhausting.
Yeah, for sure. And there are people that really feel like you owe them. I remember there was a group of women who came all the time so they think they know you. They would be like, "Listen, my daughter's here, so . . ." and they would just grab me and pull me down the street and make me have a fifteen-minute conversation with someone. There's a lot of entitlement and a lack of boundaries, but that's up to the performer to say.

Etiquette in the theatre in general is becoming increasingly challenging.
Yeah. I'm not one of those people who is super great at just ignoring the guy that's filming in the second row, or the lady that's texting, or the man that's slowly opening his candy. I don't have the wherewithal to be like, "Hey, this isn't TV. I can see you." I definitely go inward, and I loathe them from inside.

Other than adoring working with Kerry Butler, what can you tell me about her.
Oh, my God, Kerry's dressing room is so messy. I would always tease her. She was just a messy, messy girl. What I love about Kerry is that she's unflappable. She's not super emotional. That isn't to say she's not caring and wonderful, but she's not fragile. Kerry is solid, and you know that no matter what happens, she's going to catch you. If you miss a line or whatever, she's there with you. Sometimes you can look at your costar and they're like deer in headlights. Not Kerry. Sometimes my skate wouldn't come off or whatever, and we would have to improvise. I always felt safe with her. She was easy, and she's fun. It's fun to be with somebody on stage who doesn't have a lot of weird, emotional baggage. Not that I'm not—I'm very empathetic. I'm actually too empathetic. If I'm in a group of people and there's ten people, and one person's having a rotten day, I immediately can tell who it is. I home in on it, and I fixate.

That's actually lovely.
It can be a nice thing. I've learned to love that about myself, but when you have a job to do, and you have a leading lady who's emotionally fragile, you're like, "Which version am I going to get today?" Luckily, I've had super solid Kerry Butler, Kate Baldwin, who's like—talk about unflappable. She's a broad in the body of a Rita Hayworth. She's got it. It's so fun to be onstage with her and that's why I'll continue to do this.

Have you felt, as the leading man, a responsibility to lead the company?
Yeah, yeah. I remember *All Shook Up* was the first time that I knew that I was looked at to kind of be the dad, really. You inevitably look up to the principals, and for a long time it was a hard thing to be like, "Oh, it's me." Even if people in the ensemble are older than you, if you're all in a meeting, and you say something, all the heads turn to you and people listen to what you say. It's important. So if there was correspondence with the producers, if we had a concern about a Macy's Day Parade thing [for example], it was the first time in my life that I ever really started stepping up, standing in my strength. You do set the tone. And we've all seen it happen where the person at the top sets a tone and it's not great. But it can be wonderful. There's a lot of emotion. People's livelihoods are riding on the fact that the show is a success. There's politics. There's all kinds of stuff happening. I can't believe there are not reality shows of what happens behind Broadway musicals because it's nuts. I've definitely been in companies where there are a few rotten eggs, and that can be contagious. I try to lead by example, and I try to be

kind to everyone. Know people's names, respect people's time. I'm very big on time. I'm always on time. I think your attitude is everything, and I try to have a great attitude all the time because it's nice. I like to be around that. I don't love super broody, pessimistic people. It's not my fav. And I worked with my share on *American Horror Story*, let me tell you.

Your Sonny in *Xanadu* was that. He was . . . sunny.

I thought of him as a huge child in the best way. He is always unbelievably positive. He can't believe that there's not going to be a roller disco. If I didn't fully believe this guy, it would crumble. If you didn't buy it, then you're like, "What the fuck am I watching?"

You finally did get to share a stage with Jane Krakowski in *Damn Yankees* at Encores!.

I did *Damn Yankees* toward the end of *Xanadu*. That was actually one of my favorite things I've done. I love that part, and I love his relationship with Meg. Randy Graf played Meg and I had the hugest theater foot-in-mouth with her. I loved her, she loved me. We had this great

Taking in that "Old Devil Moon" with Kate Baldwin in *Finian's Rainbow*. (Joan Marcus)

relationship. We were singing "Near to You" one day, and the timbre of her voice was so specific and clear and gorgeous. I said, "God, you would have made the best Fantine." And she goes, "Darling, I was the original Fantine." I didn't know. I was cracked, as the drag queens say. Cracked. But that was great. It was really fun. Sean Hayes and I immediately became friends, and he was just hysterical. I hadn't laughed like that since Tyler Maynard. Somebody who is just naturally funny. Anything they say makes you laugh. And it's funny because he's kind of a serious person in real life. He's not always on. I adored him. And I loved working with Jane. She was so hard on herself with that. She did the original Gwen Verdon choreography, and she worked so hard. And Tina Fey came to see Jane and [saw me and] I started on *30 Rock*. Television started for me.

Your subsequent musical stage outings were both Encores! productions: *Finian's Rainbow* and *The Most Happy Fella*.

Finian's Rainbow was so sweet. What a simple, sweet story and the most-glorious score. I did it to sing that music. It certainly wasn't Woody's arc. It was great. Chris Fitzgerald was hysterical. And at one point [once the show moved to Broadway] I remember I was doing *30 Rock* all day and then going to the theater at night. I would get up at 5 AM, I would shoot *30 Rock*, and we worked it into the contract where I'd have to go at a certain time to make sure I was on time for the show. I was exhausted. It's a different type of brain stuff: technical, and marks. And then you get to the theater and you're in Rainbow Valley. Kate was just awesome with me because there were a couple of shows where I was just a fricking zombie. My brain was so fried. But you have to keep going. You keep doing it. It was actually a really fulfilling experience, and I really didn't expect much from it. I really wanted to get in great vocal shape. I wanted to have a great cast album where I was in my vocal prime. In my mind, it was for my kids. I wanted to be able to show them when my voice was really croony. Who knows what's going to happen to my voice later?

That's something you think about? That you might lose this . . .

Not lose, but everybody's voice changes, and it's fun to have a snapshot, a record of when your voice was a certain way. My voice has definitely changed from *Millie* to *Xanadu* to *All Shook Up* and *Finian's Rainbow*. When I just did the *Magic Mike* workshop, it was a totally different, rough kind of sound.

When *Finian's* went to Broadway . . .

It was a smash hit over at Encores! and everyone was going crazy. What was happening in the economy made it relevant. So when they said, "We're going to go," I thought, "Wonderful." It was really fun. And Kate was just glorious. I've been put with these women who—it's their moment, and I feel like it's my job to help them facilitate that. I knew it was all happening for Kerry during *Xanadu*. It was her Tony nomination and it was fun to be a part of that, and to help her and support her and to watch her fly. And with Kate, everyone knew this was Kate's moment. I mean, no one can sing that score more beautifully or have the most perfect Irish accent and look like that in those costumes, and have it be so effortless. To be a part of that moment with her was really great and really fulfilling. That show wasn't about Woody. It was about her, Sharon. And I was perfectly fine to be her leading man.

Were you sad to see it end so quickly?

Yeah. It was a strange time because on one hand I was happy to be back on Broadway. I was happy to be reprising this part that we had done so successfully at City Center, and just digging deeper. But I didn't have delusions of grandeur. I knew that I wasn't going to be winning any awards for this performance. It was really a mediation on taking a great job, singing the most beautiful score, and just working.

It was a full five years until *Most Happy Fella*. You moved to Los Angeles in that time.
I just really wanted to give television a go because I like it. I like the hours. I like the medium. And it was something new. I had done so much in such a concentrated time in New York, and I was going through major changes emotionally, personally: the end of my marriage, getting sober. It was just time, and I needed a new, fresh start. It just seemed like time. It didn't feel like "Goodbye, New York." It's always there. I go back a few times a year. I see a bunch of shows. I flirt with doing a show probably every year. There's been one almost every year where I'm like, "Maybe that's the one," and it's great to still even be in the conversation. It's great that I still have producers and people calling and interested in what I have to offer now. I'm just in a different place now with my life and with my kids, and what it would take [for me to do a run], you know?

So do you see yourself focusing primarily on TV and film now?
I have major financial responsibilities now. I have two mortgages, I have two kids and school. I can't be wondering where my next Broadway show's going to come from or be doing a Broadway show at night and then during the daytime doing workshops for another thing and hoping that's going to happen. It's just too stressful. I love television though. I have learned to really love the art form of it. The difficult things are the waiting, the downtime in between the work. You spend so little time actually shooting and so much time waiting, so, to maintain a performance and to build a performance, especially if it's shot out of order, it is really up to you to do your homework. I love that challenge. I'm a student. I like to absorb everything. I do a lot of research, and I've learned to really love the business. I think it's because I've been working with people who are so good at it, and they love it so much. Namely, Sarah Paulson. She's so meticulous and has binders for every character. I was looking at her one day and she's like, "I know I'm crazy. It's just what I need to do." And obviously it's working. Also, when I started TV, I don't think I was very good at it. I definitely needed to calibrate my work. I learned this from Kathy Bates: If you are really in the scene and truly listening, if you have a thought the camera will catch it. It took me a long time to trust that. On stage you've got to do other stuff. You have to project it. You have to indicate it with the body language or with a vocal projection. You have to get that point across to the back of the theater. I remember doing a scene with Kathy Bates during *Roanoke*. Angela Bassett was directing. It's a big, juicy scene and I was really prepared. You take your preparation, and you throw it out and try to be in the moment. And the little voice in my head is saying, "You're not good enough, what are you doing here, they're going to find out that you don't really know what you're doing." All of that stuff. I just pushed it aside and tried to be in it. It was the most alive and most crackly I've ever felt in a scene because every single time I would give her something, she would shift it just slightly. It was just so masterful. Every take was just slightly different but all perfect. That is so inspiring to me. I strive to do that more. I know that I'm going to be doing television for a long time. I've done twenty-something TV shows now, and I'm getting better and better. I'm getting more confidence. I'm getting to do all kinds of different things. Now, I'm dads, now I'm bad guys. The dumb hunky guy, it's done. It's a great living. It's not without its challenges. I'm still looking for my next gig. As far as theater, I mean, I miss it, and I definitely struggle with my first love of singing and live performing. I worry, "Does anybody remember me? If I came back, would anybody care?" So I try to do at least one thing a year that will scratch that itch. Like *Into the Woods* at the Hollywood Bowl was that. It was so amazing to be with Sutton Foster again! And Patina Miller, Sierra Boggess, these amazing artists. So yeah, if the right opportunity

comes, I'll do it again, but there is a world in which I may never do Broadway again, and I know that that is a possibility.

How does that make you feel?
A little sad. I definitely would love to do it again. I definitely feel like an outsider, though. When I look at a Broadway website or something now, I don't know who anybody is. It's all a new crop of people. I miss it for sure. When I heard they were doing *Into the Woods*, I got my manager on it immediately. I pursued it so, so hard. I don't really lobby hard for roles. I really feel like if it's supposed to be mine, it will come to me, and I'll do what I have to do. But when I heard this was happening, oh my gosh, I got on the horn right away. Initially the word back was that they were going for giant, giant stars. They have to shoot for the stars and then land on the people that are supposed to play the parts. We worked so hard. Let me tell you what Sierra did: So, my kids love, love, love *Little Mermaid*. She came over while we were rehearsing, and I told the kids we were going to swim with Ariel. She came fully in Ariel drag. It was so unbelievably magical. And then that night as I was putting the kids to bed, Willow is just smiling in her crib. I said, "What's going on?" She said, "I'm so happy. I swimmed with real Ariel today." And Sutton—I mean, she's a fucking Carol Burnett. We took a two-and-a-half-hour car ride one night. We had to go to our sitzprobe, and it was the craziest traffic. We just went deep, talking about our moms, and our pain, and our deep shit. It's great to have that kind of unpacking with your leading lady so then when you're onstage, there's just more of a well to pull from. I can't wait for *Music Man*. I can't wait for anything she does because she's one of the greats.

You got to do another musical, this one on film: *Hello, Again*.
I'd never seen the play. I didn't know the music, but I knew that there were great people in it, and I would be playing opposite Audra McDonald. "Yeah, absolutely!" That's the fun of getting to do what we get to do. You never know where you're going to be. I'm getting murdered by Angela Bassett and having sex with Lady Gaga and then three days later I'm in New York and naked with Audra. Nice work if you can get it. Sometimes I look at my life . . . I don't want to be too heady about it, but if I look at the landscape, it's pretty wild. [I was] this fat, gay, thirteen-year-old kid from Idaho who was obsessed with jazz-singing ladies in the woods.

You always strike me as someone who remembers being that kid. You've never gone Hollywood.
I've always just been so conscious of being humble and not wanting to talk about what I'm doing or being show-offy. Jason has come down on me because sometimes that can come across as [false modesty or aloofness]. I'm trying to find that balance. I think it's a matter of owning what you are doing, being grateful and gracious for what you have and the work that you get to do, but also just not apologizing for it. Sometimes I feel like if I'm not in the public eye for a while, I don't know if people even know who I am anymore. But several months ago I was asked to do an episode of *The Morning Show* with Jennifer Aniston and Reese Witherspoon. They said, "Would you be a singer in the party scene? You'd be playing yourself." So within the confines of the show, Jennifer Aniston's character is having a party and she's hired Cheyenne Jackson to sing? It was so meta and weird. I did it, and it was amazing. I'm singing, I'm myself, and Jennifer says, in her character, "Thank you, everybody thank Cheyenne Jackson." It's so wild to me. I really like where I am. I love to be able to go anywhere with my family. I just want to work, and I want to provide. I have some good stuff cracking, but then there'll be down times. I think Hal Holbrook said, "I've been up and I've been down. Up is better." So I'm just enjoying it while it's up.

19

JONATHAN GROFF

March 2020

"I'M NEVER HAPPIER THAN WHEN I'm riding my bike to the theater," says Jonathan Groff, expressing a simplicity unexpected for a star of his caliber. He has, after all, been the male lead in two TV series and has been featured in several others. He's got a major role in a forthcoming big-budget Hollywood feature, *The Matrix 4*, and he is, of course, the voice of the male hero, Kristoff, in the two most successful animated films of all time, *Frozen* and *Frozen 2* (not to mention on the *Frozen* ride at Disney World). But his heart, says Groff, belongs to the theater. "Even when I was doing the TV show, *Boss*, in Chicago," he tells me excitedly, "I hired Sutton Foster's understudy to teach me the tap dance from *Anything Goes*," which he performed at a benefit. "In my world, in my mind, and in my heart, I am always thinking about theater."

That was even true when Groff was a child, growing up in Amish country—Lancaster, Pennsylvania—on a horse farm. Cast albums were a gateway to theater and Groff wasted no time moving to New York right out of high school, after he completed a non-union tour of *The Sound of Music*. He made his Broadway debut in the infamous flop, *In My Life*, before hitting (and scoring a Tony nomination) with *Spring Awakening*. His sensitive portrayal of the yearning Melchior Gabor was the emotional anchor of this unlikely smash (a rock musical set in nineteenth-century Germany). Another sensitive portrayal followed with *Hair* at Shakespeare in the Park before Groff defied expectations and performed in a series of straight plays off Broadway, in Los Angeles and on the West End. The TV and film roles kept Groff pretty busy until his auspicious return to musicals in *Hamilton*, for which he received another Tony nomination. Most recently, he won raves for the rapturously received revival of *Little Shop of Horrors*.

Sitting outside with me on a quiet San Francisco street, blocks from the bay with the occasional interruption of the street trolley's clanging bell, Groff is infectiously sunny, unguarded, and smiley. He certainly doesn't look like a guy who has been training in martial arts for this *Matrix* movie in the couple of weeks since he left *Little Shop*. When he describes the joy he felt being back in a musical, I ask what made him leave. "I was looking for the next mysterious, unknowable thing," he says. "As always."

When did the theater bug bite?
When I was in fourth grade, the high school production of *Annie Get Your Gun* . . . my parents had taken me to see theater before, but that was the first time I was really conscious of it, and the first time it really got me. I was blown away by how great it was. I went to the library and got the Ethel Merman record. I was probably about ten years old. It's funny, isn't it? How Ethel Merman somehow gets a young gay at ten? I don't know what that power is. I became

With Lea Michele in *Spring Awakening*, the show that would propel them both to stardom. (Joan Marcus)

obsessed with that show. I was really into *I Love Lucy* as a kid around that same age. I was typing up scripts from memory. Watching episodes and then typing up the script. I wanted the lines down on paper for some reason. With a cover and everything. And I read them with my friends, my poor friends. Yeah. We would do table reads. Then in eighth grade was the first time I did a school play. Got really into it. And then in high school, I did the high school theater, but I also started working in the community theater. We had two different community theaters in my hometown, and that is really when my whole life became all about theater. It's all I ever thought about. It's all I ever wanted to do.

Given that you grew up on a farm, was there a context for your parents?
My parents didn't have the logistical knowledge to get me into it. They didn't put me in acting classes as a kid or anything. My dad was a horse trainer, my mom was a gym teacher, but they were really good at listening with both me and my brother. When we would say we wanted to do something or were into something, they were good at supporting it. I remember my dad asleep in the parking lot of the community theater at like 11:00 PM when I was coming out of rehearsals. And they were really confused by what it was—all of the performing stuff—but the more I did it, they were just happy to facilitate. And then when I wanted to move to New York after high school they were completely supportive of it.

Did you ever study?
I've never formally trained in performing. When I was working at the Fulton Opera House in Lancaster, I learned so much from watching. I would sit in the wings of the shows. I was such a sponge. I remember being in *The King and I*, if you can believe it, and I would tuck into the wings, and watch. I was just obsessed by watching it and hearing the audience and watching the actors.

The King and I had to have been full of other kids who were likely playing backstage. Did you perceive yourself to be an anomaly?

Yeah. I was not interested in the hanging out in the dressing room. I would just so much rather be watching it from the side. To me that was the reason to be there. It excited me and got my adrenaline going. I wanted to be as close to being onstage as possible.

Jonathan Groff	
In My Life	Broadway, 2005
Spring Awakening	Off-Broadway, Broadway, 2006
Hair	Off-Broadway, 2007
Hamilton	Off-Broadway, Broadway, 2015
A New Brain	Encores!, 2015
Sondheim on Sondheim	Los Angeles, 2017
Little Shop of Horrors	Off-Broadway, 2019

So, watching that much, were you able, to the best of your recollection, to discern the differences in performances from day to day?

Yes, that's part of what I was fascinated by. Some actors would evolve their performances over the course of the run. Some would do the same thing. Some were phoning it in; some of them weren't. It was fascinating to observe. And then when I did *The Sound of Music* tour, I'd never done a run of more than a month in the community theater, so I couldn't wait to get reps in. I remember being so blown away by the idea that I was going to get to do the show over and over again for a period of nine months and how much I would learn from the beginning to the end of it. I remember a month and a half in, feeling like a robot and breaking through to try to learn my own kind of performing; even though you're doing the same lines and the same show, we were always in different theaters and trying to embrace the different energy and the different audiences. I would still sit in the wings every day and watch the rest of the show. Rolf was only in maybe twenty minutes total of the show. That really was a whole other kind of education.

A role like Rolf is essentially a scene in a song. There are only so many variations you can hit . . .

It's almost like yoga or a meditation or something. Some of the differences probably wouldn't be noticeable from the audience's perspective, but for me it was just a desire to remain present onstage and open for whatever might happen in the smallest way. It's not like Shakespeare where there's such profound poetry that it's impossible to ever get to the bottom of it, but as an eighteen-year-old getting his legs, it was more a practice in being present. That same year I went to see Sutton Foster do a concert in Philadelphia. At that point, I'd already seen *Thoroughly Modern Millie* six times and I'd noticed the evolution of her performance in the two-year span. I waited for her backstage and interviewed her of my own volition. I wonder if part of the idea I had about wanting to achieve that [evolution] was, in large part, due to watching her those times and seeing her so . . . there. She still is that way. Even when other people are singing, she's so there for it. She's just really there, and I was so drawn to that. She talked about how, if she's having a bad day, letting her fellow actors lift her up, and vice versa. You feel differently every morning when you wake up, so wouldn't that be a part of what would affect the show? I was really fascinated by that idea. Continue to be fascinated by that idea. *The Sound of Music* was the first time I was able to really put it to use. I love a long run. I really love the ability to show up every day, and it's why I keep coming back to the theater. It's my favorite way to act. I just love it.

So you come off that tour, and you decide you're going to move to New York?

Yeah. I had deferred a year from Carnegie Mellon to go on the tour. I made $10,000 in the entire year that I was on the tour, and I was a saver. Carnegie Mellon, at that time, would have been $40,000 a year, and I thought, "I'll never be able to pay it back." And also, emotionally I wasn't feeling ready to sit in a classroom after having nine months of experience onstage. I was just starting to get confident. Starting to sing eight times a week, having never trained, was also really challenging and interesting. I was finding my way. So I thought, "I'll go to New York for a year. College will always be there." I moved to New York with a friend, I got a job, and then I went to open calls. I was waiting tables at the Chelsea Grill on 9th Avenue, and I was so happy. I was so excited to be living in New York at nineteen.

I heard you talk once about being a good waiter.

Yes. That was such a good skill to learn. That ended up being a good audition skill. Knowing, when a table sits down, if they want to talk, if they want to talk for five minutes, if they want to be entertained for the entire lunch or dinner, if they don't want to know that you're there, if they do want to talk and then it shifts—I would take that skill into the audition room and think, "Okay, this is a room where you want to be charming and talk to people because they seem receptive to that." Or, "This is a busy day for them, and they just want to hear you sing and then leave. Don't try to be memorable." Reading the room is such an important skill. I also met Tom Viola [executive director of Broadway Cares/Equity Fights AIDS] my first month working at the Chelsea Grill, and he got me a volunteer job for Broadway Cares. I was with the buckets collecting [donations from audiences, post-performance, during the annual Broadway Cares fundraising drive]. I would show up early and watch the ends of the shows. He actually said to me, when *Spring Awakening* was happening, that mine was the fastest transition from bucket collector to speech giver! I met great people. I waited on Christina Applegate when she was doing *Sweet Charity*. The whole cast of *Spamalot* would come in and I waited on Christian Borle and all of them.

Were you starstruck?

Yeah, totally. I wouldn't say anything. At that time, when I was at the Chelsea Grill, I also waited to be seen on the non-Equity lists, didn't get seen, didn't get seen, didn't get seen. And then I got into an audition for the North Shore Music Theatre where I did *Fame* and got my Equity card.

***Fame* is a dance-heavy show. Were you just an intuitive dancer?**

No. The way that I got that was my secret boyfriend at the time. I was in the closet, but I was dating a guy from my hometown who was in the *Radio City Christmas Spectacular*. He still is, actually. He would go to the dance calls for shows and he would teach me the combinations so that when I went in for the singer call, if I got called back, I would already know the dance. I got *Fame* because I had already learned the combination from my boyfriend at the time. In retrospect, [I guess that's] a very over-the-top thing to do. But it worked.

And then after *Fame*, the casting director from *The Sound of Music* called.

Rachel Hoffman was casting *In My Life*. She called me in for Christopher Hanke's understudy, and I was desperate to get it because it would have been my first Broadway show. And I got it! It was the perfect experience because I could watch again. I remember thinking, "Wow, this is really funny how it keeps happening that my first taste of something is as a fly on the wall observer." I was basically being hired to watch and observe. It was the greatest gift.

Watching how the actors worked and watching them put together a show, watching them deal with the criticism—it was such a great first experience. I was the dance captain so I had to write down all of the blocking, and I was forced to really look at every aspect of the show and learn so much about the ins and outs. I was just so excited to walk into the stage door of the Music Box Theatre every day. It was so cool.

This particular show was such a mess. Did you have any sense of that? Or did you think that this is just how shows evolve?

I don't think I knew. I didn't have any sense if the show was good or bad at all. It was so off the wall. The [rehearsal] room was really creative, and David Turner, who played the character of Winston, is a comedic genius. He would come in and think of all this shtick to do to comment on the material. He's brilliant, a brilliant actor. It was an insane story; the lead character had Tourette's and his first line was, "Fucks up duck." Everyone had such a good attitude, actually. We all have stayed in close touch. It was such a bonding experience. No one was negative. Maybe I was seeing it through a twenty-year-old's excitement eyes, which is why I have a memory of it in a romanticized way. But from my recollection of it, everybody threw their hands in the air, didn't expect the show to last that long, and made the most of it. Went for the ride. There was a lot of laughter and silliness, and it was fun. It was totally fun. And I was just so excited about walking into a Broadway theater every day. It was a very buoyant experience. I sit under the poster at Joe Allen and look at it with great pride and delight. I moved to New York on October 21, 2004, and I think the opening night of *In My Life* was October 20th of 2005, so it was a year later. It was all so surprising to me that it was happening how it was happening. I was in total, joyful shock. And then I was auditioning for *Spring Awakening* at the time that *In My Life* was ending and got cast in that in December of 2005. We did a workshop of it at Baruch College in March of 2006, and they fired five kids from that workshop, and then we did the Atlantic from April through the beginning of July of that year and then moved to Broadway in November of 2006.

You said that you thought that Melchior was beyond your level?

It was just very much a lucky moment. They happened to be looking for people that could sing and also act classical text who were raw and untrained. I was certainly raw and untrained, and the perfect age. I remember dying to be cast in it. When I was auditioning, I remember telling my dad that I knew I had so much to work on with my voice and my acting, but I knew if I got the part, I could get there. And I knew that it would change me. I knew that it was just out of my grasp of abilities, but I knew that I could get there if they just gave me the shot to really practice and work towards it. They brought me in for Hänschen, and [director] Michael Mayer was like, "He's a Melchior. Let's have him read the Melchior scenes." I read the scenes and then he asked if I could sing in falsetto, and I said, "Yeah, I can," and I sang, "Let It Be." He said, "That's your falsetto?" And I laughed at him. He put [my picture] on the "no" pile, and I left. And then Tom Hulce put me on the "yes" pile—Tom told me this story years later—because I had laughed at Michael. He thought, "This guy's right physically, he can act, and we're going to need a lead who can handle Michael's personality and is able to laugh with him as opposed to be devastated by things that he says." And then I had a session with [musical director] Kim Grigsby where she was like, "You've got a lot of work to do." She gave me the music and gave me stuff to work on with my breathing and stuff. In that month and a half period of time, I knew that I could get there. And I knew that it would be a life-changing, life-altering experience if I got to do it.

There were some big personalities there to deal with.
That always came naturally to me. I had perfect boy in the world syndrome.

You were a pleaser?
Pleaser, total pleaser. Not wanting at all for anybody to ask me about myself, so always deflecting to the other person, always wanting to know more about them and to not really look at myself. And certainly not have anybody else look at me. I would deflect and be present for the other person, which allowed me to connect with people with big personalities. I was drawn to them because I could hide behind them. Lea Michele's the perfect example. We were like country mouse and city mouse. We were so opposite. Same thing with Michael Mayer, really. So opposite that we got along so well and we found each other really amusing. I've always gotten a kick out of really opinionated [people]—it's like Cliff and Sally Bowles in *The Berlin Stories*. "I am a camera," just capturing everything around me. Partially because that's just how you're natured and then there's the added element of "I don't dare turn that camera on myself at this particular moment in my life." It allowed me to have really amazing relationships and great experiences with people with personalities that were so different from mine. It was a very interesting time for me personally because we were all so—it was the college experience that none of us were having. We were having the *Spring Awakening*. I specifically was in the closet, living with my boyfriend but neither of us were out. We were both having our relationship in the context of the four walls of our apartment, and we were roommates outside of that. Everyone knew what was going on, but no one ever talked about it and I never gave space for there to ever be a conversation about it. That was happening at the same time as I was having this personal explosion of growth and excitement. It's very rare that you get an amazing career opportunity and an amazing creative opportunity that co-exist. I was getting to do this show—it still may be the best role I've ever had. It's a phenomenal part in a phenomenal show with a group of people that were just discovering all their talents. We were all doing it together, and that was so exciting and so special. Every dream I ever had of being on Broadway was happening, and it allowed me to feel successful in the eyes of my family. So, having that feeling, "I came here to do something, and it happened . . ." It was just an incredible time. And then the weird compartmentalization of the personal life thing was, in retrospect, so bizarre. It's very weirdly in tune with the themes of the show, which was repress, release, repress, release. That was the life that I was living at that time. I was repressed in so many ways but then also with my boyfriend having an amazing time when we were alone together in the apartment.

You met the person you call your best friend, Lea Michele.
I FaceTimed with her yesterday, just talking about stuff. She taught me so much. She really knew the business, and she knew what was at stake in *Spring Awakening* in a way that none of us knew. And she knew how to present herself. She knew the importance of the press, she knew about the discipline of doing the show eight times a week, and she knew the value of taking a week's vacation and how important that was. She was really smart. I picked up a lot from her because she had so much more experience than me. We were so opposite. Also, having to fake fuck each other eight times a week, we were always delirious and punchy. It was like such an epic experience that we got to go through together that would bind us together forever, regardless if we had stayed in touch. That experience has really bonded all of us. The whole cast is still on a text chain. It's been great, that bond that we all formed.

What do you remember about the run?
Spring Awakening was a very eye-opening experience in a million ways. I never dragged my feet to the theater. Every day that I went into the stage door was an opportunity to get better.

The experience of doing it for so long completely changed me, and I also learned a sad lesson about the fact that on Broadway, there are a lot of unhappy people. People expect Broadway to fulfill them. "Once I get to Broadway, all the answers will come. I'll be set, I'll be happy." The revelation that I had when I got to Broadway was, "Oh, it's the same thing as doing a show in community theater!" Literally the same thing. It's the same drama, it's all the same. Which was exciting to me because I loved doing community theater, and I wasn't looking to Broadway as the answer to my problems. That it was more of the same was great news to me. But there is a lot of negative energy in those environments because I think people get disillusioned by the lights of Broadway, and then it's a grind. And it's really hard work. It takes a lot of effort and focus and discipline and determination, and there are people that are unhappy. Two years of doing the show, I learned about the underbelly of the Broadway community.

You also learned, I have heard, that you are a person who can be made to laugh on stage.
During performance 303, John Gallagher and I just started laughing for absolutely no reason. It was such an amazing moment. It was incomprehensible what really happened, but we just started hysterically laughing throughout the song, "Touch Me," and then it caught on like wildfire through the rest of the cast. Then [throughout the run] moments would happen like that where we would just start laughing.

Although it ultimately took off, the success of *Spring Awakening* was a bit iffy there for a while.
We couldn't sell half the house during previews. It didn't sell until *The New York Times* review came out, and that only lasted us a couple of months. We almost closed right before the Tonys, and then the Tonys gave it new life. The cast of *Spring Awakening* was kind of humbled and blown away by the success of the show. In the first nine months, every step of the way was a total surprise. The vibe was actually really uplifting. I remember being at the Tonys with *Spring Awakening*, and we were so shocked that we won Best Musical. And we were so excited to be there. I remember noticing the older actors and how nervous they were, how full of anxiety they were. Made me feel like, "Oh, I never want to take it this seriously where I'm not having a good time." There was shaking! I really remember the stress. And I also realized then that the biggest, most important thing about the Tony Awards is the commercial that you do for your show. Yes, they're about the community recognizing each other and trying to put a spotlight on great work, but more than anything, it was an opportunity for us to sell our show. When we were at the Tonys, it was not a party. It was a work event. We had to be on form and really sell the show. That was just one of those things that you learn as you go along. I was twenty-two and it was all just such an amazing lesson. You understand the business side of it. It's not just about living your dream on Broadway, it's about being a part of a business and all of the responsibility that comes along with that. I also remember journaling about [the fact that] I had my friend on the one side who is not even nominated for a Tony, Lea, and then I was nominated and lost the Tony, and John Gallagher Jr. was nominated and won. It was three different trajectories, but really what made the experience was how we all responded to those things. Just because I was nominated didn't make Lea's contribution to the show any more or less important, and just because John won the Tony didn't make his contribution to the show any more or less important. It was how we all processed those outside things and then came to work anyway. She was devastated that she didn't get nominated, of course, but came to work anyway and gave a great performance. I learned so much from that experience. And even reviews or hearing people say comments, for me it comes down to how much do I really want to do this? If a comment is going to ruin my show or a review is going to make me not want to

come to the theater, then I should just leave the theater. I should be doing it because I have to do it and because I want to do it, despite what anybody else says, good, bad, or indifferent. It comes down to the desire of wanting to show up and perform. It's easy to get neurotic. It's easy to get into a battle with your own neuroses, let alone other people's neuroses. But if that real need and desire to do it is there, then I think it's easy to handle all the stuff that doesn't really matter.

I'm struck by how conscious you were at such a young age. Some of the lessons that you're describing don't seem to me necessarily intuitive. Other twenty-two-year-olds might have missed those learning opportunities.

Spring Awakening was such an artistic show. I was suddenly being pushed and asked to do things that I never even really dreamt of doing. It inspired the desire for that moving forward. I don't know if I had it before *Spring Awakening*. That experience taught me what was possible and how much you could get from working on something that actually said something. The material was really challenging and poetic. It pushed us as actors to dig deep and try things that were scary, to be all over the place emotionally and physically. It made me have an appetite and a hunger for more of that. I definitely didn't feel the same way I felt when I moved to New York at nineteen.

Was coming out part of that? While your being in the closet is not directly germane to your career . . .

But in a way it is. When you're talking about what it means to be a leading man in . . . even though it was a recent time, it was a different time than it is now. It was a combination of growing up in a conservative community and then getting success quickly. I didn't have time to catch up to what I had found myself in professionally. I hadn't quite figured out who I was yet. I was still only twenty-two and in the closet to everyone, not even having friends who I was talking to. It was a very bizarre experience in retrospect, and the role that I was playing was this rebellious character who did not let the world define him. It was very progressive about sex and very accepting, very intellectual, and I was not any of that. Yet doing the role, playing that man, cultivated a side of my personality that didn't previously exist. I think that was also my drive to being connected to that part; I wanted to cultivate that side of myself that was not a people pleaser, that had convictions and passion and the ability to speak out and use his voice. When I left the show after two years, I really don't think that it's a coincidence that a month later I came out. My whole life changed. I broke up with that boyfriend and was on the way to living a completely different, more cohesive life. I felt safe in the context of theater because I felt like when I came out of the closet, I was probably giving up a career in television and film. I really did. I thought, "Okay, I don't really care about that. I could have a career in the theater regardless of my sexuality," and I was happy to release the desire to be in the film and television world. It was more important for me to be who I was, and that was the choice I made right after *Spring Awakening*.

Well, if you were looking for a show to support that choice, *Hair* is a good one.

Yeah, totally. The release of *Hair* was mirrored in my own personal summer of love. I smoked weed for the first time. I was coming out of the closet. I was completely released in the way that that show also expresses. It was a complete mirroring of what I was experiencing at that time personally. It was incredible.

Given how happy you were, I am surprised you decided not to continue with the show on Broadway.

It really was for me personally a very profound experience to come out of the closet, be doing that show, and feel my soul open up in the way that it did. I was uninterested in commercializing that experience. I was twenty-three, I had just done two years of a rock musical, and I didn't want to repeat myself. *Spring Awakening* was everything I ever dreamt and more come true, and when that all happened, I thought, "What artistically is the next interesting thing?" And that's when I did like three or four off-Broadway plays in a row instead of doing *Hair*. I wanted to try doing straight drama. All I ever wanted to do was musicals, and then *Spring Awakening* happened and I was like, "Okay, let me try and now expand myself and do something different." [Doing *Hair*] at the Delacorte, and the off-Broadway plays, you're exploring the ideas and the work more than you're selling a show. I was excited by the prospect of not trying to create a commercial entity. It was about the creative experience. *Hair* would have been creative and fun, but it would have been selling a product from a Broadway stage. So instead, I went the path of not selling a show or a commercial thing, but exploring and trying to push myself creatively. That was really the choice.

And that ultimately took you to TV and film, too.

I just kept following my desire for something new and different and challenging, but I never felt disconnected from the world of the theater. I read about it in the news every day. I'm always seeing shows, so in my heart and mind, I was never leaving. I am always thinking about, "What's the next play? What's the next musical?" *Deathtrap* [in London] was one. . . . I had done *Glee*, and the audition came through for *Deathtrap*, and I was like, "Yes!" And I remember my agent at the time going, "But you just did *Glee!*" At that time that was the biggest TV show in the world. Part of why the producers of *Deathtrap* were interested in me was because of how well *Glee* was doing over there. And I was like, "No, this is what I want to use that for—to go do a show in the West End." Theater has always been the ultimate thing. It always goes back to that for me. It's always a part of my thought process on the daily.

So if you could do only one medium every day . . .

Total theater. I've never cried harder than when I left *Little Shop of Horrors* in January. All the guys were in the same dressing room downstairs, and Michael Mayer came in, and I like wept in his neck, crying so hard. And then I was singing Seymour's part of "Skid Row" and I couldn't even finish it. I was a mess. Tammy Blanchard had to look at me and be like, "Pull it together. What is your problem?" Because an experience like that show is just—all I ever wanted as a kid is that. I'll always have that. That's always the number one thing in my heart. Always.

So why do you do the other stuff?

Because I love acting, and I love growing. I thought about David Fincher [and what I learned from him during *Mindhunter* when] I was doing *Little Shop*. I like doing them all because one informs the other. Taking the stuff that I learned from David or other directors I worked with and then applying it on the daily to great material—it's like every medium informs the next, and they all build on each other. It's like working out different muscles at the gym. Doing the different mediums works you out in different ways, and it's just trying to stay well-tuned in every aspect of it.

Does money play into it?

No. Never. I've fallen into lucky things like *Frozen*. I have been lucky that I haven't had to make monetary decisions when I've gone into TV and film stuff. I really don't even think about it.

So projects like *The Matrix* have nothing to do with money or stardom? It's just an interesting next thing?

It sounds unbelievable to say "yes" to that, but yeah. [The money] is great, but that's not why I'm excited to do it. The money doesn't make me feel anything. I've had the great luck that I've been able to live comfortably ever since moving to New York when I was nineteen based on the work that I did.

Let's talk about *Frozen*, because even though it's not a stage show, it's musical theater adjacent.

That was another complete lottery moment. I never would have imagined that that would happen. I put myself on a tape audition in a studio and four months later found out that I got it. And I got it because my voice paired well with Kristen Bell's voice. My voice tested well with hers.

It's so interesting that when recording those films, you didn't get to act with her. You were not in a room at the same time.

The director, and writer Jennifer Lee . . . when you're in the room with her, she's writing it, she's improvising the other characters, and you're just doing the lines a million different ways. So I'm not working with Idina or Kristen or Josh, but you're working with this writer who's making stuff up on the spot, and we're laughing a lot and feeling creative. She's pulling stuff out of you, she's the scene partner for all of us because she's got to keep the whole thing in her head.

You did two *Frozen* movies and two shorts. Is there more to come?

I hope so. I can't imagine that there won't be, just considering how successful it's been.

Speaking of success . . . *Hamilton*. The call comes from Lin-Manuel Miranda . . .

Yeah. I hadn't seen the show. They were in early previews [off-Broadway]. *Something Rotten!* got fast-tracked to Broadway at a speed no one was anticipating, and Brian d'Arcy James [who was playing King George in *Hamilton*] realized that come the end of March he was going to be doing *Something Rotten!* So Lin texted me and said, "Would you want to play this role?" I was like, "Okay." I didn't know anything about the show. He sent me no material. He and I had become friends when *In the Heights* and *Spring Awakening* were happening at the same time, and we would occasionally meet up between shows. The two of us and Karen Olivo and Lea would go to Blockheads, of all places. I always loved him because he was so nice and enthusiastic. He was really funny and fun to hang out with. And then they send me the song, and I was like, "What is this show?" It was all like so confusing to me. They sent me the script, and it was so long because it was all those rap songs. I couldn't understand what I was reading. I couldn't understand the song I was singing. I couldn't really sing the song and I was croaking, trying to learn how to sing it. It was just out of reach. I couldn't sing it until I hit the stage. That's how much of a show pony I am. I don't know what chemically it is about myself, but once I was in the costume and on the stage, then I was able to sing it. It's like that weird thing that either happens or doesn't happen. I saw the show for the two shows on Saturday and the

Sunday matinee. Monday, I had a rehearsal and then Tuesday I went into the show. It was, like, so bad. I had no sense of character. I still had no British accent. Lin said that when I walked out and did the show for the first time it looked like I had won a contest to be in *Hamilton* because I was just, like, in this outfit, singing the song with no character choices—it was hilarious. But the song killed, and that was such a lesson because I thought, "Wow, I'm bad. I'm legit bad at doing this song." I was like, "My mom could come out and do the King and get the laughs." It got all the laughs. "This is what it's like to be in a really amazing show in a really amazing part. You don't have to do anything!" The song is so brilliantly written, it's just all pure genius in the writing. And then as the run went along, I hired this lady to help me do an accent. It was like I was rehearsing in real time in front of an audience, just slowly layering in—that was my rehearsal process. And then I started to learn how minimal I could be based on how good the writing was. How one eyebrow raise—I just happened to be watching all these Barbra Streisand videos at the time. There's the video of her singing "When the Sun Comes Out" on *My Name Is Barbra*, her first black and white TV special, and it's like she's fucking herself with her own voice. She's got this, "You may worship me now" energy. I was like, "Oh! that's going to be my [approach]." I just found the feeling of it and this cat-like minimalism that was my way into the character, and then I could play with it, and then I became in control.

What can you say about being in such a massive hit?

It's so cool. Alfred Molina, when I was doing *Red* with him in L.A., said there's no better feeling than being in a hit on Broadway. There's just no better feeling. It's like the entire city opens up to you. In the first year of a show like *Hamilton*, people from politics and music and art and world leaders and the entire culture were coming to that show. It was just the most phenomenal experience, and it really makes you feel small. It's incredibly humbling because you realize how much bigger the show is than any one person's contribution. Except Lin's, of course. You really feel a part of something massive. I think everybody in that company was so admirable in their ability to take all that in and ride the wave and then also do the show. The director was really great about, "When you come into the theater, you're here to do the show." Everybody in that cast was so connected to the story they were telling that the doing of the show never changed for anyone. Everybody was really disciplined about the show that they were executing, and then the outside stuff was just a whole other insane, wonderful experience. The stage [after the show] every night for an entire year was like a cocktail party with no alcohol. Everyone would have forty-five minutes at least of this mingling period where it would be like Tom Cruise and Emily Blunt and Joe Biden and Pharrell. It was like that every single day. It was complete mayhem.

And was that mayhem magical, exhausting, or both?

Both. Totally both. This was another one of those observing jobs within my life; I would sneak into the theater dressed as King George and stand in the box right behind the people who were sitting there. They would never see me. I would peek behind the curtain. For the first three months of the show I watched every performance from the box. The experience onstage was great, and I loved playing the part, but it was nine minutes of my day. The rest was observing the kind of insane experience that was *Hamilton* and watching everybody's life change. When I signed up, it was to do it off-Broadway, and I thought that this TV show I was doing, *Looking*, was going to go for a third season. I never imagined that I would be able to do *Hamilton* on Broadway. Then *Looking* got cancelled and they asked me to do the show with them on Broadway. I wanted to spend a year breathing that air. I wanted to be a part of the experience, and I wanted to take the ride with that group. I wanted to be in that bus.

You wanted to be in the room where it happened.

Yeah. Literally in the room where it happened, that's where I wanted to be. And it was really crazy. And you have to be disciplined to stay happy and to stay present. It takes work. When something becomes successful and any sort of entity becomes commercially viable, people start to break down in their minds, "Well, who's getting the cash?" The business side of everything starts to open up, and that can get really complicated with people wanting to feel their worth. This is still the case with Broadway dancers. They are not paid what they're worth. They're just not. The level of talent and the expertise that it takes to do what they do versus how much they're getting paid to do it? It's incongruous. Same thing with teachers. Compared to the skill that it takes to be really great at what they do, it doesn't match. So there's tension there. I mean, they wrote a whole show about it. *A Chorus Line* is all about what you're sacrificing. And some people get caught up in that grind, understandably.

Between the off-Broadway and Broadway runs of *Hamilton*, you had the opportunity to do *A New Brain* at Encores!

Oh, my God, that was so cool. Working with James Lapine and Bill Finn and Anna Gasteyer. It was fast and furious. We made a recording. That was a really special theatrical experience. We also performed it the weekend that gay marriage became legal so there was all of this celebration that weekend. I remember riding my bike home from the theater on the Friday night and there were fireworks along the water. I used to listen to that CD when I was in high school and think about two men singing love ballads. And then to be able to perform it and

With Rema Webb, Quentin Earl Darrington, Josh Lamon, Jenni Barber, and Alyse Alan Louis in *A New Brain* at Encores! (Joan Marcus)

have it be that historic weekend, and then do a recording of it was really just fucking cool. I had just also done a one-night only *How to Succeed in Business* in London.

You were shooting *Mindhunter* when Michael Mayer called and says *Little Shop of Horrors*...

I never would have expected that that was what he was going to say when he said he'd found the next project for us. But when I listened to the music, I was like, "Oh, yeah, this is actually who I am." I immediately felt it. He mentioned it and it seemed a little out of left field, but then when I put on the music, I was in immediately. I listened to the entire [original cast] album at least once every day until I left the show. I just became obsessed with it. There is kind of an *I Love Lucy* element to it even though it's the sixties. There's that old-school comedy, something really throwback about the show. I'd never gotten the chance to do that but that was the reason I got into musical theater in the first place. It really sent me back to my childhood and was really satisfying to do every day. And then there was the Tammy Blanchard aspect of it. She was just so amazing to be onstage with. And you're in a perfectly written show, a perfectly written character with perfectly written music—you can't help but be good, and you can't help but improve as the run goes along because there's nothing extraneous in the writing. You can't drive the train off the track.

Actually, you can. I've seen it go off the track.

Yes, I guess the whole conceit of this production was that it was going back to its original format [in an intimate theater], and so in that format, you're inside something that is safe and perfect. So in that way, whoever plays those parts in this particular theater, in this particular production, I think, will have a similar experience. It is like a Swiss watch. The show is so tight. People just don't write with economy like that anymore. In the song, "Feed Me" the song starts with a plant talking and then six-and-a-half minutes later the protagonist is going to murder the dentist. That all happens in six minutes! It's just amazing storytelling.

So having just experienced this, your first long run in a while, did anything change for you in terms of your goals?

It did. It really reminded me that when you do really good writing eight times a week, it can't help but make you better. I knew that that was going to happen with *Little Shop*, but I didn't know the extent to which I could lose myself in the show and be so supported by the structure. I could start to really let go and really lose myself in scenes. I could start to really fly a little bit. It gave me so much confidence. Doing theater gives me so much confidence as an actor because you're in charge of what's happening. You're onstage doing it, and it really sharpens your knife. When I come off of something like *Little Shop*, and I'm here in San Francisco doing *The Matrix*, and the schedule is always up in the air, it's almost like precision acting; suddenly you're called into a set and suddenly the camera is on you, and suddenly you're forced to act and be brilliant. I can do that with greater ease and agility because I've sharpened my knife so much doing *Little Shop*. I'm feeling so confident in my ability to act and be movable and present. I got the muscle back that it makes me able to come into an environment like this and have those chops. Then, after a period of time, I'll be ready to go back and sharpen the knife again. I'll go back and definitely do something in the theater.

Are you sad when a show continues on without you?
Yeah, it's a weird mourning process. It all exists without you. I think the first time I felt that was when I went back to see *Hair*. When I went back to see *Spring Awakening*, I had done the show with so many different actors that that already felt like it had morphed. But with *Hair*, I left and then I went back and I felt jealous and sad, like I was watching my boyfriend with somebody else. I felt cheated on. But I've seen *Hamilton* a million times. I don't feel ownership of anything. The whole point is that the role gets picked up and owned and then dropped back off again, and then somebody else picks it up and owns it and drops it back off again. When I'm doing it, I feel like I own it, and I feel like I live and breathe it; it is an extension of who I am. And then it's somebody else's.

You have told the story of being an easy mark for people trying to get you to laugh on stage. So working with Christian Borle . . .
I know, I know. I just laughed. He used to call it my "stroke face" because I would start to laugh with whatever side of my mouth was upstage. I didn't even know I was doing it. He is such a genius. He's such a genius. And he's so analytical and so present on stage in a way that's totally opposite from Tammy. Christian is like a technical genius. He's just analytical about every moment while it's happening. What can he do to get a laugh at any moment? I learned so much from him, and it was so fun to be onstage with him because he was so present and always investigating everything at all times. And then Tammy is the polar opposite. She does not have the technical desire to ever do the same thing twice, but emotionally she can't fake it. She can't phone it in. She's like this kind of living, breathing, emotional organism. They just balance each other out on the show so perfectly. It was so fun to share the stage with them because they were both hyper-present but for two completely opposite reasons. He was all analytical and all about the laugh, and she didn't give a fuck about the laughs and was all about her ability to only tell emotional truths regardless of what was happening.

And there's you in the middle?
Yep. Bouncing back and forth.

What do you think you want now?
I don't feel that I won't be an actor for the rest of my life in some way, shape, or form. The mystery of not knowing what the work is will haunt me every year of my life, I think. You never know what the thing will be, but I do feel like—well, hopefully—there'll always be something, but you never really know what that thing is. If I couldn't get work, if years and years went by where I didn't have an acting job, I would go do something else. I would become a teacher. I feel lucky to have worked as much as I've worked, and I just intend to continue to try and cultivate and embrace opportunities whenever they come along. I remember Matthew Broderick talking about this when he was doing *Nice Work if You Can Get It*. "I'm trying to get these musicals in while I'm still physically able to do them." It gets harder as you get older, and I want to do that while I can.

Having grown up on Broadway albums from the library, and now knowing you are part of that world, do you still have "pinch me" moments of disbelief?
Oh, yeah. That is why I love living in New York; I'm addicted to the talent. It's where shows get made to then tour the world. New York is the incubator. All the brilliant minds are there. Being in rehearsal for *Little Shop* with the entire creative team, being in rehearsal with

Backstage at a rehearsal for *Little Shop of Horrors*. (Jonathan Groff)

someone like Michael Mayer, who is a creative genius . . . Nobody has his specific point of view. Nobody has Bart Sher's specific point of view. Nobody has Hal Prince's specific point of view. There are these great creative minds that you want to make stuff with. It's so cool. Those are the "pinch-me" moments, when you're firing creatively and collaborating with other people. Like the experience I had with Tammy in *Little Shop* I'll hold with me for the rest of my life. I just wrote her a letter to tell her what it meant to me. It was about an exchange, and I know it was for her, too. What I gave to her and what she gave to me was a really special combination that changed each of us a little bit. Wow! Someone that's so gifted, and we're going to have a back and forth with each other, and a little bit of us is going to rub off on the other one and vice versa, and we're going to make something together. That's cool to me. That's like what I live for now: the spreading of the creative virus from one person to another.

ACKNOWLEDGMENTS

IN THE ACKNOWLEDGMENTS OF *NOTHING Like a Dame*, I mentioned the village it took to make that book happen. That village now has new neighbors and I am so very appreciative of all of them.

Jennifer Keller continues to be the moral and intellectual compass by which I try to navigate. She served as a constant sounding board, occasional proofreader, and the best dispenser of tough love that I know. Her contributions to the ways I approach these conversations (and my life) were invaluable.

Melinda Berk proofread this book's every word and many that, thanks to her, aren't included. Once again, she showed unwavering support, objective perspective, and perpetual good humor.

There are a number of friends and colleagues whose help to me included their feedback and ideas, and there are others who jumped in to help me reach out to some of the book's more elusive subjects. And there are some wonderful people who work with or are married to this book's men and who dealt with my myriad communications. Thank you, Molly Barnett, Rosie Bentinck, Jesse Blatt, Christian Borle, Will Chafin, Frank Conway, Pamela Cooper, Gavin Creel, Emily Cullum, Raúl Esparza, Jeffrey Epstein, Charlie Finlay, Elin Flack, Judy Kaye, Tom Kirdahy, Norm Lewis, Ryan Oboza, Michael Paternostro, Geoff Soffer, Michael Urie, Lillias White, and George Youngdahl.

Then there are the people who worked directly on the book.

Rob McQuilken at Massie & McQuilken is the agent and cheerleader I'd recommend to absolutely anyone.

Norman Hirschy and his team at Oxford University Press could not have been more encouraging when I said I wanted to do a follow-up to *Nothing Like a Dame*, and they made the process so incredibly easy. I am grateful to have a home at Oxford.

Colleen Donley, thank you for all your transcription help.

Thank you to all of the incredibly talented photographers who allowed me to use their work: Catherine Ashmore, Bruce Glikas, Paul Kolnik, Carol Rosegg, Craig Schwartz, the estate of Raymond Jacobs, and most especially Joan Marcus.

Thank you to Laura Benanti, whose humbling, lovely, and hugely appreciated foreword was worth every penny.

And of course, thank you to all of the men whose words fill these pages. They gave me hours and hours of their time, their wisdom, and their candor. And in a few cases, their romantic advice.

Finally, my family. My parents exposed me to Broadway musicals from the time I was five. Of course, they didn't know they'd be creating a monster. But once that die was cast, they were nothing but supportive. My sisters, too, tolerated my Carol Channing impersonations when I was small, and, who am I kidding, they still do. And my nieces, for reasons I will never fully comprehend, think I can do (almost) no wrong. Seriously, it's like they are a pair of Jewish mothers and I just graduated med school with honors. And then there are the spouses and partners who love me even though it isn't a biological imperative. Thank you all for believing in me, Ann, Donald, Arlene and Rona Shapiro, Emma Morgan, David Franklin, Paul Erlich, and Noa and Hallel Shapiro-Franklin.

INDEX

For the benefit of digital users, indexed terms that span two pages (e.g., 52–53) may, on occasion, appear on only one of those pages.

Note: b indicates box and f indicates pages with illustrations.

Abraham, F. Murray, 226
Addams Family, The, 91b, 101–2, 103
Ahrens and Flaherty, 133–34, 158, 196–97, 204–5
Aida, 206, 208b, 210–11, 212, 316, 318, 321–22
Alexander, Jason, 96–97
All Shook Up, 316, 318b, 322–25, 324f, 326–29, 330
All That Jazz, 54, 56–57, 60–61, 80
Allen, Debbie, 74, 79f, 80, 81
Altar Boyz, 316, 318b, 321–23, 326
Amour, 186, 188b, 196, 254, 256b, 257, 259
Angels in America, 254, 263–64, 265, 266
Annie Get Your Gun, 53, 208, 333–34
Andrews, Julie, 24–25, 26–43, 83–84
Anyone Can Whistle, 171, 174, 292, 298b
Anything Goes, 3–4, 5b, 15–16, 105, 106b, 111–12, 224–25, 318, 333
Applause, 37, 38f, 38–40, 39b, 41, 43, 49
Apple Tree, The, 29, 144b, 164b, 174
Arima, Stafford, 85–86, 322–23
Aronson, Boris, 7, 12
Ashford, Rob, 294–95, 320
Ashley, Christopher, 137, 284–87, 294–95, 326–27
Aspects of Love, 17, 19b, 33
Assassins, 91b, 97, 98f, 98, 144b, 155–56, 162, 164b, 169, 171–72, 173–74, 184, 209, 281–82, 283, 288

Baby, 70b, 86, 188b, 193, 195
Bacall, Lauren, 37, 38f, 38–39, 40, 111, 117–18
Baldwin, Kate, 328, 329f, 330
Baranski, Christine, 155, 284–87

Barnes, Clive, 29
Barnum, 89–92, 91b, 93, 100, 103
Bart, Roger, 226
Bassett, Angela, 331–32
Bates, Kathy, 331–32
Bean, Shoshana, 54, 66f
Beauty and the Beast, 89, 91b, 96, 98–99, 100, 101, 103, 142, 144b, 146, 149–50, 157, 222, 224b, 228–29, 322
Bechdel, Alison, 183
Bed and a Chair, A, 188b, 202
Bells Are Ringing, 142, 144, 153–54, 208b, 219
Benanti, Laura, ix, 229, 313
Bergen, Polly, 287
Berlind, Roger, 225, 308
Bernstein, Leonard, 100
Big Deal, 62, 80–81
Big Fish, 238, 240b, 251–53
Billy Elliot, 206, 208b, 212, 214, 215, 216, 217, 220
Blakemore, Michael, 82–83, 134, 135
Blanchard, Tammy, 341, 345, 346–47
Blankenbuehler, Andy, 158–59
Blazer, Judy, 167
Block, Stephanie J., 160, 209, 217–18, 271
Bobbie, Walter, 12, 145–46, 196, 215
Bock and Harnick, 114, 117, 174
Bogardus, Stephen, 68, 69f, 78, 82–83, 271
Boggess, Sierra, 193, 195, 197–98, 200, 203, 331–32
Book of Mormon, The, 269, 299, 301, 301b, 302–3, 305, 306, 309, 310f, 311–12, 325

351

Boosler, Elayne, 226
Borle, Christian, 86, 156, 217, 218, 219, 230, 231–32, 254–56, 255f, 264f, 269f, 313, 321, 336, 346
Bosco, Phillip, 156, 157, 289–90
Bounce, (see also *Road Show*) 105, 106b, 120–21, 299, 301b, 302–3, 307–8
Boyett, Bob, 230–31
Brantley, Ben, 48, 87, 245, 254, 275, 316
Brigadoon, 22–23
Britton, Connie, 210–11
Broadway and the Bard, 39b, 49, 50
Broccoli, Barbara, 288, 289–90
Broderick, Matthew, 346
Brown, Ashley, 309
Brown, Jason Robert, 245, 246
Buckley, Betty, 74–75, 85f, 109–10, 226, 258
Bundy, Laura Bell, 261–62, 263
Burton, Richard, 17, 23–26, 27, 28, 33, 44, 56
Busch, Charles, 105–6, 117–18, 287
Butler, Kerry, 324–25, 326–27, 328, 330
Butz, Norbet Leo, 238–40b, 239ff2, 238 f3, 275–76, 316
Bye, Bye Birdie, 125–26, 128, 142, 144b, 145–47, 207, 318

Cabaret, 3–4, 5b, 6–10, 8f, 11, 12, 48, 73, 240b, 243, 275, 277b, 280, 283, 289–90
Cage aux Folles, La, 222, 224b, 234–35, 299, 301b, 302–3, 308, 309
Caird, John, 95, 197–98
Camelot, 17, 19b, 23–27, 32, 104, 302
Campbell, Mary-Mitchell, 178
Cariou, Len, 37–39, 38f, 42f, 46f, 137, 175, 183, 292
Carlyle, Warren, 217–18, 264
Carmello, Carolee, 86, 101, 151–52, 258
Carnival, 126b, 136
Carpinello, James, 316, 326–27
Casa Valentina, 17, 35
Catch Me if You Can, 238, 240b, 250–51, 309–10
Cats, 48, 89, 90f, 91b, 91–93, 94, 95, 96, 100, 103
Cerveris, Michael, 45, 162–64, 163f, 175f, 181f, 288, 290–91
Champion, Gower, 70–73, 74, 80–81, 87–88
Channing, Carol, 4, 67, 79
Charlie and the Chocolate Factory, 156, 254, 256b, 271, 272–74
Chase, Will, 114, 206–8, 207f, 213f, 218f, 316, 321–22
Chenoweth, Kristin, 13, 15, 16, 117, 149, 174, 193, 246, 247, 288–89, 325

Chess, 48, 277b, 297–98
Chicago, 3–4, 5b, 12–14, 13f, 16, 51–52, 51b, 64–65, 67, 188b, 196, 222, 222b, 230, 234–35
Chitty Chitty Bang Bang, 142, 144, 153, 156–58, 156f, 275, 288, 289–90
Chorus Line, A, 90, 91, 93–94, 344
City of Angels, 68, 70b, 80–81, 82–83
Clark, Victoria, 122f, 167
Coca, Imogene, 30, 33
Cohan, George M., 9, 14
Colella, Jen, 215, 257
Coleman, Cy, 31–32, 54, 80–81, 82–83, 90
Coleman, Johnnie, 63–64
Colette, Toni, 194
Colker, Jerry, 78, 81–82
Comden and Green, 16, 19, 38–39, 40, 110, 117, 153–54
Come Blow Your Horn, 3, 6
Company, 43, 193, 198, 205, 224b, 275, 277b, 290–92, 293, 294–95
Connick Jr., Harry, 87, 244–45
Cook, Barbara, 16, 110, 117–18, 170–71, 198, 199–200, 205
Cooper, Chuck, 203–4, 213
Crawford, Michael, 112, 118–20
Creel, Gavin, 114, 230, 258–59, 299–301, 300f, 310f, 312f, 316, 319–20, 321
Cullum, John, 17–19, 31f, 34, 124, 126–27
Cumming, Alan, 1, 12, 243
Curry, Tim, 100, 260
Cymbeline, 17, 178

D'Amboise, Charlotte, 89, 94, 97, 101–2, 104, 196
Daldry, Stephen, 212
Dale, Jim, 91–92, 288–89
Damn Yankees, 23, 37, 106b, 316, 318b, 329–30
Dance a Little Closer, 37, 39b, 47–48
Daniele, Graciela, 83, 85–86, 95, 133–34, 158, 193, 196–97, 211, 292
Davis Jr., Sammy, 51, 55, 56, 58–59, 60–61
Dear Evan Hansen, 296
Deathtrap, 17, 278, 341
DeLaria, Lea, 280
Dessa Rose, 188b, 196–97, 292
Diggs, Taye, 245, 247
Dilly, Erin, 156, 289–90, 307
Dirty Rotten Scoundrels, 238, 240b, 247–50, 249f
Do Re Mi, 126b, 136
Doyle, John, 174, 178, 202, 288–89, 290, –92
Drabinsky, Garth, 49, 84, 131, 133, 192–93
Drake, Alfred, 124, 126–27
Dylan, Bob, 160–61

Ebersole, Christine, 225, 226
Edelman, Gregg, 82–83, 229
Egan, Daisy, 113
Egan, Susan, 146, 226, 227f
Elegies, 70b, 85f, 86, 256, 258
Elliott, Scott, 104
Ellis, Scott, 114–15, 146, 149, 216, 217, 220, 303–4, 306
Emick, Jarrod, 280, 282, 322–23
Encores!, 5b, 12, 19b, 39b, 91b, 106b, 126b, 136, 144b, 164b, 174, 188b, 196, 208b, 219, 224b, 254, 256b, 264, 268, 277b, 292, 301b, 316, 318b, 329, 330, 335b, 344
Errico, Melissa, 284–87
Esparza, Raúl, 156, 184, 275, 276f, 285f, 295f
Eustis, Oscar, 185
Evans, Peter, 176
Evita, 162, 164b, 178, 180, 277b, 279, 291–92, 321

Falsettoland, (see also *Falsettos*), 68, 69f, 78, 82.—68, 83
Falsettos, 68, 70b, 78, 83, 254, 255f, 256b, 268, 271–72
Fame, 162, 299, 301b, 306, 336
Field, Ron, 38–39, 70b,
Fielding, Harold, 48–49
Fierstein, Harvey, 1, 222, 234–35, 309
Finding Neverland, 91b, 103, 144b, 160
Finian's Rainbow, 316, 318b, 329f, 330–31
Finn, William, 68, 77, 82–83, 86, 258, 271, 344–45
Fitzgerald, Christopher, 257, 259–60, 313, 330
Flashdance, 306, 311
Flora, the Red Menace, 7
Follies, 105, 108, 110, 139, 292
Footloose, 254, 256b, 256
Ford, Paul, 58
Forever Plaid, 147
Foster, Hunter, 216
Foster, Sutton, 15, 16, 215, 230, 233, 258–59, 260–61, 263, 270, 292, 299, 304–5, 307, 314–15, 320, 321, 323, 331–32, 333, 335
Fosse, 51–52, 53b, 65
Fosse/Verdon, 60
Fosse, Bob, 10, 12, 13, 14, 51, 54–55, 56, 57, 58–59, 60–61, 62, 63, 65, 68, 74–75, 80–81, 93
Frozen, 156, 333, 342
Full Monty, The, 70b, 77, 87, 206, 208b, 210–11, 212, 220
Fuller, Penny, 42, 193
Fun Home, 162, 164b, 166, 170–71, 172, 179–84, 181f, 185, 295

Gaga, Lady, 287, 332
Gaines, Boyd, 114
Galati, Frank, 85–86, 133–34
Gallagher, John Jr., 339–40
Gambatese, Jennifer, 303, 322–23
Garber, Victor, 97, 98f, 155
Garland, Judy, 73
Gemignani, Alex, 178
Gemignani, Paul, 41, 97, 146, 229
George M!, 3–4, 3b, 4f, 9, 10–11, 14
Gershwin, George, 200, 202, 282
Gets, Malcolm, 193, 214, 257
Gigi, 105, 106b, 122f, 123
Girl From the North Country, 144b, 160–61
Gleason, Joanna, 248
Glorious Ones, The, 143f, 144b, 158
Glover, Savion, 140
Godspell, 75, 126, 309–10, 311
Gold, Sam, 182
Golden Boy, 19–20, 53b, 56, 188b, 196
Golden Rainbow, 73–74
Goldman, William, 10
Goodtime Charley, 3–4, 3b, 11, 12, 14
Gormé, Eydie, 73–74
Goulet, Robert, 24, 26, 68, 70, 71–74
Graff, Randy, 96, 150–51, 329–30
Graham, Martha, 52–53
Grand Tour, The, 3–4, 3b, 11
Grandage, Michael, 179
Green, Adolph (see Comden and Green)
Greif, Michael, 266
Grey, Joel, 3–16, 4f, 8f, 13f, 128–29
Grimes, Tammy, 40–41
Grind, 51, 53b, 61f, 62–63
Groener, Harry, 93, 110, 227
Groff, Jonathan, 310, 316, 333, 334f, 344f, 347f
Guys and Dolls, 53, 254

Hair, 51, 53b, 56–57, 58, 59, 200, 299, 300f, 300, 301, 301b, 303–4, 309–11, 333, 335b, 340–41, 346
Hairspray, 307, 321–22, 326–27
Half a Sixpence, 3, 3b, 6
Hamilton, 67, 92, 140, 333, 335b, 342, 346
Hamilton, George, 234–35
Hamlet, 17, 19–20, 21, 22, 25–26, 28, 29, 30, 37
Hammerstein, Oscar, 170–71, 200, 284–87
Happy Time, The, 37
Harnick, Sheldon (see Bock and Harnick)
Harris, Barbara, 27–29, 32

Harrison, Gregory, 128–29, 225, 226
Hart, Moss, 23–24, 25
Haworth, Jill, 7
Hayes, Sean, 329–30
Headley, Heather, 136, 195, 212
Hedwig and the Angry Inch, 162, 164*b*, 166, 168–69
Hello, Again, 332
Hello, Dolly!, 72, 79, 144, 299, 300, 301*b*, 303–4, 309, 313, 314
Henry V, 17, 22–24, 38–39, 40, 44, 49
Hepburn, Audrey, 73, 74, 117
Herman, Jerry, 11, 72, 116–17, 309
Hewitt, Tom, 280, 308
High Fidelity, 206, 208*b*, 213*f*, 214
High Society, 144*b*, 149, 150–51
Hilty, Megan, 66, 67, 160, 267
Hines, Gregory, 63–64, 130
Hirschfeld, Al, 3, 16, 89
Hirson, Roger, 58–59
Hoebee, Mark, 77
Holliday, Jennifer, 196
Holm, Ian, 4, 16
Horton, Robert, 34
Houghton, Norris, 19–20
How to Succeed in Business Without Really Trying, 16, 344–45
Howard, Stuart, 145–46
Hudson, Rock, 106, 108
Hughes, Langston, 53
Hulce, Tom, 337
Hunt, Gordon, 74–75
Hunt, Peter, 30, 100

Idle, Eric, 230–32, 259–60
In My Life, 333, 335*b*, 336–37
Into the Woods, 111, 224*b*, 229–30, 316, 318*b*, 331–32

Jackman, Hugh, 1, 205, 251–53, 288–89, 327–28
Jackson, Cheyenne, 316–18, 317*f*, 324*f*, 329*f*
Jacoby, Scott, 73–74
James, Brian d'Arcy, 165, 218, 233, 257, 270, 342–43
Janney, Allison, 160
Jay-Alexander, Richard, 209
Jbara, Greg, 215, 233–34
Jelly's Last Jam, 52, 53*b*, 63–64, 65, 124, 126*b*, 130
Jerry Springer, The Opera, 91*b*, 98, 104
Jerome Robbins' Broadway, 91*b*, 96–97
Jesus Christ Superstar, 51, 53*b*, 57–58, 67, 104, 204–5, 254, 256, 256*b*

Johns, Glynis, 40–41, 42*f*
Jones, Davey, 225
Jones, Rachel Bay, 144–45, 154
Jones, Richard, 166, 167–68
Joseph and the Amazing Technicolor Dreamcoat, 144*b*, 147, 190
Jourdan, Louis, 27, 28

Kahn, Madeline, 30–32
Kander, John (see also Kander & Ebb), 6
Kander and Ebb, 3–4, 7, 12, 70–71, 72, 73, 74, 108, 116, 146, 149
Katzenberg, Jeffrey, 98–99
Kaye, Judy, 16, 17, 30–32, 103
Keenan-Bolger, Celia, 306
Kelly, Laura Michelle, 264*f*, 265
Kelly, Paula, 54, 55
Kert, Larry, 6
Kid, The, 222, 224*b*, 234
Kiley, Richard, 30, 124, 126–27
Kind, Richard, 121
King and I, The, 52–53, 150–51, 239, 334
King Hedley II, 136
Kiss Me, Kate, 124, 126*b*, 134–36, 135*f*, 206, 207*f*, 208*b*, 216, 219, 220–21
Kiss of the Spider Woman, 105, 106*b*, 107*f*, 114–17, 124, 126*b*, 130, 133–34, 166, 191, 216
Kitt, Eartha, 152, 194, 195
Kline, Kevin, 32, 33
Krakowski, Jane, 312*f*, 313, 325, 326–27, 329–30
Kron, Lisa, 182
Kudisch, Marc, 105, 142, 143*f*, 156*f*, 159*f*, 230, 289–90, 301, 307, 316, 319–20
Kuhn, Judy, 94, 170

La Boheme, 105, 106*b*, 108
LaChanze, 86, 190, 193, 195, 196–97
LaChiusa, Michael John, 152, 157–58, 194
Lane, Nathan, 101, 136
Langella, Frank, 291–92
Lansbury, Angela, 22–23, 26, 32, 44–45, 46, 46*f*, 47, 73, 99, 100, 110, 232, 292
Larson, Jonathan, 242, 281–82
Lapine, James, 68, 77–78, 81–82, 83, 84, 87–88, 108, 109, 112, 196, 227, 229, 271, 344–45
Last Five Years, The, 238, 240*b*, 245, 246
Law and Order: SVU, 275, 280–81, 297–98
Lawrence, Carol, 100
Lawrence, Peter, 210, 211
Lawrence, Steve, 73–74
Layton, Joe, 10–11, 48–49, 89–90, 91, 93, 101

INDEX

Leach, Wilford, 108, 109–10, 112–13
Leachman, Cloris, 49
Leap of Faith, 275, 277b, 292, 293–95, 295f, 296–97
Lee, Gavin, 241–42, 265
Lee, Jennifer, 342
Legally Blonde, 68, 70b, 86–87, 254, 256b, 259, 261–62, 263–64
Leigh, Mitch, 137–38
Lennon, 91b, 100, 101–2, 208b, 213–14
Lenya, Lotte, 7, 177
Lerner, Alan Jay, 22–25, 27–28, 37, 47, 48
Les Misérables, 48, 89, 91b, 95–96, 100, 101, 103, 186, 188b, 197–98, 200, 201f, 203–4, 209, 211, 317–18
Lewis, Norm, 86, 186–88, 187f, 199f, 201f, 220, 257
Lieberson, Goddard, 41
Linney, Laura 232
Lion King, The, 133–34, 136, 192
Lithgow, John, 247–48, 249f, 250
Little Me, 254, 256b, 264, 268
Little Mermaid, The, 186, 187f, 188b, 197–98, 325, 332
Little Night Music, A, 37, 39b, 40–44, 42f, 46, 155
Little Shop of Horrors, 254, 256b, 333, 335b, 338, 345–47
Loewe, Frederick, 23, 25
Logan, John, 46–47
Lloyd Webber, Andrew, 33, 57, 58, 117, 118, 179, 203
Longbottom, Robert, 100, 192
LoveMusik, 162, 164b, 177–78
Luft, Lorna, 73
Luker, Rebecca, 170, 219–20
Lumbard, Dirk, 91–92
LuPone, Patti, 95, 103, 105, 111, 112, 117–18, 171, 174, 175–76–, 179–80, 185, 261, 290–91, 318
Lynne, Gillian, 91–92, 93, 203, 289–90

Mackintosh, Cameron, 83, 200, 210, 311
MacLaine, Shirley, 55, 57, 243
McAnuff, Des, 150–51, 170–71
McClure, Rob, 219, 272
McDonald, Audra, 34, 34f, 35, 134, 136, 140, 170, 171, 174, 186, 193, 195, 200, 202, 245, 280–81, 332
McDowell, Roddy, 17, 23–24, 27
McGillin, Howard, 105–6, 107f, 119f, 122f, 217, 219–20
McKechnie, Donna, 186
McMartin, John, 33, 170–71

McPherson, Conor, 161
Mack & Mabel, 106b, 116–17, 118
Madam Secretary, 17, 219
Mail, 68, 70b
Malone, Beth, 173
Mame, 22–23, 26, 73–74
Mamma Mia!, 244
Man of La Mancha, 19b, 30, 124, 126b, 136–38
Mann, Terrence, 89–91, 90f, 98f, 102f, 213, 235
Mantello, Joe, 158–59, 160, 246
March of the Falsettos, (see also *Falsettos*), 68, 69f, 70b, 77–78
Marre, Albert, 30
Marshall, Kathleen, 15, 197
Marshall, Rob, 100, 114, 243, 283
Martin, Barney, 12
Martin, Ricky, 179–80
Mary Poppins, 254, 256b, 264f, 265, 266, 299, 301b, 304–5, 309–10
Matilda, 222, 224b, 235–37, 236f
Maxwell, Jan, 156, 156f, 157–58, 289–90
Maxwell, Mitch, 153–54
Mayer, Michael, 225, 226, 259, 307, 319–20, 337, 338, 345, 346–47
Maynard, Tyler, 234, 321–22, 329–30
Mazzie, Marin, 135
Mendes, Sam, 12, 243, 283
Menken, Alan, 98–99, 293, 294
Menzel, Idina, 14–15, 16, 155, 224–25, 239f, 245, 246, 247, 288–89, 342
Merrick, David, 34, 71, 72, 74, 129
Merrily We Roll Along, 283–87, 298b
Michaels, Frankie, 73–74
Michele, Lea, 334f, 338, 339–40, 342–43
Midler, Bette, 300–1, 303–4, 309, 313, 314, 315
Miller, Arthur, 32, 48
Miller, Patina, 309–10, 331–32
Minnelli, Liza, 10, 51, 67, 73, 190
Miranda, Lin-Manuel, 1, 342–43
Miss Saigon, 186, 188b, 190, 191, 195, 206, 207–8, 208b, 209–11, 212, 220
Mitchell, Brian Stokes, 82, 115, 124–26, 125f, 132f, 135f, 171, 247–48, 284–87
Mitchell, Jerry, 86–88, 96–97, 250, 261–62
Mitchell, John Cameron, 168–69
Moore, Jason, 232–33
Monk, Debra, 97, 244
Morse, Robert, 14–15, 43
Moses, Burke, 149–50
Moss, Larry, 323
Most Happy Fella, The, 316, 318b, 330, 331

Mueller, Jessie, 205
Murphy, Donna, 16, 22, 177, 225, 292, 314
Music Man, The, 188b, 205
My Fair Lady, 23, 25, 144, 238, 240b, 251–53, 252f
Mystery of Edwin Drood, The, 105, 106b, 108, 109–11, 114, 206, 208, 213f, 217–18

Nashville, 206, 209, 217, 218
Naughton, James, 12
Neuwirth, Bebe, 80, 101, 251
New Brain, A, 179b, 188b, 192–93, 344–45, 344f
New York Times, The, 12, 48, 105, 124, 162, 200, 226–27, 234, 238, 251, 254, 270, 275–76, 326–27, 339–40
Newman, Paul, 78, 160
Nice Work If You Can Get It, 208b, 219, 325, 326, 346
Nicholaw, Casey, 103, 260, 261, 270, 292
Nichols, Mike, 230–32, 248, 259–60, 261
9 to 5, 142, 144b, 157, 158–60, 159f
Normal Heart, The, 3–4, 240–41, 288
Nunn, Trevor, 93, 95, 101, 197–98

O'Brien, Jack, 86–87, 247–48, 250, 272
O'Connor, Caroline, 116–17
O'Donnell, Rosie, 167–68, 205, 287
O'Hara, Kelli, 173, 216, 219, 220, 259–60, 325, 326
O'Hare, Denis, 184, 288–89
O'Horgan, Tom, 51, 56–57
Oedipus, 21, 22
Oh, Kay!, 124, 126b, 129
Oliver!, 225
Olivo, Karen, 297–98, 342–43
On a Clear Day, You Can See Forever, 17, 19b, 21–23, 27–28, 29, 30
On Borrowed Time, 3, 5
110 in the Shade, 17, 19b, 34–35, 34f
On the Town, 70b, 87, 256b, 264
On the Twentieth Century, 17, 19b, 30–33, 31f
Once on This Island, 188b, 190, 204–5
Ono, Yoko, 100, 213–14
Orbach, Jerry, 321, 322
Oremus, Stephen, 158–59
Oscar (Academy Award), 3–4, 16, 232
Osnes, Laura, 185, 220
Ostrow, Stuart, 58–60, 74–75, 76

Paige, Elaine, 105, 112
Panaro, Hugh, 118
Paper Moon, 224b, 225–26, 227
Papp, Joseph, 22–24

Parton, Dolly, 158–60
Pascal, Adam, 212, 242, 321–22
Passion, 164b, 169, 170, 171
Patinkin, Mandy, 109, 110, 113, 144–45, 185, 194, 195, 219–20, 279
Paulson, Sarah, 331–32
Paulus, Diane, 75, 101–2, 103, 200, 235, 299, 311
Peter and the Starcatcher, 254, 261, 262
Peter Pan, 68–70, 105, 106b, 121, 267–68
Peters, Bernadette, 11, 16, 109, 144–45, 180, 185, 202, 302, 314
Phantom of the Opera, The, 48, 105, 106b, 112, 117, 118–20, 119f, 121–23, 186, 188b, 193, 203–4, 211
Pierce, David Hyde, 165, 230–32, 259–61, 272, 300, 304–5
Pinkins, Tonya, 195, 196
Pippin, 51, 52f, 53b, 58–60, 65, 66, 68, 70b, 74–76, 78–80, 91b, 101–2, 102f, 222, 224b, 235–36, 287, 311
Porgy and Bess, 186, 188b, 193, 195, 200–2, 203
Preston, Robert, 27, 28, 72
Price, Lonny, 171, 268
Prince, Faith, 82, 153–54
Prince, Hal, 4, 6, 7, 8, 9, 12, 16, 30, 32–33, 39–41, 43, 44, 45, 49, 61f, 62, 81–82, 105, 114–15, 116, 117–21, 175, 177–78, 203, 279, 308, 333
Prince, Judy, 115, 279
Private Lives, 17, 25–26
Prodigal Son, The, 52–53, 53b, 55
Prom, The, 222, 224b, 236–37
Prowse, Juliet, 54
Public Theater, The, 3–4, 105, 106–8, 157, 178, 179, 182, 183, 241
Purlie!, 19b, 186–87, 240–41
Putting it Together, 68, 70b, 83–84

Rags, 91b, 94–95, 100
Ragtime, 68, 70b, 84–86, 124, 126b, 131–35, 132f, 136, 138, 192–93
Raitt, John, 124, 322
Ramirez, Sara, 230–31
Rando, John, 33, 87–88, 268
Rannells, Andrew, 271, 302
Rashad, Phylicia, 173–74
Reed, Alyson, 12
Reinking, Ann, C1f3, 12, 14, 65, 74, 80, 81, 142, 146–47
Remick, Lee, 110
Renshaw, Christopher, 150–51
Reynolds, Burt, 160

Rice, Tim, 58, 112
Rich, Frank, 12, 105
Richards, Jeffrey, 200
Riedel, Michael, 167, 287
Ripley, Alice, 192, 280, 284–87
Rivera, Chita, 12, 13, 52, 55, 63–65, 115, 130–31, 139–40, 191, 217–18, 218f
Rivers, Joan, 117–18
Road Show (see also *Bounce*), 162, 164b, 178
Robbins, Jerome, 52–53, 96–97, 210–11
Robertson, Liz, 47
Rocky Horror Show, The, 91b, 100, 103, 104, 275, 276f, 280, 281–82
Roger, Elena, 179–80
Ronstadt, Linda, 108
Roots, 51, 54, 128
Rose, George, 109
Ross, Herbert, 110, 112
Roth, Robbie, 306
Roth, Robert Jess, 98–99, 228
Rubin-Vega, Daphne, 280, 281–82
Rubinstein, John, 74–75, 76, 274
Rudin, Scott, 205
Rupert, Michael, 68–70, 69f, 79f, 85f, 125f, 129, 271

Saint Joan, 19–20, 21, 22
Saks, Gene, 94, 145–47
Scanlan, Dick, 153, 255–56
Scarlet Pimpernel, The, 91b, 100, 144b, 151–52, 192
Schaefer, Eric, 194, 284–87
Schreiber, Liev, 175–76
Schwartz, Stephen, 58–60, 67, 75, 95
Scott, Sherie Rene, 246, 247–48
Scottsboro Boys, The, 17, 19b, 35
Secret Garden, The, 105, 106b, 113, 114, 116
See What I Wanna See, 144b, 155
Sella, Robert, 156, 289–90
Selleck, Tom, 50
1776, 17, 19b, 29, 30, 104
Shakespeare, William, 19–20, 23–24, 29, 40, 48, 49, 90, 93, 99, 162, 164, 165, 175, 219, 248, 254, 260, 269f, 270, 271, 276–77, 282, 303, 335
Shakespeare in the Park, 19, 22–23, 162, 197, 333
Shakespeare's Cabaret, 70b, 76–77
She Loves Me, 106b, 114–15, 299, 301, 301b, 304, 312–13, 312f
Shelley, Carol, 33
Shenandoah, 17, 18f, 19b, 29, 30, 36
Sher, Bartlett, 139, 253, 346–47

Shields, Brooke, 283, 293–94
Show Boat, 19b, 33, 39b, 49, 104
Shrek, 222, 224b, 232–34
Shuffle Along, 124–25, 126b, 134, 138–39, 140, 141
Side Show, 186, 188b, 191–93, 196
Sieber, Christopher, 222–37, 223f, 227f, 236f
Simon, John, 29, 144–45,
Simon, Neil, 3, 37, 61, 63, 81, 277
Skeggs, Emily, 172
Smash, 206, 217, 254, 267, 268
Smith, Alexis, 30
Something Rotten!, 184, 206, 208b, 218, 219, 254, 256b, 259, 260, 261, 262, 266, 269f, 269–71, 272, 342–43
Sondheim, Stephen, 9, 16, 40–41, 43, 44, 45, 68, 81–82, 83, 84, 97, 99, 105, 109, 111, 117, 120, 121, 136, 137, 155–56, 169, 170–71, 173–74, 177–78, 183–84, 185, 194, 198–202, 208, 220–21, 229, 245, 259, 281–82, 283–87, 290–92, 307, 308
Sondheim on Sondheim, 186, 188b, 198–200, 199f, 335b
Sound of Music, The, 83–84, 104, 105, 267–68, 333, 335, 336–37
South Pacific, 239–40
Spamalot, 222, 223f, 224b, 228–33, 254, 256b, 259–62, 263–64, 265, 270, 336
Spring Awakening, 307, 333, 334f, 335b, 336, 337–40, 341, 342–43, 346
Steel Pier, 146, 148–49, 150–51
Steele, Lucas, 234
Stephenson, Don, 167
Stewart, James, 17, 111
Stewart, Michael, 117
Stone, Peter, 167–68
Stop the World—I Want to Get Off, 3, 3b, 6
Story of My Life, The, 208b, 214, 216
Stritch, Elaine, 33, 77, 110
Stroman, Susan, 35, 146, 149, 244–45
Strouse, Charles, 37, 38–40, 47, 95
Sunday in the Park With George, 105, 106b, 108, 109, 207–8, 275, 283, 284–87, 285f, 290
Sweeney Todd, 37, 39b, 43, 44–47, 46f, 50, 81–82, 90, 104, 126b, 136, 137, 139, 162, 164b, 169, 172, 174–77, 175f, 178, 181–83, 184, 188b, 193, 194, 203–4, 205, 207–8, 256b, 259, 268, 290–91
Sweet Charity, 51, 53b, 54–56, 63, 66, 68, 70b, 74, 79f, 80–81, 336
Swit, Loretta, 109–10

Taboo, 184, 275, 277b, 280, 287–88, 294–95, 296
Taylor, Elizabeth, 26, 28, 37, 43–44, 56
Teddy and Alice, 37, 39b, 48
Telsey, Bernie, 241, 290
Tesori, Jeanine, 170–71, 182, 259
Testa, Mary, 193, 326–27
Thoroughly Modern Millie, 142, 144, 152, 153, 154, 157, 215, 224b, 230, 256b, 258–59, 265, 299, 301, 301b, 303, 307–8, 316, 318b, 319–20, 321–22, 326, 330, 335
Thou Shalt Not, 238, 240b, 243, 244–45
Three Guys Naked From the Waist Down, 78–79, 81–82
tick, tick...BOOM!, 275, 280, 281–83, 294–95, 298b
Time and Again, 118, 121
Titanic, 162, 164b, 166–68, 171
Tony Award, 3–4, 3b, 9–10, 11, 14, 16, 17, 19b, 25, 28, 29, 33, 37, 39b, 40, 43, 46, 46f, 51, 53b, 57–58, 59–60, 68, 70b, 72–73, 81, 82–83, 99, 101–2, 103, 105, 108, 110, 112, 124, 126b, 128–29, 133–34, 136, 142, 154, 157, 162, 164b, 165–66, 167–68, 169, 171, 172, 173–74, 179–80, 184, 191, 195, 196, 217–18, 219, 220, 222, 225, 232, 233–34, 238, 240b, 245–46, 247, 249, 250, 251–53, 254, 256b, 259, 260–61, 262–63, 269f, 270, 275, 288–89, 290–91, 299, 301b, 303–4, 307, 311–12, 314–15, 319–20, 321, 324–25, 326–27, 330, 333, 339–40
Torti, Robert, 147
Townshend, Pete, 166, 190
Trapper John, M.D., 124, 128–29, 131
Triumph of Love, 222, 224b, 226–27, 227f
Tuck Everlasting, 91b, 101–2, 103
Tune, Tommy, 1, 11, 142, 145–47, 254
Turner, David, 337
Tveit, Aaron, 250
Two Gentlemen of Verona, 188b, 197

Up From Paradise, 48, 50b
Urinetown, 19b, 33–34

Verdon, Gwen, 12, 65, 80–81, 329–30
Vereen, Ben, 43, 51–53, 52f, 61f, 66f

Victor/Victoria, 83
Viola, Tom, 336

Waitress, 17, 19b, 35, 212, 299, 301b, 315
Walton, Tony, 111
Warchus, Matthew, 235
Wayne, David, 70, 71–73
We Take the Town, 27, 28
Weber, Bruce, 124
Weidman, John, 121, 155
Weissler, Fran and Barry, 14, 65, 145–46, 234–36, 311
West Side Story, 53, 291–92
Westenberg, Robert, 109, 219–20
Wheeler, Hugh, 40, 43
White, Lillias, 195
Who's Tommy, The, 162, 163f, 164–66, 164b, 167–68, 170–71, 173, 181–82, 186, 188b, 190–91, 256
Wicked, 3–4, 5b, 14–15, 16, 51–52, 53b, 66f, 67, 238, 239f, 240b, 246–47, 307
Wild Party, The, 142, 144, 152–53, 155, 186, 188, 194–95, 196
Wildhorn, Frank 151–52
Wilkinson, Colm, 96
Williams, Allison, 80
Williams, Vanessa 115, 130–31, 198, 199–200, 229, 230, 302
Wilson, Lester, 55, 62
Wiz, The, 60, 187–88, 240–41
Wolfe, George, 63–64, 134, 140, 152, 153, 194, 195
Women on the Verge of a Nervous Breakdown, 124, 126b, 139–40, 141
Woodward, Joanne, 78
Wopat, Tom, 82–83, 198, 199–200

Xanadu, 316, 317f, 318b, 324–25, 326–27, 329, 330

Yeston, Maurey, 167–68
York, Rachel, 83, 196–97
Your Arms Too Short to Box With God, 241

Zaks, Jerry, 97, 112–13, 308, 313, 314
Zambello, Francesca, 197–98
Ziegfeld, 37, 39b, 48–49
Zien, Chip, 68, 77, 78, 156, 193, 289–90